Revelation

Written from a semi-preterist point of view, Dr. Kelly provides both theological and pastoral insights of great consequence to John's apocalyptic vision that often puzzles its readers. Highly recommended.

DEREK THOMAS,
Minister of Preaching and Teaching,
First Presbyterian Church, Columbia, South Carolina

With Douglas Kelly's commentary in hand, there is no longer an excuse for pastors and other teachers to neglect the teaching of Revelation. Kelly's clear, forceful, and Christ-centered exposition deals skillfully with important questions of interpretation and eschatology, so that the light of Christ's glorious reign may shine fully upon the reader's mind and heart. What a great blessing it is for the church to regain clarity about the message of Revelation! Kelly's commentary will prove invaluable in restoring this vital message to the pulpits of our churches and the lives of suffering believers."

RICHARD D. PHILLIPS,
Senior Minister, Second Presbyterian Church,
Greenville, South Carolina

One of the most neglected books in all of the Bible contains some of the most pastoral, warm, and theologically important messages for the Christian church today. That book is the book of Revelation. I thank God that Dr. Douglas Kelly has now applied his years of Biblical study, rare theological insights, and broad pastoral experience to this book. He is not coming to us as another expert to unlock secret codes (which is how some treat Revelation and why it is so sadly neglected) as he is a wise, pastoral guide who welcomes us to read it for ourselves. The Church, including the Western church and the global South in the global Eastern Church, need to read the book of Revelation now more than ever. Let Douglas Kelly be your guide. I commend the book and I commend the publisher for this commentary on Revelation for such a time as this."

MICHAEL A. MILTON,
Chancellor/CEO elect,
The James M. Baird Jr. Professor of Pastoral Theology,
Reformed Theological Seminary

Revelation

A Mentor Expository Commentary

Douglas F. Kelly

MENTOR

Douglas F Kelly is the Richard Jordan Professor of Theology, Reformed Theological Seminary, Charlotte, North Carolina.

Copyright © Douglas F. Kelly 2012

ISBN 978-1-84550-688-9

First Published in 2012
in the
Mentor Imprint
by
Christian Focus Publications
Geanies House, Fearn, Ross-shire
IV20 1TW, Scotland
www.christianfocus.com

Cover design by moose77.com
Printed by MPG, Cornwall, England
The photograph on page 7 is used with the kind permission of Robin G. Atkins.

All rights reserved. No part of this publication may be reproduced, stored in a retrieval system, or transmitted, in any form, by any means, electronic, mechanical, photocopying, recording or otherwise without the prior permission of the publisher or a license permitting restricted copying. In the U.K. such licenses are issued by the Copyright Licensing Agency, Saffron House, 6-10 Kirby Street, London, EC1 8TS www.cla.co.uk.

Contents

Author's Foreword   9

Thanks   13

1. Introducing Revelation   15
2. The Glorious Christ Speaks to His Church
   Revelation 1:1-20   23
3. The Church at Ephesus
   Revelation 2:1-7   31
4. The Church at Smyrna
   Revelation 2:8-11   39
5. The Church at Pergamos
   Revelation 2:12-17   47
6. The Church at Thyatira
   Revelation 2:18-29   55
7. The Church in Sardis
   Revelation 3:1-6   63
8. The Church at Philadelphia
   Revelation 3:7-13   71
9. The Church at Laodicea
   Revelation 3:14-22   77
10. The Throne
    Revelation 4:1-3   87
11. Around God's Throne
    Revelation 4:4-6a   93
12. Praises Around the Throne
    Revelation 4:6b-11   99
13. Heaven's Song
    Revelation 5:1-14   105
14. The Breaking of the First Four Seals
    Revelation 6:1   111
15. 'Farther Along, We'll Understand Why'
    Revelation 6:3-8   119
16. The Fifth Seal: Prayers of the Martyrs in Heaven
    Revelation 6:9-11   125
17. The Shakings of History
    Revelation 6:12-17   131
18. An Interlude Between the Sixth and Seventh Seals
    Revelation 7:1-3   137
19. The Saints in Heaven
    Revelation 7:4-9, 14   143
20. The Songs of the Saints in Heaven
    Revelation 7:9-17   149
21. An Amazing Contrast
    Revelation 7:13-17   155
22. How God has Chosen to Run the World
    Revelation 8   161
23. The Key of the Bottomless Pit
    Revelation 9:1-2   167
24. How God Uses Evil by Opening the Demonic Pit
    Revelation 9:3-12   173
25. The Connection of Prayer and Judgment
    Revelation 9:13-21   179
26. Judgment on Unbelieving Israel
    Revelation 9:13-21   185
27. Get the Gospel Out
    Revelation 10   191
28. Principles at Work in History
    Revelation 11:1-13   199
29. Two Hymns in Heaven
    Revelation 11:14-19   207
30. The Holy War
    Revelation 12:1-6   213
31. Warfare in Heaven: A Good Result
    Revelation 12:7-12   219
32. The Dragon Attacks the Church
    Revelation 12:13-17   227

Contents

33 The Church's Enemy
Revelation 13:1–10 235

34 The Mark of the Beast
Revelation 13:11–18 241

35 The Lamb and his Fair Army
Revelation 14:1–5 249

36 The Victory of the Everlasting Gospel
Revelation 14:6–7 257

37 Messages from the Angels
Revelation 14:8–13 265

38 A Double Harvest
Revelation 14:14–20 271

39 The Sea of Glass Mingled with Fire
Revelation 15:1–2 277

40 The Song of the Victor
Revelation 15:3–4 283

41 The Opening of the Tabernacle of Heaven
Revelation 15:5–8 289

42 What about Judgment?
Revelation 16:1–7 295

43 The Disaster of Impenitence
Revelation 16:8–11 303

44 Anatomy of Collapse
Revelation 16:10–21 309

45 God's Strategy to Defeat Evil
Revelation 17:1–2 317

46 Babylon the Great, Mother of Harlots
Revelation 17:3–6 323

47 Angelic Explanations
Revelation 17:7–11 329

48 The Fall of Babylon
Revelation 18:1–8 335

49 Two Reactions to the Fall of Babylon
Revelation 18:9–24 341

50 Heaven's View of International Disasters
Revelation 18:20–24 345

51 Hallelujahs in Heaven
Revelation 19:1–5 351

52 World History Concludes with a Wedding
Revelation 19:6–9 355

53 The King Conquers the Nations
Revelation 19:10–16 363

54 The Terrible Reality of Hell
Revelation 19:17–21 369

55 The Millennium
Revelation 20:1–6 375

56 Two Deaths and Two Resurrections
Revelation 20:4–6 381

57 When Things Look Worst, Victory Is at Hand
Revelation 20:7–10 387

58 The Last Judgment
Revelation 20:11–15 391

59 A Final and Sweeping Victory
Revelation 21:1–8 397

60 How Generous God Is with His Glory!
Revelation 21:9–17 405

61 Our Future Is Filled with Beauty and Light
Revelation 21:18–21 411

62 The Light that Will Fill Our Future
Revelation 21:22–27 415

63 Forward to the New Garden of Eden
Revelation 22:1–5 421

64 The Last Thing Jesus Said Before He Comes Back
Revelation 22:6–17 427

65 The Last Words of the Covenant
Revelation 22:18–21 433

Endnotes 439

Subject Index 441

Scripture Index 459

REEDY CREEK PRESBYTERIAN CHURCH AT COTTON HARVEST TIME

This book is dedicated to the Session of
Reedy Creek Presbyterian Church, Minturn, South Carolina:
Earl Rich Alford, James Little Alford, John Manton Alford,
Neill E. Alford, Roy Baxley, Jr., T. Curt McSwain.

My prayer for them, as for myself, is that
we may be in that company that 'follow
the Lamb whithersoever he goeth' (Rev. 14:4).

Author's Foreword

'The beauty of the Lord our God' is spoken of by Moses (in Psalm 90:17). The book of Revelation is pervaded by the sheer beauty of God. From the rocky shores of an island concentration camp, through distressed churches; from scenes of famine, war, and blood-shed; from fiery destruction of armies and navies; from painful plagues, and the slaughter of holy witnesses; from demonic attempts to destroy God's people, and on through pestilence, sores, and the downfall of the world's greatest economy and city; from united (and then, divided) political and religious harlotry, through the final destruction of the last desperate outburst of universal evil, the beauty of the Triune God, who sits on the rainbow-circled Throne of universal power and righteousness, casts its serene light over it all. That serene beauty and infinite power, joined to unbounded love and grace, overcomes all the horrendous corruption caused by sin in all aspects of the universe; putting the reprobate eternally away, where they need to be, and transforming everything else in the beauteous light that comes from the face of Jesus Christ: 'making all things new'.

Revelation is an overarching survey of the final victory of purity and beauty of the Triune God over the impurity and ugliness of sin, death, and hell. This remaking of a twisted creation into the beautiful rightness of a renewed one, was, is now being, and finally shall be, fully accomplished through the blood of the Lamb 'slain from the foundation of the world' (Rev. 13:8). The Lamb was the original agent of the creation of the heavens and the earth, and he is the only one who can redeem it (Rev. 14:7). The Lamb, who shed his blood and rose from the dead to save his people, and redeem the entire cosmos to its original pure loveliness (Rev. 5:9), along with his Father, and the Holy Spirit, who unites them in ineffable bonds of life and love: this one Triune God alone is worthy to receive: 'power, and riches, and wisdom, and strength, and honor, and glory, and blessing' (Rev. 5:12). The eternal Godhead, and stupendous incarnation of the Lamb, the Holy Son of God, equipped him to become 'a ransom for many'; to make voluntary and loving self-sacrifice, of such infinite worth and might, that it once-for-all redeemed in principle the whole world, and in due time, will complete its glorification. The goodness and beauty of this Lamb of God overcomes the last evil and ugliness of a fallen cosmos. So certain are the final fruits of victory of the Lamb, that the angels and translated elders are already singing: 'Amen: Blessing, and glory, and wisdom, and thanksgiving, and honor, and power, and might, be unto our God forever and ever. Amen' (Rev. 7:12).

In the Song of Solomon, after the beloved maiden describes the beauty of her lover by saying, 'he is altogether lovely' (S. of S. 5:16), the daughters of Jerusalem immediately cry out, 'Show us where he is!' (S. of S. 6:1). In the light of such beauty shown to us in Revelation by the altogether lovely Lamb, the Son of the Father, in the bonds of charity of the Holy Spirit, let us join the company of 'those who follow the Lamb whithersoever he goeth' (Rev. 14:4). The ultimate beauty of the entire universe draws us out of self, up to himself! Let us gladly follow. Nowhere is this beauty more vividly displayed, and nowhere are we more tenderly and mightily called to follow, than in the shining passages of Revelation.

These sixty-five expositions of the Book of Revelation were delivered at Reedy Creek Presbyterian Church, in Minturn, South Carolina, between November 2001 and November 2003. Several reasons prompted me to prepare this series. First, in 2001, I had just turned 58 years of age, and was mindful of the relative shortness of time that is left to me in this earthly pilgrimage. There were still a number of things I hoped to accomplish, and one of them was to preach through the Apocalypse. I had hesitated previously, owing to the complicated nature of the book, and also had remembered that John Calvin, who preached through most of the Bible, had not dealt with this book. My previous thoughts had been: if Calvin did not preach on it, who am I to attempt it? Yet I also remembered that John Calvin died at age 55, and perhaps if he had lived much longer, he would have expounded Revelation.

A second reason for preaching through Revelation is that since the early nineteenth century, many good Christians have held views of the end time, according to which they postpone into the future several events that most of the Church traditionally believed to have been fulfilled in history many centuries ago. It causes them to hold a rather pessimistic viewpoint of what happens on earth in terms of the mission of the Church between the two comings of Christ. (Of course, all of them believe strongly in the final victory of Christ, after history has ended). Although most of them faithfully uphold the full inspiration of Holy Scripture, still, in accordance with their way of looking at 'the Church Age', they generally ascribe far more influence to the work and influence of Satan than is warranted in a clear reading of the apocalyptic passages in the synoptic Gospels, and in Revelation itself.

Their postponement of most of Christ's victory to the end makes it difficult for them to take seriously enough the many texts dealing with the shortness of the time before some of the great things that are predicted would happen. Many of these events (though certainly not all of them) could be understood to have been fulfilled in the destruction of Jerusalem in AD 70, as most Church commentators generally believed before the nineteenth century. If, for instance, one postpones 'the Great Tribulation' into the remote future, then a shadow of presumed Satanic power hangs over the Church during its passage to the Last Day, and raises questions about the on-going triumph of Christ during world history. Isaiah says that Christ 'shall see of the travail of his soul, and shall be satisfied' (Isa. 53:11). The fruits of his travail are offered up, not just at the end of time, but every day, as people through faith in the suffering Servant and resurrected Lord are being justified, for 'by his knowledge shall my righteous servant justify many…' (also verse 11). Psalm 72 (a Messianic Psalm) predicts that 'he shall have dominion also from sea to sea, and from the river unto the ends of the earth' (v. 8). It could not be right to postpone that ever increasing dominion of the Lord through his gospel to the end of the age, for it has been going on for some two thousand years.

Part of the problem in unnecessarily postponing already fulfilled events to the far distant future seems to stem from the failure to interpret the images and symbols used in Revelation in light of their contexts in the Old Testament. The way they are employed there gives us significant guidance on how to understand them when they are taken up into the apocalyptic sections of the New Testament. One illustration would be the pictures of the falling of stars, the going dark of the moon, and other strange happenings in natural phenomena. These images must be understood in terms of how they were originally used in Old Testament prophecies, such as Isaiah, Ezekiel, and Daniel. There, they do not mean the literal falling of the stars to earth, but rather the down-coming of governmental powers (such as Joseph's dream of the sun and moon, and twelve stars bowing before him, meaning his parents and brothers). Not to take this into account makes it hard properly to interpret Revelation.

It is, to say the least, a poor principle of interpretation to postpone to the future what has either been fulfilled in the past, or is in process of being fulfilled. A prime example is how we understand the millennium. Should its victories be postponed to shortly before the end of time, or does it refer to the increasingly wide and victorious reign of Christ in progress since his resurrection and ascension? An important question is this: what did Christ mean when he said, upon the return of the seventy from their successful mission, 'I saw Satan fall like lightning' (Luke 10:18)? And what is the significance of Christ's 'having spoiled principalities and powers, making a show of them openly, triumphing over them in it [the cross]' (Col. 2:15)? This, along with many other considerations, indicates that Satan's power has been severely limited since the atonement and resurrection of the Lord Jesus Christ, for Christ was 'declared to be the Son of God with power, according to the spirit of holiness, by his resurrection from the dead' (Rom. 1:4).

The Messiah's death, resurrection, and ascension are how his Church has been enabled from above to carry on with considerable triumph in the winning of lost nations to Him, for the praying Church is already 'seated in heavenly places in Christ Jesus' (Eph. 2:6). Raised with him above, she now has the divinely given authority, says Christ, '[to] ask of me, and I shall give thee the heathen for thine inheritance, and the uttermost part of the earth for thy possession' (Ps. 2:8). The exercise of this heavenly authority over all lesser powers is the main thing that is happening in this age between the two comings of the Lord; which, as we shall seek to demonstrate, is the prime meaning of the millennium. The millennium is not a literal period of only one thousand years that will occur much later; rather, it is that period of victorious outreach of the Gospel to the nations: a time that lasts from Jesus' first coming to his last. Hence, it is out of accord with the rest of the Scriptures to limit it to one thousand literal years, and to postpone it to the future.

It is clear to me that devout Christians can hold to varying understandings of millennial questions, without it affecting their love for Christ, belief in Scripture, and holy obedience to Him. At the best, '...now we see through a glass darkly...', so, charitable consideration is always necessary towards different points of view on a complex matter, such as the end of the age. Yet I do think that it is important for our world-view, and hence for our confidence to labor for the Lord, that we seek to make the best sense of these matters, in light of the whole of Scripture. For example, the millennium (already mentioned) is named in only one place in Scripture; thus, it accords best with sound principles of interpretation to consider one place, in a highly symbolic book, in light of the vast number of clearer, didactic passages that treat of the same subject elsewhere, rather than to seek to fit the large number of clear, didactic passages into only one symbolic one. I well know that I could never get everything right, but I have sought to follow sound principles of interpretation, as they have long been worked out by the faithful scholars of the entire Christian tradition, East and West.

A third reason why I decided to preach through this demanding book is because of the seven blessings, or seven beatitudes, it pronounces on those who take its message to heart. Since one of the expositions in this volume discusses all of the beatitudes, I will mention here only one of them: 'Blessed [that is, truly and lastingly happy] is he that readeth, and they that hear the words of this prophecy, and keep the things that are written in it, for the time is at hand' (Rev. 1:3). Owing to the benedictions promised to faithful reading of this last books of the Bible, I have been eager to make constant application of its truths to our lives and duties as messengers of the transforming gospel in a desperately needy world. I have sought to take into account our contemporary situation, and to be practical in applying these truths.

In conclusion, working through this last book of the Bible has uplifted me in a way I scarcely thought possible! The beauty, fragrance, majesty, grace and omnipotent power of 'the Lamb of God, slain before the foundation of the world' has at times all but overwhelmed me! Revelation is primarily about Jesus Christ; he is the hero of all ages. Satan, though real enough, is finally a minor note in this divinely orchestrated symphony. My zeal has never been so much for any millennial theory, as it is for HIM, and going through this Apocalypse has only increased that zeal. 'his Name is as ointment poured forth' (Song 1:3), and 'All his garments smell of myrrh, and aloes, and cassia, out of the ivory palaces, whereby they have made thee glad' (Ps. 45:8). May the sweet fragrance of that Name, which God the Father loves the most: 'having exalted it above every name' (Phil. 2:9), waft out to many a person through the pages of this volume. This is the humble prayer of the author.

Thanks

I gladly thank the many Christian friends, who have helped me along the way with this project, which has stretched over several years. My fear is that I shall omit some helpers, given the length of time over which it has lasted. I am grateful to the congregation of Reedy Creek Presbyterian Church, who first listened to these sermons attentively, and prayed for me as I was preaching them. The session largely financed the typing of the sermons from the audio-tapes and CDs. Several others provided significant financial encouragement: Mr. Tommy Peaster of Yazoo City, Mississippi; Dr. Michael Brown and Mr. Jim Atkins of Dillon, South Carolina (all of them Presbyterian elders). My excellent typists were my aunt, Mrs. Ruth Parker Mayers of Lumberton, North Carolina, and my friends: Mrs. Holly Moody of Dillon, SC, and Mrs. Karl (Linda) Rudolph of Greenville, South Carolina. What a wonderful job they did! My friends, Mrs. Earl (Linda) Alford and Mr. Jim Atkins organized the recorded messages, and my wife, Caroline, and friend, Mr. Alex Mark, helped me with computer issues. The Rev. Matthew Miller, of Greenville, SC, revised one of the sermons. I am also very grateful to the team at Christian Focus, particularly to Dr. Philip Ross for his help and friendship.

Douglas F. Kelly,
Dillon, South Carolina
21 August 2010

1

INTRODUCING REVELATION

This last book of the Bible is sometimes called the apocalypse, which means unveiling. Revelation comes from the Latin (pull back the veil) and Apocalypse comes from the Greek (with the same meaning—to unveil). In both cases it is as if you are in an auditorium at a primary school, where the pupils are going to give a play. The audience cannot see the scenery or the children up on the stage and then somebody pulls the curtains so that you see the stage and the scenery, the actors and actresses, and the lights upon them. That is a sort of revelation or apocalypse, that is to say: unveiling. That is what is happening in the last book of the Bible. There is so much about our life, about the world, and about history, so much about the past, present and future that we cannot see or understand, so in this book God pulls back the curtain and shows us the essential meaning of many of these most important things.

Revelation Shows Who is in Charge

What we see behind the curtain is Jesus Christ, Lord of history, Sovereign God in control of all events in heaven and on earth. Revelation lets us see Jesus in charge and where he is leading all things that are happening. We received a fund raising letter from Charles Colson's organization and on the envelope was this question that somebody had asked Chuck Colson: 'Where was your God on September 11th?' Revelation has an answer for that. Our God was and is in sovereign control of everything in heaven and earth, the seas, the sky, the land, including Satan and his evil minions. That is where God was, the same place he was when he told John the meaning of life and history, the same place he is now as he pulls back the thin curtains separating our physical sight from the spiritual meaning of events.

Revelation or the Apocalypse is the last book in the Bible. There is a certain finality to it. These are God's last words to his church until we see Jesus coming with the Saints and the Angels.

Why Such Contemporary Interest in Revelation?

Revelation is a picture of the basic outline and meaning of what has happened since the Lord Jesus Christ came down and spoke to John in the first century and gave him the message of this book. It explains in principle what it all means and what will happen till the end of time. I think this is why there was an increase of interest in Revelation in the twentieth century. For centuries nobody seemed to have given much attention to Revelation, then as the last century passed, ever more interest focused on this book.

Why is that? One reason is the amount of change that we have seen in our lifetime. Changes occur so fast and often so violently that we must ask, what does it all mean? This question has been raised even by secularists, such as Alvin Toffler, who wrote a book entitled 'FUTURE SHOCK'. He notes that since the 1950s and 1960s, everything has changed so much that people almost feel in shell shock. Traditional ways and customs, especially since the radical sixties, have been rapidly displaced by an increasingly brutalized culture. It feels sometimes like strong winds are blowing against us and the tent pegs are not down in the ground very deep; the ropes are loose and the wind is so strong that the flaps of the tent are blowing out of control and you wonder how long the tent will last in this wind of change. What can we expect in the future?

Two Contradictory Movements
Sociologists have noted, especially since the 1980s (and there was a lot of comment on this at the beginning of the new millennium), that the world seems to be in the grip of two tremendous and contradictory movements, which is one reason there is so much trouble amongst the nations and within the nations. On the one hand, you have the movement to centralize everything, to give more power to the governments and come up with a one-world government maybe like the United Nations. Along the path of centralization, one sees the multinational companies, which are so powerful everywhere you go, or the World Banking System trying to centralize all finance. On the other hand, you have another contradictory movement that is pulling in the opposite direction and that is what one historian has called 'retribilization'. Great unities that were forced together, like the Soviet Union, began breaking apart in 1991, and have gone back to smaller historical units, not unlike large tribes. Especially, they have been going back to the basic religious loyalties that people had formerly. These older religious loyalties have to some degree determined how the former Czechoslovakia and Yugoslavia have divided up. In the Middle East, Sunni and Shiite loyalties have much to do with conflicts in Iraq and elsewhere. From one point of view, it is a retribilization. We do not know where it will end, but we do know our world is shaking because of these contradictory movements.

What next? No wise person would claim to be able to predict. It makes you wonder, are we just corks tossed about in a hurricane on the Atlantic coast? How can we make sense of what is happening? Hence, that is one of the major reasons that millions of people are turning afresh to Revelation where God unveils the unknown in terms of his overarching, eternal purposes.

Introductory Questions
In this chapter, we are going to deal only with introductory matters to Revelation. It would not be profitable to jump right into the first chapter until we look at some important questions about this book. The way we answer these questions helps determine how the book is understood and preached. We understand that any ancient text was written in a different historical situation. This means that we have to ask what it meant in that situation before we can correctly apply it to the times in which we live. I want to look at three questions and then make some concluding remarks of encouragement. These three questions will determine the outline of the sermon.

1. Who wrote the Book?
2. To whom was the Book written?
3. When was Revelation written?

Who Wrote Revelation?

First, who wrote this Book of Revelation? In a sense there are two answers. The first answer we are clearly told in Revelation 1:1–2, 9–10, and 19 is that it was the beloved apostle John. The Church has always believed that this is the same John who wrote the Gospel of John, the one who leaned on the bosom of the Lord at the Last Supper and also wrote the three Epistles of John.

John was one of the three disciples who were close to our Lord Jesus Christ in his earthly life. Years later, he was banished to Patmos, an island off modern Turkey, in what was called Asia Minor. John was banished there because of a terrible persecution against the Christian Church at that point in the first century. Much of the Church leadership was martyred (as were the apostles Paul, Peter, and James). But for some reason the persecutors did not kill John; they shipped him off to this desolate island, where apparently he was made to work in the mines. It was probably a sort of concentration camp. The church had spread rapidly; the Holy Ghost had come down and saved thousands and thousands, probably millions of people, so that the Roman Empire was getting uneasy. The Jews at that time appear to have been stirring up the Roman authorities to come out against the Christians. When the early Christians saw their leaders shipped off, beheaded, or crucified upside down, they began to wonder if the Church would survive.

In time of severe persecution, we naturally begin to think that God is not happy with us. Maybe God is uncaring. Sometimes people can even start to feel that way if they begin to loose their health. Has God turned against me? Am I losing everything? So, in this time of hard testing, God Almighty from the Throne sends down the presence of the Lord Jesus Christ to that concentration camp with a message or a vision of glorious encouragement to John and through him to the churches. Let me make two points about this.

Two Authors

First, although John is the author, the one who put pen to paper and wrote this book, it was truly the Lord of Glory who was telling him what to write. In this hard time, it was none less than the Divine Presence who was encouraging the persecuted John. That is clear in verses 8, 11 and 18. "'I am Alpha and Omega, the beginning and the end," saith the Lord "which is, which was and is to come."' Alpha is the first letter in the Greek alphabet and Omega is its last letter (as we would say in English 'from A to Z'). From Alpha to Omega means that everything that can ever happen at any point in history is encompassed in my plan and power, 'for I am he who was and is and is to come'. The Lord Jesus Christ is speaking here, so it means Jesus is God of God, the Eternal Son of God, as much God as his Father is God. Therefore, God of God in total sovereign charge is giving his beloved disciple a message of encouragement. Notice that he is saying, 'I want you to write this and give it to these seven churches because it is not just for you, it is for the churches' (v. 11).

The words of Jesus in verse 18 show us what the glorious news of Easter means for all our history: 'I am he that liveth and was dead and behold I am alive for evermore, Amen; and have the keys of hell and of death'. Jesus is standing there and saying, I am in sovereign control of everything that is happening, even of John's persecution; I am in control of it; I won't let it go but so far, and I am going to dispose it in a certain direction. I want you to remember that I died for your sins. I took on human nature, I became as human as you are without ceasing to be God; I endured the cross and I did victorious battle with the evil powers. In my resurrection, I conquered the one who has brought about this persecution. I defeated him. I won the victory and now I am going to share this victory with you, but you will have to trust me even before you see precisely how that Easter victory will be applied to your situation. So, it is the risen Lord who is behind the writing of this book of Revelation. It is his mighty message of encouragement to the church.

Christ Speaks
Secondly, these verses show us not only that the Lord himself directly inspired Revelation, but they also show us what Christ says he is doing and will be doing. In verse 7 he is going to come in judgment on the persecuting enemies of the Christian church. He says that he will do it soon. I will come back to that shortly.

Then we notice that he is walking in the midst of the earthly churches; those churches that are being persecuted. Verse 13 says that the splendid, beautiful, glorious, sovereign Christ with the very prerogatives of God Almighty, God Eternal, is walking in the midst of the seven candlesticks. It is like the church is a flame on top of the candle and Christ who is the light of the world is moving about in the flames, and thereby directly reigning in his churches.

Conquest by the Word of Christ. Ultimately, through the church Christ is going to conquer the unbelieving world in his own time and way. One of his ways of conquering will be by his tongue: his tongue came out and it was like a sharp two-edged sword (v. 16). That is a way of saying that he speaks the living word of God. In other words, when the word of truth is preached, the Risen Christ is moving about in his church. That word overcomes every lie; the word of love overcomes all hatred; the word of salvation overcomes all losses; the word of resurrection overcomes all deadness; the word of grace overcomes all unrighteousness and all opposition. Thus, as the word is proclaimed to the church, the face of Jesus begins to shine; his countenance is stronger than the sun (v. 16). The face of Jesus shines where the word is truly preached. The face of the Son of God begins to shine in people's souls and then begins to reflect in the world and drive back the devil. So, the one who wrote it was John, but the ultimate author of the book is the Lord of Glory. Verse 1 makes that clear; it is the Revelation of Jesus Christ that God gave unto John.

The Necessity of Listening. Along these lines, Revelation 2:7 states: 'he that hath an ear let him hear what the Spirit saith unto the churches'. The Holy Spirit is saying this; Jesus is saying this. Then notice Revelation 22:18–19, where something important about the concluding authority of this book is proclaimed:

> For I testify unto every man that heareth the words of the prophecy of this book, If any man shall add unto these things, God shall add unto him the plagues that are written in this book; and if any man shall take away from the words of the book of this prophecy, God shall take away his part out of the book of life, and out of the holy city, and from the things that are written in this book.

John certainly wrote it, yet Jesus, the Holy Spirit and God the Father ultimately authored it. Hence its immense, binding authority is specified.

To Whom Was Revelation Addressed?

The second question can be answered briefly. To whom was the book written?

First, it was clearly written to the seven churches of Asia—Ephesus, Smyrna, and the others in modern day Turkey (Rev. 1:11), which the Islamic people violently conquered many centuries ago. Before that time, it was a Christian area. Although there were many more than seven churches in the world, those seven churches with all their particularity, represented all the people of God, all the true congregations in various parts of the world, who were suffering under awful persecution. This is a message for all the early churches in difficult days.

Secondly, even though I shall suggest later that the message of Revelation to these churches was at least partially fulfilled in the first century in the destruction of Jerusalem, it nonetheless contains eternal truth that comes through the experience of those early churches of the way God handled their suffering and enabled them (and us) to overcome the world. What God does in that historical situation in the first century is a picture of what he will do through the ages for his Bible believing church, especially when the church falls on hard times. He is just as mighty, active, interested, and intervening when the church is under duress today.

When Was Revelation Written?

When was Revelation written? This is a complex question over which excellent Christian scholars disagree. The historical Christian church for the most part, until the 1830s, believed that much (though not all) of what is predicted in Revelation was fulfilled about 70 AD when Jerusalem was destroyed, the temple was burned, and the Jews were scattered out of their land. You can go through Revelation and look at specific things that Jesus told John would happen to the persecutors of the church, and see that many of them happened in 70 AD.

Later, we must compare the predictions made in Revelation to the predictions Jesus made in Matthew 24, which speaks of 'the great tribulation'. Across the ages, many Christian scholars taught that those predictions were fulfilled in principle when the Roman armies destroyed Jerusalem in 70 AD. We will later discuss why the date of the writing of Revelation is so important to this issue. Here I will only note that if Revelation were written before 70 AD, then it is all the more reasonable to hold that much of it (though not all of it) was precisely fulfilled in the destruction of Jerusalem. But if it were written much later, then far more of it was (or is) still future.

Nevertheless, even if Revelation is thought to have been composed after the destruction of Jerusalem, it is clear that Matthew 24 was written before 70 AD, so that 'the Great Tribulation' still should be seen as finding its primary fulfillment in the destruction of the Temple and the scattering of the Jewish nation. From this point of view, the major issue in interpreting Revelation is this: have most of its predictions been fulfilled in the events of the first century AD, or are most of them still in the future? I shall suggest that the former approach is most fitting, but in a way, I hope, that is charitable and fair to those who hold the latter.

For the present, let us look at Revelation itself, to see if it would indicate a date of composition before the fall of Jerusalem in 70 AD. There are six indications to hold that it does so.[1]

Coming Soon in Judgment. First, the victorious Jesus tells John that he is coming soon in judgment to deal with the situation oppressing the Christians in those seven churches. In verse 1, it says 'which shortly must come to pass'; verse 3, 'for the time is near or at hand'. 'I am coming to you quickly' (2:16). 'I am coming quickly' (3:11). 'The third woe is coming quickly' (11:14). 'The things which must shortly take place' (22:6). 'Behold I am coming quickly' (22:7). 'For the time is nigh' (22:10). 'Behold I am coming quickly' (22:12), and 'Yes, I am coming quickly' (22:20). And if this book was written in the middle sixties, and the Lord came in the destruction of Jerusalem and the death of Nero in 70 AD, then he came within three or four years of it being written. He did what he said he would do. He came quickly. That is one reason to think that this book must have been written before 70 AD. These are what Gary DeMar calls significant 'time texts' in the book of Revelation.² They indicate when many of its judgments would happen.

'Coming in Judgment'. Second: what is meant by his coming? We shall later see that 'coming' can be used either as the last coming at the end of time or coming in judgment. It is used as 'coming in judgment' in many places in the Old Testament and in the Gospels. Thus, it is likely that in verse 7, it means 'Coming in Judgment.' The judgments come from Christ's direct intervention, in which Christ in a sense rides upon the judgments against the enemies of his people.

'This Generation' Shall Not Pass. Thirdly, in Matthew 23:36 and 24:34, it says 'this generation shall not pass until all these things be fulfilled.' He talks about the destruction of the temple, and the great disaster among the Jewish nation, so that the Lord coming in this generation means that the people who were alive when Jesus was speaking, around 33 AD, would experience it themselves. In other words, before that generation had died a natural death, the Lord would have come in great judgment on his enemies, but also in great mercy on his people. Certainly there will be a final and ultimate coming of Christ on the last day (and Revelation speaks of it clearly), but we do not need to read the coming of the last day into every mention of his coming in judgment during the lifetime of this generation.

The Jerusalem Temple Still Standing. Fourth, Revelation 11:1-2 seems to consider the Jerusalem Temple as still standing when Revelation was written (as we find in Matthew 24, Luke 21, and Mark 13). The Christ whom so much of Judaism officially rejected will judge them and their now apostate temple worship as his judgment descends by means of the Roman army in 70 AD. There is no scriptural reason to postpone this historic judgment to some future rebuilt temple. We shall give detailed attention to this issue later.

The 'Sixth King' Seems to Have Been Alive. Fifth, Revelation appears to have been written during the life of the sixth king (or Roman Emperor). Revelation 17:9-10 states: 'And here is the mind which hath wisdom. The seven heads are seven mountains on which the woman sitteth. And there are seven kings: five are fallen, and one is, and the other is not yet come; and when he cometh, he must continue a short space.' If one counts from Julius Caesar (as the first emperor), then the sixth would be Nero, who started the first official Roman persecution against the Church in 64 AD. Nero died in 68 AD, so it appears that Revelation was written before his death.

Military Imagery Fits the Jewish War of AD 70. Sixth, the military imagery used in Revelation fits with the Jewish War of 70 AD. Horses and swords are used, not tanks, airplanes, and missiles. It takes a violence of interpretation to get the military equipment spoken of to mean anything but typical first century hardware. There is no compelling reason to resort to such interpretation when the events of 70 AD literally fulfill the kinds of battles spoken of in Revelation (and Matt. 24).

Seven Benedictions and Six Promises

Let us conclude this introduction to Revelation by listing seven benedictions and six sweet promises offered to all believers who study this book.³

Seven Beatitudes of Revelation

1. 'Blessed is he that readeth, and they that keep the words of this prophecy, and keep those things which are written therein: for the time is at hand' (1:3).
2. 'And I heard a voice from heaven saying unto me, "Write, Blessed are the dead which die in the Lord from henceforth: Yea," saith the Spirit, "that they may rest from their labors; and their works do follow them"' (14:13).
3. 'Behold, I come as a thief. Blessed is he that watcheth, and keepeth his garments, lest he walk naked, and they see his shame' (16:15).
4. 'And he saith unto me, "Write, Blessed are they which are called unto the marriage supper of the Lamb." And he saith unto me, "These are the true sayings of God"' (19:9).
5. 'Blessed and holy is he that hath part in the first resurrection: on such the second death hath no power, but they shall be priests of God and of Christ, and shall reign with him a thousand years' (20:6).
6. 'Behold, I come quickly: blessed is he that keepeth the sayings of the prophecy of this book' (22:7).
7. 'Blessed are they that do his commandments, that they may have right to the tree of life, and may enter in through the gates into the city' (22:14).

Six Promises to the Saints

1. God sees their tears (7:17; 21:4).
2. Their prayers are heard and used to rule the world (8:3–4).
3. Their death or suffering leads to glory (14:13; 20:4).
4. Their final victory is assured (15:2).
5. Their blood will be avenged (6:9; 8:3).
6. Their Christ lives and reigns forever and is victorious in time and eternity (5:7–8; 21:22).⁴

These seven benedictions and six sweet promises come to us in and through our union with the Lord Jesus Christ, 'For all the promises of God in him are Yea, and in him Amen, unto the glory of God by us' (2 Cor. 1:20). Revelation is primarily about him and what he is doing for his people.

2

The Glorious Christ Speaks to His Church

Revelation 1:1–20

In Isaiah 21:11, a question is raised that the early Church under terrible persecution must have been asking. Believers today in various nations that are hostile to Christianity must be asking the same question: 'The burden of Dumah. He calleth to me out of Seir, "Watchman, what of the night? Watchman, what of the night?" The watchman said, "The morning cometh, and also the night: if ye will enquire, enquire ye: return, come."'

Revelation answers that question about the darkness and hostility of this fallen world, and what lies in it and beyond it. We notice three sections in the introductory chapter:

1. Introduction from the Risen Christ to his church (v. 1–8).
2. Christ's glorious appearance (v. 9–16).
3. His message (v. 17–20).

Introduction from Christ

If you receive a letter in the mail, you notice who it is from and to which member of the family it is addressed. Verse 1 gives the authoritative return address: it is the revelation (or unveiling) of Jesus Christ, through a holy angel. It also specifies the ones to whom it is addressed: the servants of God through Christ's servant, the apostle John. This message came from Christ through John to the seven churches of Asia (v. 4). Although it came from the risen Christ, John the Apostle saw it and wrote it down (v. 2). Thus, it has the authority of an eyewitness.

True Happiness

Verse 3 encourages us to open this envelope to read the letter, by giving us the first of seven benedictions in this book. It says 'Blessed is he that readeth…' 'Blessed' means something like our current word, 'happy'. First Timothy 6:15 tells us that God himself is 'the only and blessed (or 'happy') Potentate. This implies that readers of Revelation can share God's happiness through the truths conveyed in it, as the Spirit wings home their reality. Ultimate happiness is not in material possessions or physical pleasures (that is the world's fleeting and, finally, disappointing happiness). Rather, true happiness or blessedness lies in reading about and being in relationship with the One who wrote this letter. If you who happen to be reading this message are 'down', it could be very different as you get into the divinely inspired realities of this book.

The Entire Trinity

Verses 4 and 5 give the qualities of the ultimate Author of this letter: the risen Lord Jesus Christ. Indeed, the entire Trinity is listed here. In the phrase: 'who is, and was, and is to come,' 'who is' takes us back to Exodus 3:14, where the Lord God spoke to Moses, who had asked him his name: 'I am that I am.' That is, I depend on nothing; everything else depends on me (including Pharaoh and Egypt, from whose power God had just commanded Moses to deliver the enslaved Israelites). The term 'seven spirits' refers to the Holy Spirit of God. The number seven stands for completeness or fullness, so the seven spirits refer to the fullness of the Holy Spirit (cf. Zech. 4:2, 6), and to Christ, through whom this blessed Spirit comes from the Father.

Six Qualities of Christ

These verses then list six qualities of Christ.

(1) 'faithful witness' (cf. John 1:18; John 14:8–9);

(2) 'first-begotten of the dead' (cf. Col. 1:18). This takes us to the two Adams in 1 Corinthians 15:45, 'The first man Adam [the father of all humanity] was made a living soul; the last Adam [Christ] was made a quickening spirit'; to 1 Corinthians 15:23, 'Christ the first-fruits; afterward they that are Christ's at his coming', and to Romans 5:12–21, where we are shown that Adam's sin brought all of us into death, whereas the obedience of Christ brings all who believe into pardon and new life. That is, Christ is the covenant head of a new, resurrection race.

(3) 'Prince of the kings of the earth'. Christ is the head over all human government, as we see in Ephesians 1:10–11, 'That in the dispensation of the fullness of the times, he might gather together in one all things in Christ, both which are in heaven, and which are in earth; even in him…who worketh all things after the counsel of his own will.'

(4) Christ's infinite love: 'Unto him that loved us and washed us from our sins in his own blood…' (v. 5). Elsewhere, John explains that 'the good shepherd giveth his life for the sheep' (John 10:11). How can we human beings be sure that we are loved? Many seem to spend a furiously active lifetime seeking it, and die disappointed and sad. Paul answers this question of supreme importance to us all, that the Father 'spared not his own son, but freely delivered him up for us all' (Rom. 8:32). This divine, and therefore truly infinite love, has made us 'kings and priests unto God' (v. 6). Exodus 19:5 and 6 give us the background: 'Now therefore, if ye will obey my voice indeed, and keep my covenant, then ye shall be a peculiar treasure unto me above all people: for all the earth is mine: And ye shall be unto me a kingdom of priests and an holy nation…'

Simon Kistemaker in his fine *Exposition of the Book of Revelation* shows how Revelation 1:6 expands and deepens the words of Exodus 19:

Jesus' kingdom differs from a worldly kingdom, as he told Pontius Pilate (John 18:36). He has citizens in every area, sector, and segment of life. These citizens seek to live obediently by the rules of Christ's kingdom: they pray for those who are in authority and conduct themselves peaceably in godliness and holiness (1 Tim. 2:2). They demonstrate the love of the Lord Jesus by helping the poor and feeding the hungry (Matt. 25:37–40); they defend the rights of the disadvantaged (Deut. 24:17; 1 Tim. 5:16); they care for needy people (Gal. 6:10); and they proclaim and teach the gospel of Jesus Christ (Matt. 28:19–20). As citizens of the kingdom, they testify to the present reign of Jesus in the world today. Christ's followers, who make up his kingdom, honor him as Lord of hosts and King of Kings and utter their daily prayer, 'May your kingdom come' (Matt. 6:10; Luke 11:2).[5]

Two other qualities of the risen Lord are given to us in Revelation 1.

(5) His soon-coming vindication of his suffering church (v. 7). Later, we must deal with this question of the meaning of 'soon'.

(6) This Christ whom John saw is of the same being as God Almighty (v. 8). Here his eternity, Godhead and power are proclaimed, and we shall in future chapters explore these issues. Hence, this risen Son of God is the key to future world history. That is the message of this introduction to Revelation.

THE GLORIOUS APPEARANCE OF CHRIST

Jesus appears to the Apostle John, who seems to have been in a sort of concentration camp on the Isle of Patmos (off the coast of present day Turkey). No doubt, Jesus was unexpected. John found him in the place of duty and suffering, and that is where we usually find Jesus. We are less likely to find him in the dramatic and pleasant, but in the humdrum path of duty, the Lord has a way of showing up when we least expect him.

Significantly, the risen Christ appears on the Lord's Day; the Christian Sabbath. (The Jewish Sabbath, which took place on the last day of the week was changed to the first day of the week; the first day of the new creation as opposed to the old creation, whose last day, the day of rest, was on Saturday). That is because Jesus was raised on the first day of the week. John was 'in the spirit on the Lord's Day' (v. 10). In the place of worship on the Christian Sabbath, the Lord's Day, we normally find the Lord manifesting himself to his seeking people.

To understand Revelation, one has to interpret Christ's appearance to John (v. 12–16) not literally (like an exact photograph), but symbolically (in terms of the Old Testament symbols used to express divine realities). It is impossible for John to express a heavenly appearance on earth in exact human proportions, so he uses the comparative term 'like' (e.g. v. 13—'like the son of man') to convey the reality he saw. Here we think of Paul's inability to describe just what he saw in heaven (cf. 1 Cor. 12:4).[6]

The Surroundings

First, John saw the surroundings, rather than the divine speaker (v. 12).

The Seven Golden Lampstands. In particular he saw the seven golden lampstands. This is reminiscent of Zechariah 4:2: 'Behold a candlestick all of gold with a bowl upon the top of it, and his seven lamps thereon, and seven pipes to the seven lamps, which are upon the top thereof…' The sevenfold candelabra in the Jewish tabernacle and temple, seems to follow the general biblical sense of seven as equaling completeness. So the point from the imagery is this: the most important place of the shining of the light of God into this dark world takes place in the church. In good time, the light of the risen Christ shining through his church will eventually scatter much of the world's darkness, and lead history in a new, divinely ordained direction.

The Church at the Center of World History. In the surroundings that John saw is an important message about world history that pagans cannot understand (until they are converted): the Christian Church is at the center of everything that God is letting happen in the world scene. The world naturally thinks that only the world they can see of time and space matters. Spiritual realities are either non-existent, or of marginal importance, at best. All else is supposition or perhaps dangerous fanaticism, as the materialist sees it. In fact, the typical humanist may not even realize how blinded he is by his own culture to nearly every area of spiritual reality.

Shortly after the fall of the Berlin Wall in 1989, a recently retired US Naval intelligence official (Rear-Admiral Marmaduke Bayne of Norfolk, Virginia) wrote that the intelligence networks of the West (well-funded and staffed with bright men and women) had been caught unprepared for the downfall of the Wall in 1989, as well as for the theocratic revolution in Iran in 1979, or the political significance of the religious right and the religious left in the 1970s and 80s. Why this blindness by educated, often brilliant people? Rear-Admiral Bayne suggests that the reason is the functional materialism of our culture, which severely discounts the significance of religion in the real world of political realities, whether of national or international scope. Because of their blindness to the importance of God and religion, these experts missed some of the most important trends and movements to occur in the world since World War Two.

It would be salutary for the 'enlightened' people, who are blinded to such large swaths of reality by their 'practical atheism', to take seriously what John saw when he gazed with awe upon the risen Lord walking in the midst of the light he gave to his churches. From Him, through them, light is to come to the rest of the darkened, fallen world culture.

The Person in the Midst of the Lampstands
Next, John's view moves from the surroundings (of the divinely illuminated lampstands) to the Person who is speaking to him: 'And in the midst of the seven candlesticks one like unto the Son of man...' (Rev. 1:13a). This indicates that the churches are full of light, only because the risen Lord himself (the source of natural light, intellectual light, and saving, soul-transforming light) is walking in their midst.

The Son of Man. This term 'Son of Man' so often used of Christ in the Gospels, comes from Daniel 7:13–14, where he is prophetically shown to have 'a kingdom that all people, nations and languages should serve him: his dominion is an everlasting dominion, which shall not pass away, and his kingdom that which shall not be destroyed.' Elsewhere, Daniel shows him to be the sovereign Master of an indestructible kingdom that is going to crush all others. We read the details of this by prophecy in Daniel 2:35, where he is the stone that smote the proud image of autonomous, humanistic government, crushing it to powder, and in its place 'becoming a great mountain that filled the whole earth.' And in Daniel 7, the four coming world empires are represented under the forms of various wild beasts (i.e. Babylon, Medo-Persia, Greece and Rome), all of which will have 'their dominion taken away' (Dan. 7:12), to be replaced by his everlasting kingdom.

Hence, John would understand that this taking away of humanistic dominion to be supplanted by that of Christ was already beginning to happen. That is, the Rome that placed John in exile and that was killing many in the church during the persecution under Nero, would itself be crushed through the power of the invisible Sovereign, who increases his beneficent reign through his seemingly humble, helpless church.

His Priestly Robe. Then the stunning appearance of the glorified Christ is presented by pictures taken from the Old Testament. He had an ankle-length robe with a golden sash (Rev. 2:13). This recalls the garments of the Jewish High Priest. Christ is the final and ultimate High Priest, whom all the earlier ones imperfectly, but truly, represented. Christ is that great High Priest who gets us through to the blessed Throne of the Father, as we see when—upon the earthquake that occurred at the death of Jesus on Calvary—the veil of the Temple was 'rent in twain', so that access to 'the holiest of all' was now open (Matt. 27:51). His final blood sacrifice fulfilled all of God's holy requirements for the total forgiveness of all sin, so that no other sacrifice will ever be required for sinners who seek his mercy to be eternally pardoned, and to have immediate fellowship with God himself.

His White Hairs. 'his head and his hairs were white like wool, as white as snow...' (Rev. 2:14). Again this bright, shining whiteness takes us back to Daniel, where we see a throne upon which 'the Ancient of days did sit, whose garment was white as snow, and the hair of his head like the pure wool...' (Daniel 7:9). This speaks of antiquity and absolute purity. The one who is in charge of all of the events of the rise and fall of nations is eternal (not subject to the limitations of space and time as are merely earthly kings), and he is absolutely pure in heart and character, so that he is always to be trusted.

His Flaming Eyes. 'his eyes were as a flame of fire' (Rev. 1:14b). That is, his divine vision penetrates beneath the surface, seeing all things precisely as they are in all their complex connections. This is expanded in his later message to the church at Thyatira, where he says: 'I am he which searcheth the reins and hearts...' (Rev. 2:23). This quality of penetrating vision is attributed to the word of God: 'For the word of God is quick and powerful, and sharper than any two-edged sword, piercing even to the dividing asunder of soul and spirit, and of the joints and marrow, and is a discerner of the thoughts and intents of the heart' (Heb. 4:12).

When the Holy Spirit of Christ comes into a worship service, he does this very thing: 'But if all prophesy, and there come in one that believeth not, or one unlearned, he is convinced of all, he is judged of all: and thus are the secrets of his heart made manifest; and so falling down on his face he will worship God, and report that God is in you of a truth' (1 Cor. 14:24-5). And one day from his final judgment throne, he will assess with unfailing accuracy and infinite perception everyone who has ever lived (Matt. 25:31-46). All nations, men, angels and demons will bow before him on that day, and some will cry for the mountains to fall upon them to hide them from the face of him that sitteth on the throne, and from the wrath of the Lamb (Rev. 6:16).

What a privilege you have to be alive and reading these truths about what you must inevitably face! How much better now to cast yourself on the mercy of God, seeking his pardon of your sins through Christ, than screaming for the rocks to hide you on that awful day! Ask God for the grace to bow to Christ voluntarily with all of your heart now. Do not wait until you must bow down out of terror from his flaming, holy presence on the day of judgment against unrepentant sinners, and be sent irrevocably to a place of outer darkness. The gate of his mercy is still open, but do not presume upon it.

His Feet Like Brass. 'his feet [were] like burnished brass, as if they burned in a furnace' (Rev. 1:15). The idea is that of the brightness of his coming to trample underfoot his church's enemies. As the old adage goes, 'the heels of God have lead in them, and are slow in coming. But when they come, they crush completely.' It is a bit like the flashing blue lights of a police car behind us, or the ringing siren of a red fire truck: one must get out of the way! God and his coming judgements seem unreal to us now, but one day that will be the most real thing we ever faced. Nothing else then will matter.

His Voice Like Many Waters. 'his voice was like the sound of many waters' (Rev. 1:15b). John on the rocky coast of Patmos could hear the slam of the rough waves beating on the rocks: loud, clear and powerful. So when the Lord of the church comes in judgement, nothing can resist his coming. This imagery takes us back to Ezekiel 43:2, where the prophet describes the glory of God as many waters: 'and his voice was like the noise of many waters: and the earth shined with his glory.' That voice, preceded by the sound of the angelic trumpet, will literally raise the dead (1 Cor. 15:52). That same voice is still raising the spiritually dead from sin and selfishness into a life in union with God in Christ (John 10:3). The 'many waters' they hear are those of river of eternal life, flowing from the throne of God and of the Lamb (Rev. 22:1).

His Right Hand. John then describes three physical features of the risen Lord: right hand, mouth and face (Rev. 1:16). His right hand holds the seven stars. The right hand is the place of power and protection. Christ occupies this honored place on the throne with his Father (cf. Psalm 110:1; Heb. 1:3). And in Christ's right hand are the seven stars. Stars could be the angels or messengers of the churches. The idea is that Jesus never forsakes his own (for they are in his right hand), even when they pass through 'the valley of the shadow of death'. Every Christian who has died passed through physical death into the fullness of eternal life in the sheltering right hand of God Incarnate.

His Mouth. 'Out of his mouth went a sharp two-edged sword...' (Rev. 1:16). This is not to be taken literally, as though a steel blade protruded from the mouth of the Lord. Rather, it means that Jesus fights his enemies (and those of his church), not with material weapons, but with his word. Ephesians 6:17 speaks of 'the sword of the Spirit, which is the word of God.' This word is constantly going forth with supernatural power to execute judgment and to destroy the works of the evil one. That alone may explain the fierce antagonism to the preaching of the gospel in unbelieving, modernist churches. They feel its sharp power cutting through their falsehood and pretence. One old country preacher in North Carolina once said that the sword of the Spirit which is the Word of God, is the only sword that you can stick into a dead man, and he becomes a living man.

His Bright Face. Revelation 1:16 also mentions the brightness of his face: 'his countenance was as the sun shineth in his strength.' It seems that it was the brightness of the face of the risen Lord who met Saul of Tarsus on the Damascus road that blinded him (cf. Acts 9:1–9). Some have understood Paul's allusions to his eye problems in Galatians to mean that he had continuing ocular problems ever after he saw the brightness of the Lord (cf. Gal. 4:15). One day our eyes shall behold him: either in speechless joy and glory, or in absolute terror.

Christ's Message

In the intense, transcendent light of the presence of the risen God–man, the Apostle literally fell flat on his face at the Lord's feet like a dead man (1:17). This is like the experience of the Prophet Daniel before the holy angel: 'Now as he was speaking with me, I was in a deep sleep on my face toward the ground: but he touched me, and set me upright' (Dan. 8:18). Like the holy angel did to the prostrate Daniel, the Lord tenderly touches John and raises him up. By this touch, Jesus gives him strength to face the future, and utters this command for all Christians, no matter what they have to face: by 'Fear not!' he means, do not concentrate on the scary circumstances: Look at me; I hold the future and every possible circumstance in it!

The Significance of 'I AM'

Then the risen One gives John (and us) a reason why we are never to live our lives in fear: 'I am the First and the Last...' The name Jesus takes—'I am'—recalls the name God gave to Moses at the burning bush, when he commissioned him to tell Pharaoh to let the Israelite slaves go free. 'In whose name shall I tell powerful Pharaoh to do this tremendous thing that will wreck his economy?' asked Moses. God replied: 'I am that I am' (Exod. 3:14). This means: 'I depend on nothing; everything else depends on me.' Thus, Pharaoh, his army, Egypt, the Nile River and the Red Sea all depended directly on the God who was sending Moses.

Christ is the First and the Last

Christ is 'the First', for he was the agent of creation (cf. John 1:3) and now it all 'holds together' in him (Col. 1:15-17). He, therefore, allowed the Roman Empire to rise; it depends on him, and cannot go beyond his specific plans. Roman persecution of the church can go no further than will advance the purposes of the God, 'who loved us and gave himself for us' (Gal. 2:20). This is because our Lord is 'the First' and 'the Last', and so is in charge of everything in between.

We are to focus our hearts on him when bad times come, not on the painful circumstances (as though they were the ultimate factor). No matter what we ever have to face: loss of job, hatred of enemies, betrayal by family members, loss of health, war or even religious persecution, and finally, physical death, the risen Jesus says to every believer exactly what he commanded John, 'Fear not!' Because the One who died for us and rose for us is who he is, we are forbidden to live our lives in fear.

Christ Has the Keys

Revelation 1:18 gives us the key to victory over all our fears: 'I am he that liveth, and was dead; and behold, I am alive forevermore, Amen; and have the keys of hell and of death.' Christ in his office as the agent of creation, by definition has the keys to all reality, including the realm of departed spirits. But more particularly, in his office as Redeemer, he has the keys to hell and to death, for in paying the price of our sins he went into both realms, and conquered them both, 'breaking the gates of brass, and cutting the bars of iron in sunder' (Ps. 107:16). In so doing, he 'spoiled principalities and powers...triumphing over them [in the cross]' (Col. 2:15), and thereafter, 'When he ascended up on high, he led captivity captive, and gave gifts unto men' (Eph. 4:8).

The 'Key keeper' went through death himself, and came back alive forevermore: 'I was dead; and behold, I am alive forevermore.' Death awaits us all, but it holds no ultimate terror for believers, because the once crucified, now risen one, knows how to handle it well on our behalf, having the very keys to it and through it. That is why Hebrews 2:14-15 says, 'that through death he might destroy him that had the power of death, that is, the devil; and deliver them who through fear of death were all their lifetime subject to bondage.' But once we are anchored in the 'love of God shed abroad in our hearts by the Holy Ghost which is given unto us' (Rom. 5:2), that 'perfect love' of the one who showed himself to John, and still comes to those who seek his face by faith, 'casts out fear with its torment' (1 John 4:18).

Rightly Ordered Priorities

When the huge issues of death and eternity are settled, so that the heart is resting in union with the Lord, then terrible issues such as poverty and persecution, are second place, not first place, for he alone 'the first and the last' has the highest priority in our thoughts and affections. That ordering of priorities enabled a suffering, persecuted church to triumph over the mighty empire that sought to stamp it out. The risen Lord has brought down many another evil empire since the fall of Rome. He will continue doing so until at last he gets his church where he wants her to be. The destiny of the church is always controlled by the Lord, not primarily by political and economic orders, however powerful they be. Hence, John teaches us to keep our eyes on this risen Christ, who has the keys, especially when the world around us is hostile to those who own his lordship.

John is instructed 'to write the things which thou hast seen, and the things which are, and the things which shall be hereafter' (v. 19). Since the risen Lord, whom John saw, is in control of all things as the ultimate key keeper, he therefore is in control of all things that will follow, so he reveals enough of the future for John and the church to face every evil of their time with confident assurance of a joyful outcome.

A Message of Pardon to Opposers

This message of pardon and eternal life for all who bow in faith to the risen Lord goes out with its gracious and glorious offers to the rest of the world through the light of the candlesticks of the churches, for the illumining Christ walks in their midst, and has them in his hands (Rev. 1:20). Through their lives and message, saving light shines on a dark, dying world with the light of life. Many of the persecutors of the church have themselves seen that light, and have been translated 'out of darkness into his marvelous light' (1 Pet. 2:9). What Isaiah foresaw is constantly coming true as Christ shines through his church: 'The people that walked in darkness have seen a great light: they that dwell in the land of the shadow of death, upon them hath the light shined' (Isa. 9:2).

3

THE CHURCH AT EPHESUS

Revelation 2:1–7

Revelation chapters 2–3 are composed of letters to seven important churches in Asia, which is mainly what we call Turkey. The first of these is at Ephesus. Through John, the risen Christ sends them a message that could be summarized with an important question: can lost love be regained?

If a first love grows cold, is it possible to get it back? That has been one of the questions of some of the world's greatest literature, not just the Bible. Think of the classical Greek story, *Homer's Odyssey*, in which the hero Odysseus was away from his wife Penelope for twenty years. They had a baby when he left to go to war with Troy, and when he returned, the baby was a young man. If you have not seen your wife in twenty years and other men had been wanting to marry her because of her wealth and property, could you rekindle a love for her? Can lost love be regained? This passage gives an encouraging answer. We note two major points:

1. The significance of the church to history.
2. The covenant structure of the message.

THE CHURCH'S SIGNIFICANCE TO HISTORY

Before addressing the renewal of love, I want to mention the significance of the Church to world history. The first thing we notice is the structure of Revelation. In chapter one you have this glorious vision that John had on the Isle of Patmos of the risen Lord Jesus Christ. In his glorified body, Christ left heaven for a time and showed up on this rocky, wave-beaten island, and John sees him in all his splendor and glory as the risen Lord. Thus, chapter one starts with a vision of the Lord.

In chapters two and three, we find the seven letters or messages to the churches of Christ in many different settings. These settings are so various that every church in the world across history will find something of themselves in one (or all) of these seven historic churches of Asia.

Only after you have looked at Christ in chapter one and the seven churches of Asia in chapters two and three, can you move to world history in chapter four. The very structure of this book—God's last chapter in history—is in itself highly instructive. It teaches that Christ is first in the entire cosmos, and thus, of first importance in all history. He is of utmost importance when you think about the future and what history means, when you think about what your life means, and where you are going to end, where any and every nation is going to end. To make sense of it all, you start with Christ; you end with Christ.

The next thing Revelation leads us to consider is what world history really means. What about the rise and fall of nations; the economies, banks, and the military; politics, wars and peace? These are important questions that occur to all God's image bearers because they dwell in this constantly changing world. What is God going to do next? Where will it all end?

Christ, the Key to World History
The structure of Revelation gives us the right approach to such questions. Before God takes you to the details of world history, he first shows you the risen Christ. And in that light, he makes you go by way of the Christian church. The clue to world history is that the most important thing God is ever doing at any stage in history is preparing his church for what he wants it to be. So unless we pay attention to God's working in the church, we cannot understand the meaning of all the other things going on throughout history.

One of the oldest writings that comes from the Christian church is a strange little book called *The Shepherd of Hermas*, which has this line in it: 'The world exists for the Church'. It does not mean the world is unimportant, but that the world is serving a higher purpose that the world does not even know about. This world is to be the nursery and the training ground out of which God will draw the church together for his final purpose on earth.

This is confirmed if you look in the last two chapters of Revelation, which speak about the marriage supper of the Lamb. That is a way of saying that all history is a preparation for the greatest event of history, which will be when Christ returns in his power and glory, raises the quick and the dead, and divides the sheep from the goats in final judgment. He takes them to the new heavens and new earth where there is the most wonderful ceremony that ever occurred, which every other ceremony is looking forward to; the marriage supper of the Lamb. It is as if the rest of history is the dressing room for the bride.

You would not expect the writer of a text book on world history to know that (unless it is written from a specifically Christian perspective). Yet though it is generally unknown by the intellectual leadership, you will never make sense of world history unless you see that the development of the Church is the key to it. Everything that happens—all the wars, all the empires waxing and waning, rising and falling, every kind of change and movement whatsoever—makes sense when we see that God was using all of world history to get his church ready to be the bride of his Son.

You might object, 'Isn't that taking things too far?' No, because we remember what we see in Revelation 4:11: 'Thou art worthy, O Lord, for thou hast created all things, and for thy pleasure they are and were created.' God created the material universe, the stars, the various constellations such as the Big Dipper and the Little Dipper. From the stars down to the moths, from the elephants to microbes, from the mountains and seas down to the soil composition of the smallest field—all races, all people, God has created them through the agency of Christ for his pleasure.

The Father's Gift to His Son
The best gift from the Father to his Son is an exquisitely beautiful bride—the church. So everything that is happening, (if we can understand it from the viewpoint of the goal and end of all world history), is the tender and costly shaping: the calling, quickening, justifying and sanctifying of the church to be the immaculate bride of Christ on the last day of history. The work of God in the church is the only thing that can make sense of what God is doing in the big

picture of the world. From the perspective of Revelation, the church is the prime factor for understanding the meaning of the past, present and future of world history.

Covenant Structure of the Message

These seven letters within the bigger letter of Revelation have what scholars call a covenant structure.[7] If you look at the form of the letters to these seven churches, starting with Ephesus and going down through Laodicea, you will find a definite structure, based on what is called a covenant. We find covenant structures throughout the Bible. For instance, if you look at Deuteronomy 8 or 28, you find a specific covenant structure (related to 'Suzerainty Treaties' of the ancient Middle East). The covenant structure is similar to the Ten Commandments in Exodus 20, where the Lord says 'I am the Lord thy God, therefore thou shalt have no other gods before me'. God identifies himself and then he speaks to his people and thereafter, he lays the requirements upon them and gives warnings and promises.

Israel, the covenant people of God in the Old Testament, is fulfilled in the church as God's covenant people after Christ becomes Incarnate, atones for our sins, rises from the dead, and pours out his Holy Spirit at Pentecost. I shall speak later of how God still has a future for ethnic Israel, who will once again be engrafted into the Church before the end of time. But for the present, it will be sufficient to think of how the biblical concept of covenant is the structure of the life of Old Testament Israel and the New Testament Church.

One scholar called a covenant 'a bond in blood, sovereignly administered'.[8] A covenant is a relationship that God sovereignly sets up to make us his people, so that we are saved by his grace, and live thereafter, as enabled by his Spirit, in terms of his holy character (as in Jeremiah 31:31-4). In this relationship he gives us stipulations: requirements of obedience, with promises and warnings. He alone is sovereign, but we his creatures, are responsible.

We find elements of this structure in all seven letters to the churches of Asia. Ephesus is the first. Generally, there are five parts of the covenant structure, although some do not have that many parts. We are going to look at these five things.

1. Identity of the Covenant Lord

The first element of the covenant structure is that the Lord identifies himself (Rev. 2:1). He says, 'this is who I am', as he does in Exodus 20. 'I am the Lord thy God'; therefore I give you these commandments because they are reflections of who I am in my character.' In much the same way here, the risen Lord starts off his message by showing the church who he is.

Each of the seven letters takes a different aspect of the risen Jesus from chapter one. Interestingly, Jesus shows each one of them something different by his appearance to John in his resurrection glory. Why was it that Christ would take just one aspect of himself and show it to that particular church, and then to another church several miles away in a different historical and cultural setting, he showed them a different side of himself? Then, he would go down the road another thirty miles and show them something yet different about himself. Why each particular focus? Christ focuses on one aspect of who he is, because he knows that is what that local church needs to know about him more than anything else.

What Christ Shows of himself to Ephesus. What he focuses on for the church at Ephesus is himself holding in his hand seven stars and walking in the midst of the seven candlesticks. We have already looked at that symbolic language. The stars are either the seven churches or the leadership of the seven churches who represent the church. They are in the Lord Jesus Christ's right hand. Remember the song that was popular in the late fifties, 'He's Got The Whole World in his Hands'. What he is saying here is, 'I've got the church in your perhaps dangerous historical situation in my hands and I am walking in the midst of the seven candlesticks (including yours).'

Those candlesticks represent the church and the flame is the life of Christ shining through the lives of the people. Jesus is moving amidst those candlesticks and he chooses to give his light to the world through the church. I do not doubt that God could do it some other way, for who can limit what God can do? Yet, the scripture says the Jews were to be a light to the nations, to the Gentiles. In the New Testament form of the people of God (the Christian church), God does not shine his saving light directly on the pagans. Rather, he has chosen to shine his light on the pagans through the lives of Christians; the true believers. That is what the risen Jesus wants Ephesus to remember above everything else: they are in his hands and under his protection on the one hand, and on the other hand that the light they have to reflect in a pagan society comes from Him.

We think that modern America and Europe are difficult, and they are. Over the last century our Western society has declined a great deal, yet it still is a picnic compared to what the Ephesian Christians had to endure in their pagan culture. Jesus is saying that you have all the light that the dark and corrupt world needs. You have all the light to transform lives if you will remember that the light comes from Him and stay close to Him.

The Risen Christ Holds the Churches in his Hand. Remember that the risen Christ is always holding his church, that is, the true believers, in his hand in every generation. This was true then, and it is equally true now. Jesus teaches that the Lord has his people in his hand and nothing can take them out of it (John 10). You have the absolute security of being a true believer. You are in the hand of the omnipotent, sovereign, majestic God. For something to get you out of God's favor and make you miss eternal life, it would have to be a power greater than God himself. There is no such power.

The devil and all of his imps and demons out of hell are creatures. They are more powerful than we are, but they are infinitely less powerful than God. Jesus is reminding the Ephesians, who have grown cold on him, that they are in his loving hands of infinite, wonderful protection.

Solzhenitsyn's Experience. We have seen this truth carried out in some of the worst situations of the twentieth century. Christ's continuing care of his elect people enabled Alexander Solzhenitsyn, the Russian novelist, to do things of world-shaping significance, particularly as he courageously showed the horrors of Communism, and helped to bring it down. He was a convinced Marxist, a bright intellectual, and a member of the Communist party. He never understood why, but the Communist authorities had him imprisoned, though he was loyal to them. They deported him to the frozen waste of a Siberian concentration camp. If that were not bad enough, he then developed cancer and they put him in their cancer ward. In that ward, he met a young medical doctor who was a real Christian. He got to know and respect this doctor who was dying of cancer. The Russian author experienced the breaking apart of his world view when he saw the beauty of Christ in that dying doctor. He saw his face, his bravery, joy and peace. In a word, Solzhenitsyn saw God's love in this young man, and he was converted. It was the plan of God that Solzhenitsyn survived through the cancer; he was healed and lived until 2008. Eventually he was deported from Russia, and lived for several years in the United States, from which he returned home to Russia after the collapse of communism. His powerful witness continues.

That is a picture of the church even under persecution; this man's experience is a picture of how we are in the hand of God in concentration camps and cancer wards. He did not feel he was in the hand of God, but he was. When God came into his life under the worst circumstances, he used him to be a prophet to the twentieth century. Jesus said, 'I've got the stars in my right hand.'

What Ephesus Needed to See of Christ. The risen Jesus is speaking to the Ephesians. They were part of the Roman Empire, in which persecution was being unleashed by imperial proclamation, putting them in great danger. Naturally, they would ask, when will they get us? Jesus was saying something like this: 'Yes, you are in the church at Ephesus, which is under the temporal authority of Rome, but you are in a higher hand. It is invisible, but it is a hand that is able to control the machinations of the Roman Empire.' That is the hand of Christ.

Why would Jesus have picked out this aspect of himself in chapter one to tell the Ephesians in chapter two? Was it because they were growing cold in their devotion to Him? Nothing will rekindle love better than realising how kindly someone has treated you, or how much they care for you. Even unbelievers appreciate the love of a mother, a good father, or a bountiful neighbour.

Jesus is essentially saying, 'Look, you believers are getting cold on me, but consider what I am doing for your church. You are in my hands and nobody can get you out. I am in charge of it all, and you can absolutely depend on me'.

The next thing that he mentions is that Jesus is walking in the midst of the lampstands. 'I am the light of the world', said Jesus in John's Gospel, and he chooses to shine his light into this world through men and women of faith.

2. The Stewardship of God's People

Next we focus our attention on the stewardship of God's people at Ephesus. Their Lord is surveying the situation beneath the surface. His assessment shows two positive factors and one negative.

Hard Work. The Lord appreciates hard work and the believers at Ephesus were hard workers (v. 2–3). For his name and character, they had done great work and made sacrifices to reach out and build a congregation, as they went about among the lost. God does not like laziness, and his Word rebukes it. He never rebukes the Ephesians for laziness, for they had been very zealous.

Purity. A second positive factor is that God appreciated their purity. They were a true, 'Bible believing church'. They stuck to the Word of God; they were not a group of Modernists, who said: 'We will take the parts of Scripture that fit in with the modern world view, and not affirm the other parts.' They would not have watered down the biblical doctrines of creation, election, the incarnation, atonement, and resurrection of Christ, nor his saviorhood as the only way to the Father. They would not soft-pedal the divine call to youth to retain their purity before marriage. They were solid, Bible-believing Christians.

Furthermore, they had dealt faithfully with evildoers and liars, including a group called 'the Nicolaitans'.[9] Many scholars think that this group may have been trying to merge Christianity with pagan religions. But the sound Ephesian Church would have none of this religious syncretism.

As other religions take root in the Western world through the intermingling of populations, the Christian church may be under pressure to tone down the differences between Christianity and religions, such as Islam. A new religious syncretism seems to some the best way to preserve peace in an increasingly apostate Europe and America, which have seen migrations of Muslims and many others. It will come as no surprise if Christian evangelistic efforts towards lost people in other religions are considered unpatriotic trouble-making by the cultural elite, whose only concern is economic and political power.

The Ephesians, to their credit, did not go along with the first century forms of that sort of thing. That was a positive factor in the Lord's assessment of that Church. They worked hard and stayed true to the foundations of the faith.

Negative Assessment. Like an excellent diagnostician, the Lord, points out a serious negative. He considers it a deep problem that needs urgent attention. Something is drastically wrong in their heart and they must deal with it immediately. It is not the kind of diagnosis one likes to receive, but they must act while there is still time.

He says, 'You have lost your first love' (v. 4). 'You have been getting cold on me'. They had lost the early zeal of their conversions or maybe their parents' zeal. At one time the church at Ephesus had been full of love for God and for his people. Paul spent three years in Ephesus (Acts 20), which is probably why the church was so solid and did not cave in to liberalism or to moral compromise.

There is a touching scene in Acts 20, when Paul was going to see them for the last time on his way to Jerusalem. From there he was convinced he would be carried to prison in Rome and be beheaded. He called for the Ephesian elders to come down to the shore at Miletus to meet with him, so that he could give them closing words of exhortation. They all knelt down on the shore and prayed together and Luke says that they were weeping with great sorrow because they would never see his face again, at least not in this world.

Signs of Losing One's First Love. These people did have great love for God and his apostles, but it had slipped away. They had backslidden. Do you know that this could happen to a conservative Evangelical who would never tolerate the unbelief of Modernism? I have known of men, who would stand on the floor of a Presbyterian Assembly and fight hand, tooth, and nail any Liberalism creeping into the church. They are to be honored for it; there is a time to stand up and speak out. That is good, yet if you are in close quarters with them and know something about their personal and familial situation, you may realize that something has gone from their lives.

Fragrance, sweetness and zeal for soul winning has gone. They wanted to keep everything technically correct, but they lost something precious. The spiritual power and divine presence is not completely gone, but it is burning very low, as evidenced by a lack of sweetness and drawing power in them, so that you know they have lost something. I have seen that in the ministry. Maybe the hurtfulness of a difficult church situation led them to the point of despair and finally to cynicism (which is often a sort of retreat to the possibility of being hurt again).

One sign of backsliding is loss of zeal for reaching out to others. I have known of situations where an older minister, a once zealous evangelical conservative, has become cool on the Lord and lost zeal for winning souls (or sharing his true life with others). A younger minister will come to the area on fire for Christ and the older minister will speak disparagingly of his zeal. They imply: 'Given time, you will cool off and not rock the boat, for after all, I learned better.'

Our prayer for young ministers who are on fire for the Lord must always be: 'Lord help him never to cool off.' Cooling off and becoming 'an arm's length professional' is a loss of first love, a sign of backsliding. It usually goes along with a decrease in sacrificial giving of time and money—safeguarding one's wallet, a rubber band around the check book, or cutting down the numbers of zeros we write in a check for missions or for poor people. We did not even think of doing these things when we were filled with a fervent love for Christ. Then we realized what we were to him, that we were in his hand and his light was in us, and how gladly did we give.

Another sign of losing first love is finding fault with others and announcing those faults rather than getting on one's knees with love that covers a multitude of sins and praying for them. That is one of the surest signs of backsliding in an otherwise solid Christian person. Such backslidings of otherwise true believers occur because they no longer feel the power of Christ's death for them, the beauty or his love for them, and the exquisite care that God has for them.

3. A Covenant Requirement and Solution

We notice a third thing, the covenant requirement (v. 5a). In it, God offers a solution. This wonderful God reveals the negative, but at the same time, he also mercifully gives the solution. He is not out there to hurt these people. 'He does not afflict willingly nor grieve the children of men' (Lam. 3:33). He offers a way out. The negative is only in order to a greater positive. The solution, given in one word, is a commandment which has glorious healing in it. The 'healing commandment' is a simple, imperative verb: 'Remember.'

Remembrance is the Key for Returning to Blessing. That is good news. If we have gotten out of the place of blessing, we can get back to the center of it, if we will but remember. That is how you recover a first love that has grown cold. Remember. This remembrance, calls to mind the Person of Jesus Christ, our loving Savior and Lord: what he has done for us; how he has never ceased to care for us; how he can restore us; how he wants to shine through us. He willingly sacrificed everything for us by his death in our place on Calvary; he rose again for us, ascended to the Father to make heaven our home, and he and the Father send the Holy Spirit to inhabit us for time and eternity. That kind of remembrance brings the power from heaven. It may not come in the feelings first, for usually it goes down deeper into the subconscious, into the deep cavernous chambers of the saved personality, yet the remembrance is like opening a trap door from our dark cellar all the way up into the light of heaven, through which the divine fire streams and begins to warm us. As you remember, a higher power sets you on fire to do the first works. That power is God in his gospel.

Such remembrance is found in 1 Corinthians 15, where Paul talks about the resurrection and the glorious life that lies ahead. He tells them what to remember: 'Christ was crucified for our sins according to the scriptures and was raised according to the scriptures…and was seen of five hundred'. Such remembering of the crucial truths of the gospel is a divinely appointed way to keep us connected with Christ's resurrection power.

4. God's Covenant Warning

Fourth, is the covenant warning (v. 5b). He solemnly warns that if we do not remember and have our first love rekindled, then 'he will come and remove our candlestick'.

In Revelation, sometimes God's coming means the second coming at the end of time. But there are times when 'coming' means that Christ is coming in historical judgements (before the final coming on the Last Day). The context of each passage must show us what kind of coming he means. Here he says: I will come quickly and remove you from the living churches, so all opportunity for renewal is finished.

This book does not tell us what happened to the church at Ephesus in later history. But we know from early Christian history that there was a wonderful bishop, Ignatius of Antioch, who about fifty years after this was written, was on his way to be martyred and during which journey he wrote letters to several churches. Some of these letters were sent to the same churches that are mentioned in Revelation. Among these ancient letters of Ignatius is one to the Church at Ephesus.

From what this good bishop says, something wonderful had happened at Ephesus. They had regained their first love. They were back in the center of God's blessings. Is that not something? They had accepted the rebuke; they were realistic about how far down they had slipped, how cold they had grown. They remembered the Lord; they remembered Calvary and the empty tomb; they remembered the Holy Spirit and the fire came back down in force into they lives, bringing them back to the place of blessing. Apparently, the Church at Ephesus lasted until the conquest of the Turks in the late Middle Ages. Their remembrance of the Lord kept them alive for hundreds of years.

What is going to happen to the church in China? It is going to depend on how well the believers remember Christ. He will handle the harsh circumstances around his people in China as the Church keeps its heart focused on the Lord. What is going to happen to the church in America with all of its secular humanism and materialism, with the rotting corruption of so much of its popular culture, and the near atheism of many of its schools and media? What is going to happen does not depend on what the pagans can do to us; it never does. It depends on whether the believers remember and the remembering becomes an open door into heaven through which the holy fire falls, rekindling their first love.

5. God's Covenant Promise

Then, finally, note the covenant promise, 'I am going to give you access to the tree of life' (v. 7). This image is taken from the Garden of Eden in Genesis 3, yet what is said here is, happily, its opposite. Our first parents after their sin were expelled and thus not able to eat of the tree of life. Here is how it is different. Jesus is the tree of life. In this world, as we believe his gospel, we come to him and we eat and live. He puts abundant and eternal life into us. After that, the more we remember him and his grace, the more we give ourselves up to it, the more sense of the presence of Jesus we have, and the more we begin to experience the reality of the heaven to come. This Christ-focused life engenders by its constantly remembering, a greater devotion to the Lord, and along with it, an increasing generosity and compassion to the people around us. In that sense, we already begin to partake of the tree of life, of him who said 'except ye eat my flesh and drink my blood, ye have no life in you' (John 6:53). When he is restored to his rightful place in our affections, it is certain that one day we will see him 'face to face' and 'we shall be like him; for we shall see him as he is' (1 John 3:2). God's message to the Church at Ephesus shows that we truly can regain our first love.

4

THE CHURCH AT SMYRNA

Revelation 2:8–11

Several years ago there was a best selling book written by a Jewish rabbi, a liberal thinker, as I remember, but his book seemed to strike a cord of response in the American people, so that it sold in large numbers. It was entitled, *Why do Bad Things Happen to Good People?* I could not accept the answer he gives, but he raised a good question and dealt with that important issue.

You will not find a better answer to that question than what the risen Lord Jesus Christ says to the suffering church in Smyrna. It was one of the best churches ever and it went through some of the toughest times. We learn much about what God may be doing in our lives and in the lives of those we know who are going through heavy waters as we look at this risen Lord Jesus Christ giving insight and encouragement to the suffering Christians in Smyrna.

We note three points from Revelation 2:8–11:

1. The identification of the covenant Lord: this shows them who he is (Rev. 2:8).
2. The covenant assessment of the church, shows them where they are and helps them understand what is happening (Rev. 2:9).
3. He gives them a covenant promise, or grant, a great encouragement (Rev. 2:10–11).

IDENTIFICATION OF THE COVENANT LORD

In all of these churches to which Jesus is speaking, the first thing Jesus says to them is 'look at me'. We were already given an amazing description of the risen Christ in the first chapter. Now in each of the seven churches, he takes one aspect of what he looked like, and then he emphasizes that aspect to the situation of the particular church.

What Smyrna Needed to See of Christ

Here, to the church in Smyrna, the side of the risen Christ that John presents to them is Christ's everlasting godness and his victory over death. Why should this particular aspect of who the risen Christ is be pointed out to the Church at Smyrna? He says, 'Look at me and remember what I am like, I am everlasting God and I triumphed over death'. Why did he want to call this to their minds in the crucible of suffering? It was what they needed most because of their difficult situation.

They were under 'tribulation'. The Greek word for it can be translated into English as 'pressure'. We often speak today of stress and pressure, and they were under some of the most severe stress and pressure that humans can experience in this life. The Christians there in Smyrna had this pressure of tribulation from two sources, and with these in mind, Christ showed them that keeping in mind who he is would give them the ability to handle these two sources of pressure with dignity and with hope.

Sources of Pressure
Let us look at these two earthly trouble makers or sources of pressure and then the one heavenly problem solver. Jesus says, 'the devil shall cast you into prison' (v. 10). Yes, the devil lay behind the pressure, but in our lives the evil one has to use human hands to do his ugly work. You do not normally meet the devil directly, but through other humans or institutions whom he is using.

Pagan Government. Whom was Satan using in Smyrna? One of the two major sources of pressure or tribulation that was causing these believers to suffer so much was the powerful Roman government and the pagan society that supported that government. The pagans in Smyrna had built, many years before, a huge temple in which they literally said, the government is God. They worshipped the Roman Emperor. Many of them looked to the government as the solution to all of their problems and the government liked it that way. They did not like it when Christians said 'the government is not God, there is somebody who stands above the government and we are loyal to the one who stands above the government'.

The clear message of Jesus to Rome and to the pagans who think that the government is the chief end of life, is this: 'I am the first and the last' (v. 8). The Roman emperor is not. In light of the endless ages of God, 'Eternal Rome' is a temporary blip, a mere vapor that rises in the morning and quickly passes away.

Also, in Smyrna was a pagan population who worshipped the pagan false goddess known as Cybele.[10] She was something like what has been spoken of over the years as 'Mother Nature'. The general idea was that from this false goddess, Cybele, (for whom they had a big temple and carried out immoral rituals), from her all humans had sprung. She was their origin.

But Jesus is the sovereign agent of creation. (John 1:3). He is the creator of all human life, as well as of the whole cosmos. Everyone springs from his activity, and not from 'Mother Nature', or from 'Father Time'. There is no such thing as 'Mother Nature', there is no such thing as 'Father Time'. The Lord Jesus Christ is the agent of creation. He alone is in charge and deserves our loyalty. Jesus tells the Christians not to worry too much about those pagans in Smyrna, with their impressive temples and well-attended, immoral rituals. Soon enough, because they worship idols, they will lose everything they have: soul and body. 'You believers in the Church in Smyrna, though you are heavily oppressed by the Roman government and the pagan idol worshipers; you are already on the winning side and it will not be long until it all gloriously changes for you.'

Unbelieving Judaism. The second source of tribulation or pressure against the believers in Smyrna was the unbelieving Jews who were active in encouraging the Roman government, wherever they lived, to persecute, and even to kill, those who followed Jesus. The Jews in Smyrna were in league with the pagans (v. 9). This Jewish encouragement of the Romans to persecute Christians is part of a larger pattern. Many passages in Acts indicate this. In a particular part of Greece, the unbelieving Jews actually went to the pagan authorities (Acts 14:2-6), and said 'these Christians are disloyal and dangerous. They deserve to be punished by the Roman state.'

What a devastating charge the risen Christ levels against the persecuting Jews of those days! He accuses them of belonging to 'the synagogue of Satan' (v. 9). The way they were acting here was in line with the attitude of the Pharisees, who had long been their leaders. Remember from the Gospels how the Pharisees could not deny that Jesus was doing miracles. He was causing the blind to see and the lame to walk. Finally, he raised Lazarus from the dead. The raising of Lazarus was what brought on the crisis leading to Jesus' crucifixion. The Pharisees were superb Old Testament scholars (at least of the letter, though not of the spirit or meaning). They should have known that those miracles that Jesus was doing were the fulfilments of Old Testament prophesies as to what the Messiah would do when he came to earth. Hence, they should have bowed to him and acknowledged him as Messiah and Lord.

What did they do? They willfully rejected the objective evidence. They argued that he was doing it by the help of the devil, and finally they set out to kill Christ. After he was raised from the dead, they could no longer get at him, so they sought to kill his followers to avoid the need to change their lives by admitting their sin and bowing before him as Savior and Lord.

Whenever a person denies the evidence they are given as to who Jesus Christ is as God and Savior, and will not accept it, but attributes it to the devil, God says that they belong to Satan. Now in the face of these unbelieving and persecuting Jews in Smyrna, the risen Lord Christ shows himself to be the God whom the true Jews had worshiped in the Old Testament.[11]

Look at Christ

The words the Lord uses, 'I am the first and the last' (Rev. 2:8), are used of God Almighty: 'Thus saith the LORD the King of Israel, and his redeemer the Lord of hosts; I am the first, and I am the last; and beside me there is no God' (Isa. 44:6).

But Christ adds even more encouragement to that part of the church at Smyrna, which will soon be thrown into jail and perhaps be killed (see 2:10, which speaks of being 'faithful unto death'). The risen One does so by adding a phrase to what Isaiah said about him as 'the first and the last': 'I am he which was dead and is alive' (v. 8). Jesus is saying something like this: 'I am going to allow the forces of evil enough rope so that they will take some of you, my most beloved children, and throw you in the jail, from which some of you will not come out alive. You will be taken to the chopping block. But do not worry', says Jesus, 'I do not ask you to go anywhere that I did not go, nor do I ask you to go even one step alone. I have passed through the territory of death already. I have taken all of its terror away for believers. Now, the only thing that awaits you on the other side of death is holding my hand as we walk together into the new beauties of resurrection joy.'

So the risen Christ identifies himself to these good people, to whom were happening some bad things. The main aspect of his character that he shows them here is this: no matter how pressurized, or even how terrible are your circumstances at present, the first thing that Christ will say to us is, 'Look to me, remember who I am for you, remember what I have done for you, concentrate on me and then these difficulties and pressures will relax their grip on your spirit and you will have a poise and ability to face tomorrow with more than human confidence. Look at me, I am the covenant Lord, "the first and the last"; the one who went victoriously through death with you in mind: remember me in times of trouble and immense pressure.'

A Covenant Assessment of Smyrna

In verse 9, the risen Lord says 'Now here is where you are; I know exactly what you are going through'. I have sometimes perceived over the years that when some suffering or anxious person comes to you for 'advice', what they really want is for some Christian to listen to them, so that he or she may know where they are and what it is like. That is all they need and it may be harder for us to give the troubled one a listening ear than we think, but let us follow Jesus, who in this ninth verse is saying: 'I know exactly the pot of boiling water that you are in. I understand it fully and I care, and I am involved in this trouble'. That is the main thing that all of us often need. How tenderly the Lord does that here!

No Criticism of Smyrna

Smyrna is one of the two churches of the seven churches of Asia that is offered no criticism whatsoever by the one whose eye penetrates hidden motives in the deepest place in the heart. This Jesus, now glorified, has nothing but praise for these suffering ones. What an honor! Five of the other churches are given frank and sometimes stern criticism, but not Smyrna.[12]

Christ honors them for three things: for their works, for their tribulation, for their poverty! We do not usually think of the last two, as being honors, do we? Anyone might think of good works as being an honor, but how many people normally think that it is an honor to pass through tribulation? And who in the world, particularly in our rich, materialistic society, normally thinks that being in poverty for the faith is an honor?

On the contrary, we have many people teaching that if everything is not going right for you; if you are not healthy and prosperous, then you do not have faith. Well, here is the Biblical answer. Listen to the risen Christ: 'I honor you greatly; I have nothing but praise for you because of your works, because of this tribulation that you are in, and because of the poverty that being faithful to me has caused you presently to experience'. Should the modern Church not honor those whom Christ most honors? How dare anyone accuse them of lacking faith, when they are living in poverty out of self-sacrificial love to Jesus and to the needy? Those who use aspects of Christianity for selfish gain are the ones who lack faith! One can only hope and pray that before it is too late, they will meet that 'Man of sorrows', through 'whose stripes we are healed' (Isa. 53:3-5).

The works of the believers in Smyrna obviously implies their zeal for doing good, for getting the gospel out, for helping others, for letting the rest of Smyrna know who Jesus really was by the way they lived their daily lives, including their responses even to those pressures. The people in Smyrna were finding out what Christ was like, through these self-sacrificial people, who were motivated by a higher power that simply could not be explained away in human terms. It was the sort of thing that forced a change of 'world view' on many of those who saw it.

No Escape from All Tribulation

'Tribulation' or 'pressure' was upon them every way they turned. It is not a true doctrine of the Bible that the church will be taken away before great tribulation comes on her. Smyrna was not raptured out of tribulation. Jesus said something else about tribulation here. Smyrna flourished with good works, holy lives and victorious testimonies in the midst of tribulation.

A famous evangelical tract of many years ago, said 'Out of the presses of pain cometh the soul's best wine'. Part of the immense pressure on these

Christians in Smyrna was economic poverty. That never feels good. Possibly Christians had been fired from their jobs or had their businesses boycotted, resulting in no salary or meagre wages. They were probably unable in many cases to purchase goods at the grocery store or its ancient equivalent. Perhaps many of them had to move from decent housing to tiny, dingy apartments or slum houses, with little to eat, few necessities, and no luxuries. They were poor, not because they were lazy or unintelligent, but simply because of their identification with Jesus. How proud he was of them. A good question today would be: who within our churches is Jesus most proud of? We gladly leave that assessment to him alone. But we may have a clue when he says that 'many that are first shall be last, and last first' (cf. Matt. 19:30).

I have seen this kind of thing in Romania and Ukraine. Christians up until the communist regime unraveled in 1991, had not always been able to study at the universities, which controlled access to many of the good jobs and important positions in those countries. They often could not get into the university when it was found out that they were Christians, as long as the Communists were in charge of it. Many devout Soviet Christians were given low paying jobs, and not infrequently, the breadwinners in the family were arrested on trumped up charges and jailed, leaving behind impoverished wives and hungry little children in depressing, cramped apartments.

That is probably what it was like to some degree in Smyrna, but through it all, these suffering Christians who were held back economically because they loved the Lord, were given something more beautiful than any treasure in this world. They were radiant with the light that comes from the face of the risen Christ; they were bearing the fruit of the Spirit from a higher world (love, joy, peace, self-control, etc.). The more they were pruned, the more luscious fruit they bore; making their lives things of rarest beauty. (Jesus reminds us of this process of pruning in John 15).

Three Truths about Christian Suffering

Never Alone. Christians never suffer alone. They may feel alone; they do not see the Divine presence, and that is part of the pain, but they must remember that Jesus said, 'Look at me in your suffering. Do not be distracted by your grief or by those who cause it; look at me, for you are not alone.' The Christ of Calvary is in the midst of a believer's pain, secretly strengthening them and getting them through it. It is a God who has suffered, who went through the most exquisite pain; he understands us and comes to us at such times and never will allow us to suffer alone. 'In all of their afflictions he was afflicted' (Isa. 63:9).

Never Fruitless. Christians never suffer without fruit being produced by their suffering: good fruit, beautiful results, either in their own lives or in the lives of others. The risen Christ uses their wounds, sorrows, and pressures somehow to shine out. This divine shining out is invisible to us; we do not know how he is doing it, when he is doing it, to whom he is doing it, but he is doing it. He shines out with a certain power and grace and glory; sometimes to unbelieving eyes, or to weaker Christians, transforming entire situations. God never wastes any Christian's suffering: not even one tear. As Psalm 56:8 says, 'he collects the tears of the saints in a bottle.'

The Best May Suffer the Most. Sometimes, (though not necessarily all of the time), strong Christians may be called to go through worse circumstances than weak Christians or pagans. Why is it that such spiritual Christians as in Russia, China, and Africa have suffered for the faith so much more during the twentieth century than most Western Christians? No doubt, at least one of the reasons is given to us by Jesus in John 15:2, where he is speaking of the branches abiding in the grapevine: 'Every branch that beareth fruit, God pruneth it, that it may bring forth more fruit.'

Look at the apostles. John who writes this book was exiled in a concentration camp, once or even twice. Peter was crucified upside down. Paul was beheaded in Rome; James the half brother of the Lord was slain with a sword at Jerusalem. Look at some of the Scottish Covenanters in the seventeenth century 'killing times', such as two women, one in her early twenties and the other in her late seventies. They were radiant Christians, who would not give in to the persecuting British government of that period, which wanted them to say that the king was head of the church. Soldiers put them on stakes in the Solway Firth, which has a tide that comes in very fast. As the tide was coming in, the soldiers held them down on the stakes and let the water cover their heads so they could not breathe. Then they would cruelly lift up the stakes and say: 'Admit that King Charles is the head of the church.' These godly women refused, and started singing a penitential Psalm, to the fury of the soldiers, who held them under until they were drowned. It is well for us to remember what they endured.

One could mention countless others. A godly covenanting minister in Edinburgh in the same period of time, James Renwick, had his head and hands cut off and put on a pike in Edinburgh. Later his hands were taken to his father, who was also in prison for the faith. The soldiers said: 'Do you know whose these are?' The noble ministerial father replied: 'They are the hands of my own dear son. Good is the Lord, who will do nothing but good to his children!' How do you explain things like that? This old minister had deep in his heart the truth we find in Revelation 2: God works beautiful things through the sufferings of his children: 'every branch that bears fruit, he prunes it that it may bear more fruit.'

A Covenant Promise
From this gracious covenant grant, there flow two great encouragements to Smyrna, and then one general encouragement to all churches of all ages.

Fear None of these Things
The first encouragement to the suffering Christians in Smyrna is something every believer needs to hear, especially if we are facing serous trouble. Jesus says 'Fear none of these things.' After the September 11th bombing in New York, many throughout the Western world have become aware of the potential disaster that could come to them because of terrorist activity. While it would be foolish to discount this danger, nevertheless, the risen Lord says to all of his people: 'Fear none of those things.'

Why Fear Does Not Predominate the Christian Life
A second encouragement is given in the last part of verse 10, by providing a reason why, if we keep this divine command in mind, we will not be controlled by fear: 'I will give thee a crown of Life.' The one who cannot lie, the one who fills to the fullest every promise, says 'I will give thee a crown of Life.' In other words, one split second past possibly painful death, you will have something so beautiful it will outshine all the treasures of the known world.

A once-popular, rural gospel hymn from the 1950s or 60s said:

> Acres of diamonds, mountains of gold,
> rivers of silver, jewels untold;
> All these together, couldn't buy you or me,
> Peace while we're sleeping,
> or a conscience that's free.

What Jesus has waiting for you far outshines any of that. But here is our problem: because of the materialism of our culture, we tend to think that the only thing that matters is what we can see now, and what we can measure now, as in a test tube or scales in a laboratory. How foolish for us who are embodied spirits to think that the only thing that matters is the body which soon enough we are going to leave anyway! How the Devil has our culture deceived! We give up rivers of eternal pleasure for a shallow cup of temporary water. That was how the pagans of Smyrna were deceived, whereas the Christians there saw through the pretense of the often silly passing world into the lasting beauties of eternity. Thus, Jesus says, 'I will give you a crown of life'.

The Crown of Life. The ancient city of Smyrna (now Izmir in Turkey) had a beautiful hill that was known as 'the Crown', with stately public buildings constructed all around 'the Crown'. This made it appear from the harbor if you came in on a ship, or if you were coming in on camels or horses from the distant plains, like the points of a crown. So Smyrna itself was often called 'the Crown'.[13] But Jesus said to the church in Smyrna, 'I will give you something far more lovely than the Crown of Smyrna. What I give you will shine brightly in endless eternity when all the buildings of Smyrna have mouldered into the dust.'

This crown of life that Jesus has waiting for all of his servants once past the door of physical death is, in a sense, the crowning of life: that which at last makes life completely worth while and fills it with gold. Do not ask God too many questions about your life now: why he let you go through this, why you did not get that, why somebody disappointed you, why this thing did not work out. Do not ask him now; when he crowns you with life, everything that ever happened will be filled with golden meaning, so that you will be praising the Lord, that he led you that way, rather than an easier way.

GREAT ENCOURAGEMENT

Then the generous Lord gives a covenant promise not just to Smyrna, but also to all Christians in all ages, in verse 11: 'he that overcometh shall not be hurt of the second death.' What does this mean? Obviously, the overcoming means standing with Christ by faith, no matter what. Then comes the promise: 'he shall not be hurt of the second death.'

Scripture speaks of two deaths. The first death is physical death, which is the temporary separation of the body and the soul. Even that solemn reality has no terrors for the believer. Through the sacrifice and victory of Christ, physical death has become for us the opening of an invisible door into the glorious presence of our heavenly Father.

But there is a second death immensely to be feared. The second death is that terrible and final separation of body and soul of unbelievers from the living God, so that they are put into the lake of fire. That eternal separation from God has nothing to do with the believer; it can never touch them. So on the other side of this bodily life, the believer has nothing whatsoever to fear. Is that not wonderful? Think of that. What a treasure!

Two Resurrections

Then the scripture speaks of two resurrections. The first resurrection is spiritual. When a sinner believes in Christ, he or she, is raised in their spirit into union with the Lord. You read about that in Ephesians 2:1, 'You who were dead, he hath quickened.' In other translations, you who were dead spiritually, he has resurrected you spiritually. A believer has experienced an internal, inside spiritual resurrection. They are alive with Jesus for evermore. They can never be split from the risen Jesus. That is wonderful. A Christian is a resurrected man or woman in their spirit. That is the first resurrection. Only Christians experience that resurrection.

Then the second resurrection is bodily. When the last trumpet shall sound and the bodies of the saints, and also the bodies of the lost (though for them, it is a resurrection of shame, not of glory—Dan. 12:2), shall come out of the graves and out of the oceans, as their bodies and souls are reunited by the miraculous power of God. The second resurrection is when the reunited body and soul of the believer will be 'forever with the Lord'. You can read about this in John 5:24–9, and also in Revelation 20:6. Revelation 20:6 teaches that the believers at Smyrna and, indeed, all believers, will never be hurt by the second death.

That is, those who are not hurt by the second death are the same who partake of the first resurrection. The true Christian is in every age always a partaker in the first resurrection. We have eternal life, according to John 5:24, and so we cannot, will not, come into judgment. The judgment is the second death of eternal separation of body and soul from God. But this cannot touch us who trust in Christ, because we have passed out of death into life in union with Him, the crucified, risen Lord.

That is all that really matters in the light of eternity for God's people who are presently suffering—'good people to whom bad things are happening'. What matters? To trust Christ, to commit our earthly life and endless future into his care and thus to experience the first spiritual resurrection. Thereby we avoid the only thing really worth fearing: the second death, and at the chosen time, we shall be lifted up body and soul, into the second resurrection, to the lasting glories and beauties of heaven for which this world was really created in the first place. The bad things that happen to good people are less than nothing in light of the ocean of bliss given them in exchange for one drop of suffering. What a generous Christ he is and how well we may trust him.

5

The Church at Pergamos

Revelation 2:12–17

The risen Christ says something to the church at Pergamos, which is not unlike a famous observation of Baron Von Hugel of Germany in the nineteenth century: 'The secrets that God keeps are at least as good as those he reveals'. That is the point made by the letter of Christ to this church at Pergamos. Pergamos, a large city in what is now modern day Turkey, was not too far northeast of the great city of Ephesus. It was a Christian area at one time, until the Muslims took it many centuries later.

Jesus is saying to that church, 'If you will be faithful to me and follow me and avoid the moral compromise with the culture that you are living in, I am going to show you a secret so wonderful that you wouldn't give it up for ten worlds'. The secrets God keeps are at least as good as those he reveals in his Word.

Notice four major points in this covenant letter to the people of God at Pergamos:

1. The covenant identity of the risen Christ: what he looks like, who he is, what he is doing for them (Rev. 2:12).
2. The covenant assessment or examination of that church's spiritual standing (Rev. 2:13).
3. A covenant warning from Christ (Rev. 2:16).
4. A covenant promise or a wonderful grant of a special secret (Rev. 2:17).

Covenant Identity of the Risen Christ

As in all of the letters to the seven churches, Christ says: 'I want you to look at me so that I can show you a particular aspect of who I am.' Here he shows another unique aspect of what he is like to this church.

A Sword From his Mouth

Because of the situation that the Christians of Pergamos were in, and the temptations they felt, Jesus shows them something gloriously significant about himself that he had already shown to John—his identity as the one 'out of whose mouth goes a sharp two edged sword' (1:16), the most powerful weapon in all the world.

In these days of terrorism, much of the world is thinking about suicide bombings and 'dirty bombs'. Though the radical Islamists are a minority, yet they are thought to have access to powerful and deadly weapons. But this sword that goes out of the mouth of the Eternal Son of God is massively superior, supreme in power to the most awful weapons sinners can amass on planet earth. This mighty, spiritual sword is what

Jesus showed the church at Pergamos, which was in a situation of persecution. No doubt, they felt tempted to compromise with paganism to avoid their wrath. In that situation, Jesus says 'Look at me, from my mouth comes the sharp two edged sword of the supernatural power; it is the Word of God by which worlds were created at an instance.'

Maybe this would ring clearly in the ears of the church at Pergamos, for in that place the Roman Emperor (possibly Nero) had constructed a huge temple on the major hill in the city. You can still see its ruins. It was a vast temple to Caesar, whom the pagans of Pergamos (like the whole empire) worshipped as being the final authority on earth. While they looked to the Roman Emperor as the highest power on earth, that did not keep them from worshipping other false gods. Thus Pergamos had several pagan temples, including one to the wine god, Bacchus, whose worship seems to have involved ritual drunkenness. Then there was another god called Asclepius, who supposedly had healing powers, so that his temple was a bit like a hospital.[14] Many sick people would go there, hoping for healing. They would lie down during the night, and allow the priest, who had a basement full of non-poisonous snakes, to have the snakes crawl all over the patients during the night. Supposedly, one might get healed if a snake went across one's body.

They worshipped such false gods as Asclepius and Bacchus, but the top power that they worshipped was the Roman emperor. He claimed to be divine, so he took in Latin the title, *Dominus et Deus*, Lord and God. He claimed that he was God on earth and that he had the final power of the sword. Now that is the issue. It says in Romans 13 that the state 'beareth not the sword in vain'. Human governments do have the legitimate power of the sword, but there is a higher power, a higher sword—God's sword, God's authority over life and death. Rome claimed that they had the final say over life and death, hence they were threatening the Christians that if they did not worship the Roman emperor, they could put them to death. Indeed, they had already killed some of them. Antipas, a Christian to whom they had taken the sword is particularly mentioned (v. 13). One can appreciate the difficulty they were going through.

In such a situation, it would be hard not to wonder: is it worth standing against emperor worship, when they have already killed one of our people? So the risen Christ, to encourage these people and help them get back to basics says, 'I am the one who has all sovereign power in Heaven and on earth'. You remember how Jesus said this before he gave the Great Commission in Matthew 28. 'All power in heaven and on earth is given unto me'. The ultimate sword of authority over life and death comes out of my mouth. Jesus means that although the Roman Empire does have a lesser or subsidiary authority, all of its power is finally under Him. All the sovereign One would have to do would be to speak the word and Rome would be gone forever. The emperor would be dust.

Fear Only God
We know that is what would eventually happen in history. The risen Christ says 'remember who really is in charge. Do not fear the lower powers'. As Jesus said himself in his earthly life in Luke 12, 'Fear not them that can kill the body, but after that have no more that they can do. Rather I say unto you fear him who after death hath power to throw both body and soul into hell. Him, I say, fear'. In other words: fear only God. The devil can motivate people to kill Christians. He is doing it in many parts of the world right now, but the devil has no authority to do anything to your soul

or spirit once you leave this body. Only God can put a person into outer darkness in torment.

So Jesus says that we are to think differently from the worldly people. A worldly person thinks the worst that can happen to you is physical death, that that is the end. It is not the end. It is sobering when we think of our own physical death. Anybody with good sense would feel solemn, but it is not the end, it is just a change—a great change and if you believe in the Lord and trust in God, you have nothing to fear the other side of death. God will take you to the home of happiness, the land of light and joy. It will be fine, so do not live in fear of physical death.

The only thing to fear is being unfaithful to God, who alone is able to get you into heaven and to keep you out of torment. Fear him only, and you will not compromise with paganism. The eye of the Lord is watching you, he is protecting you, and ordering your pathway. Remember that the risen Christ has all power, including the sword wielded by pagan governments.

Covenant Assessment of Pergamos

Before people have serious surgery, the physicians carry out an examination of their internal organs, so as to take corrective action. In a sense, that is what was happening with the church at Pergamos. Jesus shows them their strong points. He shows that in many ways they were in good health. At the same time, he gives a frank assessment of a serious disease in that church, so that they—with his help—could take healing action.

The Lord never criticizes us to hurt us, only so we can take positive action and get things right. Some people live their life gossiping, and seem to take a perverse delight in hurting others. It is a twistedness of spirit; a failure to have appropriated the grace of God for themselves. But the Lord is not like that. Any kind of critique or assessment from the Word of God is not primarily to hurt us. On the contrary, when God pierces us with 'the sword of the Spirit', he is really saying: 'I am going to help you do something about it, if you are willing. It must change; it can be better.' That is what he is saying to this church.

The Strong Point of Pergamos

In this assessment, Jesus honors them for their strong point, which was that they had kept the faith in hard circumstances. They had been faithful even though one of their church members, Antipas, had been hacked to death with a sword because he would not bow down and worship Caesar. They said: 'We believe that Jesus Christ is Lord'. Rome wanted them to say: 'Caesar is Lord.' 'No', they replied, even if it costs us our life, we are going to say that Jesus only is Lord and God. That is our stand. We believe in Christ as our Lord and Savior, we believe in his Word, and that is where we stand whatever it costs us. Jesus greatly honors them for that.

China is a wonderful illustration in modern history of a church like Pergamos. When the Communists took China under Chairman Mao with his great march in 1949, there were about a million Christians in all of China, yet when China opened up, we found out that these Chinese lay people had multiplied to as many as fifty or sixty million believers, with churches still growing every day. If, indeed, there are sixty million Christians now in China, that is a larger number than the population of the British Isles. I am sure the Lord would commend these Chinese Christians as he commended the believers at Pergamos, because they had stood firm when it was very hard to do so.

That raises a serious question. If Jesus Christ the risen Lord has all power in Heaven and on earth, as he says he does, he thereby also has the final power of the sword. If Rome is nothing compared to God, then how was it that he allowed the governmental authorities at Pergamos to slay Antipas with a sword? How do you explain that? It may be that some Christians in Pergamos were beginning to wonder, 'Well if the Lord has the sword, why is he not using it to protect us? Why is he letting the Romans kill us?' Would that not be a painful question in Sudan, and among the Christian minority in Iraq?

There are mysteries here that none of us are able completely to understand. Without attempting to explain evil, at least we learn something important about God's allowing Christian suffering. As we look at Christians being killed for the faith not only in the time of the church at Pergamos, but also in Darfur, China, India, and elsewhere today, we do well to call to mind Colossians 1:24. What Paul says of his own experience could rightly be said of the sufferings of God's Church in all times and in all places: 'I rejoice in my sufferings for you.' Then he gives the reason why he can rejoice in such pain, for this way, he is 'filling up (by those very sufferings) that which is behind of the afflictions of Christ in my flesh for his body's sake, which is the church'.

How to Think of Christian Suffering

Through the ages the sufferings of Christians are in a certain (secondary) sense 'redemptive'. Our primary redemption comes from the blood of Christ alone. He, and he alone pays for our sins, and fully redeems us through his sacrifice and resurrection. Christian suffering can never be redemptive in that primary sense, for that belongs to 'the Lamb of God, slain from the foundation of the world' (Rev. 13:8). But the sufferings of Christians do advance the cause of Christ, for they are divinely used to make redemption real for those who see believers going through hard times and even death for the sake of their Master, and in the spirit of their Master. Therefore, in this secondary sense, Christian suffering is a significant way the Lord uses to advance the gospel cause. We do not seek for it, if we have good sense, but the Lord knows when it is our time. There is much mystery here, and we do not know exactly how it works in detail, but all Christian suffering has a positive value. It is redemptive, it touches other lives and brings those that the Lord wants into the church, getting everything ready for the marriage supper of the Lamb. It makes the reality of the love and grace of God apprehensible to other humans in a way that nothing else can. But most of the time we do not see exactly how, and it is best to leave it to the Lord, who as our Shepherd, is with us 'in the valley of the shadow of death' (Ps. 23; John 10).

Joseph Țon, a Baptist pastor who ministered during the terrible period of harsh anti-Christianity in Romania under the Marxist dictator, Ceausescu, wrote *A Theology of Martyrdom*. Much of this book is a meditation on Colossians 1:24, which indicates that in the over-arching purposes of God, the sufferings (including martyrdoms) of the believers as ordained by the Lord and allowed into their lives are an eternally precious stewardship. They are a divinely appointed way to spread the love, mercy, and grace of Jesus to others, and thus, to hasten the coming of the King.

Think of suffering for the Lord as a strange kind of stewardship! Money and good health are kinds of stewardship; something given us by God so that we can invest it for the salvation of souls and the glory of God. But God also gives us at times a stewardship of suffering, and the returns on this investment will be incalculably great! This might be the only way that some people will be reached with the salvation of the Lord.

Another kind of strange stewardship for the Lord, and one that is peculiarly uncomfortable, is to be willing to listen to criticism about ourselves. Unlike righteous suffering, painful criticism is something that we can bring upon ourselves for our own inconsistencies. Hence, we are to seek the grace to handle it with honesty and humility.

Old Alexander Whyte, the great preacher in nineteenth century Edinburgh, used to say that only two kinds of people will tell you the truth about yourself, and that you should listen to both kinds. The first kind hates you, or at least is angry with you, so he blurts out some unpleasant truths about you. The other kind loves you very much and is willing to risk your wrath by telling you something about yourself that you really do need to hear. They care too much about you to wrap you in flattery, and let you go on as you are.

The risen Jesus is in the category of those who massively love us, and have every right to be strictly honest with us about our serious failings. Because of that, he told them that they were on the verge of severe moral compromise. The Lord says that people in the church at Pergamos are doing the same kind of thing that the Moabite Prophet, Balaam, did in Numbers 23-4.

Temptations for Believers to Compromise
When the children of Israel had come out of Egypt and were marching through the wilderness on their way to the Promised Land, they tried to go through Moab, but their king refused. The king of Moab, Balak, hated the Israelites (who were his distant cousins through Abraham and Lot), and he hired the prophet Balaam to put a curse on the Israelites. Every time Balaam tried to curse the Jews he would go into a trance in which the Holy Spirit took over his mind and mouth. Up on a hill he (and King Balak, who was paying him) could see all those thousands of tents below. Instead of cursing Israel, as the king had instructed, the spirit of God would come on Balaam so that his tongue would fly loose with blessings upon the enemy, much to the fury of the frustrated king.

We read elsewhere in Scripture that Balaam wanted that money and promotion, so he tried to please the rich king another way. He knew that God would not let him curse the Jews. But he offered this stratagem to the angry king. Balaam suggested that Balak make arrangements to corrupt the morals of the Israelites. He seems to have sent out large numbers of scantily clad, young Moabite women to lure the Israelite men to commit fornication with them, and thousands did so. Thus we read in Numbers 25 that God had to punish them by sending a plague that wiped out 25,000 Israelites. He wipes them off the map because of their moral compromise and Jesus says there are people in this church at Pergamos who are thinking of serious compromise. Perhaps they began thinking that it would do little harm to show up where they worship the emperor of Rome and eat some of the meat that was offered to the idols, or to take part in their unclean rituals.

The church is often tempted to share in the moral compromises of its generation and culture. A major denomination in the United States recently had its lower judicatories voting on whether or not to ordain homosexuals and lesbians as pastors in that church. One can only assume that the denominational officials wish to be part of an ever more corrupt culture. They are saying if everybody else is doing it, it must be okay. The Bible is outdated and we do not want to be out of date. The proper answer to that would be what the risen Christ says to Pergamos.

A Covenant Warning
The risen Christ says to the Church at Pergamos: 'Repent or I will come and wipe out those who

are compromising'. Did the Lord of Love say that? Yes. This is the Lord of Love, of whom we rightly sing: 'The King of Love my Shepherd is, whose goodness faileth never.' But his holy love is jealous love. God will not tolerate our trafficking with idols, and with the immoral practices of paganism that always accompany them.

Why do you think so many of the great cathedrals in Western Europe are empty? In some cathedrals that hold three or four thousand people inside their beautiful stone edifices, you will usually not find on most Sundays more than thirty or forty people at worship. Why is that? Why did Western Europe abandon Christianity? It is in large part because their ministers were immersed in anti-Christian humanistic education, and as a result, stopped preaching the gospel of Christ between the two World Wars (or even before), so that the churches emptied. Profound repentance is called for in Europe, and it is called for in America, which is rapidly following the apostasy of Europe. Repentance always leads to blessing.

A Covenant Promise, or Grant

The risen Lord makes two wonderful covenant promises to the church at Pergamos and not only to them but also to all true believers. He says: 'To him that overcometh will I give to eat of the hidden manna, and will give him a white stone, and in the stone a new name written, which no man knoweth saving he that receiveth it.'

An Overcomer

Now what is it to be an overcomer? It is somebody who looks out of self, sin, and weakness, and looks up to Christ, saying, 'Lord I trust in you and I give my life to you'. That is an overcomer. A loser looks to self and the culture around him. He depends on what he can accomplish by worldly means. That means you are certain to lose even if you are sitting on a throne like Nero. But an overcomer says, 'It's not in me, Lord, to do right; I have broken the law; I am weak, I can't do right, so I am looking to Jesus to clean me up by his blood, and then to empower me to follow him with his own gracious resources.'

'This is the victory that overcometh the world, even our faith,' says 1 John 5:4. Renewed faith in Christ is precisely what is needed to win battles against the ungodly pressures against us. That was what was needed in Pergamos, as some of the church there felt tempted to go along with the insistent demands of their ungodly culture.

Notice this carefully: although the Lord openly rebuked them for their sins, he offers them the path to victory, for he gladly buries the sins of the penitent in the seas of his forgetfulness. It is still true: no matter how terribly we have failed God, if we will now exercise faith and its 'twin sister' repentance, God will start with us afresh; forgive us, and put us on the road to victory. Along that road, he offers us two wonderful things:

Hidden Manna. First, 'I will give you hidden manna'. Remember about the manna God provided the hungry Israelites in the wilderness, where there was no food. The Lord rained down a kind of sustaining substance like small bits of corn or wheat, with which they could make good bread. It was called in Hebrew 'manna', which means 'what is it?' That is the secret of God's provision for overcomers, for people who exercise faith in Christ. God provides for them, and they do not know where it came from, nor how it got there. It has a heavenly explanation. God is going to take care of you as long as he needs to. His supernatural, overruling providence will take care of you physically and spiritually.

Let me give you one illustration. I know of a ministerial family in the deep South several years ago that had to have $500 by Tuesday. On the preceding Friday they had nothing in the bank and no way to get the sum (that to them was large). The minister, his wife, and their children went down on their knees on Saturday night and simply said: 'Let's ask God to send us the money the first of the week.' Before five o'clock on Monday afternoon there was a check in the mail for exactly five hundred dollars from somebody who had absolutely no way of knowing what their need was. Was that mere coincidence? Of course not! They knew that it was God's manna. It comes in many different forms, as God sees that his people truly need it so as to honor him in meeting all their commitments on time.

A Stone with a Secret Name on it. Second, 'I will give you a stone with a secret name on it'. Probably behind this symbol lies the breastplate of the High Priest which had twelve stones on it, representing the twelve tribes of Israel. When he went to the holiest place of all to confess the sins of the people, and then to pray down the benediction, those twelve stones must have been glittering in the light, so that the light of the divine countenance would shine upon all of those twelve tribes.

It seems that God is saying something like this: 'I am going to add a new stone to the High Priest's breastplate, not the Jewish High Priest now, but the Great High Priest in Heaven! I am going to put your name on a 'personalized' stone that Jesus takes in to the Father. Every time he is in there, you are in there. Your name, your personal name is on Jesus' heart before the Father and he is talking about you. And I am going to give you something else. I am going to give you a new name that is secret between you and the Lord. That means, Christ is saying, 'I take your name up in a little stone on my breastplate up to my Father and then I bring down a sweet secret just between you and the Lord; something that is so wonderful that it is better than the whole world. You know how it is in a lifelong love relationship, in a good marriage. None of them is perfect, but there are certainly many very good ones. A husband and wife have certain secrets between themselves that bond them close together and they never share with another person. It is something like that between a saint and the Lord. God deals with you in a personal, secret way, different from anybody else and it is so valuable that you would readily give up your life for it.

The familiar gospel hymn, 'I come to the garden alone', has a line in it that says: 'and the joys we share as we tarry there, none other has ever known'. That is exactly right, even though the hymn is not one of my favorites! That secret has kept me going through many years of ordained ministry. For this secret, you will put up with anything to sustain you.

I went to see someone recently, who is in the final stages of cancer, apparently near the end of a long and valiant battle. He is still triumphantly going on; even though his mortal body is about to fail him, he is triumphant, not least, because of the secrets between him and the Lord. It is not a human explanation, it is supernatural. Another hymn (ascribed to Bernard of Clairvaux) says: 'The love of Jesus, what it is, none but his loved now'. Psalm 34:8 gives the invitation: 'O taste and see that the Lord is good: blessed is the man that trusteth in Him.'.

6

The Church at Thyatira
Revelation 2:18–29

This is one of the seven churches of Asia to whom the Lord in his risen glory sends a message that is as relevant to the situation that we face in our Western culture today.

In the late 1980s, one of the most widely read books was by a professor at the University of Chicago, Allen Bloom: *The Closing of the American Mind*. In the first chapter of this interesting book, he said that for the thirty or more years he taught at the University of Chicago, he could count on one thing from the freshmen who came into his class. Nearly every one of them would say, 'You cannot know ultimate truth. If you think you have the absolute way of truth, then you are very dangerous.' It is what we call relativism, and Bloom thinks that this relativism (nobody knows what is finally right and what is finally wrong) has brought our culture down in the moral, spiritual, and social sphere, wrecking so much of family and personal life.

It would not be far wrong to suggest that something like this is the problem that the risen Christ pointed out would destroy the church at Thyatira, if they did not deal with it and deal with it fast. The culture in Thyatira in many ways is reminiscent of the culture the Christian church is now facing throughout Western civilization.

Jesus said this falsehood is of utmost seriousness. You must deal with it fast. I believe he is saying to the churches today the same thing. We notice in this little letter to Thyatira four points as we have in most of the letters. They are all structured alike, although there are different contents depending on what each church needs.

We consider four points:

1. The Appearance of Christ (Rev. 2:18).
2. Covenant Assessment of the Church at Thyatira (Rev. 2:19–20).
3. Covenant Warning (Rev. 2:24–5).
4. A Covenant Promise to Overcomers (Rev. 2:26–8).

The Appearance of the Risen Christ

In verse 18, the Lord shows himself to the Church at Thyatira. Each church, as we have seen, was shown a different aspect of the risen Lord that they most needed to see because of their peculiar situation. To the folk at Thyatira it was what John described: 'the Son of God who hath his eyes like unto a flame of fire, and his feet are like fine brass' (1:18). Christ with flaming eyes sees through the externals to the heart of the matter. His eyes are something like an X-Ray or a MRI scan that uncovers everything and discloses what the health or problems of our body and soul are really like. Something bad had to be uncovered and cut out for the good of that congregation in Thyatira. His feet 'like polished brass' probably refers to the swift coming of his judgement upon Thyatira, if they refused to submit to an operation to cut out this spiritual, moral cancer.

Does Jesus Judge?

For some reason much of modern Christianity never seems to think of Jesus as judging people. We only attribute love to him, and Jesus is the King of love—supremely so. It is wonderful and should be preached constantly. It is true that God is love, but the divine love is holy love, a jealous love that therefore involves judgement when that unique love to us is violated by idolatry. We do not hear judgment spoken of much today because we have forgotten that God is holy and by his character has to deal firmly with unrepented sin. A 'user-friendly' God, who makes everybody feel jovial and comfortable, is not the God of the Bible. He is an idol, popular though he be. In fact, the user-friendly God is more like the God of the Thyatiran form of Jezebel.

A COVENANT ASSESSMENT

The flaming, all seeing eyes of the Holy One find good things and also a very serious problem.

Strong Point of Thyatira

First, the positive assessment (v. 19). Looking into the body life and into the spiritual reality, Jesus finds something for which he is full of praise. Paul says that faith works by love. James says that good works prove faith. No doubt the church at Thyatira had a heart of true faith in the Lord, because their lives expressed God's love by means of practical deeds of kindness, generosity and helpfulness. Indeed, the Lord said that far from having lost their first love like the church at Ephesus, their good Christian deeds, motivated by the love of God, were increasing all of the time. Jesus thanks them for it.

This is no small thing. God is pleased whenever we show practical love to other people for the sake of his Son. James tells us that words are never enough. They have to be backed up by practical kindness and helpfulness to demonstrate the love of God to others. One of the greatest values of good deeds in Jesus' name is that they show people in daily life who God really is. To care for another person, especially if they cannot pay you back, makes them feel the power of love as a reality even greater than the power of evil which, perhaps, has hurt them. In other words, a Christian life that is zealous for good works demonstrates the existence of the God of the Bible in this life.

Some people never read the words of the Bible; but they can all read with close attention good works, especially when it touches their own life with encouragement in the Lord's name. They understand that instinctively, and we are thereby given an avenue to tell people who God is, by being good to them. Isn't that amazing? It is wonderful to be involved in things like this and the risen Christ is pleased to see it in the church in Thyatira, as he is pleased to see it today.

MEDICAL MISSIONS

Spiritual Disease of Thyatira

Then there is a negative assessment, the locating of a cancer (v. 20-23). It is always scary to be told that you have cancer, but it may not necessarily be bad, if they find it soon enough to deal with it. At Thyatira, the Lord points out this moral, spiritual cancer beginning to work in their vitals. He

JAF

points it out in time, so that it could be operated on and they could recover their health. That is the good news in this otherwise negative assessment.

Here is what the holy eyes of the risen Lord saw. A good, kind, helpful church that believed in Christ, was for some reason or other tolerating an influential woman, who claimed to be a big Christian, but she was corrupting many in the fellowship with 'relativism'. God took this cancerous corruption so seriously that he calls this woman, (we do not know what her real name was), by the Old Testament name of the wicked queen of Northern Israel, Jezebel.[15] Jezebel was Ahab's wife, who mixed Pagan Baal worship with Old Testament religion, and then tried to kill the Prophet Elijah when he killed her false court prophets. We know what became of the original Jezebel. She was thrown out of an upper window by palace servants and the dogs ate her body except for part of her hands and skull.

A First Century AD Jezebel

The first century AD 'Jezebel' in Thyatira was like the eighth century BC Jezebel, in that she encouraged her many followers to compromise true Christianity with Pagan practices in the culture around them. That way it seemed they could please the world and keep everybody superficially happy. That is what happened in many of the Protestant churches in the twentieth century. The original Jezebel and her husband, Ahab, had their people pretend to worship Jehovah and Baal at the same time. They encouraged them to participate in feasts at the idolatrous Temple of Baal, to eat and to drink with idolaters. The influential church-woman in Thyatira was doing something like that. She must have said, 'Let's mingle with these people during the week; let's go to their religious services, and participate in their feasts. Then they will realize that we too know how to have fun, and are not judgmental of them. It's fine to be in the Christian church, but do not go narrow minded'. If everybody else is doing it, why do we have to be different? If she was right, then you can serve Jesus and please the world at the same time. This is what the Jezebel at Thyatira was teaching.

This kind of disastrous compromise always attracts a certain following and if it is not rebuked firmly, soundly and bluntly, it will attract an even bigger crowd. History tells us that Thyatira, while not a strong military city, was an important commercial center because of ancient trade roads that ran through Thyatira, which was about forty miles southeast of Pergamos. This city was controlled by wealthy trade guilds. It was an ancient form of the modern labor union. These powerful guilds or labor unions controlled everything. They were the establishment. At this period of time, the members of those guilds who controlled the economy and the social life of Thyatira, were expected to participate in Pagan feasts at the temple (which frequently involved illicit sexual activities with the idol worshipers there). Apparently, if you refused to do so, it could cost you your job. They would not kill you, but they would take your job, so that your family might go hungry.

No doubt, many Christians in Thyatira would have felt the pressure of this, and would be tempted to go along with this modern Jezebel and her call to compromise. She and her group held that there are sufficient economic and social reasons for compromise with the idolatrous system in this city. Perhaps our reasonable compromise will win some of them into the Church. That was the argument, and the church was beginning to give ground. In light of the friendly easiness of what

Jezebel called for, what Christ said in pointing out the disastrous sin of this compromise would not have been popular in all quarters, and never is.

Think of how harshly Franklin Graham was criticized in the media and in some of the churches, when he dared to state the plain truth that Islam is not the same thing as Christianity, and is not noble and peaceful. People today, not just the media but many in the church, do not like you to say things like that, but surely the question is never what does the public like or even what does the church leadership like. The question is: what does Jesus say?

Here is what Jesus said then to Thyatira, and what he says now: 'Repent or else'. Verse 21 says that the Lord graciously gave this woman, who had grabbed leadership and was using it for her own corrupt purposes, plenty of time to repent. Yet she adamantly refused.

The High Cost of Refusing to Repent

Then verses 22-3 tell us the 'or else'. She and her compromising followers who enjoyed getting into bed with somebody that they were not married to, would be cast by the power of God into a bed of disease and death (v. 22). I can think of a modern illustration of that, can't you? It makes me think of the fatal disease of AIDS, for which there is still no known cure, as the recompense for so awfully violating God's law for human relationships. The homosexual movement seems to be getting ever more aggressive and brazen. In more than one American state, they have sought to use the schools to teach their perverse philosophy of life. But AIDS rages on, and in a few short years many of these strident activists will be laid low in a hopeless bed of death from which, unless they repent, they will be hastened into the grief of eternal blackness and feel the lasting fires that give off no light. I do not say that with any joy.

I hope they will repent and I pray for them. Yet the truth has to be told of what happens if such do not repent. That is what the Bible says, isn't it? And yet God, as Micah says, 'delighteth in mercy', 'God rejoices not in the death of any sinner', and so gives these people in Thyatira one last chance to repent. And this same merciful opportunity of repentance is being sincerely held out by God today to those who have violated his moral standards.

One could figuratively think of repentance as being like a thin invisible door, leading into heaven. It is not really an iron or wooden door, but is more like a curtain that is hanging between two worlds. You go to the door of repentance in faith; lean on the thin door, and the curtain gives way so that you are right into the presence of God's blessing and pardon. Repentance is like that. The invisible curtain of repentance quickly flies back, no matter how many horrendous sins we have engaged in, if only we come in faith in the crucified, risen Lord.

A Covenant Warning

Many in Thyatira still believed, and had not gone along with this sinful woman, yet apparently were wavering. Maybe they didn't know how they were going to handle the pressure of not compromising. We know they were wavering because they had not disciplined this Jezebel. They had not put her out of the church. So Jesus says to these people this word; 'hold fast'. Hold on to the one true saving gospel, hold on to the one way to heaven through the atoning blood of Christ as the only way. Don't let the allurements of this present outwardly attractive world cause you to loosen your grip on Jesus and on God's truth. Do not try to mix Christianity with false religions, regardless of how popular they are. Make sure you stay sexually pure and faithful to your husband or wife, in spite of all allurements to the contrary. If once you say, 'all roads lead to God; all religions are probably equal,' you leave yourself open to the pressures that are sure to come on us from secular governments, in their eagerness to avoid conflict, as for instance, between Islam and Christianity.

Of course, no sane or honorable person would wish to provoke religious war, but to deny the finality of God's truth is too high a price to pay. Indeed, is it even certain that moral and religious relativism actually leads to greater peace? The sort of theological compromise in which you stand for nothing but material advantage does not seem to have provided a safer world.

Jesus tells his people in all ages to be careful not to deny the basic truths by which they are saved. To give in to the pressures of the day, to be well liked and go along with everything, you will wind up losing everything that matters.

A COVENANT PROMISE TO OVERCOMERS

The risen Lord concludes with a promise, or really, two promises. He is encouraging to those who are wavering. We saw in the last message what makes an overcomer: one who simply looks away from self and the current world system up to Jesus for salvation, and for all of life. The human idea of overcoming is to look at self, and say, 'I am strong and can be anything I want to be'. No! The Bible says that God's overcomer looks away from self, up to Jesus. As the hymn puts it: 'I am weak, but Thou art strong.' The world's weakest people can become victorious overcomers by simple faith. Faith, as one of the English Puritans said, is like an eye looking out to someone else for help, that's what it is, or at least, that's where it starts.

The Source of Being an Overcomer

Hebrews 11, the great chapter on faith in the Bible speaks of those who, 'out of weakness were made strong'. Is that not wonderful? All we have is our moral weakness, intellectual weakness, and various kinds of personal weakness, but with faith in Jesus 'out of weakness we can be made strong'. It is an imparted strength that is sent down from outside ourselves by God himself. Ask for the strength to be an overcomer in times of widespread compromise. Look up for it and it will be given as a gift.

1. First Promise: Power over the Nations. Verses 26-8 make two wonderful promises to overcomers. Both of the promises are what the risen Christ will give. The first promise is 'I will give you power over all nations'. Revelation 2:26-7 are direct quotations from Psalm 2, a Messianic Psalm that is speaking about Jesus Christ, written a thousand years before Christ was on earth. This Psalm gives the assurance that the incarnate Son of God, once he comes to earth, will conquer all the proud secular nations of this impressive, but sinful and condemned world system. Psalm 2 and then Revelation 2:27 compare the haughty nations to clay pots and the gospel of Christ and the ministry of the Christian church to a rod of iron bashing against those clay pots.

It is the opposite of worldly thinking, which believes that what really counts would be money, political power and prestige. God, that true reality, is entirely different from this evaluation of true power. It is as though he were saying: 'I want to show you beneath the surface, so you can tell how things really are. The nations, with all their wealth and military power, are clay pots. The gospel committed to the church is a rod of iron and once bashed against the brittle pots, what do you think will happen?

The poor Christians at Thyatira had probably been fired from their jobs because they would not eat food at pagan temples or play fast and loose with their bodies with people to whom they were not married. The world of trade guilds and pagan religion surrounding them must have seemed all powerful, as it was cutting them down to size economically and socially.

But the risen Lord of Glory says, 'Dear children, wait a little while. Recall my truth, and keep looking up with expectation, then you will start partaking of an invisible strength sent from somewhere else. Wait a little bit. I will cut these proud, immoral, idolatrous nations down to size in due time.'

As Paul has instructed us, 'we walk by faith, and not by sight' (1 Cor. 5:7), especially since God's sovereign power is usually hidden from the physical eye. The power brokers of the world do not see it. But this power of Almighty God that created the heavens and the earth out of nothing, and keeps them rotating, is infinitely greater than an iron fire poker whamming against a fragile clay flower pot! Proud Rome and its pagan supporters like Thyatira would be shattered into dust by barbarians in due time and the church would emerge and create the blessings to the Western world for hundreds of years to follow.

That is why we are here in this twenty-first century. The Church will always endure, because Christ is risen from the dead, and is in charge of everything. The Messiah is in charge; he is on the throne. After a number of years every pagan, Satanically-inspired kingdom, powerful though it seems at the time, with power to hurt God's people, every one of those kingdoms is eventually in the passage of history shattered to slivers and the Christian faith rides on stronger than ever.

In our own life time, in 1991 the USSR went down and there are still a lot of problems, but the Christian church is stronger than ever in Russia and Ukraine. Those who oppose Messiah will always lose over time, though God takes his time, and it is not ours. He works according to his own clock and if we keep asking, 'when are you going to do it, Lord'? He says, 'Look up, wait a little bit; when you are weak, I will make you strong as you keep looking up'.

I cannot know the future, but I suspect that the materialism of the West, if unrepented of, will eventually collapse our economic system. It will do so (we know not when) because of the greed and lies and inhumanity of it, that refuses to take moral issues into consideration. I wonder if we already see small signs of this imminent collapse in some of the companies that are going bankrupt, almost like a house of cards. But the gospel will keep spreading, even when these regimes and multinational firms have been broken like clay flower pots shattered by an iron fire poker. The real question is not, When will God bring down this country? When will he bring down that country or this system or that system? We cannot know that. Those are not the real questions for God's Church.

Here is the question we need to answer today: Am I on the winning side or not? That is the question we can answer. That is the only one that matters.

2. The Gift of the Morning Star (Rev. 2:28). Jesus makes the second promise to overcomers, to those who refuse to compromise for temporary gain with the world's crowd. He says 'I will give you the morning star'. The morning star is Jesus himself. That beautiful star emerged triumphant from the dark night of death out of an empty tomb and will shine evermore brightly until the sun and moon and stars are no longer needed. The whole universe will be bathed in the light of the face of Jesus. It is certain. It is coming. When this risen Lord promises, 'I will give you, the faithful ones at Thyatira, (or the faithful ones today), the

Morning Star, no matter what pressures you are under,' here is what he means: 'I will give you myself, my own life, my resurrection, with all the grace of my presence. I will put all of this inside of you so that I will shine through you into a dark world by my overcoming light.' That must have been well received in suffering Thyatira as it would be today in places where Christians are persecuted.

All that the persecuted saints at Thyatira needed to overcome the stifling darkness around them was the resurrection light personally received from the Lord of Glory. That light then and now, by the power of the Holy Ghost, shining out of Christian hearts and eyes could break down strongholds of Satan, transform opponents into friends, and do every kind of wonder that would be needed to sustain the beleaguered Christians in Thyatira and make them 'more than conquerors', until God moved to adjust the whole situation for their benefit and for his glory. That same rod of iron, that same bright and morning star is freely and gladly available to the humblest believer today who will turn his back on all compromise and offer himself, both soul and body, whatever the cost, to this Lord Jesus Christ.'

7

The Church in Sardis

Revelation 3:1–6

The major ministry of the invisible Holy Spirit is to shine the light upon Christ, so that believers can be caught up in his glory (cf. John 16:13). But when the church is lacking in the power of the Holy Spirit, she forgets how spiritually impoverished she is, and thus fails to address Christ for all he could be to her. We looked at several of the other churches and we saw that the risen Christ gives a special message of encouragement, and a rebuke to each one of these churches. We see the same pattern at Sardis in Revelation 3:1–6.

A Church in Need of Revival

The position of the church at Sardis can be summarized this way. Often when the church is in need of revival, she does not know it and thinks everything is fine, which is part of the problem. You could use an analogy from human health. Someone that I knew of seemed to be in the prime of health. Everything looked fine outwardly when he went to the doctor to be checked. It was a shock to find out that he had terminal cancer, with possibly a month or six weeks to live. It was a bit like that at Sardis. The malignancy was far gone in an impressive looking body, but the difference here is that the Lord Jesus speaks to them with the promise that if they act, there will be just enough time to take care of the cancer and then to live a normal and healthy Christian life. But whether or not the underlying spiritual condition proved to be terminal would depend upon that church facing her desperate need of revival, and thus, humbly turning to God and seeking his face. Their whole survival depended upon receiving and acting upon the word of the risen Jesus.

We notice four points in this text:

1. The identity of the Lord.
2. An assessment of the church at Sardis.
3. A Warning to Sardis.
4. A promise.

The Identity of the Lord

As in all the different letters to the seven churches, this letter presents the identity of the risen Lord (v. 1). As we have already seen, the Lord shows an aspect of his Person that is particularly appropriate to each church in its own situation. It seems as though Christ says, 'look at this side of my character as your risen Lord because that is what you need to concentrate on. If you will look at me and what I am like, your problem, your malignancy can definitely be healed'. Thus Jesus continues to show something different about himself in accordance with the weakness or the need of those various churches. How like the Lord that is! How particularly he deals with his people in bringing home to their situation his Word. It is just what we need in accordance with where we are at the time. He seems to be saying to each one, 'If you will look up and receive this, it doesn't matter what state you are in, it can be different, it can be put right'.

Sardis is Shown Christ as Dispenser of the Spirit
He shows himself to Sardis in Revelation 3:1, and they behold the same thing that John saw in Revelation 1:4. First of all, they are shown seven spirits coming out from the Lord. That does not mean that the Holy Spirit is seven persons; he is only one person, but seven is a Biblical number for totality and fullness. This perfect biblical number seven is a symbolic way of saying that everything you have ever needed is in the Holy Spirit, and Jesus is in control of who gets the Holy Spirit.[16] Did you realize that? You do not have a relationship with the Holy Spirit apart from faith in the risen Jesus.

In John 20, after his resurrection, Jesus shows up in his risen body to his shocked and bewildered disciples who had seen him killed. He is physically alive out of the grave, and they are quite bewildered. At that point of their bewilderment, they see the risen Jesus, who breathes on those disciples and says, 'Receive ye the Holy Spirit.' He is the baptizer in the Spirit. So when the Lord Jesus ascends back to the Father in his resurrection body, what he does from the throne on the day of Pentecost, is to send down the Spirit in immense measure. He baptizes his church with unique fullness and power so that she will be gloriously equipped to do all that she needs to do until the end of time, to accomplish the Great Commission. Thus, Jesus is personally in charge of sending the Holy Spirit (see John 16:7). Why do you think he says particularly to Sardis: 'Remember me as the one who is able to send you the Holy Spirit'? Surely it is because that church needed revival, new life from God, new life from heaven, and Jesus is the one from the Throne who can see our need, hear our prayer and then send down exactly who we need, that is the Holy Spirit. This is what we would expect from Hebrews 7:25, 'he ever liveth to make intercession for his saints.'

The Full Sufficiency of the Holy Spirit
In the coming of the Holy Spirit, there is what we need physically, as we see in James 5:14-16, for instance. When the elders of the church anoint the sick and lay on hands, praying for their healing, the anointing oil they use is symbolic of the Holy Spirit, who is the healer from the Throne. The same Holy Spirit is able to come with financial provisions and other needed blessings. The Holy Spirit is able to come and change people, softening attitudes, and sweetening bitterness.

To summarize, the Holy Spirit is able to open every door that is for the glory of God in our lives and service. He goes beneath the surface, and gives us what he knows we really need. Perhaps what Sardis needed was the warming of a cold heart—rekindling a love whose flame had burned low. Most of us Christians can at times become cold on the Lord; lose much of our loving zeal for Him. To this moribund state, the Holy Spirit can come from Jesus, bringing fire from the altar of Heaven, setting it aglow deep inside us, filling us with a new devotion, desire for purity, and zealous service. What God made every human being for is to directly experience the divine love, which focuses our life on the Lord's glory, and is the final source of every joy worth having. We see this in Romans 5:5, 'The love of God is shed abroad in our hearts by the Holy Spirit who is given unto us'.

Sardis had grown cold on the Lord; their love had gotten dim, and they had lost any enthusiasm for the things that mattered most. In that situation, Jesus effectively said to them, 'Look at me, I am the one that can send you the Holy Spirit and the supernatural provision to make everything right. Look into my face, and as you look at me who has done so much for you, be repentant'.

The Stars are in Christ's Right Hand

Then verse one mentions that the risen Christ 'holds the seven stars in his right hand'. Revelation 1:16 has already explained that 'the stars are the churches'. This means that Christ is in charge of what happens in the churches. Especially, he can give authority and anointing to the preaching and the praying. It appears that Sardis had gone along with the externals of nominal Christianity, but they had lost the power. Remember how Paul says that many will have 'a form of godliness, but deny the power thereof' (2 Tim. 3:5). In that sad case, what is the solution? It is looking to Jesus (Heb. 12:2), who holds the seven stars; he has the churches in his hand, not only the churches of Asia at that time, but also in all times all of the churches throughout the world. He says 'Remember, I am in charge'. That means that he is saying: 'If you want things to be different, first of all look to me; do not worry about your enemies; do not count your resources, but instead, before you do anything else, look up into my face (see Ps. 27:8). I am in charge and I can give unction to the ministry of the church, to the preaching, to the praying, to the sacraments in such measure that the congregation experiences something of heaven on earth'.

Where Revivals Come From

The history of revivals are a demonstration that Jesus keeps the stars in his right hand. One vivid illustration occurred on 21 June 1630 in a rural, village church not far outside Glasgow: the Kirk of Shotts. A visiting minister, John Livingston, preached at a communion season attended by a vast concourse of people from the district. Thousands were converted; far more than during his entire ministry up to that point. He later wrote that it was 'the one day in my life wherein I got most of the presence of God in public.'

A similar thing occurred over 200 years later in Charleston, South Carolina, in a largely black church (Zion Presbyterian), whose minister was the great John L. Girardeau (who happened to be white). The mighty revival there started with a prayer meeting:

> That constantly increased until the house was filled. Some of the officers of the church wanted him to commence preaching services, but he steadily refused, waiting for the outpouring of the Spirit. His view was that the Father had given to Jesus, as the King and Head of the church, the gift of the Holy Spirit, and that Jesus in his sovereign administration of the affairs of his church, bestowed him upon whomsoever he pleased, and in whatever measure he pleased. Day after day he, therefore, kept his prayer addressed directly to the mediatorial throne for the Holy Spirit in mighty reviving power.[17]

In both revivals, they immediately knew that God had done it. They knew on the inside that the fire had come from the altar of heaven. The risen Lord, who has the stars in his right hand had dispensed his blessed Spirit to them.

I have never seen anything like that, but I did see a certain 'quickening' when I was a PhD student in the University of Edinburgh back in the late sixties and early seventies. For three or four years, there was a definite movement of the Holy Spirit amongst the students in the Scottish Universities. During weekly Bible studies (especially in the Inter Varsity Fellowship), God had been greatly using some evangelical ministers like James Phillip and William Still. They asked some of the older students from time to time to address groups of seeking students on Sunday nights at various universities. Large crowds attended, many of them never having heard the gospel, but they had been invited by Christian friends. After the preaching, the speaker would stay to answer questions (often until midnight). It was obvious that the Holy Spirit was making crowds of young people seek the Lord. The risen Christ was communicating his Spirit in the preaching. At nearly every meeting, students professed conversion. They had heard what Christ was like, and wanted him now, no matter what changes it would entail in their lives. During that time, I almost never preached in Scotland without there being conversion, and the same was true of the other speakers.

Keep On, Even When There Seems No Response
But then I graduated and came to Dillon as minister, where for about the first five years, I could see very little response to Word and sacrament. I talked to the Lord about the discouraging lack of response. I knew that my life was the same; I hadn't changed anything in my life; the essential message was the same. But what kept me going was the knowledge that Christ holds the stars in his right hand and he is the one that gives or withholds the Spirit. We have to be faithful and see what he will do. How glad I was later that I did keep going, seeking to 'walk by faith, and not by sight', for I later found out that there had been considerable fruit being born. God had been working, unknown to me; several had been converted, but did not make it known for some years, since they were long since church members. Even in a hard ministry, we will keep going so long as we keep in mind the identity of the Lord shown to Sardis in Revelation 3:1. The key is to keep looking to Christ to send down the Holy Spirit so that every congregation will be quickened from spiritual deadness to vital faith and repentance towards the Lord.

DIVINE ASSESSMENT
In the later part of verse one and particularly verse two, he gives an assessment of their health, and an honest evaluation of where they stand. Of the seven churches, the toughest criticism comes on Sardis and Laodicea (as we will see later). Basically you could say that the root of the problem in Sardis was what is called 'nominalism.' A nominal Christian describes somebody who has the name of being a Christian, is a member of the church, has been baptized, and sometimes attends, but for them God, Christ, the Holy Spirit, and genuine, personal Christianity are no more than names, or theoretical concepts. Such people would say: 'I am not a Muslim, a Buddhist, or an atheist, therefore I am a Christian. I am a respectable member of Western culture. But I do not want to get too religious.'

The Tragedy of Nominal Christianity
But that is not the same thing as being saved by Christ; it is not the same as having been baptized by the Holy Spirit into union with Christ. If we only have the merely formal name of Christian, when we die physically, then tragically we shall lose our soul, and go into a lost eternity of woe.

The risen Jesus says you must have the reality on the inside of your life; your cold, selfish heart must be set afire with the love of God, which is demonstrated through faith and repentance, as the continuing basis of a holy life (holy in Christ; not in yourself). The risen Jesus told the nominals at Sardis that they must get the reality of his life in them to be real Christians. That is precisely what he means when he says at the end of verse one, 'Thou hast a name that thou livest, and art dead.' That was the divine assessment of many church folk at Sardis: they simply did not know Jesus in the way that he speaks of it in John 17:3: 'This is eternal life, that they know thee, the only true God, and Jesus Christ whom thou hast sent.'

Unlike the other churches that we have looked at, Sardis was not being persecuted. Is that not interesting? People who are just nominal Christians, whose lives are not different from the rest of the world, do not (by their lack of reflection of the Holy Christ) rebuke the sinfulness of a selfish world. Nobody persecutes them. Evidently, the devil does not mind it if somebody is a nominal Christian, for he has not been born again, and therefore does not have the life of God in his soul. He could not be living for Jesus, so why would the devil bother to persecute him? He has him anyway. Nominals are not doing him any damage. They are not winning any of the lost out of his prison or breaking down strongholds of evil. They are not light in a dark place or salt to preserve society from putrification. They are just like the world, so the evil one leaves them alone.

This next point is only speculation, but I wonder if Sardis had deceived herself on this matter. She well knew that other churches were being persecuted, such as Thyatira and Ephesus. Sardis may have felt superior to the others, for her own lack of persecution by the world. I have wondered if part of the immense attraction of Modernism in the twentieth century in the once Christian countries of the West was a determination to be accepted by a secular society, who looked askance at anything like 'enthusiasm' or 'fundamentalism'? The moderate nominalist refuses to take religion too far; they will never wish to offend powerful unbelievers and their selfish culture. Could Sardis have thought: 'the other churches that are being persecuted have taken Christianity so far that they have offended the nice people in worldly power? But we have been much more moderate and careful, and look at how well we are getting along in this multi-faith culture! We have not lost our jobs, and we are looked up to by the world.'

A sociologist said some forty years ago that the big Protestant, 'mainline' churches in America had become mere appendages of the American culture by World War I. They were not seriously different from materialists, and within fifteen or twenty years, one could count on these churches to reflect everything the culture was doing. No doubt, they avoided the criticism and disdain of ungodly secularists.

But what was it worth? Where did the souls of their nominal members go after they died without a saving knowledge of God in Christ? How long did their once impressive influence last after they quit believing the gospel and loving Jesus? How long before their empty lives were indeed, inoffensive to the lost (but also, unhelpful to the eternal interests of the unconverted)? Once you lose the offensiveness of the gospel, the church also loses the beauty of Jesus. Then it is good for nothing to a needy, perishing world! That is why, within 25–50 years, large numbers of nominalistic churches become abandoned, even by the world which they so courted! Why should the world go to a place where there is nothing for them?

Warning to the Church

Not unlike the seriousness of a concerned surgeon who tells the patient that his only chance for survival is immediate and radical surgery, Jesus warns Sardis that their condition will be fatal unless they come to terms with his divine warning. The risen One warns them of two actions they must take immediately in order to survive.

Christ says: 'Wake Up'

His first warning is a command: 'Be alert! Wake up!' Why did Sardis need this specific warning from Jesus? Perhaps it was because Sardis was a remarkable military fortification and a very rich trade center in what is now modern Turkey. This city was located on the brow of a very high hill, so that it was hard to take by military action. They had the protection of this rocky, stony cone sticking out of the plain upon which the proud city rested, behind a strong wall which was virtually impossible to get through.

But in addition to their military security, Sardis was a rich trading area. We could say that they were secure and rich, not unlike the rich fool, who lost his soul (see Luke 16). The famous King Croesus used to live there, which is the area known as Lydia. Croesus was the man, according to the ancient myth, who gained the power to turn everything he touched into gold. But finally he touched his daughter and she turned to gold, so he lost the love of his life. Well, at least the myth does accurately reflect the ancient memory that gold was there in plentiful supply. Sardis was still a wealthy place in the first century AD. It was rich, secure, and asleep.[18]

But their feelings of security, and their lack of watchfulness worked to their disadvantage on two historical occasions, when the enemy climbed over the wall and killed the secure, but foolishly sleeping people of Sardis. When the risen Christ said, 'Wake up, Sardis', he was probably bringing to mind that they had been asleep in their security and lost their city twice in the past. But Jesus is warning that they are going to lose far more than that! This wealthy, moderate, inoffensive church with its good-looking, well-connected people had no idea how close they were to imminent judgment—the soon losing of both body and soul for all eternity! The risen Christ spoke the unpleasant truth in love (v. 3), that if they do not make a change, by moving from this spiritually dead nominalism to a heartfelt trust and love for him, he would come 'like a thief in the night'.

Now Jesus says, 'if you do not change, I will come'. When Christ says in Revelation, 'I will come', it can be used in two different ways. It can mean the very end of time; he is coming at the end of the age: the Last Day. But his coming does not always mean the Last Day. Often when he says 'I will come in judgment', it means: 'now, in your lifetime'. At particular times, the Lord 'comes in judgment' upon an unbelieving, sinful church, (although the judgment can come through armies, pestilence, famine, and other reversals, it is the Lord himself who is coming by their means). But he does not come in this way without giving his people plenty of warning. That is the way the 'I will come' is used in Revelation 1:7, 2:5, and 2:16.[19] 'I will come' in these passages means 'in this lifetime, while you are alive I am going to come if you do not make some changes'.

So, he says, 'Be watchful, wake up'. The problem in Sardis, and in many declining churches, is that in their lethargy, they are unaware of their true spiritual condition. Such a church must ask itself: do we have the love of God in our hearts, accompanied by genuine faith, trust and obedience? Otherwise, judgment is coming and all will be lost. That is the message when Christ says, 'Wake up!'

Repentance Is the Only Hope for the Nominal
Secondly, he commands: 'Remember and repent!' Remember the gospel! Remember 'that Jesus died for sins according to the Scriptures' (1 Cor. 15). Thereupon, you may say: 'I feel condemned; I know my sins; I have done wrong; I have failed the Lord, and I do not believe there is any hope'. 'No', he says, 'of course there is hope'; your sins and my sins are not greater than the death of Jesus. Our worst failures can be made whiter than the snow under the blood of the cross.

The real problem of any sinner is not finally their sin, so much as it is holding on to it like a pet snake in one's bosom; refusing to confess it and seek God's help to forsake it. Our real problem is holding on to what has pulled us down. Jesus says, 'Let it go under the blood. I will be gracious to you'. Think of the woman taken in adultery (John 8). She was a sinner, but Jesus forgives her and says 'I do not condemn you. Go and sin no more'. So remember the gospel promises to the most unworthy, no matter what they have done, and therefore, repent.

A Promise
The Lord gives a wonderful promise in verses 4–5. Earlier he had given a stern warning about their critical disease. He had done so out of his tender love for the compromising people at Sardis. But now he makes a sweet promise. He says that there are some in Sardis who have been faithful and who have not soiled their garments with worldly compromise. They have not forgotten the gospel, and have been unashamed of an enthusiastic faith in Jesus before a skeptical, disapproving public.

The Promise of White Robes
Then the Lord promises two things. First, 'I am going to let you walk in white garments'. God himself puts upon his saints the 'beautiful robes of white'. These garments have been washed white in the blood of the Lamb, slain for the pardon of sinners. Have you ever thought at a church wedding, when the bride comes down the aisle that it is a pale reflection of that last day, when 'the marriage supper of the Lamb' takes place? How beautifully and brightly the ransomed church will shine, as the Lord comes out to take her to be his forevermore!

Although we are meant to take literally the beautiful white robes that will be placed upon the saints (see Rev. 6), a sort of 'moral' description of them (or of those who wear them) is given to us in Colossians 3:1–10: 'When Christ, who is our life, shall appear, then shall ye also appear with him in glory.' The glory is the brightness of the white garments, shining out with the beauties of the Savior's indwelling presence in the believers. 'Mortify therefore your members which are upon the earth; fornication, uncleanness, inordinate affection, evil desire, and covetousness, which is idolatry; for which things' sake the wrath of God cometh on the children of disobedience…'

The Names of True Penitents Not Blotted Out
The second promise from the risen Lord to Sardis is: 'I will not blot his name out of the book of life' (Rev. 3:5). We read in Isaiah 49:16 that our names are engraved on the palms of God's hands. Similarly, he says here that he will not blot out our names.

From the rest of Scripture, I do not think this implies that all of the descendants of Adam are born into the world with their names in the book of life, and that then because of their sins, God blots out many of the names that were originally recorded. It is simply saying that if you come to Christ in faith, he has given you his life in the Holy Spirit, who unites you to your Savior forever, so that your name is recorded in God's book of life, never to be taken out.

The Perseverance of the Saints

Sometimes this is spoken of as 'the perseverance of the saints'. The true meaning of perseverance is not that anyone who makes a nominal profession of faith is automatically a Christian, and no matter how much he or she sins, is eternally secure. That is a dreadful perversion of the truth of perseverance. What perseverance really means is that God puts eternal life into sinners, thus regenerating them. He gives them new hearts that are focused on him (see Jeremiah 31 and Hebrews 8). They keep 'looking to Jesus in faith' out of a God-given desire to please the Master. They are imperfect, so they still have to keep repenting; yet they are profoundly depending on the Lord. These things show that they have the life of God in their souls, and thus that their name is in the Lamb's book of life, (or with Isaiah, their name is inscribed on the palm of God's hand, where it will always remain. As Augustus Toplady wrote in his hymn:

> My name from the palms of his hands,
> Eternity will not erase;
> Impressed on his heart it remains,
> In marks of indelible grace;
> Yes, I to the end shall endure,
> As sure as the promise is given;
> More happy, but not more secure,
> The glorified spirits in heaven.

One of the Puritans said: 'The life of faith is made up of ever new beginnings.' That is, if we are granted true faith in God's miracle of regeneration of sinners, then we have the inner disposition from the continued influence of the Spirit of Christ to keep repenting, to please the heart of our Savior. Sardis was warned, as many of us need to be warned, that final refusal to repent from nominal Christianity means our names will not be recorded in the book of life. It is our human responsibility not to ask to peer into the book of life in heaven, but to seek the grace of the Holy Spirit of Christ to trust in our Savior, penitently and gladly following him to the end.

8

THE CHURCH AT PHILADELPHIA

Revelation 3:7–13

We generally think of the judgment of God as a very awesome and frightening matter, and certainly it is, given God's complete holiness and our imperfections and sinfulness. To think of standing before him is most sobering, if we really believe the Bible. On the other hand, there is another side to the judgment of God that we sometimes forget, and that is that the judgment of God can also be very good news. It can be just as happy news as the gospel itself. Imagine what it will be like, standing before the awesome Throne, with God smiling upon us and saying, 'Well done thou good and faithful servant'.

The Smile of God Upon Philadelphia

Now this latter reality of God's smiling upon his people is exactly what is happening as the risen Christ talks to his church at Philadelphia. Most of the other churches we have studied are given some praise and a good bit of criticism, but Philadelphia and Smyrna are the only two that before the assessment of the Lord received nothing but commendation. So God's favorable judgment is given to those who are faithful to him, for with all of their weakness, they hold on to his promises. For such, God's judgment is glorious good news, which is why the Saints are taught to pray, 'Even so, come quickly, Lord Jesus'. For them, Christ's assessment is going to be the greatest pleasure of their entire lives.

There are three matters in this text:

1. The Identity of the Covenant Lord (v. 7).
2. The Assessment of the Church (v. 8-10).
3. Divine Promises (v. 9-12).

IDENTITY OF THE COVENANT LORD

In all of these letters there is a similar structure in each one of the letters to the different churches, although this one is a little different because there is no section on rebuke from the risen Christ. Jesus lets John see what he looks like now in his glory, but the glory he shows John varies somewhat from church to church. The Lord shows each particular church what it needs to remember about him, to help them to get where they are going. Specifically, Jesus shows Philadelphia that he is as perfectly pure and holy as God the Father Almighty is holy in the highest heavens. He shows them that he is absolutely true, without any mixture of falseness or lying. Jesus says, 'Look at my holiness and purity'. Those are what theologians call the attributes or qualities of God. Two of the most important attributes of who God Almighty really is, are his holiness and truth. Jesus says, 'I am like that'.

Why this Emphasis on Christ's Holiness and Truth? Now why would he have shown that aspect to this church at Philadelphia? He did it because the church possibly came the closest of any other church to reflecting those two attributes of God's own character, namely this church was filled with the holiness of the Lord and the truth of the Lord. It is hard for us to realize how pleased God is when he sees his own character reflected in his children, especially when they are in a difficult situation.

God is interested in his children on earth, and in our specific responses to the trials that he lets come into our life. With all of God's greatness and majesty, we tend to feel that God is not interested in us little creatures. But that is not right! If we could say God has the telescopic view of everything, we must at the same time say, God has the microscopic view of everything, so that he is interested in the smallest details of his children's lives. Furthermore, when God, the Father on the throne, is looking down here and sees the likeness, the qualities of Jesus Christ reflected in some of the believers' lives, then his heart is gladdened.

That seems impossible to our human thinking. Since God has everything, what does he need? Why bother with us? Of course, as Almighty God, he needs nothing. He is not dependent on us. And yet he made us and longs for us to be like Christ, and so when the Father sees that some of his children are being faithful and reflecting the holiness of Jesus in their lives, he is just as happy as a human parent when they have reason to think that their children are carrying on the faith and are living as real Christians. That is who God with all of his greatness really is. We must remember that God has a very tender, Father's heart, so that you and I have the honorable possibility of making our heavenly Father's heart glad. You might not be able to change the world, but you can do something more significant than that. You can make the heart of your Heavenly Father glad!

Yes, it is all by grace, but still, when he sees the likeness of Jesus in us he is pleased. That is why he was very pleased with this church at Philadelphia.

Christ Wears the Keys on his Belt
Then Jesus through John shows Philadelphia something else about himself. It is like what we find in Revelation 1:18, with its splendid vision of the risen Lord. There we see that the risen Lord was wearing a belt, a high priestly sash, and hanging on this belt were some keys. In this picture Jesus is saying to Philadelphia, 'I want you to remember that I have a set of keys hanging at my belt, and that I am using those keys to open some important doors for you. So do not worry about what the opposition, particularly in the Jewish Synagogue, will be able to do against you. Do not worry about the doors they seem able to slam in your face. They cannot close any doors against you, without my permission, because I have hanging by my belt, as the risen Lord to whom the Father has committed all authority in heaven and on earth, these invisible keys. I am using them right now to open the very doors that you need passage through.'

The picture of this risen Christ with the keys at his side comes from Isaiah 22:22, where there was a man who had the keys to the king's treasury, by which he could get in and out, to provide all that was needed. In similar fashion, we are told in Revelation 1:18 that the Lord Jesus Christ has the keys to death and to Hades, (to the other world), to the most important issues that affect every soul. He has the key to every other door that is related to the most important affairs that a human being deals with in his life. He has those keys. The wonderful thing is not just that to Jesus is committed the keys of the most important things that ever happened in world history and in human life, but Jesus uses those keys for the advantage of his servants in the believing church.

How actively the risen Christ has been employing these invisible keys! Only one thing is necessary for the church to go forward and for the gospel to work, and that is for the risen Christ to use the keys. From the 1780s to the 1830s there was a tremendous movement of the risen Christ coming to South Carolina and North Carolina, up and down the East Coast, using the keys to open the doors to the hearts of sinful men and women. It was a time known as the Second Great Awakening, which lasted on and off for about fifty years, when one revival after another came along. In the Carolinas it swept through with hundreds of thousands being saved. God went up and down the Carolinas using the keys. Again in 1858 and 1859 the Lord was moving up and down the Carolinas and in other places like New York, as well as across the Atlantic in Scotland, Northern Ireland, and England, opening the doors of the souls of men and women, ushering hundreds of thousands into the Body of Christ.

So the Christ says to Philadelphia, 'Don't worry about the situation you are up against; what they think they can do to you; how they think they can stop your influence. I have the keys and I know how to use them. At the right time I will open the doors because you have been faithful and true. Stick to my gospel, for I am going to get you through all kinds of trials in which your holiness and truth will spread to many another'. That's the risen Christ and the aspect that he showed them.

Assessment of the Church

Secondly, there is the divine assessment of the church at Philadelphia (as there is of all of these seven churches of Asia). But in this assessment, there are no words of criticism. Instead, he mentions four things that he is very happy about.

They Took Advantage of Opportunities

First, he says 'I know thy works'. You are faithful and busy. These works are not specified, but probably he means good works in the name of Christ; giving the message of salvation; ministering to the poor; letting the love of God flow through them in practical ways to the community. They did whatever they could, however limited their resources, so that others could know the same blessing of Jesus that they knew.

Philadelphia at this time was a crossroads of the world, a big trading center where major highways came together. All sorts of trading meant that people of many languages, countries, and beliefs were flooding into Philadelphia to trade in the markets. That church was out there getting into the market, doing what they could to tell people about Jesus.

Maybe they weren't able to go over the world, but the world was coming to them and that is one of the things that America and Britain need to be aware of, with all of these foreigners coming in to live, work, and study. We need to be thoughtful and active towards the foreigners who are here. We must consider that one of the reasons the Lord may be letting so many foreign workers come into our countries is to give us an opportunity to reach them with the grace of Christ in a way that we could not in their home country.

The church at Philadelphia was grasping this opportunity, and the Lord was pleased. Something that counted for eternity was happening, because Christ was opening the door for them. As

Christians increase their efforts to touch people's lives, Christ is actively opening the door.

Why Weak People Can Do Great Things
Then next, Christ says, 'you have a little strength'. That was not a criticism, but a realistic comment. He is saying, 'you are up against tremendous odds'. It appears that the Jews at Philadelphia had influence with the upper echelon of pagan leadership of the Empire, and through them were trying to get the church shut down. In light of this strong opposition, Christ said: 'you do not have much strength over against them, but use what you have, and I will open such doors as the opposition has never imagined so that your little strength will become supernaturally mighty.[20]

God never asks us to worry about how small our strength is and how great the opposition is. Yet many Christians do so as they contemplate the aggressive secularism of modern America and Western Europe, with systematic unbelief in high places, such as the universities and the media. Add to that the entrenched Modernism of the educational system, and the precipitous moral decline in once-Christian populations. It is true that over against them our strength is small. But Jesus says that we are not anxiously to worry about it. 'You have a little strength; use what little you have, and I am going to supernaturally multiply it by opening the right doors'. He tells us to use what little strength we have; to lay hold by faith of what portions we know of the Scriptures, and then turn them into particular prayers. He instructs us to do whatever good we can do for the poor and the needy. Even the weakest of us can make some visits to those who are discouraged. You cannot buy a needy family a new Mercedes-Benz, but you can give them a cup of cold water or a loaf of bread. Through these humble actions, Jesus will open invisible doors. On the solemn Judgment Day we will find out the majestic power of a giant was in the scanty strength we had insofar as we used it for the Lord.

A Church That Kept to the Bible
Then thirdly, Christ says to Philadelphia: 'you have kept my word'; that is, you have stuck to the Bible. That is what Philadelphia did. They stuck to the Bible (or the parts of it that they then had). One of the churches we looked at recently had gone away from the Bible as far as their real heart was concerned. But the people God uses for his glory to transform sinners and to bring in the kingdom of beauty and light are the ones who simply believe that the Bible is true and give their heart and soul to the Lord who inspired it.

The reason that hundreds of American presbyterian churches from about 1973 pulled out of the denominational connection that we had all been born and raised in was because we believed that the denominational connection of our forefathers had departed from the faith of our forefathers. They were not teaching in the seminaries the Virgin Birth, the Deity of Christ, his bodily Resurrection, or following his Blood Atonement. They had quit believing the Bible and teaching ministerial students the Bible. That is the reason why almost twenty years ago I left the parish ministry to teach in Reformed Seminary, because it was committed to the Bible.

They Were Proud of the Name of Christ
The fourth thing he says is 'you have not denied my name'. One of the other churches that we have looked at began to backpedal on the Deity of Christ and the one way of salvation in and through Christ Jesus, in order not to offend the other religions. That is to deny his name. I suspect that Christian people in this country are going to come under more and more pressure as the years

go by to accommodate themselves to Islam, to keep Islam from being offended as we teach the Holy Trinity and salvation by grace. But in my opinion, the only way you can keep Islam from being angry with you is to convert to Islam. Nothing less is likely to satisfy them.

But the risen Christ commends Philadelphia precisely on this point. He said 'You didn't do that. You didn't backpedal. You have said Christ is God, he is the way to the Father and I am pleased with you and I am going to use you, for you have not denied my name'.

Divine Promises

Finally, we see the divine promises in verses 9–12. Christ promises some great and practical blessing to Philadelphia. In verse 9, he first of all promises that he will deal with the enemies of the church. In this case, the greatest pressure was coming from a very powerful synagogue of people who said they were true Jews, but they really rejected the message of the Old Testament which comes to its fulfillment in Christ the Messiah. On the contrary, they hated Christ the Messiah, and hated his people and so were using all the political and financial influence they had to destroy the church. But Jesus said, 'do not worry about that. I will deal with them'.

Let God Deal With Your Enemies

He doesn't tell them how he will deal with them and we never know ahead of time how he will deal with our own enemies. When facing some kind of enemy who is making your spirit feel troubled, Jesus says, 'If you will keep your eyes on me, and seek my holiness and truth, I will deal with your enemies'.

When facing difficulties, the first question we normally raise is, 'Lord, how are you going to deal with them? What are you going to do? When are you going to do it?' He won't tell you. It is not your business. He says, 'I will deal with them, if you will put it in my hands, keep on doing what you are doing with faithfulness and truth; be zealous to do good works, and I will handle your enemies at just the right time'. That is why Romans 12 says, 'Do not seek to repay your enemies on a personal level. Vengeance is mine; I will repay, saith the Lord'. Jesus says 'Don't be disturbed in your heart over your enemies. Leave them to me, I will take care of them, so you keep your energy for faith and good works. I will handle it'. But he does not tell us how. We have to walk by faith, not by sight.

Secondly he says, 'I will keep you in the hour of trial'. We do not know exactly whether it meant under the coming persecution of Nero, or later persecution from the Roman Empire, or when Islam came in about six hundred years after this letter was written. I would say that it applies to all of those times. 'I will keep you in the hour of trial'.

The Church at Philadelphia Endured

It is very interesting to note that Jesus fulfilled his word to this church at Philadelphia. The great New Zealand scholar, Blaiklock, brings out in one of his books, that at the time of World War I, the only one of the seven churches that still had lineal descendents and that had never closed down, even under the horrors of Islam and the Turks, was Philadelphia. Upon the outbreak of World War I, it still had five congregations.[21] So the Lord Jesus Christ literally kept his word across nearly two thousand years. This is the only one of the seven churches that never ceased to be a church of worship and witness. Jesus kept his word about being faithful to them in the hour of trial over many a century.

Humble Folk Are Made Pillars in God's House

Then finally, 'I will make you pillars of the house of my God.' He says to the faithful folk, many of them just humble ordinary shopkeepers or fishermen, or street sweepers, with some of them higher up in society, 'Keep the faith.' He promises that one day they are going to be furniture in the heavenly temple of the New Jerusalem. They are going to be part of the temple. Think of these beautiful Gothic cathedrals, such as Westminster Abbey in London or Notre Dame in Paris. One of the glories is the gorgeous columns and the arches and the fretted vaults on the inside of the marvelous structures. Without the columns, those cathedrals could never have been erected.

He is saying that part of what the glory and joy of heaven is going to be is you, just this ordinary person out there selling fish on Monday morning, a little wife with a kerchief on. I can see her with a basket of fish, selling fish in Philadelphia on the streets. One day she is going to shine brighter than the stars in the firmament for ever and ever. She is going to be like a cathedral pillar; a constituent part of the temple of the Lord God Almighty.

But how is that possible? Jesus says, 'I will make you pillars'. Every person who believed in him and sought to follow Jesus will make heaven brighter. The true believer is actually going to make heaven brighter than it would be otherwise and thus bring pleasure to the heart of God the Father Almighty. That is why he says in conclusion, in verse 13, 'He that hath an ear let him hear what the Spirit saith to the church'.

How very different this is from worldly thinking! The world says, 'this is all there is and you lose if you do not get into the world system and cooperate with them and become part of them, then you lose everything'. But the risen Lord says, 'Do not listen'. Instead, listen to what the Holy Spirit says. The Spirit beautified the work of creation. Listen to the spirit who says, 'If you concentrate on Jesus, and give your life to him, I will make you one day pillars in the House of God. You will be more beautiful than any columns in the most gorgeous cathedrals of Europe. You will be lovelier than the most beautiful Georgian mansion, the most wonderful palace or castle, than the loveliness of snow capped mountains, the beauty of the foaming seas, and the green meadows of the forest. All of that will be nothing compared to the beauty that our whole universe is going to admire when I get through with making you what I have planned for you to be. Keep that in mind!'

9

The Church at Laodicea

Revelation 3:14-22

This church at Laodicea is the last of the famous seven churches of Asia to whom the risen Christ sends a message.

We have an expression in English, 'from the sublime to the ridiculous'. While the word, 'ridiculous', does not apply to God's churches, nonetheless you go from the top to the bottom as far as true Christian spirituality is concerned when you place Philadelphia, which was probably the best of the seven churches, right beside Laodicea, which was the worst. It is a strange contrast: Philadelphia was the finest, and received nothing but praise from God, but Laodicea was the worst, and received almost nothing but rebuke from God, who nonetheless rebuked them because he still loved them.

I wonder which one of these two churches, most accurately reflects who you really are spiritually? As for me, I can see a little bit of all seven churches in me; at times, some good aspects, some bad, and some indifferent. But there is good news in what would otherwise be a devastating passage.

God's grace reaches us whether we are like Philadelphia, or Laodicea or any of the seven churches. God's grace reaches out to us in love and says, 'It can be different if you listen to me.'

The message to Laodicea contains the same three points that we see in the letters to all seven churches:

1. The identity of the Covenant Lord (v. 14).
2. An assessment of the Church (v. 15-17).
3. A Gracious Promise (v. 18-22).

Identity of the Covenant Lord

John shows to Laodicea what he himself saw (Rev. 1:5) when he was knocked flat on the ground with the splendor of the glorified body of Jesus Christ. It was that aspect of the risen Christ that they most needed to see and it was different from what the other six churches needed to see.

Laodicea is now shown three truths about the risen Christ, and these three truths are all really one truth. Different words are used to convey the one truth that Laodicea really needed to hear.

Christ the Amen

Christ says I am 'the Amen', second, 'the faithful witness' (which is another way of saying 'amen'), and thirdly, 'the true witness' (which is yet another way to say 'amen'). He effectively says: 'I am Amen; yes, I am Amen, and yes I am Amen'. Then he gives a reason that backs up why he is 'the threefold Amen'. At the conclusion of the service, some congregations sing 'Amen, Amen, Amen'. That is very Biblical. Christ is the threefold Amen and he says the reason that I can be the 'Yes' (another biblical way of saying 'Amen') to you is that I am the origin and the complete controller of everything in created reality; I am in charge of it all, and that is why I am able to work it all out where at the end of your life, there is a loud ringing 'YES', if you look towards me.

Christ is God's 'yes' to all the promises of the Bible that apply to us. He establishes the reality of those promises. He puts wheels on it and gets the blessing right into your body and soul. Jesus is able to do that; he is the 'Amen'. This is precisely what 1 Corinthians 1:20 says: 'All the promises of God in him (that is, in Christ) are yes, and in him are Amen'. Here is the key to get any appropriate promise in the Bible we need. We go to Jesus and when he deems it to be right for us, he says 'yes'.

You do not sign the check in your own name, and take it down to the bank, because we are spiritually bankrupt. Instead, we go to Jesus, who signs the check for heaven's bank, making over to the believer any promise that the Lord decides he needs for that day. Thus, Christ is the 'Amen', the 'yes' to the promises of God.

Christ the Faithful Witness

Christ is 'the faithful witness'. 'The faithful witness' is a rendition of the Hebrew 'Amen'. In Hebrew the word they employ for 'to have faith in God' and 'to trust in God' is the same word from which we get 'Amen'. In Genesis 15:6, when it says 'Abraham believed the Lord, and the Lord reckoned it to him for righteousness', a literal translation of the Hebrew text is as follows: 'Abraham amened the Lord and God said you are righteous before me for all eternity'. So Jesus is the 'Amen', the one who believes God in our place, as our Covenant Head, and then his belief flows over into us and we believe.

Christ the True Witness

Jesus Christ is 'the true witness'. Again, 'true witness' is another translation of the Hebrew word for 'Amen'. 'Amen' literally means 'let it be established, let it be counted true'. That is, 'let it be totally carried through'. This is opposed to false, empty religious talk that does not carry through.

How often we hear of men who married a young woman in church, and during the ceremony took the vow 'until death do us part'. Yet in a very few years they abandon the wife to whom they are bound by lasting, holy vows before God, and take up with someone else. Our society is full of people taking all kinds of vows and not meaning them. They get under pressure and temptation and they break their vows, leaving devastation behind. Jesus is not like that. He carries through to the death and into the next world every promise he ever makes to you. You can rely on him to the end. He is not the false witness, not the prevaricating witness, he is the true witness. Some of the old gospel hymns express well this confidence, such as 'How firm a foundation', and 'Standing on the promises'.

Then he gives the reason that he is the threefold Amen, faithful witness, the true witness; he explains why he is able to carry out everything he said he would do. It is because he is the origin and the controller of the whole creation of God. We read in John 1:3 that the Father created this whole cosmos, with everything in the oceans, and everywhere else. He created them through the agency of the Lord Jesus Christ. And in addition to that, Colossians 1:15–18 tells us that 'All things hold together (cohere) in Christ', who brought it into being in the first place. The significance of that shows us why Christ is able to carry out whatever promise we can validly claim from God's Word in faith. Jesus controls everything you will ever walk through.

Think of the international organizations trying to empty out mine fields. We are to remember that Christ is in control of all of the mines in all of the fields that we can ever go through. He is in total charge. He has the power and the heart to see you through, and he will do exactly that.

Why did Laodicea need reminding of that aspect of truth about the risen glorious Lord? The reason is clear from this passage. Laodicea had become largely unfaithful and untrue, and was acting in a false and dishonest way. Instead of looking to Christ as God's answer for their needs, they were looking at lower realities. They were trusting in various aspects of the created order. They were trusting in the wealth that they had collected. This was probably the richest of all of the seven churches and instead of looking to the one who owns all the gold and silver and the cattle on a thousand hills, they were looking to their created wealth. Their hearts had grown cool or lukewarm, and their hands and feet very inactive in doing good. They had lost zeal for God, they had cooled off and were rapidly becoming a church that is an empty shell.

God rebukes them for their falsehood, because God still loved them and was offering them a way back. That is the wonderful thing about the rebukes of the Lord. If God goes finally silent on you, everything is finished; you are past the point of no return. Hell is certain. But as long as God is speaking and chastening, there is still a wonderful opportunity offered that can make an eternal difference.

Assessment of Laodicea

All seven churches of Asia were assessed. The one immediately before Laodicea, the 'sublime' one, if I may call it that (Philadelphia), received nothing but praise from the risen Lord Jesus. But this one receives nothing but rebuke, except for an all-important offer of grace. In verses 15–17, we are shown what that church at Laodicea was really like. We notice three things in this reading of the internal organs and the functions of the people, who called themselves the people of God, in Laodicea.

First of all, he says, 'I know thy works'. What he means is clear. 'I know your lack of good works. The fact that you are not doing anything to help people, to encourage them in the name of Jesus, shows that you are no longer hot. You are not on fire for God with burning love for people. Yet you are not totally cold, you have no excuse that you have never heard the gospel. You are not hot and you are not cold'.

Lukewarmness of Laodicea

Historians and archaeologists tell us something very interesting about the city of Laodicea. The ruins of it are still there. The reference to Laodicea as being lukewarm would be like calling Chicago the 'windy city', or London 'the foggy city', or Paris 'the city of lights'.

Laodicea was called 'lukewarm Laodicea' for this reason. Two nearby cities had a wonderful water supply. One was called Hierapolis. It was about six miles from Laodicea. Hierapolis had piping hot springs, literally springing out of the earth, with mineral elements in the water. Then another city, Colossae, to which one of Paul's letters was written, was eleven miles away from Laodicea and it had cold springs that poured out pure almost icy water for the needs of the public. Laodicea did not have much of a water supply but it was a big, wealthy, commercial center so that the Empire built a Roman Aqueduct to carry water to it through its long pipes upon arches.

An aqueduct ran to Laodicea from the hot water supply of the mineral springs of Hierapolis. When the water would leave those hot water sources in the caves of Hierapolis, it went through the Roman Aqueduct and by the time it traveled those six miles, the water had become lukewarm.[22] Medically, lukewarm water can induce vomiting, whereas hot or cold water in general does not. Now Jesus bluntly says that the Christians of Laodicea are as lukewarm as the city water supply. They are not truly cold, that is without any knowledge of the way of salvation. They have at least got it in their head and can talk good talk. Nor are they hot for God, but they are disgustingly lukewarm. They have cooled off from the fervency of vital faith in Jesus and the accompanying hopes of heaven, which make believers eager to bless others. They are lukewarm because their heart is really focused on the paltry pleasures and honors of this passing world. Their lukewarmness is shown by their lack of good works, with no effective witness to the lost, no zeal for prayer meetings, little or no visitation of the sick and imprisoned, and no organizing of collections to relieve the needs of the poor. In other words, lack of zealous, loving, caring lives is one of the sure signs of loss of true faith in Christ. It is a warning post from God—'Danger Ahead'— if we have cooled off in our desire out of love for Jesus to be a blessing in other lives. Jesus says, 'Watch it. You are about to run into quicksand, into the rapids that will take you down'. As the Lord assesses his church quite honestly, he is blunt in order to help them, to let them see where they really are, so that they can act.

Material Wealth No Substitute for Spiritual Wealth
Next, he who sees beneath the surface right into the heart, says 'You say you are rich and need nothing'. That would be the case, I suspect in many prosperous places in our own wealthy nation. Christians who engage in evangelistic door-to-door visitation are often told by people, 'Thanks for coming but I really do not have time to talk. I am fine, thank you very much; if I need you I will call you. Don't call me, I will call you, for everything is alright with me'. So they thought they were rich and needed nothing because they foolishly thought that they already had everything.

Do you know what that means? It means that the church people at Laodicea failed to perceive the difference between material wealth and spiritual wealth. That is one of the greatest problems in America and Britain today, for people inside and outside the church in this well off culture. The danger is that because we are materially well off, at least as compared to other countries, we will think we are spiritually well off. We can begin to think, 'Because I am on top physically, materially, and economically, when I get into the next world, obviously I will be on top there, because I am on top here. I deserve it'.

We know from secular history that there had been a terrible earthquake in that part of the world a few years before John wrote this letter. Afterwards, the Roman government had to help rebuild several cities which had been damaged by the earthquake, but Laodicea refused any help from the central government. Laodicea was still so rich that even though the walls and many buildings had been shaken down, they told the government ,'We do not need any of your money, we have all the gold and the silver banked up, so we will take care of ourselves'.

There is nothing wrong with having wealth. Abraham was rich, and Joseph became rich, but the question is what do we do with it? Do we still trust in God? Do we use it to bless the needy and to expand the Kingdom, after taking out what we really need? Or, do we start trusting in the wealth, in the stocks, in the lands and go lukewarm on Him, who alone should be the trust of our heart? That is the question. They thought they were rich and needed nothing.

Freedom from Persecution and Spirituality
These Laodicean Christians were not under any persecution from the Roman Pagans, nor from the Jewish Synagogue,[23] yet they were in the worst shape spiritually. We might foolishly think that we must be very wonderful because we are not being persecuted, whereas Christians are being killed in Sudan and Indonesia. Laodicea was not being persecuted by the pagans or by the Jews because they had lost the offensiveness of the gospel. Their lives were no longer salted to preserve from corruption. They were no longer the light of the world to shine with the beauty of the purity of Jesus and thus offend pagans. Once you grow cool on the Lord, you lose the offensiveness of the gospel and the devil has no interest in persecuting you.

Only a foolish person sets out to be offensive. To act towards the world with unnecessary offence is wrong; it is a bad testimony. But on the other hand, the price of being universally liked by a sinful world is to lose the reality of having your life full of God. That is often a temptation for preachers. If you get your eyes too much on a congregation and want everybody to like you, you get your eyes off God, and thereby lose the offensiveness of the gospel. You will be no good to those people. The basic trouble is that we become more concerned with what people think of us, than with their eternal welfare. In other words, what we really love is self, rather than the people. The risen Jesus says that to become lukewarm on the Lord means that the real focus of your emotional life is on the assessment of the world around you rather than on the face of Jesus. That is to enter the danger zone of being nauseating to the Lord God Almighty and spewed out of the place where you can be divinely used.

Wait on God Rather Than Exalting Self
Now the self-satisfied religious person, like many in Laodicea, thinks, 'I have need of nothing, I can cope with the world and make whatever reasonable compromise may be necessary to cope and to be well thought of. So I can keep my pride, I can have the world and I will handle it with skill.' But even while his possessions and honors are increasing, his soul is shriveling up on the inside. What spiritual blindness it is when we are no longer able to discern our own true standing before God! Proudly to say: 'I have need of nothing, everything is fine' is the opposite of Psalm 62, where the Psalmist cries out: 'My soul, wait thou only upon the Lord, for all my expectation is from Him.'

In Andrew Murray's little devotional book, *Waiting on God*, there is a meditation for each day in a thirty-one day month. He brings out the profound truth that the essence of true Christianity is dependence on the Lord, waiting on God for everything, large or small, for forgiveness, strength, life, and hope. But it would appear that the folk at Laodicea, far from waiting upon God, were depending on their own abilities to get out of the world system what they needed.

No Awareness of their Fatal Condition
A third assessment of Laodicea is this: Jesus says, 'You do not realize that you are wretched, miserable, poor, blind, naked'. Let me summarize just two of these words.

Miserable. Had you passed them on the street, wearing their fine clothes, and going to their well-appointed homes, you would not have thought that they were in the category of 'miserable'. But the all-seeing One says that they were empty on the inside; they were trusting in the externals of that culture and their considerable part in it. Therefore, Jesus says, 'You really are miserable'.

The same Greek word for 'miserable', is found in 1 Corinthians 15:19 that says, 'if Jesus is not risen and we do not have a share in his resurrection, then we are of all men most miserable'. Perhaps we should connect these two passages from Revelation and 1 Corinthians to discern what an awful reality this word 'miserable' conveys. On resurrection day, there are two classes of those who will come out of the graveyards. There is the resurrection of the just or 'the resurrection unto honor', by which the bodies of the justified will be resurrected to honor, glory and beauty. But there is another resurrection, one so awful that Paul does not give a description of it in 1 Corinthians 15. It is the resurrection of the lost, the resurrection of those who were not justified through faith in Jesus. They indeed are raised, so that they receive back their bodily form in which they must experience the never-ending consequences of life separated from God. Holy Scripture does not give us a description of the resurrected bodies of the lost, other than to describe it as 'shameful' and 'miserable'. I take it that the Risen Lord is saying, 'You are miserable now, so watch out, or you will not have a part in the resurrection of the just if you remain as you are. Jesus warns them while there is still time for repentance. It is a warning given out of the love of God.

Spiritual Blindness. Then Christ utters this word, 'you are blind'. That was particularly appropriate historically for Laodicea. We are told that it had the most prestigious eye hospital in the ancient world. People came from all over the world to the hospital at Laodicea. Ancient writers say that they had a particular eye salve made of certain plants and flowers, mixed with dust ground from particular stones. Apparently, they had learned to concoct a wonderful eye salve that would relieve various ocular diseases, and at times actually restore sight. Naturally, Laodicea was proud of its wonderful eye hospital. It would seem that Christ was saying something like this: 'Although you are the world's best in giving people help with their physical eyes, you are blind to your own potentially disastrous spiritual state.'[24]

A GRACIOUS PROMISE
When we have to rebuke offenders, we will do well to seek the divine grace to do it as the Lord did it to Laodicea. He administered a very stern rebuke, but it was mingled with hope, and given in love. He makes a gracious offering to a church that was in bad spiritual condition, and in imminent danger of being literally spewed out of the mouth of God. Isn't it like Christ to offer sinners and hypocrites something infinitely better than they deserve? That is the meaning of grace!

Essentially, the Lord offers to supply them freely at his own expense with absolutely everything they needed, but only if they—like the prodigal son in the mire of the pigpen—'came to themselves' so that they would see their miserable condition, and admit their need. That is the price: stop hiding in the bushes (like fallen Adam and Eve); face yourself as you are, and then face me. When we do so, we will find that—as the hymn writer says: 'There's a wideness in God's mercy, like the wideness of the sea; there's a kindness in his justice, which is more than liberty!'

Do Not 'Wait Until You're Better'
It is significant that the risen Lord does not require several months or years of improved life

before he makes this offer of grace. No; he first and foremost calls for renewed faith and heartfelt repentance. No doubt, amendment of life will follow; but it is the fruit of grace, not the condition of it.

Over twenty-five years ago, a woman came to see me in the church office, where I was serving as minister. It was widely known that her life was out of line with true godliness. She would vaguely admit that she had a spiritual problem, but made it clear that she was unwilling to seek God's gracious intervention into her life. Her words were something like this: 'Well, I know my life is not just right, but by and by I am going to do better, and then everything will be fine with the Lord'. I looked her straight in the eye and said to her, 'No, what you are saying is not right. You seem to think that you can reform yourself without God's grace, and in that way commend yourself to God. But that is a hopeless, counterproductive attitude.' Then I quoted to her a verse from a Welsh hymn: 'If you wait until you are better, you will never come at all; not the righteous, not the righteous; sinners Jesus came to call'. I earnestly besought her to cast herself just as she was on the mercy of Jesus. But she left our meeting, still vainly hoping to commend herself to God. It was a sad day.

Seek For True Gold
Would that she could have heard what the gracious Lord offers to Laodicea and to every repentant compromiser in any church, in any age, on any day! He offers four things: First, 'buy of me gold tried in the fire'. What did he mean by 'refined gold'? Obviously he is not speaking literally. He is speaking allegorically. Look in 1 Peter 1:7: 'That the trial of your faith, being much more precious than of gold that perisheth, though it be tried with fire, might be found unto praise and honor and glory at the appearing of Jesus Christ'. That is what is meant by 'the refined gold'.

Well there is gold and gold. I have a friend in Mississippi who had a very wealthy uncle. After this wealthy uncle died, my friend was asked to go with his widowed aunt to the bank to help her clean out the many deposit boxes in the vault. My friend said that they took out drawer after drawer that was packed full of South African gold pieces. The Clerk of Court stacked up those gold pieces on a big long marble table in the vault of the bank—over a million dollars worth of gold, plus all else that he had. Then the Clerk of Court picked up the gold and put it back into the drawers, and my friend said that there was gold dust on the marble table, so that he was tempted when nobody was looking, to scrape it off in his hand and put it in his pocket. It was gold. When the uncle died, he left all that gold. He could not take it with him where he went. But the true gold, Jesus says, can be taken with you.

Do you know what true gold is? It is refined by fire. It is Holy Ghost character, or true Christ-like character, worked into the depths of our soul by a life of depending on Jesus through thick and through thin, not looking at our own character, but looking to him, so that something truly supernatural happens on the inside.

Romans 5:3-5 describes this: 'We glory in tribulations also; knowing [Laodicea was not in tribulation, they had lost the offensiveness of the gospel] that tribulation worketh patience; and patience, experience; and experience hope: And hope maketh not ashamed; because the love of God is shed abroad in our hearts by the Holy Ghost which is given unto us'. Jesus says, 'Above everything else in this world, get hold of this gold that you can take with you, which is a godly Christian character.' It comes from looking to Jesus. He says 'Buy it.' We reply, 'But it is too expensive. I cannot even buy five Krugerrands; how could I get this refined gold that goes with me into heaven?' Jesus says, 'You have to buy it on my terms'. What are his terms? You will find them in Isaiah 55:1: 'Ho, everyone that thirsteth, come ye to the waters, and he that hath no money; come ye, and buy and eat; yea, come, buy wine and milk without money and without price'.

You know the line in 'Rock of Ages': 'Nothing in my hands I bring, simply to Thy cross I cling'. But the Laodiceans did not know how naked they were, so they could not say: 'Naked look to Thee for dress, helpless look to Thee for grace; foul, I to the fountain fly, wash me Saviour ere I die'. Realize your need, and look up to him with empty hands. Fine gold worked deep into your character through a life time of looking to Jesus.

Beautiful White Garments

In offering us 'refined gold', he offers us, unworthy people, some of the finest things in the world. He offers 'white garments' to cover the shame of sinful nakedness. We remember how Adam and Eve realized they were naked after they had sinned, and went and hid in the bushes because the holiness of God scared them. It is like that with unsaved people or compromising Christians, when God's presence becomes apprehensible. But Jesus says, 'I will cover you and clean you up with my blood, no matter what you have done. Not one thing, no matter how bad, no matter how rotten, no matter how compromising, can keep you back'. He says, 'I will clean you up with my blood, so that the purity and whiteness of my holy life will be put upon you like royal robes that you receive through faith in me'.

We are told that if you would walk the streets of Laodicea at the time that this letter was written, you would have been surprised. Most of the people would have been wearing black clothing. That is because they bred a tremendous number of sheep with black wool, and all over the city there were mills that made this black wool into nice clothing, which was then shipped all over the world. So the people of Laodicea wore black woolen garments (except the pagan priest wore white).[25] Jesus says, 'What you need to be in is white, a spiritual white and beauty that gives you entrance to heaven, access when you pray, and hope when you die. You can get the white garments from me, because I have done everything that needs to be done to make you white and pure, but you are not going to have it until you look to me and ask for the blood to be applied.'

Eye Salve

The risen Lord then offers 'salve to anoint the eyes'. We have already said that what they called the Phrygian salve was especially made in Laodicea. Many doctors wish we knew today what the formula was, because it was so wonderful to cure pink eye and to help with glaucoma. It seems that they were ahead of their time medically. Yet they were spiritually blind, and Jesus says, 'I am offering you something for your spiritual blindness, I offer you a salve that will take care of it so that you can see your way to heaven. It is the unction of the Holy Spirit to heal the eyes of your soul, so you can recognize your need and look to me, to Jesus'. He speaks in this manner in 1 John 2:20: 'But you have an unction from the Holy One, and you know all things'. That unction from the Holy One, from the Holy Spirit, is the salve that penetrates deeply, not into the physical eye, but into the spiritual eye of the soul, so that it can then see, and in seeing, know God and be eternally saved. This is the divinely appointed salve to anoint the eyes.

God Invites Spiritual Failures to Enter his Door

Finally, we notice verses 19–20: 'As many as I love, I rebuke and chasten: be zealous therefore, and repent. Behold, I stand at the door and knock: if any man hear my voice, and open the door, I will come in to him, and will sup with him, and he with me.' The risen Christ says that the church people in Laodicea are lukewarm, but promises that they can catch fire again, and be full of the love of God, and full of good works. But they must open the door of their innermost values to the risen Jesus (v. 20). That is what they are asked to do, open up afresh to Jesus.

Here is a mystery. Calvinists and Arminians have debated for a few hundred years concerning which side of this proposition is true. On the one hand, God's sovereign grace is the only thing that can change a sinner's heart. John 6, Ephesians 1, and Romans 8 all with one accord teach this truth. But on the other hand, here and in texts such as Isaiah 55, we are told 'Come and buy'. One side of truth is God's sovereign grace; the other side of the truth is that the Lord holds us morally responsible to open the door whatever our situation. Now which side is true? My answer is both sides are true!

Think of it this way: if you do not have the sovereign grace that has done something in the soul, how could you look to see Jesus? How could you possibly open the door? It's like the miracle at the tomb of Lazarus. He was dead and couldn't make a human response. He had been dead four days. But the voice of Jesus went through the stone tomb into that cave where the rotting body of Lazarus lay still and lifeless, and said 'Lazarus, come forth'. The voice of Jesus chose to go to that dead man and speak the word and in the command of Jesus, there went forth supernatural life-giving power, so that Lazarus got up, still bound in his grave clothes. That is the kind of miracle we are talking about. It passes human understanding to put it all together.

You could take Luke 24:28–32, where the risen Christ unexpectedly shows up to some little-known disciples. At first, he does not let them know who he is, as he talks to them, explaining what his death and resurrection really meant. They were bewildered, but then it was about supper time, so they invited the unknown stranger into the house for supper. The risen Son of God waited purposely to see if they would invite him into their house and they did. When he began to break the bread, they saw the nail prints in his hand and said: 'Did not our hearts burn within us, while he talked with us by the way, and while he opened to us the scriptures?'

That was God's plan for us before the world was made; yet he waits for the elect to open the door to him today, and as he draws near, they will do so.

10

The Throne

Revelation 4:1–3

To grasp the message of this text, we consider three points:

1. The larger structure of the first two visions (chapters 1–8).
2. An Open Door and a Familiar Voice (4:1, 3).
3. The Throne: Its Inhabitant and its Appearance (4:2–3).

The Structure of the First Two Visions

In this second vision is a majestic view of the throne of God, which controls everything in our lives and everything that will ever happen. Our vision of this throne, and our understanding of it, is of utmost importance for the attitude with which we face daily life, and the attitude with which we die in the face of eternity. Let me give you two absolutely contrary illustrations of those who know the throne, and of those who do not.

A number of years ago when the disease of AIDS first became known, I read about a once-famous, handsome movie star (from the 1950s and 60s). He was dying of AIDS in Hollywood, and had contracted the dread disease for obvious reasons. A newspaper related that a Christian actor had visited him to witness to him before it was too late. Without the slightest repentance for how he had lived, this dying movie star said 'I have decided that life doesn't make any sense whatsoever', and that nothing is fair. That is one attitude held by many in times of adversity. Sadly, this famous actor did not have the view of the throne that John shows us here.

Back in the 1680s in Edinburgh, we meet someone who had the opposite viewpoint, because—by faith—he had seen the Throne. And indeed, his circumstances were far worse than those of the once-famous, almost idolized actor facing death by AIDS. An elderly Scottish Presbyterian minister (a Covenanter), Alan Cameron, was in Edinburgh, where he awaited execution for refusing to deny 'the crown rights of Jesus Christ' as understood by the Scottish Reformers. Only hours before, his son, Richard Cameron, also a Covenanter minister, had just been put to death and hanged, after which they cut off his head, his hands, and his feet. The authorities, very cruelly, brought to the prison cell of his elderly father the head and hands of his son, who had been executed earlier that day. They showed them to the saintly old man, and asked him: whose head and hands are these? Both of the Camerons were of very fair complexion. Instantly he said, 'I know them, I know them. They are my son's, my own dear son's. It is the Lord. Good is the will of the Lord, who cannot wrong me nor mine, but has made goodness and mercy to follow us all our days.'

Alan Cameron was a man who by faith had seen John's vision of the Throne. What a difference it makes when we have seen the throne! We can never be defeated in the good cause!

The Structure of This Part of Revelation

First, we must recall the outline of this part of Revelation. It is necessary to consider the structure of this book in order to interpret it properly. We begin a new section with chapter four, where we enter the second great vision John had in the Book of Revelation. The first vision (in chapters 1–3) concerned Christ's appearance to the seven churches of Asia and his assessment of those churches. The second vision (beginning in chapter 4) moves from the earthly seven churches up to heaven, where we are given glorious visions of God's throne, which controls everything in heaven and on earth. This second vision of the sovereign throne runs from chapter 4–8.

Understandable, but not Literal

But before we enter the details of these first three verses and this amazing picture of the power of God, let me say two things about this second vision as a whole. First of all, the message of the first vision to the seven churches was direct and fairly simple, using plain, understandable language, but the message of the second vision, that is of the throne ruling over the whole universe, is given in symbolic language. It is not direct, literal language; it is highly symbolic. Why has the kind of language used between the first vision and the second vision changed so radically?[26]

The reason is that we cannot see God with the human eye, nor with merely human understanding. God is infinitely great. He massively surpasses our limited, finite capacities of seeing and understanding. The Bible says 'no man can look on God and live'. When Paul was taken up to the heaven of heavens, he was not allowed to relate plainly in human words just what he saw in the immediate dwelling place of God. Yet John is allowed to convey tremendously important and greatly needed truth about what the throne can mean in our life and the history of the world from its beginning to the last day. Since God as Spirit is invisible, and infinitely mighty, he cannot be described literally like a photograph or a portrait. To do so is impossible. But the Bible, through saints such as John, can give us the basic meaning of God's throne through symbols and pictures, and these symbols and pictures are all taken from various books of the Old Testament and then filled with light and with meaning to uplift our hearts as we too grasp what the throne is all about.

The Throne and God's Power

That brings me to the second remark about this second vision. Above everything else in these chapters, it conveys this vision: that God's personal power from the throne is in supreme control of everything that ever has been or ever will be allowed to happen anywhere in the universe. That would be important for those seven churches of Asia. They were facing a great deal of hatred, persecution and evil. We do not know how many Christians are in jail today, nor just how they feel about what has happened to them. How would you feel if you were in their place? This vision of the throne teaches us that evil, the worst that Satan can manipulate governments and individuals to do against believers, is always hemmed in by God's power, and ultimately is never allowed to prevent God's predestinated purposes from being carried out in our lives.

Romans 8:28 gives all imprisoned ones great comfort, in saying: 'for we know that all things work together for good to them that love God, to them who are the called according to his purpose'. That is true only because of the throne which controls everything, good and evil. The very structure of the first two visions in this book helps us grasp this aspect of the message given by Christ through John.

An Open Door and a Familiar Voice

The second point of the message comes from verse one where we look at an open door and a familiar voice. First, there is a door between heaven and earth, but it is usually invisible as far as our human eyes are concerned; it is closed to natural observation. We have some tremendously powerful observatories in the USA, like Mount Palomar in California, whose telescope can see far out into remote regions of the solar system. But even the strongest observatories cannot see this heavenly door. You may remember a Soviet Cosmonaut, who went up into space and orbited around the earth in the late 1960s. When he came back to Moscow, he reported to the newspapers that he did not see heaven and he did not see God; therefore, he concluded, there is no God.

What a foolish observation! This door to heaven is closed to natural investigation, except on rare occasions when God himself opens this door and lets somebody see the realm that is the control chamber of everything else. God did so at least four times in the Old Testament; he opened the door between earth and heaven. He did so for Jacob in Genesis 28:17. This young man had fled from home to avoid his brother who wanted to kill him. He must have been very disturbed camping out in the desert, using a stone for a pillow. God opened the door to heaven and Jacob saw a ladder reaching from heaven down to earth and angels going up and down that ladder. We do not know all that he saw, but it would be the basis for the transformation of his life and the establishment of Israel, the forerunner of the church. Jacob learned that heaven is just as real as the earth is real. The ladder leaned on them both. But most of the time, although it is always there, you cannot see it with the human eye.

Centuries later, Isaiah had the door opened to heaven and saw the throne, when he saw the Lord 'high and holy and lifted up and his train filled the temple' (Isa. 6:1). Ezekiel saw it, as we shall discuss later. Daniel saw it (Dan. 7:9). But the Apostle John is even more privileged that any of the Old Testament saints. He is not actually seeing the throne from earth, but rather he is taken up through that invisible door into heaven, where God's throne is. God, and God alone, can open that door to the place of fabulous beauty and sovereign power.

The Future Controlled by the Throne

Anytime you talk about the Book of Revelation, people think of the future. We have history books about the past and in a sense, Revelation is a book written about the future, before it happens. The only way a mortal can know what the future holds would be to go through this hidden door to the control room above, like John, or else, like us on earth, he would have to talk to somebody who has been there. That is how it is with us. That is the major point of this second vision; only at the throne will John be shown precisely what is really going to pass, things that have not yet happened, but are certainly going to occur. He sees it at the throne, because the throne is in charge of everything else. And then he shares a certain amount of it with us in Revelation.

Next, note a familiar voice that John heard. It was the voice of his Lord, the voice of the risen Jesus. It was he who got him through that door. A voice rings out and the door opens, so that John is caught up in the spirit. We do not know exactly how it happened, but somehow, John in the spirit heard the familiar voice of the risen Lord Jesus Christ sounding like a trumpet, (we have already read about that in Revelation 1:10, where the risen Jesus' voice spoke like a trumpet). Now the voice rings out to John, 'Come up hither.' How did John get through this invisible door that the Soviet Cosmonaut could not get through, and that the telescopes cannot see through? The command of the voice of the risen Jesus took him through, right up to where the glorified body of our Lord Jesus Christ is.

The Voice of the Risen Lord tells us of the Future
The way we get access to this throne that controls the future is also by hearing the voice of the risen Jesus. Our concern should never be so much to know what our immediate future is like those unwise people who go to fortune tellers to find out what will happen to them. That is forbidden by scripture. That is dealing with Satan. God does not reveal the precise details of your life between now and the time he calls you home, but you can get in touch with the throne that controls all those details through this voice of our risen Lord Jesus Christ.

A Definite Plan for the Future
Then his voice tells the Apostle John: 'I will show the things which must be hereafter.' As far as John and the churches on earth are concerned, Jesus is saying, 'I am going to show you all you need to know about the future between now and the end of your earthly course, and indeed, end of space-time history. Notice the words 'must be'. God's plan must be carried out. It is not indefinite. It does not mean 'if you do well, things might work out'. Certainly not, it 'must be'; it is going to happen. In other words, Jesus shows John God's plan for the future.

Note that God has a definite plan for everything. That is what the Hollywood movie star did not understand. That is what the Covenanter minister in the prison in Edinburgh, who was shown the chopped off hands of his son did understand. God, who has all the power and tender love, for us and for ours who believe in him, has a definite plan that includes even the painful things in our lives. Ephesians 1:9–11 speak of this plan: 'God works all things after the counsel of his will.' That means that God doesn't merely work out most things, or just the good things; God 'works ALL things after the counsel of his will'.

'The counsel of his will' means his predestinated plan. Everything is being worked out by the one who controls that throne, so the plan will come to pass exactly as God said it would, as God determined it would before he made this universe. For instance, the Old Testament saint, who walked with God, Enoch actually saw the second coming of Christ before he saw the first coming. That was way back in the Book of Genesis. Or take Abraham, before any of his descendants were born. God opened the future to him, and showed him their going down into Egypt and their coming back out hundreds of years later. God let him see the future and it occurred with the greatest precision. God let Isaiah foretell the captivity of the Jews to Babylon and their coming back home, many years before it occurred. That is because the plan had already been worked out. Or consider the details of the sufferings of our Lord Jesus Christ in Psalm 22 and Psalm 69. These were described in literal, precise detail some thousand years before Jesus was born on earth.

So how can a human being accurately know and foretell what is going to happen in the future? God has a plan, and when it is in his will, he opens that invisible door and lets some of his saints see parts of how this plan is being carried out across the centuries.

The Inhabitant of the Throne and his Appearance

This heavenly throne is the place of final power, from which every detail of God's predestinated plan is executed with unerring, exquisite care. From the beginning of history to an endless eternity; everything that happens is an outworking of the program that proceeds from the heart of God, who sits on this glorious throne. In the fourth chapter, the word 'throne' is used thirteen times in eleven verses. It shows the truth of what Daniel once said in the Old Testament, 'the heavens do rule'.

How strong a person may we become? The weakest of us, the frailest of us, can become very strong in character when we have a vision of that throne that rules everything else. What a deep rest and happy trust it brings to the soul who exercises faith in this throne!

Let me say a word about the inhabitant of this throne, who is God Almighty. God cannot ever be directly described. Exodus 20:4 (the second commandment) does not allow 'God who is Spirit' to be directly represented by human images. But, the Bible in general, and especially this book, does convey truth about God's being and activity in terms of certain Old Testament symbols. With God, the invisible has to be represented somewhat indirectly by the visible. This is in accordance with what Paul says in Romans 1:19–21, that we cannot see the invisible God, but we can see the visible things he created and these do show us something about the invisible God.

The Old Testament symbols used here (Rev. 4:2–3) to describe what God is like on that throne come from the breastplate of the high priest. The high priest had a breastplate over his heart when he went into the holiest place of all. There were twelve precious stones on the breastplate, and different precious stones represented each one of the twelve tribes of Israel. Three of those stones are mentioned here. The Authorized Version calls them: jasper, sardius and emerald. It is difficult to know exactly what the stones were, but probably jasper is about the same thing as a diamond; sardius is deep red; emerald is green.

Precious Stones
What do these three precious stones mean when applied to God's throne above? First, the jasper, or diamond, tone of the throne is referred to in Revelation 21:11, which speaks of the glory of God in the New Jerusalem, whose brilliance is like jasper or diamond. In other words, this is speaking of God's shining purity, of his matchless holiness, and white holy glory. 'God is light and in him is no darkness at all'. That is what John saw: the jasper, diamond, tone of that glorious throne reflected God's unsullied holiness.

Next was sardius, sometimes called carmelian stone. This was a beautiful, dark red stone. Here you seem to have the idea of sheer beauty of God's splendid presence. Perhaps it conveys something of the beauty and fascination of fire, without the burning and without the hurt in most fire.[27] This burning beauty is also mentioned in Ezekiel 1:26–8. Ezekiel saw this beautiful red sheen that proceeds from the throne of God. It must have been something like the glory cloud over the tabernacle; apparently a dark, red, splendid beauty.

Where God's immediate presence is, there is always glory and beauty. We do not consider often enough the beauty of God, the source of all created beauties in the world. We are all made to long for beauty, to appreciate beauty wherever we see it: whether it be rivers, trees, an attractive human face, or splendid buildings, beautiful cotton fields, herds of deer, woods covered with snow or a thousand other created beauties. God himself is the source of all this beauty. Augustine, in his *Confessions* speaks of God as 'O Thou ancient beauty, always new, always old'.

Then the Emerald stone, which is obviously something like a greenish rainbow, circling that majestic throne. This seems to speak of the loveliness of eternal life; fresh, pure green in the spring that life triumphs over death. The rainbow is probably speaking of God's Covenant with Noah, the Covenant of the Bow, guaranteeing the orderly continuance of all creation.

These three lovely jewels from the breastplate of the High Priest help describe the out-rayed beauty that the Apostle John saw from God's enthroned presence.

This is to say that all the massive power behind this vast universe is concentrated in an absolutely beautiful Throne. Why then would we feel uneasy to think that God is omnipotent and that 'his kingdom ruleth over all'? Here is the right question: where would you wish the ultimate power to be? Do you want it in the hands of foolish mankind? Do you want it in sinful human government? Do you want it in the hands of the devil? Do you want it in a fortuitous combination of atoms? Where do you want it to be? Would not you want the supreme power to be exactly where it really is: in the throne of this majestic, beautiful and loving God? That is where the final power is, as Noah saw long ago in the Covenant of the Rainbow, and as John saw in his visions on the Isle of Patmos. Like Noah, may we all find grace in the eyes of the Lord, as we exercise faith in the Son whose sacrifice opened the way for us to see and enter this realm of glory and beauty!

11

AROUND GOD'S THRONE
Revelation 4:4–6a

Thirty years ago, I along with my family, was flying on a Boeing 747 from California to North Carolina, and for some reason the plane had to sit on the ground at the airport for about an hour. The pilot, to entertain the children, announced that he would be glad to have any of them come to the cockpit to see how the plane was controlled. We had five little folk with us, but they all lost nerve and would not go in the cockpit. Thus they missed visiting the control chamber.

Who Is Behind Everything?

In a sense, Revelation 4:4-6 invites us into the cockpit, into the control chamber of the entire universe. That is an amazing concept! With the incredible complexity of this vast cosmos, there is a profoundly simple truth behind it. From one point of view, the physical sciences have long been motivated to find out ultimately simple principles behind the vast complexity of the universe.

More knowledgeable people than I tell me that the great physicist, Albert Einstein, in working out his General and Special Theories of Relativity was seeking to reduce the complex laws of nature to one or two basic principles. These would then explain all material reality, along with the functioning of space, time, and all natural forces. Exactly how he worked it out is beyond me, but I gather that he was seeking to simplify complex realities into simple, but universal constructs that would make sense of everything else. The universally simple principle that the physical sciences go on seeking, is given to the eyes of faith in the teaching of Scripture on God's throne.

What Lies Behind Everything

Revelation 4 shows us, from God's perspective, what lies behind everything that ever has or ever will occur in the whole space time universe. It is brought down to one crucial point and that is the vision of the throne of the omnipotent God. The eternal throne of the Triune God is behind the bringing of space, time, matter and motion into existence. It is behind how history is running its predetermined course. It is behind what is going to occur at the end of time on the very last day and from there on into eternity.

We are privileged to be given a little bit of access to the highest authority of all, to the ultimate supreme court. That is happening in this chapter. It does not necessarily answer some of the questions we might like to ask, but it gives us the basics of that which lies behind everything else, and shows us what it all means.

We note three points from these verses:

1. The elders of the church (v. 4).
2. The voices and light (v. 5).
3. The crystal sea (v. 6).

These three things are the companions of the glory-throne, of the sovereign majestic power that runs everything else. Three things around that throne give us some insight as to what life means, why we are here, and where we are going.

The Elders of the Church

Is it not interesting that when John was taken through the invisible door into heaven, the first thing God showed him was the twenty-four seats around the throne of God. Some people say, (I do not know exactly how they know), that twenty-four seats were thrones or chairs arranged in a semi-circle next to the throne of God. In this holy semi-circle of twelve smaller thrones on one side of the majestic glory throne and twelve smaller thrones on the other side of the majestic glory-throne, we see the twenty four elders.

Why Twenty-four Elders

Why twenty-four? It is almost certain that the twelve on one side represent the twelve tribes of Israel, the twelve sons of Jacob who constituted national Israel, the forerunner or the Old Testament counterpart of the redeemed church of God. The twelve thrones on the other side of God's majestic presence represent the twelve Apostles. Jesus' disciples became Apostles, although Judas was replaced by Mathias. So here we see the twelve Old Testament tribes and their counterpart in the New Testament, the twelve Apostles. This same number seems to be carried out in the foundations of the New Jerusalem, with the names of the tribes of Israel and the twelve Apostles on the twelve foundations of the walls and on the twelve gates.[28]

Why are elders important to time and to eternity? In the early part of the Old Testament, Moses selected elders, and even before his time there were the tribal elders, who adjudicated disputes. The elders represent the people of God, all who will ever be saved through faith. Since the elders make it to heaven, then those whom they represent will also make it to that glorious place.

Whom Would You See and Hear in Heaven?

If you could ask God to let you look into heaven for five minutes, what would you ask to see? Many of us would think of our loved ones who have gone on above; we would like to see what they look like, what they are doing, and how they are rejoicing in the presence of God. That is what I would like God to let me see, if in his providence I could look into the other world. Others might like to see the mansion that the saints are going to inhabit. Those of you who love music, might like to see the angelic choirs and to hear the ringing of the golden harps. Won't that be wonderful?

In the Welsh Revival of 1904, one of the strangest supernatural events was what people called 'the singing in the air'. Believe it or not, many responsible Christian people, upon leaving the chapel that had been filled with hundreds of people, would walk through quiet rural paths to their cottages and hear angelic music ringing in the air above their ears. It became known as 'the singing in the air'. Evidently in the Welsh revival of 1904, God's presence drew so close that the songs of the holy angels were actually heard by human ears in the beautiful hilly county in Wales. It has never been forgotten.

So we might say, 'Lord I would like to see and hear the angelic choirs that sometimes have been even heard on earth in the singing in the air.' But the first thing God shows us in this chapter is not any of those things, legitimate though they are. The first thing he wants you to see in heaven is that the church is there. Its representatives who have died in Christ are close to the throne of God.

In our next study we shall think about the angelic hosts at the throne, but it is interesting that before the Lord describes these majestic, holy angels, he wants us to look at the human beings who have safely made it to heaven. This is the Lord's church. So the most important thing to God in heaven is his church, his people. What do you think of that? If you are having a bad day and you think this through a little bit, you will have a good day, no matter what you have to face when you go home or what you have to face next week.

Angels and Believers

Look at it this way. The holy angels are more powerful beings than humans. They excel in wisdom and strength, as Hebrews 1 says. They can do amazing things, such as become invisible, and move like the wind and fire at the commandment of God in a split second. God loves and values his blessed, holy angels. But there is something that God loves even more than his blessed, holy angels, and that is his redeemed people.

When Jesus came to earth, as we are told in Hebrews, he did not become an angel, he became a man. 'He took not on him the nature of angels: but took on him the nature of the seed of Abraham' (Heb. 2:16). Jesus became a human being, and lived and died as a human person. The most precious thing to God in the universe is his Son, and the next most precious thing would be formerly sinful, weak, and frail human beings who through the blood of his Son have been redeemed and washed whiter than snow.

That is why when John takes us into the control chamber in heaven, the first thing we see beside the throne is the representatives of the Old and New Testament church from beginning to end, from the gates of Eden to the day when the last trumpet shall sound and the church is gathered into the glory world.

It is hard to know exactly what Paul means when he says in 1 Corinthians 6:3, that the saints will judge the angels. Certainly the angels are above us in power, wisdom, and holiness, but at the end of time when we have been transformed into the likeness of Jesus (1 John 3:2), somehow the saints will be given the task of assessing how well the angels did in serving the church through the ages. At present, we are not competent for that work. But it will be different when we have seen the King face to face. Then the saints will judge the angels. Hebrews 1:14 tells us that the angels are ministers to them that shall be heirs of salvation. Presumably that is their major task. They help us. They serve us. Most of the time they are invisible to us, so that we have no idea of what they are now doing for us.

Invisible Help of the Angels

I knew a wonderful man, now in heaven, who was a professor of theology in Philadelphia for many years. One time he mistakenly failed to slow down for a stop sign. A possibly fatal wreck would have been entirely his fault. But suddenly before he went through the stop sign, his brakes slammed on and his car stopped within a few inches of another car. A very courteous man, he got out of his car and apologized profusely to the man that he almost ran into. The man said, 'Don't worry about that. It is amazing that you stopped'. How did you stop? He said 'I do not know. Something caused my brakes to slam on'. He knew what it was that slammed on his brakes. It was a holy angel. The gospel of Matthew speaks of the angels that look after children; the angels of children always behold the face of the heavenly father. Could you and I have made it out of childhood without the angels? If we realized one percent of what the angels do for us in a given week, we would be full of praise.

The angels are ministers to them that are heirs of salvation, helping us in many different ways. But wonderful as these glorious beings are, they are servants to poor, sinful, plain, frail, inconsistent men and women like you and me.

The Beauty of Heavenly Clothing
The saints in glory had on white raiment, beautiful white clothing, evidently shining with the splendor of God. Formerly poor humans, all the sin is purged out of us before we get to heaven, and then God clothes us with beautiful white heavenly linen. We are told elsewhere that the white linen of the saints is the righteousness of Christ given to them. What the saints have is not just enough to keep them from being embarrassed, but something splendid and beautiful like a king or a queen would wear; majestic robes that are literally radiant with beauty and light. We are asked in Revelation 7:13-14, 'Who are these that are clothed in white raiment'? And the answer is, 'These are they that came out of great tribulation and have washed their garments white in the blood of the lamb'.

The fact that the saints who have left earth and gone to heaven are so beautiful is not because they were perfect in this world or did all they could have done. They had many imperfections. But their beauty is a beauty of grace. It is a gift. Jesus lived and died for them. He arose for them and he has the moral authority to put on them all this beauty spoken of in the white raiment of the saints. Their dignity and nobility is a gift they received through the grace of Jesus Christ.

Golden Crowns of the Saints
We also read that they have on their heads golden crowns. Queen Victoria succeeded to the British throne when she was nineteen years old. The crown of England weighed thirty-nine ounces. She, a small, slender, nineteen year old sitting on the throne had on her head a heavy crown with all its solid gold, diamonds and rubies, emeralds, and sapphires. You can still see it if you go to the Tower of London. This majestic crown is the frailest shadow of the beauty of the crown that will be put on the head of the saints.

The crown means authority and dignity—the highest position under God. The saints reign with Christ (Rev. 3:21). They have been made kings and priests unto God (Rev. 5:10, 20:4, 6). Revelation goes on to say that they shall reign on the earth.

We can understand the saints reigning in the beautiful presence of God, but how in any sense do ordinary Christians reign on the earth? Here is one of the many ways the saints even now are reigning. It is through exercising this scepter of Christ, which is prayer. Paul speaks in Ephesians 6 of 'the weapon of all prayer'. If we knew the authority we have to take charge of a bad situation through believing prayer in Jesus' name, you could not keep us from the prayer meetings.

Dignity of the Saints
Some years ago I was in Romania and a Baptist pastor took me to speak to Baptist ministers in that area. We went by an imposing government

building. He said, 'Every time I walk by that building, I almost get the shivers, because until 1991, the communist government would take Christians, particularly ministers, elders and sometimes their wives into that building, where a particular room served as a sort of a torture chamber.' The authorities would make it as cold as possible, then require the Christians to take their clothes off, and if they would not renounce their faith and curse Jesus, they would shock them with electric rods or tie them in a place where they would sit in terrible cold. Then they would pour icy cold water on their heads. What terrible things these faithful Christians went through! But like the saints who suffered in the first century in some of the seven churches of Asia, the believers in Romania were on their way to a glorious crown!

So the elders around the throne represent the church and show that to be a true member of the church, your ultimate destiny is next to the elders around the throne. Where are our loved ones who have died and gone ahead of us? That is where they are. They are somewhere around this absolutely splendid throne in union with 'the church triumphant'. God may let church people get persecuted and killed, but their existence always ends in the highest victory.

Heavenly Voices and Light

Secondly, heavenly voices and light come from that splendid throne (v. 5). John saw something like flashes of lightning and heard crashes of thunder. If I took you back to Exodus 19:16 when the law was being given on the top of Sinai, when Moses went up to receive the Ten Commandments, you would find that the whole mountain was shaking and trembling with lightning and thunder. These awesome natural phenomena represent the power, splendor, and tremendous majesty of the holy God. The same lightning and thunder that literally shook the desert with its mighty mountain were proceeding from that throne.

Light From the Throne
Then light was shining from before the throne. The light came from a seven-fold candlestick. Again, we could look at Exodus 25 and Zechariah 4. The seven-fold candlestick represents 'the seven spirits of God', which does not mean that God has seven different Holy Spirits. There is only one Holy Spirit, but seven means fullness, plentitude. The seven-fold candelabra that was in the tabernacle, and in Solomon's temple speaks of the fullness of the Holy Spirit to turn our darkness into light. Everything we need in our moral darkness to overcome temptation, fear of the unknown, and safe passage through the challenges of earthly troubles—bad health and finally death—is provided by this light. The light-bringer, the Holy Spirit shines in a dark world, into our otherwise darkened soul. We are told in Psalm 119 that 'The entrance of thy word giveth light' because the Bible is inspired by the Holy Spirit.

I have seen people on the verge of sheer ruin; people addicted to drugs, or other illicit habits. They seemed beyond hope or help. Yet some humble Christian started telling them the truth of God's Word (maybe for the thousandth time!). If you can get somebody into the truths of the Bible; especially the stories about Jesus, sin, and redemption, something supernatural may well begin to happen. Into the darkest, most confused soul in turmoil, divine light begins to shine, as the Holy Spirit turns on the light inside them. The shining of this divine light begins to bring supernatural healing inside a person, with eternal transformation of the personality. Yes, 'the entrance of thy word giveth light'.

The Crystal Sea

In front of the throne there was a sea of glass like crystal. I remember as a child how delicate crystal was, for on two or three occasions without meaning to do so, I broke some of my mother's and grandmother's wedding crystal—beautiful, thin glass. Crystal is truly delicate and something you can see through.[29]

We See Through the Crystal Sea

The saints above, the twenty four elders and all the Christians who are gathered with them, can look through the crystal sea and look into the rest of the universe. I do not know how much God lets them see on the earth. Apparently looking through the crystal sea makes everything plain in light of the wisdom and goodness of God.

The truth of Revelation comes to us through symbols, and the crystal sea is one of those, but that does not mean that we should think of it as unreal. It is simply that one cannot completely describe such transcendent realities in human language, and therefore the beloved apostle and others, such as Ezekiel, employ symbols to help us understand how wonderful all of this is.

Keep in mind that this throne is absolutely real, and from its viewpoint we are enabled to make sense of everything else. When John was taken through the invisible door up in heaven, he was enabled to look down through the crystal sea and see the brightness of God's future. From the throne we see with clarity that the Triune God is in control of all things past, present, and future.

Some six hundred years before that, the same throne and same crystal sea was seen from the bottom by the prophet Ezekiel (Ezek. 1:28). Right after the strange vision of the wheel within a wheel, Ezekiel from planet earth was given a vision in which God rolled back the curtain that separates eternity from time so that Ezekiel could look up. What John had seen from the top, Ezekiel saw from below. It was the same throne from different perspectives. From bottom and top it looked like crystal, with pure white transparency. From the bottom, Ezekiel saw the throne with angelic beings around it. He reports that the throne had a bluish tinge. Six hundred years later it has not changed, relaxed its power, or slowed down in executing its purposes.

These two complementary visions of the eternal throne show us that from God's perspective, everything is clear and will ultimately turn out for beauty, goodness, and blessedness for all those who walk by faith, trusting God in the dark places of life in this world. Everything will one day be perfectly clear. Until then we walk by faith, even when it is dark, illumined by the beautiful clarity ahead of us. We are able to walk by faith in the light of the clarity that one day is coming.

The well-loved hymn, 'Be still, my soul', set to music by Sibelius, expresses faithfully what Ezekiel's and John's vision of the throne means for the struggling church on earth:

> 'Be still, my soul: thy God doth undertake
> To guide the future as he has the past.
> Thy hope, thy confidence, let nothing shake;
> All now mysterious shall be bright at last.
> Be still, my soul: the waves and winds still know
> his voice who ruled them while he dwelt below.'

12

Praises Around the Throne
Revelation 4:6b–11

In Revelation 4, God calls us to walk by faith in things we do not yet see clearly. In this supernatural way—walking by faith—we can share through the inspired Word of God the clarity of the vision that John saw of the angelic creatures and the translated elders of the church. The revelation of this vision enables us to experience clear guidance, hope, and joy in a dark world. This is one of those amazing Bible passages that in effect says, 'Come up here and share in the vision of the glorious activity of these heavenly beings. Your life can be marked by joyful seeing, rather than grieving and complaining'.

Let us note three things in these verses:

1. How the world looks from the throne (v. 6b).
2. The ones who see and praise (vss. 6–10).
3. We hear the song of the translated elders (v. 11).

How the World Looks from the Throne
It is impossible for us mortals to know how this world really looks with all the hundreds of millions of complicated lives in different nations; with constantly changing events of nature and history. How complicated and confusing this world is. But it is a different matter when we are given a glimpse of it from the Throne.

The keyword here is 'clarity'. Two images in Revelation 4:6 convey this sense of clarity. The first is the crystal sea. The holy angels and saints above are able to look through this crystal sea down to earth and see everything with beautiful clarity. From that perspective, it all makes sense from beginning to end.[30] The next imagery given is that of the living creatures full of eyes. To the best of my understanding, John is speaking in symbolic language (like Ezekiel), to convey the truth that the angelic beings see everything as clearly and completely as if they were full of eyes. This means that they look in every direction in the whole universe, both in the unseen heavenly world and in this visible material world. As they look up and down heaven and earth, everything makes sense to them from God's throne. They see clearly. You and I cannot yet see in this clear and full way. But one day, in a better world, we will share their vision. Whether then or now, everything is clear from the vantage point of God's throne.

In 1 Corinthians 13, Paul tells us, 'But now we see through a glass darkly'. At best, we see through a glass darkly all the years we are on earth. Much always remains unclear to us: why did certain things happen? Why did God not answer certain prayers? But then, says Paul, we shall see 'face to face' and it all comes clear.

What the Authorized Version, calls 'the beasts' means 'living creatures' (not necessarily horrendous ones). These living creatures are face to face with God, where everything makes perfect sense. The total scene is beautiful and wonderful. Everything they can see, from beginning to end, from North to South, East to West, about human life and world history, is perfectly right and clear and they are happy over it.

Life is not Accidental

While I was studying this chapter, I happened to visit a relative by marriage, who is a good Christian man. He spoke about the medical condition of one of his granddaughters, a young lady in her twenties, and a consecrated Christian girl with much talent. Since a young age she has been suffering from serious medical disabilities, through no fault of her own. It caused me to think: I am thirty years older than her and I have never suffered like that. This relative was saying, 'Sometimes I wonder why the Lord lets someone who loves him like my granddaughter go through this suffering, while there are pagans who hate God and it looks like everything is fine with them. They seem to get everything they want.' I said to this kinsman, 'Well I do not know why, but when we get up to the throne, everything is going to be absolutely clear. We'll know why. It'll make sense. Until then, we have got to walk by faith, knowing God loves this child and God is going to bring wonderful things out of this suffering so that we'll be able one day to praise him for it.' This is walking by faith, and not by sight.

The key to this passage is that the throne of a thrice-holy God, who plans and executes everything that ever happens with perfect propriety and exquisite care, is always moving towards a glorious conclusion that all the powers of hell, sin, suffering, death and sorrow cannot hinder or stop. I wonder if the living creatures around the throne, these angelic beings, can already see the end of time, since they are so close to the Throne? If so, they understand why God allows his people to experience temporary defeats and long sufferings. Already, those holy angels see that everything has turned out with absolute victory and beauty for every soul and every angel who will ever love God. Therefore, these four angelic intelligences with this remarkable form know that no part of life is accidental.

Humanist Philosophy Sees Life as Accidental

If you go by the man-centered philosophy that we pick up in school and college, or from the culture around us, you tend to think that what happens to us is purely accidental. This humanist philosophy can make us feel uprooted and hopeless. But the holy angels know that life is not accidental when you take it from beginning to end from God's perspective. Blind, impersonal fate, as we find it in much of the ancient Greek and Roman philosophy, is not what causes things to happen. Nor is independent, iron-clad natural law the main thing that drives the world to its conclusion. Nor is chance, materialistic evolution behind all that finally happens.

The holy angels at the center of execution of every fact that will occur, know better than any of these short-sighted human philosophies. They know that blind fate, independent natural law and fortuitous evolution are not what drives the world on and what is encompassing our lives. From the throne, the holy angels can see with 'clarity'. They see clearly through all the perplexities of the changing events that are always passing over our heads and they know that nothing that has ever happened is meaningless, blind, chance, or harsh.

Everything that occurs serves a God-guided, beautiful purpose. That clear reality which the angelic creatures are able to see makes them burst forth in praise and rejoicing. If we could see as clearly as they now see, we too—even in the midst of an often dark and painful world—would join them enthusiastically in their praises of the Lord! That is how the world looks from the throne.

The Ones Who See and Praise

The second point of the text is about the ones around the throne who see. The text indicates that there are two classes of beings around the throne who see clearly and are full of joy.

'The Beasts' Near the Throne

First (v. 6–8) we have 'the beasts' (or living creatures) and then (v. 10) the church elders. The 'living creatures' seem to be some kind of angel.[31] We do not know too much about the angels, but they are a different order of creation from mankind. Mankind dwells as soul and body (or spirit and flesh); the angels are nothing but spirits, although they can take on a certain form when the Lord wants them to do that. They are highly intelligent, massively powerful spirit beings, of which there are different orders. In humankind, we have but one order. We are a combination of flesh and spirit. Either we human beings are saved or we are still lost, but we all share the same order of humanity. We are descendants of Adam.

But the angels appear to be in different ranks, levels and orders. Apparently at the top are the archangels, Gabriel and Michael. They are in charge as mighty captains of the Lord's host. Then slightly below these mighty archangels are those heavenly beings called cherubim and seraphim (the 'im' is Hebrew for plural). These four living creatures around God's throne are probably in the order of cherubim and seraphim.

We meet some of these cherubim and seraphim some six hundred years earlier in the prophecy of Ezekiel. They do not fade with the passing of the years. They do not get old. They do not get tired. They are just the same. Ezekiel describes them (Ezek. 1:4–7):

> And I looked, and behold, a whirlwind came out of the north, a great cloud, and a fire infolding itself, and a brightness was about it, and out of the midst thereof as the color of amber, out of the midst of the fire. Also out of the midst thereof came the likeness of four living creatures. And this was their appearance: they had the likeness of a man. And every one had four faces, and every one had four wings. And their feet were straight feet; and the sole of their feet was like the sole of a calf's foot; and they sparkled like the color of burnished brass.

Ezekiel adds, 'As for the likeness of their faces, they four had the face of a man, and the face of a lion on the right side; and they four had the face of an ox on the left side; they four also had the face of an eagle' (v. 10). I gather that these same living creatures appeared in the Temple of Jerusalem when God gave Isaiah his call (Isa. 6:1–3). These are a special order of angelic intelligences below the Archangels and evidently above the ordinary angels subject to serve us day by day, who are somewhere in between.

We might ask, 'Why four?' We know that there are ten thousand times ten thousand holy angels below these. But why are four of these living creatures mentioned specifically in Ezekiel and Revelation?[32] Some commentators think it is because of their connection with the created order of the four winds that blow on earth, and the four points of the compass. If that is correct, it would be a way of saying that these angelic beings have a close connection with earthly life, with everything that happens, even in the animal realm as well as in the human realm. So whatever direction you go on earth, these angels would be there. Many church fathers thought that these angelic beings are directors of the other angels, and since they see so well all that is occurring, they know exactly how to direct them.

Some of the church fathers (such as Augustine) have said that the four faces that you see on these living creatures in Ezekiel and Revelation stand for the four different gospels. According to this idea, you find the face of a lion in Matthew (specifically written to the Jews, where Christ is the conquering Lion of the tribe of Judah). Then Mark presents us with the ox: that is, Christ's solidity, quiet obedience and his strength, as he suffers and serves, bearing the yoke of the law. Luke, which takes the family tree or genealogy, not merely back to Abraham, but all the way back to Adam, the first man, the father of all mankind, speaks of Christ Jesus, as the perfect man for all men. Finally, we see the face of an eagle in John, where the deity of Christ is so emphasized. I would not push these analogies too far, however.

The Four Angelic Creatures ('Beasts')
More important, these angelic creatures all aspects of human life and animal life. John Calvin in his commentary, which he never lived to finish, on the prophecy of Ezekiel said that in these faces (a man, a lion, an ox and an eagle), the whole created order, both animal realm and the human realm, was encompassed. What it meant was that these angelic beings have vibrancy and the power of God to give direction and strength, not only to the humans but to the animals, and to cause all intelligent life to move in a certain direction.

This view of the running of the natural order is very different from the Deism that many of us were taught in school. We Western people were educated to think that maybe God created and wound up the world like a clock, but then he left it to run on its own strength. The Bible does not say that. The Bible says that every gust of wind, every drop of rain that falls, the power of all intelligent beings to think and do anything is directly communicated from the throne of God so that God is in direct charge of all that occurs.

You say, 'Isn't that a bit extreme?' Whether or not it is extreme, depends on whether or not you take the full balance of the Biblical teaching on this mysterious matter. The Bible presents God's sovereignty in conjunction with the reality of natural (or 'secondary causes') and the importance of responsible, human choices. Look in Acts 17:25 at what the Apostle Paul says to the pagans in Athens, 'that God, the Lord of heaven and earth, dwells not in temples made with hands; Neither is worshipped with men's hands, as though he needed any thing, seeing he giveth to all life, and breath, and all things.' Every breath, even of the pagans, comes directly from God. This God is in charge and in someway, these unseen angels seem to be involved in every intelligent motion that occurs here below. There is a lot of mystery in that, but the Bible says at least that much. The point here is: do not worry; God is in charge. These living creatures indicate that the most appropriate thing to do, when from the vantage point of the throne, you are able to see everything clearly is to burst forth in triumphant praise to the one who is in charge of it all.

The Twenty-four Elders Around the Throne
Then there is another group up there, the twenty four elders, who immediately join them in this grand doxology ringing around the throne. These twenty four elders represent the twelve tribes of Israel (the Old Testament form of the church) and also the Apostles (the New Testament form

of the church). It is the same church; the twenty four represent all who will ever by saved. The church elders represent what we are going to be when we get home and show us what in a sense we can do a little bit now by faith, even while we are on earth. But once we get home, to our Father's house, we will sing the same praises as the holy angels. Isn't that wonderful? That is what we are going to talk about when we enter into his immediate presence. Even now, when we cannot see clearly so many things, by faith we can still take a kind of journey in the spirit to where we really are going, and start praising God, along with the most glorious intelligences. We can already join the holiest angels in lauding him.

That is what the four living creatures are doing, and by faith, we are invited to join them. Every day we have a choice, we can complain and criticize, but to do this is to walk by sight. Yet you can make a choice: I am going to walk by faith. The first thing to do is to start praising him whom the four living creatures and the elders above see and laud. When you do so, Satan has absolutely no choice but to flee the camp of your life.

Singing the Grand Doxology
Now we find the angelic beings and church elders above singing the grandest doxology of all. Two doxologies are being lifted up around the holy throne. One is sung by the Cherubim and Seraphim and the other is sung by the church elders. The angels are singing what Isaiah some seven hundred years earlier had heard with awe in the Temple of Jerusalem, 'Holy, holy, holy, Lord God Almighty'. What they are celebrating is God, and then life truly becomes a celebration.

The Right Kind of Worship
This hymn is celebrating God. He is the center of that song. Several books have come out dealing with 'Worship Wars', different theories about how you ought to worship God. Often the fight is over whether the service is to be contemporary or traditional. I'm not going to say anything about that except this: whatever else you say about worship, for it to be a Christian worship service, it ought to be centered on God. It ought to celebrate God. It ought to turn people's hearts towards God. It ought to lift them out of their selves towards God. A true worship service, whether traditional or contemporary, should do far more than focus on man and his needs. The power and the glory, the strength and the life of a worship service is to celebrate God, to center on him. That is what the angels are doing and their song particularly is lauding in various words his holiness, power and eternity. Let us take three of its central concepts: his holiness, power and eternity.

Holiness. Habakkuk says that 'God is of purer eyes than to behold evil'. The New Testament says that 'God is light and in him there is no darkness at all'. Since God is in charge of all things, and God is perfectly holy, then why do bad things happen? Does God directly make evil occur? James says that 'God cannot be tempted with evil, neither tempteth he any man'. For God to do evil would be contrary to his own righteous character. Yet, here is a mystery. I like what the Reverend William Still, the late minister from Aberdeen, used to say: 'God uses sin sinlessly.' God, the holy one, is able to allow sin and evil, and indeed, to include them in his plan, without causing them directly. He creates moral beings, and it is they who choose to go in an immoral direction (a choice included in the divine plan, without being directly caused by it).

Power. Next, the song celebrates the divine power (Rev. 4:11): 'Thou art worthy to receive power'.

Immediately after this, the text says—as a prime illustration of God's infinite power—'for thou hast created all things, and for thy pleasure they are and were created'. The angels and saints above articulate in their songs how 'the heavens declare the glory of God and the firmament shows forth his handiwork' (Ps. 19:1). They are praising the sheer miracle of creation out of nothing. God spoke worlds into existence and he has absolute control over all that he spoke into existence: all the amazing cosmos, solar systems, galaxies, planets, microbes, and dust, and all their interrelationships.

Eternity. The heavenly doxology praises him for his eternity (Rev. 4:9—'who liveth forever and ever'). They say to God: 'You were, you are, and you are to come' (Rev. 4:8); everything that occurs depends on you. In Exodus 3:14, God told Moses at the burning bush that his name is 'I AM'. The four Hebrew letters of the divine Name 'I AM' (JHVH) are the consonants of the verb 'to be.' In other words, it is God's nature always to be. He needs no origin. He has no cause. Everything less than God needs an origin and explanation, and requires a cause. That is to say, everything else depends on God, but God depends on nothing. Even the passage of time depends on him who inhabits eternity, for by his creative power, he brought time itself into existence. When we begin to think of God's eternity, we shall find it easy to praise him. As Faber sings:

> How dread are Thine eternal years,
> O everlasting Lord,
> By prostrate spirits day and night
> Incessantly adored!

Then finally, the song of the church elders concludes (v. 11). They are praising God, who is worthy because 'he created all things for his pleasure'. On the contrary, humanistic history says that the world makes sense in light of itself. Rome thought that everything made sense in terms of the Roman state and its emperor. But the Roman Empire is long gone. Many today think that the world makes sense in terms of its modern multinational economy. That too will break down. This song tells us that the creation makes sense in light of the Creator. It is for his purpose. My life makes sense, not in light of my little purposes or my convenience, but in light of God's purposes for the entire created order including myself in some way. To know this is to set the soul singing.

13

Heaven's Song

Revelation 5:1–14

Revelation 5 sounds out a wonderful hymn of praise that rings down from heaven. You can almost hear it. This fifth chapter needs to be taken with Revelation 4. In both chapters we overhear how much singing and praising and delight there is in heaven over what God is doing on the earth. The inhabitants of heaven can already see things from God's perspective, and thereby know how it will all turn out. As they think about the church on earth, past, present and future, they burst forth into glorious, triumphant song. That is how heaven looks at the future of the world.

I do not know if it is natural for us to look at it that way. It is more natural for us to focus on signs of trouble in our lives, and in the larger world, so that we hang our heads down. These chapters do not deny that there can be terrorism, persecution, trouble and death in the experience of the saints on earth. We see much of that in the next chapter, but from God's throne, looking down through the crystal sea and knowing God's Book, which has everything in it from beginning to end, the saints in heaven and the angelic beings rejoice as they consider the whole picture, even when the short term seems very bad.

To that end, let us note three things about the glorious song of praise in Revelation 5:

1. How this hymn of praise fits into the structure of the Revelation (Rev. 4–6).
2. The theme of the hymn of praise (Rev. 5:9, 12–13).
3. Who is singing this hymn (Rev. 5:8–14).

How This Song Fits into the Structure of Revelation 4–6

Here is the basic structure, rather simply stated. In chapter 4, as we saw one has a vision of God's throne at the beginning of the chapter, by which it is made clear that God is in control of everything. Then at the end of that chapter, all heaven is full of praises, because of him who is running all things.

Similarly in chapter 5, one sees the vision of God's Book. It is the book of history; the Lamb's Book of life. In it are the predestinated purposes of God, from the foundation of the world until the consummation when all the elect are gathered together. You have a vision of the scroll or Book being opened, of the working out of God's predetermined purposes, and of their being wonderfully concluded, when all heaven bursts forth in hymns of praise.

John Calvin once said that not one drop of rain falls outside the expressed plan of God, and hence everything that happens is comprehended in it.

We are going to look at some bad things in the Book of Revelation, as well as many good things. Everything that transpires is included in the Book some way or another. Everything is working in accordance with this Book of God. The throne is in control, the book is being fulfilled and therefore, the saints and angels are so happy, that they are full of praise.

God's Rule Comes Before the Saints' Suffering
Concerning the structure of Revelation and the praises you find in chapter 4 and 5, one old commentator said: 'It is a very beautiful arrangement that puts Chapter 4 and 5, namely the Rule of God, before Chapter 6 which is the sufferings of the people of God.' As though to say, 'You must first look at Christ and at what he has done for you and at how he is controlling all things in your interest; look at that before you concentrate on your own sufferings'.

The Bible talks frequently about Christian suffering, and Revelation does not hide the brokenness, the pain, the grief and the defeats that come to the lives of God's people. It is a very realistic book for hard times. But here in Revelation, before it speaks in great detail about the suffering and the terrible things that happen to God's people, it first takes us by way of the throne and the Book, thereby reminding us that an all powerful God is in control and that he has a heart full of love for us, by which he is working everything out, things including the suffering he allows in the church's life on earth.

An old Southern hymn says: 'Tenderly he watches over me.' It is an uplifting thought that the Almighty God, who is in control of every puff of wind and every drop of rain, every microbe and every motion of every atom, has a most tender heart. He employs all his mighty power in the most tender love to the least of his children. Yes, 'Tenderly he watches over me.'

That is the perspective found in Revelation when the Christian church undergoes dreadful persecution and individual believers experience deepest hurt, that otherwise would seem inexplicable, if not senseless. Paul and Silas had this perspective after they had been beaten and bound in the Philippian jail. With blood running out of the stripes on their backs, they began singing hymns of praise to God, because they already knew by victorious faith that the glory of God comes down through the wounds of his saints, when they suffer in accordance with his magnificent purposes.

God Spared Not His Own Son
The tender loving care of God, who sent his Son to die for us sinners on the cross, can always be trusted to bring something good out of every kind of suffering, hurt and defeat. I have always remembered an experience related by my professor of preaching at Union Seminary in Richmond, Virginia, Ben Lacy Rose. He had been a pastor in a small rural Presbyterian Church in Eastern North Carolina, where one of his elders lost a fine young son in his early teens to some kind of disease. Dr Rose preached the boy's funeral sermon from Romans 8:32, bearing in mind this elder and father who had lost his only son: 'He that spared not his own son, but delivered us up for him all, how shall he not with him freely give us all things?' Here is a grieving father whose son is now enclosed in a coffin, soon to be lowered into the ground. But the truth of Romans 8:32 lifted up this grieving father, for he could trust in the God who held not back his own Son. We can trust God when he takes the dearest thing from us, because he held not back

the greatest treasure of his own heart: his well-loved Son; the One in whom he delighted.

That is at the very heart of the message the risen Jesus has given to the church as he showed himself to John and brought the apostle up to heaven so he could see the throne and find out about 'the Book'. The only one who can open the Book is the one who was slain for John's sins and our sins, and he is now on the Throne. This one is tenderly watching over a suffering church and is sending that church encouraging news, far beyond what they could now see.

The Theme of the Song
The theme of the song is heard in Revelation 5:9-12:

> Thou art worthy to take the book, and to open the seals thereof: for thou wast slain, and has redeemed us to God by thy blood, out of every kindred, and tongue, and people and nation; and hast made us unto our God kings and priests: and we shall reign on the earth...Worthy is the Lamb that was slain to receive power, and riches, and wisdom, and strength, and honor, and glory, and blessing.

Its theme is the Lamb of God. Through Him, the government of the throne and the purposes of the Book are carried out. For us who believe in Him, that is very good news. Everything that happens in our lives, everything that will happen in world history, can be understood only in terms of the Lamb of God and what he is doing in history to get his church and bride into the shape that he wants her to be in and to get her to where he wants her to be.

The Lamb of God
It is normal that Christ should be the center of this song in which the angelic beings are joined by the representatives of the church, the holy elders of the Old and New Testament. It is natural that he should be the center of this song, because he is the center of the Book of Revelation itself. In chapters 1-3, he is in the center of the church, walking in the midst of the candlesticks. As we saw previously, the candlesticks represent the seven churches of Asia (and all true Churches) and also he has the stars of the Churches in his right hand. It is all centered on him.

In chapter 6 and following, we are going to see that history is centered on what the Lamb is doing. The events of history are not accidental, although from our earthly viewpoint they may often seem to be so. The Lamb is the center of everything that he is allowing to happen. He is riding forth, 'conquering and to conquer'. He is the center of history. In chapters 21-22, the Lamb is the center of eternal glory. After the heavens have rolled back like a scroll, and the sands of time flowed down, so that we are at last into the glorious consummation, the Lamb is in the center of heaven. There they need no sun, moon or stars, because the Lamb is the light. They need neither temple nor tabernacle, because the Lamb, whom both represented, is there in his embodied and glorified Person to be worshipped. The words taken from Samuel Rutherford by Mrs. Cousins, and turned into a hymn, say it well: 'The Lamb is all the glory, of Immanuel's Land'.

Why the Lamb is Worthy
In this heavenly song to the Lamb, which is echoed in verses 9-12, we are given two marks of the Lamb's worthiness, which constitute two lasting grounds for praise. First, he was slain for us and secondly, on the basis of his being slain, he has redeemed us. This redemption puts every kind of hard circumstance we can ever face into

its proper place. It does not matter what you are facing, nor what terrible things we fear may lie ahead. Facing such potentially (or actual) hard times, this glorious redemption gives us ground for singing even in such times! No matter how we feel, God immensely cares about us, and will help us through it, so that absolutely nothing can keep us from singing the praises of the Lamb. Our singing will be all the better if we remember the two marks of his worthiness: that he was slain for us, and that by his being slain, he has redeemed by his blood.

Who Could Open the Book?

Before we listen closely to the choir rendition above, we need to think about verses 2–7, which give us the background. These verses show us the unique, incomparable worthiness of the one the choir is singing about. He is the only one who could have offered himself up to be slain and thus redeem the world. He is the only one who could have accomplished our redemption. In verse 2, a strong angel states a question that seems to baffle the Apostle John: 'Who is worthy to open the scroll [or Book] of coming history so as to unseal its seven seals?' That is, who can open the Book of Life so that sinners can be saved? To be written in the Lamb's book of Life is to be assured of pardon for your sins, and thus of eternal life. Who can open that book? We are told that only one can open it. According to Revelation 13:8, 'Christ is the Lamb that was slain from the foundation of the world'. This was written in the book. It means that when God planned the world, he knew what Adam and Eve would do; he knew that sin would bring death, and that the human race, that had been planned to be the bride of the Lamb, would be condemned to death and condemnation in hell. But God already had a plan ahead of time.

At the center of his plan, was the one spoken of in chapter 5 as 'the Lamb that was slain'; only he could open the Book of Life out of which you got the roll of the true church.

An old gospel hymn says:

> No angel could his place have taken,
> high, of all the high, though he;
> The loved one on the cross forsaken
> was one of the Godhead three.
> Who saved us from eternal loss?
> Who but God's son upon the cross?
> What did he do? Died for you.
> Where is he now? Believe it thou;
> in heaven interceding.

Why Our Redeemer Had to Be Man and God

'No other could his place have taken'. No angel could have done it. Moses could not have done it. David could not have done it. Like ourselves, they are all descendants of Adam and all encompassed with sin. Only a sinless one could have done it. He had to be identified with God, so his suffering would be great enough to pay the penalty of infinite sin. We cannot get rid of that stain of endless, infinite horrendous guilt brought on by our sin against an infinitely holy God. So God sends his son who is the second person of the trinity, 'God of God', into human nature, so that he could fully and truly represent our humanity. For sin to be forgiven, it had to be punished in the place where it was committed; that is, in human nature. Hence the Lamb is able to represent God as infinitely worthy, and at the same time represent humanity. By this means, he can take our human nature and be perfectly holy in it, and then take the penalty of sin upon himself, thus taking it up from sin and death into the marvelous light of God. He represents God;

he represents man. Only he could do it. No angel or human being could have done it. It had to be someone who is God and man. It is the worthy Lamb; he came down here and did all this.

Praise the Cleansing Blood!
It must be glorious to hear this hymn of praise with its two themes. He was worthy because he was slain. Hebrews 9:22 says that without the shedding of blood there is no remission of sin. Blood had to be shed for Douglas F. Kelly to be forgiven of his sins to get into heaven, and also for you. Blood had to be shed from his pierced body. Isaac Watts' hymn reminds us of this:

> See from his head, his hands, his feet,
> sorrow and love flow mingled down;
> Did 'ere such love and sorrow meet,
> or thorns compose so rich a crown?

From what I understand of Luke 24, on resurrection day, the risen Christ walked with some disciples on the road to Emmaus (though he kept them from recognizing him at first), and then waited for them to invite him in for the evening meal. On the road as they talked, he explained the Scriptures as to why the Messiah would have to suffer before he could enter into his glory. Inside the house, the stranger was asked to offer the evening blessing over the food. Suddenly they recognized him, for 'he was known to them in the breaking of bread'.

He spread his hands out to bless the bread and they saw that his hands had nail prints in them. Evidently, up on the throne of God Almighty, the nail prints in some way are still there. Another hymn speaks of it this way: 'rich wounds, yet visible above in beauty glorified.' When we come to die, we do not deserve to get into heaven, but the Father looks on the wounds of the nail prints in his Son's hands, which prove that all my sins have been paid for, and I am eternally and totally acceptable to God. This is no small matter! Who would not wish to join the saints and angels above as they sing: 'Worthy is the Lamb that was slain!

The Good Shepherd leaves the ninety and nine sheep, to find the sheep that was lost. Then he brings him home rejoicing.

Who is Singing this Song?
Two categories of beings are singing this heavenly song: particular angelic beings (the four living creatures), the other angels, and also the redeemed church. Twelve elders and twelve apostles, both phases of the Church join together praising the Lamb, who saved them both. Hence, he is the one on whom all history centers. He is in the center of the throne; he is in the center of the Book. He unleashes the seals and he precisely determines what world events shall follow after other world events, until it finally reaches that glorious day.

Two Contradictory World Views
What a world-view is given here! It is certainly not materialism, which foolishly holds that the only thing that really matters is physical bodies, natural forces and nuclear structure. Then there is another worldview called deism. It admits that there was a God who somehow started everything, but they deny that he now controls the world. They fondly pretend that he is radically separated from it. Thus, he doesn't really answer intercessory prayer, nor is he able to do miracles, for that would require his reaching into this world, from which these people separate Him. But in neither deism nor materialism will you hear them praise the Lamb, nor will you see their

lives filled with joyful singing. But Bible believers realize that this glorious and wonderful God is on the throne. Christ is in the midst of the throne; the very one who loved us and gave himself for us! God's Book is being carried out day by day.

> God is working his purpose out,
> as year succeeds to year;
> God is working his purpose out,
> and the time is drawing near,
> nearer and nearer draws the time,
> the time that will surely be,
> when the earth shall be filled
> with the glory of God,
> as waters cover the sea.

The Saints Reign Through Prayer

The Book is being opened and is being administered through the Lamb in exactly the right way. An amazing phrase in Revelation 5:10 shows us that the saints are reigning through prayer (for they are 'kings and priests'). The saints are reigning with Christ already through prayer. The saints are making a difference in how history unfolds by their prayers. God says that their prayers are shaping the future and in this sense they are already reigning with Christ. That is the kind of world we live in—with a direct connection between heaven and earth by means of prayer—and thus the saints and the angels join and 'praise him from whom all blessings flow'. God invites us to join in these prayers of saints and angels above, and so through Christ to take part in the reign which is bringing blessing where there was cursing, which is bringing victory where there was defeat, which is bringing glory where there was pain, suffering and shame. Through praying and praising of the Lamb, our lives can be moving things in that direction. God invites us to join the choir by faith.

The Unworthy Can Pray

We feel unworthy to join that choir, for our lives have too often denied its message. But the very point of it is this: the Lamb is worthy. The heavenly beings do not say, 'WE are worthy'. Rather, they say, 'Worthy is the Lamb that was slain'. He invites the unworthy to come and join the choir. A former prostitute will be in that choir, for Jesus forgave her, and she anointed his feet with precious oil, as she wept and dried his sacred feet with her hair, as a preparation for his crucifixion. Murderers are there, such as David and Moses. Through the blood of the Lamb, they are all there. Liars are there. Simon Peter lied, and denied his master. Former homosexuals are there. Paul names this category, and says: 'such were some of you, but you are now washed, you are now justified through the Lamb' (1 Cor. 6:11). Absolutely nothing we have done in our life that is wrong, unworthy, nasty, unclean or impure disqualifies us to apply to the blood of the Lamb. You are invited to sing the song that they sing.

In his book on *The Life of Elijah* A. W. Pink shows that Hebrews 11, the great chapter of the heroes of the faith, never mentions the sins of the Old Testament saints. Although mentioned in the Old Testament, they are never mentioned in the New. Pink explains that it is because their sins are all under the blood of the Lamb, who now has come. That is how we can join this white robed choir. Let us put off our dirty, nasty clothes, and by faith, wash in the blood of the Lamb. In exchange, he will give us the fine, white linen righteous garments of the saints, in which we may happily join that singing above!

14

The Breaking of the First Four Seals
Revelation 6:1

Revelation 6:1-8 is a solemn and sobering portion of scripture. It shows us a crucially significant truth about our life in this changing world. The basic premise from which it is working is this, that the history of the world, including what seem to us terrible disasters such as war, economic breakdown and famine, are not just accidents. The way most history has been taught, for maybe 200 years, is that life is a fortuitous combination of atoms in some sort of evolutionary process, without transcendent direction. In this undirected process, it so happens that various nations arise and develop, and then they weaken and are replaced by another nation. A variety of environmental and economic forces are in the equation, but finally there is no overall meaning to it. World history is more or less like a boiling cauldron with bouncing atoms. Whatever happens, happens on its own without following any sort of divine program.

But on the contrary, this passage and, indeed, the entirety of the book of Revelation, gives us a completely different viewpoint on what makes history happen, including the waxing and waning of the kingdoms, the rise and fall of empires, with the myriad of human lives that are involved in all of that constant change. According to Scripture, history is anything but an accidental combination of impersonal forces.

So, we notice two points in this text:

1. The Lamb is in charge of history (Rev. 6:1).
2. The Lamb opens the seals that control the future (6:1–8).

The Lamb is in Charge of History

The Bible directs our attention to the mighty One who stands behind what is happening. He is called in verse 1, 'the Lamb'. We know who it is of course; he is the One whom John the Baptist announced before his baptism in the River Jordan, with these words: 'Behold, the Lamb of God that taketh away the sin of the world'. He is called in Revelation 13:8, 'the Lamb slain from before the foundation of the world'. He is behind the unleashing of historical forces that bring devastating and munificent changes in our lives and in the history of the world; the Lamb is behind them, for Rev. 6:1 shows him opening 'one of the seals' that controls the future.

How Could a Lamb be in Charge?

This is most amazing, for we rightly think of the lamb as a sacrificial animal. Along this line we are given a wonderful description of Christ as the sacrificial lamb in Isaiah 53, where it says: 'Like a lamb before her shearers is dumb, so he openeth not his mouth'. Christ stood in for us as the sacrificial lamb to bear away all the sins of all who will ever trust in Him, and he took all the wrath of God upon himself—all the just indignation of the Holy God against sin was borne by that lamb on Calvary's tree. That had been in God's plan before the world was even made, according to Revelation 13:8—the Lamb slain before the foundation of the world. So that's the Lamb who is directing world history.

But the same Lamb has been resurrected. We saw in Revelation chapter 5 that this mighty, victorious, risen Christ is described 'as a lamb that had been slain'. Evidently, in the beautiful, glorified resurrection body of this Lord Jesus Christ, there is the continuance of the nail prints in his hands and in his feet, as well as the print of the spear in his side. We sometimes sing, 'Crown him with many Crowns', which has a line that speaks of the continuing wounds in the now victorious, risen, conquering Lamb, who has become the Lion. It says: 'Rich wounds, yet visible above, in beauty glorified'. One day we shall see, face to face, the marks of our salvation in the glorified body of him who is the suffering Lamb and conquering Lion of the tribe of Judah.

This Lamb, upon his resurrection, said in his Great Commission to the church in Matthew 28, that we should go into all the world, to preach the gospel, to disciple the nations and to baptize them. He prefaces this Commission with this immense authority claim: 'All power in heaven and on earth is given unto Me'. He has all power. Everything that happens on earth now goes through the Lamb. We are told in the Acts of the Apostles that 'God hath appointed a day on which he will judge the earth by that Man whom he hath ordained'; that Man is the God-Man, the one Mediator between God and man, the Lord Jesus Christ. So all power flows through the Lamb and thus, he is in charge of letting loose the forces that shape what is going to occur in the history of the world between his death and resurrection and his second coming. He is in charge of the entire process. The direction of power and purpose do not come from a fortuitous combination of atoms, nor blind fate; rather, it is a Person who is in charge—the Lamb.

The Wrath of the Lamb

Another amazing thing is said here about this Lamb; it speaks of 'the wrath of the Lamb'. That seems to be almost a contradiction in terms: on the one hand, a gentle, meek Lamb who submitted to all the abuse that Satanically-inspired humans could pour on him in his passion and death—that Lamb 'who opened not his mouth before the shearers'—now is spoken of by Revelation as the source of awesome and infinite wrath! The same word used elsewhere of the holy, omnipotent God's wrath against sin is employed here in Revelation 6 of the wrath of the Lamb.

Let us think what that means in the outworking of history. The basic idea is this: as far as the wrath of God against sin is concerned, I think that the theological liberals and even the atheists (because for all their sin and unbelief, they are still created in the image of God), cannot completely get rid of that deeply embedded concept of divine wrath against sin. For all of the so-called modern man's resistance to Scripture, it does seem that one point that everybody somehow understands deep down inside, is that sin is wrong and merits the wrath of God against it.

Why do people of goodwill have to speak of the wrath of God? Simply because God is holy; he has to be consistent with his own character. For God not to go out against sin, which is a contradiction of his character, would be to deny himself; that is impossible. So God's wrath, in a moral universe—which after all, he made—must deal justly and firmly and thoroughly with sin, which leaves violators guilty for violating his holy law, for going against his character.

But the good news is this: all of the wrath of God against sin and filth and shame and rebellion and atheism and wickedness, every kind of sin in the book—financial, sexual, societal, personal—all of that was poured on the Lamb on Calvary's cross. That is why Jesus could say before he dies, 'It is finished!' Anyone who looks in faith, out of self, to Christ for salvation, will never have a problem with the wrath of God. It has all been poured out on the Lamb; it has all been taken care of; God's law was magnified in what Jesus went through.

What Satan Does not Want You to Know about Prayer

When we come to pray, one of the reasons we can pray and get answers to our prayers, even with all our imperfections—is that all the righteous wrath of God has been poured out on Christ, so that now God Almighty and All-perfect sees us as righteous in Christ. He has taken our sin and placed it on the head of the Lamb. At the same time, in this infinitely mysterious transaction, God takes the righteousness of the Lamb and puts it on our head. That's why prayer works.

The devil doesn't want you to know that, because if he can keep you from praying, he can keep much of God's blessing out of your life and out of your family circle; he will tell you it depends on how well you are doing, so do not pray this week—you have not yet reached a holy enough position to get prayers answered, the evil one will keep reminding you. How do you answer him? The Biblical answer is clear: you never pray in your name; that's why we say 'in Jesus Name,' or 'through Jesus Christ our Lord.' All the wrath of God that would keep him from answering my prayers has been poured out on Christ, so that if I'm truly in Christ by faith, God sees me as righteous, and on that basis is delighted to answer my prayers (though, of course, always in accordance with his holy will).

But let us take the outworking of God's righteous wrath against sin a step further. We have just seen that for all who are in Christ, the holy wrath is forever averted; their Judge is their Father! Yet what about the rest of the world that willfully remains outside the grace of God in Christ? Insofar as they manifest sinful contradiction to the holy character of God, the wrath of the Lamb must necessarily go forth; partially, in the judgments of history, as we see in Revelation 6:1–8, and then totally, in the final judgment. The wrath of God must necessarily go forth against those who reject the saving work of the Lamb; to reject Jesus Christ as Savior and Lord means I'm not covered in his sacrifice; it means I am bearing my own sin and guilt. A holy God must punish that which is contrary to his character and will do so, even before the end of time in the movements of history, and then will do so totally on the last day.

To be in the Lamb is to know no wrath; to reject the Lamb is to experience the wrath of the Lamb. An illustration of this is given in Hebrews, which speaks of those 'who trample under the blood of the covenant', who trample on the mercies of the Son of God; they must experience that wrath for themselves. And so the biggest question in human life is always this one, when I come to pray and then when I come to die: am I in the Lamb? Am I trusting in Him, so that the Holy Spirit is uniting me into his death and resurrection? If so, all will be well, here and hereafter.

The Lamb Opens the Seals of the Future

Most specifically, this passage shows us that the Lamb opens certain seals (6:1, 3, 5, 7, 9). We dealt with the seals in the last message, and must do so in yet another message. But for the present, we can note that the Lamb has the initiative in unleashing historical forces. You may say the banks have the power, or some cabal has the power, or the big governments have the power. Yes, they have limited power, yes; they'd like to have all power, but they can't, they do not, they won't. All power goes back to a Person, it goes back to the once suffering, now triumphant Lamb. This passage in Revelation tells us that when the right time comes, (no human knows when that time is), he opens a certain seal, and then amazing things begin to happen in the space/time history in the real world. An invisible world controls the forces that are let loose in the visible, natural realm; that is the teaching of Scripture. The Lamb is behind the letting loose of these forces.

Four Horsemen of the Apocalypse

Thus, what we have described for us in chapter 6 of Revelation is the moving forth of what we call 'the four horsemen of the apocalypse'. As we have seen, 'apocalypse' is another word for revelation or unveiling—of the future. When these horsemen are let loose by the Lamb, devastating events then occur in history. At this point, the mighty, victorious Christ tells John some of the major things that are going to happen between the time he is speaking to John on Patmos, and his second coming. It appears that what he has in view here, when he says 'these things must shortly happen' will be the ending of the Jewish economy, the destruction of the temple, the scattering of the Jews and the passing of the torch of salvation from what was left of Old Testament Judaism (which had become largely apostate), to the early Christian church. The ending of the Jewish economy and the rising of the Christian economy would make possible Christian missions to the rest of the world. The Lamb is in charge of all of this, and to accomplish this change, he sends forth four horses with very amazing riders on each horse. Each rider does something different to let forth the wrath of the Lamb on those who have rejected his atonement. In this case in particular, it appears to have focused on national Israel, which was persecuting the church (along with the Romans). Jesus himself had said during Passion Week, as he grieved over what would happen to the Jews for rejecting Him: 'Oh Jerusalem, Jerusalem, how oft would I have gathered thee unto me as a hen gathers her chicks under her wings; and you would not! The day is coming when your house will be left unto you desolate and there will not be one stone left upon another in the temple'. Here Jesus grieves over what would come to pass about forty years after his sacrifice, in the fall of Jerusalem. Of course, many of the Jews accepted his sacrifice; Acts says that many of the priests and Levites became obedient to the faith. But nationally, they rejected it and the horsemen are sent forth to let out the wrath of the Lamb on those who had rejected Him. Yet this national judgment would have a very positive end in view: to prepare the way for the spreading of the gospel to the rest of the world.

Old Testament Background of the Four Horsemen

The Old Testament background of these four horsemen of the apocalypse is found particularly in two chapters in the Old Testament; one is Zechariah 6, where these same four horses appear, and then in Habakkuk 3.[33] The Habakkuk passage was a prophecy of the military invasion of Judah by the Chaldeans (the Babylonians), who were God's instruments of wrath on the people for having become idolatrous and apostate. And so Habakkuk and Zechariah taken together show the going forth of the horsemen—that is looking at it spiritually from God's perspective—and then it shows what this looks like physically, by the devastation of the country and the deportation of the people. Under similar imagery, the Apostle John prophesies first century Israel's destruction by the Roman armies and the same woeful horsemen are let loose once again, about five hundred years after Zechariah and Habakkuk.

The horses and their riders show us God's means of controlling and bringing judgment upon the disobedient covenant people. It shows how he did it in the Old Testament and again how he will do it after the New Testament is completed. The colors of these four horses and their riders indicate their work in space/time history. The first one is white; the second one is red, (blood red in the Greek); the third one is black; the fourth one is pale, or sickly-greenish. Only the fourth one is given a name, and that's 'death,' although we can discern who the first one really was by noting this same image of a white rider on a white horse being taken up in Revelation 19. His name is Christ, whereas the two in the middle are not named, but they are adequately and solemnly described.

The Rider on the White Horse

Let us look at the first horseman of the apocalypse. We see a white horse with a rider, who has a bow in his hand and a crown on his head. That is the Lord Jesus Christ. Some commentators have said that it is the antichrist, but that is not possible. It is none other than the victorious Christ, whose crown shows that he was vindicated after his finished work, by his coronation in glory above. The bow he carries is the instrument of God's judgment against his own enemies. This is taken over in Revelation 19:11–16, where it is clearly indicated that it is Christ, the Word of God. Similarly, that passage shows Christ riding a white horse, but with this difference: a sword is coming out of his mouth (whereas in Revelation 6, he carries a bow). It is the same basic imagery, though with a significant difference that we noted. This indicates that the first rider on the white horse is our Lord Jesus Christ[34]. And, indeed, in the Old Testament, Psalm 45:3–5 prophetically sets forth what Christ would do on the white horse (in Revelation 6 and then in a different way in Revelation 19). This Messianic psalm speaks of what Revelation calls 'the wrath of the Lamb' in verses 3–5:

Gird Thy sword upon Thy thigh, oh most mighty, with Thy glory and Thy majesty. And in Thy majesty ride prosperously because of truth and meekness and righteousness; and Thy right hand shall teach thee terrible things. Thine arrows are sharp in the heart of the king's enemies; whereby the people fall under Thee.

If it is correct that Revelation could be dated before the fall of Jerusalem in AD 70, then what the victorious Lord would do in riding forth in judgment during that time is set forth, not only in Revelation 6, but also in Hebrews 10:26–31:

For if we sin willfully, after that we have received the knowledge of the truth, there remaineth no more sacrifice for sins, but a certain fearful looking for of judgment and fiery indignation, which shall devour the adversaries. He that despised Moses' law died without mercy under two or three witnesses; of how much sorer punishment, suppose ye, shall he be thought worthy, who hath trodden under foot the Son of God, and hath counted the blood of the covenant, wherewith he was sanctified, an unholy thing, and hath done despite unto the Spirit of grace? For we know him that hath said, 'Vengeance belongeth unto Me. I will recompense,' said the Lord. And again, 'the Lord shall judge his people.' It is a fearful thing to fall into the hands of the living God.

In this light, we remember that 1 John 3:8 says that one of the things Christ came to do was 'to destroy the works of the devil'. Christ came, Jesus was manifested, to destroy the works of the devil. The main way he did it was in dying for our sins and rising for our justification and glorification. We are thereby transferred from the realm of Satan to the realm of the risen Christ. But in another sense he also carries out this destruction of the works of the devil in the sending forth of these apocalyptic horses, for they play a potent role in destroying the works of the evil one.

'When the Devil Is Active, God Is More Active'
The Rev. William Still of Aberdeen, Scotland used to say: 'When the devil is active, God is more active.' Let that encourage us. Sometimes we say, 'The devil's after me this week'. I've felt that many times, haven't you? And then I think of what Mr. Still said, 'when the devil is active, God is more active'. He is ultimately working to destroy the works of the devil, even by means of the judgments he sends into history.

The chapter in Habakkuk 3, along with the one in Zechariah 6, is the background to Revelation 6, which speaks of God moving forth in vengeance against his enemies. Listen to Habakkuk 3:3–8:

> God came from Teman, and the Holy One from mount Paran, Selah. His glory covered the heavens and the earth was full of his praise. And his brightness was as the light; he had horns coming out of his hand; and there was the hiding of his power. Before him went the pestilence and burning coals went forth at his feet. He stood, and measured the earth; he beheld, and drove asunder the nations; and the everlasting mountains were scattered, the perpetual hills did bow; his ways are everlasting. I saw the tents of Cushan in affliction; and the curtains of the land of Midian did tremble. Was the Lord displeased against the rivers? Was Thine anger against the rivers? Was Thy wrath against the sea, that Thou didst ride upon Thine horse—and Thy chariots of salvation?'

Psalm 46:8–9 says, 'Come and behold the works of the Lord, what desolations he hath made in the earth. He maketh wars to cease unto the end of the earth; he breaketh the bow, and cutteth the spear in sunder; he burneth the chariot in the fire.'

Psalm 2:9–12, another Messianic Psalm speaks prophetically in much the same vein. These passages show us that the Lamb is fully in charge of the judgments and changes of history.

Different Images of the Rider in Revelation 6 and 19 (Judgment and Salvation)
Let me make a further point about this Christ riding forth on a white horse to conquer God's enemies. There's a big difference between the vision of Christ mounted on a charger in Revelation chapter 6, and then the same Christ mounted on a charger in Revelation chapter 19.[35] In Revelation 6, Christ has a crown and a bow, a bow to destroy the enemies that have rejected the blood of the covenant. But in Revelation 19, he has a sword going out of his mouth; that is not meant literally, but it is a way of saying that the sword out of his mouth symbolizes his word. We remember from Ephesians 6 'the sword of the Spirit, which is the word of God'.

The very similar, and yet very different images of Christ given us first in Revelation 6 and later in Revelation 19, show us what is to happen in salvation history. In Revelation 6, Jerusalem is to be destroyed, the Jews scattered, and their power to persecute the Church, broken. That prepares the way for what follows in Revelation 19, where Christ is riding forth to the nations with the gospel. From this perspective, every time the gospel is preached, it's like a sword coming down from Christ. Years ago I heard an elderly minister say that 'the sword of the Spirit which is the word of God is the only sword you can stick into a dead man and he becomes a living man'. The gospel is like that. Christ, riding forth with the sword out of his mouth, means the gospel shall be conquering the nations after the destruction of Jerusalem and the temporary end of the old covenant with Judaism ('temporary', for Romans 11 and 2 Corinthians 3 show that God still has covenant blessings waiting for the Jews). The sword is active as history moves on until the last of the elect are gathered in and the Lamb comes back as the conquering Lion of the tribe of Judah. That's Revelation 19, but that's not in view yet in Revelation chapter 6 during the breaking of the seals.

Here Christ is coming against his enemies in judgment and truly it would be the last days for apostate national Judaism which had seen his miracles and rejected them, and ascribed them to the power of Satan. And so the wrath of the Lamb would come, as we're told in the first chapter and the second chapter and the third chapter of this same book of Revelation; 'shortly, very shortly'— probably not more than three or four years after this prophecy was given of the white horse of the apocalypse going forth (if indeed, Revelation be dated before AD 70). He came, but what we must remember is that he came forth in judgment in Revelation; but after that event, he is still coming forth in mercy, by means of the sword of the Spirit which is the word of God proceeding from his mouth, and the Holy Spirit proceeding from him and the Father. Every time this book is faithfully preached, the Holy Spirit is there and is going forth with the word of life, with the gospel and saying, come into Him; hide in Him; He's in charge of all that will ever happen in the history of the world; He's in charge of all that will ever be allowed to happen in your life; come to Him; live! Let this gospel penetrate you; let it stick in you; instead of killing you it will make you alive, and you shall live.

15

'Farther Along, We'll Understand Why'

Revelation 6:3-8

This pictorial text brings before us three matters:

1. The last three horsemen carry out the Lamb's work (6:4-8).
2. How to understand the elapse of time (6:6).
3. What the last three horsemen do (6:4-5, 8).

The Last Three Horsemen Carry Out the Lamb's Work

We now look at the last three of 'the four horsemen of the apocalypse', as they are popularly known. These frightening horses come out of the heavenly stable, and they are loosed with their riders to execute a work of the judgment of God. In the previous chapter, we saw that the first horseman of the apocalypse, the rider with the crown and the bow on a white horse, was the Lamb of God. Now the Lamb is moving forward like a lion; the Lord Jesus Christ is exercising the authority given to him to control history that he rightly obtained, first, as the agent of creation, and then as Redeemer of creation. As redeemer, he entered creation through the womb of the blessed virgin, becoming a man without ceasing to be God, and living a holy life and atoning for the sins of all who will ever believe; after which he rose from the dead, whereupon God the Father committed all power and authority to Him, as we see in the Great Commission in Matthew 28. To this once suffering Lamb, now triumphant Lion of the Tribe of Judah; to him and him alone, is given the final disposition of all that occurs in world history, from the time of his resurrection to the time when he returns.

While many details in Revelation are very hard to work out, this much is perfectly clear: the Holy Spirit is using the visions of the apostle John in Patmos, to lift him up into the heavenly realm, into the control chamber of this universe. Christ's main work is that of redemption, yet part of his activity between his first coming and his second coming involves a certain amount of judgment. The judgment is in order to bring a greater blessing for the spread of the gospel; but Scripture does not hold back that the holy God, at particular times and seasons in history lets loose forces to work judgment amongst mankind to avenge unbelief and persecution of the church, and in so doing prepares the way for the spread of the gospel. This passage deals with such a period of judgment that prepares for greater blessing.

How to understand the elapse of time in Revelation

To make sense of the going forth of the last three of the four horsemen of the apocalypse, we must consider the issue of time. That is to say, it is necessary to look within Revelation itself and see what it may indicate concerning the particular period of time between the two comings of the Lord. Without being certain about a very complex issue, there is something to be said for the belief that this book was written perhaps as early as AD 66 or 67 AD. If that is correct, then some of the things that he predicted were going to come to pass very shortly, actually did so. That would mean that a number of the judgments indicated as 'coming shortly to pass' took place by the year AD 70 (only 3 or 4 years after the vision was given to John, according to this early dating).

What are some indications within Revelation of a date before AD 70? Let us start with Revelation 1:1—'The Revelation of Jesus Christ which God gave unto him to show unto his servants things which must shortly come to pass'. Either that means what it says or it doesn't. Then notice Revelation 1:3—'Keep those things which are written in this book for the time is at hand'. These two time texts seem to indicate by any plain reading only a very few years. There are other time texts in Revelation which indicate the nearness of fulfillment of the prophecies of the risen Lord to John.

DeMar has assembled several of these texts:

> Every time *near* is used in the New Testament, it always means 'close' in terms of distance (Mark 2:2; Luke 15:1; John 11:18; Acts 1:12) or 'close' in terms of time (Matt. 24:32; Luke 21:30). *Shortly* is used in a similar way (Acts 24:4; Phil. 2:19, 24; 3 John 14). Thus, the events of Revelation were near—close, at hand, right around the corner—for those who first

read and heard this prophecy...The hour of testing (Rev. 3:10) was 'about to come', that is, it was near for John. In the middle of Revelation, its first readers were told that the 'third woe is coming quickly' (11:14). On ten separate occasions in Revelation, at the beginning (1:1, 3, 2:16; 3:11), in the middle (11:14), and at the end (22:6, 7, 10, 12, 20), the nearness of a series of prophetic events was on the immediate horizon.[36]

So in Revelation 6, Christ predicts that the going forth of these horsemen of the apocalypse must shortly come to pass. Jesus was promising the suffering church of that time, which was suffering under Nero (around AD 65–66), and discouraged by Jewish opposition that relief was coming to them soon, by means of the impending judgments to be unleashed by the other horsemen of the Apocalypse. To put off this relief for the first century persecuted church for two thousand years would make no sense of what Jesus promised the suffering church, represented by the seven churches of Asia.

Hence, the time text is clearly that which 'must shortly come to pass'; the time is at hand. Revelation chapter 6, with its opening of the seven sealed book and the sending forth within that opening of the four horsemen of the apocalypse, indicates a soon letting loose of historical forces that would bring judgment on the apostate Judaism that had rejected the Lord.

Comings of the Lord

At this point we must consider another significant issue raised by this, and other, chapters of Revelation. It is the question of the soon 'coming of the Lord.' He seems clearly to be saying in several of these texts that his coming is to be soon, yet we who read this book would say that some two thousand years after Jesus was speaking to John, the world has not ended. I shall address the details of this important matter later, for the present, let me give a broad overview of the question. When we compare Revelation in its entirety to certain chapters in the Gospels: Mark 13, Matthew 24–5; Luke 21; and then many places in the Old Testament, some of which we noted in the previous chapter, it's clear the phrase 'the coming of God,' or 'the coming of the Lord with his angels,' can, depending on the context, mean 'coming within history' in either powerful judgments or powerful blessings.

There are, of course, two major comings of the Lord; that is, when our Lord Jesus Christ was born—his life—his death and resurrection. And the next major coming ('the Second Coming') will be at the end of time, on the Last Day, when the trump shall sound and the dead shall be raised for the final judgment. So there are two major comings of the Lord.

Other Comings of the Lord in Historical Judgment
But, if you take into consideration some of the passages just mentioned in Revelation, along with other connected texts from the Old Testament (such as Psalm 18:9; Isa. 19:1; 31:4), as well as 'the apocalyptic' passages in Mark (13), Matthew (24 and 25), and Luke (21), you find that the Lord can be spoken of as 'coming' at times when major nations fall and judgment is unleashed. When great nations and their political and religious systems are knocked down, it does not happen without, in some sense, the Lord coming to exercise his power in history, since he is in charge of disposing all events. And after that sort of coming (not the major, final second coming on the Last Day), but rather after that sort of historical coming in judgment, you always find an increase of the blessing of the gospel in the earth, after the removals effected in these judgments or 'comings' of the Lord. When God's Son comes forth and unleashes historical forces that bring down religious and political systems, with their great cultures, what happens is not that everything is therefore ruined. On the contrary, mighty walls are reduced to rubble to provide building blocks for the highway along which the truth of God goes forth to the nations.[37]

Let us notice an illustration that is in chapter 6, the horsemen of the apocalypse are not referring to the final coming of the Lord on the last day, but rather to particular interventions in history long before the end. Look at verse 6, '*and I heard a voice in the midst of the four beasts,* (that is, the four heavenly creatures surrounding God's throne), *say, a measure of wheat for a penny and three measures of barley for a penny, and see thou hurt not the oil and wine*'. We notice in this particular 'coming' of the Lord (which happens in his sending forth of these horsemen), a distinction made between a yearly crop and a perennial or a permanent crop. It's like the Lord says to this angelic creature, 'I'm giving you authority to let loose forces of economic chaos, so that there will be a shortage of grain for a year'. The mention of the penny seems to indicate a massive price increase because the crops of grain had been destroyed that year. But what is the significance of 'not hurting the oil and the wine', which are what we call perennial, or on-going crops? The Lord says, 'I do not want you to destroy the olive trees; I do not want you to destroy the grape vines'.

What that indicates is that he leaves the olive trees and the grape vines because after this judgment of one year, in which the loss of one crop is lost, then there is going to be a time of blessing , during which the Lord's people will be moving forward, and will need to use the grapes and the olive oil. Thus, the Lord instructs those leading the soon-coming judgment to spare that which is perennial, so that it will be available to his people after the time of temporal judgment with its destruction of the yearly crop. This apparently minor detail of apocalyptic judgment indicates that this is certainly not at the very final end of history. Instead, it is speaking about a particular event of judgment soon to come, in which there will be a shift from the older Jewish economy, which rejected its Messiah, to the new Christian economy with its focus on the entire world.

The Right One to Handle Vengeance
Previously we saw how Christ is the first of the horsemen who rides forth, and in so doing, he has the leadership in dispensing these judgments to be unleashed by the other three horsemen. And the detail about not hurting the oil and the wine shows that the Lord fine-tunes every judgment, only letting them go so far as will serve his larger purposes of grace and glory! He lets judgment go far enough, but not too far. This should make us think of the principle in Romans chapter 12, where God says that we believers are not to take vengeance on our enemies. He immediately gives us the reason, '*Vengeance is Mine, saith the Lord; I will repay*'. When God lets forth vengeance and judgment he always does it right. He does it in the highest moral way. It never goes too far; it just goes to the exactly right degree, because he is a sinless, infinitely wise and good Being. He knows precisely how far the destruction should extend. God will never allow it to go any further than will remove evil powers to open the way for fuller gospel blessing. Whereas if we took vengeance to ourselves, we wouldn't know where to stop; we'd go too far.

So Christ, riding forth, the first of the four horsemen of the apocalypse, the white rider on the white horse with the glorious crown, shows that he is leading in these judgments that from time to time are let loose, and that he will do it right. Therefore, we can have great confidence even if we see things beginning to collapse. The Lord is leading. We never need take vengeance in our hands, we never need be vindictive persons; but we must trust in him who is (even when we do not see him) 'riding forth conquering and to conquer'.

What the Last Three Horsemen Do on earth

With this in mind, we must turn our attention briefly to the last three horsemen of the apocalypse. The Lamb then sends out the second horsemen, the blood-red one (Rev. 6: 3-4).

The Blood-red Rider

This grim rider takes peace from the land, (this could refer to the Judean land), that men should slay one another and a great sword is given to him. This rider stands for something that makes us all tremble, and that is war. What this shows, as the second horseman of the apocalypse goes forward and then war ensues, as one commentator said, is how utterly depraved mankind is.[38] How little it takes to get people to fight! This commentator adds that God does not have to stir up men to fight one another, he simply orders his angels to take away the conditions of peace; that's all He's got to do. God doesn't do evil directly; it's impossible—He's holy. But when it is in his will, he can remove restraints and let human nature take its course, and then it's disastrous. Then Chilton asked, 'In a sinful world, why is there not more bloodshed?' he answers that it is because there are divine restraints on man's wickedness, on man's freedom to work out the implications of his hatred and rebellion against the Lord. These invisible, divine restraints keep people from being as bad as they would be, if they could. But once God removes the restraints, man's ethical degeneracy is revealed in all its ugliness.

Some commentators (though far from the majority) have understood this particular horseman to have removed peace and employed a huge sword in the destruction of Jerusalem in AD 70, some three or four years after Revelation was written (if one accepts the early dating—also an open question). But if that be the case, then the first-hand description that the Jewish historian, Josephus, gives of the siege and destruction of Jerusalem would certainly be a lurid picture of the removal of invisible restraints against the almost incredible evil exercised by depraved humanity.[39]

Loraine Boettner a number of years ago wrote a book dealing with this, and brought out the fact that more people were killed in the destruction of Jerusalem than when the Americans bombed Hiroshima and Nagasaki.[40] In Jerusalem, the population was swollen about ten times over (perhaps to a million people) because multitudes of Jews had come to celebrate Passover. At precisely this time the Roman army surrounded Jerusalem, and put it under siege. Jerusalem could handle that great increase in population for a week, but not for years!

It came because the Jewish leadership refused to accept the truth of their own Scriptures, in their precise description of what Messiah would be like when he appeared among them. It was true then, and it is true now, rejecting the Scriptures that you claim to believe, brings the most devastating kind of judgment. God sends far worse judgments on unbelief when you had the information and rejected it, than on somebody that didn't have the information. The devastations that occurred in Jerusalem (including cannibalism) certainly look like what happens when a blood-red horse goes out and removes the restraints on wickedness. There's a certain principle here that is always true, not just in AD 70. All God has to do is not to encourage people to do wrong—he would never do that, for 'he tempts no man with evil'—all he has to do for judgment to break out in any generation is to remove angelic, invisible restraints and let self-centered, egocentric human nature begin taking its course. What a disaster! That's the second horseman. And he has been seen many times since the Fall of Jerusalem.

The Black Rider

The third horseman is an angelic rider on a black horse holding a pair of scales in his hand. This is a symbol of famine from the prophecy of Ezekiel (4:10): this horseman introduces economic hardship, massive food shortages based on agricultural breakdown, inflation of prices for food and, of course, financial depression. Verses 5–6 indicate, as scholars tell us, perhaps a thousand-fold increase in price for wheat for a loaf of bread. A thousand-fold increase, say, in a week's time—how could you afford bread? It is said that it would cost a workman at least an entire day's wages, or maybe two days' wages, now, to get a loaf of bread and there wouldn't be any money left over for oil, for meat, for the rent, for any other thing. So a disobedient culture that rejects God's truth ultimately loses its economy. That's what happened in Egypt. It was the richest nation on earth, the most sophisticated, wealthy, distinguished, powerful nation in history up to that time, but Egypt's economy was destroyed by the ten plagues in Moses' time because of their rejection of the many opportunities the Lord gave them. And that's what would happen to Israel in AD 70 shortly after Revelation was penned by

John (if we accept the early date). But whether we do or not, we find that it is a principle always at work throughout all history.

The Pale Rider

Finally, the fourth horseman is perhaps the scariest of them all—a pale rider, or death, followed by hell for those who are killed. In Revelation 1:18, Christ is described as the keeper of the keys of death and hell. He is described as an absolutely glorious being, who has a big belt with keys hanging on it. And amongst these keys, which indicate authority to control what happens in history to the lives of men and women, are the keys of death and hell. Here, as the pale horse and the pale rider go forth, the Lord is using the keys to open the invisible door of death, and hell beyond that, for the rejecters of the gospel and the persecutors of the church.

Some might question, whether God is good, if he does such terrible things? The answer depends on whether you are talking about the only true God, the One who is described in scripture, or whether you wish to fabricate a little god that suits your purposes. The god of Modernism, who never judges, is an idol, a figment of people's imagination that they can handle without having to change their life by submitting to Him. But the true God is described in scripture. Yes, God is wondrous love, holy love, generous love, forgiving love—but his holiness requires judgment upon sin; particularly, after many opportunities have been given, one crosses an invisible line, a point of no return, where holy judgment is certain.

We never know when an individual has crossed the line of no return; we cannot judge such a thing. All we can do is, looking back on the judgments of God in history and the comings of Christ in those judgments, realize that a certain culture passed the point of no return, when a holy God said 'enough is enough', and sent forth the pale horse and the pale rider. In such cases, an invisible door is opened by the authority of the Lord and many will be taken through it to their irreparable judgment. This awful rider is given authority by God to bring four plagues on the disobedient land: the sword, famine, death and wild beasts.

Blessing Follows Terrible Judgments

After these judgments brought by the pale horse and rider, there will be a tremendous going forth of the gospel, when persecutors and other hindrances are out of the way. In the meantime, many more will be saved, and pass through the invisible door of life and eternal blessing.

Everything, even the judgments that occur around our heads—the timing and the outworking of them—are under the control of his throne. This gives us a great calm, for even though we cannot understand everything about the evils we see around us, we know whose Throne is in charge, and that is sufficient, in good times and in bad times. Hence, in the words of the old Southern gospel hymn, we can wait now in patience and faith, until 'Farther along, we know all about it.'

> 'Farther along, we'll know all about it;
> Farther along, we'll understand why.
> Cheer up, my brother, live in the sunlight;
> We'll understand it all by and by.'

16

THE FIFTH SEAL: PRAYERS OF THE MARTYRS IN HEAVEN
Revelation. 6:9–11

The prayers of the martyrs in heaven bring down ungodly nations and make way for fuller gospel blessing to the world. That is made clear in this passage.

We see here:

1. The supernatural connection between two worlds (Rev. 6:10–11).
2. The part the martyred saints play in determining world history (Rev. 6:11).

THE SUPERNATURAL CONNECTION BETWEEN TWO WORLDS

This passage demonstrates very clearly the close connection between the unseen, heavenly realm and this realm of flesh, blood, nature, and world history. Owing to the rank materialism of our Western culture (which foolishly holds that only physical matter and natural forces are real), even Christians tend to discount the most important factor of all in making things happen here below: the usually invisible, but all-powerful heavenly world. This text shows us that the biggest events in the history of mankind are initiated in that powerful and unseen realm.

The opening of this fifth seal (Rev. 6:9) lies behind the historical downfall of evil systems that oppose the gospel. If Revelation was written early, then this would first of all apply to the downfall of Jerusalem in AD 70. In that case, the prayers of the martyrs in glory (perhaps like Stephen) would have been effective in bringing down the unbelieving and persecuting Jewish economy of that time, thus making way for the fuller expansion of the gospel. But even if one holds that it was written later, the principle holds true, that the prayers of the heavenly martyrs make changes in the course of world affairs.

THE MARTYRS' PART IN DETERMINING THE COURSE OF HISTORY ON EARTH

Once the saints have been martyred, they do not lose their effectiveness in changing the course of world history. Their continuing ministry in this regard is hidden from us on earth, for they are now beyond the range of our physical observation. The 'worldly wise man' would say that once someone (like a martyred saint) has been torn apart by animals, stoned, shot or burned, he has gone out of existence. But the God who is truth tells us that their souls or personalities are as vibrantly alive as ever (indeed, more so), and they are dwelling in the immediate presence of God in the realm of joy and light.

Since the soul or personality of the sons and daughters of Adam is in the direct image of the eternal God, it is not possible to kill their spirit or soul. (I am using spirit and soul interchangeably). All the powers of Hell could not blot out one soul. It is impossible that the soul of one human person could be annihilated or extinguished because it is in the likeness of eternal God and hence the soul goes on existing somewhere forever.

Focus on Martyrdom

The focus of Revelation 6:9–11 is on those who loved Jesus, those who testified to his gospel and lost their lives because of their testimony for Him. Many of us have visited the ancient coliseum in Rome, where such large numbers of the early Christians were put to death to entertain the crowds of pagan spectators. The cruel authorities would sometimes put the Christians in animal skins, and then from under the floor of the coliseum, they would let out fierce lions, bears and other wild animals that would claw and tear the Christians to shreds, so that there would not have been very much left of their physical bodies. Others of them were burned in various ways (as in the time of Nero); some were hacked to death, with probably very little left to bury.

This text specifically shows, and the whole word of God backs it up, that those Christians who were put to death for the Lord, had their spirit immediately released from the physical body and now they have been received into the highest Heavens, into the presence of God. The death of the body, in no sense whatsoever, indicates the cessation of existence of the spirit in us, for it is in the image of God.

Description of the Martyrs in Glory

Three things are said about the martyred saints in this text. First, the martyred saints now in heaven are very near Almighty God; they are said to be 'under the altar' (verse 9). Secondly, they are clothed in the beauty of white robes (verse 11). Then thirdly, as they are enjoying this wonderful rest, they are talking to God (verses 10–11).

(1) The Martyrs are near God. The saints according to verse 9 are under the altar. They are close to the throne of God, from which comes forth the carrying out of all the divine decrees for God's program in the history of the lower world. These martyred saints who have died and been taken above, are about as close as a human being could be to the center of all the power, for blessing and judgment, as concerns the future in heaven and on earth. This is precisely the opposite of what the evil powers who took the lives of the saints of God would have intended. To rid themselves of the testimony of these believers, who were showing up the darkness of the evil works of sinners by their humble and holy lives, the world system said: 'Let's dispatch them. Then we shall be rid of their annoying influence, and our lives will no longer be disturbed by their Christian testimony.' But look at what actually has happened: they have only dispatched them to a place of tremendous authority that they can now exercise near their heavenly father's heart in heaven, as they are praying. Is this not an illustration of Psalm 76:10, 'Surely the wrath of man shall praise thee', and of Romans 8:28, 'For we know that all things work together for good to them that love God.'

(2) They are clothed in garments of white. Secondly we are told the martyred saints, those who have died in the Lord and for the Lord, are clothed in beautiful white robes. The destruction of their physical body on earth does not mean that they do not have a beautiful shape above. The white loveliness of their heavenly garments comes from

the red blood of Christ shed for their sins, as that altar that they are under will eternally remind them and us. The life of those saints flows from Christ's death on Calvary in their place, just like ours does. Once we believe in Christ, we are forevermore bound in a bundle of life with the risen one. Absolutely no power in heaven, earth or hell can annihilate us because we are bound up with the ever living Christ who is the very image of God himself. So passing through the gates of death, even when people's bodies are hacked up in terrible ways, does not deprive us of a beautiful likeness once we pass through the slaughter. On the contrary, we are given marvelous white robes.

This is connected with 2 Corinthians 5, where it says that 'we know that if our earthly house of this tabernacle be dissolved, we have a building of God, an house not made with hands, eternal in the heavens.' Paul is not speaking here about the resurrection of the body at the end of time. What Paul is saying in 2 Corinthians 5, is that immediately after we leave this earthly body, we have a beautiful shape, somewhat like we are now, but purged of any defects. John Calvin said that we could think of it as a down payment, a first installment on the resurrection body we are going to receive on the last day.

What is described for us in Revelation 6, that we are not told in 2 Corinthians 5, is the supreme beauty, the bright shining, heavenly glory of the garments that God so tenderly and gladly puts on his saints when they come into their heavenly home. This dressing of the martyrs brings to mind a blue-grass gospel song, that was popular in the 1940s in the American South. It helps us contemplate the joys and beauties that now belong to those who have been slain for the Lord.

'Beautiful robes of white, Beautiful land of light,
Beautiful home so bright,
Where there shall come no night;
Beautiful crown I'll wear,
Shining with stars o'er there,
Yonder in mansions fair, Gather us there.'[41]

(3) They are Communicating with the Lord. The third thing that is said about the martyred saints in the glory of that serene realm, where they enjoy the bliss of rest and the refreshment in the green pastures beside the still waters of the crystal sea, near the rainbow circled throne is they are communicating all the time with the Lord God Omnipotent. Isn't that wonderful? At times we think of our loved ones who have left us, and perhaps feel that we would like to be able to talk to them. Well, we need to remember that they are talking, communicating with the one who loves them more than anyone ever loved them; with God himself. They have immediate access to God. In some cases, they may have been considered nothing while they were on earth, absolutely powerless, with no access to the corridors of money and political power, but now they have the ear of the King of Kings and the Lord of Lords. He is very attentive to what they are saying to him and what they are asking him to do. Truly to them, as Paul says elsewhere, 'to die is to gain'.

The Content of Their Discussion

Notice what they are talking to the Lord about in verse 10. They are praying for God to vindicate his Church on earth and in this way they add their intercessions for the bringing down of corrupt, evil, political polities that are opposing Christ. They say, 'Lord, bring them down so that the mighty gospel can take eagle wings and fly across the face of needy nations with great effect and liberation'. In particular, they are calling on God to deal with those who are persecuting his people and hindering the outreach of the Church. And then notice, that not only do they talk to God, God also talks back to them. The gracious Lord answers them and has something to say to them. What he says is in the latter part of verse 11. They say, 'Lord, now move in and deal with this evil that is hindering the spread of the truth'.

Maybe we can think of what opposition to God's truth there is in the schools and in the government bureaucracies and in the media, and sometimes even in certain churches who want anything but submission to Scriptural truth. Could the saints above be asking: 'Lord, break down the satanic opposition so that these people can be liberated'. Think of the Islamic countries where to be baptized literally means beheading, if the person was previously a Muslim and the government finds out. The martyred saints above are asking: 'How much longer until the truth gets out and these people can be saved?' Yes, he hears them. Notice how tenderly the Lord of glory answers them here in verse 11, that they should rest yet for a little season until their fellow servants also, and their brethren that should be killed as they were, should be fulfilled.

The Divine Response Given Them
What is God saying? God is saying, 'yes I am going to answer your prayers for the Church and I am going to deal with the evil powers that are preventing their outreach to the lost, but I want you to wait a little while'. He doesn't say that they have to wait until the end of time, to the last day, but he says, 'Wait a little season and then I am going to do something'. Well, we know how he brought down Jerusalem in AD 70. We know how the Roman Empire fell about three hundred years after that. We know how the USSR unraveled in 1991. God says, 'Yes, I will answer your prayers. Your prayers are important to me and I am hearing them and will move as you ask, just at the right time, so that these prayers are going to make a huge difference. But I am the one who knows the right time to release these judgments and then blessings from the altar that will break down wickedness and turn lose righteousness upon the earth.

Why God's Answers Do not Come Immediately
In this setting of the times and the seasons, the Lord says, 'Keep on praying for a little season; I am hearing you, but I alone must determine when to move.' Factored into that 'little season', there must be more martyrdoms, more believers must be killed on earth by the opponents of Christ, before the Lord will be ready to send certain blessings in certain places.

Colossians 1:24 tells us something closely related to this. The Apostle Paul says, '[I] now rejoice in my sufferings for you, and fill up that which is behind of the afflictions of Christ in my flesh for his body's sake, which is the Church'. This verse indicates that our heavenly father has ordained and is using the suffering of Christians on earth to fill up a certain measure, so as to get everything ready. From this it would appear that a certain number of believers have to be killed for the faith, and then their holy deaths are used to get everything right for God radically to change certain things on earth so as to let loose his blessings. In other words, a definite number of saints have to suffer. Some will suffer and die a natural death, some will actually be martyred before everything is ready for God to wipe out evil powers and then extend his Church.

The Suffering of the Saints Is Like
Sands Filling the Hour Glass
The idea of waiting for a certain fullness before divine action is taken seems to be reflected in a very different context in Genesis 15:16, where

Abraham is promised that his descendants would return triumphantly from bondage in Egypt after 'the fullness of the iniquity of the Amorites' in the fourth generation of the time of the children of Israel in Egypt. God would wait for a fullness of iniquity to occur among those pagans, in which he would let them reach a certain condition of wickedness, then, it would be the right time to let his people come in and take the land of the unrepentant pagans, who had turned down every opportunity from the Lord.

Vast Martyrdoms in the Twentieth Century
As we look at what has happened in the twentieth century, various statistics show that there have been more Christians killed for the gospel in the twentieth century than any other century since our Lord was on earth. What does that mean? According to this text, it means, that they are going up into the heavenly realm and their prayers are being added to the prayers of the other saints beautifully robed in white and the cup is being filled up of the necessary suffering to honor Christ, to take part in his sufferings so that others can receive the message. God must be getting ready to do absolutely tremendous things, maybe in this twenty-first century. Of course, no one knows times and dates, for as God said to the saints up there, rest now 'a little season', and I am going to keep working while you pray, but leave the exact time in my hands. According to this promise, one day we will see an in-gathering of souls for the Lord Jesus Christ, such as we haven't seen in untold centuries.

Perhaps the amazing growth of the Church in China at present is the fruit of the martyrdoms during the Red Guards purge. Perhaps the explosive growth of Anglican Christianity in Uganda is the fruit of the time of killing under Idi Amin. If so, it is the fulfillment of what Tertullian said in North Africa in the early third century, that the blood of the martyrs is the seed of the church. It is not without significance to the expansion of Christianity that when the martyrs are dispatched from earth to their heavenly intercession, their prayers work great things for the suffering church on earth.

One of the old Puritans said that 'The prayers of the saints are the beginnings of the execution of the predestinated purposes of God.' The prayers and suffering of the saints on earth, and the prayers of the saints above are all playing their part in filling up the cup of necessary suffering and martyrdom. At certain times in history the cup fills up and spills over with mighty blessing; bringing down unbelief, immorality, and wickedness, making the way clear for the spreading of Holy Ghost revival, renewal of the culture and the gathering in of vast numbers of the lost. Judgments are always preludes to mighty blessings. Our prayer is: Lord, send down the blessings that will gather in the lost and honor our Lord Jesus Christ.

17

THE SHAKINGS OF HISTORY
Revelation 6:12–17

Revelation 6:12–17 is the explanation of what lies behind the shakings of history, what controls the occurrences amongst the nations. You could put it very simply if you wanted to summarize this whole passage: when the saints pray, there come tremendous shakings on the earth. Two major points:

1. What lies behind the shakings of history—the rising of some nations and the falling of others; the movements of peoples, wars, prosperity, failure and so forth on a large and small scale.
2. What this shaking on earth looks like.

WHAT LIES BEHIND THE SHAKINGS ON EARTH

Here is the key to what we noted in the last chapter. The saints are praying. In this case, it is the martyred saints—the ones whose souls have temporarily left their bodies and are near the throne of God in heaven. There they are praying to God to do certain things upon the earth. But we would also wish to take into account here Revelation 8. It speaks of the prayers of all saints ascending before the throne, and that means the saints in heaven, as well as the ones who are still fighting on earth. The result of all these prayers—from heaven and from earth—Revelation 8 tells us 'fire *comes down from heaven to earth*'. But here in Revelation 6, the saints are praying, and tremendous shakings, something like earthquakes, occur in the nations of the world.

But this praying takes time to build up its effects. God controls the times and the seasons. He waits for the prayers, like water coming into a pond that backs up behind the dam, and then just at the right moment, he opens the sluice gate and lets the water through so that the mill wheels begin turning. So the saints were praying, and in due season their prayers will be effective in bringing down evil powers. That happened at the right time with unbelieving Judaism, and later with the Roman Empire. God said, 'I've heard you; I'm going to answer you; your prayers are effectual, but you must let Me choose the moment when I execute the answer to your prayers'.

WHAT THIS SHAKING LOOKS LIKE

In the next section, verses 12–17, a mighty shaking occurs on earth. It is difficult to be exact, but if Revelation were written as early as AD 66 or 67, then this tremendous shaking occurred within three to four years of the time those prayers of the saints were being raised. In that case, God waited three or four years; it was not long, and fits in with what you read in Revelation 1 about 'a short time', and 'the time is near'. Yet it is difficult to be certain. But here is the point, whether an early or a later date for Revelation is correct: the saints pray and the earth, by and by, begins shaking. History is changed.

The Prayers of Believers and God's Purposes
Verses 12-17 show that prayers of believers cause the Lamb to open another seal on the book of predestinated history. One might object and reply: but if things are predestinated, it makes no difference what you do, as far as praying is concerned. But according to Scripture it does matter: exactly the opposite is the case, because predestination—that is, God's sovereign control of all things from beginning to end, including the means to accomplish what God has written in the book which the Lamb opens, seal by seal—unfolds in accordance with the prayers of the saints. Prayer is one of the major means to accomplish the eternal purpose of God. The Lord has written the effects of the prayers and sufferings of the saints into his book. That is why when the saints pray, in due season tremendous shakings and amazing events occur in history.

Stellar and Geological Conveys Historical Events
What does this shaking on earth, these mighty earthquakes, look like? Descriptive words are used like *shaking* and *stars falling* and *heavens departing as the scroll is rolled up*. What does all of this mean? Verses 12-14 especially, use imagery taken from the Old Testament to describe this shaking in non-literal symbols and images. One has to trace these word pictures back to their Old Testament sources to understand their meaning, which—in general—is not absolutely literal[42].

Sports writers, for instance, may say: 'one football team creams another', or 'wipes up the floor with another', or financial writers tell us that 'the stock market has gone south.' The news writers did not mean what they said to be taken literally, but they were conveying in dramatic language a certain truth: one team, by a large number of points, beat the other team decisively, or the stock market has fallen seriously. Everybody gets the point. To a certain degree, that's how it is with these Old Testament symbols. They're taken over from the Old Testament and employed, as in Matthew 24, Luke 21, Mark 13, and Revelation to state dramatically important truths.

Old Testament Background to Imagery
This requires us to look into the Old Testament images to see how these word pictures such as 'stars falling' are used. It is a way of the good principle of interpreting scripture in light of scripture. Augustine and others have long ago shown us that we must interpret the symbolical parts in light of the plain, historical parts, the hard parts in light of the easy parts, the few parts in light of the many parts, and then we are on more solid ground to understand what God is saying through the inspired apocalyptic writers.

With this principle in mind, let us look at these ancient symbols used in Revelation 6:12-14. Some of the symbols are 'fire falling to earth' after the saints pray; the land shaking; the sun turning black; the moon becoming as blood; the stars falling and heaven being rolled up like a scroll. These images convey a message that Jesus wanted the early church to see through the apostle John.

Mountains and Earth Shake
First, geological structures are said to 'shake.' One could go to Exodus 19:18 (where God called Moses up to Mount Sinai to give the law. We

learn that the mountain was shaking when Israel was being constituted a covenant people. It is significant that the same imagery is taken over in Revelation 6, when unbelieving Israel, which had rejected their Messiah is being de-constituted as the major covenant people, and their covenant status is being transferred in significant ways to the suffering church.[43] So Exodus 19:18: 'And Mount Sinai was altogether on a smoke, because the Lord descended upon it in fire; and the smoke thereof ascended as the smoke of a furnace, and the whole mount quaked greatly'. Or you can take verses in Isaiah 24: 'Behold the Lord maketh the earth empty and maketh it waste and turneth it upside down, and scattereth abroad the inhabitants thereof' (v. 1). Then verses 19-23:

> The earth is utterly broken down; the earth is clean dissolved, the earth is moved exceedingly. The earth shall reel to and fro like a drunkard, and shall be removed like a cottage; and the transgression thereof shall be heavy upon it; and it shall fall, and not rise again. And it shall come to pass in that day, that the Lord shall punish the host of the high ones that are on high, and the kings of the earth upon the earth. And they shall be gathered together, as prisoners are gathered in the pit, and shall be shut up in the prison, and after many days they shall be visited. Then the moon shall be confounded, and the sun ashamed, when the Lord of hosts shall reign in mount Zion, and in Jerusalem, and before his ancients gloriously.

Nahum 1:2 and 5 speaks in similar fashion:

> God is jealous, and the Lord revengeth; the Lord revengeth, and is furious; the Lord will take vengeance on his adversaries, and he reserveth wrath for his enemies... The mountains quake at Him, and the hills melt, and the earth is burned at his presence, yea, the world, and all that dwell therein.

In Revelation 6, these images seem to indicate the destabilization of the land of Israel, then under the control of the Pharisaic Jews. The principle would be the same with reference to the Roman Empire, or to other great national entities. But its primary reference was to the establishment of covenant Israel and then the imagery was used for God's judgments as they were taken into captivity, when the land was shaken down. That is why many (especially those who propose an early date for Revelation) hold that the original reference of these same terms in Revelation 6 would be to the most important nation in God's plan up to that time, which was Israel. It is a defining moment in the history of the nations and in the history of redemption when Israel is being shaken down to be replaced by something else.

The Sun Turns Black

Another image borrowed by Revelation chapter 6 from these Old Testament passages is that 'the sun turns black'. In Exodus 10:21-3, we see the same sort of imagery. By the way, the early church, so many of whom were Jewish, understood these terms, for they knew their Old Testament. Exodus 10:21-3 occurs during the plagues in Egypt. 'And the Lord said unto Moses, stretch out thine hand towards heaven, that there may be darkness over the land of Egypt, even darkness which may be felt'. The imagery of darkness is used also in Isaiah 5:24-5, which refers to God's judgment against corrupt judges: 'Therefore as the fire devoureth the stubble, and the flame consumeth the chaff, so their root shall be as rottenness, and their blossom shall go up as dust; because they have cast away the law of the Lord of hosts, and despised the word of the Holy One of

Israel. Therefore is the anger of the Lord kindled against his people, and he hath stretched forth his hand against them, and hath smitten them; and the hills did tremble, and their carcasses were torn in the midst of the streets.' For all this his anger is not turned away, but his hand is stretched out still. And then in verse 30: 'And in that day they shall roar against them like the roaring of the sea; and if one look unto the land, behold darkness and sorrow, and the light is darkened in the heavens thereof'.

We find this sort of imagery in Ezekiel 32:2, 7–8:

> Son of man, take up a lamentation for Pharaoh king of Egypt, and say unto him, Thou art like a young lion of the nations, and thou art as a whale in the seas; and thou camest forth with thy rivers, and troubledst the waters with thy feet, and fouledst their rivers.... And when I shall put thee out, I will cover the heaven, and make the stars thereof dark; I will cover the sun with a cloud, and the moon shall not give her light. All the bright lights of heaven will I make dark over thee, and set darkness upon thy land, saith the Lord God.

To take these images literally would be to miss the message. By means of referring to astronomical changes, the truth is conveyed that Egypt, (and then later, it is applied to the Jewish nation), Egypt's light, as the bright shining leader of the nations, would go out and down she would go. This fall is spoken of in solar terms to help us understand its significance.

It is much the same with the little prophecy of Joel: 2:1, and 10: which speak particularly of the holy nation of the Jews:

> Blow ye the trumpet in Zion, and sound an alarm in My holy mountain; let all the inhabitants of the land tremble; for the day of the Lord cometh, for it is nigh at hand... The earth shall quake before them; the heavens shall tremble; the sun and the moon shall be dark, and the stars shall withdraw their shining.

Or Amos 8:9: 'And it shall come to pass in that day, saith the Lord God, that I will cause the sun to go down at noon, and I will darken the earth in the clear day...'

Astronomical Phenomena Represent Nations

What is being said is this: by speaking in astronomical and cosmic terms, we are shown that the former brightness of God's blessing on a nation is removed when they consistently, for generations, reject the clear meaning of his Word, and must undergo his severe judgments. After a certain period of time, their light will go out. The restraint against the powers of darkness that God held back from getting that nation will be removed, and thereby evil powers are allowed to overwhelm that now apostate nation. The nation sinks, as it were, from being the top of the lighthouse, with its broad and bright beam shining out over the waters, to the very bottom of the blackness of the churning sea. And their national sinking is in such passages spoken of in these cosmic terms.

The Stars Fall

Another image in Revelation 6 is that of the stars falling. Again, the faithful Bible interpreter must note that this is not being used literally; if a star fell to the earth, the earth would be vaporized immediately, for stars are massively larger than the earth. The sun is a star, and there are stars that are much larger than our sun. So if a star literally fell to earth it would be all over—nothing! That can't be meant, because in the immediate passage following this one, the angelic messengers are instructed, 'see that you do not hurt the trees'; so the earth is still there. The picture of a star falling is therefore being used in another way.

Stars in the Old Testament are often used as emblems of governing powers. You remember how the dream that really got Joseph in trouble and made his brothers hate him was when he told his father that he had seen the sun and the moon and the stars bowing down before him. His father rebuked him, and said: 'Shall your mother and I, and your brothers bow down before you?' Jacob immediately got the point, that sun and moon and stars were used as emblems of ruling powers; that is to say, Jacob and his wife and the twelve patriarchs. So when it says that the stars fall, it's a way of saying that the time for national Israel (and other nations at various times) has run out. The clock has ticked its last. Thus it says: 'the stars of heaven fell unto the earth, even as a fig tree casteth her untimely figs, when she is shaken of a mighty wind'. Such language is used in Job 9, Ecclesiastes 12:1–2 and Daniel 8:9–10. The fig tree, we are told in Matthew 21:19, is speaking of Israel. Israel would be shaken down; that's another way of saying that Israel's star is fallen, to be replaced by something else. We are told elsewhere what that something else is: he is sometimes spoken of as 'the Bright and Morning Star'; sometime as the 'Sun of Righteousness rising with healing in his wings'; he would replace Israel when her star fell.

The Heavens Are Rolled Up Like a Scroll

Then we notice that 'the heavens are rolled up like a scroll'. We find this imagery used in Isaiah 34:4: 'And all the hosts of heaven shall be dissolved, and the heavens shall be rolled together as a scroll; and all their host shall fall down as the leaf falleth off from the vine, and as a falling fig from the fig tree'. This is the origin of the image used in Revelation 6. Similarly in Psalm 102:25–26, we see the same thing: 'Of old Thou hast laid the foundation of the earth; and the heavens are the work of Thy hands. They shall perish but Thou shalt endure; yea, all of them shall wax old like a garment; as a vesture shalt Thou change them, and they shall be changed'. The heavens being rolled back as a scroll, waxing old, being removed and replaced by something else, is a way of saying that Israel (and various Gentile powers as well) are going to be shaken down so that God can replace them with something better in his redemptive purposes. We are told what that 'something better' is in Hebrews 12:26–7: 'Whose voice then shook the earth; but now he hath promised, saying, Yet once more I shake not the earth only, but also heaven. And this word, Yet once more, signifieth the removing of those things that are shaken, as of things that are made, that those things which cannot be shaken may remain'. The next verse says that it is the kingdom of grace. God is shaking nations down, particularly in answer to the prayers of the suffering saints. God was going to shake down national Israel (in collusion with the Romans) persecuting the churches. And then in due time, he would shake down the Roman Empire. Indeed, in due time, God will shake down everything else that opposes his church to make room for the kingdom of love and grace.

Finally, notice that people hide as mountains are moved. Job speaks similarly: 'Which removeth the mountains, and they know not; which overturneth them in his anger. Which shaketh the earth out of her place, and the pillars thereof tremble' (9:5–6). Nahum uses the same imagery: 'The mountains quake at Him, and the hills melt, and the earth is burned at his presence, yea, the world and all that dwell therein. Who can stand before his indignation? And who can abide in the fierceness of his anger? His fury is poured out like fire, and the rocks are thrown down by Him' (1:5–6).

Old Creation and Old Covenant Give Way to New

If you take all of these cosmic and geological images together, what do they mean? It means initially that God's old creation, that is to say, covenant Israel, is to be shaken down; she had rejected the law, she had rejected the gospel, she had crucified and abused the Son of God and had not repented. God says, I must darken your position as the head of the covenant, as the light to the nations. I must shake you down. The temple will be destroyed, for I will remove the restraints that kept the Romans from doing to you what they could well do. Then you will be scattered among the nations to make room for the new creation. Political and national powers will be shaken down to make room for God Almighty to transfer his kingdom through Christ to the gospel-preaching church, the missionary church. Yet this principle holds true long after the destruction of national Israel. The principle is true throughout history. Other nations and empires must also be shaken down, have the light of their stars fall, to make way for the expansion of the gospel of light.

In due time, God answers the prayers of the saints above and below; at various junctures in world and redemptive history, the Lamb does come in judgment, but one day the Lamb will come for the last time, and all will be over. Whether in AD 70, or when the Roman Empire fell, or at other turning points for the nations, and above all, at the very end of time, none will be able to hide from God's face, brilliant and burning with holy light. Malachi 3:2 asks: 'But who may abide the day of his coming?'

Today's Shakings Will Make Room for Something Better

Today we are living in a day of profound shakings. Hebrews 12 says that Almighty God is using these shakings, as he did when he removed Israel to be replaced by the new Israel, and as he did when he removed Rome, and at other times; God is removing all obstacles that stand between the face of the sovereign Lamb and every human being on earth. One day all will be gone; we shall see nothing but the face of the Lamb. C. S. Lewis, in a remarkable essay, entitled *The Weight of Glory*, said that in the end of the day, the only thing that matters in every human being's life is their looking at the face of God in Christ, the face of the Lamb. He pointed out that for the saved it is exactly the same face as for the lost. But for the saved it is a face of beauty and supernal light and benediction and blessing and healing and joy, as in 1 John 3:2, 'We shall be like him for we shall see him as he is'. But we must remember that it is the same face of God Almighty in Christ that the unsaved person will see, and will scream out to the mountains, 'Fall on us, hide us, crush us; we had rather anything happen to us than to see that face of holiness and power and glory that we have rejected and hated and cursed. Hide us from the face!' It's the same face. Whatever else our life amounts to, the real question is, which category you and I will be in when nothing can hide us, as one day nothing will be able to hide us, from the face of God in Christ.

But for those of us who 'love his appearing', who long to see his face, we are amazed to realize that even now, God is using our feeble prayers. Because we are in Him, unworthy and weak as we are, our prayers have supernatural efficacy. God is taking our prayers to fill up the pool of water behind the sluice-gate of history, so that the Lamb gives word to unloose certain seals, which begin the shaking down of the strongholds of Satan, leaving room for the march of the beautiful feet that advance the Gospel of peace. With this in mind we are encouraged to pray on!

18

An Interlude Between the Sixth and Seventh Seals
Revelation 7:1–3

These verses may be as clear an explanation as you will find anywhere in the Bible of why God, our heavenly Father, seems so often to delay answering some of the most important prayers of his saints. You know how in some long movies, plays, or concerts, there is an interlude, a pause in which to rest before the final or the second half. The two visions in Revelation 7, that is, verses 1–8 and then 9–17, are like two parts of a larger work, between which we find an interlude or an intermission; a period of delay, between the sixth seal and the seventh seal.[44]

This Interlude Explains God's Delays
This interlude helps to explain the period of waiting, which the saints found hard to understand in the previous chapter (Rev. 6:10), when they were crying out and asking God why it was so long till he answered their prayers. They say with a loud voice, 'How long O Lord, holy and true, dost Thou not judge and avenge our blood on them that dwell on the earth?' That was the question addressed to the throne. God heard their question and provided the reason for his delay. Thus, this section explains one of the major reasons why, throughout history, God delays answering the prayers of his people. Yes, he clearly will answer the prayers that are right—and these were right prayers. We see God beginning to answer in the next chapter. But God is the one and the only one who carefully decides the right time to answer. Good farmers do not pick cotton until the right time. God, the heavenly Husbandman and Lord of the harvest, does not send the blade of cutting judgment on the world until his elect are ready and safely set apart. It's like the parable of the wheat and the tares. The tares are not pulled out before harvest time, lest it uproot the wheat. God alone knows when everything is ready; he does not send judgment too early, lest it disturb the growth of the wheat. For that reason, God delays answering the prayers of the saints for relief and vindication of his people until all is ready. Then the right moment comes, and he lets loose the angels of judgment.

It is possible that this passage is setting before us a Divine judgment that came primarily at the end of the old covenant Jewish age in AD 70. But whether that is true or not, we can observe here a spiritual principle that is in operation till the end of time; it's in operation right now.

Let us look at these two periods of waiting before devastating judgment (which occurs once the number of saints is filled up):

1. The first period of waiting could be considered that which came before the end of the old Jewish age, and
2. The second period of waiting, that which lasts until the very end of time.

Waiting Until the End of the Old Jewish Age

The first period of waiting can be thought of as the delay before the fall of Jerusalem, that is, the end of the old Jewish age in AD 70. Why was what happened to Jerusalem so important to the early Christians? Christianity came out of ancient Judaism. In a sense, it is a reformation of true Judaism. Jesus said to the woman at the well, '*Salvation is of the Jews.*' Jesus was the promised Messiah to the Jews and to the whole world. He precisely and perfectly fulfilled the Jewish Scriptures, namely the Old Testament, in every detail. But the Jews as a nation rejected and murdered their true Messiah, the very Son of God in the flesh. Thus in due time, they brought disastrous judgment on their nation, their capital and their temple. Yet many individual Jews, indeed thousands on one day, were saved through believing in Jesus. Indeed, the first church was Jewish. The early Christian mission in the various parts of the Roman Empire first of all went to the Jewish synagogue to preach the gospel; they very properly wanted to give Israel the first chance, because the message was first to the Jews, and then to the Gentiles, as the apostle Paul says in the epistle to the Romans.

But here was the problem faced at the time John wrote Revelation for the suffering church: while many members of the thousands of synagogues throughout the known world were being saved through faith in Jesus Christ, those who rejected the message were using their influence (and some of them were highly placed) with the Roman government to persecute severely the young church. This fact is mentioned more than once, as we have seen, in Revelation 1 and 2. So the saints, especially the martyred saints above, were crying out to God to vindicate his church by dealing in judgment with the persecutors, especially apostate Israel. God said in Revelation 6:11 something like this (and I paraphrase it): 'Yes, I hear you; your prayers do have influence with Me. I will answer them. One day you will be very glad you prayed like this, but wait a while; right now I must withhold serious judgment on this unbelieving nation that is hurting you, until the right number of them are saved; then it's all over for the unbelieving national system.'

Do not Hurt the Seas and the Trees

Then the apostle John hears a mighty angel command four lesser angels not to hurt the earth, the sea or the trees (Revelation 7:3), till they had done something else first. The angels had to do something else first before judgment could come. The doing of this 'something else' is why God delayed for a while the answer to the prayers of the martyred saints. What is this 'something else' that had to happen first before the prayers could be answered? Here is the key to why God waits so long in answering the prayers of his people. 'Don't uproot the crop', says the leading angel, so to speak, 'till we have sealed the servants of God in their foreheads.'

This imagery is taken from Ezekiel 9:1-7:

He cried also in mine ears with a loud voice, saying, 'Cause them that have charge over the city to draw near, even every man with his destroying weapon in his hand.' And, behold, six men came from the way of the higher gate, which lieth toward the north, and every man a slaughter weapon in his hand; and one man among them was clothed with linen, with a writer's inkhorn by his side; and they went in, and stood beside the brazen altar. And the glory of the God of Israel was gone up from the cherub, whereupon he was, to the threshold of the house. And he called to the man clothed with linen, which had the writer's inkhorn by his side; and the Lord said unto him, [essentially the same thing that this possible archangel is saying to the four lower angels], 'Go through the midst of the city, through the midst of Jerusalem, and set a mark upon the foreheads of the men that sigh and that cry for all the abominations that be done in the midst thereof.' And to the others he said in mine hearing, 'Go ye after him through the city [that is, do not go ahead of him; do not go with him, but go after he's finished his work] and smite; let not your eye spare, neither have ye pity; slay utterly old and young, both maids, and little children, and women; but come not near any man upon whom is the mark; and begin at my sanctuary.' Then they began at the ancient men which were before the house [that means the elders, the leadership.] And he said unto them, 'Defile the house and fill the courts with the slain; go ye forth.' And they went forth, and slew in the city.

So the elect had to be sealed with the seal upon their foreheads; that seems to mean in New Testament language, 'the seal of the Spirit'. We read about it in Ephesians 1:13 and 4:30. This seal is applied to true believers; first of all, to the right number of true believers, before the other seals—the seals of wrath—are let loose on the wicked. That is why God waits.

If it be true that Revelation were written about the year AD 66 or 67, the angels of judgment would be held back for only another three or four years until they were let loose on unbelieving Jerusalem in the year AD 70 through the fury of the Roman army. Why were they not let loose, let us say, just a few days after John wrote Revelation (assuming its early date)? Why wait three or four years? It's because God said there must be a pause or intermission from divine judgment. This was needed to allow the elect to be sealed with the blood of Christ through the power of the Holy Spirit. Looking back, we can see that this was happening in three ways at that time.

Good Things Happen during God's Delay
First, tens of thousands of Christian believers, history teaches us, safely escaped besieged Jerusalem in the year AD 65. Jerusalem was sealed up for some time and the Roman armies came with idolatrous banners, as Jesus had predicted in Matthew 24 and Luke 21. He had told the Christians, 'When you see Jerusalem surrounded by armies, know that the time of the end is near; when you see those armies surround Jerusalem, get out before destruction comes.' But how could the Christians have gotten out of Jerusalem, if the armies already surrounded the city? The answer is simple. History teaches us that for some reason in AD 65, the Roman armies, under the commandership of Cestius Gallus, suddenly left. The early Christians knew what Jesus had said in Matthew 24 and Luke 21 in particular, and so they fled from Jerusalem across the river, as soon as the Roman army moved away. Ancient history reports that not one Christian was slaughtered when the Romans came back. They came back a short time later and surrounded Jerusalem again, reducing it to famine and finally breaking it down in AD 70, in which they killed over a million people. The Christians had gotten out in that little interlude to safety in another place.[45] That is one thing that God was doing.

Secondly, outside Jerusalem in the other parts of the ancient world (the Roman Empire), tens of thousands were being converted day by day, through the preaching of the gospel, sometimes in the Jewish synagogues themselves, and later outside the synagogue in other places. Judgment could not come till the full number had been sealed, which was known only to God. Then the seventh seal could be broken and the four angels of judgment turned loose; and so it happened.

Then thirdly, in God's overarching providence, (and this is something we do not usually talk about), God honors a chosen number of saints with martyrdom. We moderns may not think that it is an honor, but in fact, it's one of the greatest honors a Christian could ever have. The God who loves his people more than anyone else, appoints a certain number of them in his secret providence at particular times of persecution, to be killed for the name of Jesus Christ. This may seem hard to us, with our limited vision, for them 'to die', as Paul said, 'is gain'. They fill up the number above and they're given white robes and rejoice around the throne. This reality is spoken of in the last half of chapter 7. Some saints are set apart to be slain for the honor of Christ. Others, like the true believers who escaped Jerusalem in AD 65, are set aside to be spared. In both cases, God keeps them from the ultimate evil which would be the sin of denying God, and safely lands their souls on the other side of the river in the heavenly realm.

Illustrations of how God works both ways are not lacking. You may have read Corrie Ten Boom's autobiography, *The Hiding Place*. Corrie Ten Boom and her sister were Dutch Christian maiden ladies, who had sheltered Jews from the Nazi persecution in Holland during the early years of World War II. These good ladies were put into a Nazi concentration camp, a terrible place. Near the end of the war, Corrie's sister, Betsie, had a dream, which she related to Corrie, that they would soon get out of the Nazi concentration camp, and it would be all right. Within two or three days, Corrie's sister Betsie, died peacefully in her sleep in the camp. Only a day or two after that, because of a mix-up in the office of the commandant who ran the concentration camp, Corrie was released. Thus Betsie's dream was fulfilled to a 'T'. Both of them got out of that awful camp: Betsie through a happy death and Corrie through a bureaucratic mix-up. Eventually, both of them safely reached their Father's house, and soon enough God brought down the Nazis. Similarly, not one prayer of one saint was wasted before Jerusalem came down; not one prayer of one saint was wasted before the Nazis were brought down; not one prayer of one saint today will ever be wasted before the next evil systems come down. All right prayers will be surely answered; but, on God's timetable.

Waiting Till the End of The Age

We turn now to the second period of waiting: waiting till the very end of the age, when the Lord Jesus comes back in power and glory. And also it would be proper to mention here, our waiting for the intermittent judgments between the Fall of Jerusalem and the end of time. In the previous chapter, we referred to Hebrews 12:27, which speaks of 'the shaking of the things that can be shaken, as of things that are made, in order that that which cannot be shaken—namely the kingdom of grace—may remain'. Yes, in AD 70, old covenant Judaism was violently shaken down. No doubt, the prayers of the saints played their part in that. Then in the fifth century, the Roman Empire was shaken down so that the Christian church had 1,000 years of freedom to spread the gospel throughout all of Europe. In the sixteenth century, the Protestant Reformation took place as the oppressive, Medieval Catholic synthesis was shaken down, after which the gospel truth spread throughout northern and western Europe, and across to these colonies in North America, and across the entire world. In 1991, the USSR, the Soviet Union, was shaken down—giving Christianity tremendous new opportunities in eastern and central Europe.

God's Delays Today are the Church's Opportunity

Today we face an atheistic Chinese government which, in spite of its persecution of the church, has still been unable to stop the massive growth of Christianity in their land. Some say that there may be as many as a hundred million house church Christians in China. But they're under duress, no doubt. We also face Islam, which forbids even a Bible or a cross to be brought within its realm, and some of its adherents have attacked us in our own countries. At this same time, we face immoral, materialistic control of much of our economic and cultural life by powerful multinational companies that control the media and influence governments, often in anti-Christian ways. In the meantime, true Christians, even today are being killed across this world. Hundreds of thousands have been slaughtered in recent years in Sudan, Rwanda, Liberia, Indonesia and elsewhere. Many have been imprisoned and some put to death in China.

The Number of the Elect Must Be Filled Up

The number of the elect, those being sealed with the seal of the Spirit on their foreheads, is filling up. Many are being clothed in white robes in the glory of God. This means that God is busily working, although he seems invisible and far away when we hear of Christians being put to death. Where is God? Answer: God is working! Great things are afoot if this book of Revelation is true. When will China's atheistic government be shaken down? When will Islam with its iron-like grip over the souls of millions be broken down? When will God bring down the multinational, immoral plutocrats? Only God knows the right time; we do not know that. But there are two things we know: first, every obstacle to the spread of the gospel of Christ will in due season be shaken down, to prepare the way for the fuller establishment of the kingdom of grace, as Hebrews 12 says. And the prayers of the saints—the ones above and the ones below—will hasten that glad day. Thus, beloved Christians, keep on praying. Pray big prayers. Pray for the world; pray for the nations. Your prayers shape God's future for this world more than you can possibly realize in your present circumstances. Keep on!

Here's what Andrew Murray wrote about this matter in his wonderful book, *With Christ in the School of Prayer*. Murray says this:

> Real faith can never be disappointed. It knows how, just as water, to exercise the irresistible power it can have, it must be gathered up and accumulated until the stream can come down in full force. So there must often be a heaping up of prayer until God sees that the measure is full and the answer comes. Faith knows how, just as the plowman has to take his 10,000 steps and sow his 10,000 seeds, each one a part of the preparation for the final harvest, so there is a need be for oft-repeated, persevering prayer, all working out some desired blessing. The answer will be given in due time to him who perseveres to the end.

He goes on to say,

> There may be in those around us, there may be in that great system of being of which we are a part, there may be in God's government, things that have to be put right through our prayer, ere the answer can fully come. The faith that has, according to the command, believed that it has

received, can allow God to take his time. It knows it has prevailed and must prevail; persistent and determined perseverance, it continues in prayer and thanksgiving until the blessing comes. Let no delay shake our faith—a faith that holds good: first the blade, then the ear, then the full corn in the ear; each believing prayer brings a step nearer the final victory. Each believing prayer helps to ripen the fruit and brings us nearer to it, fills up the measure of prayer and faith known to God alone, it conquers the hindrances and unseen world; it hastens the end. Child of God, give the Father time; he is long-suffering over you; he wants the blessing to be rich and full and sure. Give him time. While you cry, day and night, only remember the words of Jesus: *I say unto you, he will avenge his elect speedily.*[46]

Faber wrote in the 19th century:

> Workmen of God, O lose not heart,
> but learn what God is like.
> And in the darkest battlefield
> thou shalt know where to strike.
>
> Thrice blest is he to whom is given
> the instinct that can tell
> That God is on the field
> when he is most invisible.

Yes indeed, God seems 'most invisible' when Islamic militants surround Christian villages in Indonesia, and are allowed to go in and slaughter the people. God has seemed terribly invisible for the last ten years in Sudan, when thousands were literally crucified or slaughtered in other gruesome ways. Where was God? God is busily working, filling up the number of the elect; taking them home to glory, giving them white robes, talking with them—and at the right season, God will move to vindicate, to make everything right:

> He hides himself so wondrously
> as though there were no God;
> He is least seen when all the powers of ill
> are most abroad.
> Ah, God is other than we think;
> His ways are far above,
> Far beyond reason's height
> and reached only by child-like love.
>
> Then learn to scorn the praise of men
> and learn to lose with God,
> For Jesus won the world through shame,
> and beckons thee his road.
> For right is right, since God is God;
> and right the day must win;
> To doubt would be disloyalty;
> to falter would be sin.

19

The Saints in Heaven

Revelation 7:4–9, 14

This text shows us that when Christians are martyred for the Lord, something is happening in two different realms: that of the seen, and also that of the unseen. By sight, we only see the visible taking of life, but by faith we are able to see something else of highest importance, that helps us make sense of the visible tragedy.

In the southern Philippines during 2002, a devout missionary couple from Kansas, who worked with New Tribes Mission, were captured and kept hostage by Muslim militants for many months. Eventually the Philippine army went in to rescue them. During the rescue, Richard Burnham was fatally shot, and his wife was shot in the leg, though she lived. Through the news media, we saw the tragedy that occurred visibly. But something was going on at the same time above that the media could not possibly know about, for it was invisible, though every bit as real as that which the news cameras showed us.

This text tells us that God, the holy angels, and the saints, received him into the number of the blood-bought, rejoicing and redeemed ones, in the immediate presence of God. To him were given white robes and a voice with which to praise the Lamb, through whom he was redeemed, and for whom he was working when his life was taken.

In Revelation 7 there are four points, but in this message we shall deal only with the first two points:

1. The numbers of the martyrs in heaven (Rev. 7:4–9).
2. When do these numbers of saints get to heaven? (Rev. 7:14).

The Numbers of the Martyrs of the Faith now in Heaven

How many Christian martyrs will be congregated in heaven? We do not even know how many may have died this very week, much less how many have been martyred over the last two thousand years. In verse 4 a precise number is given in symbolic form, and then in verse 9 the real meaning of that number is explained. The number is 144,000, out of all the tribes of Israel. Let us consider the derivation of this number.

Derivation of 144,000

Twelve in scripture indicates perfection, and we know that Jacob had twelve sons who constituted the twelve tribes of Israel. It is generally believed that the number 144 comes from the twelve sons of Jacob (i.e. the twelve tribes of Israel), multiplied by the twelve apostles. Also we are told that the heavenly city will have twelve gates. If you multiply the twelve sons of Israel times the twelve apostles of Christ, you have 144.

Significance of One Thousand

In scripture the number ten stands for fullness and the way scripture indicates a multitude is 10 x 10 x 10, or a thousand. In the Old Testament the basic unit of the armies of Israel, the host of God, was 1,000; you find that in Numbers 10, and 31 and Psalm 68:17. Indeed, in Micah's prophecy that Christ would be born in Bethlehem, it says that the Messiah will be born in Bethlehem of Judah, and though it is very small amongst the thousands of Israel, yet out of it will come the one whose goings forth have been of old, even from everlasting. It was that very text that Herod's scribes used to instruct the wise men as to what precise location the star was standing over; that it would have to be in Bethlehem that the Christ, the Messiah would be born. So they use *thousands*. Thus, as Kistemaker says: 'Twelve tribes of Israel times the twelve apostles (21:12, 14) times a thousand equals perfection times perfection times a multitude.'[47]

Unusual Listing of the Twelve Tribes

Revelation 7:5-8 lists the twelve tribes, but it is different from the regular listing of the children of Israel. It's a listing after the work of the Redeemer; that is why it is different. After the work of Christ is accomplished, there is a certain difference in the listing. Notice three differences:

First, Judah is listed ahead of the true firstborn, that is, Reuben. This is because Jesus Christ, the Messiah, is born of the tribe of Judah. Secondly, two tribes are missing: Dan and Ephraim. They are left out because they were the first tribes to commit apostasy, to bring in official idolatry to replace the worship at Jerusalem by the golden calves. Thirdly, normally Levi was not numbered because of their priestly duties, but Levi is now considered a regular tribe, rather than being set apart. Because the priesthood has been fulfilled in Jesus Christ, the Levites have no more work to do as priests.

Hence, the number of those who are sealed by God, who after tribulation have been taken up to glory, is: twelve tribes times twelve apostles times a multitude: 144,000. The next verse (9), shows us that this number is symbolic, rather than literal, for it says here: 'After this, [after giving the numbers], I beheld, and behold a great multitude, which no man could number, of all nations, and kindreds, and people, and tongues, stood before the throne and before the Lamb, clothed with white robes, and palms in their hands.'[48] But if the number 144,000 is not literal, then why did John and the angel who was speaking to him, use this exact number, rather than simply saying, 'a countless multitude'?

What 144,000 Demonstrates

The reason was to show that all of the saints in heaven are part of God's church, formed of Old and New Testament components. Or as the New Testament says, 'the church is built upon the foundation of the prophets and the apostles': prophets in the Old Testament, and apostles in the New Testament. This means that no man will ever get to heaven except as part of the church, whether in its Old Testament phase or its New Testament phase. Becoming a part of the church, being in the blood-washed multitude through saving faith in Christ, is the only door in heaven. That is why the so-called multi-faith approach is so severely flawed. Its proponents hold that if you are sincere, whether Muslim, Buddhist, Hindu, or even atheist, you will certainly get to heaven. But this text, and many another in God's Word, tells

When Do These Great Numbers of Saints Get To Heaven?

Revelation 7:14 pictures the time when these uncountable numbers get to glory, and receive white robes and palms of victory. But when does that occur? Two things are to be kept in mind here: (1) There is a short-term, primary fulfillment of the number, and then (2), there is a long-term, secondary fulfillment of the number.

Primary (or Short-Term) Fulfillment

David Chilton writes: 'God will not destroy Jerusalem and make the once holy places desolate until he first chooses and seals a select number as the beginning of the new Israel. The first Christian church was formed out of the chosen servants of God from 'the twelve tribes of the dispersion' (James 1:1), and the end of the Jewish age was not to come until by the ministry of Jewish Christian apostles and prophets the gospel of the kingdom had been preached for a testimony unto all the nations (Matt. 24:14).'[49]

From this perspective, we could see a primary fulfillment in what happened in the destruction of Jerusalem in AD 70, several years after the coming down of the Holy Spirit at Pentecost, which equipped the Church for its gospel mission to all tongues and all tribes on earth. But there is a longer term way to look at it.

Long-Term Fulfillment

There is, I believe, a longer term, secondary fulfillment that is still going on, of this particular text that deals with visible tribulation and invisible victory. In previous chapters, I have presented various lines of evidence to indicate that 'the great tribulation', spoken of in Matthew 24, Luke 21 and Mark 13, was literally fulfilled in AD 70, and that the believers in Christ got safely out of Jerusalem in AD 65, shortly before the deadly siege. But all over the empire at the same time, tens of thousands of Christian believers were being killed for their faith, particularly under the terrible Emperor Nero. Of all those numbers that were being killed (often mentioned in the letters to the seven churches in Revelation 1 and 2), not one failed to get home to heaven. What John saw was in a primary sense fulfilled in the first century. Yet the principle will operate to the end of the age, for as long as there is tribulation and martyrdom in this world. Even though the great tribulation is in one major way fulfilled, there is still tribulation. Many are still being killed. As long as that happens, saints are going to be translated to join the white-robed multitudes in glory.

How Long Does Tribulation Last?

How long does tribulation last, even after 'the great tribulation' has been long since fulfilled? Jesus says in John 16:33: 'In the world ye have tribulation; but be of good cheer, I have overcome the world'. Paul says in 2 Timothy 3:12, 'Yea, all that live godly lives in Christ Jesus shall suffer persecution'. Peter says in his first epistle, 'My brethren, think it not strange concerning the fiery trial which is sent to try you'. God, therefore, is allowing this persecution and tribulation. Why is he allowing it to the people whom he loves the most? God allows it because through this pressure he is busily saving the world, even by means of this sometimes tremendous pressure that comes on the bodies and souls of his beloved children. This is one of the ways he spreads the redemption purchased by Christ to the needy multitudes; it is not the only way, but it is indeed one of the ways he does it.

What Does Tribulation Accomplish?

The most basic overview of the plan of salvation for the world is given to us in John 3:16–17:

> For God so loved the world that he gave his only begotten Son that whosoever believeth in him should not perish, but have eternal life. For God sent not his Son into the world to condemn the world, but that the world through him might be saved.

Christ commissioned the Church to spread this knowledge to the entire world.

Many Biblical passages cast light on how tribulation upon the people of God is an instrument to spread among humankind saving knowledge of the Son of God. Isaiah 49:6 gives a clue as to why God allows tribulation and persecution after Jesus has come:

> And he said, 'It is a light thing that thou shouldst be My Servant to raise up the tribe of Jacob and to restore the preserved of Israel. I will also give Thee for a light to the Gentiles, that thou mayest be My salvation unto the end of the earth.'

Long before Isaiah, this promise was made to 'the father of the faithful', Abraham, in Genesis 15:5: 'And the Lord brought him forth abroad and said to Abraham, "Look now towards heaven and tell the stars if thou be able to number them." And the Lord said unto Abraham, "so shall thy seed be."' Scripture teaches that God would save the world through this chosen seed of Abraham, as we see in Galatians 3:8: 'And the scripture, foreseeing that God will justify the heathen through faith, preached before the gospel unto Abraham saying, "In thee shall all nations be blessed."' We put such passages together and see that God uses the tribulation and martyrdom of his saints to hasten saving faith among the heathen.

It would be very uncaring, and out of accord with the Spirit of Christ, not to be deeply moved and grieved over the killing of the saints by the powers of evil. Yes, we do care; yes, we do weep; yes, we do want to see them vindicated. But at the same time, we strive to remember by faith that this is one of the ways that God is at work saving the world. Many believers from Christian tribes in Sudan have literally been crucified, while numbers of Christians were hacked to death with machetes in Rwanda. Large numbers of believers were cruelly slaughtered by the government of Amin in Uganda several years before that. Reliable statistics indicate that the twentieth century had the highest number of martyrdoms in all of history. No century, even when the Roman Empire was at its worst, ever compared with the twentieth century in numbers of violent deaths meted out to believers in Christ.

We do not know what it is going to be like in this century, especially with violent conflicts between branches of Islam and Christians in various parts of the world. Common sense would indicate that many more true saints of God will have to lay down their lives before the knowledge of salvation by the grace of God in Christ extends to the Middle and Far East. But, here's what we are to keep in mind: the devil does not gain the victory through any of these anti-Christian persecutions. With the eyes of faith, we can discern an unseen Sovereign God, busily occupied in saving the world by calling in the elect to faith in Christ. Not infrequently, the elect are called in through many a bath of Christian blood, and that will keep happening in this 21st century.

Two Benefits of Tribulation

This works in two ways: first, the saints get safely home when they are put to death by evil powers on earth. Satan would like to get their souls, but he cannot do that. The angels are sent to accompany them across the great divide. Satan cannot finally get them as they are persecuted and killed; all he can do is to get at their body (as he did the body of Job); he can never get at their spirits. Psalm 34:9 makes the point: 'O fear the Lord, ye his saints, for there is no want to them that fear him.'

When the saints are put to death, it is not a loss for them. On the contrary, as the apostle Paul said in Philippians 1:21, 'to die is gain'! Look at what Jesus says to Peter in Matthew 19:27-30:

> Then answered Peter and said unto him, 'Behold, we have forsaken all, and followed Thee; what shall we have therefore?' And Jesus said unto them, [to Peter and the other apostles, who, along with the prophets, are the foundation of this symbolic number of 144,000], 'Verily, I say unto you, that ye which have followed me in the regeneration when the Son of man shall sit in the throne of his glory, ye also shall sit upon twelve thrones, judging the twelve tribes of Israel. And every one that hath forsaken houses, or brethren, or sisters, or father, or mother, or wife, or children, or lands, for My name's sake, shall receive an hundred fold, and shall inherit everlasting life.'

And then Jesus says—in a radical reversal of the world's common sense—'But many that are first shall be last; and the last shall be first'. So, in this text, we are first presented with the way God is busily saving the world, through allowing the killing of his saints; thereby getting them home to the heavenly realm.

And then the second way he is saving the lost multitudes is also connected to the deaths of the saints. Tertullian was a great church writer from North Africa in the early third century. He was a lawyer, who appears to have been converted when he saw two young women, named Perpetua and Felicitas, martyred. When he witnessed the constancy of their faith, love and joy, he realized he didn't have it, and soon he turned to Christ. Later he became one of the greatest writers and theologians of the early Christian ages (although he did have problems in his later thinking). Tertullian used this phrase that you have probably heard: 'The blood of the martyrs is the seed of the church.' Some of my scholarly Chinese friends indicate that in China there was blood of the martyrs from 1949 with the Communist takeover, perhaps reaching a crescendo in the Red Guard purge in the 60s. In 1949 there may have been something like one million Christians in China, but after the bloodshed of so many martyrs, some think that there may be as many as 100 million believers in China at present. The blood of the martyrs is truly the seed of the church.

Let us go back to Philippians 1:21, 'to die is gain'. But we need to notice something else in the previous verse (v. 20): 'According to my earnest expectation and my hope, that in nothing I shall be ashamed, but that with all boldness, as always, so now also Christ shall be magnified in my body, whether it be by life, or by death'. When Paul was put to death at Rome, no doubt God answered this prayer, so that Christ was magnified in his body by death, even as he had been magnified by Paul's life, when he was writing these epistles and preaching the word. Somehow, the Christ of the gospel is magnified in the death of his saints, as their very bodies wear out or are destroyed. It is basically the principle that we find in Jesus' words in John 12:24: 'Except a corn of wheat fall into the ground and die, it abideth alone. But if it die, it bringeth forth much fruit'.

Isn't it passing wonderful, that the humblest, the weakest, the most inconsistent of us, once we are in Jesus Christ through the bonds of faith and the Holy Spirit, we cannot possibly lose to the powers of evil! Even the bad things that happen to some of us may be one of the ways God is using to extend the redemption of Christ to the world. Satan would like to get us; those manipulated by Satan and a sinful, world system, would like to get us. But once we are in this crucified, risen Christ, nothing can get us, for John 10 tells us that 'nothing shall be able to take us out of the Father's hand'. We cannot lose when we commit all we have and all that we are to this Christ, 'because whether by life or by death', we shall always pray that either way: by life or by death, in our body, 'Christ shall be magnified', and the message of the saving gospel shall somehow be extended to the needy world.

20

The Songs of the Saints in Heaven

Revelation 7:9–17

These verses portray what awaits us in heaven. The passage shows us:

1. The importance of meditating on heaven (7:9).
2. The songs that the believers are singing in heaven (7:10–12).

The Importance of Meditating on Heaven

If it be true, which it surely is, that our time on earth is very short and our 'time' or experience in heaven is not only very long, but never ends, it is well to think about where we're going to pass most of our time, since we are creatures with immortal souls.

For instance, if you went camping for a week, you would have some concern about the tent that would be set up so that you could survive for a week. But you wouldn't be nearly as concerned about that tent as you would be about your residence where you'll live the rest of your natural life. Any intelligent person is going to put their thoughts on where they'll be most of their life. It's like that concerning heaven. Earth certainly is important; it's where we make the final decisions. But in the light of eternity, our time in this world is very, very short. And according to the Bible, we're making a serious mistake if we give most of our heart to this rapidly passing world. We're told in Colossians, 'set your minds on things above, where Christ dwelleth'.

God wants us to think about where we're going to be for the vast majority of our everlasting experience, because when we are more heavenly minded, we are more realistic concerning the days we spend on earth. This passage, as well as any in the Word of God, puts our minds on heaven, where many of our loved ones already are and where all who are saved will soon be.

The Songs They are Singing in Heaven

One of the significant things we are told about heaven is that it is a place of beautiful, wonderful singing. We also notice that the singers, the saints have white robes on, with palm branches in their hands. It's interesting that the Apostle John wrote Revelation, and also the gospel of John. This particular Greek word for palm branches is used only twice in the New Testament; it's used here in Revelation and it's used in John's gospel. John is the only gospel that tells us that in Christ's triumphal entry to Jerusalem on Palm Sunday (as we call it) that the crowds, including the children, had cut down palm branches and were waving them as the triumphant Lamb of God passed through the streets. The crowds with their palm branches were saying 'Hosanna in the highest; blessed is he that cometh in the name of the Lord'. And the palms, as we shall see, speak of victory.

The first thing we are told about the saints when—to use an earthly word—they die, or in this case it is when the martyrs are killed, is that they are dressed in beautiful robes and are singing with beauty! The first thing they do is to laud, praise, and honor, to articulate the glory, wonder, kindness and the beauty of the Lamb of God, who got them to heaven in the first place. The first thing the saints are doing when they get to heaven is not worrying about having been killed; not at all. They are too full of praise for that; they are too thrilled with the sight of the One who died for their sins and sustained them and got them home; they are praising Him. White robes and palms of victory speak of paradise restored. Adam and Eve were put out of the beautiful Garden of Eden, and we will not get back to its equivalent until we get to our heavenly home. The palm branches seem to speak of the victory that God gives us, when he restores us to the paradise that through our sin we forfeited.

Let us notice what they are singing. We do not know exactly what the tune sounds like; we will hear it soon enough. But we are given the words of some of the singing in heaven; here we are shown part of the hymnal of heaven, in Revelation 5 and 7. Salvation is the theme of the first hymn that the saints raise immediately they get home to the presence of God from this sinful world. What they are doing is celebrating the work of redemption through the Lamb. In other words, the people around the throne know and recognize that they are able to be there in this matchless place only because of what the One who is now seated on the throne did for them, through his suffering on earth. They are so full of gratitude that somebody of such splendor, possessing the very being of God the eternal Son, should have come down off that throne and mounted the cross to get them home. Hence the first thing they want to do is to praise him and to articulate the gratitude of their hearts in this paean of praise.

The Themes of the Songs
Well should the saints tune their hearts and lift high their voices. The Lamb crucified and risen, the Lamb now and always triumphant, is the theme of the first song. You see it here in verse 10, 'Salvation to our God which sitteth upon the throne and unto the Lamb'. It's much like Revelation 5:12, 'Worthy is the Lamb.'

Then a second hymn is sung to the whole Godhead, to the entire Trinity—'Unto our God'—this time, not only by the saints who lived on earth, who were sinners, who became saved, and then suffered with and for the Lord, and in due time were called through death to the other side. Now the saints are joined by the holy angels. Saints and angels join together in verses 11–12 and sing the second hymn, of which we hear the tones falling from the height of heaven down to the Isle of Patmos on earth.

The Order of the Songs
The order of the hymns teaches us something important. First, they praise the Lamb for salvation, and after that they praise the whole Trinity: the Father, the Son and the Holy Ghost. The reason they started out with salvation is simple; we would not be in a position to praise God the Father, if it were not for what Jesus did for us; that he took hold of us and cleansed us, turned us around and gave us a heart of praise. Without that gift of a new heart, instead of praising God the Father, we would be fleeing God; we would, like the people who die and go to hell, be hating

God. So there is no praise of God the Trinity even in heaven, until first of all you experience through faith and the Holy Spirit what the Lamb of God did in your place.

Ephesians 2:18 makes this clear; 'For through him [Christ], we both [Jew and Gentile] have access by one Spirit unto the Father.' That is, it is through Christ that Jew and Gentile have access; the door is open so that they can get to the throne, for in the new birth they have been given hearts to praise. Only through Christ, in the Holy Spirit, who brings rivers of living water inside of you, cleansing you, changing you, filling you so that you will praise God; only that way do we get to God the Father Almighty.

Only One Way to God
Various Protestant Churches, many of them formerly evangelical, no longer wish to say that Jesus Christ is the only way to God. To say the least, their information is not the same as what the saints know in heaven! Part of the problem comes from the politically correct movement that has taken over some Christian educational institutions. It is based on what we call relativism, the basic idea that you cannot say anything is definitely true, so you cannot say there is only one way to God, for everything must be equal or relative to every other thing. If that is right, then of course, Islam, Hinduism, or even sincere atheism will get you to God.

On the contrary, the Bible says that 'There is a way that seemeth right to a man, but the end thereof is the way of death'. God has said that sin cuts us off from Him. The only way we can get to him is to have our sin completely forgiven. Only Christ, who is God and man at the same time, only he by his holy life, his suffering and his resurrection, can open the door for us to get into heaven, where we join the songs of the saints and angels. Jesus talks about the people who will be surprised at the end of time. In Matthew 25, the people who are told by the Lord that they are among the goats and must forevermore depart from Him, so that they will not be in heaven, are taken aback! They thought that they were in the leadership of the culture, perhaps even top people in the churches, where they can claim that they did wonderful things in his name. To their utter surprise, Jesus will say to them: 'Depart from Me you workers of iniquity, for I never knew you'. 'Know' means to be in a loving relationship, an intimate trust, between my soul and Christ. Jesus said that on the last day, many who will not get in thought they were going to make it, and will be the most shocked of all.

Amen the Covenant Response
In the next hymn (v. 12), we hear 'Amen', which is a covenant word. It means, 'Lord, we come through Your covenant of grace; through Your provided way, through all Your promises, we stand on them, and thus we sing: "Blessing, and glory, and wisdom, and thanksgiving, and honor, and power, and might be unto our God for ever and ever."' Here again is the covenant response, 'Amen'—'so be it Your way, Lord.' Essentially what this second hymn is about concerns the attributes of God, the qualities of God. Both of these hymns, the first one about Jesus the Lamb, and the second about the whole Godhead, are focused on who God is; not on our feelings, not on what we've done or what we've been through, but on God himself.

If the devil wants to make a person depressed, or even atheistic, he seeks to get their eyes off of God and onto themselves. But on the contrary, this hymn is focused on some of the attributes or qualities of what God is like, and there are seven mentioned. God has far more attributes and qualities than that, but seven is a number meaning fullness. Seven things are mentioned.

Seven Themes of Praise

1. Blessing. The saints and angels look at God, see what he is like, and say 'Blessing!' In other words, 'Praise'. Psalm 103 expresses that so well: 'Bless the Lord, O my soul, and all that is within me, bless his holy name'. To see him with the eyes of faith that Jesus gives us in the new birth, is to love Him, to appreciate his qualities, and then we can only praise God. One sign of the new birth is a heart that praises God. We never praise him as much as we want to, but there is a real sense of gratitude and gladness that we want to express as we contemplate how wonderful God is. God in all his greatness, the majestic One, 'the Star-maker', likes it when he hears a little creature of dust praising Him. He bends his ear over and listens; the great, mighty, awesome God is touched and pleased when the least of his children starts praising and blessing Him. They have an audience in heaven; the majestic, Sovereign God is interested!

2. Glory. The second part of the hymn is 'glory'. 'Glory' is something like splendor; the outshining of his light, radiance, and beauty. The *Shorter Catechism* asks, 'What is the chief end of man?' It responds: 'Man's chief end is to glorify God and to enjoy him forever'. 'Chief end' means the primary purpose for which you were made. Why did God make you? If you could get rid of everything that is secondary, what would be the primary purpose for which God caused you to be born? Above every secondary purpose, the primary one is that you might glorify Him. That means that you might express in your praises, and let shine through your life, something of the beauty of the God who created and redeemed you. God's glory is such a wonderful thing that it comes down and glorifies us, and illumines us with his light! The New Testament says: 'You who were sometimes darkness, are now light in the Lord'.

This is profoundly different from the worldly way of thinking, which is that if you are to be a good humanist, what you need to think about is self. The chief concern is how can I make myself happy; how can I get out of life what I wish? How can I avoid any more pain than necessary? How can I have the maximal, physical or emotional pleasures? How can I use other people to give me that pleasure? In other words, the humanistic position is glorify self. But once you set as the goal of your life to make yourself happy, you are assured of misery! Self-seeking of my own pleasure and glory brings more psychological, relational misery than anything you can imagine. It is the lie of the devil. I remember hearing some wise words of an old Fundamentalist preacher: he said, 'You do not find happiness; you stumble over it in the pathway of duty'. That is psychologically and spiritually true. In human relationships it is the people who are the most caught up in the glory of God and seeking to honor him who will be the kindest to others and will finally have done the greatest good to themselves. They are liberated personalities; free and open-hearted. When you seek something outside yourself, particularly the glory of God, it brings happy insight and deliverance into your own soul! The saints and the angels know that better than anybody else, and so they're singing 'Blessing and glory'.

3. Wisdom. Then they sing of 'wisdom'. I will not unfold that immense concept, but even the most superficial thought should give us grounds for endless praise. Think of the brilliance of the eternal counsel of God, that we were lost and the devil thought he had us, and God outdid him by sending his Son in our place to be God and man at the same time, thereby redeeming us and restoring us and renewing us. It was accomplished through the wisdom of God, by which he originally made this world out of nothing, with all its harmonies and complexities; a world which from beginning to end he totally controls by his exquisite providence. What surpassing wisdom! Who could make an eye to see? Who could make skin with sense of touch? A nose that could smell fragrance? A mind that outlasts the body? He is even now superintending every aspect of reality to get all things without exception exactly to where they will bring him the glory and endless blessing for his people. Once thought of, who would not praise him for his wisdom?

4. Thanksgiving. We are told in 1 Thessalonians, 'in all things give thanks'. William Law, a devotional writer of England in the early 1700s, asked, 'Do you know who is the greatest saint in the world? It is the person who has a thankful heart'. He adds:

> If any would tell you the shortest, surest way to all happiness and perfection, he must tell you to make a rule to yourself to thank and praise God for everything that happens to you. For it is certain that, whatever seeming calamity happens to you, if you thank and praise God for it, you turn it into a blessing. Could you, therefore, work miracles, you could not do more for yourself than by this thankful spirit, for it heals with a word speaking, and turns all that it touches into happiness.[50]

This text shows us how full of thanksgiving are the saints in heaven. Even while we are still on earth, the easiest person to live with is the person who is thankful. A thankful spirit and an attitude of praise plays a part in establishing the atmosphere of heaven. That is probably one of the characteristics of the Christian Church and of individual saints which most draws an unbelieving public into their fellowship, and finally into fellowship with the living God.

One thing lies within our power as believers in a sinful world, and that is to practice stopping our mouths from complaining, and learning to express verbally thanksgiving to God all through the day. In so doing, we are in some sense joining in the fellowship of saints and angels in the realm of light and joy, and in some way helping to reflect that same heavenly atmosphere here below.

5. Honor. Then the heavenly choir sings of God's 'honor', and that means the sheer holiness and integrity of God, such as we see in the Biblical phrase: 'God is light and in him is no darkness at all'. God never did any wrong; God never thought any wrong, and so the Lord Jesus Christ could ask: 'Who convinceth Me of sin?' He was 'holy, harmless, and undefiled, separate from sinners'. There is not one blot in the character of God. There is nothing but rightness. That is a major theme in the praise now being sung above.

6. Power. Then the glorious choir sings of 'power'. At the first creation God used his infinite power to do an amazing thing. There was nothing; God speaks, and the solar systems spring into existence. God used the same mighty power after the vicarious sacrifice made by his Son in the flesh. Jesus was dead; his abused body had lost its blood; his heart had quit beating; his brain waves had gone flat, and he was dead as any corpse has ever been. They had stuck a spear in his side, and thereupon coagulated blood and water came out. Then he was laid in a borrowed tomb: 'crucified, dead, and buried'. But God Almighty put forth the power of heaven into that tomb and raised the body of his Son from the dead. He transformed it into a resurrection body of splendor, glory, power and honor, and out he came alive forevermore! The power of God! The power of God to create the world out of nothing, the power of God to raise his Son from the dead! That same power is put forth into a sinner who is undone in his lostness, condemned and without hope. Somehow, God secretly and invisibly puts forth his power into the personality of the sinner who is coming to faith and repentance in Jesus. The Holy Spirit is the invisible, secret power of God. The amazing thing is that he joins with massive power an incredible gentleness, so that we feel that it is we who are doing it, for from deep inside of us comes this desire to believe and be saved through this wonderful Savior. As Psalm 110:3 says: 'Thy people shall be willing in the day of thy power…'

That same divine power makes us through the new birth a new creation: 'If any man be in Christ, he is a new creation; old things are passed away; behold, all things are become new' (1 Cor. 5:14). When you have come into touch with Jesus through faith, you have experienced a spiritual resurrection, so that now you are risen with Christ. No wonder the saints are praising God!

7. Strength. Finally, the heavenly chorus ascribes to the Triune God: 'strength', or might. Psalm 21:1–2 gives us a clue here: The king shall joy in Thy strength [the same word], O Lord; and in Thy salvation how greatly shall he rejoice! Thou hast given him his heart's desire, and hast not withholden the request of his lips.' The idea is that the saints (here it is especially King David, who represents true believers), sinners though they are, joy in the strength of God, for this God has been strong enough to give us such desires as are right. We read in another Psalm to 'delight thyself in the Lord and he shall give thee the desires of thine heart' (Ps. 37:4). When we are seeking God's glory, it gets us into an atmosphere where we want things that really are good for us and for others to have. God's power is able to release those divinely approved blessings we pray for. Hence the saints praise him for his strength to carry through all of his promises.

As I was looking at this text, I remembered a burial plot in the old cemetery of Lumberton (Meadowbrook), where my grandmother and parents are buried. When I was a child, there used to be a playhouse that had been built over a little girl's grave. It had a tricycle and toys inside it. I asked my mother and father, 'Why is this playhouse built over a little girl's grave?' They told me that the man who built it after his little girl died had been very busy practicing law. His daughter often said: 'Daddy, build me a playhouse'. And he promised to do so, but with legal duties never got around to it. Sad to tell, a sudden disease came upon his beloved little daughter and in just a few days she had died, at the age of six or seven. The devastated father in his grief had her a playhouse built after it was too late. Most of us parents can think of things we wish we had done for our children, or perhaps that we had not done. We often enough fail to carry out our resolves to do good; we lack either the strength or the resolve.

God is different. He is able to carry through every aspect of every gracious promise he has made to his children. In due time, he will carry through everything he ever said he would do for us. God has no regrets when his children must leave this world. He gave us what we needed down here, and he took us up to the realm of joy and light. Everything he has promised he fulfilled in the precise way and degree that was right for us, because he has the might to do it. In that land of light, the saints now realize just how much his strength has been put forth for them and is going to be put forth for all eternity. They are praising him for it, and we join our praises with theirs.

21

An Amazing Contrast
Revelation 7:13–17

One of the most amazing contrasts in any chapter of the Bible is found in these verses. This chapter starts with a description of some of the worst kind of treatment that an unbelieving, hostile world can mete out to Christians: violent persecution that entails their immense suffering and physical death. Later in this same chapter, the scene shifts and shows the same ones who were abused and put to an unjust and cruel death, experiencing a beautiful reception and being given tender treatment by God Almighty, a split second after they have been released from the sufferings of this world. It is a scene that has sustained the pilgrim people of God through all the centuries. This sudden shift from the world of hard suffering, with its great tribulation, to the calm green splendors of the hills of heaven to which they go, calls to mind Psalm 121: 'I will lift up mine eyes unto the hills, from whence cometh my help; my help cometh from the Lord which made heaven and earth'. These verses of Revelation 7 lift up the eyes of God's embattled people to the hills of heaven to which they are going.

There is something about knowing where you are going that gives your steps firmness and your will a fixedness and unvarying determination; it gives your heart a certain quiet joy when there are many things all around that could make you afraid. So, I believe that God has his reasons for letting us see as closely as he does into heaven. Interestingly, the Bible does not tell us a great deal of detail about heaven, but does make it clear that it is our home and that it is a wonderful place. Probably these few verses, along with Revelation 22, are among the most detailed explanations to be found in Scripture of what heaven is like. It is significant that these lovely details about our heavenly home were given to the Church when she was under great pressure. At such times it is particularly helpful to be reminded of where we are going, for it provides strength and hope for the pilgrimage before us.

The Experience of the Saints in Heaven

We noted in the previous message the content of the hymn-singing, or the heavenly psalms of praise, by the now translated saints above. We now turn our attention from what they are singing in the supernal realm, to what the life that believers experience when they leave this physical body is now like. The special focus of Revelation 7 is on the martyrs, those who have shed their blood for Christ. It is an honor to them that God will certainly use their blood to raise up others. Yet valuable as the blood of the martyrs is, it is not their own blood that makes them clean and gets them home into heaven. It is always and only the blood of the Lamb. Jesus alone gives us the white garments, the wedding garments needed to get in to the feast, to the marriage supper of the Lamb.

Here are the saints who have left this world, some of them having paid a high price to honor the One in whom they believed. They have been made perfectly, spotlessly beautiful and pure, and their ransomed spirits are up into the most desirable place in all the universe: the very Throne of God, something that surpasses the ability of our human language to express.

The great evangelist, Dwight L. Moody, who was a plain, fairly uneducated shoe salesman in Massachusetts, was wonderfully converted and filled with the Holy Spirit to spread the saving gospel to America and Britain. God got hold of him and made him one of the greatest evangelists of history, winning hundreds of thousands of lost souls to Christ. Towards the end of his life, Moody said shortly before he died in Northfield, Massachusetts: 'One day you're going to read in the newspaper these words: "D. L. Moody dead."' he said, 'Well do not you believe it; I'll be more alive when I have left this frail body than ever I was while I was on the earth.' Moody had it right, and this passage gives us some description of what it is then like for the translated believer.

We notice in verses 13–14, four details about our heavenly life:

1. Beautiful clothing (Rev. 7:13 and 14).
2. Wonderful fellowship (Rev. 7:15).
3. Absence of pain and distress (Rev. 7:16).
4. Tender care rendered by the Lord himself (Rev. 7:17).

BEAUTIFUL CLOTHING

Verses 13–14 are like a telescope through which we can see a little bit of heaven. We probably are not shown much about heaven, because if we saw all of its wonderful, desirable and gloriously beautiful details, it might be hard for us to be content to stay here on earth and do what we must do. He lets us see enough to allure us, but not so much that it would make us discontent with our earthly lot. Through this 'telescope' we see that beautiful white clothing has been given to the ones we call 'deceased'.

Jesus' parable of the wedding feast shows that those who were invited, for the most part, refused to come (referring to the Jewish nation at that time), but then the Lord sends out his messengers into the highways and byways to compel people to come in. A big crowd finally turns up with all kind of nondescript people, whereupon the master of ceremonies said to some of them, 'Why are you here without wedding garments? Depart! Get out!' We might think this strange, for he had invited everybody to come in. Yes, but the custom in the ancient Middle East at that time was to give to everyone at the door of the feasting hall the wedding garments, which had been freely provided by the father of the bride. Even if you came in off the streets as a very poor person, the lord of the feast offered you the appropriate garments to put on. It appears that some of those who came to the wedding feast off the streets must have said, 'I do not want to wear his garments; I'll go in like I am'.

'Post-Funeral' Garments

This parable of the wedding feast relates to this passage in Revelation 7 as follows: those who get into heaven when their physical body dies have been given by God their wedding garments, which are provided through the life, death and resurrection of their Savior. They received these benefits through faith in Jesus Christ. They were given spotless holiness through the blood of Christ; it was not of their own doing. Unlike the people who were ejected from the wedding feast in the parable, they gladly received the gift of the Lord's gracious provision; they did not try to come in on their own merits, in their own clothing. The blood of Christ received through faith cleansed their souls, and that got them ready to receive on the other side of physical death these beautiful, shining white garments that we see them wearing in heaven.

When we die as Christians, we are not naked, bare spirits. Too many people feel that our experience in heaven before the final resurrection is the abstract existence of a naked, bare, and half-unreal spirit. Even some Christians seem to dread death because they think that on the other side of it, their existence will be inferior in every way to their present embodied existence. But in fact, Paul says 'to die is gain'. He says in another place, 'to depart and be with Christ is far better.' It would not be gain, it would not be better, if you were just a naked spirit, a ghost floating about with little sense of personalized existence, perhaps even unable to experience bliss and joy and share in communication. In that case, to leave our physical bodies certainly would be worse than what we know now.

Some ancient Greeks, such as Plato, tended to look at it that way. In reality, when we leave this world, and our bodies are temporarily laid in the ground, God gives us something in exchange for it that is massively better than what we laid down. In the case of the martyrs, their bodies were taken from them by burning, stabbing, hanging, drowning, or whatever. Certainly they lost something very valuable: their embodied physical life. But 2 Corinthians 5 tells us that the heavenly Father gives them something more valuable than what he asked from them as they bore testimony to his grace. Death for the believer is not a dead-end street, it is a wondrous exchange, in which they are given something tremendously better than what they previously had.

Death is an Exchange, not a Dead-End Street

The nature of this exchange when we lay down our body, is such that we do not live a ghostly disembodied existence; we go to an even fuller existence than we had in this physical body. 'For we know that if our earthly house of this tabernacle were dissolved we have a building of God, an house not made with hands, eternal in the heavens' (1 Cor. 5:1). God has another building for us. According to Paul, our earthly body is like a tent or tabernacle, a temporary, moveable tent like the Tabernacle during the Old Testament wilderness wanderings. In exchange, we are provided with a more permanent building, not make of skins, but rather like the stones of the temple in Jerusalem: something more permanent and valuable. In death, we lay down the temporary, and God gives us something permanent, something of more substantial quality than what he asks us to lay down in the dust of death. Like the old Tabernacle constructed of animal skins, anything made by the hands of man will fail; anything constituted merely of dust will fail, and break apart, resulting from the second law of thermodynamics, the law of entropy. But here is something to which the law of entropy does not apply: 'an house not made with hands, eternal in the heavens'. This is because God made it, so that it is framed to be eternal in the heavens. Verse 3 tells us: 'If so be that being clothed we shall not be found naked'. No saint that leaves this world goes to heaven naked; they receive beautiful wedding garments—'an house not made with hands'.

Certainly, there is mystery here. John Calvin says in his commentary on 1 Corinthians that what Paul is speaking about in chapter 5 (and also here in Revelation 7) is a down-payment on the resurrection body. Calvin says that it is like the first installment on our final resurrection bodies. According to Scripture, one day our bodies will be raised out of the dust. We will all come out. But we will already have had a first installment on the resurrection. The split second our spirit is no longer embodied, there is a building of God for us, eternal in the heavens, something that looks very much like what we are going to get when our bodies are raised out of the dust. It will express elements of our own shape, but without sin, deformity, or pain; it will prepare us for the final resurrection of our body on the Last Day. Until that grand time, all translated saints are clothed in beautiful robes of white.

Wonderful Fellowship

Secondly, we notice in verse 15, another characteristic of the life they are living in heaven. It is the most wonderful fellowship they ever experienced. It is the fellowship of which all other good relationships are just a mere picture or shadow. The most important thing in our life is our relationship with God and with other people. My high school class had a fortieth reunion last fall and at that stage people look back, when they are well up into their fifties. They think about what they may have accomplished or, if they are Christians, what God did for them. It is a normal time for people to ask: was it all worth it? I can think of some of my classmates who have done extremely well financially. But with a few of them, the major relationships they had seemed to be in a shambles. In your fifties, you realize that no matter how solid your bank accounts, how large your house, and how solid your professional accomplishment, what really made life worth living was your relationships. The quality of life is more about relationships than anything else.

There is a reason for that: we are persons, created in the image of God, the Father, the Son and the Holy Ghost, three Persons, one God. God made us to know Him, first of all. Without knowing God, who he really is in Christ, we cannot be satisfied in our other relationships. To know God is to be related to the supreme personal reality, and this is what gives created existence its stability and its meaning. Everything else is secondary: houses, land, career, money, education—those are all important blessings, and we must have them while on earth. Yet they are finally in second place.

Augustine may have said it best in his *Confessions*: 'Lord, Thou hast made us for Thy self, and our hearts are restless until they find their rest in Thee.' Once the saints of God are at home, this fellowship for which they were created: primarily to know and love God, and then to know and love one another is being fulfilled more splendidly than ever. What a family reunion it is, with the other believers in glory!

Absence of Pain and Distress

In verse 16, we notice an absence of all pain and distress in their heavenly existence. While we are still on earth, God, in his providence, allows us to be disciplined by pain and distress in accordance with his plan. These are necessary for us to get to where he is taking us (Romans 8:31–9). The saints below experience from time to time great pain and distress in this sinful world, so influenced by Satan. They often know 'tribulation, distress, persecution, famine, nakedness, peril and sword.'

Believers cannot expect a pain-free, difficulty-free existence here below. These painful realities in this world are part of God's discipline to shape us in a Christ-like direction. But the split second after we leave this world, we experience absolutely no pain, no distress and no tribulation, ever again. In verse 16, how much is included in the phrase, 'they shall hunger no more, neither thirst any more; neither shall the sun light on them, nor any heat'. No internal, nor external lack will distress us.

Christ said in Matthew 5: 'Blessed are they that hunger and thirst for righteousness, for they shall be filled'. At length, there is no more painful lack. Instead a bountiful feast is provided, so that there is contentment and fullness that is part of God's gift to us. Also, Revelation says that 'no heat shall light upon them, nor the sun burn them'; there is nothing that could cause distress externally. There is an external blessedness; environmental, ecological blessedness with no extreme heat.

This is the opposite of what the unbelievers experience: the fires of hell—great distress, as we see later in Revelation, and also described by Jesus in Matthew 25. Some will object: 'Why do you believe in hell? Are you a vicious person?' We believe it simply because the Bible so clearly teaches it. Jesus taught it, and God showed it to the apostle John. But that is not in view here, for in hell there is heat. Hell has its mysteries, but by any measure, it is a very unpleasant, undesirable place, with heat and no water. But in the glory realm, there is no extreme heat; it is the opposite of the fires of hell. It is perfect weather—gorgeous, cool, lovely; like a delectable spring morning. Happy Paradise!

Tender Care Divinely Given

A fourth detail here is perhaps the most touching of the whole description. It is almost hard to believe, except that it is part of the scriptural text. I suspect that most of us do not often think of the tender, loving care given to the least of the brethren by the highest authority in the universe. Can you imagine that? Notice the amazing tenderness conveyed in verse 17: the Son of God, who was the agent of creation of all things out of nothing, the mighty creator Word, who was holding all things together even when he was on earth; the One who was crucified for our sins, and raised from the dead for our justification; the One who is the final judge and disposer of the destiny of men and angels; the very Son of the Father; the One who is as much God as the Father is God and the Holy Spirit is God: this One, the Lamb with the nail prints still in his hand, who is now raised, with all the glory of God within him and upon him and around Him; no less than he gets up from the throne and goes down to take care of the humblest saint that dies on earth and goes to heaven. The Lord does not send a servant to take care of us when we cross the great divide. He does not even send an archangel. Once we get there, the angels step aside and God the Son gets off the throne like a loving mother would for a baby or a hurt child. He leaves everything aside, picks up the child, and cares for the child.

Even if you have a nanny in the home, if a child gets hurt, they do not go to the nanny; they go the mother or the father, when possible. God himself will wait on us. Can you imagine that? Do you remember how shocked Simon Peter was when Jesus took a towel, put it around his waist, took a pan of water and began washing the feet of the disciples? Simon Peter said (and he knew who Christ was, because he was the first one to confess Thou art Christ, the Son of the living God), 'Lord, be it far from You to do this [it wouldn't be proper for you to wash my feet]. But Jesus said to Simon Peter, 'If I do not wash your feet, you have no part in Me'. Jesus was showing that it is in the very heart of God to serve his people. Do we find it hard to believe that?

The 'Humility' of the Sovereign God

When I teach the attributes of God each year in the seminary, we go through a section of the divine attributes that many theologians seem to leave out. One of these neglected divine attributes is the humility of God. Some of the students are shocked. Then I remind them what Jesus said, 'Come unto Me, all ye that labor and are heavy laden, and I will give you rest. Take My yoke upon you and learn of Me, for I am meek and lowly of heart; and ye shall find rest unto your souls'. Jesus brings the very meekness and lowliness of the heart of God Almighty to bear, when he washes the disciples' feet on earth.

And then, as if that were not enough, when they get up to heaven, he goes down and dries their tears! Perhaps he takes a linen cloth (like the face cloth that was laid on his own face in the tomb), and wipes their tears away. Jesus is not going to let anybody welcome his saints to heaven but himself, so the Son of God comes and tenderly takes care of their every need. Then he leads them to a banqueting table. I do not know what is on the banqueting table, but the Bible speaks of milk and honey and things like that. As one brought up in the American South, I would like to think that the table might have roast beef, barbeque, scallops, oysters, and pecan pie! (Strictly speaking, of course, in the new world, it will be like the pre-fall world; we shall eat things other than meat). This banqueting table will be just right for us, like the best and the finest from home! A great Scottish theologian named Thomas Boston once said something like this (in *The Fourfold State of Human Nature*): 'Is not God generous? You gave a cup of cold water to a child that was in need while you were on earth, and when you get home to heaven God gives you a river of pleasure in exchange for that cup of water that you handed out.' What a God!

We conclude with this text from the end of the great resurrection chapter, 1 Corinthians 15:57-8: 'But thanks be to God, which giveth us the victory through our Lord Jesus Christ. Therefore, my beloved brethren, be ye steadfast, unmovable, always abounding in the work of the Lord, forasmuch as you know that your labor is not in vain in the Lord'. To this glad assurance of where our future lies we are called for the rest of our time on earth.

22

How God has Chosen to Run the World
Revelation 8

How God has chosen to run the world: that is what is explained to us in this passage in symbolic fashion. During the British civil wars in the 1640s the greatest military leader was Oliver Cromwell.[51] He took shepherds, fishermen, small shopkeepers and farmers, and made them into a great army, a victorious fighting force, that swept the king's armies before it. While these wars were going on, a distinguished military person from France had heard so much about Cromwell's armies, that he requested permission to come to England to visit the troops. In his biography of Cromwell, Christopher Hill of Balliol College in Oxford, records that this French general was amazed as he went through the Puritan armies. Everywhere he went in the camps, they were holding prayer meetings. It was very surprising for a Frenchman, even before the revolution in France, that an army should be doing that much praying. So he came back in the evening to Cromwell's headquarters and told him how impressed he was with the organization and all that they were doing. Then he said, 'I would like to ask you one question: Why are you allowing or even encouraging all these prayer meetings of the troops?' Cromwell answered him without even having to think: 'Sir, I have learned that those who pray best, fight best.'

This text shows us:

1. God has ordained prayer as a major way to get his purposes accomplished (8:3-13).
2. The saints' prayers connect the two realms (8:5).
3. The Perfume of the Angels (8:3-4).
4. Fire is Cast into the Earth (8:5).

God Has Ordained Prayer as a Major Way to Get his Purposes Accomplished

Why is it that prayer, far from disconnecting you from the responsibilities and the accomplishments of the real world, confirms you in it and very often is the winning factor? The reason is because of the way God, the Creator of the heavens and the earth, the judge, the controller, sustainer, governor and redeemer set up this world to work. In God's eternal plan, prayer is like a highway between the physical world and the unseen, transcendent, heavenly realm.

We could think of prayer as what brings down the huge 18-wheeler trucks or long trains full of divine blessing, strength, and help. The empty trucks or trains first go up with our requests and then come back down this invisible highway, filled with the blessings that the camp needs. Prayer is the highway between the two realms in which we live. God set up the world that way, for God created us in his image as persons, so that we are more than this body; we are also spiritual beings, having the possibility of contact with the unseen realm.

Materialism is not required by Science
One of the great mistakes of so much of modern culture is that according to various forms of evolutionary theory or materialism, we are nothing but physical bodies. Indeed, the animal rights movement, or the extreme greens, think we are not even as good as the animals. Many cultured people have been under that sort of materialistic thinking, whereby they think that all they are is an accidental combination of atoms. They are just a higher primate, a higher form of animal, but that is all. They are born, they live, they suffer, they die, and they rot; and there is no world but the one you see. If that is true, then of course, prayer would be a ridiculous waste of time. That sort of theory has been increasingly shown to be bogus scientifically, for true scientists (such as Michael Polanyi) have shown that every level of reality has to be open to a higher level of reality for the lower level to make any sense, so that ultimately the world, and especially persons, have to be open to God for it all to make sense.

THE SAINTS' PRAYERS
God made us in his image, so that we are not only physical bodies, but also spirits, embodied spirits, or divinely created personalities. God has made us so that we would wish to communicate with the One who made us. That is what is happening in prayer. God put us into a world where we are very limited, and unable to do it all ourselves.

Sometimes it takes a crisis in our life for us to realize our weakness and our limitations and that we need help from a higher realm. Then we begin to pray to the Father through the Son, so that the help comes down the highway of blessing. Our needs go up, the help comes down, by which blessed traffic changes are made, and our life begins to fit into the purpose for which God put us into this world.

This text is a pictorial representation of how God moves world history and particularly the history of his people, the church, from one point to another. It is through letting his people come under pressure, so they talk to him in prayer, and then he sends down the strength and makes the necessary changes. That is how it works. If the action in this text were a stage play, you would have two different scenes. You have the earthly realm, for it talks about the sea and ships, trees and green grass, people and the fish in the sea, then the fire burning things up, giving us a picture of the world of nature in which we live.

But then there is another realm that is more powerful than the natural realm; indeed, it controls what happens in nature. The realm that we cannot see with our eyes is called the transcendent, or the invisible world. One day we will see it with our eyes, but even though we do not see it now, it is far more powerful than what we do see. That is no more unreasonable than to note that because we do not directly see electricity or forces of gravity does not mean that they do not exist, for we see and experience in our known world their powerful results. The most powerful things are things that we do not see; even the material is finally a function of energy. So there is more than the world we live in and see. Scripture says there is something else; it is the spiritual realm that brought the material world into being out of nothing: specifically, God the

Father, the Son and the Holy Spirit. Prayer is the interconnection between those two realms.

Notice how this works. In the last verse of chapter 7, and in the first two verses of chapter 8, we are shown the Lamb of God, the eternal Christ, who became a man and still is a man. He still bears the marks of how he suffered to pay for our sins and to make us able to get into God's presence in prayer and also when we die. The Lamb at the end of chapter 7 was tenderly caring for the saints who have died and gone above, but now in chapter 8, he is shown to be very active in what is happening to the saints who have been left on the earth.

The Predetermined Scroll of History is Opened Through the Prayers of the Saints

We see the Lamb here opening the seal; that is, the scroll of history, by which God's purposes work out in time. As the Lamb opens one seal after another, certain events in the eternal plan begin to occur. When he opens this particular seal, we are told that there was silence in heaven about the space of half an hour. In other words, when the Lamb acts, when the eternal Christ acts, the universe goes silent to await his orders. Then notice an amazing thing: two sounds come next. There is the sound of the trumpet of the angels, sounding forth particular judgments that change the course of history. The noise of the angelic trumpet sounds out the message for such and such to happen that has been written in the scroll of history. But then there is another sound: it is the prayer of the saints.

This shows us that the most significant things in world history: for instance, a naval battle, is determined by the prayers of the saints. Revelation 8 speaks of fire falling from heaven and burning up a third part of the ships. Of course, it is symbolic language, but it means something. It means that military battles can be determined by prayer. The same is the case with the reference to trees being burnt up; all sorts of physical, natural changes take place in this real world in answer to something that is invisible (or generally, even inaudible to the world): the voice of the saints praying.

The Perfume of the Angels

Before we go any further, we must ask: what is a saint? The New Testament gives us a different picture from what we would get from the popular idea, going back to the early Middle Ages, that a saint is a particularly holy person, possessing heroic virtues, far above ordinary believers. There are such people, and I do not mean to make light of it, but the New Testament tells us something different. It does not deny that there are some people who are particularly holy and unusually close to God. The New Testament usage of 'saint' means a sinner, a sinful man or woman, a normal human, with all their flaws and imperfection, who has asked Jesus Christ to forgive them of their sins, to save them and to make them his people. That is a saint. Their sainthood is not in themselves; it is in Christ.

'We are sanctified in Christ Jesus', says 1 Corinthians 1:2, and in verse 30 that 'he is made unto us wisdom, and righteousness, and sanctification, and redemption.' To be a saint means that a sinful person has trusted the Lord for forgiveness, and God by his grace has miraculously done it, regenerating us in and through Christ, so that many holy changes start coming in our lives, although while on earth we are still never completely where we need to be. One of these God-induced changes is that we are granted an authority to talk directly to heaven, to send there an empty truck with our needs and those of others. Then, in accordance with God's wise and gracious plan, the answer comes down with the particular blessing for others and self.

Saints, Though Imperfect, Have Supernatural Power
Another remarkable point in verses 3–4 indicates that a believer, who is holy in Christ, though still not perfect, has the divine authority to make a request to God, with expectation of a divine response to divine promises to them in his Word. Certainly, our imperfect requests bear upon them the dust of our earthly imperfection, so how could we think that anything we pray is going to have any influence in the highest court of all, in the holy of holies, from which God will send down this power and—in this case, his holy fire?

The Use of Incense in the Old Testament
How the prayers of imperfectly sanctified believers work is explained in verses 2–3, which draws upon Leviticus 16, where the high priest sprinkled perfume upon the worshipping people of God in the tabernacle. It shows that the people of God are imperfect in themselves as they worship a holy God. Because of this the high priests were told to take a censor filled with steaming incense. The traditional censor was something like a ball, or an empty globe with little holes in it, and was suspended on the end of a chain. The High Priest would take hot incense in this empty ball, and then would walk around the congregation where the praying and praising was going on, swinging the censor all around. It was a way of showing that human worship and prayer is not acceptable to God, unless it is perfumed by the grace of God, by the presence of God himself. Then the worship of the imperfect believer is acceptable in heaven.

Perfume on the Saints' Imperfect Prayers
Revelation 8:3–4 tell us that this is what happens when Christians pray. Our prayers go up with all the dust of the earth upon them, because they come from imperfect people. But before they get to the throne of God, the place from which the predestined purposes of God are planned and executed, the place where prayers are answered and from which Jesus will come again, something has to happen to our prayers. An angel takes perfume or incense and sprinkles it on the prayers of the saints, so that our prayers are transformed. They become pure, sweet, and fragrant, like bunches of beautiful roses; they become worthy to be taken to the throne of the King.

This perfume is the worthiness of the sufferings of Christ, of his holy life and atoning death. As a Lamb before his shearers is dumb, so he opened not his mouth; and with his stripes we are healed (Isa. 53). It is as if the saints' prayers go through the wounds of Christ, through the nail prints in his hands and feet, and the wound in his side. The perfume of his perfection, worthiness, and devotion to the Father is added to our prayers as they go up to the Father, who has infinite power.

An imperfect illustration of this is given by Robert L. Dabney, a Southern Presbyterian theo-logian who wrote the biography of Stonewall Jackson, having served as his chief of staff for a while during the War Between the States. Dabney relates a touching scene at the lying in state of Stonewall Jackson, who had been accidentally shot late in the evening by his own soldiers. A few days later, his body was laid out in the Capitol in Richmond, Virginia, designed by Thomas Jefferson. His coffin was open, and tens of thousands of Confederate people came in trainloads to pay their respect. Thousands marched through, then came the time to close the senate chambers where the coffin was placed. The marshal of the day gave orders to the troops to close the great bronze doors to the senatorial chamber in Richmond. But a battered old soldier, a rough looking man with a beard, in a tattered, gray uniform, brusquely pushed his way past the crowds and the marshal. The marshal was about to push him down the stone steps, but the governor of the Commonwealth of Virginia was standing by and put his hand on the marshal to leave the old soldier alone. Then this old soldier lifted up the stump of his right arm and said: 'With this right arm, which I lost for my country, I demand the privilege of seeing the general under whom I fought one more time.' And the governor of Virginia said, 'Open again the doors; let this one man go in; he has won entrance by his wounds that he suffered for the Confederacy.' It is something like that when we pray. The wounds of Christ for sinners win us access to the immediate power and grace, love and mercy of God, with all the provision that we could ever need. So the saints pray, but their prayers do not go to God until they go through the wounds of Christ, which is pictorially represented by the angels sprinkling perfume upon them. They are purified and made fragrant through the merits of Christ.

Fire is Cast into the Earth

The next movement shown between the heavenly realm and the earthly realm, is that fire is cast into the earth. Real physical changes come about in answer to the prayers of the saints. When the saints pray, fire is cast into the earth. The larger context is connected with chapter 6, where the martyrs were crying out to God under the altar asking God to vindicate them and to deal with the evil powers who were attempting to lay waste Christianity. And God said essentially, 'Wait a little while, and I'll answer.' Now in chapter 8 they are doing some more praying, undoubtedly joined by the saints on earth, so God says to the angel, 'Blow the trumpet; send down fire in answer to their prayers; I am now answering'.

The fire coming down is a picture of God vindicating his cause at particular junctures in history. When the time is right, the saints have prayed enough, and everything is in position, he sends down fire and burns away that which is destructive to the advancement of his kingdom.

The Fire Still Comes Down

While we cannot be certain about all the details, it appears that the coming down of the Berlin Wall in 1989 and the implosion of the Soviet Union in 1991 were the answers of God to the prayers of his suffering people on earth. It was as though fire was cast into the earth and burned away the Berlin Wall and broke up the horrendous power of the Kremlin. Some media reports indicate that the final events of the coming down of the Berlin Wall were directly connected to prayer meetings. Lutheran young people in the huge Leipzig church where Johann Sebastian Bach had been *kappelmeister* had begun having prayer meetings four or five nights a week. Then the Roman Catholics joined them, as well as youth from other denominations. Eventually the parents started coming, so that they filled up the church and spilled into the town square, praying for God to do something about this terrible regime under Erich Honecher. Word spread to what was then East Berlin and another Lutheran church filled up the same way, and then the city square around that church. The government became very worried. It was illegal to have a meeting in East Germany of more than ten people without government permission, but here were assembled over 5,000 people, four or five nights a week, praying for God to do something about the government. The government taught in the schools that there is no God, but they got very nervous when the Christians started talking to God about them!

The dictator of East Germany called out the troops to surround this prayer meeting. In doing so, he made a mistake; he called East German troops instead of foreigners. He had not taken into account that a lot of the soliders had children, wives, mothers, and fathers who were in the prayer meeting. Furthermore, they knew that no moral law had been broken by these people who were praying. Thus, when the dictator gave command to the troops to open fire, the troops refused to obey. The dictator was out of a job immediately. The next day the wall came down. Revelation 8 says that when the saints pray, fire is cast into the earth.

That was not only true in the time of Revelation when the early church was suffering under Rome, fire would fall again in consuming streams two and a half centuries after Revelation 8 was written. The fire had brought down the unbelieving Jewish state in the first century, and then it brought down the Roman Empire when the Lord deemed that the Church was ready and that the saints had prayed sufficiently.

Some of us in the Presbyterian Church in Dillon saw a remarkable illustration of intercessory prayer bringing down the fire of God in the year 1977. The World Literature Crusade used to send out prayer requests to be given to weekly prayer meetings. One Wednesday night I shared a request with the Dillon prayer meeting. We were asked to pray for God's work in Fukien Province in China (a coastal province), specifically that the coastal defenses of Fukien Province would be confused. I asked who would pray for it. Retired General Henegan raised his hand and said he would pray. That was on Wednesday night. The following Tuesday on the third or fourth page of the newspaper, there was an article headed 'Fukien Province.' It said that one of the top pilots in the coastal defense of Fukien Province had absconded from China, and flew to Tokyo, where he requested and was given political asylum. On the plane that he took away were military secrets that were turned over to Japan. I immediately looked up what would have been the time difference between China and South Carolina, since the article told exactly when the plane had successfully eluded the other Chinese aircraft and made it to Tokyo. As best I could tell, the pilot who absconded from Fukien had left within three or four hours after General Henegan had prayed in Dillon for God to do something in Fukien. According to Revelation 8, this is not a strange coincidence; it is how prayer works. When the saints pray, fire is cast into the earth.

Why do we need to see the fire come down? What is it in ourselves? What is it around us that needs the fire of God to melt it, to purge it, change and renew it? If we want it to happen, God's way is: send up the prayers in the name of Christ, commit our selves to the work of God, let him take his time, keep praying till he does it, and in due season 'we shall reap if we faint not'. 'He that has ears to hear, let him hear what God says to the church'.

23

THE KEY OF THE BOTTOMLESS PIT
Revelation 9:1–2

The heart of this brief text pictures a holy angel opening the bottomless pit. It is a preparation for what follows, which shows us that not even the worst evils that can occur in the world are outside the control of God. It is a very comforting doctrine for the believer.

To understand these two verses, we consider:

1. The structure of Revelation as the background for historical shakings (Rev. 6–9).
2. As a prelude to these shakings, evil spirits are unleased from the deep pit (Rev. 9:1–2).
3. How could a good God let loose foul spirits?

THE BACKGROUND TO HISTORICAL SHAKINGS

The structure of Revelation 6–9 provides the background for understanding how the principle of evil is overruled in the permissive will of God, and allowed as a way of advancing the Kingdom of Light. We find this principle exemplified in Hebrews 12:26-7, and in Revelation 9, we see a tremendous shaking in world history. We can think of shakings on earth as history moves on—the shaking down of countries, tearing up of institutions, massive population migrations, risings and fallings of different political and economic powers, victories and losses of armies, and other major movements. If you get behind the shadows and see what is really happening as the judgments of God march through the earth, these are seen to be in answer to the prayers of the saints. We must always remember that when evil is unleashed, God is using it and overruling it according to his hidden will.

The Big Picture from Chapters 6–9

We must look at the big picture, provided for us by the movement of action from Revelation 6–9. The first strokes of the big picture appear in chapter 6, where the martyred saints who were killed for the faith, have gone up before the presence of God. They cry out to him for vengeance on evil-doers, for God to take action against the worldly powers of unbelief who are attacking the church here on earth. They are praying that way in Revelation 6. And God says to them, 'I am going to answer, but you will have to wait a while.'

Then in chapter 8 the prayers of the saints for God to take action are answered as fire falls into the earth. When the saints pray, their prayers are perfumed by the angels with the merits of Jesus Christ, and fire is cast unto the earth. Now, chapter 9 is a graphic way of describing the judgmental fires of God falling into the earth. In chapter 8, a third part of the creation is burned up. Here in chapter 9:18, we read that a third part of mankind is killed. Both of these are in answer to prayers of the persecuted.

You might wonder: does prayer really have that kind of power? Yes, indeed, for in order for the kingdom of Christ to advance further into this difficult, sinful world, evil powers from time to time have to be shaken down from their stronghold. That sometimes includes the death of many humans who are totally sold out to evil. In other words, when wars break out among the nations, when seemingly senseless disasters occur across wide swaths of various countries, something behind the scenes is happening: things that can be shaken are being shaken, in order that that which may not be shaken may remain. These shakings that bring down governments, destroy armies and navies (Rev. 8), are ordained of God in answer to the humble prayers of his dear little saints, who were counted for nothing, as mere trash, in the eyes of the worldly elite.

Spiritually, that is the background of what is happening in world history in Revelation 9. These things are occurring on the basis of Christian prayers in Revelation 6 and 8. The fifth angel sounds his trumpet, and sets loose these terrible events. He blows the trumpet in answer to a long time of hard, fervent praying of the believers. That is the reason I always stress the importance of prayer meetings; God has ordained that whatever good thing is going to happen in the future, comes always through humble, constant, believing prayer in the Name of the Son of God. Could not God have done it another way? We cannot limit what God can do; of course, he can do what he wants to. But the real question is, what does he say he will do, and how will he do it? He will bring down evil powers and bring about the good, shaking up the nations to do so, but it will be in answer to the constant prayer of the saints.

The Lord Temporarily Hands Over the Key of the Pit to Satan

Revelation 9:1 shows us what lies behind the horror and cruelty of earthly wars and destruction that usually accompany great shakings. At a given point in time, the evil in a place reaches a certain peak, then the prayers of the saints reach a certain intensity. In a holy way, hidden from our eyes, God turns a precise amount of destructive power over to Satan to let loose upon the earth. Satan is spoken of in this verse as a star that fell from heaven to earth. The Old Testament calls him Lucifer, son of the morning, who at the dawn of time rebelled against God. God cast him down and a large number of angels that became demons, with him.

But the work of Christ has greatly limited what these fallen, evil angels can do. Look in Luke 10:17-19. 'And Christ said, I behold Satan as lightning fall from heaven. Behold I give unto you, the believers, power to tread on serpents and scorpions and over all the power of the enemy and nothing shall by any means hurt you'. These scorpions may indicate terrible, demonically driven attitudes that can drive unsaved people to a deranged condition, in which they do awful things. But this text from Luke states that those kinds of scorpions would never be allowed to bite believers. When the devil is able to let loose his evil powers on parts of mankind, still the scorpions can never come on the minds and hearts and attitudes of the people of God.

Opening the Dwelling Place of Evil Spirits

From time to time, as a way to shake up powers that grow increasingly atheistic and materialistic in their work against the truth, God, in answer to the prayers of his suffering people, temporarily hands over a key to the Prince of Darkness, and says 'You can open this invisible door that is at the top of the shaft.'[52] It is like the abyss, or the bottomless pit which is the haunt of unclean spirits; a prison of demons and the realm of departed, wicked beings, a real place, although we cannot see it. Generally it is kept locked up.

People can get in; evil persons who die are sucked in, but down there, they generally cannot get out. Yet at certain seasons in history, God says 'All right, here's the key'. The shaft from that foul realm runs to this real world; it is invisible, but as real as anything you ever see. God says, 'I'm going to let you open this shaft leading down to where the powers of evil dwell in the realm of darkness. You can let these tormenting spirits out through the shaft for awhile. God is very patient and long-suffering, but when things reach a certain point, God lets Satan open this door and let loose evil spirits into the minds and bodies of unbelieving humanity. Every thing changes; terrible shakings occur, so that things which cannot be shaken—namely Christ's Kingdom of holy light—actually advances over the rubble of destruction when the powers of evil are let loose on one another.

In the next chapter, we must think about how this happened to apostate Judaism which crucified Christ and rejected him in the first century. The demons were let loose about AD 66. In that message, we will see how Rome destroyed Jerusalem in AD 70 after Jerusalem had more or less destroyed itself from the inside. At that time, these evil spirits were let loose, in answer to the prayers of the martyred Christians. Then over the rubble of destroyed Jerusalem, the early church was able to advance the Christian mission to the rest of the world.

Times When Satan is Let Loose in History

For now, we will consider the broader principle that at various times in history, great international evils must be seen as the letting loose of Satan by God to wreak destruction amongst unbelievers for the advancement of the kingdom of the One whom Satan hates the most: the Lord Jesus Christ. The bad news is that we have to cope with evil. The good news is that it works exactly the opposite to what Satan would hope; it actually decreases his vile crowd and increases the kingdom of God.

As we think of Islamic terrorism confronting so much of the world, we wonder if we are on the verge of seeing the evil one opening the shaft to the dark pit and letting loose hell on the modern world. If so, many things that we count on for our daily comfort could be shaken down very fast. But remember that even in the worst times, the kingdom of Christ will somehow invisibly be advancing over the rubble of materialism and unbelief, as the towers of human pride tumble down. We are taught here in Revelation 9:4, that the evil spirits who are let loose cannot ultimately harm—that is to say, get into the minds and cause to commit sin—those who are sealed, those who believe in Jesus. The powers of evil cannot sidetrack them from the heaven to which they are going. Certainly, at times, God does let the powers of evil kill his saints to fill up the number of the elect who are in glory. That cannot be ruled out. But the one thing he will not allow is this: he will not let the powers of evil get through to our minds, to our souls and spirits, so as to cut us off from faith in Jesus and the love of God in Christ. That can never happen, and it is a great comfort to us, no matter what may be ahead in the uncertain days ahead.

The real issue is never to predict the future. God does not give us that ability; we do not need it. But we can keep in mind that as believers, we are already and always on the winning side. Although we cannot be certain of the physical issues, we can deal with the things that matter. We cannot deal so much with the things that may be shaken because God may shake down all our worldly confidence, but everything that can be shaken in accordance with the will of God, will always work to the advancement of the true cause of Christ. The issue for us as we face the future is to be certain that we are on the right side now.

How Could a Good God Let Loose Foul Spirits?

One final question arises from the text: how could a holy, loving God turn over to the evil one the key to the bottomless pit, so that he can let loose these foul spirits, who then affect the minds of the unbelievers and cause great destruction?

We know that God is good; the Bible teaches that all the way through. Jesus said that 'there is none good but God'. When I was in kindergarten at the First Presbyterian Church in Lumberton, a little cup of orange juice was brought to us at recess in the morning and they would have us sing: 'God is good; I know that he is good'. That belief in the sheer goodness of God has stayed with me all of my life. The God who is good hates sin. So how could such a God give, at times, authority to the powers of evil to manipulate sinful people to carry out huge acts of destruction?

John says that 'God is light, and in him is no darkness at all'. James 1:13 says, 'Let no man say when he is tempted, I am tempted by God. For God cannot be tempted with evil, neither tempteth he any man. But every man is tempted when he is drawn away of his own lusts and enticed'. Habakkuk 1:13: 'God is of purer eyes than to behold evil'; that is to say, God is of purer eyes than to look with favor on anything that is wrong.

God is nothing but purity, light and truth. You will find no darkness in God. Psalm 45:6–7 tells us: 'Thy throne, O God, is for ever and ever; the scepter of Thy kingdom is a right scepter; Thou lovest righteousness and hatest wickedness; therefore God, thy God, hath anointed thee with the oil of gladness above thy fellows'.

Yet, other places in scripture make it clear that God has set the world up in such a way that he takes into account and includes in his planning, the choices of men, angels, and demons. God never directly makes a person do any thing wrong; certainly not! If we stand before the throne of God and say, 'God, you made me commit adultery, you made me hate,' it would be a lie. God never makes any one, including Satan, do what is contrary to God's character. Indeed, God warns us of the consequences of moral rebellion against Him. Yet, as William Still of Aberdeen in Scotland used to say: 'God uses sin sinlessly.' In a holy way, God allows rebellion and sin, but he hems it in with his omnipotent power. He will only let it go so far. According to Revelation 9, God uses this evil that he allows and hems in; he uses it sinlessly to shake down wicked institutions and advance the unshakeable kingdom of love and light and truth. All the while, he has everything in control. His heart is yearning over the humblest of the humble who believe in Him. Throughout history, God is protecting his believers, and advancing his cause.

The Wrath of Man Is Made to Praise God

Psalm 76:10 exemplifies this principle: 'Surely the wrath of man shall praise Thee; the remainder of wrath shalt Thou restrain'. That is to say, God will never let the anger and hatred, unbelief and moral rebellion, wicked plotting and conspiratorial actions of the worst of fallen humanity do anything but what will ultimately redound to his praise. Even if you do not see it for 100 years, it will bring praise to the Lord. If it would not bring praise to the Lord, then he will restrain wicked actions so they cannot occur. No wicked action is ever allowed but what somehow, from the perspective of the end of time, will have brought praise to the Lord. That is because God is omnipotent and omniscient; God is sovereign and God is good. One day we will be able to thank God for what he allowed, even when it cut us very deep. We will know at the end of time that the greater blessing we shall have for eternity came because of what he allowed.

The Greatest Good Came from the Greatest Evil

The greatest of evils could never be so bad as the awful taking of the life of the incarnate Son of God. Acts 2:23 shows us that: 'Him, (that is Christ), being delivered by the determinate counsel and foreknowledge of God, ye have taken and by wicked hands, have crucified and slain, whom God hath raised up'. Two things are said here: first, that the death of Jesus was in the predestinated plan of God. He foreordained that the wickedness of the Pharisees and the complicity of the Romans should slay his beloved Son. And yet God did not approve of what they would do, because it says 'with wicked hands' you took and slew the Prince of Life. God never does evil himself; but it is in the plan. We must remember that this foreordained evil above all other evils brought the greatest good that has ever occurred: the salvation of the elect, and the renewal of the entire cosmos. This foreordained death has made the forgiveness of sins available, so that anyone who says, 'Lord, I am a sinner; forgive me; fill me; change me,' can be utterly pardoned for all eternity. Indeed, salvation came to some of the very ones who slew the Prince of Life, for later in Acts we are told that many priests and Levites became obedient to the faith. Presumably some who had cried out 'Crucify Him' asked for forgiveness, and they got it.

Because of the supreme evil of his death, the world itself will be totally renewed in holiness and beauty. No matter how solemnly we feel the presence of evil in our society, all evil will one day be removed and cast off into that bottomless pit. Then the door will be shut for all eternity, and evil will never get out from the lake of fire. Everywhere else in all of creation will be renovated, cleansed, purified and beautified. As it says in 2 Peter, 'There shall be new heavens and a new earth, wherein righteousness will dwell.' Then we will thank God, even for how he allowed and used evil, and how he kept it from ever getting the best of the very least of his children.

24

HOW GOD USES EVIL BY OPENING THE DEMONIC PIT
Revelation 9:3–12

When we see large-scale immoralities sweeping through the cultures of America and Western Europe, it tells us something. God has allowed Satan to lift the lid off the pit and to turn demons loose on those who have rejected the Word of God for several generations. One particular question faces us: why are certain types of perversion increasing in America and Europe, apparently reaching into high levels of government, universities, and the media? Why is there so much of it now that we did not see several years ago?

Revelation 9 provides the answer: God has let the fallen angels open the pit for a time as a judgment on the unbelief of our materialistic society. They have loosed demons into people's minds and bodies, causing them to do unspeakable and perverse things. In June 2004, Swedish pastor, Åke Green, was sentenced to one month in prison for preaching that homosexuality is a sin. He was eventually acquitted following two appeals, but after two thousand years of Biblical influence in the Western world, how could a prosecution like that even have begun? It makes no sense. There is only one explanation. It is the letting loose of demonic powers into a culture that is destroying itself from the inside out.

The issue is not whether we may experience the judgments of God for our sinful materialism at some future time—these judgments are already upon us. The fact that such things can happen legislatively is a sign that we are already under serious judgment. The demons have been let loose for several years already. But before we say more about our own day, we must consider:

1. An historical example of opening the Pit, AD 66–70 (Rev. 9:3).
2. A Continuing principle of divine judgment on evil generations (Rev. 9:4–12).

AN HISTORICAL EXAMPLE OF OPENING THE DEMONIC PIT

Some scholars believe that this prediction was, in one sense, carried out in the Holy Land in the late first century AD as a punishment of the Jewish nation for its rejection of Jesus Christ as Savior and Lord. The Roman Procurator of Judea, a man named Gessius Florus, slaughtered 3,600 innocent citizens of Jerusalem, hoping to incite the Jewish nation to rebellion, so that he could violently put it down and destroy them. He carried out his slaughter over an exact period of five months, the same period mentioned in Revelation 9, in which the locusts could harm the human spirits of the unbelievers for five months. The Jewish historian, Josephus, was alive and writing at that time as an eye-witness in Jerusalem. He reports that this five months' killing of 3,600 innocent citizens was the beginning of the end for Jerusalem and for the Jewish nation. He says that what happened in Jerusalem was like the letting loose of evil spirits from the abyss into the minds of that nation.[53]

Unclean Spirits Let Loose on Unbelieving Jerusalem
This terrible turn of events seems related to what Jesus predicted in Matthew 12:43–5, which gives the underlying principle:

> When the unclean spirit has gone out of a man, he walked through dry places, seeking rest and findeth none; then he said, 'I will return into my house from whence I came out;' and when he is come, he findeth it empty, swept and garnished. Then goeth he and taketh with himself seven other spirits more wicked than himself, and they enter in and dwell there; and the last state of that man is worse than the first.

'Even so,' says Jesus, 'shall it be unto this wicked generation', the very generation that rejected Him. In other words, Jerusalem had been swept clean by the ministry of Jesus, but now, according to Revelation 18:2, Jerusalem had become 'the dwelling place of every unclean spirit and hateful bird'. Josephus, who saw it all, describes how this letting loose of wicked spirits into a Christ-rejecting population, actually worked in *The Jewish War* (Book 4, pp. 246–7). Satanic gangs of murderous zealots preyed on the citizens of Jerusalem, so that the citizens of Jerusalem had more to fear from their own Satanically-inspired gangs of zealots, than from the Romans outside the city walls:

With their insatiable hunger for loot, they ransacked the houses of the wealthy, murdered men and violated women for sport. They drank their spoils with blood and for mere satiety they shamelessly gave themselves to effeminate practices, plaiting their hair and putting on women's clothes, drenching themselves with perfumes and painting their eyelids to make themselves attractive. They copied not merely the dress, but also the passions of women, devising in their excess of licentiousness unlawful pleasures in which they wallowed as in a brothel. Thus they entirely polluted the city with their foul practices. Yet though they wore women's faces, their hands were murderous; they would approach with mincing steps and suddenly become fighting men, and whipping out their swords from under their dyed cloaks, they would run through every passer-by.

Evil spirits. Locusts with scorpion-like stings in their tails, indeed! In a sense, Revelation 9:1–12 was fulfilled as the letting loose of these spirits came to an end when Jerusalem was razed to the ground and reduced to rubble and dust.

A Continuing Principle of Divine Judgment

Secondly, notice a continuing principle of Divine judgment on evil generations. This helps us understand much that happens in world history, and possibly some things that are going on now. Even if this prediction of judgment was fulfilled in one sense in past history, there are further fulfillments at work until the end of time.

This passage likens evil spirits to horrendous locusts. Revelation 9:7 refers to their having human faces. This means that these invisible beings project evil with a human face that is turned away from God.[54] That is, they work through depraved persons, who for all that, may be physically alluring (as perhaps, in the pornography empire). Verse 9 says of these terrible locusts, 'they have stings in their tails like scorpions'. In this case, God's judgment on unbelievers is not final, but preliminary. Verse 4 indicates that 'the locusts' can sting only 'those who have not the seal of God in their foreheads.' We are told here that the evil spirits can harm unbelievers for five months—a limited time. But the torment they inflict is terrible while it lasts, so the people wish to die but cannot. The five months seem to refer to five months' growing season in Judea, more or less from May to September, which was the time when locusts ordinarily did their destructive work on the crops.⁵⁵

The Eighth Plague on Egypt and Revelation 9

This demonic plague differs from the eighth plague in Egypt because these 'locusts', who are evil spirits, not physical locusts, do not harm the vegetation, but cause grief and torment in the human spirit. Physical suffering is difficult, but in general, it is nothing to compare with mental, spiritual, and emotional anguish or torment.

Believers are not always protected from physical danger and harm. We see in these early chapters of Revelation that God had allowed many of his saints to be put to death, yet these evil spirits, 'locusts', cannot get into the minds and hearts of true believers who are sealed in their foreheads with the seal of God (v. 3). That refers to belonging to Christ, to having professed the gospel and to what we call the baptism of the Holy Spirit, that is regeneration, or the new birth. In that miraculous action, the Holy Spirit seals you in Christ, when he baptizes you into the death and resurrection of Christ, so that evil spirits can never get inside your mind and soul, much as they would love to, for they are powerless.

The Value of not Giving in to the Culture

The passage is not teaching that true believers are always sheltered from persecution by the forces of wickedness. It is teaching something more important and wonderful that ought to give us great joy as we contemplate and wonder what lies ahead. This passage teaches that the simplest, humblest, true believer is always kept safe from having his or her soul invaded by evil spirits. Did you ever think that might be one of the reasons why true Christians seem out of touch and out of date with a society that is ungodly and is rejecting basic morality?

'Do you mean to say we are out of touch?' Of course we are! Believers do not share the spirit of the age any more than Daniel shared the spirit of Babylon or Joseph shared the spirit of Egypt. Being a peculiar people is one of the greatest protections of the saints from harm in the judgments already falling on a rotting culture. This is not the same as a narrow and harsh separatism that denies all aspects of human culture. A Christian attitude seeks to affirm and further the goals of honorable and uplifting culture. But there are dark and sinister strands of culture that have demonic aspects to them.

The description of evil spirits under the form of locusts, who have hair like women and teeth like lions', may have reference to the allurement of illicit sexuality in an age where immorality is widely accepted. Kistemaker gets right to the point: 'Female hair is pleasing to the eye; the contrast between its charm and the ferocity of the teeth is striking in its symbolism…for demonic forces seek to entice human beings and ultimately destroy them.'⁵⁶

From the point of view of the unclean and ungodly aspects of human culture, we ought to teach our children never to be worried about not fitting in with what the popular mob is doing.

That is one of your strongest protections: to be definitely different in moral issues. In such times, when the spirit of evil envelops a once godly land, we remember what Revelation 9:3 teaches, as well as what Jesus said in Luke 10:19: 'Behold I give unto you power to tread on serpents and scorpions and over all the power of the enemy, and nothing shall by any means hurt you', meaning, in your spirit, in your true personality. We will not always be kept from persecution by evil forces on the outside, but we will always be kept from being demon-possessed, and spiritually tormented. We will always be kept from rejecting God and going into the bottomless pit.

Thus Paul says in Romans 8:35–9 these words:

> Who shall separate us from the love of Christ? Shall tribulation, or distress, or persecution, or famine, or nakedness, or peril, or sword? As it is written, for Thy sake we are killed all the day long; we are accounted as sheep for the slaughter. Nay, in all these things we are more than conquerors through him that loved us. For I am persuaded that neither death, nor life, or angels nor principalities, nor powers nor things present, nor things to come, nor height, nor depth, nor any other creature shall be able to separate us from the love of God which is in Christ Jesus our Lord.

These locusts, or evil spirits, let loose from the pit of hell at particular times in history, can attack only those who have rejected the truth of God and have refused his grace.

This is exemplified in Romans 1:21: 'Because that when they knew God they glorified him not as God, neither were thankful, but became vain in their imaginations and their foolish heart was darkened.' Then verse 24, 'Wherefore God also gave them up'. Do we not see that written across modern American society right now? 'God gave them up'. Do we not see it in Sweden, Canada and many places in the world: 'God gave them up… to uncleanness, through the lust of their own hearts, to dishonor their own bodies between themselves.' Verse 26 adds: 'For this cause God gave them up unto vile affections, for even their women did change the natural use into that which is against nature.' Verse 28: 'And even as they did not like to retain God in their knowledge, God gave them over to a reprobate mind.' How could intelligent, educated, cultured people think like this? Here's the reason: 'God gave them over to a reprobate mind, to do those things which are not convenient'.

The Corruption of Western Culture

Much of our Western society looks as if it has already been given over to lust, greed, and evil. It has been a slow process, which has taken several years for us to see how destructive it would be, but now it is upon us! The once famous evangelist, Billy Sunday preached a well-known sermon, 'The chickens are coming home to roost.' He had it right: worse judgments are sure to follow. Signs of impending economic collapse in rich countries, and unrest in the Middle East may be only the beginning of sorrows. But there is a safe and mighty refuge in the storm to come. The storm, far from destroying every thing, will only destroy what God feels needs to be brought down, and will make room for the spread of the truth of the grace of the gospel. This mighty refuge is found in faith in Christ, and consecration to his Person and Word.

Martin Luther wrote a hymn based on Psalm 46 during a time when it seemed that the demons had been turned loose in the moribund Catholic church and throughout Europe. Yet, after the judgments and conflicts, something good emerged because a few men stood and claimed God as their refuge. We might see a new day coming, if like Luther, Calvin, and Knox, come what may, we claim Christ as our refuge and stand. This is what Luther says:

> And though this world with devils filled
> should threaten to undo us,
> We will not fear, for God hath willed
> His truth to triumph through us.
> The Prince of Darkness grim;
> we tremble not for Him;
> His rage we can endure,
> for lo his doom is sure.
> One little word shall fell him.
>
> That word above all earthly powers,
> no thanks to them abideth.
> The spirit and the gifts are ours
> through him who with us sided.
> Let goods and kindred go;
> this mortal life also;
> The body they may kill;
> God's truth abideth still.
> His kingdom is for ever.

And if we are in his kingdom, all will be well. That is the only thing we need to be concerned about. He will take care of us as we move forward into an unknown future with confidence, trust and hope.

25

THE CONNECTION OF PRAYER AND JUDGMENT
Revelation 9:13–21

A man whom I knew as a child who had worked in the media, used to say, 'We need to know the story behind the story', and then he added: 'but in most cases we do not'. That is, he believed that the news media presents us with the results of world affairs, but not necessarily the true causal factors.

This passage in Revelation does get behind the scenes. In the next chapter, we look at what happens when these demonic beings are let loose out of hell to influence humans to do devastating things (such as destroying one third of the people). But Revelation 9:13–15 tells us what made it happen; in a sense, 'what lies behind the story'. Thinking about that opens a much bigger view of how God is running the world, and of our place in the purposes of God as we see time rushing on. What part do we have to play in how God is standing, as one of the hymns says, 'standing in the dim unknown, keeping watch upon his own', controlling and working all for his glory?

Notice three things in these three verses:

1. The connection of prayer and judgment (v. 13).
2. The connection of the visible and invisible world (v. 14).
3. The precision of God's clock (v. 15).

THE CONNECTION OF PRAYER AND JUDGMENT

We all think of prayer and blessing, and that is proper; it is the major truth about prayer: a source of blessing. But the Bible also teaches that there is a direct connection between the prayers of the saints and judgments that fall from time to time in world history, so we must look at that connection.

The Golden Altar is the Place of Power

First, verse 13 speaks of 'four horns of the golden altar', which is before God. By means of picturing the Old Testament tabernacle or temple with its golden altar, with horns on the four corners of it, we are taken up into the highest heavens. This is not the altar of incense which stood outside the place of worship, but the golden altar which stood in front of the most holy place.[57] It shows that everything has been removed that would keep the saints from immediate access to the favorable presence of a prayer-hearing God. We have already seen this altar in Revelation 8:5, and in various verses in chapter 6. It is the place where God receives the prayers of the saints and turns them into Divine action, that then releases tremendous forces on earth. They are often forces of blessing, but sometimes, to make room for even larger blessings, the saints have to pray for God to release from that altar forces of destruction to tear some things down, to make way for that which is right and good.

The control chamber behind what happens in this case of terrible wars, insurrections, and other large or small breakdowns of society, must be traced to the unseen realm of the heavenly altar of a sovereign God. That is the last word in the universe, the supreme bar of judgment, the final place from which the decrees are issued that this shall happen and that shall happen.

We who believe the Bible can certainly accept that. Either God is God or he is not. If he is God, he is in total control and even the bad things that happen have to fit into his plan. This is generally held by all true believers. Yet this passage speaks of something that we do not always think about: the specific timing of the sending forth of the decrees of God to make big changes in world history and in people's lives is in specific accordance with the prayers of believers. Of course, God is in charge of the timing, not the believers, yet he has worked into his plan their seasons of much prayer, which will then release judgments and blessings, as appropriate to God's overall purposes.

The Prayers of the Saints Usher in Judgment
Secondly, notice that the prayers of God's saints—those who are already above (ch. 6) and those who are still below (ch. 8–9)—sometimes usher in devastating judgment on an unbelieving culture. Verse 15 tells us that in answer to the prayers of the martyrs and of the Christians still on earth, one third of mankind is killed. So prayers of believers can also stand behind judgments that are let loose in this world. That may not be popular to preach about, but it cannot be excised from the Bible.

Do you think it is ever right to pray against the powers of evil and to ask God to bring judgment down upon those powers? Is that really Christian? Let us go to the scriptures, for instance, the book of Psalms, where the pious believer is calling out to God to do something about the forces of wickedness that are working against righteousness. These are known as the imprecatory Psalms.

Psalm 5, for example, gives a terrible description of the enemies of God, who are trying to bring down what is good and true. In verse 10, the Psalmist prays, 'Destroy thou them, O God; let them fall by their own counsels; cast them out in the multitude of their transgressions, for they have rebelled against Thee.' We hear a similar plea in Psalm 10:15: 'Break Thou the arm of the wicked and the evil man; seek out his wickedness till Thou find none.' It is similar in Psalm 35:4: 'Let them be confounded and put to shame that seek after my soul; let them be turned back and brought to confusion that devise my hurt.' Then the Psalmist requests that an angel get these evil doers (v. 6): 'Let their way be dark and slippery, and let the angel of the Lord persecute them.' Psalm 68:1 is much the same: 'Let God arise; let his enemies be scattered; let them also that hate him flee before Him.' Psalm 140:1 asks for deliverance from the evil man and to be preserved from the violent man, then verse 8 prays: 'Grant not, O Lord, the desire of the wicked; further not his wicked device lest they exalt themselves'. Think of the wicked designs that are out there. The Psalmist is praying specifically, 'Lord God, let them not carry out this evil that they intend to do.'

So I gather from what is said in Revelation 6, 8, and 9, in addition to many Psalms, that the prayers of believers against evil—evil causes, wicked persons, corrupt systems, oppression, lies and wickedness—will be used by God in due time as a way of bringing down evil. Prayer really works against evil.

Is the Church Praying Enough?

It may be that the church is not praying enough against evil powers, which may be one of the reasons they are now exalting themselves to the degree they are. Prayers are great weapons against what is wicked. According to Romans 12 and the Sermon on the Mount, we are not to take personal vengeance. So what do we do? You may feel powerless against so much of what is happening in the world. Even so, we gather from these psalms and chapters in Revelation, that our prayers against evil will be massively and triumphantly effective in due time. Praying against the evils of our age is never a second best, nor a way to make ourselves feel better. It puts us on the front line of world change, for in doing so, we are using some of God's most effectual weapons (invisible and humble though they are).

A Modern Illustration

Sometimes I visit Romania where I met Cornel Iova, a pastor whose first wife got a particular form of cancer in her thirties. It was treatable, and Christian friends in Great Britain sent word to Pastor Iova that they would pay for him and his wife to fly to London. They lined up treatment for her at a hospital, where all their needs would have been gladly taken care of by British Christians.

At this time, however, Ceausescu was exercising total power as president of the country. He hated Christians, and did everything he could against them, so when the Pastor Iova and his wife applied for a passport, the authorities sent word to the minister that he would receive no passport whatsoever, unless he and his wife would renounce their faith. In that case, the government would gladly issue him a passport to go to London and get the treatment. The decision of this devout Christian couple was clear; they honored Christ, and the minister's excellent wife suffered through for several months until the cancer got her.

But in the same month she died, Ceausescu was brought down. Christians had prayed and prayed and prayed, and near the end of 1989, he was brought down. In fact, it was on Christmas Day that Ceausescu and his wife were executed, and it was shown on television. In the providence of God, the minister's wife lived one week after the dictator's execution. Her mind was perfectly clear, so before she left her earthly home, God let her see that prayers had been answered against the great persecutor of the church in Romania. She lived to see this man brought down. The prayers of the saints have a way of bringing down evil persons and structures, if one persists in those prayers.

Is it Right to Pray Against Wickedness?

Do you think, in that sort of light, it would be right to pray against Al Queda? Or against the Taliban? Islam denies that Jesus is God; he is a prophet, but not the Son of God. Is it right to pray against it? The attitude in which we pray for evil to be defeated and judgment to be let loose, is always one in which we desire that those who are involved in evil should be brought to repentance. Who could have been acting in a more evil way than Saul of Tarsus, laying waste the church, helping to kill the first Christian martyr, Stephen? No doubt the early Christians were praying against what Saul of Tarsus was doing. Yet some of them must have been praying for him to be converted because one day the risen Christ came down and met him and he was turned around.

When we pray against evil, it does not mean that we hate the people we are praying against; that is never appropriate. It is right to pray against wickedness, but we always do it with a heart of love, beseeching God for the ultimate welfare of those who act wickedly, that it would be his will that they turn to Him.

James 4:2 says: 'Ye have not because ye ask not'. And the question comes to mind, are the people of Christ praying as they should against the materialism and the unbelief of their countries, not to mention the evil religions and atheistic systems in other places? James says, 'Ye have not because ye ask not', but we could state that positively this way: you will have it if you ask, which is what Jesus says in the gospel: 'Ask and ye shall receive'.

No one could ever write a true world history, for so much of what happens is directly connected to the prayers of unseen, suffering saints. God has chosen the weak and foolish things of this world to confound the mighty, so we cannot write even a comprehensive history of the church or the world. It may be that the crucial factor in great events coming to pass is some sick widow, whose prayers may have massively more power than the greatest, most consecrated preacher. Prayers going up from some shack in Sao Paulo may be the very thing that goes up to the golden altar to release blessing and judgment.

Four Horns on the Golden Altar
Thirdly, we see that this golden altar in heaven has four horns on it. What does that mean? If you trace this back to the Old Testament, which you always have to do to understand Revelation, you find many of these images in the Old Testament, which gives you a clue as to what they mean in Revelation. If you go to Leviticus 4:13–21, you find it speaking of the four horns, one on each of the corners. The High Priest would smear blood on these horns, as a symbolic picture of covering the sins of the saints, so that the power that comes out of the altar would not devastate believers, but turn into a blessing for them. Revelation 9 takes this picture from Leviticus 4, in which our sins are covered in the blood of Christ, so that the decrees of God which issue from the control chamber, will not devastate you.

It is important to remember that the people who pray to God to bring down wicked dictators and break up evil systems are themselves not perfect. We see this truth in such places as Psalm 14: 'There is none righteous, no not one'; and Isaiah 53: 'All we like sheep have gone astray, we have turned every one to his own way'. 1 John 1:8: 'If we say that we have no sin, we deceive ourselves and the truth is not in us'. The best of Christians have to fight daily with personal imperfection, but in the eyes of God, we are sanctified perfectly in Christ, for he 'is made unto us wisdom, and righteousness, and sanctification, and redemption' (1 Cor. 1:30). In ourselves there is much weakness, but the weaknesses of those who pray are taken care of by the blood that the High Priest smeared on the four horns of the altar. We appropriate cleansing which removes the judgment of God from our lives by the fact that Christ stands in for us. So when the judgments come in answer to the prayers of believers who are sincere and trusting in Christ, yet not perfect themselves, those judgments will not fall on the people of God.

THE CONNECTION OF THE VISIBLE AND INVISIBLE WORLDS
We see in verse 14 the connection of the unseen world and the natural, physical world. This verse helps us to get behind the events of history. It shows us a sixth angel, who is commissioned to

release four angels who had been bound in the River Euphrates. Thus, we notice a real physical river full of water, and then angelic beings, who in this case are evil. Notice how Scripture presents without hesitation aspects of the two worlds together: visible and invisible. They are distinguished, but not totally separated. One is no more or less real than the other. Deism with its axiomatic separation between the spiritual and the physical is not found in the Bible.

It should come as no surprise that in this actual, physical body of rushing water, are contained four supernatural beings with massively more power than any human could ever gauge or imagine. These four angels are fallen angels or powerful demons who, though usually invisible to human eyes, can become visible, or inhabit humans or other creatures who then turn into weapons of widespread destruction. These two worlds, the physical river and the evil angels, are together. God has power over both. When it is in accordance with the purposes of God, he answers his saints' prayers for vindication, and lets loose unseen powers from the mysterious realm to cause devastation in the normal human world of daily life.

The Precision of God's Clock

Verse 15 shows us the precision of God's clock. The major clock in the United States to keep other clocks straight is at the United States Naval Observatory in Maryland, but supposedly the clock to end all clocks, and by which all other clocks are to be set, is in the Greenwich Observatory, near London. Without speaking literally, we might say that God has a clock, not in Maryland or Greenwich, but near that heavenly altar, and it is a very precise clock. It does not lose time; it does not gain time; it is just right. As the hymn says:

> God is working his purpose out
> as year succeeds to year;
> God is working his purpose out
> and the time is drawing near;
> Nearer and nearer draws the time,
> the time that shall surely be,
> when the earth shall be filled
> with the glory of God
> as the waters cover the sea.

Hence, verse 15 mentions a precision of chronological measurements: an hour, a day, a month and a year. Forty years ago, in the state of South Carolina, when family estates were being settled, you settled an estate one year and one day after the person died. In the divine realm, God gives a precise measure for the length of time that he will allow these evil spirits to be let loose in judgment upon those who refuse to repent. It is an hour, plus a day, plus a month, plus a year. That much time: no more, no less. There will be a beginning and a termination in the historical kind of time that humans experience, and it will come in answer to the prayers of the saints.

God's Time in Old and New Testaments

We find a certain reference to this element of divinely measured time in Genesis 49:10, where Jacob is giving a prophetic blessing to Judah, in the larger context of his parting benedictions upon his twelve sons. He says about Judah, that such and such will be the case, 'until Shiloh comes'. 'Until Shiloh comes' means until the descendent of Judah, the conquering Lion of the Tribe of Judah, the Lord Jesus Christ appears in the flesh. It was a time precisely set. One can read about it in Daniel 10, which calculates the precise number of years from the time Daniel was on the earth giving his prophecy in captivity in Babylon, until Messiah would be slain in

Jerusalem. Scholars can work this number out exactly from the year that Christ was baptized in Jordan, and then count it down to the time that he was crucified outside Jerusalem; it is the precise number of years revealed long before to Daniel in his prophecy. God's clock is very precise.

Paul writes in Galatians 4:4 that, 'In the fullness of time God sent forth his Son'. Jesus was conceived in the womb of the blessed virgin and born in the fullness of time; it was the right time, set before the world was even created. God's clock is just as precise today as it ever was, which is why we must never despair if evil seems out of control. It is not out of control. God sometimes lets evil reach a certain point like a painful boil or sore before it can be lanced. I believe the powers of evil are like that. God in his wisdom lets it reach a certain stage of wickedness, and at the same time that this wickedness is increasing, the prayers of the saints who are suffering and concerned, are increasing, and then God says 'That's it! Let them loose; let them loose!' Unless you repent, the judgment comes inexorably.

Judgment Is not an End in Itself
Let us remember that judgment is not an end in itself. Isaiah said that judgment is 'God's strange work'; his normal work is blessing. The judgment is real, but it is a prelude to ever wider blessing, because he is a God of mercy, love and grace. Yet God has set up the world and planned history in such a way that he does not release his predetermined judgment and blessing except in answer to the intercessions of the saints which go up to that golden altar with its four horns smeared in the blood of Christ. This predetermined connection of historical events with the intercessions of the saints does not in the least make the coming judgments and blessings uncertain; rather, it is God's way to hasten them.

An old Puritan said something like this: 'The prayers of the saints are the beginning of the execution of the predestinated purposes of God.' These intercessions are, in a sense, the first ticking we can hear of God's precise clock. We frail, limited humans cannot say whether the 'ticking' we hear of the prayers of believers has reference to a particular a day, plus a month, plus a year. That is God's business. But we know that at precisely the right time, God will release these supernatural powers, and they will do a work that needs to be done in that generation. And we have our own part to play in it. That may be a more powerful way to shape the future than any thing else we can do, although obedient action to God's revealed will must always accompany our prayers. He that has ears to hear, let him hear what the Spirit says to the church.

26

Judgment on Unbelieving Israel
Revelation 9:13–21

In many ways this passage is grim, yet in other ways, it is encouraging. One commentary on Revelation has spoken of this particular passage as 'All hell breaks loose in human society.'[58] At the same time that there is, figuratively speaking, hell on earth, God provides the safe sanctuary in which all his people may take refuge. How that works is what we want to look at in this chapter.

As this passage starts, the hour strikes, the angelic trumpet blows, and supernatural beings are set loose to work destruction on unbelievers. We saw in the last chapter how spiritual judgment is a divine answer to the prayers of the saints. Here we want to look at what this strange answer to prayer, this devastating judgment on unbelievers and their nations, involves.

We must consider three points in this text:

1. Interpreting the question of fulfillment (Rev. 9).
2. An historic fulfillment (Rev. 9:14–21).
3. A continuing fulfillment (Rev. 9:20–21).

The Question of Fulfillment

We must face an important question of interpretation concerning this passage. Has this judgment already occurred, or does it still lie in the future? That is the question of interpretation that is most important here. It would appear that this passage is both past and future; that is, in one sense already fulfilled, but also in another sense its principles can still be in the future. It is not 'either/or,' it is 'both/and.' Sometimes Revelation is like that. This and the next point may demonstrate this 'both/and' character of chapter 9.

If we assume that John wrote Revelation around AD 65 or 66 then there are remarkable parallels between this predicted judgment of demonic hordes being let loose to devastate a nation, and what actually happened in the fall of Jerusalem and the destruction of the Jewish nation between AD 66 and 70. Therefore, in one sense, this prophetic judgment has already been fulfilled in the first century.

Yet there is another sense in which God lays out lasting principles here that still operate in world history. That is to say, the terrible destruction of Jerusalem four or five years after Revelation was written fulfilled Revelation 9, but that fulfillment also gives us a foreshadowing of events that may well come upon unbelieving nations in the future.

An Historic Fulfillment

If we assume an historic fulfillment of awful judgment against unbelieving, Christ-rejecting

Israel, it helps us to make sense of this symbolic and complex text. We find clues to the validity of this understanding in geographic locations mentioned in these verses, as well as numbers of the enemy and types of strange weapons.

Precise Geographic Location
The first geographic location seems to provide a definite clue as to what is meant here by the River Euphrates. It is a real river, so this is talking about something real, although it uses Old Testament symbols to convey what happens.

We know that fearful pagan forces somehow get across the Euphrates River, which ideally had served as the northern boundary of Palestine. God had said as far back as to Abraham in Genesis 15:18 that the Euphrates would be the northern boundary, and that is reaffirmed in Joshua 1:4 and in other places. Scripture often forewarns the Jews about enemies coming from the north, and the Euphrates was its northern boundary. Jeremiah 6:1 and Ezekiel 26:7 speak about the pagan enemy coming from the north across this river. In past judgments in Old Testament history, Assyrians, Babylonians and Persians had always come from this direction, from the north. They had to cross the Euphrates River to take over and oppress the people of God in Israel.[59]

Revelation 9 warns that a similar crossing of terrible enemies was soon to occur, perhaps not long after John wrote Revelation in the mid-sixties. Josephus tells us that eventually a huge Roman army came from the Euphrates area and devastated the inhabitants of the land, possibly killing as many as one third of the Jewish inhabitants, which would fit in with what we are told in Revelation 9:15. The Greek word used here for 'land' can mean the Holy Land, or it could mean the whole earth. If it refers to the Holy Land, it would mean the destruction of one third of the inhabitants of this particular nation, so central in the purposes of God.

Numbers of the Enemy
Other facts mentioned in these verses also lead us to think seriously about the likelihood of historic fulfillment. These are numbers of the enemy and the strange type of weapons that they employed. Revelation 9:16 speaks of two hundred thousand thousand; it is probably not so much an exact number, as a way of saying that with such a vast army, that they could overwhelm any country. This number of thousands of thousands, or myriads of myriads as some translations state it, comes from Psalm 68:17, which says 'The chariots of the Lord are double myriads, thousands of thousands'.[60] In other words, when the angel gives word to the hosts of evil, the number of troops that they can raise up against any nation is more than enough to overwhelm any nation, as though the chariots of God were fighting from the heavens against an unbelieving multitude.

Strange Weapons
Notice the characteristics of the enemy and their strange weapons. We see this in Revelation 9:17–19; breastplates of fire and brimstone, heads of lions issuing fire, smoke, and brimstone, with tails that actually have serpent heads to bite and kill. The characteristics of hell itself are some way in these particular hosts of enemies. What we know from the text is that one cannot exactly describe them; there is mystery here. But we know that these 'horses and riders with power in their tails to sting and kill and mouths of lions with fire issuing forth,' are not of the earth; their power cannot be explained merely by human terms; they belong to hell, as do the riders on these terrible horses, whatever they are.[61]

This is a demon-inspired force. Once the sixth angel blew the trumpet, at the Lord's command, this demon-inspired force seems to have gone ahead of the Roman army into the souls and bodies of hundreds of thousands of unbelieving Jews in Jerusalem who had rejected Christ and were persecuting the early church. These people who once seemed rational and in control of their lives literally become wild men and women, turning on each other for three or four long, terrible years. Moses had predicted something like this in Deuteronomy 28:34, that after an evil generation had finally rejected the Lord's covenant, 'You shall be driven mad for the sight of what you see'. Josephus says that after AD 66, demonic madness caused the Jewish nation to start fighting one another; civil war broke out inside the city and cruel actions were taken by the different factions of Jews on one another. The things that they did to each other were as bad as being stung by a scorpion and bitten by a snake, ripped open by a lion or burned by fire from a dragon's mouth. Resistance was largely broken down on the inside, so that when the Roman army, mounted on thousands of horses from the Euphrates, finally charged in and finished the predicted devastating judgment in AD 70, there was nothing like the kind of resistance they would have had. The devil had turned the people against one another; 'a house against itself cannot stand'. The devil always brings division. Thus Revelation 9 was a few short years after the book was written.

A Continuing Fulfillment
Divinely given moral principles in operation throughout world history, indicate that there can be many fulfillments of prayer and judgment upon evil cultures across the ages, not unlike what took place in the first century. Jesus Christ is 'the same yesterday, today and forever'. God changes not; his principles do not decay. He does not depend on a vote as to how he will operate this world; it is determined by his character from all eternity. So though this passage was fulfilled long ago, near the River Euphrates in the historic Holy Land, the principles of the government of Christ among the nations that brought about that judgment are still in operation.

A time comes when unbelieving nations have at last filled their cup of disobedience and perversion to the full. A time comes when the prayers of the suffering saints have gone on long enough against pagan persecution, and God tells the angel to let loose the demons out of hell to cause the pagans to begin destroying themselves. This blast of the sixth angelic trumpet, which unleashes malign, demonic hordes into the souls of proud, powerful pagans only occurs after a nation or the nations have finally and resolutely refused all repentance. God is slow to anger and of great mercy. Judgment is always God's strange work; his normal work is blessing. He never unleashes devastating judgment until he has given repeated opportunities for people to repent and to avert that judgment. That is the kind of gracious God he is. Yet he is holy. There comes a time after all repentance has been refused, that God's holiness requires him to unleash the demonic forces of judgment.

Refusal to Repent Makes Judgment Certain
We read in verse 21 a sobering phrase: 'Neither repented they of their murders nor of their sorceries nor of their fornication nor of their thefts'. The vile thing they refused to repent from is identified in verse 20 as idolatry: putting things in front of God. Notice the kinds of activities that have to be permeating a society before God allows the angel to blow the trumpet and send out the

judgments. These things could be summarized in modern English in this way: violence, sexual immorality, economic dishonesty and oppression.

Devastating judgment seems not to fall when you have only one or two of these societal sins. But when a culture accepts all of these things listed as part of its everyday existence, and voices are no longer raised against them as they used to be, when the church will not deal with it, and good people go along with violence, sexual immorality, economic dishonesty and oppression, when it all comes together and continues a certain number of years, something terrible must happen. These forbidden practices do not become prevalent in a land until idolatry takes over.

What Does Modern Idolatry Look Like?
One could object that in our country we do not worship idols, but the Bible says that idolatry can permeate a nation even when you are not literally bowing down to graven images of false gods. What is an idol, according to the Bible? An idol is any thing less than God, some aspect of the created order, that you put in place of God. It might be money. When it becomes the focus of your life and the love of your heart, when you think about it day and night, when it determines your decisions, and how you relate to other people, it is a false idol. In other instances, the idol of the heart may be politics. Politics is always important, but it should never be the focal point of our lives and affections. With some, the idol may be sex. Certainly, there is nothing wrong with sex, it is a good gift of God. There is nothing wrong with money, it's a gift of God. There is nothing wrong with politics, you need government to make decisions so as to keep good order. But when you reject God in Christ and put those things in front of God, it is idolatry.

In a country where vast numbers of the population have given themselves over to these different idols, then the horrible practices listed in verse 21 will take place on a wide scale. Peter warns us all when he says, 'Be sober, vigilant, for the devil goes about as a roaring lion, seeking whom he may devour; whom resist steadfast in the faith'.

This passage that predicts severe judgment for such willful idolatry and the wicked practices that always follow idolatry, reminds us of what Francis Schaeffer used to say, 'Adultery follows idolatry.' There comes a time when it gets so bad, that like the flood of Noah, God says, 'That's it! Send forth the judgment.' This terrible sequence occurred in first century Jerusalem, and it can occur from time to time, until our Lord returns.

Mercy Mingled With Judgment
But this certainty of societal judgment upon widespread idolatry and wickedness should not depress or discourage Christians. For the terrible devastations let loose by evil spirits cannot really touch the Christian. That is made clear in Revelation 9:4: 'And it was commanded them that they should not hurt the grass of the earth, neither any green thing, neither any tree, but only those men which do not have the seal of God in their foreheads'. God gives those who belong to Christ a place of serene security in national and international judgments,.

How does this work? We know that the early Christian church was able to get out of Jerusalem before the final destruction came. They saw certain signs that Christ had predicted in Luke 21 and Matthew 24, the abomination of desolation, which seems to have been the idolatrous banners of the Roman armies that surrounded Jerusalem. Yet the Roman army withdrew for a short time, leaving the Christians time to get out, before the Army returned the second (and last) time. Hence,

God sheltered his first century church from the devastating destruction that was predicted in Revelation 9.

How will he do it in the future as terrible judgments fall? Well, God has not told us how he is going to shelter his people if judgment should come and stalk the land in our lifetime. God does not tell us how he is going to look after us when the bad time comes, so we will have to trust in him alone. The most important thing in our Christian life that God wants from our hearts is that we trust in him. The Psalmist says, 'In Thee, O Lord, have I trusted; let me never be confounded'. God does not give us the details of how he will take care of us; he says 'Look to Me; trust in Me.' It is the same with provision for our financial needs and all other needs. God does not tell you how he will provide for you in a month or a year; he says, 'Trust in Me.' The Lord is the place of security to which you are to look.

We may well keep in mind Romans 8:38–9: 'For I am persuaded that neither death nor life nor angels nor principalities nor powers nor things present nor things to come [including future judgments on the land] nor height nor depth nor any other creature [even these horrible creatures spoken of in Revelation 9] shall be able to separate us from the love of God which is in Christ Jesus our Lord'.

When through fiery trials thy pathway shall lie,
My grace all-sufficient shall be thy supply.
The flame shall not hurt thee
I only design thy dross to consume
And thy gold to refine.

The soul that on Jesus has leaned for repose
I will not; I will not desert to his foes.
That soul, though all hell should endeavor to shake,
I'll never, no never, no never forsake.

27

GET THE GOSPEL OUT
Revelation 10

If you saw the film based on Tolkien's book, *Lord of the Rings*, you may have noticed that it had no interludes where you could rest. In the book, there were interludes in the exciting military action and personal dangers, but not in the film. It was constant action all the way through.

Revelation is a book of tremendous action, of massive things happening, in sky, and sea, in earth and the nations of men. But there are certain pauses or intervals, in which you can rest a little bit and stand back from the action, where God is saying, 'Now here is what lies behind all this. Be still a while from the action, so I can show you what is behind the action'.

Intervals in Revelation

That was the case in Revelation 6–7, where we had an interval from tremendous activity on earth to see what the martyred saints were doing in heaven. Chapter 7 says, 'Let's pause from the unfolding of world history, so you can see something that lies behind world history.' What he showed us in chapter 6 was the believers who had gone into heaven praying to God to complete his purposes on earth, to bring down evil and to bless the gospel expansion of the church. Then in chapters 8–9 we have tremendous activity once again; God's purposes are being carried out.

In chapter 10 we come to another pause to see what lies behind the action. As chapters 6 and 7 were interludes in heaven, chapter 10 is an interlude of what is occurring for the believers on earth, and their relation to the word of God written.[62] And that is a large part in what is making it happen. Hence in chapter 10 and in chapter 7 you do not have an advancement of the action as far as the fulfilling and the ending of world history, but you go back into the control chamber. In chapter 7, the saints are praying; in chapter 10 you see believers and their relationship to the word of God written. It is the prayers of the saints and the word of God written being carried out that are the two most important factors in everything that occurs in Revelation. The most important, of course, is God and his decree, but God works his decree in accordance with the prayers of the saints, and their believing and carrying out the word of God written.

So, in this interlude, we are taken behind the scenes and off the battlefield for a while, where we may be still and contemplate what is causing these things to work out the way they do. We are given an amazing vision that only comes to the eyes of faith. We cannot see it without faith, although it is absolutely real whether you see it or not. The grand reality is the glory of the Word of God arching over the whole activity of this frenetic world. What we see is a mighty angel representing the Word of God, with one foot on the sea and one on the land, and in his hand an open book. This shows us that it is the words of this book, and the power of God behind it and through it that carries forward the truth of this book; that is at the absolute center of all that is happening. Bringing everything to its focus makes sense of it all.

We look at four points in this text::

1. The mighty angel and Who he is (10:1–7).
2. Where this angel stands (10:2–3).
3. What this angel refuses to tell us (10:4).
4. What this mighty angel does tell us (10:5–7), which will conclude our interlude, the pause in all this stupendous action.

The Mighty Angel and Who he Is

First, in Revelation 10:7 we see the mighty Angel spanning the sea and the land. Who is he? Who is this special Angel? Commentators have differed, but I think it likely that, given the way this mighty angel is described, he is the Eternal Word of God, the Lord Jesus Christ. Sometimes in the Old Testament Christ is prophesied under the name 'The Angel of the Covenant.' This Angel especially represents the Word of God. We are told in John 1:1 that Christ is the eternal Word: 'In the beginning was the Word, and the Word was with God, and the Word was God'. He is the eternal Word in the bosom of the Father, in the ineffable life of the Trinity. Then in John 1:14 we are told 'the Word was made flesh and dwelt among us'. He is the incarnate Word; he is the enfleshed Word; he is the mediator between God and man, the Man Christ Jesus. This Angel that has the open book in his hand is the Eternal Word, the incarnate Word of God.[63]

Who Is the Mighty Angel?

The description of this mighty Angel in the first seven verses compares closely to the description of the risen Christ in Revelation 1:14-16. There John says what the risen Christ was like when he saw him on the Isle of Patmos. Many of those same characteristics are related of this mighty Angel in Revelation 10 and if you go back to the Old Testament, Ezekiel 1:25–8, you have a description of God himself on his throne as Ezekiel saw Him, when Israel was being deported.

Ezekiel seems to have experienced another interlude, in which he looked to God on his throne as the One in total charge, even as Israel seemed to be on the losing side, as they were being deported for the next seventy years. But the Lord said: 'Look up here, I am on My throne.' The same characteristics that are ascribed to the mighty Angel in Revelation 10 are shown to Ezekiel, as he glimpsed the Mighty One on his throne. In other words, the mighty Angel is none less than God himself: God, the eternal, incarnate, ruling, reigning Son.

But some have wondered if it might not have been an archangel. Let us note six reasons why this mighty Angel with the Word is none less than Christ himself.[64]

1. The Angel is Clothed with the Cloud. No doubt that means the glory cloud that covered the tabernacle in the Old Testament, the fiery, cloudy pillar. Then when the temple was built and Solomon was dedicating it, the glory cloud so filled that temple that Solomon and the priests had to run out. The splendor of the glory cloud of God's presence from heaven that had been over the tabernacle, filled that stone temple in Jerusalem, and nobody could stand for the holy, majestic God to be that close. They had to run! There is a description of this glory cloud in Exodus chapter 40. What it means is that the mighty Angel, Christ himself, is clothed with the entire majesty of the heavenly court. When Christ comes down and does his work on earth, he has the majesty of the angelic armies surrounding Him, with all their power and wisdom.

2. He Has the Rainbow around his Head. The rainbow was a sign of the covenant to Noah, that in judgment there is mercy; God would not judge the world again by a deluge. We see this covenant rainbow again in Revelation 4:3 encircling the throne of God. This Angel brings the authority of the rainbow-circled throne as he stands on sea and land. There is a description of this in Ezekiel 1:27-8, with the rainbow circling the throne of the Triune God.

3. His Face Shines Like the Sun. The face of this mighty Angel was like the sun shining in its strength: the bright noonday sun. That is said of Christ in Revelation 1:16. In Matthew 17 and the other gospels, when Peter, James and John were with Jesus in the days of his humility on that Mount of Transfiguration, God's presence began to shine out from the skin of his face. The disciples had to drop to the earth, since the glory that was shining out and his face became like the sun in the darkness of the night. In 2 Thessalonians 1:7-9, the apostle Paul describes the flaming fire of judgment at the end of time against unbelievers as being Christ's face and glory. It is an amazing thing: the comfort of the fiery, cloudy pillar to the saints will be the burning, destructive, consuming fire of God to those who reject the gospel.

4. His Legs were like Pillars of Fire.
The fourth reason we believe this mighty Angel had to be Christ is that the text says that his legs were like pillars of fire. The pillars seem to refer to the pillar of fire and cloud in Exodus 14 that brought the children of Israel through the wilderness. We are told in Exodus 13:12-21, that the Lord himself was walking in that fiery, cloudy pillar in the wilderness with his people. It is wonderful that though Christ's body has ascended into heaven, there is a real sense in which in all of his power and grace he is walking with his people. He walks in the midst of his people on earth even now, covering and protecting us, leading and sustaining us, though he will not be seen by the eyes of unbelief.

5. He Has the Book Open in his Hand. Verse 2 gives us this fifth reason we consider him to be Christ. Think of Revelation 5:3-4: 'No man on earth and no man in heaven was able to open the book'. But then in verse 5: 'And one of the elders saith unto me, "Weep not, behold, the Lion of the Tribe of Judah, the Root of David, hath prevailed to open the book and to loose the seven seals thereof."' No angel could open that book; the only one who could open it has it spread out in his hand, and that is the Lord Jesus Christ, the mighty Angel of the covenant. He alone can open the book of the future, the book of the decrees, for God determines and executes all that will transpire.

6. He Roars Like a Lion. The sixth reason it must be Christ is in verse 3: 'he cried out with a loud voice as when a lion roareth'. We have seen in

Revelation 5:5 that he is 'the Lion of the Tribe of Judah'. Since it is the voice of God that goes out from this mighty Angel, it has to be God who is personally in Him.

Psalm 29 tells us something about the voice of God; it is the same voice in this Angel, who must be God's Son. In Psalm 29:3: 'The voice of the Lord is upon the waters; the God of glory thundereth; the Lord is upon many waters [this Angel, had one foot in the water]; the voice of the Lord is powerful; the voice of the Lord is full of majesty; the voice of the Lord breaketh the cedars, yea, the Lord breaketh the cedars of Lebanon.... The voice of the Lord divideth the flames of fire; the voice of the Lord shaketh the wilderness; The Lord shaketh the wilderness of Kadesh; the voice of the Lord maketh the hinds to calve and discovereth the forest and in his temple doth every one speak of his glory'. This is the voice of the Son of God ringing out over the sea and the land with a supernatural and majestic tone, that is responded to in a seven-fold peel of thunder.

He is the mighty Angel who is behind everything that is happening on the sea and land. There is a lot of anxiety in the countries of the world which are facing terrorism and other conflicts. But one thing we have to keep in mind, is that it is the Angel of the covenant, the mighty Christ, who has charge of the sea and the land and the skies. We are under his sustenance.

WHERE THIS ANGEL STANDS

Second, verses 2–3 tell us that this mighty Angel stands over sea and land, which indicates his direct supremacy over them, and another verse adds, the heavens. He has a little book in his hand, and he places solidly his two feet on planet earth. One is on the sea, and the other on the land. Some say that the sea is mentioned first because the oceans cover about 70% of the earth's surface, and the continents cover about 30%, so water is the most extensive. This mighty Christ has his foot on the waters, the most extensive portion of this planet, but also on the continents.

Christ's Colossal Greatness

This demonstrates his colossal size in his glorified state. Quite rightly we think of a tiny Christ, who was born from the womb of the Virgin Mary. Yet at the same time, while he was in that cradle, there is a sense, according to John 1 and Colossians 2, that he was still in control of heaven and earth. It's a mystery! But do not think he's very small now. Do not think he lacks total ability to run everything God's way. He is colossal in the size of his strength and his far-reaching, all-encompassing control. That is our Christ; that is the Christ of Revelation, and of the Bible. He has in his hand the Word, and it is opened.

The Lord Jesus Christ with his spoken and written Word has absolute priority in determining every thing that shall take place on sea, on the land, and in the skies. The Word of God is still as much in charge as the split second that John saw this mighty Angel of the covenant standing on the sea and on the land. The Word is the greatest power of all. He alone makes sense of everything. His is the final program that is taking every thing else down the path it must go.

Secularism Utterly Discounts his Greatness

That does not seem obvious to our materialistic Western culture. In the 1960s the Bible was largely taken out of the public schools of the United States of America. Since then there has been a concerted effort by many to take any influence of Christianity out of public life. Father Richard John Neuhaus wrote a significant book, *The Naked Public Square*, about this strong drive by the secularists some years ago.

It would be easy to multiply examples of aggressive secularism's pushing Christianity out of a culture that was once largely Christian, but why do so? Is not the best answer to aggressive secularism the explosive truth of Psalm 2, which talks about the humanistic plot to get rid of God and his word in the culture. Psalm 2 replies: 'He that sitteth in the heavens shall laugh; the Lord shall have them in derision'. As desperately as the atheists wish to get the Ten Commandments out of the court house, prayer out of the schools, and the Bible out of any public discourse, the factor that matters most and that will determine everything else is something that they do not see. It is the sovereign Word standing with one foot on the sea, one foot on the land, and his hand in the cloud, exercising ultimate control, even over atheists and devils.

Even here, we must remember that a holy God never makes an atheist do wrong. He does not approve of their wrongdoing; he will bring them to account for it, yet in some way he is able to use the wrongdoing of the most vicious persons in society to advance his cause. I do not know how he does it; I would have to be as big as God to be able to explain that. The sovereign, mighty Angel, standing with one foot on the sea and one on the earth is in charge of everything; he is even able to use evil things without ever approving of them. That is why Romans 8:28 is universally true, and thus gives us great comfort in evil times as well as in good ones (Rom. 8:33–9).

He Is Sovereign Even Over Secularism

Therefore, even as we see so much of Western culture coming down around our ears, we should still be a people of comfort and internal peace because of Romans 8:28: 'All things work together for good to them that love the Lord, to them that are the called according to his purpose'. All things includes evil things—atheism, hypocrisy, and the movement of the very devils. We must never forget that the Word of God has as much sovereign sway over world history in times of apostasy as it does in times of revival. I have tried over the years to convey to ministerial students whom I teach what a privilege it is to preach this Word of God, because it is the major factor overarching every thing that happens in this world. The biggest thing to be in on is the Word of God. I fear that people who cut their sermons to ten minutes do not believe that.

What the Angel Does Not Tell Us

Third, notice what the Angel does not say, or what he refuses to let us overhear. John the apostle heard seven thunders that responded to the lion-like roar of the mighty Angel. Those thunders brought words, articulate expressions of truth. John got out his quill and dipped it in the ink, the scroll was open and he started to write, but a voice said 'No, John; put your quill back in its place; do not write this down. Seal up this information. I'm not going to let the church hear it.'

The same thing had happened to the prophet Daniel; concerning certain things God said 'Daniel, seal up the vision until the end. I'm not going to let the church hear it.' What was the information conveyed in those seven thunders? Of course we do not know, because he sealed it up! It may have been specific details of what was going to happen between the time John was standing there on the Isle of Patmos, seeing the mighty Christ overarching the sea and the land, and the return of this Christ at the end of thousands of years. It is impossible to be certain.

We have noted that much of Revelation seems to have been fulfilled during the first century with the destruction of Jerusalem, the fall of old Israel, and its replacement with the church. A considerable portion of Revelation is contemporary with the time in which it was written, but not all of it. Some things in the last book of the Bible are far into the future and cannot have been fulfilled in the first century. Was the message of the seven thunders a sort of outline of what would transpire between the first century and the last day of earthly history when Jesus comes back? Whatever it was, the Lord said, 'Do not tell it to My people.'

God Keeps Many Secrets
There are many things that God will not tell his beloved, blood-bought church beforehand. He keeps us in the dark about several things. It is not unlike the status of your own life when you get saved. God does not tell you whether you will get married at such a time, or enter this profession, or live this long, what your health will be like, or how many children you will have. All that is fixed, but it is known only to God. The fact that he knows it does not remove your responsibility or the meaningfulness of your actions and your choices, for all of these things are in his plan. But how long we shall live, or what our lot will be is not our business. Similarly, there are many things about the future of the church in world history that God simply will not tell us.

So many Christian people are digging into Revelation to try to get specifics about the future, when God said to John, 'Seal it up; do not tell'. We are not to be too curious about the specifics of the future. We must be fully satisfied with what is written in the open book in the Angel's hand.

Why is that? Listen to Deuteronomy 29:29: 'The secret things belong unto the Lord our God, but the things that are revealed belong to us and to our children that we may do them'. God calls for obedience to what we know, but what is not clear in his word is no ground for speculation.

The old hymn, 'Trust and Obey, for there's no other way to be happy in Jesus, but to trust and obey' gives us the right attitude. God does not tell you the specifics of your future, but he does promise that if you are His, he will take you home to be with him and that he will be your Shepherd all the way through. That is enough to know about your future! That is enough to enable you to live to the glory of God. He keeps most of our future and much of the world history to himself. Perhaps that is so that we will keep our hand in his hand, and our face upward toward Zion, step by step with Him.

What the Angel Does Tell Us
Fourth, we hear what the mighty Angel does tell in verses 5–7. The Angel of the Covenant lifts up his right hand as a witness in the court of law. When I had to settle my mother's estate, I had to go to the Robeson County Courthouse in Lumberton and, as is their rule under North Carolina law, put my left hand on the Bible, lift up my right hand, and swear in the Name of the Trinity that I would settle this estate, give all honest information to the best of my knowledge and ability, so help me God.

At that point, North Carolina law (which is older than American law, since it was one of the original English colonies) comes from the Bible, where one lifts up the right hand and swears on the book. In the Old Testament, God swears by himself in the prophecy of Amos, and raises his hand to heaven in Exodus 6:8 and Deuteronomy 32:40. God swears by his own book, which is swearing by his own integrity and character. How solemn that is—God swearing by the book. How encouraging it is, that the character of God stands behind everything that is said in this book. Everything in the book is backed up by his holiness, truthfulness, power, and being. If

God failed to keep any of his promises (such as granting full forgiveness to a sinner who repents), he would have to deny himself. It is impossible! God will forgive any one if we repent—he swears by the book (see Isaiah 1:18 and 1 John 1:9).

No More Delay

Then he says there will be no longer time—that means no longer delay, which is in accordance with what the saints were praying in Revelation 6:10-11. The mighty Angel says, 'Now your prayers are full, and I am going to move; I am going to do something'. Then he commands John to take and eat the book that he was holding in his hand. There is an earlier picture of this in Ezekiel 2-3, where Ezekiel is told to take and eat the scroll of truth, that it would be sweet in his mouth and bitter in his belly. What is the book? Some believe it is the book of Revelation; some believe it is the gospel; most think it is not the whole Bible because it says 'little book'. Maybe it is the gospel or Revelation, but I am not sure about that and I am not sure it matters.

Sweetness and Bitterness Are both in the Book

What we do know, is the revealed truth of God in words that we can understand, and therefore, can take and eat, which means personally, intellectually, morally appropriating its words for your life, inside and outside. It has sweetness and bitterness. Sweetness is gospel joy; there is nothing so wonderful as going to bed knowing your sins are forgiven, and that if you were to die in the night, you would wake up in heaven! That is a large part of the sweetness of the book: God will be faithful to you in life and in death.

But there is also a bitterness. No matter how sweet and wonderful the gospel is in your heart, there will be people around you who do not accept it and who may even hate you for where you stand. In some cases, if they can, they will try to make your life miserable. The Apostle John was in exile, and no doubt it grieved him to see his own Jewish nation rejecting Christ, and certain to come in for judgment. It was bitter. But the sweetness is that the church will go forward. Sweetness and bitterness—you cannot have one without the other.

It is an unrealistic kind of preaching that says, 'If you love Jesus, every thing will always be sweet and wonderful and every one will always like you.' Such is never promised in Scripture. Sweetness surely predominates in the Christian life, but there is also this element of bitterness.

An illustration of the inevitable mingling of sweetness and bitterness was the godly life of the great theologian and man of revival, Jonathan Edwards. I do not know that I have read anything more sweet than *Charity and its Fruits*, sermons he preached from 1 Corinthians 13 during the First Great Awakening in Northampton, Massachusetts in the late 1730s. Large numbers of people were savingly brought out of darkness into the kingdom of beauty, love, and light, but the devil reacted strongly, so that it was not many years before he was fired by his own church, which had been revived under his faithful ministry. Sweetness and bitterness.

I could tell stories about my own life, especially my early ministry when people were getting saved. It took me a while to perceive a pattern in the bitterness that nearly always followed the sweetness of a new conversion. Eventually I noticed that after somebody would come and say, 'God has saved my soul', in nearly every case, on the same day there would come some kind of attack or trouble, in the church or larger community. Then I began to understand what was happening. The devil was angry because people who had been in his camp were being saved, so that they were no longer under his control. Thus, he would attack. Once I perceived his strategy, I felt better, and was encouraged to carry on with it. I realized that with the sweetness, also comes a certain amount of bitterness.

The Church Must Spread the Word

Finally, this mighty Angel commands John, and no doubt the church through him, in Revelation 10:11, 'Thou must prophesy again before many peoples and nations and tongues and kings'. God commands us to get the word out. While some are spending their time in prophetic speculation, this mighty Angel, this glorious Christ, says to John, 'Get the gospel out! It's their only hope.' It is the thing that matters the most. Talk of the gospel. Tell people. Live the gospel. Pray it out. Support those who take it. Give all your energies to get out the Word, because the thing that is controlling history is this Word; get it out to the people! Then they can get in touch with the God who alone can take beneficent charge of their life and give it the most wonderful meaning!

Unbelieving materialists seem to be in control of America and the Western world, but that is a superficial viewpoint. They are out of touch with the source of power: the Word of God. The more they get out of touch with the One who is in charge and is really running things, the more they lose discernment, and are unable to see clearly even worldly reality, so they make bad decisions. Unless they repent, they will be crushed by events of which they can make no sense.

So do not worry too much about whoever you think is in charge of our cultural disasters. God says, 'Get out the word; I will handle everything else. I will let them destroy themselves, except those who are marked for faith and repentance. But as for you, get out the word, and in that light you may walk a safe path.'

28

Principles at Work in History
Revelation 11:1–13

Revelation 11 is a history of what God did to unbelieving Jerusalem in 70 AD, and a prophesy of how God will care for his true church and judge unbelievers from 70 AD until Jesus returns at the end of time. The stories of the Bible do this: they give a true event that occurred in history, and then that historical event becomes a token of what God will do in the future.

Biblical Events are Tokens of Greater Events to Come

The Exodus in Egypt was a token of the greater exodus at the time of Christ, that Christ himself should accomplish. The Passover, when they were getting ready to leave the land of Goshen and go to the freedom of the wilderness, was a picture of the Last Supper. Think of how David, as a shepherd boy, slew a lion and a bear with his own hands. That really happened, but it was also a picture of something more significant: David as a king would slay tens of thousands of the enemies of the Lord amongst the Philistines and the Ammonites. God was preparing him. It even becomes a token of God's future principles and blessings in Jesus. He feeds the 5,000 with just a few loaves and fishes; it's a miracle, but it's a picture of a greater miracle, of how God, through the gospel that the church will preach, will feed the hungry souls of those that are willing to be fed on the gracious truth, with the bread of life and the living waters.

But to understand Revelation 11, we have to keep in mind that while it refers to a particular historical event that was soon to happen, it is also a way-token. God lets unbelieving Jerusalem be trodden under for forty-two months by the Gentiles, but he has John measure the true saints, that is the real temple. To measure them means to number them in God's book and set a seal of protection upon them, until he gives them the victory in world history.

Thus, we note four points in this text:

1. A Historical Event (11:2).
2. Measurement of Temple, Altar and Worshippers (11:1–2).
3. The Two Witnesses (11:3–11).
4. Altar of Incense and Call to Intercession (11:1).

A Historical Event

Let us look at the historical event that is alluded to in this rather complex chapter. Verse 2 speaks of an outer court of the temple, and we notice that through the angel, the Lord tells John not to measure the outer court; that is, not to put the protecting seal of God on the enemies of the Lord who are outside the temple. This refers to faithless Jerusalem that rejected Christ and crucified Him. We know from Josephus that the Roman armies took precisely forty-two months, three and a half years to devastate and annihilate Jerusalem and the old Jewish nation. But God, in that time, kept his protecting rod, his rod of measurement, upon his own people, although he had not measured or protected the old order. In that sense the old order, as unbelieving Jerusalem was, passed out of the center of God's purposes.

'Not to Measure' Means 'To Cast Out'

One commentator has helped us understand this word: 'Do not measure them.' Literally, this verb means to 'cast them out' (in Greek, *ekballo*), and apparently it refers to the outer court.[65] It means: do not include them in God's protecting measurement. This Greek verb is generally used in the Gospels in the phrase: 'to cast out evil spirits'. It is also used for Christ's ejection from the temple of the money changers. Jesus had warned that unbelieving Israel as a whole would soon be cast out from the church (that's what the true temple means). The unbelieving Jews would be cast out, while believing Jews and believing Gentiles would stream into the kingdom and receive the blessings promised to the seed of Abraham.

Luke 13:24–9 may make clear what John means in Revelation 11 about not measuring and the casting out. Jesus says:

> Strive to enter by the narrow door; for many, I tell you, will seek to enter and will not be able once the head of the house gets up and shuts the door and you begin to stand outside and knock on the door saying, 'Lord, open unto us.' And he will answer from within and say unto you, 'I know not where you are from.' Then you will begin to say, 'We ate and drank in your presence; and you taught us in our streets.' And he will say, 'I tell you, I do not know where you are from; depart from me, you workers of iniquity.' There will be weeping and gnashing of teeth when you see Abraham, and Isaac and Jacob and all the prophets in the kingdom of God, but yourselves being cast out (*ekballo*), and they will come from the east and the west [Gentiles or whoever believes]—and from the north and the south, and will sit at the table in the kingdom of God.

MEASUREMENT OF TEMPLE, ALTAR AND WORSHIPPERS

Attention is drawn here to the temple itself, of which only a small part is included in the outer court (meaning that both the Gentiles and unbelieving Jews would not be protected, but cast out from the church, except upon faith and repentance). The true temple and the true altar are put under Divine protection from all Satanically inspired activity.

Meanings of Temple

Temple can be used in different ways, of course. But here it is most likely that the temple means what Paul says in 1 Corinthians 3:17 and 6:19, that believers are the temple of the Holy Spirit. God would finish his dealing with the physical temple in Jerusalem which, with its priesthood and system, rejected his Son, for it was crushed in 70 AD. The true temple of God on earth is the church; it is the body of true believers who are indwelt with the Holy Spirit, thereby making them the actual dwelling place of God in union with Christ (as we see in John 15, Romans 6:3–6 and Galatians 2:20). Also in Revelation 21:3, we are told: 'Behold the dwelling place of God is with men'. So the ultimate temple is God living in human personalities, dwelling with them, bringing them into union, communion, and everlasting fellowship with the Lord himself. That is the temple—the temple which John is told to measure and put a protecting seal on its souls. The Devil can never get to the personality, to the soul of the regenerate: thus, the true temple of the Lord is divinely protected.

Two Altars
Revelation 11:1 speaks of an altar inside the temple. What does that mean? There were two altars in the original temple at Jerusalem as there had been in the Tabernacle that preceded it. One, the altar of burnt sacrifice, was in the outer court. It is not spoken of after the ultimate sacrifice of the Lord Jesus Christ on the cross of Calvary. That altar has no more relevance because all that it stood for is perfectly, completely, and eternally fulfilled. This whole burnt offering—this holocaust offering—was made in the soul and the body of Jesus when he paid the supreme price for the sins of all who ever believe. So that altar is done away with.[66]

An Altar that Is Still Functional
The altar spoken of here still functions in the heart of the church and in the heart of the believers. What is it all about? It is the altar that was inside the temple, known as the altar of incense, where incense was sprinkled, which speaks of the prayers of God's people going up and the incense being the beauty of the fragrance of the death, resurrection and merit of Jesus Christ that makes their prayers acceptable in heaven. That altar is still functional in Revelation 6; thus, that is the altar here which John measures. It refers to the place of prayer in the name of Jesus, which avails to the highest heavens.

We do not see that altar on earth. But there is an altar: it is the altar of incense in heaven, and the martyrs are very near it. When we pray in Jesus' name on earth, those prayers become a powerful reality. The major instrument given to the true temple, to the people of God who are measured, is the reality of intercessory prayer that takes them to the supreme court, to the Commander in Chief, to the final Word in all the universe. We will come back to that in a little.

We see how important this altar of incense, this place of prayer, is for the advancement of God's cause in a hostile, wicked world system, especially as we look at the two witnesses described in verses 4–13. One reason it is difficult to get it all together is that two or three different images, or events and personalities, are taken out of the Old Testament and put together to try to convey the fact that when the church is preaching and praying, when God's people are trying to live Christian lives in the midst of all this hostility and difficulty, God is working and ultimately winning, although there may be many temporary defeats. God is working just the way he did with what is spoken of as the two witnesses. The most important thing that we learn from the two witnesses is the principle of how God is working right now, and what he will do between the time that John was writing and the time that Jesus comes back.

THE TWO WITNESSES
Originally these two witnesses stood for Moses and Elijah. Moses represented the law; Elijah represented the prophets. Those were the two that came from the Old Testament economy and stood with Jesus to encourage him, stood with Christ not long before he was crucified, on the Mount of Transfiguration. Moses and Elijah are the summary of the whole Old Testament, and by

their standing with Jesus say 'he is the One; he is the fulfillment of everything we were talking about and went through; he is our hope.'

Moses and Elijah

Verse 6 makes this identity clear. It speaks of shutting up heaven against rain. That refers to the judgment of drought that Elijah, by his prayers, brought in the time of wicked, idolatrous King Ahab and Queen Jezebel, whose name is synonymous with wickedness. Then verse 6 speaks of plagues, such as turning water into blood, and any Sunday school child would be able to tell you that it refers to what God did to the Egypt that was persecuting his people, and to high-handed, arrogant Pharaoh, along with the other nine plagues announced by Moses.

Verse 3 confirms that these two witnesses, Moses and Elijah, and all that they stand for, belong to the Old Testament; they summarize its testimony.[67] Their being clothed in sackcloth is a sign of the deep need for profound repentance for ungodliness, breaking the covenant, and idolatry. If you look in the prophets of the Old Testament, such as Amos and others, you will see that they would often put on sackcloth and cover their heads with ashes. In other words, those who wear sackcloth are calling for repentance and renewed faith. Something like that was seen in the ministry of John the Baptist. Jesus Christ himself says that John the Baptist is like a new appearance of Elijah. John the Baptist wore garments not unlike sackcloth, and the main point of his ministry was repentance: 'Repent, for the kingdom of heaven is at hand. The axe is laid to the root of the tree. Except you repent you shall likewise perish.' Later John says, 'Behold the Lamb of God that taketh away the sin of the world' as Jesus comes to his cousin to be baptized in the Jordan. John the Baptist, in a sense, summarizes the witness of Elijah in calling the Jewish nation and even the Roman soldiers, many of whom repented, to change their ways in order to turn back to God, because Jesus is here.

Killing of Witnesses

Verse 8 speaks of these witnesses being killed, and we must combine several things from the Old and New Testament to make sense of it. The witnesses being killed was, in one sense, literally fulfilled when wicked King Herod chopped off the head of John the Baptist after John had taken a stand against the incest that Herod was committing with his brother's wife. Perhaps the killing of the other witness, may be a reference to putting to the sword the half-brother of Jesus Christ, James. Both of these witnesses were literally killed at Jerusalem, John the Baptist and James.[68]

Others have thought that the witness that stands in for Moses was literally the Lord Jesus Christ. According to the New Testament, he is the sealing prophet, the final prophet, who was pointed to by Moses himself in Deuteronomy 18:15, which speaks of the 'prophet that shall come'. The New Testament takes what Moses said of the final prophet in Deuteronomy 18:15 and applies it clearly to the Lord Jesus Christ. You say, but is not Christ more than a witness? Yes, he is more than a witness, but he also calls himself a witness and says his Father witnesses to Him.

Whoever these figures are that represent Moses and Elijah, they point above all to what Jesus had come to do, and he was slain no where else but outside the city walls of Jerusalem, on the cross of Calvary. Indeed, the last chapter of the Old Testament confirms this. Malachi 4:4-5, which is quoted in the New Testament: 'Remember ye the law of Moses my servant, which I have commanded unto him in Horeb for all Israel, with the statutes and judgments' (that is Moses), and then verse 5: 'Behold, I will send you Elijah the prophet before the coming of the great and dreadful Day of the Lord'. The last passage in the Old Testament speaks of Moses and Elijah as being the prelude to the fullness of what God is going to do. If you accept what God is going to do, to which Moses and Elijah witnessed, you will be eternally saved, included in the church, the true temple, measured, and protected forever. If you reject it, you will be in the crowd in the outer court that will be cast down, excluded from salvation. You will receive the consequences of that rejection of the One to whom the Father witnesses; the one that Moses and Elijah summarize in the Old Testament, saying, 'Here he is.'

Revelation 11:9–10 describes the temporary joy of unbelievers (for there is always 'pleasure in sin for a season'). It shows the wickedness of the unregenerate human heart when the satanically inspired pagan authorities slay godly witnesses. We cannot imagine how much unsanctified joy there was when John the Baptist was killed, when the Lord Jesus Christ was crucified, and when the apostles were put to the sword.

Then the text speaks of three and a half. It may not necessarily be literal in this text, but many commentators think it could be referring to the three days of Christ in the tomb as it took him about half a day to get the clear witness that he was out of that tomb.

So the witnesses to God's truth are killed. The world system is often able to persecute the church. Think of what they did to large numbers of Christians in Sudan in the 1990s, while the Western countries did nothing to protect these innocents. On the surface, it seems that evil is winning in such places. And so it seemed that evil had won when Jesus' body was put into the tomb. But that was on Friday. Then Sunday morning came, and evil had not won an ultimate victory. The victories of evil are always limited and temporary. Three and a half seems to speak of that. Seven speaks of perfection or fullness. Three and a half speaks of that which is limited and temporary.

The Principle of Death and Resurrection

So here is the principle: ever since Jesus' death and resurrection, every victory of evil over good is always limited and temporary. We need to keep that deeply within our minds as we try to understand what's happening in the world today, which seems to be going in such as secularist direction. This principle continues to work till the end of time in the witness of the church in this way: as evil powers stamp out Christian testimony for a time, then the witness of the Christians through the resurrection providences of God comes back stronger than ever. Remember how Tertullian said, 'The blood of the martyrs is the seed of the church.' On that basis it is probable that one of the greatest Christian churches in all of history is going to be the church in Sudan, for the blood of those martyrs will not have been shed in vain. If we were alive in one hundred years, we might well see the rich fruit of their blood in multitudes of saved men and women. One day it will be a flourishing church.

The same principle is true in China. Some of the Christians are in jail, and under all kinds of persecution, yet the church is increasing in spite of official duress by the atheistic authorities. One day the Chinese church will be one of the most flourishing churches since Pentecost. That is how it works; that is God's principle.

Paul talks about this in 2 Corinthians 4:8–12: 'We are troubled on every side, yet not distressed'. He has a long-term view such as the one we find in Revelation 11. Both passages are to keep us from being distressed when things are bad, and we pass through deep troubles. We can be troubled, but in the worst times, God can keep us from being so distressed that we lose heart by such truths as 2 Corinthians 4: 'We are perplexed, but not in despair; we are persecuted, but not forsaken; cast down, but not destroyed; always bearing about in the body the dying of the Lord Jesus, that the life also of Jesus might be made manifest in our body'. Then these verses show how God advances his church, when are we willing to pay the price: 'For we which live are always delivered unto death for Jesus' sake, that the life also of Jesus might be made manifest in our mortal flesh. So then, here's the principle, death worketh in us, but life in you'.

What is the principle? It is this: God calls us to mortify the self-life, and then we shall experience resurrection life in those around us, those whom we seek to influence for good. This principle then refers to all true Christian witness in a sinful society till the end of time. Death first, then resurrection. C. S. Lewis has wonderful things to say about that in his book *The Great Divorce,* and also in his essay *The Weight of Glory.* Read those, for they wonderfully show how the principle of death–resurrection is the mode by which God grows his Church and transforms society.

How can we face death to our self interest? Verse 4 explains how, again, under symbols taken from the Old Testament. We go back to the two witnesses, who are spoken of under the images of two olive trees and two candlesticks. That imagery takes us to Zechariah 4:1–6:

> And the angel that talked with me came again and waked me as a man that is waked out of his sleep, and said unto me, "What seest thou?" And I said, "I have looked, and behold a candlestick, all of gold, with a bowl upon the top of it, and his seven lamps on it, and seven pipes to the seven lamps which are upon the top of it. And two olive trees by it, one on the right side of the bowl and the other on the left side of it." So I answered and spake to the angel that talked with me, "What are these, my lord?"

Then in verse 6 the meaning is provided: 'Not by might, not by power, but by My Spirit, saith the Lord'. This refers to the lighting in the tabernacle and the temple, where the candlesticks had two olive trees behind them, from which the olive oil flowed to keep the light going. Zechariah says that the light that God asks us to reflect to the world does not come from us; we are not expected to be able to keep shining on our own paltry resources. No, the Holy Spirit is the oil, and he flows into us from another place. He pours his personal presence and unction into the 'olive trees' of all the witnesses of the risen Jesus to keep their light shining, so that our Christian witness does not depend on human might, on personal power, but on 'My Spirit, saith the Lord'. It is the Spirit who raised Jesus up from the dead (Rom. 8:11). He still raises up the witnesses to God's truth in a world that seeks to knock them down. He is available to help every Christian be the kind of witness that is spoken of in this passage.

Altar of Incense and Call to Intercession

Let us summarize this chapter. In verse 1, God has the apostle John measure the holy people, and then measure the altar of incense. That altar of incense, as we see in Revelation 6:10, is the place where the prayers of the saints are transmuted into power. It is the engine that lies behind what happens in world history. That is one of the reasons why Paul says in Romans 12:19 that Christians are not to take personal vengeance. The Lord says, do not avenge yourself: 'Vengeance is mine, saith the Lord; I will repay'. And in Revelation 6:10, the martyred saints in the glorious home above are calling to the Lord in his time and his way to send vengeance on those who are laying waste his church on earth. This means something very important, namely, that for the church to win over evil, we must keep coming back to the altar of incense: that is, intercessory prayer in the Name of Jesus. From that place, God sends down fire against his enemies on earth, as Revelation 8 says. From that place, in answer to the prayers of the saints, God stops the rain and causes all kinds of things to happen in nature.

One thinks of the massive Spanish Armada, which in 1588 sought to crush Protestantism in England, and force them back into obedience to Roman Catholicism. But all over the British Isles, believers were fasting and praying. Suddenly tremendous storms came up, and all but devastated the Spanish Armada. The English ships were small, and could manoeuvre better than the huge Spanish galleons, by which they were greatly outnumbered. The prayers of the British saints went up to the altar of incense, and God changed the weather to something like a hurricane that devastated the majority of the Spanish Armada. And Reformed Christians, or Protestants, exist in some places today because the saints prayed in 1588 in Britain at the altar of incense. They could not do everything, but they could do that. And God changed the weather.

What is our duty today? We may feel overwhelmed at the constant attacks of atheism trying to get a stranglehold on public life against any kind of Christian testimony. We feel tossed about. According to Revelation 6, 8, and 11, according to the teaching of Jesus and Paul, according to Daniel, Samuel and Abraham, all the way through, our duty is to go to the altar of incense, always available to the Church. What about possible war and economic crises? Go to the altar of incense ahead of time. Go to the place of intercession and pray in Jesus' Name. How about burdens that we personally bear, or that our families bear? What can you do? Go to the altar of incense, because as those prayers go up in the name of God's worthy Son, Jesus makes you worthy. He makes your prayers acceptable in heaven. Go, therefore, to the altar of incense and from that altar God can send down the fire and earthquakes; God can shut up rain or send rain; God can send prosperity when he wants to. Above all, he will enable us to bear witness in our generation to those who may not want to listen. All that we proclaim and all the stands we take will avail little or nothing, unless we are covering it all in intercession at the altar of incense, in the secret place of the Most High, believing that prayer in the name of Jesus will bring every change that God wants to be brought. He that has ears to hear let him hear what God says to the church.

29

TWO HYMNS IN HEAVEN
Revelation 11:14–19

This passage takes us near to the heart of God. It lets us see, through the heart of God, what our lives with all their conflict, and the history of the world with its constant change, really mean.

In 2002, a terrible fire in Colorado burned down thousands of acres of wonderful timber. If you watched it on the news, you would have noticed that they sent airplanes above the fire, so they could see which way it was spreading in the hope of taking action on the ground to hinder its advance. These verses in Revelation 11 are somewhat like that. The passage takes us above the battle fields and fires of this world, right to the presence of God, and lets us see what is happening from God's perspective.

Notice three things from the text:

1. The structure of Revelation.
2. The sounding of the seventh trumpet (11:15).
3. The songs of Revelation 11 (11:16–18).

THE STRUCTURE OF REVELATION

Revelation is filled with busy details—tumultuous battles, wicked persecutions and divine judgment occurring on earth. It is the scene of whirling, stupendous activity, and at times it can all but wear you out. But periodically we are given breathing spells when we can go up to the holy quietness of heaven and take stock of what is happening on the earth. Verses 14–19 constitute such a breathing space, where John lifts us up with him to our Father's home. There he calms us and encourages us by showing heaven's perspective on the whole pilgrimage of the church through a hostile world.

All Events Have Reference to the Church

This brief passage shows us the end from the beginning—the final, irrevocable victory of Christ over everything else, from the perspective of the inauguration of his reign after he ascended on high and poured out the Holy Spirit at Pentecost. Now the risen Jesus is running everything on earth with reference to his church, which fulfills and surpasses the Old Testament Israel and is composed of believing Jews and Gentiles in one body. The early part of Revelation 11 spoke of the downfall of apostate Judaism and the destruction of the Jerusalem temple. This coming down of the old form of Judaism would be preparing the way for the new and worldwide kingdom of Christ to spread victoriously throughout the earth. The coming down of Judaism, as such, would be the beginning of the fulfillment of Ephesians 2:12–15:

That at that time ye (that is, we Gentiles) were without Christ, being aliens from the commonwealth of Israel, and strangers from the covenants of promise, having no hope, and without God in the world: But now in Christ Jesus ye who sometimes were far off are made nigh by the blood of Christ. For he is our peace, who hath made both one, (that is, Jew and Gentile, one body) and hath broken down the middle wall of partition between us; Having abolished in his flesh (that is, on the cross) the enmity, even the law of commandments contained in ordinances; for to make in himself of twain one new man, so making peace.

That is what God is doing in the tumult and changes of history, and in our little lives, from the time that Jesus is risen and ascends into heaven, until he returns. From this heavenly perspective, all the battles and struggles of God's people on earth, from the persecutions of the early church to the last gasp of Satan's host on this planet, are beautifully made sense of in Revelation 11:14–19. It is as though these verses cast a massive burst of light on everything else. Then, in the midst of the battle, because of that light, we understand what the battle means and where we are going.

Sometimes the Highway Department does major road works through the night. They reduce several lanes of traffic to one or two lanes, where one must drive slowly, under the incredible brightness of huge, beaming spotlights. Their glaring light enables drivers to see the highway workers, and to discern what is happening on the road. This passage is something like that, except that the light does not shine on what is presently happening beside the road. Rather, it takes our view down the road into the long future. From the time Jesus reaches his Father's throne after his work is completed, until he comes back, this light is shining to show us what it all means.

Thus we, in the midst of our own struggles, can rest a while, and by faith, join in the happy singing of saints and angels above. If this section of Revelation 11 casts light on the long future, enabling us to see into the far distance with joy, we note that this spotlight with its huge beams is focused on the singing of the saints. Their heavenly songs, containing two hymns, make sense of everything that is transpiring on earth.

The Sounding of the Seventh Trumpet

Before we look at the two hymns of praise, I want to note that the heavenly singing is an immediate response to the seventh trumpet that the angel blew. We must interpret the seventh trumpet out of the Old Testament. Each of the Jewish festival months was introduced by the blowing of trumpets, as we can see in Numbers 10:10. In the Mosaic economy, the festival year had various celebrations for seven straight months. At the beginning of each of those festival celebrations was always the blowing of the trumpets by the Levitical priests. The seventh month, the month of *Tishri*, was the last time in the liturgical year that a trumpet would sound. It was known as 'the last trump.' You can read about it in Leviticus 23:24 and Numbers 29:1.[69]

The Significance of 'the Last Trump'

Some of the kings of Israel counted the inauguration of their reign as beginning on the first day of *Tishri*, the seventh month, when the last trump was sounding. That is the case with King Solomon (1 Kings 1:34) and Jehu, who was king in the north (2 Kings 9:13). The sounding of the trump, the last trump, in the seventh month, announced that this king has taken authority, and that now his reign is proceeding.

In Revelation 11, the seventh and the last trump of the angel celebrates the victorious, never-ending reign of the enthroned Lord Jesus Christ. It is a celebration of the new creation which starts with the expansion of the Spirit-baptized church. This is good news, for once the seventh trumpet, the last trump, is sounded it means that no power, Satanic or otherwise, can stop the expansion of the glorious reign of the Lord Jesus Christ on earth. That is why we can be certain the year will come that Communism will fall in China, just as the Berlin wall came down and the USSR came apart—the trump has sounded and evil systems that seek to stop the expansion of the gospel will eventually fall. That will be the case with Islam, which seems so powerful with all its oil money and wishes to use it to stop the gospel. Down it must go, because the seventh trump, the last trump, has sounded at the glorious reign of Christ; he will be victorious over all his enemies.

So it will be with the secular humanism (really atheism) that is largely in charge of America and the Western world. It has rejected the Christian faith, and seeks to exclude every influence of Christianity from the public forum. Secular humanism, for all its strength and pride, will break apart; it will come down because the last trump has sounded, announcing that Jesus is victorious. The working out of his final victory in space and time is on God's timetable, not ours, on God's clock and God's calendar, not ours. But victory is on the way.

THE SONGS OF REVELATION 11

The third point of this text is found in the songs of Revelation 11. The spotlight of these heavenly songs makes manifest the future of the church on earth. God shows us life and history, and what it all means through the singing of his people. Is not that wonderful? To think that God would have us view what he is doing on earth in terms of the medium of singing, praise, and thanksgiving. That is how God wants you to see your life and how it fits into the rest of world history through the heavenly singing.

Singing Throughout the Scriptures

Job 38:7 tells us that from the dawn of creation, the morning stars sang together, and all the sons of God shouted for joy. In other words, soon after their own creation, the holy angels were praising the Lord for the beauty of what he was making on the last two or three days of creation. Some of the old astronomers even thought that as the planets revolve in their orbits, they give off beautiful notes of music, the so-called 'harmony of the spheres.' That, I presume, is unlikely. But we do know that God's people have always been a singing people. After the Exodus, Moses' sister Miriam led the Israelite women in singing about the miracle of the Red Sea: 'Sing unto the Lord triumphantly, for the horse and his rider hath he cast into the sea.' When the Lord Jesus was born, we know that a multitude of the heavenly host, a huge number of bright, beautiful angels, were singing all over the plains of Bethlehem. As I understand Psalm 24, and as the fathers of the church understood it, it is referring to the triumphal ascension of the risen Jesus into heaven after he had completed his atoning work on earth. As this risen Jesus passes through the gates of glory back up to his Father's throne, here is what the heavenly angels are singing from verses 7–10:

> Lift up your heads, O ye gates; and be ye lifted up, ye everlasting doors; and the King of glory shall come in. Who is this King of glory? The LORD strong and mighty, the LORD mighty in battle. Lift up your heads, O ye gates; even lift them up, ye everlasting doors; and the King of glory shall come in. Who is this King of glory? The LORD of hosts, he is the King of glory.

This is what the angels were singing as Jesus went through the holy gates of heaven.

The Doctrine of Election Calls for Doxology

Singing may be the best way to understand the significance of what God is doing in his mighty works throughout the universe. In Romans 9–11, Paul tells us that the election to eternal salvation of those who will be saved through faith, and the passing by of sinners who refuse to believe the gospel, depends on the mysterious will of God. Paul never explains exactly why this is so, but he does something else after he has talked about the high doctrine of sovereign and eternal election, which lies behind the salvation of every believer. At the end of Romans 11, he breaks out into a doxology, praising God from whom all blessings flow. He knows it is good news when we remember that God is in charge of everything, including salvation. The best way to deal with election is by singing praise to God that he knows what he is doing and will do it well. Thus Romans 11:33–6 is a doxology, a hymn of praise:

> Oh, the depth of the riches both of the wisdom and knowledge of God; how unsearchable are his judgments and his ways past finding out. For who hath known the mind of the Lord, or who hath been his counselor? Or who hath first given to him and it shall be recompensed to him again; for of Him, and through him and to him are all things, to whom be glory for ever. Amen.

In Revelation 11, there are two songs that give us much light on what is coming in world history and what has already been happening.

The First Song

The first song is in verse 15 and apparently all the voices in heaven, saints and holy angels, join in this song. It is directed to Christ and rejoices over what his newly established kingdom will accomplish: 'The kingdoms of this world are become the kingdoms of our Lord and of his Christ; and he shall reign forever and ever.' Satan tempted Jesus by offering him the kingdoms of the world, when he promised, 'If you bow down and worship me, I can offer You all the kingdoms of the world.' Jesus answered: 'Get thee hence, Satan: for it is written, Thou shalt worship the Lord thy God, and him only shalt thou serve' (Matt. 3:10).

This song makes clear that Satan no longer possesses the kingdoms of the world; they are not bound by his power. That is why missionaries can be successful. Satan is not in charge, since Jesus says in the gospels, 'I saw Satan fall like lightning'. Jesus conquered him on the cross and in the empty tomb. Yes, there is still a Satan. He has a certain amount of limited, delegated power, but he is not ultimately in charge of the nations; Jesus is in charge. Hence the saints and the angels join in this hymn. In other words, the kingdom, the real power, the total future, belongs in the hands of the Son of God. This heavenly hymn teaches us that only Jesus and his people will win. Secular humanism and Islam can only lose. Their promises to the foolish nations who believe them are vain and self-destructive promises that will end in dust rather than glory.

The Second Hymn

The second hymn (v. 17–18) is sung by the twenty-four elders, who represent the twelve tribes and the twelve apostles. The entire church until the end of time is represented by the singing of the twenty four elders. It is a hymn of thanksgiving to the Father for the redemption purchased by his Son for the church. This song looks ahead to the final judgment of the quick and the dead as though it had already happened. It rejoices that every wrong will be righted, every noble aspiration fulfilled, every tear dried, every deed of love rewarded, every evil dealt with and eternally put away, and Christ will be all in all. This hymn says that beneath all the complications of our lives and beneath all the terrifying events among the nations, we need to open our ears by faith to hear this song that will one day ring out all over the universe as the curtain falls on world history. Tune your ears by faith through the Word of God, and you will be a happier person when you hear the saints and angels singing of what is going on and what really is going to happen, contrary to superficial appearances in the media.

Quietness Follows Singing

After this concert of heavenly music, all is quiet. Then in verse 19, we are shown the open temple of God with the Ark of the Covenant, which had the Ten Commandments in it, and the mercy seat upon it. From that holy place we hear majestic and terrifying sounds, such as were heard when the law was originally given on Mount Sinai. This is a symbolic way of reminding every believer in both hard and good times, that since Jesus' crucifixion for sinners, the veil of the temple has been rent in twain. The way is always open to the holiest place of all, where you will find the mercy seat, where the atoning blood of Christ satisfies the holy law to forgive all your sins, putting you in the right with God. From the heavenly sanctuary the blood still speaks eternal peace to all who will receive it. At the same time, there is destructive lightning and shaking down to the pit, that will engulf all those who reject Christ and his merciful gospel.

That is the final outcome of world history, which we see from this vantage place near to the heart of God. It has been at work a long time. Sooner or later each one of us and all of our family must attain either peace with God through the blood of the covenant, or else be lastingly, as the phrase says here, destroyed with the destroyers.

Remember the old Sunday school hymn:

> What will you do with Jesus;
> neutral you cannot be.
> One day your heart will be asking,
> What will he do with me?

That is the issue. Will you and I join the happy, harmonious choirs of saints and angels, or will we grieve forever with the lost? Those are the only two options for any of us. He that has ears to hear, let him hear what the Spirit says to the church.

30

THE HOLY WAR

Revelation 12: 1–6

This passage draws upon Old Testament symbols, so it is highly symbolic, but rightly understood, it has a powerful, practical message. It gives us the key to understanding why there has been so much war through the history of humanity. From the beginning down to the present, there have frequently been wars between various countries and tribes, as well as other kinds of struggle between good and evil. Can we make any sense of living in a world where no matter how much they talk about peace, there is always war? Why all this war?

The War of the Ages

One gathers from this passage that there has been a Holy War going on from ancient times. According to Christian teaching, there is what we call the 'Just War theory'. It means that one should not engage in a war unless it would cause more damage not to fight it, and that if you engage in a war it should be for some compelling reason (or just cause)—the war should not be any more destructive than necessary to achieve its ends. That has been the consistent teaching of the Catholic and the Protestant churches all the way back to Augustine. At times it is hard to know whether a war is justified, but that is another issue. In the first six verses of Revelation 12, we are given a Holy War that must be fought. It is absolutely essential and right: a 'just war', indeed.

Structure of Revelation 12

Revelation is divided into two parts and chapter 12 is the beginning of the second part of the book.[70] The first half of the book is primarily the victory of the Lamb of God over his enemies, while the second part of the book covers the same ground, yet has a different emphasis. It is the victory of the Church of God, the wife of the Lamb of God, over all satanic opposition so that the bride ultimately overcomes every enemy through the Lord's power and is beautifully glorified and made ready for the final wedding supper of the Lamb.

The Big Picture

Revelation 12 is like taking a telescope and taking the big view all across the heavens. The first six verses give us a vision of what the history of the world means, with special reference to the wars and conflicts which are such an integral part of this world from beginning to the end.

If you went to the great observatories at Mount Palomar or Mount Wilson in California, you would find huge telescopes, which provide an amazing perspective of the earth, and much of the solar system. But the issue in Revelation 12 is not the stars and the constellations, but the rising and fall of the world empires, one after another, with related political changes and ensuing battles that determine the base of world history. It is as though God says, 'Look through this telescope that I have provided in the revelation imparted to my servant, John, and you will see what is motivating all this fervent activity like that going on around a beehive or an anthill.' In a sense, we are seeing world history from the struggles at the dawn of time, motivated by Satan, down to the final judgment with the victory of Christ in a holy war that took many different shapes, but was essentially the same struggle.

The Apostle John, who wrote this book, intends that you and I will understand our lives and times in terms of this larger picture of a cosmic battle between God and the devil, between good and evil. You will never understand your own life, if you look at it only superficially. Superficial matters are important (one's background by family and nation and one's changing environment). But without denying the significance of our personal and national circumstances, we can only understand what it all means, as we survey the bigger picture of the ultimate conflict between good and evil.

With this larger picture in mind, let us look at three things from Revelation 12:

1. Two real enemies in the Holy War (12:3–10).
2. The one real battle (12:4).
3. Who finally wins the battle (12:5–6)?

The Two Real Enemies

All great military commanders have carefully followed the principle: 'Know your enemy.' That is why most countries spy on other countries and a massive amount of money is allocated by governments to intelligence agencies.

The Dragon

Revelation 12:3 speaks about 'Another wonder in heaven…a great red dragon'. That is the first enemy and verse 5 describes the one against whom he fights as 'a man child'. Hence the struggle is between the great red dragon and the man child; those are the two, underlying enemies. Everything that happens in world history is ultimately related to that struggle. Various historical events are lesser aspects of that one mighty battle. If we can grasp who these two mighty enemies are, the dragon and the man child, we will have the clue to understand much of what has been going on in world history and is still far from finished.

Look first at the enemy identified by John: the dragon in verse 3. As we have seen, Old Testament symbols and pictures are taken up by John to help convey profound truths that we could not take in otherwise. The dragon in verse 3 is identified more precisely in verse 9:

> And the great dragon was cast out, that old serpent, called the Devil and Satan, which deceiveth the whole world: he was cast out into the earth, and his angels were cast out with him.

A strange thing occurred soon after the dawn of time. God had created Adam and Eve upright, perfect, and pure. He had placed them in a beautiful place, a Paradise, but soon an evil presence came into that garden and solicited them to rebel against their loving, holy Creator. That evil power which came to them is described in Genesis 3 as 'the serpent'. The serpents we see today show profound signs of the curse that God placed upon them after the evil one misled our first parents. Before they were cursed and put down on their bellies, they may have been beautiful creatures, so that this primal serpent would not have made our mother frightened when she saw him, unlike our general reaction to snakes today. Before he solicited Eve to sin against God, he walked upright and had the ability, certainly in this instance, to speak. Scholars have suggested that some of the brilliant and beautiful colors of certain snakes may reflect the ancient beauty of this creature who was possessed by the evil one.

How Did Evil Come into a Good World?

How can you have evil in a perfect world? How could the serpent (that is, the being who was in him) be evil, since God created everything 'very good'? The one in this serpent form had originally been a creature of light, possibly the brightest of the Holy Angels. His name in the Latin translation is 'Lucifer' ('light-bearer'). As a bright and beautiful angel he evidently became so puffed up with his own beauty that he decided he would like to be, not only as big as God, but bigger than God. Because of this, he was cast out of heaven. We see this in 2 Peter 2:4: 'For if God spared not the angels that sinned, but cast them down to hell, and delivered them into chains of darkness, to be reserved unto judgment.' Jude 6 also speaks of it: 'And the angels which kept not their first estate, but left their own habitation, he hath reserved in everlasting chains under darkness unto the judgment of the great day.'

Church Fathers and Protestant Reformers thought that Isaiah 14:12–15 referred ultimately to Satan's fall, although in its immediate historical context, it referred to a proud earthly king:

> How art thou fallen from heaven, O Lucifer, son of the morning! How art thou cut down to the ground which didst weaken the nations! For thou hast said in thine heart I will ascend into heaven, I will exalt my throne above the stars of God: I will sit also upon the mount of the congregation, in the sides of the north: I will ascend above the heights of the clouds; I will be like the most High (like God). Yet thou shalt be brought down to Hell, to the sides of the pit.

In Genesis 3:5, this serpent tempts Eve to encourage Adam to rebel against God by doing the one thing he had told them not to do: to eat of the fruit from the forbidden tree. God had generously given them the freedom of that garden. Everything was available to them except the fruit of one tree: the tree of the knowledge of good and evil. We assume that one thing was off limits in order to test the first couple's willingness to love and obey God. They were to trust that what God had said was right for them, and not to 'second-guess' the Lord. The evil one tempted them to decide for themselves what was right and wrong, and that thereby they could be as gods, knowing or determining good and evil themselves, without reference to a divine, sovereign agency.

The Enlightenment Was Motivated by Satan's Desire

That seems to have been the chief motivating factor in the eighteenth century European Enlightenment, that sought to replace God's written Word with the philosophy of an elite, functionally atheistic group, who claimed to speak for mankind. The nineteenth century German philosopher, Nietzsche, (who was the son and grandson of Lutheran pastors), took it further than most, when he said, 'Unless I can be God myself, there is not a God'. Insane as that sounds (and Nietzsche did end his life in insanity), it goes right back to the origin of the titanic struggle between God and Satan; between 'the dragon' and 'the man child'.

The Seed of the Woman

In Genesis 3:15, God promises Eve, our first mother: 'I will put enmity between your seed and the seed of the serpent and the seed of the serpent will bruise the heel of your seed, but your seed will crush the head of the serpent'. All the wars and struggles of this world history, and our little part in it, go back to the Holy enmity, the Holy War, between the seed of this first woman, and the seed of the evil one. The Bible is basically an unfolding of the map of this conflict.

The seed of the woman is passed down for scores of generations. From that point of view, the Old Testament Israel was pregnant with Christ for thousands of years. Israel was being used as a womb from which the Messiah would be born. That was a basic function of Israel. Isaiah 26:17-19 makes this clear:

> Like as a woman with child, that draweth near the time of her delivery, is in pain, and crieth out in her pain [the same phrase used in Rev. 12]; so have we been in thy sight, O Lord. We have been with child, we have been in pain, we have as it were brought forth wind; we have not wrought any deliverance in the earth; neither have the inhabitants of the world fallen. Thy dead men shall live, together with my dead body shall they arise.

The history of Israel is a struggle to bring forth Christ. Isaiah 54:1 speaks to the same end: 'Sing O barren, thou that didst not bear; break forth into singing, and cry aloud, thou that didst not travail with child: for more are the children of the desolate than the children of the married wife, saith the Lord.' Look at Jeremiah 4:31: 'For I have heard a voice as of a woman in travail, and the anguish of her that bringeth forth her first child, the voice of the daughter of Zion, that bewaileth herself, that spreadeth her hands, saying, Woe is me now! For my soul is wearied because of murderers'.

The seed of the woman, as given in the first promise of the gospel, comes from Israel, and ultimately the Virgin Mary, as Isaiah 7:14 prophesies: 'Behold a virgin shall conceive, and bear a son, and shall call his name Immanuel.' Matthew 1:20-23, applies these exact words to the one through whom the Holy Spirit conceives the very seed of God, the Eternal Son of God, so that he takes on human flesh[71].

The Rod of Iron

The son whom the woman brings forth will win the battle over Satan and all his hosts of evil in this long lasting holy war. Revelation 12:5, speaks of this seed 'ruling all nations with a rod of iron.' These words are taken from Psalm 2:9, which prophesies of him: 'Thou shalt break them [that is the nations, swayed by Satan], thou shalt break them with a rod of iron; thou shalt dash them in pieces like a potter's vessel'. Then Psalm 2:12 adds: 'Kiss the Son, lest he be angry'. Voluntary submission to him is the only hope for anyone's future, for he is the seed of Eve, the seed of Abraham, and the seed of David. He is the eternal son of God in the flesh and it is hopeless to fight against the King of Kings and the Lord of Lords! Submission or crushing; those are the only alternatives.

THE ONE REAL BATTLE

Behind all of the different conflicts of this world, we need to remember that Satan's goal is to abort the work of Christ, 'to devour and kill him'. Revelation 12:4 shows graphically that the dragon is waiting for this woman to bring forth this child, for Israel to bear the Messiah, at which time the dragon will be waiting to gobble up the Messiah, so the world cannot be saved and delivered from the devil. All through the ages, the devil sought either to prevent the birth of Christ, or if he were born, to kill him as soon as he was born.

A Sweep Through Biblical History

A brief sweep through Biblical history shows us that this is the underlying motivation of the battles God's people have had to fight in this fallen world, including the persecutions that the seven churches of Asia were undergoing. He is trying to help the suffering church make sense of why they are being persecuted. He does so by giving them a long term perspective on the real struggle.

Cain and Abel. The first murder in world history was when Cain killed his brother, Abel. Who could doubt the devil influenced Cain to be envious of his holy brother to the point of killing him? The evil one wanted to blot out the seed of the woman, so the good son, Abel, was killed in that interest. But we are told in Genesis 4:25 that God gave Eve another son and she called his name, Seth. That means 'appointed'; a replacement is appointed and the holy seed would come through the third son of Adam and Eve, the one who replaced the murdered son, Seth.

Seth to Noah. In the next few chapters of Genesis, the devil tries to corrupt the line of Seth by getting them to intermarry with the Cainites, the wicked descendants of Cain. The sons of Seth were in the holy line by faith, yet they started intermarrying with Pagans, which corrupted the whole line to such a degree that in Genesis 6 God said: 'I shall blot out all flesh' (with a flood). Yet the devil did not win, for one family was preserved, Noah, with his three sons and their wives. Through them the seed of the woman would come. That messianic seed would come through Noah and then through his son, Shem.

Israel in Egypt. In Egypt, Satan tried to kill the seed of Abraham, that is, the family of Jacob, who were the bearers of the Messianic line. Behind the scenes, he motivated Pharaoh to kill the first born of all the male sons of the Israelites. We might think that this was merely a governmental policy instituted to keep the Israelites from ever forming a rebel army, yet behind it was the evil one seeking to blot out the male seed, the line of the future Messiah.

Saul and David. Centuries later, the evil one encouraged Saul to kill David, of whom the seed of the woman was coming. Saul, two times, cast a spear at him. But God delivered David, so that the seed of the woman would indeed come and would defeat the seed of the serpent.

Queen Esther and Haman. Yet again, centuries after that, Satan tried to outdo God by having the Jews killed in the time of Queen Esther. A pogrom was arranged by Haman (a conniving counselor of the emperor) to kill every Jew in the empire, which would have effectively wiped out the Messianic line, so that the world could never have been delivered from darkness and hell. But spiritual weapons worked gloriously against Satan's designs: Esther fasted and prayed, and the people of God with her, and the evil plot was foiled.

Christ and Satan. This battle between the two seeds reached its climax when the Son of God was born of the Virgin in Bethlehem. King Herod was terrified when he heard the wise men ask, 'Where is he that is born King of the Jews?' Herod sent for the scribes, who told him that according to Micah 5 that the baby, the seed of the woman, would be born in Bethlehem. He then computed the time of the birth of the Christ and sent his soldiers to Bethlehem with swords to hack into pieces every male baby two years old and under. Yet Satan did not win this time either, for God had forewarned Joseph in a dream to take Mary and the Holy Child, and flee to Egypt.

So what John speaks of in Revelation 12:6 ('the woman fleeing into the wilderness, where she has a place prepared'), was fulfilled in the holy family's escape to Egypt, until King Herod died, leaving them free to come back to Nazareth.

Who Wins the Battle at Last?

Third, who wins the battle at last? Revelation 12:5 goes back to Psalm 2 and makes the final victor clear. It is Christ, the man child, who will rule with a rod of iron. All the nations with their political orders, great military systems and economies are nothing but fragile clay jars to which the man child takes his rod and smashes them to pieces if they reject God's offers of mercy in the gospel.

How Messiah Wins the Battle

How does he win the battle? His victory is based on this phrase, that the child was caught up after birth to heaven (v. 5). This incorporates all of Christ's mediatorial work, beginning with his incarnation, through his holy life and blood atonement, ending with his resurrection and ascension into glory to be seated at the right hand of the Father. Because of this successful work, the man child is caught up to safety in heaven, having paid the price of our redemption, and secured it fully and eternally for the Church.

Thus Psalm 2:8–9 is being fulfilled as wicked empire after wicked empire rises, and then he takes the rod, and smashes them to bits. The reference in verse 3 to the dragon who has seven heads and ten horns, is a summary of this long work in world history. This many-headed, many-horned red dragon goes back to Daniel's four beasts in Daniel 7:3–7: Babylon, Persia, Greece and Rome. When you put together the seven heads and the fourth beast with ten horns, you have a summing up of vast world empires, which were all stages in the serpent's attempt to establish his illicit control over the whole earth. But they were all smashed by the seed of the woman with his rod of iron!

The Fourth Beast

The fourth and last beast would have ten heads. Rome was still running things when Revelation was written, but roughly four or five hundred years later Rome would be smashed.[72] Other empires have risen since then and the iron rod of the man child on the throne still breaks in pieces, satanic attempts to establish control over the world so as to dishonor Christ and to replace God. Evil, oppressive, political orders will eventually be crushed by this rod of iron, wielded by the woman's holy Son on the throne of power.

Whatever country we dwell in, we need to remember one thing above all else: 'to kiss [the feet] of the Son' as it says in Psalm 2, 'lest he be angry'. The only hope of ultimate security and victory for us as individuals is to identify by faith with the ascended one, the seed of the woman, who sits on that throne and is ever gracious to receive us, to forgive us, to love us and to keep us.

31

Warfare in Heaven: A Good Result
Revelation 12:7–12

Here we see warfare in heaven that has a very successful result. The winning of this warfare from heaven is the basis on which we are called to live our daily lives. We are in a difficult world, but we are called to live on the basis of the victory that God has already won on our behalf. It is the basis of the Christian life, and the reason why the Christian life is ultimately victorious against every evil power that can come against it.

This war has already taken place, and the results were stupendously successful for the forces of good. So we look at three points:

1. When did this battle, presented in this chapter, occur (Rev. 12:7–12)?
2. What happened in this battle (Rev. 12:7–11)?
3. The good results of this battle (Rev. 12:12).

When Was this Battle?
This battle took place during the same time we discussed in the last chapter (Rev. 12:4-6). It occurred when Israel brought forth Christ, and immediately the devil sought to destroy Christ, and to persecute his people. Yet Satan lost, and the man child, that is Christ the Lord, now rules the nations 'with a rod of iron' from his throne in heaven. So this battle in Revelation 12 is not future. This battle is past, but it is a past that informs and shapes our future. Since the Lord won this battle, 'the woman', in other words the Church, the people of God could be protected in the wilderness, so that Satan will never stop the church in its spread of the gospel. He would love to stop it, but he cannot. In other words this heavenly warfare was taking place during the birth, life, death, resurrection, and especially the ascension of the Lord Jesus Christ.[73]

Hebrews 10:12-13 deals with this: 'But this man who is Christ, a great high priest, after he had offered one sacrifice for sins for ever, sat down on the right hand of God; from henceforth expecting till his enemies be made his footstool.'

What Happened in this Battle?
In this battle, the holy angels, led by the Archangel Michael, defeated Satan, casting him and his host from the heavenly presence of God forever. This casting out did not finally happen until Jesus shed his blood, was raised in the same body in which he was crucified, and was taken up to the throne.

From Daniel 9, we gather that the angels were battling over the coming of Messiah even before he was born. Despite Satanic opposition throughout the ages, the Lord Jesus Christ was born at exactly the predetermined time (Gal. 4:4), and in due season, won the victory, and presents his glorified body to the Father. As a result of that momentous event, Satan was finally cast out.

This helps us make sense of the role of Satan in the book of Job. At that time, Satan had the authority to appear in God's presence to accuse the brethren. In Job 1:6 and 2:1, Satan argued that the only reason Job was serving God was because God was blessing him. Satan alleged that if God quit blessing Job with such magnificent physical prosperity, Job would curse the Lord. So God gave Satan a limited authority to prove that Satan was wrong, but also to refine Job's character, and then to bless him more than he had before.

In Zechariah 3:1-12, Satan accuses the high priest of the Jews who have returned after the Babylonian captivity. Satan sneers at the dirtiness of the high priest, but God rebukes him and clothes the high priest in clean and beautiful garments. Satan is the accuser of the brethren. Before Christ completed his messianic work on earth, Satan had a certain access to God.

In Luke 10:18, seventy-two disciples returned from a successful gospel mission. Jesus told them that their success in winning the lost and healing the sick was possible only because: 'I saw Satan fall like lightning from heaven'.[74] At this stage in Jesus ministry, the tempo was increasing in the battle in the unseen realm. By the time Christ appears in the flesh, Satan has been prevented from access to God's presence, where formerly he could accuse God's people day and night. When Jesus completed his redemptive work for sinners and took his place on God's throne, Satan no longer could come before God to criticize the saints. Rather, Jesus is now there, where Satan at one time could walk in and out before God. He is there as our advocate, rather than Satan as our accuser. Hence, we have an advocate, a heavenly lawyer, pleading our case, rather than accusing us. We see this in 1 John 2:1: 'My little children, these things write I unto you, that ye sin not. And if any man sin, we have an advocate with the Father, Jesus Christ the righteous.'

The Saints are not Perfect
1 John 1 and 2 make it clear that the saints commit sin. But before the incarnation of Christ, the devil would have been there to cry out: 'Your people sinned, and so you must let me curse them'. But he no longer can do that. So when we believers sin, we have someone who says, 'Father look on the wounds on my hands and feet. It was for them'. Then 1 John 2:12 tells us that Christ is 'the propitiation for our sins, and not for ours only, but also for the sins of the whole world.'

So Jesus' earthly activity and his ascension to heaven after he had done his work, is to a degree, visible to us in the sense of what we read in the Bible. But in Revelation 12, Job 1-2 and Zechariah 12 some of the underlying action is largely invisible. Yet the Gospel accounts make clear that throughout the time Jesus was on earth doing his mediatorial work for his people, he was constantly opposed in invisible places. The evil angels were fighting against God's eternal truth and his plan of salvation.

Why So Many Demons in the New Testament?
In general, the Old Testament does not give us much information about demons (though in places, they are present: as in the Garden of Eden, and in the mental illness of Saul). But when one reaches the New Testament, it is full of demons and angels. What is the difference? Why are there so many more demons in the time of the New Testament than in the Old Testament?

Here is the reason: Jesus had come to redeem the human race from the power of the devil and so the demons came from Hell, with all their force to attempt to stop it. That is the significance of the dragon seeking to devour the child of the woman, as soon as he was born, and then to persecute the woman, the believers in Israel and the Church. Upon the coming of the Son of God in the flesh and while the Lord Jesus Christ was on earth, the demons were let loose in the most massive military action ever known.

Hence, the continuing relevance for believers of Ephesians 6:11-12, where Paul says: 'Wherefore take unto you the whole armor of God, that ye may be able to stand against the wiles of the devil. For we wrestle not against flesh and blood, but against principalities, against powers, against the rulers of the darkness of this world, against spiritual wickedness in high places….'

Daniel Battles the Powers of Evil
Revelation 12 tells us that the Archangel Michael led the holy angels against the devil and his hosts. We meet Michael earlier in Daniel 10, where the prophet is praying for God to fulfil his promise in Jeremiah 21, of the chastened people of Israel returning to Jerusalem after they had been in Babylon for seventy years. When Daniel read in the book of Jeremiah that the seventy years were about up, he began fervently pleading the promises of God. He said, in effect: 'Lord, now fulfil your word!' Or, 'Do what you said you would do!' The promises of the Bible are thoroughly reliable, and will therefore be carried out without fail. They are the basis for all our hope, the ground of our life, and the foundation of all our praying. Yet, they are not fulfilled without any exertion of the saints. God requires that these promises be prayed into execution. But the saints part in praying into execution the promises of the Lord, in no sense makes their outworking uncertain, nor God's predestinated plan indefinite. God has built into his eternal purposes the intercessions of his people. They are a means of carrying out his purposes. That is, God predestines the means, as well as the goal in his glorious plan.

The Importance of Persistence in Prayer
Knowing that, Daniel took the promises and prayed persistently. He knew exactly what to do with the promises of God. This well-instructed prophet was aware of the ancient designs of the evil one to keep Messiah from being born. He knew that there would be unseen enemies, who wanted to prevent the Jews from going back to the Holy Land. That was one of the demonic goals simply because they knew that Messiah would have to be born in Israel, as had been predicted in Micah 5. Thus, if Satan could keep the Jews in Babylon, never to go back to their homeland, then the Messiah could not have been born in Bethlehem (as Micah 5 predicted).

That is why the evil one sent out his hosts to prevent the answering of Daniel's prayers for the Jews to return from Babylon to Jerusalem. This is the background of this battle in the heavens. Though it is mysterious to us, we gather that Daniel had to keep praying and fasting for three solid weeks, so great was the Satanic opposition. And because of Daniel's prayers, the Archangel Gabriel, who had been fiercely opposed by all the forces of Satan, was at the end of those twenty-one days of Daniel's praying, enabled to get through to bring the promised blessing to the Jews. They could at last go back home.

Think of that! The prayers of a believer on earth turned the tide of a mighty battle in the unseen heavenly places. Prayer has that kind of supernatural authority. Here is how it worked. In answer to Daniel's prevailing prayer, the Lord sent the Archangel Michael, the same one we meet in Revelation 12. He redresses the balance and turns the tide of the battle, so that Daniel's prayer for the return of the Jews, in principle is answered. Shortly thereafter, the pagan emperor Cyrus issued a decree that the Jews could go home. In this way of continued intercession, Satan was defeated, and Michael, who particularly protects the Old Testament people of God, came to redress the balance. That is how powerful prayer is. God has set it up so that his people shall win the divinely predetermined victory by means of God's answers to their prevailing prayers.

Revelation 12:9 says that Satan was cast out and limited in his activities to earth after this work of Christ, who did everything God required to be done for sinners to be saved and delivered from evil powers. When the once crucified Jesus, now risen and glorified, took his seat beside his Father in the place of highest power, it delimited the access that the evil one had to God, by which to accuse the saints and to bring distress upon them.

What Cast Out Satan

Verse 11 shows us precisely the basis on which Satan was cast out. It is 'the blood of the Lamb and the word of their testimony', that is, the saints' testimony. It is the triumphal result of the blood of Christ. The infinite substitute who represented God and man in one person and two natures, who more than paid for all the sins we could ever commit, thereby declaring us forever and totally justified, by this means allows me to get into heaven through prayer. Satan used to go there, but he can do so no longer. But we who believe in Christ can go there through the prayer of faith, and then come out against Satan and his foul works. This is the result of Christ's finished work: the saints overcome Satan 'through the shed blood of Christ and the word of their testimony'.

'The word of their testimony' means that we are still overcoming the devil and his minions. Every time we preach the gospel, witness a good confession, speak to a child about the Lord, or give someone a Bible, we are engaging in a war that in principle has been already won, although there is a 'mopping up operation' to the end of time. We are helping to mop up and to overcome the forces of darkness every time we have anything to do with proclaiming the gospel. I would go further and say that every time we give money to the missionaries to make their work possible, we are overcoming by the blood of the Lamb and the word of the testimony. Most of us believers are probably not specifically called to spend our life in China, Africa, or Indonesia, but we can help those who are there. They cannot stay if we do not support them materially and pray down God's protection and success upon them. That is how we overcome Satan. It all comes back to the simplicity of the Great Commission, that we believe in the gospel, and thus we go to all nations, seeking to disciple them and baptize them in the name of the Father and the Son and the Holy Ghost. That is overcoming Satan. That is how God will finally hem him in totally, and at the right time, send him down to the pit. The evil one's final sentence is advanced as God's people proclaim the word and believe in the blood.

The Good Results of this Battle

'Therefore rejoice ye heavens, and ye that dwell in them,' says Revelation 12:12. 'Woe to the inhabiters of the earth and of the sea! For the devil is come down unto you having great wrath, because he knoweth that he hath but a short time'.

There are two responses to the results of the battle: (1) lasting joy, and (2) temporary testing.

Lasting Joy

When a war ends, there are usually big parties. Lumberton, North Carolina, where I was born and raised, was a conservative, Christian town. They did not allow alcoholic beverages to be sold until the 1970s, and had not allowed any public dances before the end of World War II, but the town council finally gave in to allow a big dance when the soldiers came home in 1945. More recently, we remember how when the Berlin Wall finally came down, thousands of people were passing around bottles of champagne and singing on the wall, rejoicing that this evil symbol of Communism was at last being knocked down. People rejoice after a war, and that makes sense.

How much more it makes sense for the people of God to be told here in Revelation 12 to rejoice at the continuing victory of Christ over Satan and his evil kingdom that so long oppressed us! It appears from this text that although we are worshipping on earth, in a real sense, our worship reaches up to the heavens. The One in whose name we are worshipping on earth has raised our souls with him already, up to the highest heavens. As Ephesians 2:6 says: '[Christ] hath raised us up together, and made us sit together in heavenly places in Christ Jesus…' Having cleansed us by his blood, he gives us full, sweet, and happy entrance into God the Father Almighty's presence. His winning of that battle gets us into heaven, even as it casts Satan out. Therefore, we have every reason to be a joyful people, and this joy of immediate access to a reconciled, smiling Father should always be reflected in our worship.

The Heavenly Sanctuary Purged by Blood. We are told something else about the miraculous effects of the blood of the Lamb in heaven itself in Hebrews. Perhaps to our surprise, Hebrews says that heaven itself has been cleansed by the finished work of Christ from the very presence of Satan who used to be, from time to time, allowed to go there. Listen to Hebrews 9:22–4:

And almost all things are by the law purged with blood; and without shedding of blood is no remission. It was therefore necessary that the patterns of things in the heavens should be purified with these; but the heavenly things themselves with better sacrifices than these. For Christ is not entered into the holy places made with hands, which are the figures of the true; but into heaven itself, now to appear in the presence of God for us.

How powerful are these words: 'To appear in the presence of God for us.' Jesus always had God as his Father because he is the eternal Son of God, bound in an everlasting communion of life, light and love with the Father and the Holy Spirit. Christ was always the beloved Son of the Father, in communion with the Holy Spirit, but after his incarnation, he enters into a different focus of life and activity. Having finished his atoning work on earth, by which he defeated sin, Satan, death and hell, he now appears before God primarily for us: 'Christ for us'. He came down for us and now as Hebrews 7:25 says, 'he ever liveth to make intercession for his saints'. Christ is there primarily to appear before the Father for us, tenderly to speak to his Father on our behalf. Instead of someone accusing us to God, as Satan once delighted in doing, Christ is there speaking to the Father for us. Knowing this, who would not rejoice?

Temporary Testing
There is another response to this successful first phase of the war: 'Woe to them that inhabit the earth and the sea, for the devil has come down and he knows his time is short'. So the second response is that we are warned of temporary testing, while we are on our earthly pilgrimage. We have the final victory, that is definite. Nothing can keep us from it.

Satan's Troublemaking Is now Limited to This Earth. The only thing the devil can do is now on earth, for he has been denied all access to heaven. Now he can only do two things against the saints. First, he can try to get a certain access to their conscience to make them feel condemned. This wretched being first of all, tempts you, and then if you give in to the temptation, he screams condemnation in your ear, as though he had never suggested it.

We know also the evil one is able to influence lost persons, inhabit them, and make them commit terrible crimes. It would seem that a high percentage of drug related crimes are in that category. For instance, a sniper who shot innocent people around Washington, DC, in 2002, left a tarot card where he had been. A young woman who burned some churches in Charlotte, NC, about the same time, was discovered by the police to have been a member of a Satanic cult. Some of the people who entered schools and shot children are said to have been into the occult. This should not surprise us, for the devil is a murderer from the beginning, and he engenders murderous thought in those whom he or his imps, inhabit.

That is why Peter warns us: 'Be sober, be vigilant; because your adversary the devil, as a roaring lion, walketh about, seeking whom he may devour: whom resist steadfast in the faith' (1 Pet. 5:8–9). James, the half-brother of our Lord, tells us 'Resist the devil, and he will flee from you' (James 4:7). The devil has no choice but to flee from any saint who resists him! When you resist the devil, you do so 'through the blood of the Lamb and the Word of the testimony'. What threw him out of heaven in the first place, will work now on earth, if you will resist the devil when he tempts you, either through evil persons or through the remnants of the flesh still within you. You overcome him by remembering and claiming in a particular situation of attack, Jesus' objective work: the blood of the Lamb and the testimony of the apostles. Then the devil has to flee from you.

Three Ways the Evil One Attacks the Saints
You are not worthy to preach. There will be few, if any, true preachers of Christ, who have not keenly felt many times before they got into the pulpit to preach: 'I am totally unworthy to be doing this'. But then we remember, 'I am not preaching myself or my merits; I am here to preach Christ who shed his blood for my sins and for all who will receive it by faith.' We are in the pulpit only to give the same word of the testimony of the apostles, that Christ shed his blood for us sinners. It was for me; God gave me the message. It is recorded in his Book; I did not write it. The effectiveness of the message, and the divine call to deliver it, do not depend on my worthiness, but on Christ's worthiness. We never preach in the foolish conception that we are wonderful, because it is not true, as God's Word tells us. But we do know someone who is wonderful. Isaiah 9:6 calls him: 'Wonderful counselor, The mighty God, The everlasting Father, The Prince of Peace.' Yes, he is wonderful, and that is reason enough for us imperfectly sanctified believers to proclaim the message, and keep pressing on one more time, whether we feel like it or not. When we do so, Satan has to flee the building.

You are not worthy to pray. The second mode of the devil's attack on believers is to do anything he can to keep them from prayer. One morning when our family was assembled for family worship, the phone rang, and later it rang two or three more times. We answered it once, and listened to it ring two more times, so we decided to take it off the hook. By this time the family was down on their knees for morning prayers. Next, a knock came at the side (glass) door of the room in which we were praying. But we prayed on, for I decided that they could wait, because we were in the presence of the King of Kings and Lord of Lords. Then I realized that the devil did not want the Kellys down on their knees seeking God's face this morning, and he sought to prevent it.

We probably do not realize how significant it is when we start praying in Jesus' name. Changes are going to come that would not have happened if we had not been praying. But Satan knows this, and desperately seeks to prevent us from doing so. One of the ways he tries to prevent our praying, even on urgent matters, is to suggest that we have already prayed long enough, and that since the Lord has not yet answered our petitions, we might as well give up asking.

It is well that Daniel did not give into this temptation, for he kept praying and fasting for three solid weeks. Great blessing would soon descend upon captive Israel, because Daniel did not give up after two weeks (which certainly feels like a long time; if that is your main activity, and especially if you are fasting). I do not know how much knowledge of spiritual realities the devil has (everything about him is limited, since he is a creature), but I suspect that he may know enough to be aware that if he can stop your intercession after only a certain while, he will be able to hinder, or even prevent your getting the answer. It may be that the devil knows enough to realize that if you persist in these intercessions for another week, you are going to get the intended blessing. Therefore, he will do all he can to make you stop short, for if your intercessions are answered, they will weaken his malign kingdom.

How will he get you to consider stopping short? He will say such things as, 'You are too imperfect and inconsistent to get these answers', or 'Someone else could do this far better than you. So, by all means, do stop praying, and stop now!' Perhaps the accuser of the brethren will use somebody in your family or church to say it.

How do we answer such deeply felt and cutting suggestions from an unseen, evil source? Two inspired texts will help us:

> For if our heart condemn us, God is greater than our heart, and knoweth all things. Beloved, if our heart condemn us not, then have we confidence toward God. (1 John 3: 20–21)

The late William Still accurately diagnoses this heart problem of Christians who are having trouble keeping at prayer in *Towards Spiritual Maturity*. He suggests, that very often it is the devil himself who sneaks into the remnants of our fallen, fleshly nature, hiding himself in the folds of our imperfectly sanctified humanity, so as both to suggest dirty thoughts, and then immediately to accuse us for them. The last thing he wants you to realize is that he, the evil one, has suggested unworthy attitudes, so that he can condemn your tender conscience for them. Mr Still gives an illustration of this 'wile of the devil' from *Pilgrim's Progress*, where the devil was whispering bad thoughts into Christian's ear, hanging just above his shoulder, and then, by grace, pilgrim looks around and sees who is the source of the trouble.

If our heart condemns us, what are we going to do? Look up to God, for 'God is greater than our hearts.' Then, in his appropriated presence we shall have confidence, as we remember all that he has done to declare us truly righteous through the shed blood of his well-loved Son. The Father reminds us through the inspired testimony of the apostles that every imperfection of every believer is covered by the blood of the Lamb. Hence, we believe 'the word of the testimony', and on that basis get onto praying ground, as we see in

1 John 3:22–3: 'And whatsoever we ask, we receive of him, because we keep his commandments, and do those things that are pleasing in his sight. And this is his commandment, that we should believe on the name of his Son Jesus Christ, and love one another, as he gave us commandment.'

Hebrews 10:19–20 and 22 speaks to this same issue:

> Having therefore, brethren, boldness to enter into the holiest by the blood of Jesus, By a new and living way, which he hath consecrated for us, through the veil, that is to say, his flesh…Let us draw near with a true heart in full assurance of faith, having our hearts sprinkled from an evil conscience, and our bodies washed with pure water.

Think of what that consecration through the pierced body of Jesus will always mean for your ability to keep getting through to God, so as to have your prayers answered. Triumphs of prayer over the kingdom of evil depend upon our keeping this at the front of our minds!

You are not worthy to witness. The devil will attack you in yet another area: that of your bearing witness to lost people. He has various ways to get at us to stop being soul-winners. One of his most effective ploys is to take part of the truth, while he hides the other side of it. We do not deny that we are imperfect in our Christian walk. But Satan hides, if not denies, the other side of this truth. I am made worthy to bear testimony, not in myself, but in and through the blood of the Lamb. So long as Satan hides the truth of your standing in the gospel, then he will be able to keep a seal on your lips, so far as witnessing is concerned.

In 1967, as a student minister, I attended a conference on evangelism sponsored by the Synod of North Carolina, at St. Andrews College. D. James Kennedy spoke, just when he was establishing Evangelism Explosion, which has won so many people to Christ. He told us that they gave Christians questionnaires to fill out, asking the question: 'Why do you not witness more than you do?' he said that the vast majority of the answers replied: 'Because of my life'.

How shall we imperfect Christians answer this question of an imperfect life, keeping us from evangelism? Of course, our life is imperfect, but God has purposely put his heavenly treasure into earthen vessels (1 Cor. 4). We are earthen vessels. We are marred and we have quirks. What are we but 'clay jars'? Yet in this work of salvation, God has put heavenly treasure, heavenly light, into us with all our human weakness. Perhaps surprisingly, it is often our very weakness that will commend us, so that the unsaved will say: 'We know you are not perfect, but it looks like there is something there to enable you to get through this difficult life with something beautiful from another place. We wonder what it is?' We then talk to them, and that is how it works. Pay close attention to 1 Corinthians 4:5–8, 10:

> For we preach not ourselves, but Christ Jesus the Lord and ourselves your servants for Jesus' sake. For God who commanded the light to shine out of darkness, hath shined in our hearts, to give the light of the knowledge of the glory of God in the face of Jesus Christ. But we have this treasure in earthen vessels, that the excellency of the power may be of God and not of us. We are troubled on every side, yet not distressed; we are perplexed, but not in despair…Always bearing about in the body the dying of the Lord Jesus, that the life also of Jesus might be made manifest in our body.

That is God's evangelism program for imperfect believers such as we are.

32

The Dragon Attacks the Church

Revelation 12:13–17

Revelation 12:13–17, is a rather strange picture, but one that explains much that is otherwise inexplicable, where the church and the world interact. It shows us that the church is being attacked by a foe who has already been finally defeated. To keep up our courage and be strong, we have to keep in mind that the worst enemies that are sent out against us are sent out by a foe who knows that he has, in principle, already been defeated.

A Defeated Foe Who is Still Breathing

The famous New Testament scholar, Oscar Cullman, said that the continuing battle of the devil against the Christian church can be compared to the action of Adolph Hitler and the Nazis after D-Day. On D-Day, the allies stormed into Normandy, where Hitler's armies had made a last stand. My father was in the troops that landed at Normandy. At the mercy of the Lord he lived through it, although it had been so rough it was clear he did not like to discuss it. At the loss of considerable life on our side, the Germans were already, in principle, defeated. World War II was all but over. Many of Hitler's top generals and admirals begged him to come to an accommodation with the allies, to make some kind of peace treaty to keep Germany from being destroyed. Yet Hitler, despite knowing he was defeated and that the Russians were pushing in on the other side, like the evil one here, he kept on fighting to the last.

In Revelation, instead of twentieth century combatants, we are given a picture of the Dragon or the serpent, the devil who is attacking the church. We see how the Lord deals with those attacks. We note three points in this text:

1. Why does the devil attack the church (Rev. 12:12–13)?
2. How does God protect the Church (Rev. 12:14–16)?
3. What does the Church do to help win (Rev. 12:17)?

Why Does the Devil Attack the Church?

This passage clearly indicates that the reason for his attack is that he was cast down when Christ was enthroned. The evil one lost all influence in heavenly places. Therefore, the last area in which he can have any influence is the earth and the sea, because Christ is on the throne with the Father, ruling over all the heavenlies. We have seen that the devil cannot have any influence in the heavenly places, as he did, for instance, in the book of Job. He cannot get at the risen Lord who defeated him on the cross, through the empty tomb and the ascension to heaven, much as he tried to do so during the life of Jesus.

What can the devil do, since he will never repent? If he cannot get at Christ, the Head of the church, the next best thing he can do is get at the body of Christ, the church, on her earthly pilgrimage. It is significant that the risen Jesus came down and met Saul of Tarsus when he was laying waste the church, getting Christians into jail and helping hold the cloaks of those who stoned the first Christian martyr, the deacon Stephen. The risen Lord confronted this persecutor, who would later become the great apostle to the Gentiles. He asked this Saul: 'Saul, Saul, why persecutest thou Me?' (Acts 9:4).

The Devil Hates Christ in Christians

Although his knowledge is limited, the evil one knows that Christians on earth are in an intimate union with the Lord Jesus Christ, who is on the throne. The devil cannot get at Christ, so he tries to get at those who are in union with Christ. Even though he is given a limited range of activity in which he can come against the church, this passage shows us something to encourage us in the midst of battle in a hostile, unbelieving world. The church, even on earth where Satan goes 'about as a roaring lion, seeking whom he may devour', is still sheltered by the providence of God. Even down here in a very difficult scene of conflict, Satan's stratagems against us will eventually, in every case, be defeated. He will not achieve the goal he has in mind when he comes out against goodness, truth, and Christianity.

John is shown this because it is easy to forget who is in charge when you are in a battle. The early church needed this kind of encouragement.

This was particularly relevant because the Roman Empire at this time, probably the AD 60s, was severely persecuting the young Christian church. Many were being imprisoned, some were being killed; John himself was in exile on the Isle of Patmos. Those believers felt small, isolated, separated and weak, especially when they considered how powerful the world-wide Roman system was culturally and politically arrayed against the Christian believers. To those who felt weak, John brings a message of incomparable strength. It is that way today. We can feel weak and beleaguered and forget that our ancient foe, who lies behind every attack against goodness, truth and honor, is in for another trouncing, even as he comes out against us with such force.

Two Contemporary Dangers

I would say that the Christian church in the world today faces two great dangers. The first is Islam and the second is Western secular humanism. Both deny that the Father sent the Son to be our Savior and Lord. Islam and secular humanism are very different, but they have in common that they are against the true Christian church. The challenges from Islam are increasing in many different regions of the world, and are likely to continue to increase.

In our Western countries, secularism, with its materialistic philosophy, refuses to accept that there are differences between the world religions. It goes against their theory of the total irrelevance of all religion and that all religions are equal, and, at bottom, the same. Underlying that, is their assumption that no religion is really valid, and that all of them are backwards and detrimental. Yet in Western culture, most secular humanists tend to be apostates to the Christianity of their grandparents (or perhaps they have rejected traditional Judaism). For the most part, there is a particular antipathy to the Christianity that they abandoned. Bernard Goldberg's book, *Bias*, effectively shows how this antipathy to the religious foundations of the West is keeping governments from facing the real dangers that are coming against our freedom and moral standards.

This assumption that religion cannot be considered as a factor in public behaviour makes it impossible for us to face the real international issues. If the guardians on the city wall are blind, who will announce that the enemy is at the gates? Paul asks, 'If the trumpet sound with an uncertain sound, who shall prepare himself to the battle?'

The devil takes many different forms over the generations by which to attack Christianity and the culture it has engendered. It is nothing new, but each time it happens in a different form, we feel it is new and that things are out of control, but they are not. Revelation 12 shows us that although the times may indeed be stressful, things are never out of control.

How does God Protect the Church?

That leads us to the second point in this text: How does God protect his church? Notice that it is not humanly elected political authorities who take care of the church (Rev. 12:14). That is rare in history, although sometimes it does happen. Most of the time you cannot depend on the political system, for it changes so fast and it can be treacherous. We have frequently noted that somebody else is taking care of the church; somebody who is infinitely more effective than any elected or despotic government.

We see that this woman, whom the devil is coming out against, is given two wings: the wings of a great eagle, to get away from the place of danger into the safety of a remote wilderness. She stands for Israel in the Old Testament and the church in the New Testament, for Eve and the virgin Mary, for all who were on God's side to reproduce the truth of Christ. What does it mean that this woman is given the wings of an eagle?

The Protecting Wings of God in the Old Testament

As always we go back to the Old Testament, particularly Exodus chapter 19:4–6, where Moses is speaking: 'Ye have seen what I did unto the Egyptians, and how I bare you on eagles' wings, and brought you unto myself'. It is like the Lord lifted the Israelites out of slavery in Egypt, and bearing them on eagles' wings, crossed the Red Sea into the safety of the wilderness; that is where the apostle John gets his picture. Or this same Moses is speaking in Deuteronomy 32:10–11:

> He found him [that is, God found him, his people] in a desert land and in the waste howling wilderness; he led him about; he instructed him; he kept him as the apple of his eye. As an eagle stirreth up her nest, fluttereth over her young, spreadeth abroad her wings, taketh them, beareth them on her wings, so the Lord alone did lead him and there was no strange god with them.

Then these wonderful verses from Psalm 91:4–11: 'he shall cover thee with his feathers, and under his wings shalt thou trust; his truth shall be thy shield and bucker, for he shall give his angels charge over thee to keep thee in all thy ways'.

I remember as a child, being on the old Blue Family property of my great-great-grandparents, where my great-aunt Maude still had lots of hens, free-ranging all over the property. I stood on the front porch watching a sudden summer thunderstorm come up, and observed one large old hen that had about twelve or fourteen biddies. This old hen was a very solicitous mother-hen. She ran around and clucked to the biddies, leading them to stand in the corner of the rock chimney, where the roof of the old house extended out, giving them refuge from the torrential downpour of summer rain. I was fascinated to see how all those dozen or so biddies took refuge under her wings. After the thunderstorm was over I stepped off the porch to see if the biddies were actually dry. Although the mother hen was wet, since the rain had poured down in waves upon her feathers, every one of her biddies was dry. God is caring for his believers at least as much in the times of their travailing, as did that mother hen. It seemed to me as a small boy, and even now as an older man, that that big, old Dominicker hen had a beam of the light of God in her nature. It was a picture of how God protects his church.

Varying Significance of Time References
God's protection of his Church is given a certain time reference in this verse (Rev. 12:14b). It speaks of 'time, times and half a time', that is, three and a half years. This time reference takes us back to Daniel 7:25. If Revelation was indeed written in the AD 60s, then we can find a literal fulfillment of this temporal promise in what happened to Jerusalem shortly before AD 70.[75]

Historic Fulfillment
In that case, there was a literal fulfillment of three and a half years when the Romans came against Jerusalem in 67 AD. We saw earlier how Christ had warned his church in his prophetic discourse in Matthew 24-5 that when they saw the abomination of desolation, that is the Roman armies with their idolatrous images and banners surrounding the city, then to get out and flee immediately to a place of safety. The Roman soldiers, led by Cestius Gallus, for some reason that history has never known, did leave Jerusalem for several days; they retreated and the Jews followed and inflicted damage on the rear guard of the Roman army. When that happened, the early Christians remembered what Jesus had said would be the sign for them to get out of the city, so that thousands of them fled out of Jerusalem across the Jordan to a place of safety. As far as we know, not one Christian was in Jerusalem when the Roman armies came back and besieged it for three and a half years, until they finally laid it waste with utter devastation. The Christians had been, as it were, on eagles' wings, lifted to a place of safety known as Pelham across the river. So there was a literal fulfillment of this for the Church in the first century.

A Continuing Principle
Without denying the literal, historical fulfillment, there is also a continuing, or 'principal' fulfillment at times in history, when the Church goes through heavy persecution. In the two thousand years since the historic fall of Jerusalem, the providence of God allows the evil one at particular periods to come out with tremendous fury against the church. Kistemaker is right in suggesting that what is spoken of here, the time, times and half a time, means that for limited periods of time before Jesus returns, the evil one can come out against a church, but God will intervene to protect his people, as they look to Him.[76] Chilton brings out the same point: 'The deliverance of the Judean Church...is representative and illustrative of the deliverance of the Church as a whole...'[77]

Different Ways God Protects his Church
There are several ways he protects his church. How does he do it? At times, civil governments, which are supposed to protect their people, can come under the influence of Satan. So how would the church be protected, if the civil authorities are fiercely opposed to it, as they were for so many years in the USSR?

The Lord has a variety of ways to do so. Sometimes he providentially removes his people to another country. That's how it was in the 1620s and the 1630s when the Pilgrim Fathers and the English Puritans left the persecution of the British government and came to the freedom of the American continent, which was then a wilderness. Many of these Puritans felt that God got his church out of persecution 'on eagles' wings'. At other times, God protects his church by bringing down a wicked government. After much bloodshed, many tears, and many prayers, providence finally brought down the Soviet Union in 1991. There are still many problems in Russia and its former republics, but there is a great deal more freedom than has been known for centuries.

The Earth Swallowing Up Evil Floods
A strange picture is painted for us in verses 15–16. The serpent casts a flood of water out of his mouth to drown the woman, and to inundate believers, but God causes the earth to open up and immediately swallow Satan's attempts to drown Christian faith and those who hold it.

Again, to understand this symbol of the earth opening up and swallowing down the enemy, we have to go back to the Old Testament. In Numbers 16:28-33, Korah, Dathan and Abiram, stood against Moses and denied the leadership that God had given him. They raised a rebellion that, if it had been successful, would have destroyed the people of God during their wilderness journey, before they ever reached the promised land. It was yet another satanic ploy to destroy the people of God. In response to this malign rebellion, Moses spoke to the congregation in Numbers 16:26-33:

> Depart, I pray you, from the tents of these wicked men and touch nothing of theirs lest ye be consumed in all their sins. So they got up from the tabernacle of Korah, Dathan and Abiram, on every side; and Dathan and Abiram came out, and stood in the door of their tents, and their wives, and their sons, and their little children and Moses said, 'Hereby ye shall know that the Lord hath sent me to do all these works; for I have not done them of mine own mind. If these men die the common death of all men, or if they be visited after the visitation of all men; then the Lord hath not sent me. But if the Lord make a new thing and the earth open her mouth and swallow them up, [that is the exact phrase used in Revelation 12] with all that appertain to them and they go down quick into the pit, then ye shall understand that these men hath provoked the Lord.' And it came to pass as he had made an end to speaking all these words that the ground clave asunder that was under them, and the earth opened her mouth and swallowed them up, and their houses, and all the men that appertained unto Korah, and all their goods... and the earth closed upon them and they perished from among the congregation.

This opening of earth and the removal of waters reminds one of how Pharaoh's army had intended to re-enslave or kill the fleeing people of Israel. But God led, on eagles' wings, his people dry-shod through the Red Sea, whereas by the time Pharaoh's army got into the middle of the channel through the Red Sea, Moses waved his staff, and the waters came back down upon them with massive weight and drowned them, every one.

It may be over-spiritualization of this principle to say that it could refer to the floods of lies and false philosophies that Satan periodically sends to drown Christian truth, so as to keep people in spiritual and moral darkness and unbelief. The pressure of the intellectual culture in Western Europe since the eighteenth century

Enlightenment against the Holy Trinity, the truth of Holy Scripture, mankind's sinfulness, and the grace of salvation through the blood of Christ has been constant and unremitting. Our cultural elites are in large numbers inundated in a flood of God-dishonoring lies.

But true Christians, whether the simplest person or the highly educated, will never be overwhelmed by such falsehoods, no matter how popular or attractive they are to the majority culture. One of the most powerful ways that God protects his church is to keep his people believing. For instance, Isaiah 43:2:

> When thou passest through the waters [even through the waters of the false philosophies of the reigning elite] I will be with thee; and through the rivers, they shall not overflow thee. When thou walkest through the fire thou shalt not be burned, neither shall the flame kindle upon thee.

What does it mean that the earth opens up to swallow the floods of destruction that Satan is sending against the people of God? Sometimes it can be taken literally, like Dathan, Korah and Abiram, being literally swallowed up, or the sea literally closing in on Pharaoh's army, so as to drown it. But at other times it could be much more subtle.

God controls everything with an exquisite network of his divine providence that takes every little fact and connection, even atomic connections, into account, because he is God. At times, the Lord lets things get to a certain point where the devil overreaches himself by a surfeit of evil within society. Things can get so bad within the basic creation ordinances of society: the family, marriage, church, government, schools, and honest economy, that God sends devastating judgments to remove great evils so as to clean up the earth. That may be an illustration of what Revelation 12:15–16 can mean when it says that 'the earth swallowed them up'. There may come many judgments to swallow up those elements that have violated the most basic commandments of God, and if they continue, would overturn the moral structures that sustain society.

What does the Church Do to Help Win the Battle?

Although God's superintending providence is our protection, nevertheless, the Church has a part to play in winning the struggle against evil. That is made clear in Revelation 12:17: '...the remnant of her seed, which keep the commandments of God, and have the testimony of Jesus Christ.' This shows us the important part we have to play.

Here is the background of our chosen role in the battle against the kingdom of evil. The devil seems to be particularly enraged against the Church, because something in the behavior of the true church infuriates Satan. What is it that he particularly hates to see in the church, that sends him into paroxysms of anger and fury? What he hates to see more than anything else is the likeness of Christ in a man, woman, or child. It grieves him to the heart.

Two Battle Actions for the Church

The two things that so grieve Satan are summarized at the end of verse 17, and these same two things are precisely what the church can do to help win this battle: namely, to keep the commandments of God and the testimony of Jesus. One of the signs of the new birth will be, not total perfection while on this earth, but over the course of our lives, a sincere desire and effort to please God, to keep his commandments, and to honor his character in our conduct. The basis of this heart-felt desire to please the Lord is our relationship to Jesus, which is summarized in the words 'keep the testimony of Jesus'; that is, hold to the saving gospel. Those two things are the greatest weapons you have against Satan: keeping the commandments in your life and enthroning Christ in your heart. Satan cannot handle that.

Obeying the Lord
These two life-motivations speak of obedience, as do 1 John 1:2–4, 'And hereby we do know that we know Him, if we keep his commandments', and 1 John 5:3, 'For this is the love of God that we keep his commandments. And his commandments are not grievous'. 'Grievous' means a burden to your spirit. On the contrary, they are liberation to the spirit. Figuratively speaking, it helps defeat the devil whenever you deny the self-life to please Jesus. He can't stand it! It sets him back! For instance, when you restrain anger in the stress of traffic, and show courtesy; when you refrain from critical words against an offensive, annoying person and instead pray for him, the devil hates it when you do that! But he is most pleased when you complain and fuss and harbor anger.

The Power of Praise
One of the worst things you can do against Satan is, instead of complaining, start praising the Lord. Merlin R. Carrothers wrote a book entitled, *From Prison to Praise*. He shows that although you cannot always change your circumstances, you can decide to stop complaining, and instead to articulate praise to God for he is in charge of all things, and has promised to bring you through. This change in attitude trips the devil. He wins when we complain; he loses when we praise. It is that simple!

From that point of view, the quiet, humble, unnoticed daily obedience of ordinary Christian men and women is as significant in winning major spiritual battles in the long-term providence of God. The brilliant leadership of such officers as General MacArthur, walking the decks of ships in the South Pacific during World War II, or General Eisenhower leading the troops into Normandy was extremely important. But we will be shocked at the end of time to see how major to achieving the overall victory was the unobserved service of ordinary little Christians in a corner that nobody knows about; denying self and praying instead of worrying, praising instead of complaining.

That may well be part of what Jesus means when he says: 'The last shall be first, and the first shall be last'. On the Judgment Day, when it is all over, some of the humble ones who were largely unknown during their lifetimes will probably be much closer to the throne than the great ones. God has arranged human life and the progress of the Church so that we have to be little, we have to be small, for God to let loose his mighty power through us. God does not like to release his fragrance, blessing, and power through a proud, self-important person. Those who are nothing in their own eyes, like David was as a shepherd boy and when he first went to be king, are the ones through whom Jesus can let loose major power and win major victories. They do not see it. We do not know. We trust him in the small, and all the time he is winning big victories. As David once sang out in the Psalm: 'Thy gentleness hath made me great!'

Holding to the Gospel
The basis of seeking to please the Lord by denying self, is that we continue to hold to the testimony of Jesus. The basis of all this is:

Jesus loves me, this I know;
for the Bible tells me so.
Little ones to him belong;
they are weak, but he is strong.
Yes, Jesus loves me.

Jesus died for my sins. He took my place. All that I deserve, he took on his head on Calvary. For the rest of my life, until the sweetness of an everlasting, never-ending eternity is fully mine, He—in exchange for my sin and guilt—is giving me all that he deserved at the hands of his Father. That is the gospel. And as we hold to that gospel, there is no power from hell or on earth that can stop us from accomplishing what God has planned for our lives; and in our own little way, though it may be much bigger than we know, in having a part in winning these victories that he has in store for his church.

33

THE CHURCH'S ENEMY
Revelation 13:1–10

One of the most important things in any kind of warfare is to know who your enemy is and what he plans to do to you, if he gets the opportunity. One of the difficult tasks of the United States and British governments has been to identify who of its citizens are members of terrorist cells, seeking to blow up targets in their own countries. They are expending considerable resources on this question, for it is hard to take out an enemy, if you do not know who he is or where he is. That is what Revelation 13 is all about; it identifies the enemy of the believer and of the Christian church, and that is a great benefit. We notice three things in Revelation 13:1–10.

1. Who is the enemy (Rev. 13:1–3; 5–7)?
2. The disaster of following superficial opinion (Rev. 13:4–8a).
3. The security of the saints (Rev. 13:8b–10).

Who Is the Enemy?

Revelation 13:1–3 and 5–7 identify the enemy of the Church. The Holy Spirit seems to have brought John down from the throne of God, and stationed him on the seashore. Perhaps at low tide he was standing on the sand between the sea and the land, and here on the seashore, John could see clearly the church's enemy. There on the beach, John sees this terrible beast rise out of the sea. What he saw helps us face the opposition and sometimes open persecution that Christians find from the first coming of Christ to his triumphant second coming.

Meaning of 'the Sea'

It will help our understanding of this pictorial event to look at the usage of the term 'the sea' in Holy Scripture. That gives us the clue as to who the church's enemy is, because it shows us what context he is rising out of. In Revelation 9:1–3, the sea is associated with 'the abyss', the dark, ugly, horrible, satanic pit where the demons are locked up for a time, and on occasion they are allowed to get out. We see this in Luke 8:26–33, where the Lord Jesus set a man, who was demon-possessed with a whole legion of demons, free from these unclean spirits. They had demonized him so that he was naked, dangerous, and did himself violence. The large host of unclean spirits besought Christ that he would command them to go out into the deep, and so Jesus released them to go into a herd of swine, who were feeding in a pasture overlooking the sea. These unclean animals (according to Old Testament law) then rushed down into the deep, where they drowned and the demons went back into the deep place.

In Isaiah 57:20, this phrase is used about the sea, 'The wicked are like the troubled sea that cannot rest; it casts up mire and dirt'. Later, in Revelation 17:15, we are told something else about the sea: 'And he said unto me, the waters which thou sawest where the whore sitteth, are peoples and multitudes and tongues and nations'. Therefore, in Scriptural usage, 'sea' can mean literal sea, where the demons were cast down on their way into the deep places where they are locked up, and it can also mean unregenerate, ungodly nations that are being manipulated by Satan and his foul realm of spirits.

Out of this chaotic, demonic realm sometimes called 'the sea', referring to unregenerate peoples who are motivated by the devil, there emerged the powerful government of Rome. At the time of John, it was being used, and would be for several generations, to persecute the church. This beast that comes out of the seas with ten horns and seven heads can take different forms in different periods of history. He was an image of the dragon, the evil one himself, in Revelation 12:3, and he appears again in Revelation 17.

Ten Horns

Revelation 17:12 suggests that the ten crowned horns of the beast relate to the ten provinces of the Roman Empire, which was the world empire at that time. It had ten provinces. Many scholars believe that the seven heads refer to the line of the Caesars who reigned over that empire. One of those Caesars, about whom we will see more in the next chapter, was the terrible, perverted emperor, Nero.

History indicates that Nero set up a 120 foot statue of himself, and wanted people to worship it. Coins were struck, some of which still exist, in the time of Nero and some of the other emperors, on which is inscribed the name of the emperor in Latin: 'Dominus et Deus'—'Lord and God.' Their pretensions reached the point of wanting to stand in the place of God; they wanted to be worshipped.

Because the early church worshipped God alone and refused to worship anyone else, they brought terrible persecution on themselves. Many take 2 Thessalonians 2:3-4 to be referring to what was happening in the time of Nero, when John and Paul were living:

Let no man deceive you by any means, for that day shall not come except there come a falling away first, and that man of sin be revealed, the son of perdition; who opposeth and exalteth himself above all that is called God, or that is worshiped; so that he as God sitteth in the temple of God, showing himself that he is God.

Others consider it to be sometime in the future, but the main point to consider here is the blasphemous pretension of many political systems. When they get enough power, some of them want to put the government into the place of Almighty God. Scripture teaches that civil government is ordained by God, and that believers are to honor it insofar as we can (Rom. 13). The difficulty is, that the evil one gets into civil governments, particularly the stronger they become, so that they want to become like God, replace his laws, and take oppressive action against any who oppose their pretensions to total lordship. The Roman Empire was doing that.

Four Beasts

Rome was pictured later in Revelation 13 as acting like ravenous, predatory animals, which takes us back to Daniel 7, with the lion, the bear, the leopard, and then a fourth beast, a terrible creature with iron teeth and ten horns. It seems that Rome combined all the worst features of the previous three pagan empires: Babylon, Persia, and Greece. Yet Rome is stronger and, if possible, has more pretensions to divinity than the first three.[78] Under Nero's Rome, the first official persecution of the Christian church was launched. It appears to many scholars that it was in the light of that Neronian persecution that Revelation was written, when the seven churches of Asia were being laid waste by this terrible emperor, who evidently saw the church worshiping Christ as a threat to his own desire to be worshiped.

Age-old Struggle between the Two Seeds

We are told a strange thing in verse 3: 'And I saw one of his heads (this terrible beast that rose out of the sea) as it were wounded to death, and his deadly wound was healed. And all the world wondered after the beast'. What can 'the wounding of the head of the beast to death' mean?

To find out, we have to go all the way back to Genesis 3:15, which is the first promise of the gospel. After Adam and Eve had sinned and brought death upon our race, putting us under the judgment of God, because Eve had heeded the temptation of this dragon, God nonetheless was not through with the human race. He makes a promise to Eve, our first mother, in Genesis 3:15. In this first promise of the gospel, the Lord promises Eve that she would have a seed, and this awful serpent who had been judged by God would be thoroughly broken down and brought to naught under 'the seed of the woman'. The serpent would bruise her Seed's heel, but the Seed of the woman would crush the serpent's head.

We have already traced this struggle between 'the two seeds' all the way through the Bible:

the seed of Eve, the seed of Noah, of Shem, of Abraham, of David; and finally, the Seed of the Virgin Mary—our Lord Jesus Christ—God and man: two natures in one person. The New Testament makes clear that the life of Christ was the ultimate battle royal between the two seeds. Through the substitutionary death of Jesus on the cross of Calvary, all the sins of all who would ever be identified with Christ by faith were paid for. By his resurrection, all believers in principle were exalted in him above all the powers of Satan, the opposing seed. Particularly when the risen Christ ascended to the Father's throne, Satan was cast down, and limited in what he could do. The grace of God appearing in Christ Jesus in the gospel reversed the powers of Satan, and, in principle, did him in.[79]

The Disaster of Following Superficial Opinion (Rev. 13:4 and 8a).

The second part of these first ten verses of Revelation 13 shows us the disaster of following fickle public opinion (v. 4, 8a). How quickly public opinion seems to change, even before the kind of ubiquitous media we experience today. Though the evil one was, in principle, defeated by Christ, nonetheless he was not completely removed from the scene, and will not be until the last day. Only then will he be completely cast down into the Lake of Fire. Until then, he has a limited range in which he can go about as a roaring lion, encouraging the wicked persons and their evil governments to sin, so as to do harm to God's people.

The Wounded Beast Gets New Power

In verse 3, the situation suddenly changes after the head of the evil beast was wounded to death. Something strange happens. It seems that the beast gets new power; somehow he rises up, and, according to several interpreters, while he is rising up, the Jews in Jerusalem (before it was destroyed) began persecuting and killing the church.⁸⁰

You may have read during 2002, that a very strange coffin—what they call an ossuary—a stone box that contains bones, had been discovered, possibly going back to the first century. Inside of the lid of the box it says (in Hebrew): 'Jacob, [James] son of Joseph, and brother of Christ—brother of the Lord.' The authenticity of the box was debated, but whether it is authentic or not, the death of James, one of the leaders of the Church in Jerusalem, shows that the beast seemed to come back from his defeat for a while. He got power from the abyss to release demons and to do great harm against the church.

We read that the world wondered after the beast after he got this power. On the earlier dating of Revelation, the beast refers to apostate Israel, who was able to manipulate the authorities of the Roman state to persecute the Christians. There is a question as to how you would translate 'the world wondered after the beast'. Some have restricted that to the land of Israel wondering after the beast,⁸¹ although I am not sure that it should be so restricted to that one time and place.⁸²

One might plead in its favor John 19:15, 'And Pilate said to the Jews, behold your King (that was Christ.) But they cried out, "Away with Him! Away with Him! Crucify Him!" Pilate saith unto them, "Shall I crucify your King?" The chief priest answered, "We have no King but Caesar."' In that case, the religious authorities were compromising and making themselves one with the people who had the raw power in their day: the Roman Empire. When the beast (the powers of evil) seem to be running the land, it is surprising how quickly decent people will go along with the most wicked political regimes; they tend to worship the beast. One could use 1930s Germany as a tragic illustration.

Three and a Half Years of Persecution
Nonetheless, we are not to be discouraged, because Satan's time to persecute Christians and to win limited victories is fairly short. Verse 5 speaks of forty-two months, 'Three and a half years'. Again, how do you interpret that?

Many commentators point out that Nero's persecution of the early church endured for exactly forty-two months, from November 64 to June 68. Yet it is saying more than that, because there were other persecutions later in the century, from Domitian onwards, and later in AD 250, Decius, and then others. Persecution has continued at various intervals until today, but the periods of time that the evil one is allowed to make open war with the saints by using wicked governments to do terrible things to those who profess the gospel are always limited. Ultimately, God hems in the devil, even in this fallen world. Persecution and dark times are always limited.

The Lamb's Book of Life
Who refuses to go along with Satan's program during the times when evil appears to hold sway? Revelation 8:8 makes it clear that those who do not go along with it are those whose names are written in the Book of Life. On the contrary, those who do go along with demonic movements against God, Christ and the holy gospel, are said in the same verse to be those 'whose names are not written in the Book of Life of the Lamb slain from the foundation of the world'.

In other words, we are given here a telescopic view from the throne of God, when the whole universe shall be assembled before God at the end of time. Much that is now a mystery will then be made plain. We will see that those who refused the gospel and participated in persecution of those who loved God did so of their own volition, against many calls to repent. At the same time, we will see that their names are not written in the Lamb's Book of Life. This knowledge is now hidden from us, but it is all recorded in God's Book, and one day we will see that he carried out his Book with truth, justice, and goodness. None will be able to criticize Him.

We creatures are limited by the time series of past, present and future. But God inhabits eternity, where past, present and future are all spread out to Him. He can work with them anytime, anyway, for he is not limited like we are. Future and past are as much in his sight and control as is the present. Those whose names are not written in the Book of Life adamantly refused to accept the offers of the gospel; they compromised with the evil powers for their own self-interest; they refused to discipline their lives and give their hearts to Jesus. Indeed, some used religion to advance their own interest while disbelieving in the Lord and in his Word. Some of them actually taught in theological institutions where they openly denied the truth of the Scriptures.

Jesus tells us in Matthew 25 that many of those who used religion, but rejected the Savior will be surprised on the last day that they are not going into heaven. Many who will be cast away into outer darkness, says Jesus, will protest: 'But Lord, did we not in Thy name prophesy and in Thy name do many wonderful works?' he will reply: 'Depart from Me, you workers of iniquity; I never knew you'. Those who finally and fatally compromise with evil are those who never knew the Lord, those whose names are not written in the Book of Life. They have only themselves to blame, given the rich opportunities that were offered them of faith and repentance. Instead, they chose to follow superficial public opinion, and it finally landed them in the pit.

The Security of the Saints

By 'saints', the New Testament does not mean a sinlessly perfect person; it means a true believer, as we see in 1 Corinthians 1:2: '...sanctified in Christ Jesus, called saints...' 1 John 1:8–10 indicates that these saints need to keep confessing and forsaking sins.

Who Is in the Book?

The saints will always be given grace to hold out, because their names are written by God in the Book of Life of the Lamb slain from the foundation of the world. You might say, 'The good people get in the Book'. No they do not. The saints are only in the Book because Jesus' blood was shed for them and they accepted the gospel. They are not good; no one of us is good. We need the shedding of his blood; we need Christ to be our Savior. The only way any of us were written in that Book is in view of the grace of God in Christ, planning what Jesus would do, and including us with grace sincerely to receive that gospel.

The real question is not to be able to discern ahead of time who is in the Book of Life and who is not. That is none of my business. Such matters belong to God alone, for 'The secret things belong unto the Lord our God, but the things that are revealed unto us and our children that we may do them' (Deut. 29:29).

The Only Right Question

John Calvin, who had much to say about predestination and election, is a safe guide for us here. In his *Institutes of the Christian Religion* (III, 24:4–5), he wisely says that we are not to ask questions about who is elect and who is not elect. That is not the question for a sinner to raise; God will take care of that. The question is, Do I receive the gospel that Jesus died for sinners? Do I confess that I am a sinner and unworthy to get into heaven, to stand before God, to bow down and say, 'Lord, I receive as best I am able the atoning sacrifice of Your Son; I do not deserve it, but I ask that You would deal with me as You deal with Your Son; impute his death to me; impute his holiness to me. Then when the time comes, take me home to be with You'? When the books are opened, and the names are read out, all who do that will find that their name is written by God's grace in the Lamb's Book of Life. Calvin says that we are never to seek for assurance 'outside the way' (that is, the simple way of the gospel). Instead, we are to look for assurance in the only certain way offered to sinners: believing in the gospel that Jesus died for my sins.

Perseverance of the Saints

Certainty that the saints, the elect, will always hold out, even when it looks like everybody is going against what they stand for, is found in 1 Peter 1:2–7 (only a few of the words):

> Elect according to the foreknowledge of God the Father…by the blood of Jesus, born again…kept, by the power of God through faith unto salvation, ready to be revealed in the last time…Wherein you greatly rejoice, though now, for a season if need be, ye are in heaviness through manifold temptations…that the trial of your faith, being much more precious than of gold that perisheth, though it be tried with fire, might be found unto praise and honor and glory at the appearing of Jesus Christ.

Along these same lines, Revelation 13 contains a paraphrase of Jeremiah 15, 'he that leadeth into captivity shall go into captivity: he that killeth with a sword must be killed by the sword; here is the patience and the faith of the saints'. Scholars ask if verse 10, which picks up from Jeremiah 15, refers to the unbelievers, or to what the saints have to go through? I tend to think it may be speaking of times of persecution of believers because it does say, at the end of verse 10, 'Here is the patience and the faith of the saints'. In other words, when it is difficult, the saints will not throw in the towel and give up; they will hold out, even when it involves captivity, as it did for so many.

That is precisely what John means in verse 10. 'Here is the patience and the faith of the saints', and the evil one, and all his minions and all the most evil governments and false religions can not conquer such patience and faith. God give it to us as we need it, and we will see, I believe, some major turnings in years that lie ahead should Christ tarry. Amen.

34

The Mark of the Beast
Revelation 13:11–18

The identity of the mark of the beast is one of the most controversial passages in Revelation. Before we look at that identity, we need to summarize the overall meaning of the passage, and then concentrate on the details.

The meaning of the passage is basically this: the only way for believers to live the happy life, especially in difficult times, is to look their worst enemies in the face, then look up to God and trust him to take care of us and our enemies. That is simple, yet profound. It is much easier said than done. Be realistic about the difficulties of life. Do not hide from them, but when you face the worst, look to God, trust in Him, and he will take care of it all.

John tells us about two horrendous enemies that the early church would have to face. We looked at the first beast in the last chapter, 'the beast from the sea'. We saw that 'the sea' represents the ungodly nations with their political, military, and economic power, which is arrayed against the Church of Christ. Revelation 13:1–4 showed us how God will take care of that enemy.

In this chapter, we look at a companion of the first beast, the second beast: 'the beast from the land'. Like the first beast, this 'beast from the land' hates believers and will exercise all the power he gets from Satan to break down Christian belief and those who hold it. But, the good news is, that both of these terrible enemies: the beast from the sea, and then this ominous, terrible beast from the land, have already been dealt a fatal blow by the Lamb of God. The evil one who has been fatally wounded still has some power, but it is limited, and ultimately he must fail, whereas Christ and his people must win.

So we note two points in this text concerning this beast from the land, whose number is 666.

1. Who is this beast (Rev. 13:13–17)?
2. What does his mark mean (Rev. 13:18)?

Who Is the Beast?

One must be careful in interpreting a Biblical symbol such as this number. I have heard sermons from men who were not careful to compare Scripture by Scripture; they immediately jumped from a symbol in Scripture to the front page of the newspapers, as though by this they could identify who this individual was. Some of these preachers actually named modern political figures and said they were the ones with the mark of the beast.

For this reason, it is important to consider the proper methodology for understanding this, and other difficult, symbolic or obscure passages in the Holy Bible. Otherwise, to use a famous expression, a difficult or figurative passage becomes a 'nose of wax.' Without some kind of objective principle of interpretation, you can take your finger and shape a nose of wax in any direction you want, particularly to fit into the political or cultural events of the time. Many have done this with 'the mark of the beast': 666.

One of the ways properly to interpret the Bible is this: we interpret the difficult passages of Scripture in light of the more simple passages. We interpret the symbolic passages in light of the plain passages. We interpret the few in light of the many. These clear principles go back at least to Augustine, who followed 'The Rules' of the fifth century Donatist of North Africa, Tychonius.

To state it another way, we must always seek to understand the Bible in the light of the rest of the Bible. That way we will come the closest to having God's mind on what these things mean. As *The Westminster Confession of Faith* (1.7) states:

> All things in scripture are not alike plain in themselves, nor alike clear unto all, yet those things which are necessary to be known, believed, and observed for salvation, are so clearly propounded and opened in some place of scripture or other, that not only the learned, but the unlearned, in a due use of the ordinary means, may attain unto a sufficient understanding of them.

With these principles of interpretation in mind, we can now seek to identify this terrible and sinister figure for the early church, described as 'the beast from the land'. Elsewhere in Revelation (16:13 and 19:20), he is described as 'the false prophet'. He is not the antichrist; that is a different being, to be discussed later. As used here, 'beast' means a powerful, horrible, exemplification of raw might and oppression.[83] Let us look at some of the characteristics that are given by John of this beast in Revelation 13.

Characteristics of 'the Beast from the Land'
Verse 11 says he has a deceptive appearance. He looks fine: a lamb with two horns. What could be sweeter, more gentle and innocent, than a lamb? What could be nobler and holier than 'the Lamb of God' slain for our sins?

But here it is a very ominous figure. No doubt, he wishes to look like Christ, so he can get your sympathy to deceive you, but he is a lamb with two horns, which means two appendages of power.[84] We are warned not to be deceived by his initial appearance, which at first glance seemed favorable. Most totalitarian dictators start out that way; they offer encouraging programmes to help masses of people get ahead, if only the people will give them the power. I could give several twentieth century illustrations of this.

In addition to his two horns (like a lamb), the beast from the land speaks like a dragon (Rev. 13:11). This obviously refers to the enemy of men's souls, who speaks with the voice of Satan, the serpent who tempted our first parents, as we have seen from Genesis 3 and Revelation 12:9. He uses deceptive speech to draw people away from the Lord. It is interesting that corrupt totalitarian political systems throughout history ultimately try to get the loyalty and finally the worship of the population away from God towards themselves. The totalitarian system does not just want your vote, it wants your worship. We will soon see how that was true in Rome.

The next characteristic of this beast of the land (Rev. 13:12-13) is that he has demonic power. He has more than human power. He is in league with the sea beast who controls the ungodly nations. Some commentators consider this unholy league between the two beasts to apply to apostate Judaism, which rejected Christ in union with pagan Rome.[85]

Assuming that Revelation was written shortly before the fall of the temple and the scattering of the Jews in AD 70, it makes good sense to identify the league between the sea beast and the land beast as the collusion between the unbelieving Jewish leadership and the Roman state to crucify Jesus. There was a certain cooperation between these two powers to try to wipe out the early church. So the sea beast represents the power of the nations organized under ungodly Rome, while the land beast represents the unbelieving leadership of first century Judaism. Those two beasts worked together against Christ and against his people. Many good commentators, however, do not agree that Rome and Jerusalem are intended,[86] especially if they hold to a late first century date for the writing of Revelation.

On either view, verses 12 and 13 show us that false prophets (or 'the land beast') can have supernatural ability to do things far beyond mere human power. This is confirmed by the words of Jesus in Matthew 24:24: 'For there shall arise false Christs and false prophets and shall show great signs and wonders insomuch that, if it were possible, they shall deceive the very elect'. Earlier in Revelation (11:3-6), it speaks of fire that they are able to control and to turn against the people of God. So Scripture teaches that the evil one is allowed, at special points in history, to give ungodly, supernatural power to those who hate the Lord, and to use this power to hurt what God is establishing. They can only go so far, but at times they do brutal things.

A third characteristic is that the beast uses this satanic power that he is given for a time, to deceive multitudes (v. 14). The text speaks of giving power to an image. Some have interpreted it to refer to a literal image, to which satanic power is given to speak. When we consider the way the Bible looks at idolatry, what is being spoken of here is more likely to be 'an image' in people's minds or affections, rather than a literal physical statue.

In our Western culture, an idol is something that you put in the place of God. That is our kind of idol. It is what you organize your thinking around instead of God. It is counting on something less than God as your ultimate point of reference. We see this in Romans 1-2, which says they worshiped the *creature* rather than the *Creator*.

Some people give their hearts to money. Others put sex above God and his moral requirements. But in this case, it seems to be a political system that says: 'Don't look to God; do not even worship God; instead, worship this government; worship what we can do for you. We will give you womb to tomb security; but do not put anything higher than human government, and we will make a paradise for you on earth'. That was the case with Roman political power, whose emperors were beginning to name themselves, 'Lord and God'. It is this idol that was given the tremendous power spoken of here.

A fourth characteristic of this beast is that it uses that power to kill believers, and those he does not kill he oppresses terribly for a limited time (v. 15-17). In other words, the beast uses this power that ultimately comes from the pit of hell to oppress those who will not worship him. Where he is able, he puts them to death.

There were foreshadowings of this in the Old Testament, as in Daniel 3, where 'the three Hebrew children': Shadrach, Meshach and Abednego were told to bow down and worship this image of King Nebuchadnezzar, set up in the plain. The drums were beating while a fire was blazing in a terrible oven, seven times hotter than a normal fire. But Shadrach, Meshach and

Abednego were true believers. Nebuchadnezzar's government wanted them to bow down and said, 'If you do not worship this government, you are engaged in treason. The only way to deal with treasonous persons, who are dangerous to the unity of the human political government, is to put them to death'.

The Mark of the Beast

Having looked at the beast, we now consider 'the mark of the beast'. Revelation 13:18 says: 'Let him that hath understanding count the number of the beast, for it is the number of a man, and the number is six hundred and sixty six'. So what does 666 mean, in light of Scriptural usage? Genesis teaches that man and beast were both created on day six of the creation, whereas God's perfect number is found on the day of rest: seven. Thus, 'six is the number of man, i.e. a human number'.[87]

To understand what 666 means in Scripture, we must consider the ancient way of counting, when the Bible was written. At that time, they did not yet have the system of numbers that we use. Our system of numbers is taken from the Arabs, but in ancient times a letter stood for a number. In Greek, *alpha*, the first letter of the alphabet, stood for 1. In Hebrew, *aleph*, the first letter in the alphabet, stood for 1. Thus, in the biblical languages, to represent a number they had to use a letter of the alphabet—'alpha numerology'. The letters for 666 in the text add up to the name Nero, Caesar.[88]

DeMar explains:

When Nero Caesar's name is transliterated into Hebrew, we get *Neron Kesar* (*nrwn qsr*: Hebrew has no letters to represent vowels). 'It has been documented by archaeological finds that a first century Hebrew spelling of Nero's name provides us with precisely the value of 666. Jastrow's lexicon of the Talmud contains this very spelling.[89]

When we take the letters of Nero's name and spell them in Hebrew, we get the following numeric values: n=50, r=200, w=6, n=50, q=100, s=60, r=200 = 666. 'Every Jewish reader, of course, saw that the Beast was a symbol of Nero. Jews and Christians regarded Nero as also having close affinities with the serpent or dragon…. The Apostle writing as a Hebrew, was evidently thinking as a Hebrew…Accordingly, the Jewish Christian would have tried the name as he *thought* of the name—that is *in Hebrew letters*. And the moment that he did this the secret stood revealed. No Jew ever thought of Nero except as *'Neron Kesar'*.[90] Those who read John's account of the Beast probably had come to this conclusion even before they made their calculation.[91]

Farrar writes: 'All the earliest Christian writers on the Apocalypse, from Irenaeus down to Victorinus of Pettau and Commodian in the fourth, and Andreas in the fifth, and St. Beatus in the eighth century, connect Nero, or some Roman emperor, with the Apocalyptic Beast.'[92]

We remember that John wrote to an early first century church that was experiencing terrible suffering as a persecuted minority in the Roman Empire, and through John, God gives them hope. He says that relief is coming in such words as: 'these are things which must come to pass shortly'.

The purpose of the Revelation was to comfort the Church with the assurance that God was in control, so that even the awesome might of the Dragon and the Beast would not stand before the armies of Jesus Christ. Christ was wounded in his heel on Friday, the sixth day, the Day of the Beast—yet that is the day he crushed the Dragon's head. At his most powerful, St. John says, the Beast is just a *six*, or a series of sixes, never a *seven*. His plans of world dominion will never be fulfilled, and the Church will overcome through her Lord Jesus… who conquered on the Eighth Day.[93]

To put this 2,000 years in the future and say that the Beast must be some political leader in the twenty-first century cannot be right. The risen Christ was saying, through John, that many things predicted in Revelation concerning the suffering of the church, and concerning the beast who was making the church suffer 'must come to pass shortly'. As we have argued, Revelation may have been written in AD 65 or 66, when Nero, the one to whom the 666 referred, was laying waste the church. In fact, he was Caesar number 6 and the first emperor who officially persecuted the Christian church. It may well have appeared that he was going to win, but the Lord promised that he would take care of him 'shortly'. Within a year or two of Revelation being written, Nero Caesar committed suicide in AD 68. About two years later, in AD 70, the unbelieving Jewish state, who, with the Romans, had sought to put out the light of the early Christian church, was destroyed.

A number of faithful New Testament scholars do not think that 'the Beast' can be identified with a particular individual, including Nero Caesar. Rather, they hold that a major principle is illustrated here, and that it was in action from the conflicts in the first century down to the end of time. Kistemaker writes in this vein:

> Although the devil has tried to eliminate all of God's people from the death of Abel to the present, he has never succeeded. In this age-old conflict not Satan but God is in charge. In conclusion, the number 666 belongs to Satan and not to one particular individual who did the devil's work in history.[94]

Even if one holds that Nero fulfilled the primary role of the beast in the first century, the principle would still hold true until the end that fallen humanity, motivated by the powers of evil, cannot finally prevail against the Lord and his Christ.

Imposing the Mark of the Beast
The mark of the beast would be put either on people's hand or on their forehead (v. 16). That raises a fair question: is the mark of the beast literal, or is it symbolic? When we say something is symbolic, it still means something very important, but not in a literal fashion. To know what it means requires some attention to the Biblical concept of imposing a mark, or branding.

One of the central texts of the Old Testament relates to this concept of marking, as we see in Deuteronomy 6:5–9:

> Hear, O Israel, the Lord our God is one Lord; and thou shalt love the Lord thy God with all thine heart and with all thy soul and with all thy might. And these words which command thee this day shall be in thine heart and thou shalt teach them diligently unto thy children and shall talk of them when thou sittest in thy house and when thou walkest by the way and when thou liest down and when thou risest up. And thou shalt bind them for a sign upon thine hand and they shall be as frontlets between thine eyes. And thou shalt write them upon the posts of thy house, and on thy gates.

Here you have the same idea of marking, placing the sign upon the hand and frontlets between the eyes. It means that one is under the Divine protection, that one has assimilated by personal faith the Word of God and who God is. One is committed to who God is in thinking and in action. The nineteenth century hymn expresses this idea:

> Take my life and let it be
> consecrated, Lord, to Thee.
> Take my hands and let them move
> at the impulse of Thy love.
> Take my intellect and use
> every power as Thou shalt choose.

Isaiah 44:5 deals with being sealed on the forehead: 'One shall say, I am the Lord's; and another shall call himself by the name of Jacob; and another shall subscribe with his hand unto the Lord, and surname himself by the name of Israel'. The ultimate seal on the forehead in the New Testament is of course, Christian baptism. We are baptized into the name of the Father and the Son and of the Holy Ghost. It is not a literal seal, although circumcision which it replaces was a literal seal. Colossians 2:11–12 shows us that the literal or visible seal has now been replaced by an invisible seal:

> In whom also ye are circumcised with the circumcision made without hands, in putting off the body of the sins of the flesh by the circumcision of Christ: Buried with him in baptism, wherein ye are risen with him through the faith of the operation of God who hath raised him from the dead.

An Invisible, but Real Mark

Thus, in true Christianity, the sign of the Holy Trinity is upon us. It is invisible, yet real. After the water of baptism has been administered, one can no longer discern the water, but what it represented. A new heart given by God, forever remains for all who are truly regenerate, and defines who we are for eternity. The initiatory seal is invisible, although you can tell it by its fruits.

So the concept of being marked or sealed is a symbolic action, though one that expresses profound reality. Ladd writes:

> It is not at all clear that John is thinking of a literal brand visible on the person of the worshippers of the beast. The seal of God placed on the forehead of the 144,000 (7:3) worshippers is surely not meant to be a visible mark; it is a symbolic way of expressing divine protection (see Isa. 4:5). The mark of the beast may be intended to be a parody on the mark of God.[95]

When God gives a mark to set apart his people, the mark is not visible to the eye. For example, in Revelation 3:12 we read, 'he who overcomes, I will make him a pillar in the temple of my God, and he will not go out from it anymore; and I will write upon him the name of my God, and the name of the city of my God, the new Jerusalem...'[96]

In summary, the mark of God or the mark of the beast is an expression of the deepest loyalty of the individual who has experienced its inner reality. Jesus said: 'No man can serve two masters...' Those under the mark of the beast will be ultimately destroyed by the hateful spirit to whom they are given over, but those who are under the mark of the Lord will be protected to eternal life.

Buying and Selling

Revelation 13:17 tells us that the powers of evil will keep those under the mark of the Lord from buying and selling. If Revelation was written before the Jerusalem temple was destroyed, then the buying and the selling probably has reference to activities in the temple. In Matthew 21:12, the temple leaders controlled the buying and the selling for any Jew to get into the temple. They started casting the believers out of the synagogue, like the man born blind whom Christ healed. To get into the temple you had to bring money and pay for sacrificial animals to have something to offer God in worship. When you were cast out of the synagogue they would not accept your money. In other words, you could not participate in the worship of God in the temple.

We read in Acts 21:26-30 of how Paul was literally dragged out of the temple. Jesus had said earlier that the temple has become a den of thieves (Matt. 21:12-13). The buying and selling probably indicates that opposition would intensify against Christ so that those who confessed Jesus could not buy and sell. They could not access the temple or what had always been believed was the holiest of all. Of course, the truth is that they did have access to the temple in heaven, for as Hebrews 12:22 says: 'You have come to Mount Zion and to the city of the living God, the heavenly Jerusalem, and to myriads of angels.'

> Revelation 13 and 14 contrast two ways of salvation: access to the temple through the mark of the Beast or through Jesus and the mark of the Lamb. Those who were circumcised in only their flesh followed the Beast, while those circumcised in the heart followed the Lamb.[97]

The Wounding and Return of the Beast

Revelation 13:3 speaks of the killing of the sixth horn: that is, the wounding of the beast, and then his coming back. What could that mean? In terms of the history of the Roman Empire and its struggle with the early Church, it could refer to the occasion when Nero committed suicide, having done horrible things to his own family, and having persecuted the Christians, falsely accused them of burning Rome. He killed himself in his early thirties. It looked as if Rome was going to fall apart. Rome had been wounded with a potentially fatal wound, and some Germanic tribes were already getting ready to move into Rome, but there seemed to be a healing. The Roman senate got things back together and the state reconsolidated its power, so the beast lived again and would be living for another two hundred or so years in which, periodically, it could persecute the people of God.

Nero, the beast, was killed, but Rome, in a sense, was healed, and lived on to persecute the Christians. Yet, ultimately the beast from the sea, and the beast from the land, were destroyed by the power of the gospel. God took his time to do it, but he did it and he did it right.

A Message to the Modern Church

What do such ancient historical events mean to the church? One thing it means is this: God fulfills his Word to the fullest letter every time he speaks it. 'God is not a man that he should lie'. God said through John that these things would 'shortly come to pass', and in five or six years, Nero was killed, Jerusalem was destroyed and the church was spreading. Some four hundred years later, the unbelieving Roman Empire was shaken down and replaced by 1,000 years or more of the growth of the Christian church. When God says 'Look at your enemies! I know it's bad. I know it's scary, but when you look at them, look up to Me. Believe in Me, I will take care of your enemies and I will take care of you.' God did it.

Even though the essence of this was fulfilled in the first century, nonetheless the devil is still on a chain. Although he still has influence, and from time to time motivates and empowers wicked governmental systems to oppress the church and kill its people, like the Soviet Union from 1917–91. But it came down. Something similar is bound to happen in due time in other countries that oppress the church. If God did what he said he would do, if he dealt with those who were oppressing the early church, he will continue to do so all through the ages—on his time schedule, not ours. The church will be victorious because Jesus is victorious. On the sixth day, and on the sixth hour, the Son of God was crucified on the cross, and he crushed the head of the serpent. The serpent is still writhing around to some degree causing some trouble, but he has lost his power to be finally successful.

In the Western world, which has to a large degree gone apostate from true Christianity, the real question is not what will happen in other nations that oppose us, but what will we do about ultimate Lordship? Will we repent and seek to come under the mark of the Lord, or will we continue in materialism, sensuality and unbelief, thereby identifying with the mark of the beast?

Remember what James promises: 'Resist the devil, and he will flee from you'. The devil has no choice; Christ has conquered. Resist the devil in your own life; he has no choice but to flee. Resist him therefore. We saw earlier that the suffering saints got the victory over a massively greater power than themselves, because 'they overcame him by the blood of the Lamb and the word of their testimony'. That is the good news for today. God says, 'Look at your enemies. Be realistic, then look up to Me, and thus you poor, frail, limited, ignorant humans can overcome things far more powerful than yourselves.' God will give us the victory as we turn to Him.

35

THE LAMB AND HIS FAIR ARMY
Revelation 14:1–5

This is a wonderful passage with a message much needed in a troubled world. Perhaps the best way to get the thrust of the passage is to consider a brief Old Testament episode in the life of Elisha, and a young servant who was helping him (2 Kings 6:15–17). They had been surrounded by a huge army, with men and chariots, wishing to put them to death. Old prophet Elisha was calm and happy, while his servant was horrified:

> And when the servant of the man of God [i.e. Elisha] was risen early and gone forth behold, an host compassed the city, both with horses and chariots; and his servant said unto him, 'Alas, my master, how shall we do?' And he answered, 'Fear not; for they that be with us are more than they that be with them.' And Elisha prayed and said, 'Lord, I pray Thee, open his eyes that he may see.' And the Lord opened the eyes of the young man; and he saw; and, behold, the mount was full of horses and chariots of fire round about Elisha.

The servant found out that when we are fighting the battles of the Lord, no matter how terrible the enemy looks, how loud the rumbling of their tanks and their planes buzzing overhead (to put this in modern times), God's invisible hosts are massively more powerful than a whole army. 'They that be with us are more than they that be with them'. In the first few verses of Revelation 14 it is as if John is praying concerning the church, which is undergoing great stress in an evil world, 'Lord, open their eyes and let them see what it's really like'.

Revelation 14 is answering a question raised by the previous two chapters: 'What about all this opposition to Christianity from this evil triad: the dragon, the beast from the land, and the beast from the sea? They manage to inflict a great deal of hurt and damage on Christians. What about it? What is the result of true believers standing fast against sin and being willing to suffer? Are we not having any effects in the world? Will we, after all, be defeated?'

This is the struggle of faith: in our life we can see the enemy against us very clearly. What we do not see is the invisible hosts that God has between us and the enemy to protect us. After meeting the horrendous enemies of chapter 13, we ask: 'How are we going to make it?' John lets us see what is really going on behind the veil, who is in charge, and what the final results will be of the battles that God lets his people go through in their earthly life.

I want us to look at four questions from Revelation 14:1–5:

1. Who has the high ground in this battle?
2. Who is with the Lamb who is on that high ground?
3. What kinds of sounds do they hear?
4. What is this ransomed army really like?

Who Has the High Ground in this Battle? (Rev. 14:1)

Several years ago, my wife and I were invited to watch the movie *Gettysburg*. The film was fairly true to what actually happened in 1863. In this battle, which helped turn the tide against the South, the Confederates were defeated, in large part because the Northern troops got the high ground at Gettysburg. The South did not move fast enough; J. E. B. Stuart was not on guard as he should have been; Longstreet did not make some of the right decisions to move up and take that high ground in time, so the North got the high ground, up on a hill. From that advantageous location, all they had to do was to mow down thousands of Southern young men in Pickett's Charge. Courageous as they were, and as hard as they tried, it is generally just a fact that the one that has the high ground usually wins.

'Lord, Open Our Eyes'

We are clearly shown in Revelation 14:1 that the Lamb of God, through his death, resurrection and ascension, on behalf of his people, forevermore possesses the high ground in every battle until the final one, when he and all of his will be totally victorious. But you have to see him with the eyes of faith, so that all the while you are going through such attacks as you find in Revelation 14, you must keep praying with Elisha, 'Lord, open our eyes.'

In Revelation 14, the Lamb of God is seen to be standing on Mount Zion. That reference brings to mind the temple mount in Jerusalem, but as to its application to the whole Church, we must ask: where is this Mount Zion? Is it on earth? Or is it in heaven? It is both. Christ is literally on the throne in heaven, which is ultimately the true Zion that the temple mount vaguely reflected (see Heb. 12:22–3). But even though he is standing in heaven looking down, he is with his people on earth, and able to surround them like the fiery angelic armies encompassed Elisha and his servant.

'Keeping Watch Above his Own'

We speak of Christ going up to the throne, and sitting down at the right hand of God the Father Almighty, as we are told in Hebrews 1, Acts 1, and in many other places. Upon his ascension, he was seated. But Revelation 14 shows that he is so interested in conducting the affairs of his church, particularly when they are in danger, that instead of sitting beside the Father, he is pictured here as standing up. We have an illustration of that in Acts 7, where the first Christian martyr, the deacon Stephen, was stoned to death by the unbelieving Jews. Indeed, Saul of Tarsus had a hand in that, which shows that people who do wrong to the church can be converted. While Stephen was being killed, his face became as it had been the face of an angel; it was reflecting the light of Jesus. Acts 7:56 tells us that Jesus was standing up and watching over Stephen's death. It is as though he was so interested, that he no longer remained seated on the throne. Instead, he stands, as though he were peering over the edge of glory, gazing with love upon his faithful servant Stephen, cheering him on, so that the light of Jesus is reflected in Stephen's face as he is being bashed to death.

So the Lamb is on mount Zion, but in this case, he is very involved, cheering on his people. Sometimes he lets them directly win the battle, and sometimes they win by losing. Had you ever thought of that?

In Deuteronomy 4:32, we are told about the high ground. 'Know therefore this day and consider it in thine heart that the Lord, he is God, in heaven above [which is where Mount Zion is] and upon the earth beneath. There is none else'. From there, the Lamb on Mount Zion is fully in charge of everything transpiring on the earth beneath. We see this high ground in Psalm 91:1: 'he that dwelleth in the secret place of the Most High shall abide under the shadow of the Almighty'. Or in Psalm 46:1: 'God is our refuge and strength, a very present help in time of trouble; therefore we will not fear though the earth be removed, though the mountains be cast into the midst of the sea, though the waters thereof roar and be troubled'. Similarly, in Psalm 27:1, 'The Lord is my light and my salvation; whom shall I fear? The Lord is the strength of my life; of whom shall I be afraid?' Or Psalm 23, 'The Lord is my Shepherd; I shall not want'. And then down to the end of that Shepherd Psalm: 'Surely, goodness and mercy shall follow me all the days of my life and I will dwell in the house of the Lord forever.'

From this high ground, the Lamb who has conquered and is continuing to conquer, attentively observes the conflict on the hills of the earth below. John is obviously drawing on Psalm 2 concerning the raging of the heathen and the desire of the kings of the earth to cast away God's law: 'Yet have I set my King upon My holy hill of Zion'

(v. 6). The Lamb is on mount Zion. The King is God's Son and he is in total charge (v. 12).

James Russel Lowell's hymn, 'Once to Every Man and Nation' expresses this truth of the divine solicitude and overruling of evil:

> Though the cause of evil prosper,
> Yet the truth alone is strong;
> Though her portion be the scaffold,
> And upon the throne be wrong,
> Yet that scaffold sways the future,
> And behind the dim unknown,
> Standeth God within the shadow,
> Keeping watch above his own.

This contrast between the enemies of God in chapter 13, and the Lamb on Mount Zion in chapter 14 shows us who really has the high ground. We can illustrate the contrast this way:

Revelation 13	Revelation 14
False lamb with two horns, devil imitating Christ (v. 11).	True Lamb.
The beast comes out of the earth (v. 11).	Mount Zion, the high place, the high ground, that's in charge of the earth (v. 1).
Worship of the beast (v. 12).	Song of the redeemed (v. 3).
Number of the beast (v. 18).	Number of the saints (v. 1).
Mark of the beast.	Name of the Father on the forehead.
Deception and dishonesty of the beast (v. 14).	No lie in the mouth of the saints (v. 5).

So who has the high ground? Christ and his saints, who by grace reflect the integrity of his pure character; that is what will turn the battle ultimately. The battle between good and evil ultimately does not primarily depend on physical resources or on places of worldly power. The outcome of this battle depends upon spiritual realities, not physical ones. So that is Who has the high ground: the Lamb of God.

Who Is with the Lamb?

In Revelation 14:1 we are told there are 144,000 on Mount Zion with the Lamb. What does that mean? It summarizes the church on earth and the church in heaven. We sometimes speak of the church on earth as the church militant and the church in heaven as the church triumphant. The number 144,000 is a way of saying, the whole church, past, present and future—the one you can see down here and the much larger church that you and I cannot see in the other world. This number, as we have seen previously, comes from the twelve tribes of Israel multiplied by the twelve apostles of Christ, then multiplied by one thousand, being the number of perfection or completeness. This symbolic number refers to the totality of all God's people who will ever be redeemed, from the gates of the Garden of Eden down to the last elect person, who will believe a split second before Christ comes back in his power. Thus, the whole church, militant, triumphant, and those yet unborn, is included in this number.

Unity with Our Relatives in the other World
Think of our deceased relatives, many of whom have lived a Christian life before us and before God, who have been taken home to heaven over the years of our lives. Is it not wonderful that they are in this number? They who are now at home with him are in the number; they are in the army of the Lamb. In that sense, we are still together! What a glorious truth.

Nothing matters in our life so much, as making sure we are in the army of the Lamb, in the number of those who confess their sins in the name of Jesus and trust him to save them. That is the most important question anyone will face in this earthly life. It's the big question. Settle that, and everything else will work out just right.

What Do the Saints Hear?

If you were in an earthly battle, you might hear planes overhead, or missiles, as was my father's experience in England during World War II. But what sounds does the Lord's ransomed army hear? These sounds indicate God's control over all the natural realm. First, they hear the sound of many waters, the tumult of the nations, the sound of thunder, and things that are rumbling around.

The Joy of a 'New Song'
But all that makes way for the sweet, beautiful sounds they hear: sounds of triumph, victory, and joy! The angelic harpers play on beautiful, melodious harps, then, as the harps are ringing with celestial beauty, they hear an angelic choir. It must have been the most wonderful singing that ever pierced their ears! The angels are singing 'a new song'. We are not given the words of that song, yet I refer you to Psalm 96: 'O, sing unto the Lord a new song; sing unto the Lord all the earth'. And then this new song goes on to specify (v. 10-11): 'Say among the heathen that the Lord reigneth; the world also shall be established that it shall not be moved; he shall judge the people righteously. Let the heavens rejoice, and let the earth be glad; let the sea roar, and the fullness thereof'. And it ends: 'Before the Lord, for he cometh, he cometh to judge the earth; he shall judge the world with righteousness, and the people with his truth'.

It is a new song because it was only recently before Revelation was written that the Lamb had been slain. He had shed his blood and paid the supreme sacrifice, magnified the law of

God, redeemed his people for all eternity, and been seated in the glory after his resurrection. Something wonderfully new has happened that changes everything in an old, dying, terrible world. Precisely *that* Lord is coming!

The Angels Are Already Singing!
Whatever this singing may have been, it did not come from the beast on the land, or the beast in the sea. Indeed, some say that Satan cannot sing a note. The singing came from somewhere else; it came from above their heads from the holy angels, who know how all this is going to turn out. The angels are already singing, for they see the way the battle will end. Even though the Christians are presently in very difficult circumstances, the holy ones know that under terrible pressures, the saints at battle are being changed more and more into the likeness of Jesus (see 1 Cor. 3:18, 4:16–18). That is why they are singing!

Is this not a word about the sheer inner joy of the Christian life? The world has no explanation for why a real born-again Christian is inwardly so happy. Although the personalities of believers vary considerably, and many of them will never be 'bubbly', every real Christian has a deep, inward contentment and joy that does not come from the world, and the world cannot take it away. C. S. Lewis, who was converted from atheism to evangelical belief entitled his autobiography *Surprised by Joy*. From a different time, Bernard of Clairvaux in the Middle Ages said: 'The love of Jesus, what it is, none but his loved ones know'.

There is something about being a Christian that the unbeliever does not hear; they do not perceive the music. Paul explains why: 'The natural man receiveth not the things of the Spirit of God, for they are spiritually discerned' (1 Cor. 2:14). When we have this opening of the ears by the Holy Spirit and this anointing of the eyes with the eye-salve of the Holy Spirit, we see, and we hear wondrous music that sets the soul singing. No matter what the earthly circumstances we will be called on to go through, our basic inner orientation is joy because it comes from God, who loves us and is ever victorious over all his and our enemies!

WHAT IS THIS RANSOMED ARMY LIKE?
What is the Lamb's ransomed army like? In a wonderful old hymn taken from the last words of the great Scottish saint, Samuel Rutherford, who helped write the *Westminster Confession of Faith* in the 1640s, there are these lines:

> The Lamb, with his fair army
> Doth on mount Zion stand;
> And glory, glory dwelleth
> In Immanuel's land.

What are the characteristics of the fair, beautiful, lovely army of the Lamb? Four are mentioned. I heard my father say that after Pearl Harbor was bombed, he soon got a telegram: 'Greetings from the President of the United States'. He knew what that meant: report to the draft board. So he did that and saw heavy service in Europe. But he was sent off to war only after the doctors had examined him.

The basic diagnosis here of the army is not of physical qualities, but of spiritual qualities: questions of faith and character. In Revelation 14, we are given a view behind the veil of what really works and what will really win. This diagnosis shows us that the ultimate question is not physical prowess, or political or economic power; it is a question of true spirituality. Those who by grace have been given the requisite spiritual qualities are in the fair army of the Lamb, and victory is assured by the King of Kings and the Lord of Lords.

Purity

Four qualities are given of the Lamb's fair army, as Rutherford would have called it. First, purity. Revelation 14:4 says that they are virgins, not defiled with women. This is a symbolic way of saying, 'They are not defiled with the whore of Babylon, the anti-God religious world system. They have not gone to bed with a corrupt system and sold out their heart to an anti-God program of religion, money, and politics. They are virgins; they are not defiled with women.

It does not mean there is anything wrong with Christian marriage, for marriage is given to us in scripture as one of the basic ordinances of God from the first creation. Hebrews 13:4 says, 'Marriage is honorable in all and the bed undefiled'. To be married in a normal relationship is in no sense defiling; it is approved by God and in every way, worthy. The idea here is that every soul who is in Christ is purged, and given a new virginity, as far as the eyes of God are concerned before the Judgment Seat. It is an imparted virginity, through the blood of Christ, and applied by the Holy Spirit. We are, in that sense, as a people, as a church, married to Christ; he is the heavenly Bridegroom and we are the bride. Hence, we are not to commit immorality against our heavenly Bridegroom, by going with another religion, by going with another way of salvation. Paul makes this clear: 'For I am jealous over you with Godly jealousy; for I have espoused you to one Husband, that I may present you as a chaste virgin to Christ' (2 Cor. 11:2). This means that our heart never goes away from our Lord; we never look to another to save us and to be the soul of our soul, but only to the Lord Jesus Christ.

Therefore, in this army, there is this immaculate purity. It is not that the members of the army on earth are sinless yet; they are not. Their purity is because they are looking to the Pure One, to Christ. They give him their heart, and they will not trust in anybody else; this is true purity.

Obedience

The second mark of the Lamb's army is obedience. 'They follow the Lamb wherever he goes'. Jesus says in Matthew 10:38 that if we do not take up our cross and follow Him, we are not worthy of Him. One thinks of the hymn by B. B. McKinley, the great Southern Baptist musician:

> 'Take up thy cross and follow Me,'
> I heard the Master say;
> 'I gave My life to ransom thee;
> surrender your all today.'
> Wherever he leads I'll go;
> Wherever he leads I'll go;
> I'll follow my Christ who loves me so;
> Wherever he leads I'll go.

This army is following Jesus. That is its strength, contrary to the worldly way of fighting, which says, 'You win, if you have enough personal resources.' In the only battle that finally matters, the person who wins is following the Lamb. That is what gets you there; not your own resources, but the Lamb whom you follow. What our life amounts to in the few short years we are given does not depend on our own resources. Thank God! It does not matter into what socio-economic status we are born; it is no disadvantage. How our life turns out depends entirely on the One we follow. Obedience to the Lamb is what wins the victory God has for us. I can win everything Jesus Christ wants me to win, without any resources in my self. Hallelujah! He provides it all!

That is why Jesus has us pray, 'Give us this day our daily bread'. He will keep us dependent on Him. He will have us keep asking every day for the bread. Why does he not say, 'Lord, give us a week ahead, a month ahead, our daily bread'? He will not show you where the money is coming from a month ahead. That way, he will keep us dependent, so we will know that anything we ever accomplish is not dependent on what we have, but on what he graciously gives us. Therefore, following the Lamb is the victory.

Unity with the 'Firstfruits'

The third characteristic of the fair army is unity (Rev. 14:4). That concept is conveyed to us in the Biblical feast of the *firstfruits*. Our Lord Jesus Christ is first of all spoken of as 'the firstfruits' in 1 Corinthians 15:20, the great resurrection chapter: 'But now is Christ risen from the dead and become the firstfruits of them that slept'. The firstfruits, the early part of the harvest, guaranteeing that the power that will bring about the harvest is working, so the rest will mature in its season.

The next chapter, speaks of the house of Stephanas, 'that it is the firstfruits of Achaia' (1 Cor. 16:15). The risen Christ is the firstfruits; the resurrection of Christ flows out and makes us become his people. Then this household of Stephanas, ordinary folk who became Christians, had the resurrection of Christ come into their lives, raising them spiritually from the dead. They are the firstfruits of that region, guaranteeing that other people of that region were going to be spiritually resurrected. This is the organic unity that is spoken of: 'raised with Christ' (see Rom. 6:5 and Eph. 2:1).

In other words, all Christians ultimately take their new life from the resurrection of Christ, the firstfruits from the dead. His resurrection power comes through the gospel, through the sacraments, and through the ministry of the church; through the lives of our parents and grandparents, if we come from Christian homes, or through a witness somewhere on the street. When somebody is pushing us towards the Lord, somehow and somewhere the resurrection of Christ comes through. With me it was through the widely connected Christian family that I was in, and through the First Presbyterian Church in Lumberton and Eureka Presbyterian Church in Moore County, North Carolina. The resurrection power of Christ was working through them to me.

Truthfulness

The fourth characteristic in this diagnosis of the Lamb's army is veracity, or truthfulness. 'No lie is found in their mouth' (Rev. 14:5). It is a characteristic of the Lamb of God in Isaiah 53:9, that no guile, no deceit, was ever found in his mouth. Then in Zephaniah 3:13, which John seems to be referring to here, 'The remnant of Israel shall do no iniquity, nor speak lies; neither shall a deceitful tongue be found in their mouth'. There is something about coming to Christ, and experiencing his resurrection in the new birth, with the Holy Spirit continuously working through you, that does make you an honest person. Honesty does not mean that you have to be tactless, nor does it excuse verbal brutality, or mean that you have to say every thing you think. That is unwise and unspiritual. But it does mean that what you say will be essentially honest. You are not trying to deceive anybody for your own advantage, but you are seeking to be a person of truthfulness and integrity. Even a sinful world cannot help but appreciate it. It is one of the characteristics of the Lord's army.

Purity, obedience, unity, and finally, veracity— all of these are personal qualities. They are not swords, tanks, missiles, or weapons of mass destruction. They are weapons of mass resurrection. These personal qualities will overcome, in due time, verbal violence, physical violence, hatred, bitterness, and lies. Ultimately, these spiritual qualities engendered by Jesus and his army, as he is standing on mount Zion orchestrating it all, will overcome all the violence and wickedness of a Satanic world system. That is why the angels are already singing. They know how it is going to turn out. God give us ears to hear them, because the Lamb's army, living this way, stands under the protection of the Lamb, who stands watching over them. Although he is unseen to the world and unseen by their enemies, the believers are already standing on the high ground with their Lord Jesus Christ, and all will work out just right (see Eph. 2:6).

36

The Victory of the Everlasting Gospel
Revelation 14:6–7

We have here, from the highest possible vantage point, a mighty angel flying midway between heaven and earth. In modern warfare, even going back as far as World War I, it seems that those who win have the planes and the missiles that can be sent high above the horizon and come down to do their work. That was the case in Serbia, in the Gulf wars, and presumably it will be the case if there are other wars. In a slightly similar way, God is saying that the highest power, the One that controls the destiny of nations and humans, is higher than anything else. He is giving this mighty message, which determines the outcome of everything else. To it you must listen, if your life is to be preserved and you are to avoid defeat.

We look at two points in this text:

1. The victory of the everlasting gospel from the high point between heaven and earth (Rev. 14:6).
2. The right response to that everlasting message (Rev. 14:7).

The Victory of the Everlasting Gospel

In Revelation 14:6–13 we have the latest news on what is going to happen to every individual who has ever lived. Nothing could be more important for what lies ahead than that we get this straight. If we saw planes coming with bombs, we would get anywhere we could to take refuge. During World War II, my father was stationed near Northampton in England, and the Germans managed to send buzz bombs when the Allied soldiers were leaving the mess hall after their evening meal, but he got down on the ground, and he was spared.

An Accurate View from Above the Earth

There is something up there that is more important for our eternal destiny than if we were prey to bombs. The overarching message about what is before all of us is given in verses 6 to 13. Three angelic voices, and then the voice of the Holy Spirit himself speaks saying, 'This is what is coming through the skies; this is why you need to get ready, and how you may get ready.' Nobody can avoid what is coming from the three angels and the voice of the Holy Spirit. In this chapter we are going to listen to the voice of the first angel flying midway between the highest heavens and the earth.

The location from which the four-fold message is given, shows its high and Divine and irrevocable authority over us. It comes not from the pit of hell, nor from a merely human source, with information on how you can face life and how to prepare for the future. Ideas that come only from a human source are not finally competent to help you face what matters most in your future.

The High Source of the Message
This message of the mighty angel does not come from a human source. Its authority is like that of the apostle Paul speaking in Galatians 1:12, where he says, 'I did not receive my message from men, but directly from the Lord Jesus Christ himself'. The divine authority of the message the first angel proclaimed is demonstrated by where he is flying as he proclaims it: in the midst of heaven, as he bears the everlasting gospel. This angel is moving above the earth where we live, where all the varied scenes of the human action play out. He is higher than the mountains, higher than any man-made structure, higher than any political order, no matter how imposing it seems to be. Thus his message has supreme authority over us. The destiny of the people in every nation will be determined by their response to this message of the angel who flies above every other factor.

What a privilege to preach this message of highest possible authority. Verse 6 tells us that this message is very good news. We get our word 'gospel' from the old Anglo-Saxon words 'god spel', which means 'good message,' or 'good tidings'. This is something to make you truly happy, once you understand it. What the angel is proclaiming, unlike the buzz bombs in World War II, is wonderfully good news—almost too good to believe. Yet in believing it, we find that it really is true.

The Apostolic Gospel
Verse 6 speaks of it as 'the everlasting gospel,' which is no different from the apostolic gospel delivered to us by the apostles. Paul delivers us this gospel in 1 Corinthians 15:1–6.

> Moreover, brethren, I declare unto you the gospel which I preached unto you, which also ye have received, and wherein ye stand; By which also ye are saved, if ye keep in memory what I preached unto you, unless ye have believed in vain. For I delivered unto you first of all that which I also received, [a higher message, directly from Christ, not from man] how that Christ died for our sins according to the scriptures; [it fulfills the Old Testament in his death]. And that he was buried, and that he rose again the third day according to the scriptures: And that he was seen of Cephas, [Peter] then of the twelve: After that, he was seen of above five hundred brethren at once; of whom the greater part remain unto this present, but some are fallen asleep.

Paul is delivering an objective message; it is not a figment of some individual's imagination; five hundred people at one time saw the resurrection body of Christ, when he came out of the stone cold tomb, eternally alive. The fact that he was seen physically (or, we might say 'empirically') proved that it really is true that Jesus died for our sins and that his death was sufficient to pay for our sins. God the Father demonstrated his full acceptance of his Son's all-sufficient sacrifice by raising Jesus from the dead (see 1 Cor. 15:17, and Rom. 4:25). By the bodily resurrection of the incarnate Son, God the Father is saying that no more needs to be done for you to be forgiven for all your sins. Nothing more needs to be added to the death and resurrection of God's Eternal Son. It is to be received through faith, which is God's gift to us (Eph. 2:8–9), although it is our responsibility to exercise it.

The great Anglican scholar, J. I. Packer wrote a wonderful introductory essay to John Owen's classical treatment of particular redemption, *The Death of Death in the Death of Christ*. In so doing, Packer summarized the essence of the five points of Calvinism by saying that what they truly mean is that 'God saves sinners.'

The Everlasting Gospel

The Apostle John tells us (Rev. 14:6) that the angel's gospel message is everlasting. Who could understand what 'everlasting' means? I think of a mighty oak tree at the old Kelly plantation house in Moore County, North Carolina, which experts say is 300 years old; it was old when our family came to this country from Scotland two centuries ago. Eventually that oak tree will have to die, to fall down and rot. Yet it is not very old compared to the huge sequoias on the northwest coast of the upper part of California. Some say that some of them may be two thousand years old. But still, they are not everlasting. We do not know exactly how old the pyramids are; they probably were built fairly soon after the flood of Noah. Depending on dating questions of the ancient Middle East, some think that the pyramids were there in the time of Abraham, which would be 2,000 BC. If so, the pyramids may be a good 4,000 years old. But even so, they had a beginning, and presumably they will have an ending.

Our earthly life is very short at the longest. I attended a cousin's funeral in Salemburg, North Carolina. He was almost 99, and possessed his mental faculties to the last. It was a long pilgrimage, but like all flesh, his physical body finally gave out. One century is not very long in comparison with the history of the world, and who could compare it to eternity? But this gospel is absolutely everlasting; it's just as fresh and new and powerful and vibrant as it was the day the angels were singing it out when Jesus was born in the manger at Bethlehem. It never grows old.

Eternity Compared to Time

Why is the gospel like that? Because it is the message of God, and God is eternal. As the *Westminster Shorter Catechism* says: 'God is a Spirit, infinite, eternal, and unchangeable, in his being, wisdom, power, holiness, justice, goodness, and truth.'[98] He has no beginning, no ending, no diminution of his mighty attributes and power. God is always there. He is the Rock of Ages. He inhabits eternity. He created time and space; they are just a little stitch in the massive fabric of eternity. Our human minds simply cannot understand what eternity really is. But God is eternal, and this gospel comes from what he has done on our behalf in Jesus Christ. Hence, this eternal gospel is able, when it is received by faith, to come into us failing human creatures, and deposit an everlasting quality inside our innermost personality, so that we are immortal. The essential me, my personality, will not then go into decay when the bodily systems cease functioning, causing a temporary separation between body and soul. God has intervened in the gospel to put into us, not temporary life, but everlasting life. 'Whoever believeth in Me shall not perish, but have everlasting life' (John 3:16).

If you could compare the length of time that your body lasts to the never-ending eternity in which your soul will always exist, it would not even amount to the comparison between one drop of water with all the waters in the Atlantic and Pacific. It would massively surpass the comparison between one grain of sand placed between your thumb and forefinger, to all the sand in the entire world. There would still be no comparison, with the length of existence that your soul will always have, and the short time that you have in your body in this fading world.

What the Substitutionary Death Accomplished

That is why the everlasting gospel announced by the angel is so wonderful. When received in faith, it supernaturally lifts us from the existence in which we are condemned to death, into eternal fellowship with the risen Christ, into vital and indissoluble union with him forever. For that purpose, Jesus came into this world. He took on our human nature. In it, he lived a holy life of devotion to the Father, thus turning it away from its refusal to face God, and bringing it back 'face to face' with the Heavenly Father. Jesus died a substitutionary death in our human nature; he raised our human nature into resurrection existence, and thereby adapted our human nature to go up to the throne of God, where, by his grace, we shall last eternally. He says: 'I am he that liveth and was dead; and, behold, I am alive forevermore. Amen; and have the keys of hell and of death' (Rev. 1:18). The ever living One uses those keys to open the gates of eternal life for us sinners who believe, for he says in John 14:19: 'Because I live, ye shall live also.' 'For since by man came death, by man came also the resurrection of the dead' (1 Cor. 15:21).

This everlasting gospel means that Jesus took care of the everlasting death due to our sins against the Lord. 'The wages of sin is death' (Rom. 6:23); 'by one man's offence, death reigned by one' (Rom. 5:17). But here in 1 Corinthians 15, Paul makes clear that the infinite sacrifice Jesus made for us, when 'he was crucified for our sins according to the scriptures,' is the first step, the foundation of the everlasting, apostolic gospel.

'How Bright these Glorious Spirits Shine'

The bad news is that sin brought death, but the good news is that Jesus goes into our death, and blows it apart from the inside out, so that death no longer has any hold on our spirits. Eventually, on the last day, death will have to let its bony fingers loose of the dust of our bodies, and they also shall be raised. This everlasting gospel is the highest authority over all human life. It means God deals with us infinitely better than we deserve. The Father treats us as he would his own beloved Son. If we have faith, he delivers us from sin and all its consequences, namely disintegration, death, misery, and hell. This is a wonderful thought, as we stand out in the graveyard by an open grave and see the dirt being clumped onto the top of the coffin of a loved one. In one sense it is hard, but in an even fuller sense, we profoundly feel that everything is all right because if our loved ones were in Christ, they lived and died forgiven, and they are forgiven forever. Sin and death has no hold on them. Death became not an end, but an open door into the presence of their Father. They are, by the sheer grace of this gospel, made as righteous as Jesus Christ is righteous, in the sight of the supreme Judge. Thus, they are bright and shining, pure and holy—not because of themselves, but because faith links them to the pure and Holy One, the Lord Jesus Christ!

A hymn by the great English Puritan minister, Richard Baxter, says *'How bright these glorious spirits shine!'* That is what I often think of when I visit the graveyard where my ancestors are buried. What a gospel! What a piece of thrilling news to us poor sinners: by simple trust in Jesus now, one day when the world is no more and the skies have been folded up, when the stars have fallen and all is changed, we shall be shining with the brightness of the stars of the firmament forever and ever (Daniel 12:3).

So the message of the first angel is a victorious message for anyone who wants it. It is proclaimed in the midst of heaven, above every other philosophy and every other power claim. This is the highest power and authority. All sinners who receive it shall shine as brightly as the luminaries of the heavens.

The Right Response to the Everlasting Message

Verse 7 points out the right response to the everlasting message proclaimed by this mighty angel. Receiving this victorious message in faith, repentance, and obedience is the only thing that can make us victorious. This has already been shown to us in Revelation 12:11, where the suffering saints 'overcame by the blood of the Lamb and the Word of their testimony'. This is the gospel, and the way to receive it! One simply looks out of self to 'Jesus' blood and righteousness'. Then one gives the Word of their testimony: 'I receive it; I stand in it, no matter what, because even if I have to pay the price possibly of losing bodily life, I can only win because the gospel is proclaimed from above; it is the everlasting reality that gives me the everlasting victory'.

For whatever reason, some people sincerely feel that they have been losers for much of their life, or all of their life. They consider that everything has gone against them, and that they cannot do anything right. While other relatives and friends always seem to be successful, everything they do is a broken dream and a disappointment. But even if someone harbors those kinds of negative feelings about themselves, there is a sure and certain way to come out of it, regardless of one's background or years of failure. If they will cast their total being onto the word of Revelation 14:7, 'Fear God and give glory to Him', they can rise up and become an overcomer. That is the way. It is open to the humblest, to the highest, to the in-between, to anyone. 'Fear God and give him glory'. Let us look briefly at those two things required by God through the mighty angel.

Fear God

First, the holy angel says the right response to this everlasting gospel is to confess that you believe the message is true: that Jesus was crucified for your sins, and that he is risen from the dead, with all authority in his hands to save forevermore those who put their trust in Him. Paul speaks of this in Romans 10:9: 'That if thou shalt confess with thy mouth the Lord Jesus, and shalt believe in thine heart that God hath raised him from the dead, thou shalt be saved.' 'To fear God' means such tender reverence towards the heavenly Father, who went to such lengths for you, that you can no longer bear not to say the same thing about the Son that his Father says! Thus, 'Whosoever shall confess that Jesus is the Son of God, God dwelleth in him, and he in God' (1 John 4:15).

The Virgin Mary speaks of this kind of fear in her noble *Magnificat*, where she cries out in Luke 1:50: 'And his mercy is on them that fear Him, from generation to generation'. She knew that the holy Redeemer in her womb would do all that was necessary to convey this boundless, divine condescension and mercy unto all who would ever cry out to him for help.

Psalm 130:3-4 poses and answers the great question concerning the mercy of God for sinners who fear Him. 'If Thou, Lord, shouldst mark iniquities, O Lord, who shall stand?' (Ps. 130:3). That is, before the strict judgment seat of God, we would all be justly smitten. But here is the good news that the mighty angel proclaims in Revelation 14:6-7: 'But there is forgiveness with Thee, that Thou mayest be feared' (Ps. 130:4). To fear God is very close to worship and is essential to it, as John Owen brings out in his treatise on this Psalm. He writes: 'By the 'fear of the Lord,' in the Old Testament, the whole worship of God, moral and instituted, all the obedience which we owe unto him, both for matter and manner, is intended… 'That thou mayest be feared,' then, is, 'That thou mayest be served, worshipped…"[99]

Psalm 34:9 attaches a rich promise to the fear of God by his saints: 'O fear the LORD, ye his saints: for there is no want to them that fear him.'

Two Kinds of Fear in the Bible

Hateful Fear. There is the fear that 'has torment', spoken of in 1 John 4:18, and it is not appropriate for the child of God, because 'the perfect love' that they know has 'cast it out'. That is what the devils have; that is what the unregenerate God-haters have: fear with torment, which means they see God only in terms of his massive power. That kind of fear torments them, making them wish that there were not a God, which is why so much humanistic philosophy and evolutionary thought will do anything to get away from the possibility of the existence of God. It is because they are tormented at the very thought that there is a God. That is why the secularizing societies of the West were so determined to take any respectful recognition of God out of the schools, and out of public discourse. They see God as a horrible, tormenting power. This is the very kind of 'faith' possessed by the demons themselves, for as James 2:19 tells us: 'the devils believe and tremble'. They know that there is a holy, omnipotent God. Only the atheists, whom they control, are foolish enough to deny it!

Jonathan Edwards discussed the difference between the faith that the saints have of God, and the faith of the demons. The saints recognize God's holy power, and they immensely love him for it, whereas the demons recognize the same holy power, but they hate him for it.[100] That kind of fear is not what is talked about here in Revelation 14:7. That bad kind of fear will drive you from God, making you despairing and bitter.

Loving Fear. The kind of fear that is talked about here, when the holy angel commands: 'fear God', means reverential trust in Him, and endless gratitude for all he has done for you. It means that you are overcome with the greatness of God, but also at the same time, with his mercy and Fatherly goodness to you. Therefore, you do not wish to do a thing that would let him down. That is 'reverential trust', sensitive fear flowing out of tender love; in a word, sweet, deep devotion.

One biography of General Robert E. Lee, the notable general so much respected and greatly loved by the Southern Troops, tells of how they would gladly go to all lengths to make his arduous life easier. At one time Lee had been up two or three days in a row, and finally in the day time some of his officers convinced him to take a much needed nap, somewhere in northern Virginia. General Lee had at last gone to sleep in his tent, and soon several thousand Confederate troops were on the road right next to the tent marching, and keeping time, with a certain amount of necessary noise to order their pace. Suddenly the word started in the front of the troops, and was rapidly passed all the way back, that the general was taking a nap. Those Southern troops, some of whom would be marching to their death in a few days, so loved their general that they quit marching in time, so they would walk by as quietly as possible, to keep from waking up this beloved general. Such was their great regard for this self-sacrificing man.

That may be a pale picture of the kind of tender love or reverential fear that the saints have for the God who has so greatly loved us, who gave the Son of his heart to save us. A few moments of contemplation of what he has done for us answers most of the moral and ethical questions of our life. Many of you will be familiar with the hymn:

> O how I fear Thee, living God,
> with deepest, tenderest fears;
> And worship Thee with trembling hope
> and penitential tears.
> No earthly father loves like Thee;
> no mother ere so mild;
> Bears and forebears as Thou hast done
> with me, Thy sinful child.

That is what the fear of God, commanded to us by the angel, means.

Give him Glory
Secondly, the holy angel says that the proper response to God's gospel is: '*give him glory*'. Jesus speaks of this in the Sermon on the Mount (Matthew 5:16): 'Let your light so shine before men that they may see your good works and glorify your Father which is in heaven.' In other words, show something of what God is like in the way you live. Is that not a noble challenge? Does that not make life worth living and doing whatever you have got to do in a manner that through the continual grace imparted to us by the Holy Spirit, shows what God is like—how pure, good, loving, and true, God is? One little life, if consecrated, can bring God great glory that way! Through the Holy Spirit, with meditation on the Scriptures, frequent prayer, and endeavors after daily obedience, even poor, frail creatures such as we are can show what God is like.

Now is the time. The angel appends two good reasons: First, 'for the hour of his judgment is come'. This takes us immediately to John 16:8–11: 'And when he the Holy Spirit is come, he will reprove the world of sin, of righteousness and of judgment; of sin because they believe not in Me; of righteousness because I go to my Father and ye see Me no more; of judgment because the prince of this world is judged.' Now that Jesus has come, and has done all this for us, it is now the hour for us to decide which side we are on. The hour of judgment is come, and the most important question we will ever face in our life, the only one that really matters, is what will we do with the One who was judged in our place, and was raised victorious? He stretches out his nail-pierced hands and says: 'Take hold of My hands by faith, and I will raise you up.'

The Creator deserves to be worshipped. A second reason appended as to why we should give the Lord glory: 'he created all things and should therefore be worshiped'. In Acts 14 and 17, Paul was preaching to the pagans of Greece, who did not have the Jewish Scriptures of the Old Testament, but had pagan myths and stories. Without the Old Testament background of creation, fall, sin, and redemption, how would Paul bring the saving gospel to these people? What does he start with? He starts with the creation. He says, 'You live in a marvelously created world; guess who made it? Our heavenly Father made this world. He created everything. He created you. Therefore, your real loyalty is no longer to be placed on the idolatrous myths you have long heard; your real loyalty can only properly be given to your Creator. He deserves your worship. He requires your worship, and he has sent his Son to do what is necessary to pay for your sins and change you, so that you can worship the One True Creator and Redeemer.

Athanasius said that it would take someone as great as the Creator to be our Redeemer. And that is exactly what happened, when Christ, the agent of creation (see John 1:3) became incarnate to carry out his redeeming work. Only the One who made everything can restore everything. He sends his holy angel midway between heaven and earth to give you a divine call to move by faith from a now-fallen, judged creation, up into a pure realm of redemption where God would never judge you and Satan can never touch you. What a gospel! And it is available to make me an overcomer.

37

Messages from the Angels
Revelation 14:8–13

When someone runs into a crowded room where everyone is talking, and says to one of the group, 'Come to the telephone, so-and-so is wishing to speak to you', the expression on the face of the summoned person may change, depending on whom you tell them is calling. In some cases, they will be very interested, and in others, they are reluctant to be bothered. But regardless of who bears the news, if they think the message may relate to life and death issues for them, then you have their closest attention. The reaction to a message depends to a degree on who is giving it, but also on how seriously it will impact our lives. In the case of Revelation 14:8–13, these messages merit our highest attention both because of who bears them, and because of the eternal impact of their news on the future of the church.

In the last chapter, we listened to the message of the first angel, who proclaimed the everlasting gospel, as the supreme reality (Rev. 14:6–13). In this exposition we look at the messages from the second and third angels, and then from the blessed Holy Spirit. Hence we note three points:

1. The defeat of unbelief (Rev. 14:8).
2. The punishment of idolatry (Rev. 14:9–11).
3. The safety of the saints (Rev. 14:12–13).

The Defeat of Unbelief

Verse 8 presents a stark contrast. Immediately after the serene, over-arching message of the everlasting gospel, we see 'the Fall of Babylon the Great'. The adjective 'great' indicates that Babylon: a political, economic, military and religious order represents the biggest edifice that unredeemed humanity can ever build. Which nation is 'great' varies with the centuries. At times it has been Egypt, Greece, Rome, China, Spain, France, Britain, America, and others. When they reach human greatness, how imposing and unshakeable they look! What could stop them?

Do not Be too Impressed by Worldly Power

That is the point of the message of the second angel, who, like the first angel flies midway between heaven and earth, so that his words cannot be missed by any ear. He says: 'Do not be overly impressed by the most massive human power. If any mighty human power consistently rejects and persecutes the bearers of the everlasting gospel, down they will fall! This is to be written on their tombstone: 'Babylon is fallen…that great city!''

Meaning of 'Babylon'

There is some question as to what is the prophetic sense of 'Babylon' in Revelation. Does it mean Rome, or Jerusalem, or some other ungodly world power? Evidence in Revelation 17–18 points in the direction of its standing for unbelieving Jerusalem (pre-AD 70). Jerusalem had rejected Christ and persecuted his church. In Revelation 11:8, the terms 'Sodom' and 'Egypt' were used to describe 'the great city where the Lord was crucified'. In Revelation 16:19, the same term 'the great city' is applied to 'Babylon' (as it is here in Rev. 14:8). Thus it would seem that 'Babylon' primarily means pre-AD 70, unbelieving Jerusalem, which perhaps three or four years after Revelation was written (assuming its early dating) would be disastrously brought down.

A Lasting Principle

Yet of equal importance with the likelihood of its primary historical reference in the first century is a lasting principle that endures to the end of time: Babylon stands for any ungodly political and military power that arrays itself against 'the Lord and against his anointed' (cf. Psalm 2:2). Throughout history, against every seeming likelihood, the Sovereign God warns that at a predetermined moment, his holy wrath will fall with disastrous judgment against ungodly powers that seek to destroy the witness to his gospel.

Verse 8 speaks of how ungodly nations corrupt others regions of the world by getting them 'to drink of the wine of her fornication.' Whenever a mighty nation willfully spreads moral corruption to other parts of the world on a grand scale, it is only a matter of time before it can be written on their tombstone: 'The great nation is fallen!'

The old adage, 'the bigger they are, the harder they fall' is proven to be true in history. One sobering illustration of this adage concerning the widespread sowing of immorality can be seen in how the United Nations (heavily financed by the USA) has encouraged abortion in third world countries, against the most basic commandment of God: 'Thou shalt not kill'. In addition to that, the elites of our nation (and of Europe) work tirelessly to force Christianity out of public life. It is surely a time to listen to the second angel, who tells us what our spreading the poisonous cup of fornication across the world will cost us. If our Western countries continue to move in an ever more atheistic direction, how long will it take for our national tombstones to read some variation of: 'Babylon the great is fallen'?

The Punishment of Idolatry

Then the third angel proclaims another solemn warning with a loud voice (Rev. 14:9–10):

> If any man worship the beast and his image, and receive his mark in his forehead, or in his hand, The same shall drink of the wine of the wrath of God, which is poured out without mixture into the cup of his indignation; and he shall be tormented with fire and brimstone in the presence of the holy angels, and in the presence of the Lamb.

Different Kinds of Drunkenness

A frightening analogy is given here between the defencelessness of being drunk and the foolish stupor that comes upon those who give themselves up to the moral blindness that follows idolatry. People who become intoxicated are unable to resist those who assail them. They stagger about, and are an easy prey for their sober enemies. Thus it is with nations who consistently reject the true God, and substitute some kind of idol in his place. (An idol is not only a graven image, but is any value less than God that replaces God, whether money, sex or power).

Idol worshippers, for all their outward differences, share this disastrous characteristic: they lose normal discernment about how the world really works, and what the true value of things is. If they carry on long enough, they will eventually reach the point where they call good evil, and evil good; they will call right wrong, and wrong right.

A recent British study of evil characters found that those whose characters became deeply depraved during a life of serious evil-doing reached the point where they actually thought that the victims of their crimes were the evil ones, not themselves. This kind of reversal of reality constitutes dreadful moral darkness, and self-imposed drunkenness of spirit. The third angel says that this kind of intellectual depravity is one of the last stages reached by a culture that is rapidly declining into divine destruction.

The Grim Reality of Hell

The description in verse 10 of the reprobate being tormented by fire and brimstone is a pale reflection of what happened in Sodom and Gomorrah. They blinded themselves to basic moral truth, implanted in all the image-bearers of God, and declared that unnatural relationships were perfectly acceptable. Then they became aggressive against the few godly who remained. Suddenly, fire and brimstone swallowed them up, and ushered them into a place of everlasting burnings.

So it will be with all humans who follow the immoral, idolatrous crowd blithely to violate God's moral law, of which they are well aware. The consequences then and now is everlasting burning in a place of darkness and separation. The Modernists who deny the existence of hell will find out all too late its horrendous reality. Those who hate God, by giving themselves over to idolatry and immorality, certainly wish to get as far away from him as possible. And that is exactly what they will get in the place of outer darkness and endless grief. But they will continuously discover that what they wanted (the absence of the presence of God) comes at a price too terrible to be counted!

During their earthly lives, they managed to desensitize themselves to contemplation of final realities by gulping down large doses of the wine of godless pleasure. For a while it served as a measure to avoid thoughts of the solemn realities inevitably awaiting those who are determined not to believe and repent.

The Safety of the Saints

The safety of the saints is found in exercising patience (Rev. 14:12), which is especially required when their surrounding culture rejects God and his Word to pursue idolatry. One of the chief ways to excuse following popular idols rather than God is the pretence of relativism. One can excuse wretchedly wrong thinking and wretchedly wrong behavior by the empty platitude: 'Who can say what is right?' The relativist spirit attacks as dangerous and uncharitable fanatics those who continue to hold that what God says in his Word is right, and what God forbids in his Word is wrong. In such an uncomfortable and mean-spirited culture, the saints faithfully carry on year after year seeking to put God first, no matter how fiercely the sophisticated resent them for it.

The Patience of the saints

Verse 12 describes two things that the saints keep doing: (1) They keep the commandments of God, and (2) They keep the faith of Jesus.

They Keep the Commandments of God. God's commandments are summarized by Moses in the Ten Commandments (Exod. 20 and Deut. 5), and these are explicated by our Lord Jesus Christ in the 'Sermon on the Mount' (Matt. 5–7). These commandments are a shining out of the beauty, purity and goodness of the character of God. They are the only basis for a happy life and a stable society. The commandments cannot save our souls; instead, their pure light points out our sin and need of divine grace. But once we are saved, then we walk in the paths they point out, for they are summarized by Jesus as consisting in love to God and love to neighbour. Christ saves us to be His, and thus, to walk in love, for 'God is love'.

The paths of love shown to us in the moral law of God, and made possible to us through the blood and resurrection of Christ, as applied in our needy souls by the Holy Spirit, are fiercely resented by the relativists. They do not want to be told to restrain either their minds or their flesh by a higher standard than self and fallen culture. These people often speak of 'love', but by it they appear to mean something like 'not holding me to a holy standard, so that I may without compunction of conscience satisfy my lusts.'

But the saints of God, for all their imperfections, carry on seeking, by the imparted grace and power of the Holy Spirit, to love God above all, and their neighbours (including their immoral enemies) as themselves. Their sincere desire is to be pure in thought, word, and deed, and they pour out their energies and resources to bring up their children in these holy paths of purity and grace. The kind of societies these saints produce is one of beauty and fragrance. It is starkly different from the ugliness and stench of the self-centered relativism that has in varying degrees corrupted so much of our Western society.

They Keep the Faith of Jesus. The saints also exercise divinely provided patience in challenging situations to keep 'the faith of Jesus'. This faith is precisely what Jude 3 calls 'the faith once delivered to the saints'. Holding to it means that they live and die on the basis of the gospel of Christ. That is: Jesus is our salvation; he alone is our righteousness; we belong to him body and soul for all eternity. Or, in the words of the first question of the *Heidelberg Catechism*: Q. What is your only comfort in life and death? A. That I with body and soul, both in life and death, am not my own, but belong unto my faithful Saviour Jesus Christ...'

John knew that in the historical situation where the churches of Asia had to live, 'keeping the divine commandments and the faith of Jesus' might well lead to persecution and death for many of these early Christians. Thus, he assures these tried and tested saints of their supreme security, no matter what goes on in the godless society around them. Even in the face of death, John bids them listen to the words of the blessed Holy Spirit himself: 'Blessed are the dead which die in the Lord from henceforth; Yea, saith the Spirit, that they may rest from their labors; and their works do follow them' (Rev. 14:13).

'Blessed' means 'Happy'
On the basis of the victorious sacrifice and resurrection of the Lamb of God, death has become an open door into the happy presence of Christ, and of all the departed saints who are now in glory. 'Blessed' really means 'happy'. Imagine this: the Holy Spirit himself is telling us that those who die in the Lord are supremely happy! God always speaks truth, and therefore, happiness is the supreme truth about every believer on the

other side of death. The early church readily took this divine definition of happiness to heart, and they out-lived and out-died the pagans around them, thus winning the jaded peoples of the late Roman Empire to true happiness.

The first major church historian was Bishop Eusebius in the fourth century. When many Christians had sealed their testimony with their blood. He wrote:

> We were witnesses to the most admirable ardor of mind, and the truly divine energy and alacrity of those that believed in the Christ of God. For as soon as the sentence was pronounced against the first, others rushed forward from other parts to the tribunal before the judge, confessing they were Christians, most indifferent to the dreadful and multiform tortures that awaited them, but declaring themselves fully and in the most undaunted manner of the religion which acknowledges only the one Supreme God. They received, indeed, the final sentence of death with gladness and exultation, so far as even to sing and send up hymns of praise and thanksgiving, until they breathed their last.[101]

The Scottish Covenanter martyr, Archibald Alison, exclaimed before his death upon the scaffold in the late 1680s:

> What think ye of Heaven and Glory that is at the back of the cross? The hope of this makes me look upon pale death as a lovely messenger to me. I bless the Lord for my lot this day…Friends, give our Lord credit; he is aye good, but O! He is good in a day of trial, and he will be sweet company through the ages of eternity.[102]

With such testimonies before us, we could well pray with Bishop Lancelot Andrews: 'Lord, give me a happy death, and a deathless happiness', and then with the mercenary prophet Balaam: 'Let me die the death of the righteous, and let my last end be like his!'(Numb. 23:10).

38

A Double Harvest

Revelation 14:14–20

This text speaks of a double harvest. Concerning the agriculture of this world, we never really know from year to year what a harvest will be like, or whether there will even be a harvest when autumn comes. Harvests gathered in by poor humans are uncertain; sometimes very good; mostly moderate, and sometimes very bad. Farming and harvesting are uncertain propositions.

But the double harvest set before us here is not uncertain. This double harvest is as certain as the original creation of the world, the exact time of the birth of Christ in Bethlehem, or the precise time of the return of the Lord, which were set before the foundation of the world. This double harvest does not depend on the weather, on the economy, or on politics. It does not depend on anything mankind can do. It depends only and entirely upon Almighty God. That is why this harvest is absolutely certain, unerring and sure.

This brings us to two points:

1. Who is it that is carrying out this harvest? Who are the reapers (Rev. 14:14–19)?
2. What is this double harvest; what does it involve, so that it's not a single crop, but a double one (Rev. 14:14–20)?

Who Is Doing the Harvesting?

This text sets before us the future harvesters. I spent many summers on our family place in Moore County, priming tobacco and hoeing cotton, so I learned something about harvesting. Every week, as I travel through a lot of good agricultural country, with wide fields, I often slow down to see who is doing the harvesting. Fifty years ago we did it by hand, with droves of us workers in the fields; today it is all done by tractor drivers. But whoever does it never knows what the outcome will be until the cotton is picked, pressed together, and hauled to the gin. But this harvest of souls, spoken of in Revelation 14, is done by the One who exercises highest authority in heaven and on earth. He is the Creator and the Sustainer of the ends of the earth. He is the God of the universe, the Supreme Governor, and the final reaper.

The Primary Harvester: The Son of Man

In Revelation 14, there are two classes of harvesters. The first is described in verse 14: one sitting on a white cloud, likened to the Son of Man, having on his head a golden crown and in his hand a sharp sickle. The term 'Son of Man,' comes from the prophecy of Daniel, which has a close connection to Revelation. The 'Son of Man' is described in Daniel 7:13-14, from which John is directly drawing as he sees the final results of the harvest of souls:

> And I saw in the night visions and behold, one like the Son of Man came with the clouds of heaven and came to the Ancient of Days [the Father], and they brought him near before Him. And there was given unto Him, [the Son of Man], dominion and glory and a kingdom that all people, nations and languages should serve Him. His dominion is an everlasting dominion which shall not pass away, and his kingdom that which shall not be destroyed.

Daniel shows that to the Son of Man, our Lord Jesus Christ, the eternal Son of God, a kingdom out of all the nations of the earth was given by his Father. Part of that donation means that the final harvesting is given to Christ. He will gather in all the chosen, all who will ever believe in him and repent from their sins. Unlike uncertain human harvests over the centuries, this harvest cannot fail.

Daniel portrays this glorious Son of Man, seated on the cloud, harvesting from all nations exactly who he has chosen to be in his church. This picture is presented before we are shown the appearance of the terrible beast—the worst that can ever happen in human government, exercising raw, brutal, ungodly political and military power. He is the beast with seven heads and ten horns, who Daniel contrasts to the Son of Man. Revelation has the same sort of sequence. What the Lord is saying through John in Revelation 14 is most encouraging. It is as though he says, 'Let the beasts do their worst, let the ungodly nations—spoken of in Psalm 2, raging against the Lord and his Anointed—let them do their worst. Let them gather their armies, navies, and air forces. Let them make all their plots to blot out the name of the Lord and of his Christ from the earth. Let them do their worst, because the Son of Man was incarnate, lived a holy life, was crucified for the sins of all his people, raised in the same body in which he was crucified, and he is now ascended up into that cloud, to the throne of God beside his Father, whence dominion over all nations has been given unto Him. The beasts can never stop, nor even slow down the harvest that the Son of Man is carrying on from his ascended dignity on the glory cloud, from the throne of heaven. He is in charge of it all.

Harvesting Between Christ's Two Advents
Although Revelation 14 has reference to that ultimate future harvest at the end of time, it also applies to all the ages between Christ's first advent and his second advent. This chapter indicates that since his first advent, Christ has been seated on the cloud, on his heavenly throne. We see this in Hebrews 1:3: 'And upholding all things by the word of his power, when he had by himself purged our sins, sat down on the right hand of the Majesty on high.' And Hebrews 1:13: 'Sit on my right hand, until I make thine enemies thy footstool'.

From that pre-eminent place, the risen Jesus, ever since he took his seat of authority, majesty, and grace, has been directing the gathering in of people. He will be doing that until the last great day, when the gospel will be preached no more, when faith will pass into sight, when the heavens are rolled back as a scroll, the stars fall, and there is a new heaven and a new earth. But until then, the Lord Jesus Christ continues to be in charge of every one who ever will be saved: of the life situation that they go through, of their genetic code, the parents they have, and the environment in which they live. He directs the opportunities they have to hear his truth, the missionaries who go out, and all good influences in their lives. The enthroned Lord is in charge of it all. Jesus is continually reaping and gathering in his church. Satan cannot stop it. Whether in China, Africa, or the Middle East, a harvest is constantly going on that cannot be stopped by any human or demonic circumstances, because the risen Jesus is in charge of it.

What is the ultimate reason that we are Christian believers? Many of us would truthfully say: 'Well my mother and father, my grandparents, aunts and uncles showed me Christianity in their lives, and told me about Christ, so that I began to believe as early as I can remember.' That is the case with me, and with my parents before me. We are also influenced by our home churches and faithful pastors. But that is not the ultimate reason. The reason we are Christians is because the Son of Man from the glory cloud of heaven, reached down his sickle and harvested us personally. That is what brought us in. We can never be discouraged throughout the passage of world history, because the great harvest is constantly going on, and its end result will be victorious, because of who is the ultimate Reaper.

Harvesting by the Angels

The primary reaper is the Lord Jesus Christ in his office as Mediator, and head of his church. But there is another class of reapers mentioned in the passage—the holy angels (Rev. 14:15–19). Certain of these angels will assist in the final harvesting of the saints ('the wheat') and others with the final harvesting of the lost ('the grapes'). Verse 15 presents the final work of the angels deputed to gather in the saints:

> Without delay, the grain is threshed. Here the time for harvesting refers figuratively to the Judgment Day (see Jer. 51:33; Joel 3:13; Matt. 13:30, 40–42). It is the time of gathering believers into the kingdom, for the sickle goes forth to reap God's people (Mark 4:29; John 4:35–38). The 'son of man' has been given the authority to put the sickle to work, though he uses his angels to assist him (Matt. 13:39; 24:31).[103]

Other holy angels have been selected to harvest unrepentant souls, who rejected the gospel, at the end of the age. This is shown in Revelation 14:17, where the fifth angel sticks in a second sickle:

> The second sickle is used not for the harvesting of grain (God's people) but for the grapes of wrath (God's enemies)…Here is the difference between gathering God's people for his glory and reaping his enemies for wrath…The judgment is the outcome of unbelievers' continued and persistent rejection of God and his revelation and is God's answer to the numerous prayers directed to him by a multitude of suffering saints on earth and by the souls under the altar.[104]

The Double Harvest

These verses set before us the double harvest. It is a way of presenting two different classes of people, who are being harvested throughout history, until the final harvest on the last great day. One class is those who will become Christians or the elect. The elect are represented by the wheat. The wheat refers to the saints, to those who will become believers. Jesus gathers them in, as Jesus gathered us in. When our loved ones die we have to remember that Jesus gathered them in the first time to make them Christians, and so he has the rightful authority to take them home whenever he chooses.

The Grapes of Wrath

But we also find a second class of people or second type of fruit, being harvested in this passage; they are spoken of as the grapes of the vine. Those are the people who, in life and in death, reject the gospel of Jesus Christ. The New Testament speaks of the 'mystery of iniquity;' it is a mystery that none of us can ever understand. How is it that the best news the world ever heard, of a loving God who will forgive our sins in Christ for the mere asking, infuriates a certain class of people? Instead of its melting their hearts with love to the God who, as it were, tore his own heart out in sending his Son and putting him on the cross, they hate God for it. They resist the gospel; they blaspheme Christ; they persecute his people. It is illogical, irrational, and suicidal that they should do this. It is the mystery of iniquity. There is no human explaining of why somebody refuses to believe such a wonderful message of tender love, of why they trample on this holy, tender, personal love. We do not know why.

These recalcitrant people are spoken of as 'the grapes'. They too will be harvested. All through history, and finally at the end, the holy angels are harvesting the grapes of wrath. Jesus harvests the elect; to the angels are given the sharp sickles to gather in those who hate God, who die unbelieving and unforgiven. Both harvests take place simultaneously; there will be a fullness and consummation of this process on the Last Day.

Jesus speaks to us in Matthew 24 and 25 of the last great assize, that final assembly of the universe. Everybody who was ever born will be there. Angels and demons will all be there. All beings will be fully conscious, absolutely alert, knowing that their eternal destiny depends on the God-Man, who is on the throne. It is he who pronounces the last sentence of judgment or of forgiveness. From that august throne, he will separate the sheep on his right hand, from the goats on his left. It is a double harvest, and one's final disposition depends directly on one's relationship to Jesus.

Is God's Judgment out of Character with his Love?
Many feel that it is a hard thing to say that some people will be among the goats, or some will be the grapes, who are pressed down into blood, and finally crushed from the presence of God. We must take our bearings here from the Bible. The only God I know of is the God of the Bible. If God is truly love, as the Bible consistently teaches, then why would anybody end up being grapes of wrath, pressed down in the winepress outside the holy city walls? It is because the God of love is also holy; our God is a consuming fire. God is holy love. If his love were not holy, it would have no character to define it. He is of the highest integrity. He built the universe on moral lines, and must always act in a way that is in accordance with his own true holy and loving character. That means that God has to punish sin, for sin is a contradiction of God's character.

Sin against an infinite God is infinite sin, and infinite sin cannot be dealt with by finite punishment, as Anselm of Canterbury said long ago. Infinite sin must be purged away by an infinite punishment. That is why Jesus bore the infinite penalty of our sins on Calvary's cross in the place of all who will ever believe in Him. We notice that the winepress was trodden without the city (v. 20). In the Middle East the winepress was outside the town, where the barefoot harvesters trample the grapes.

We are told in Hebrews 13:12 that Jesus suffered 'without the gates', outside the city walls of Jerusalem. This goes back to Isaiah 63:2-4:

Wherefore art thou red in thine apparel, and thy garments like him that treadeth in the winefat? I have trodden the winepress alone; and of the people there was none with me; for I will tread them in mine anger, and trample them in my fury; and their blood shall be sprinkled upon my garments, and I will stain all my raiment. For the day of vengeance is in mine heart, and the year of my redeemed is come.

Good Wheat or Grapes of Wrath?

Because of the gospel, we can be wheat on that final day, rather than grapes of wrath. Once I look to Jesus in faith, my sins are on him who trod the winepress alone. The infinite Son of God, made man, took all of our sins, and disposed of them eternally. Isaac Watts has a verse in 'When I survey the wondrous cross', that is left out of some hymnbooks:

> His dying crimson, like a robe,
> spreads o'er his body on the tree.
> Then am I dead to all the globe
> and all the globe is dead to me.

He has trodden the winepress alone; Jesus took care of all the sins of any who will ever ask him to forgive them. Thereby they are counted among the wheat; the winepress of the wrath of God no longer concerns them.

A famous minister of 10th Presbyterian Church in Philadelphia, the late Donald Grey Barnhouse, used to say that your sins can be in only one of two places in this universe. You can live and die leaving your sins upon your own head. If you do that, the ultimate consequence will be the crushing in the presence of a holy God in the winepress of his righteous wrath. But you can look in faith to Jesus, and your sins will be taken off your head and placed on the head of the Redeemer, the Man of Sorrows, on the cross, and you will never meet your sins again. You will be wheat, lovingly, tenderly gathered into his garner. The question comes to me and to you: how do I want it to be with my life? Shall I be wheat gathered in by the loving Lord Jesus to the heavenly home? Or, will I refuse his offers of grace, pardon, and fellowship, and live and die in my own sins and be in the grapes of wrath? Which will it be?

39

THE SEA OF GLASS MINGLED WITH FIRE
Revelation 15:1–2

The first two verses of Revelation 15 bring to mind the story of Daniel and the wicked, debauched feast of Belshazzar, where a hand suddenly appeared and started writing on the plaster, high up in the banquet hall. It wrote things that nobody could understand, so that they were terrified at this mysterious hand. Then somebody remembered that Daniel was a prophet of God, so they called him in to interpret the mysterious writing on the wall: 'Thou art weighed in the balances and found wanting'.

In the English language, if we use the expression 'to see the handwriting on the wall,' it means, figuratively speaking, that you see the end is coming. Trouble is coming—a nation is about to lose the war, somebody is about to die, or a company is going under. 'The handwriting on the wall' forewarns us of the imminent end.

In Revelation, three signs state what is going to happen in the future, especially if you take these signs together. They show you the shape of future history, and what is going to occur.

In Revelation 15:1 we read, 'And I saw another sign in heaven'. It is not on the banquet hall in Babylon this time, but in the glory realm to which John was taken, so he could see the handwriting on the wall of future history. When it says 'another sign,' that recognises that there have been two previous signs, so that this one makes three signs.

The first one was in Revelation 12:1-2: 'I saw a great sign; it was the woman': that is the Old Testament Israel and the New Testament church, all one. The woman gives birth to the man child, to Christ. That is the first thing that is going to control the shape of the future, the church, under its head—Christ, born of the Virgin Mary.

In Revelation 12:3, we are given the second sign that will also determine the future shape of world history and of our lives—the dragon, or the devil, that tried to gobble up the baby, the man child, whom the woman had borne. So the second sign is that God allows the evil one to attack the church, to try to overcome what is good, by attempting to stamp out the light.

Then the third sign is given, and it begins a new section, which is the last section of Revelation. From Revelation 15:1 to chapter 22, everything comes under the third sign.[105] To see the third sign, we have to be taken up with John to the heavenly courts, where God's beautiful, all-powerful throne is. In this holy place we see the third sign: seven holy and mighty angels holding huge chalices filled with the wrath of God. Later, God gives the angels orders: 'Take the bowls, (the chalices) and pour them out on the world' (Rev. 16:1). That divinely ordered outpouring will be the last expression of the righteous indignation of a holy God against the world.

This final outpouring of the wrath of God is actually a prelude to lasting victory. The expression of the wrath of God has a beautiful side to it; like fire, it removes dross, and makes way for a cleansed, renewed state of affairs.

In this chapter, we are considering the place from which the final wrath of God comes into this world. Our task at present is to interpret properly the outpouring of the wrath of God in world history, particularly by seeking to understand where the judgment comes from. The judgment of God comes from the holiest place of all, from the character of a holy God, and from the throne of God.

Two points concern us as we seek to penetrate the place and the meaning of divine judgment in human history:

1. The crystal sea (Rev. 15:2).
2. The victors who stand by the sea (Rev. 15:2).

The Crystal Sea

First of all, the crystal sea, or 'glassy sea', as the hymn, 'Holy, Holy, Holy', calls it. Think of the finest crystal goblets that your mother or your grandmother had. We are told that such crystal is so fine that talented women with a strong soprano voice can literally cause the crystal to break by singing high notes. From this crystal sea, the word goes forth to order all that happens in world history.

Delicate Blue

This crystal sea corresponds to the sapphire pavement, seen by Moses on Mount Sinai (Exod. 24). When God was giving the law, he opened up the heavens to let Moses see this beautiful crystal sea. From above, it is clear crystal, but from below, it looks blue. If our eyes could see what is there, we would notice a delicate, sapphire blue that is over the whole earthly and cosmic realm, leading us up to the throne room of God. Ezekiel saw it in his first vision, where it is described as glassy, with a blue tinge.

A Reddish Tinge

Here in Revelation 15, it is still beautiful and clear, yet it is no longer bluish, but reddish.[106] We are not certain what that means, but it probably refers to the lasting, all-important, cosmic significance of the shed blood of Christ and of the burning, purging fire of the Holy Spirit. The Old Testament saints saw it as blue before the blood had been shed, and the Holy Ghost had been poured out in a definitive way. 'The sea is mixed with fire', which symbolically directs attention to the pillar of fire that led the Israelites across the Red Sea (Exod. 13:20–14:31). The fire portrayed is a symbol of light and joy to all the saints who are standing next to the sea of glass. But the sea mixed with fire is also a symbol of God's wrath directed against his enemies.'[107]

This is a way of showing us that when John is by miraculous action of God taken to the upper realm, to the throne by the crystal sea, everything on earth then makes sense. It is crystal clear, in a way that it cannot be while we are on the earth.

A Sharp Contrast

It is not hard to contrast the limited vision we possess while we are on earth, with what we could see from where God lifted John. Indeed, through John, God lets us see a certain amount from this supreme place. The sharp contrast is between the crystal sea where everything makes sense, giving wonderful delight, with our experience in the dark shadows of earthly life.

Not always, but frequently, the world we inhabit seems like a dark, raging sea, or a thick London fog. Revelation, following the Psalms, often compares the raging sea to the activities of the heathen nations. It seems that we never go for long without a war. The nations are like 'the troubled sea' (Isa. 57:20), and we have to live there while we are on our brief pilgrimage down here. Therefore, we cannot see very far through the raging sheets of water from the sea, or through the thick clouds of the dark storms that surround us.

'We Walk by Faith and not by Sight'
Revelation 13:1, as we saw earlier, reports that a wicked beast arose from the sea to make war on the church. Sometimes the church feels like Noah's ark, tossed up and down on mountainous waves and torrents, unable to see what comes next.

> Tempted and tried, we're oft made to wonder,
> why it should be thus, all the day long;
> while there are others, living about us,
> never molested, though in the wrong.
> Further along we'll know all about it,
> further along, we'll understand why...'

So, throughout most of earthly history and most of our Christian experience, at best we can usually see only a few feet ahead of us. Much of our pilgrimage is dark and mysterious, yet as we face another day and another test, we face it 'by faith and not by sight'. That is how it is down here.

Most of us can think of some strong Christian people who went through painful and dark episodes, where the only thing they could do to survive for another few inches of their hard journey was to walk by faith and not by sight. I think of such a person in my early ministry, whom I had to tell early one morning of the death of his only son, a twenty-two year old law student, who had just been killed in an automobile accident. Although it happened decades ago, it is something I could never forget. None of us, either then or later, knew why the Lord had allowed this to happen to a fine young Christian. Hard as it was, the bereaved father held on to his faith in the Lord; he knew that he had to keep walking by faith, and not by sight, for he was not privileged to see yet the clarity of the crystal sea.

The Carnage of Wars
One could think of the terrible carnage of the War Between the States, in which vast numbers of young Christians, especially those from the generally evangelical South, were killed (though there were certainly Christians on the Northern side). Two of my relatives, both Christian believers in their early twenties, were killed in one battle on the same day in Virginia. They, and hundreds of others, were quickly buried in shallow graves. Some of our relatives went in two wagons to retrieve the bodies, and bring them home to North Carolina. By the time they got the bodies of these youths back home, it was impossible to bring the bodies into the house for the wake, because of the smell of decomposition. They did the next best thing. There was a six foot picket fence around the house, so they took posts and inserted them into the ground next to the fence, so they could place the two coffins on top, to keep the dogs away. This was a solid Christian family, and they never knew why, nor did they ever understand why such sacrifices did not result in final victory. But they kept trusting

in the Lord, and serving him, even though they had not yet the vision of the crystal sea.

One could think of the useless killing in the two world wars, or how many innocents were killed by Hitler, Stalin, Mao, and Pol Pot, including multitudes of Christians among them. God does not give us short-term explanations here below. Oceans roar, darkness descends, the mountains shake, but God says, 'Trust Me; explanations come later, by the crystal sea; I cannot give them to you now. Trust Me.'

Brightness of the Crystal Sea
But how different is our viewpoint when we are lifted up with John, far above the dark raging sea, to the body of clear, crystal, smooth glass. Viewed from the edge of God's throne, where John now stands, nothing is dark in all creation; there is not one dark corner, nor one unexplored cave. Every fact makes sense. That is what 'crystal sea' means. From the viewpoint of God's eternal throne, every fact is meaningful; all makes sense; everything fits into God's overall program and purpose.

Every war, grief, and defeat; every early death, tear, and martyrdom: all is clear, smooth, and transparently calm as the finest, most delicate crystal. From that place we can see with our eyes—by sight, and not just by faith—exactly why Paul would say in Romans 8:28, 'All things work together for good to them that love the Lord'. We shall see why he says in Ephesians 1:11, 'God works all things, after the counsel of his will'. From the throne we will know there has never been one loose or disconnected wire in all the intricate system of history. God was supervising absolutely everything, all the time. From that place, we will recognize that what seemed to be the craziest events, the most rambling and senseless accidents, were all the time being overruled by God to the right conclusion, in due time, according to his clock and calendar. Not one single fact or event is senseless or unclear from the crystal sea. All shines with the holy light of God streaming through the clearest, most beautiful crystal.

THE VICTORS BY THE CRYSTAL SEA
The victors stand on this beautiful glassy sea. They are the saints, many of whom, while on earth, 'came out of great tribulation' (Rev. 7:14). Some of them had a tough time. Indeed, some were slaughtered, tortured, and hacked to pieces for the faith.

Temporary Loss and Eternal Gain
Notice here another contrast. We have thought of the dark ocean of earthly experience, where so much is dark to us. Let us contrast that darkness in the experience of earthly believers with the stupendous beauty, comfort, and joy that they experience immediately they go above. In Revelation 13:7 we read that the beast: the devil and all his fallen, Christ-hating world system, 'was given power to make war against the saints and to overcome them'. Yes, they lost their physical lives, because they refused to worship the devil and bear his number to be successful in this fallen world; they refused to sell out for temporal gain. They lost, temporarily, but look at what they eternally gain! That is the contrast: temporary loss, and eternal gain.

The Apostle Paul works through this wondrous contrast in 2 Corinthians 4–5: temporary loss, eternal gain. They died, not as losers, but as victors, just like their Savior did. With Moses, they 'chose the reproaches of Christ rather than the riches of Egypt'. With the faithful in Hebrews 11:35, 'they were tortured and did not accept deliverance, that they might attain a better resurrection'. All we can see in these earthly battles is the mangled bodies and the loss. But from the crystal sea, we gaze upon what a happy, eternally generous, glorious, wonderful exchange it was.

During 2002, in Yemen, three Southern Baptist missionary medical doctors, who had been doing a noble job of ministering free of charge to tens of thousands of people, were shot to death in their clinic when a Muslim extremist walked in and opened fire. Their crime was their possible influence upon their patients to believe in Christ.

People of good will find such vicious slaughter most strange, but when you consider the perversion of the devil and what powerful influence he has in false religions and on unregenerate minds, it may not be so strange after all. Yet, in light of the view from the crystal sea, the martyred Christian doctors are victors and not losers.

No Hard Thoughts of God

From this high vantage point, the majestic, light-filled throne, shines its holy beams through the crystal sea. The supernal light will keep us from thinking hard thoughts of God for allowing the suffering and and deaths of his dearest saints, for reasons known to himself at that particular time and place. God appoints a certain number of his people to suffer severe persecution, and martyrdom. We would not think hard of God, if only we could see the glory and thrill that is theirs above, immediately after their soul is loosed from their body. We would gladly join them in 'praising God from whom all blessings flow.' That is the place in which the final sign is given that makes sense of all the struggle of world history between the church and the beast that attacks the church, until an outpouring of divine wrath brings the long battle to a final conclusion. If, by faith, we take our stand near the crystal sea, with glad hearts we can trust in God, praising him, even when here below, we are not able to understand so much that is occurring.

Be still my soul: thy God doth undertake
to guide the future as he has the past.
Thy hope, thy confidence, let nothing shake;
all now mysterious shall be bright at last.
Be still my soul; the waves and winds still know
his voice who ruled them while he dwelt below.

40

The Song of the Victor
Revelation 15:3–4

Here we listen to the song of the victors who are now in heaven. Have you ever wondered what would be the first thing that the saints do when they get to heaven after they have left this earthly life behind them? Revelation 15:3–4 tells us that they begin singing praise to God for who he is, for what he has done, and for his wondrous superintending all their experience while they were on earth. Whether that is exactly the first thing they do, at least it is mentioned here and elsewhere in the Bible as one of the first activities of the heavenly life of the redeemed. In this chapter we are to consider:

1. The hymn they sing.
2. The worthiness of the Lord to whom they are singing this song.

In one sense, every time we have a worship service, it is preparing us for a much greater worship service that one day we too shall join.

The Hymn they Sing

This hymn begins at the last clause of verse 2 and goes on through verses 3–4. The harps of God accompany this song. These harps are provided by God, and adapted so that they can be played in order to praise God. Beautiful instruments are employed in heaven to make the harmony of the redeemed voices even more beautiful than they already are. Psalm 43:4 says this 'Then will I go unto the altar of God, unto God my exceeding joy; upon the harp will I praise Thee, O God my God'. In this Psalm, David is speaking about employing his harp in the earthly tabernacle. David's playing could drive away the evil spirits that were oppressing wicked King Saul, so beautiful was the playing and the singing of the Psalmist of Israel. But we cannot imagine how much more gorgeous are the liquid sounds of the golden heavenly harps as their notes resonate from the pure glass of the crystal sea. What sounds await us! Heaven is a place of sheer beauty, not only beauty of sight, but beauty of hearing. It is a magnification of the most wonderful splendors of earth, the things we see and hear. I have heard about people who, shortly before crossing over the river of death, overheard some of the splendid notes of heaven. It has happened in my ministry to people whom I have known; they heard a little bit of heavenly music, and evidently it was the ringing of the harps, just before they went home. We ourselves will hear this heavenly music, and these golden harps, but most of us do not hear it in this life.

We have to await the glad day, when we are swept up into the grand 'hallelujah chorus'. It will come soon enough if we keep looking by faith to Jesus and trusting in his Word. Our time will come to hear it and to help make music.

The Happy Ones Sing!
What could be more natural to a person than to sing when they feel very happy? If heaven is a supreme place of happiness, then the singing of the ever-happy victors through Christ must surpass the finest music we have heard in our earthly pilgrimage, whether from a choir, an orchestra, or a huge well-trained congregation. Once a year, in early August, there is an evangelical conference in Aberystwyth, Wales, attended by about 1,500 people. It is hard to imagine anything more beautiful than those 1,500 singing in four-part harmony, some of the finest hymns ever written. It is moving, almost overwhelming sometimes, but Wales will not hold a candle to the swelling praise of the victors on the crystal sea, ringing out those golden harps that God has provided for them.

James 5 asks: 'Is any one among you merry? Let him sing psalms'. Some say the best way to get the devil in retreat is to sing praises to God from your hearts. Praise expels Satan's influence from our lives, our churches and our communities, as Ignatius of Antioch said long ago. He cannot stand Christian praises; it all but drives him out of his mind, and he will leave.

Singing Drives out Satan
Which would be more effective in changing the atmosphere of your life: complaining or praising? Wise King Jehoshaphat knew that praise was the greatest weapon he could employ against the devil, and the people who were motivated by Satan.

We read what he did in 2 Chronicles 20:21–25. Israel was surrounded by enemies, and greatly outnumbered. But Jehoshaphat had the nation to fast and to pray. He organized the army and then did a strange thing on the morning of the battle. He brought the white-robed, Levitical choirs out of their service in the temple, and lined them up in front of the army. Can you imagine how dangerous that was? Yet Jehoshaphat knew what he was doing. He told the Levitical choirs, who regularly sang the 150 psalms of David, to start praising 'the beauty of holiness'. As they lifted up their voices, singing God's praises on the battlefield, something supernatural happened. The power of God fell. Satan was routed. Israel's enemies started destroying one another. The victory was won by praising the Lord.

On that crystal sea, the heavenly victors stand gloriously singing, with all of their enemies long past and forever removed. They no longer have to deal with their own sin, for one look at Jesus was sufficient to perfect and glorify them forever. How clear now is the sight of the saints of this glorious God! How full of joyous rapture are their hearts. They see God and they begin to praise him as he deserves.

The Lord to Whom They Sing
Verse 3 shows the Lord to whom the overcomers are singing on the crystal sea. It gives us the title and the content of the song or the hymn, while verse 4 explains why this song is sung with such fervency.

The Title of the Song
What is the title of the first thing they are singing in the glory world? The title is 'The Song of Moses and of the Lamb'. Moses composed two songs reflecting on the victory that God gave Israel over

Egypt in the Passover and at the Red Sea. These are found in Exodus 15 and Deuteronomy 32. For the most part, those two songs of Moses are not much like Revelation 15. But this heavenly song of Revelation 15 does quote a great deal from the Psalms and the prophecy of Jeremiah, although it is not very reflective of what Moses wrote. So why is this song that the saints are singing called 'The Song of Moses and of the Lamb'?

Two great events in the New Testament give us the connection, and explain why what the Lamb did for us is closely connected to what was prefigured in Moses. The first event is the Last Supper and the second event is at the Mount of Transfiguration.

The Last Supper

The Last Supper is connected with the Old Testament feast of the Passover. Paul says, 'Christ our Passover is sacrificed for us' (1 Cor. 5:7). Jesus instituted the Lord's Supper at the very time that the Passover lamb would be sacrificed in the homes of Jerusalem. So the Passover, when it was instituted by Moses through the instruction of God, speaks of the killing of an innocent lamb as a vicarious substitute for each family. They would take the blood of that lamb and smear it on the lintels of the door, so that the Destroying Angel of Death would pass over. He would punish Egypt for their sins against his people, killing all the firstborn of man and beast, but he would pass through Goshen, where the Israelites were, and spare their lives when he saw the blood. The Passover lamb was speaking of a perfect lamb, 'the Lamb of God slain from the foundation of the world', that the heavenly Father would provide, so that God would pass by our sins and deliver us from death into victory. This time, not into the wilderness and then into the promised land, but into the victory of living under the power of God in this life, and then the perfect life in heaven.

The Mount of Transfiguration

The second connection between Moses and the Lamb is at the Mount of Transfiguration. Before the Passion Week, Jesus went up to a mountain and was transfigured before Peter, James and John. In that place, two Old Testament saints, who were alive in heaven came down and met with Jesus. They encouraged him concerning what he would have to go through to become the sin-bearer, in which he was separated from his heavenly Father for a time, as he entered into our hell. The two Old Testament figures that talked to Jesus were Moses and Elijah. We are told in the New Testament that Moses, Elijah, and Jesus spoke of 'the exodus which he should accomplish at Jerusalem'.

Moses is saying to the Lord Jesus Christ, 'Your exodus in Jerusalem, outside the city walls, Your blood-shedding, is the great exodus; my little exodus out of Egypt through the Red Sea, was only a foreshadowing of the great exodus which Your death and Your resurrection must accomplish. In other words, the salvation of Moses, Elijah, and of all the saints of all times, depends directly and only upon the deliverance, the exodus event through Christ in Jerusalem. So 'the Song of Moses and of the Lamb' is celebrating salvation by the shed blood, salvation by the grace of God—God intervening and doing for us what we could never do for ourselves.

The Content of the Song

This heavenly song of the victors on the crystal sea is all about God, from beginning to end. That is one of the ways to judge whether a hymn is good or not—the content should be about God.

The people in heaven are God-centered in their thoughts, so they turn their thoughts about God into praises.

People on earth, who are given the grace to stop concentrating so much on self, and begin thinking more about God, are already entering into a foretaste of the atmosphere of heaven. The word 'worship' comes from the Anglo-Saxon 'worth-ship'. It means expressing what God is worth in our hearts and on our lips; expressing the worth of God is worship. Revelation 5:12 is an illustration of this: 'Saying with a loud voice, Worthy is the Lamb that was slain to receive power and riches and wisdom and strength and honor and glory and blessing'. That is what worship is: the saints sing praise to God. Then we are told three things:

What God Has Done. 'Great and marvelous are Thy works' is the first thing for which they say 'You are worthy for all of this'. These works are not specified in this song, but we can gather from other places in Revelation that they are creation, incarnation, and atonement.

Who can imagine such a thing as creation—God making this vast universe out of nothing? The human mind cannot conceive that once there was nothing but God, then he speaks and the solar system springs into existence, and the light shines. What a great and marvelous work: God creating these things out of nothing, and suddenly, they are there.

Then we can think of the incarnation of Christ. The eternal Son of God, the agent of creation, enters the creation; he becomes a creature without ceasing to be the Creator. It is a marvel! A miracle! Maybe it is greater than the creation: the Son of God becoming one of us, without ceasing to be God. It would take somebody as big as the Creator to redeem us. That is Jesus! And it takes his atoning blood to forgive our sins. Our sins are great, but Jesus' blood is greater. I say that to people who sometimes wonder if God will forgive them. They protest: 'But you do not know what I've done.' I reply, 'Maybe not, but I know that the blood of Christ is richer and greater than the worst of your sins. God will forgive you if you ask Him.' Great and marvelous works!

Cleansing blood, and then the resurrection of the dead body of Jesus out of the tomb. Life from death, resurrection which guarantees salvation (for it shows that God has accepted the sacrifice). Great and marvelous are the works of God. If you start thinking about it a little bit your tongue will get loosed and you will praise the Lord!

'Just and True are Thy Ways'. The second thing for which the saints are praising him in 'The Song of Moses and the Lamb' is for the righteousness and the truth of how he did everything that he did. 'Just and true are Thy ways'. Some people use the existence of evil as a reason for denying the existence of God; it is for them a convenient excuse. There are mysteries about evil that no person can explain at all, but in glory we will at last understand how and why God allowed evil, and how he guided it in definite directions without approving it, or doing anything that was not loving, kind, good, and true. Then we shall gladly say: 'Lord, You are holy, and everything You did was just right!' That is what these heavenly creatures are now saying.

Ezekiel 14:13 talks about the evil that the Lord had to allow to punish Israel for its idolatry. Then God says through his prophet, 'And they shall comfort you when you see their ways and their doings and you shall know that I have not done without cause all that I have done, says the Lord God'. It will be a great comfort to us in heaven, when we contemplate every bad thing that happened in our lives, every evil that God allowed to occur, to see that God had a reason that was loving, just, and in accord with his holy character for every bad thing we experienced. We will praise him that he knew what he was doing. What a rejoicing of our hearts it will bring to see that those things that hurt us and worried us, now make sense. We will praise him for all of them.

'King of Nations'. Then the third thing for which they praise God is 'Thou, King of nations'. The United States of America is, no doubt, the strongest country in the world at present. It was not so always. In the sixteenth century it was Spain, France in the seventeenth century, and after that, it was England. Such things change. Even so, the strongest nation is mere dust in the balance beside the King of nations, God Almighty. He is ultimately in charge, and one day it will be made manifest.

John tells us in conclusion in Revelation 15:4, why it is that once the saints get home, they get busy praising the Lord. The saints are praising God like this as a way of answering the question, 'Who shall not fear Thee O Lord and glorify Thy name?' This implies that massive numbers of all who have ever lived, will one day see the holy majesty and infinite work of God, and will be converted to his glory. Not everybody who has ever lived will be converted; there will be numbers in hell, but hundreds of hundreds of millions upon millions will yet turn to Christ before earth history ends. Something like 17,000 people are converted to the Lord Jesus Christ in Africa every day. Huge numbers come to Christ every day in China and South America. Many are praying that God's Holy Spirit will come back in large effusion to the largely apostate countries of the West and be poured out on us again, like he was on our forefathers as late as 1859. I believe it is going to happen one day.

Once the Holy Spirit is poured out on our apostate countries of the West and we begin to see what God is like, and we begin to praise Him, what singing you will then hear in churches and businesses. Up and down the streets, people will be walking and spontaneously praising the Lord. Nobody will think they are crazy. What singing you will hear from families assembled for daily worship at home! If we realized afresh by faith what the saints above now see with their eyes we could not keep from bursting forth into praise. I say, 'Lord, do it again, and everything will be different'.

41

THE OPENING OF THE TABERNACLE OF HEAVEN
Revelation 15:5–8

This text is a graphic way of speaking to us of where the future comes from. Have you ever thought of that? In all countries of the world, everybody wonders what the future holds. We do not know the details of what the future holds; God does not reveal it. But this text shows us the most important thing to know as we contemplate the future, and that is, where the future comes from. It comes from the holy place in the tabernacle in heaven. The future on earth is sent down from heaven, in direct proportion to what mankind does with the testimony of God that is enshrined in the heavenly tabernacle.

We look at three things out of this text.

1. The opening of the tabernacle (Rev. 15:5a).
2. What is in the tabernacle (Rev. 15:5b).
3. What comes out of the heavenly tabernacle down into the everyday world (Rev. 15:6–8).

OPENING OF THE TABERNACLE

In verse 5, the tabernacle in heaven is opened. This well-known Old Testament fixture is termed 'the temple of the tabernacle of the testimony in heaven.' The word 'temple' refers to the holy place, sometimes called 'the holy of holies', in Latin, *sanctus sanctorum*. The earthly tabernacle, and the stone temple of Solomon that replaced it, had three main compartments: the outer court, the inner court, and a small cubical room in the middle, which was the most important holy space in Israel. Indeed, it was the most important holy space on earth before Jesus came. This was 'the holy of holies'. It is what is meant by 'the temple of the tabernacle', the innermost part of the tabernacle.

The Holy of Holies

In this holy of holies, there was very little furniture, but what was there—the Ark of the Covenant—was of stupendous importance for the life of the human race and their future. It was a remarkable sort of a box that had been made according to the pattern that the Lord gave to Moses on Mount Sinai. This oblong box, which had poles fastened to the sides, by which the Levites could carry it on their shoulders, was covered with gold. On the top of it was 'the Mercy Seat' and inside it were the two tables of the law: the Ten Commandments.

The Mercy Seat

The Ten Commandments had been inscribed by the finger of God, literally, on these stone tablets. Inside the Ark, therefore, would be the expression of who God is—the expression to us of his character, of his heart, and of his requirements upon all who are made in his image. Upon the Mercy Seat, on top of the Ark, the High Priest of Israel, once a year on the Day of Atonement ('*Yom Kippur*') would come in with a bowl of blood from the slaying of an innocent substitutionary lamb outside the tabernacle. He would sprinkle the blood on top of that Mercy Seat for his own sins and for the sins of the people whom he represented. At each end of that oblong box, were representations of angelic figures (or *cherubim*). Holy though they were, they had to veil their faces with their wings, for none can look on the thrice holy God directly and live. That was all that was in the holy place; but in a sense it was everything. It was all that mattered.

God Opens the Tabernacle

When God opened the tabernacle, he let John see it on the inside. Of course, John could only have looked inside this holy tabernacle and not been slain immediately, because when Jesus, the agent of creation, was dying in his human nature, it was as though the creation was about to shake to pieces. As he was making atoning sacrifice for the sins of all who would believe, there was an earthquake in Jerusalem, and the thick heavy velvet that shut off the holiest place from the other two compartments of the temple was split in two—from top to bottom. It was as if the finger of God himself slashed all the way through it. According to the epistle to the Hebrews, by this divine action, the way into the holiest place of all was made open by the death of Jesus. In other words, we can now get directly to God the Father Almighty in heaven through Jesus, in a way of intimate communion that was not possible in the same way, or in the same measure, before the death of Jesus. So the tabernacle was opened, so that John could see into it, because of Jesus' death, resurrection, and ascension.

WHAT IS IN THE TABERNACLE?

Within the Ark was enshrined the law of God, the expression of his holy character. The reality of the character of God reposing within the holiest place of all should have much to say about our worship today. A sense of God's essential holiness, and therefore, of the seriousness of our sins against it, cannot be absent from true, Christian worship. I know of a man who attended various conferences, which claimed to show him how to make his church much larger. On the basis of what he heard, he decided that in his worship services he was not going to allow sin to be preached. But if, to please the general public, you make worship services light and happy by not talking about sin, it is necessary that you play down the holiness of God. That may draw larger numbers, but his particular church, far from growing, shrank. It got so bad that he had to leave.

The Holiness of God Crucial to True Worship

'The temple of the tabernacle of the testimony in heaven' shows us that the holiness of God must always be central to true worship. Reverence towards God is essential to genuine worship. If a worship service is going to be truly Christian, it will be God-centered, and will tenderly remember the holiness of God. We see this in Isaiah 6, where the angels were crying out, 'Holy, holy, holy is the Lord of Hosts'. When one turns a worship service into a mere human work to make people feel good, one loses the sense of God's purity, majesty and holiness. In a word, one loses transcendence—the only thing that lifts us up from earth and makes worship worthwhile. When the tabernacle was opened, the beautiful, spotless holiness of God written in letters of light on these tables of stone was shining out.

Because God is holy, his holiness determines everything that is going to happen in my little life and in the big wide world, including the planets and galaxies. Directly related to God's holiness, there are two realities in that heavenly tabernacle. These two realities are the most determining factors for our future. One of the realities is God's mercy; the other is God's judgment.

A wonderful old Scottish hymn, drawing on the last words of Samuel Rutherford, says: 'With mercy and with judgment, my web of time he wove.' Sin is a cancer that would malignantly eat everything up, if left unarrested. Hence, the righteousness of God requires him to deal with sin. It is too big for us finite creatures to handle, so God himself deals with sin. That is the point manifested by the blood-sprinkled Mercy Seat in the tabernacle. The tabernacle is where God met man in stupendous mercy. It had the Mercy Seat that blood was sprinkled upon and the veil that had been split open at the death of Christ. In other words, any thing that needs to be done about my sin has been perfectly done by God himself in Jesus Christ. The heart of what determines the future for us all is the Mercy Seat.

Sin First Covered, then Totally Removed

God is merciful! I do not mind preaching the holiness of God because I know that allied to his holiness is his mercy. One has no conception of what the mercy and the tender loving-kindness of our heavenly Father means for us poor sinners, until we realize how holy he is. His holy justice requires him to deal to the fullest degree with every infraction against his character. If he did not, he would be less than holy. He would deny himself, which is impossible. The animal sacrifices of the Old Testament: the lambs, goats, and bulls; the holocaust and the whole burnt offering, speak of the covering of sin. But Jesus' once-for-all sacrifice accomplishes something far greater than covering. Hebrews says that when Jesus dies, sin is not merely covered; it is removed and destroyed.

Animal sacrifices had their value; they could temporarily cover sin and keep us from being destroyed. But the final and infinite sacrifice of Christ perfectly takes all sin away. Thus, the veil into the most holy place is split wide open from top to bottom, and lets us get through directly to God. It is out of this holy place that John sees the mercy of God coming down to this world. Jesus brought the mercy of God when he was conceived without sin in the womb of the blessed virgin Mary, born of her, lived a holy life, announced God's will, fulfilled the law in all its requirements, and died to pay the penalty of our sins. The Father accepted his sacrifice as having done everything that was necessary to bring mankind back to the heavenly Father when he raised his body from the dead and took him back to the Throne in Glory.

Hence, in Revelation 15:5, John sees that Jesus brought God's mercy out of the tabernacle. How important that is as we face the future! We do not know how long we are going to live. We do not know the details of the future, but this much we know: if we by faith lay hold of Jesus Christ as our Savior and Lord, the future for us will always be marked by the mercy of God.

That does not mean that God is going to make our pathway easy every day; he knows best. Again, to refer to that hymn:

> With mercy and with judgment
> my web of time he wove;
> And aye the dews of sorrow
> were lustered by his love.
> I'll bless the hand that guided;

I'll praise the heart that planned,
When throned where glory dwelleth,
in Immanuel's land.

So God mixes our cup of loss and gain, of suffering and relief, of victories and defeats. He mixes that cup by his providential mercies, so that what we are given to drink is just right. When we get to the hilltops of heaven and look back, we will see that what characterized our walk, even when we went through dark valleys and painful episodes, was the mercy of God being with us in just the right proportion. The right medicines were administered to make us ready to be like Jesus, more and more from the inside out, and to get us victoriously home to heaven.

Out of that tabernacle of holiness, mercy and grace, comes the future. For all of God's people, sinners though they were, the future that God administers for them is primarily marked by the wondrous mercy of God as the Father sees fit, and sends out the holy angels, causing particular things to happen. Divine and infinite mercy comes out of the holiest place of all in heaven.

What Comes Out of the Tabernacle?

Having surveyed the mercy that comes out of the heavenly tabernacle, we must now notice something else that comes out of the same holy place of sovereign power and grace: it is judgment. Judgment is for those who refuse to accept the judgment of Christ in their place, for their sin. I have never understood how, when the gospel is explained, and the great love of God to us in Jesus is held forth, some people are angered and will not accept it. After a fairly long preaching and teaching ministry, I have gained the impression that preaching the sheer grace of God is far more likely to anger sinners than preaching the requirements of the law. In my early years, I had assumed that it would be the opposite, but the years taught me better.

I will never forget one Sunday night, many years ago, at an evening service at the First Presbyterian Church, Dillon. I preached a rather long sermon on Psalm 22, setting forth the wonderful grace of God in Christ, who was forsaken that we need never be forsaken, whose blood is the only thing that can get any sinner into heaven. One man at that service became extremely angry. He was not angry over the length of the sermon, but over what was said. At times, I have made people angry, but I have never seen a person more infuriated than on that night. That older gentleman said something like this: 'What do you mean by saying we cannot do something to please God to help us get into heaven, and that if we do good works, they are not sufficient? I have never heard such things! You are excluding people here who are trying to do good.' I quietly and calmly replied, 'Well, do not argue with me; argue with the Lord'.

It worked out well. Time went by, and he was getting into the Word of God, attending every service and reading Holy Scripture daily. God saved his soul! Then he was very glad that grace would be preached. Sinners do not like the law, but there is something they like even less: the mercy of God in the cleansing blood of Christ, that requires them humbly to bow at the foot of the cross. But keep preaching it, for it is the only way lost men and women can get in touch with that tabernacle and the God whom it represents. Whether they like it or not, 'as many as ordained unto eternal life will in due time believe' (Acts 13:48). That is what controls the future: how you stand with Jesus Christ, whether you get under the blood by faith. Following that, you will know his everlasting mercy, and all will be well.

How Can a Loving God Judge the Lost?

But reject that, and what comes out of the tabernacle for you? Seven angels, having seven bowls or challises, full of the wrath of God. There was a modernist movement in Protestantism, and now amongst Roman Catholics, which openly rejects Holy Scripture. It picks and chooses aspects of God that it finds acceptable, while denying inconvenient truths. It wants a user-friendly God who is not holy and who has no wrath. Many of them say, 'My God is a God of love; he couldn't judge people'.

But there is only one God—the God of the Bible. How does the Bible describe Him? Yes, he is the most wonderful love; he sacrificed the Son of his heart to forgive us, if we accept Him. But it is holy love; it has character and shape to it. If you deny God's holiness, and thus his wrath upon those who reject the blood of his Son, then you deny the only true God. The God you are talking about is an idol or vanity (an empty thing), a false God who is not really there. To come to terms with reality, you must face the true God, whose holy character and infinite loving kindness led him to provide an atoning sacrifice in Jesus Christ, by which believers can get into heaven. That once-for-all sacrifice is what made it possible for John to see 'the temple of the tabernacle of the testimony'. That is why there is so much singing and praise rolling forth in heaven. Vast numbers join together on account of the divine mercy that comes out of that tabernacle to sinners on earth.

Many people say, 'I do not accept the wrath of God.' It is an unrealistic viewpoint on the world to assert that there is no such thing as divine holiness, or sin and evil, which are contradictions of it. If there is nothing wrong, and if there is no such thing as sin, then why is the world not perfect and without blotches, physically or morally?

Evidences in History that God Judges Evil

The world where there is no evil is a figment of the imagination of secular humanism and other false religions. The God who never punishes anyone is also a figment of the Enlightenment imagination. Does this world in which we live really work that way?

What do you actually find in this world? Look at the twentieth century alone. More blood of innocent persons was shed in the twentieth century by wicked dictators and corrupt politicians than in all the centuries from the time of Jesus Christ through to the nineteenth century. The wars and the genocide of huge populations in the twentieth century—the time that claimed to be the most enlightened—under Stalin, Mao, and others, have been worse than in any other period of history. It looks as if there are evidences in the last century of the coming down of the wrath of God against sin out of that tabernacle! Would not the scores of millions killed under Stalin, as Solzenitsyn's multi-volumed *Gulag Archipelago* testifies, serve as evidences of wrath upon the earth? Who could count the numbers killed in China and in large swaths of Africa? How many have starved to death in North Korea? Common sense will show that this is not a perfect world, where there are no consequences of sin and evil; where there could be no wrath coming down from above. The wrath of God is evident to anybody who has eyes open. The wrath that comes down is evidence of God's judgments against sin that has not been atoned for. To those who refuse the gospel, only wrath can come out of the tabernacle.

Have you ever thought that behind the judgments that occur in history is a divine plan to shake down evil systems to make room for the good? That was the case with the fall of Jerusalem. Wrath came in God's due season, first-century

Judaism that had rejected the Lord was shaken down, and its stronghold destroyed. There have been shakings-down throughout history. Who can imagine the judgments that may lie ahead?

God's Judgment and the Prayers of the Saints

Consider what is going on behind the scenes of every historical judgment from Revelation 8:5, and 6:9-10. Revelation 8:3-5 shows that behind the coming down of the wrath of God in future judgments on the world, lies the prayers of the suffering saints. It may be prayers of the saints on earth, or the prayers of the martyred saints now in glory, talking to the Father. In that holy realm they are saying: 'How long, O Lord, holy and true, dost Thou not avenge our blood on the dwellers on the earth' (Rev. 6:10). Then we are told that the angels are released with these judgments, in answer to the prayers of the saints.

These verses in Revelation 6 and 8 teach us that the coming down of judgments on an evil world system is from the Lord, who has heard the prayer of his saints. Thus, Revelation 6, 8, and 15 unite in teaching us that even the judgments that come out of that tabernacle are always mingled with mercy. The judgments behind destructive events proceed from the loving, holy heart of the God whom the suffering saints across the ages pray to vindicate his people and to honor his Name.

What Should You Do?

What does the future hold for you, for me? I do not know what it holds in detail, but I do know that the future is coming out of this beautiful, holy tabernacle on angel wings. At least I can know the most important thing about my future, which is that Jesus has taken away my sin and I have been given grace to look to him for forgiveness. Therefore, out of that tabernacle that Jesus controls, the mercy of God will be upon me until the time comes for him to take me to that glorious place. But those who reject the testimony of the Father to the Son, leave God no alternative but to send out the angels to visit upon them preliminary wrath, with the judgments that come on earth, and, if they are still unrepentant, final wrath at the Last Day. God gives us who hear this message of grace a choice. How wonderful to be alive! We have the privilege to have our minds working, and to have the gospel available.

Some of you may feel bewildered by this testimony as to the true state of affairs. You may even suspect that your own destiny could be determined by how you respond to the offers of the loving grace of God, through the atoning blood of Christ. Perhaps you feel unable to repent and believe in Him; you do not know how, nor what it would look like if you tried to do so. But millions of plain men and women from every part of the world, before you came onto the scene, have kept asking God to work in their lives by his Holy Spirit, so that they would be able to respond to the sweet call of the gospel. God can do it for you, but he wishes for you to ask him until you know the power of his presence, opening your innermost being to the light and joy of the Lord. Follow David in Psalm 27:8: 'When thou saidst, Seek ye my face; my heart said unto thee, Thy face, LORD, will I seek.'

42

WHAT ABOUT JUDGMENT?

Revelation 16:1–7

This is a passage about the holy judgments of God coming into history. I remember an older minister in Scotland, when I was a student, saying to some of us that one of the great values of preaching through the Word of God, passage by passage, rather than just picking out something you like, was the objective personal discipline of going straight through the books of the Bible. It would cause you to preach on things that otherwise you would avoid. Thereby, the people of God would be edified by getting the whole message, as God intended. One of the things that most pastors would avoid in their preaching, if they just go through and pick out things that they like, would be this passage on the judgment of God hitting the real world. But God has a good reason for having it in the text. Far from hurting a congregation, it helps to give them the whole range of the truth. It makes them stronger people and wakes them up to the great realities if the Holy Spirit blesses. Yet, there is no doubt that in the modern church there is a hesitation to preach on judgment.

This passage says five things about the judgment of God:

1. Judgment comes out of a holy place, not an unholy or bad place (Rev. 16:1).
2. Judgments on the earth are answers to the prayers of the saints (Rev. 16:7; 6:10–12; 8:2–5).
3. Divine judgment is horrible for the impenitent (Rev. 16:2–4).
4. Divine judgment fits the crime perfectly (Rev. 16:6).
5. A word of hope (Rev. 16:6–7).

JUDGMENT COMES OUT OF A HOLY PLACE

Notice that the terrible judgments described in chapter 16 all come directly out of the holiest place in the universe: God's temple in the highest heaven. Furthermore, each one of these horrendous judgments against a sinful, blaspheming society, is sent forth by the voice of a holy, loving God. The mighty angels of judgment that come out of that temple above dare not inflict even one of these judgments until the thrice-holy God bids them to do so.

This means that these judgments visited upon the earth serve the purposes of the holiness and goodness of our heavenly Father, he who is love in its purest and highest form. You might think, how can this be true from all we hear about the goodness of God? Could a loving God really pour out devastating judgment, even on Christ-rejecting sinners? Much of the church has decided that he does not; therefore, they never preach on it. But if we go by Scripture, we will indeed preach on this subject.

God's Character Shapes Righteous Judgment
That raises the question of why a loving God judges? In the previous chapter we considered the Biblical reasons for the necessity of God's judgment against sin. We need not repeat that here, but we do need to note the related point, that righteous judgment is shaped by the holy character of the God of the Covenant of Grace. The precise shape of the judgments of God is determined by his character, which has been manifested in his gracious dealings with his people. For instance, in Exodus 20, the Ten Commandments are introduced by 'the preface' 'I am the Lord thy God which hath brought thee out of the house of bondage out of Egypt' (Exod. 20:2). In other words, the Ten Commandments are given because of who God is; the moral law is an expression of his integrity. He made us in his image, therefore he requires this of us.

For instance, why ought I not to steal? Why ought I not to commit adultery? You could say, 'It's bad for society; it will degrade you and hurt other people.' That would be true, but the most basic reason is because of who God is, and because you have been made in his image. That is why we are not to do these destructive actions. Deuteronomy 5:24–5 adds this to the account of God giving the Ten Commandments:

And ye said, Behold, the Lord our God hath showed us his glory and his greatness and we have heard his voice out of the midst of the fire. We have seen this day that God doth talk with man and he liveth. Now therefore why should we die, for this great fire will consume us. If we hear the voice of the Lord our God any more then we shall die.

In this manner, God shows us his glory and holiness, and says, in effect: 'The law, which is the way that you love, comes out of who I am'. We sinful humans must bear in mind that God's pure holiness burns against all that is impure and dirty. His loving holiness must consume the cancer of sin in order to maintain its sterling integrity and matchless goodness.

We see that again in Deuteronomy 6:15: 'For the Lord your God is a jealous God among you; lest the anger of the Lord thy God be kindled against thee and destroy thee from off the face of the earth'. That means God's integrity, his love, is expressed in moral terms. Not to get right with his holy character requires destruction of that which is rebellious against God's purity. To leave sin undealt with, God would have to deny his own character. If he denied himself, the universe would disappear like a snowball hitting the noonday sun; all would be gone. We are told God cannot, will not deny himself; it is impossible.

Enlightenment Rejection of Judgment
Since the eighteenth century European Enlightenment, and the Modernism that followed it, some people have objected, 'But the God you're presenting is the God of the Old Testament, not the God of the New Testament.' Such objections go as far back as the heretical movement known as Gnosticism in the early centuries of Christianity. In order to deny the holy judgments of God against sin in this world, not a few have said: 'But what about Jesus? Isn't he different in this matter of judgment?'

When I was a student in Edinburgh, a fellow student had an aunt, who attended a church which denied the full truth of Scripture. She used this kind of argument against her nephew, of whose robust faith she keenly disapproved. Her nephew invited her to go to the great evangelical church we attended, but she replied:

'I'm not going to that church, because they preach about sin and judgment, and that is not the kind of religion I believe in.'

He said 'Well, what kind of religion do you believe in at that church you attend?'

Her answer was: 'I believe in the religion of the Sermon on the Mount given by Jesus and that is what the church I go to stands for. We believe the religion of Jesus, instead of all this Old Testament kind of thing.'

'Well, do you accept all of the Sermon on the Mount?' he asked her.

This caught her up short: 'What do you mean by that?' she countered.

He then put this question, 'Do you accept the part in the Sermon on the Mount where Jesus says "If thy right hand offend thee, cut it off, for it's better for thee to go through life halt and main than to be cast into the lake of fire."'

'No, I certainly do not accept that kind of thing.'

He said 'Well then, it looks like you do not really believe in the Sermon on the Mount, nor in the One who gave it.'

Here was his point: if you claim to accept part of the Bible as true, then you must accept all of it. To believe in a God of love is altogether right, but we must define 'love' as the Word of God defines it. We may not simply pick out one or two instances of God's actions that we like. In that case, we paltry mortals are the givers of the truth instead of God, something the third century Christian writer, Tertullian of North Africa, dealt with in his treatise, *On the Prescription of Heretics*.

Divine Judgments Appropriate to the Sin
The angels that bring vials of wrath out of the most holy place let loose judgments that are specifically appropriate to particular kinds of heinous sins:

- sores on worshippers of the beast (they thought he would give them beauty and pleasure);
- turning waters into death-dealing cesspools of blood (for those so punished had shed the blood of the righteous);
- burning and scorching upon blasphemers (who thought they would find cool refreshment through an alliance with the powers of hell).

These judgments are a holy way of punishing high-handed unholiness. They come from the holy place, and the saints above properly cry out, 'Even so, Lord God Almighty, true and righteous are thy judgments' (Rev. 16:7). Only the unholy have the temerity to argue that a loving God would not punish wickedness. To do so shows that one refuses to recognize who the holy covenant God really is, and such refusal merits appropriate chastisement.

God is eternally holy, and so will bring every attitude and every deed into account. That is why America should be very humble and fearful. We have legally allowed the abortion of millions since 1973. The holiness of God says that killing of the innocent is wrong, and the blood of the innocents will be fully and justly avenged by the Eternal One. That sending out of chastisement from the holy place includes serious reversals and judgments in nations that practice this, unless they repent. All these future judgments against us will come out of the holy, beautiful place in heaven. Proud sinners will be smitten to the ground in horror when it occurs, except they repent before it happens.

Judgments on Earth Are Answers to the Prayers of the Saints

Verse 7 speaks of the praises given by the saints in glory for God sending his judgments into the earth. Passages we have already seen, such as Revelation 6:10-12 and 8:2-5, indicate that God's judgments on earth are the answer of God to the prayers of his saints about evil. Judgments on earth have a background. It is not only the evil that those who rejected God committed, but also the longing, praying hearts of his saints.

'Deliver Us from Evil'

The Lord's Prayer, given to us by Jesus, instructs believers to pray: 'Deliver us from evil'. One of the ways that the Christian church gets deliverance from evil is by praying to God to vindicate the suffering of his people, and thus to deal with evil powers. Believing prayer of concerned, suffering saints, ultimately will always prevail in God's wise timing. When God finally pronounces the fearful word in Revelation 16:1, he sends forth the avenging angels to do their frightening work on earth among the nations. Their going forth is the culmination of the long, agonizing prayers both of suffering saints on earth and of triumphant martyrs gathered round the altar in heaven.

We saw this movement in Revelation 6:10-11 and then in Revelation 8:2-5. God smelled the sacred fragrance. He heard the prayer of the Church: 'Deliver us from evil'. But he takes his all-wise time to send out the destroying angels on those who are laying waste his church. At the right moment, the prayers of the saints come into full effect, and 'fire is cast into the earth!' Perhaps the suffering Church was tempted to think that God would never see and would never do anything about their powerlessness against demonic foes, but suddenly, God moves in.

God's Judgments Come in his Time-Frame

Andrew Murray in *With Christ in the School of Prayer* says, 'Satan may hinder a prayer but he can never stop it.' The most the evil one can do is to make your getting of the answer to that prayer a little longer, but if you persist, the answer will come. That is why Jesus says, 'Men ought always to pray and not to faint.' Murray adds: 'The power of believing prayer is simply irresistible.'

The only continued prayer that God will not answer from his saints is for something that would be outside his will, that would not be to his honor, nor to our good. But anything that would be to God's honor and for our good will surely be answered, if we keep on praying, and not fainting. God exercises all-wise control of the clock, with its minute hand and second hand. He is in direct charge of the turning of the calendar, month by month, and the eventful movement of the years. Yet God will use those prayers. With him who has ordained and empowers those prayers, they have irresistible power, including the delivering of his church from evil.

Let us fervently hope that the Christian church will not miss the countless opportunities to shape the future 'to deliver us from evil', by continuing to pray. Let us be a part of the solution to evil in our time by much specific and tireless prayer!

Divine Judgment Is Terrible for the Impenitent

What about those who never repent? The solemn answer to that is conveyed to us by the first three bowls or vials of wrath that these holy angels are sent to pour out on unrepentant sinners in Revelation 16:2 and 4. These judgments have something in common with several of the ten plagues that were visited on Egypt except that they are far worse: deeper and more wide-ranging.[108]

Malignant Sores

The first avenging angel puts a loathsome and malignant sore upon the people who have the mark of the beast. It is as if the mark had broken out in a deadly infection and was eating up their skin, just as God put boils upon the persecuting Egyptians in Exodus 9, as one of the ten plagues. Indeed, Moses had predicted that this would happen in Deuteronomy 28:27-8 and 35, where he says:

> The Lord will smite thee with the botch of Egypt and with the emerods [haemorrhoids] and with the scab and with the itch, whereof thou canst not be healed. The Lord shall smite thee with madness, and blindness, and astonishment of heart… The Lord shall smite thee in the knees, and in the legs, with a sore botch [a terrible eruption in the skin] that cannot be healed, from the sole of thy foot unto the top of thy head.

That is the very thing that the avenging angel is sent to unleash in God's time on those who reject the truth and persecute the Lord's people.

Dead Blood to Drink

Then the second angel pours his bowl of wrath into the sea, into the oceans, and it becomes like the sluggish, coagulated, putrefying blood of a dead man.[109] There is a remarkable passage about an actual occurrence of this sort of thing in Josephus, *The Wars of the Jews* (iii.x.9), who was an eyewitness to the destruction of Jerusalem in AD 70. He describes how several thousand Jews thought they were going to escape from the Roman armies by attempting to cross the Sea of Galilee in little dinghies so as to escape from the Roman army. But the Romans quickly came and by using long lances and swords from their much stronger boats, were able to stab them and cut off the heads of many of them. Josephus then says: 'One could see the whole lake stained with blood and crammed with corpses, for not a man escaped. During the days that followed a horrible stench hung over the region and it presented an equally horrifying spectacle. The beaches were strewn with wrecks and swollen bodies which, hot and clammy with decay, made the air so foul that the catastrophe that plunged the Jews in mourning revolted even those who had brought it about.'[110] This was an historic fulfillment of the sending forth of the second angel unto judgment, but it is not the only one, nor is it the last one!

The third angel pours out a cup of wrath that is like the first Egyptian plague in the time of Moses, when he turned the rivers and springs into blood. The New Testament, not just the Old Testament says: 'It is a fearful thing to fall into the hands of the living God'. It also says 'our God is a consuming fire' against that which is unrepented of and contrary to the divine character. Those proud false religionists who will never believe in the splendid holiness of God, and create the vain idol of a God who is comfortable with their sins, will feel the effects of that holy wrath being poured out upon themselves, when it is too late for repentance. We must pray that many who read these lines will reconsider their tenuous and disastrous position, while still there is time!

Divine Judgment Fits the Crime

We have already considered the appropriateness of God's outpouring of wrath upon specific kinds of sins and upon specific kinds of sinners. But here we must pursue further how the divine judgment fits the crime perfectly. We see this illustrated in how the angel explains these terrible judgments coming upon the people (v. 6), as when the sea becomes blood, and they have to, as it were, drink their own blood, instead of water: 'For they have shed the blood of saints and prophets and Thou hast given them blood to drink for they are worthy'. The punishment fits the crime exactly; they have shed innocent blood, and now they must drink their own putrefying blood. God's judgments are always according to truth; he does everything fairly, justly and right.

Listen to what Isaiah 49:26 says, prophesying all this: 'And I will feed them that oppress thee with their own flesh; and they shall be drunken with their own blood, as with sweet wine; and all flesh shall know that I the Lord am thy Savior and thy Redeemer, the mighty One of Jacob'. Divine judgment fits the crime and is totally just, or else God would not maintain his eternal integrity.

Then the holy ones around the altar add their testimony: 'And I heard another out of the altar say, even so, Lord God Almighty, true and righteous are Thy judgments' (v. 7). The heavenly throne is white; it shines with holiness and beauty and splendor. All that is dark and rebellious must be eternally separated from the great white throne, and from him that sits on it. Everything impure must be cast into a place of outer darkness and into a fire that gives off no light whatsoever because God, the source of light, is holy, and to be separated from him leaves one in profound darkness. Every judgment is just right, and perfectly appropriate to the sin that was unrepented of.

A Word of Hope (Rev. 16:7)

A word of hope emerges in verse 7. We are buoyed up by hope as we consider with the saints above that 'true and righteous are God's judgments.' Every last sin must and will be subjected to the totally appropriate wrath of a thrice holy God. But here is the most important question we can ever face: Did the holy wrath of God against my sin fall upon me as I am united to Christ by faith and the Holy Spirit, or must it fall upon me alone? Either way, in a moral universe, 'life must be given for life'.

'The Life is in the Blood'
Leviticus 17 shows us this truth when it says '*The life is in the blood*'. That is the significance of the blood of the animal sacrifices, and the blood of Jesus, to which they pointed. 'The life is in the blood' shows that, according to the law of the harvest, life must be given for life. We forfeit life, for we deserve eternal death when we sin against God. To make just reparation for our sins that merit death and separation from the Living God, blood must be shed in accordance with the moral principles that emanate from the character of the God who created this moral universe.

Consider this awesome grace of God that is open before us today. Whether we consider how many sins we have committed personally, or corporately partaken of living in a nation that is sinning with a high hand, both ways, everything wrong has to be paid for. A holy God cannot overlook any sin and remain who he is.

Propitiation
But listen to the same man who wrote Revelation. The same man who saw these horrendous judgments says there is hope! John writes: 'If we say that we have no sin we deceive ourselves and the truth is not in us' (1 John 1:8). Then he adds this all-important promise from God: 'If we confess our sins, he is faithful and just to forgive us our sins and to cleanse us from all unrighteousness' (1 John 1:9). We can be cleansed from sin and all its horrid consequences, totally and forever. We can be set free from all that brings the devastating judgment of God. How? If we look to Jesus and

confess our sins. John says further, 'If any man sin we have an advocate with the Father, Jesus Christ the righteous; and he is the propitiation for our sins; and not for ours only, [not just the Jews, but for them first] but also for the sins of the whole world' (1 John 2:1–2). The cross of Calvary is the place of the shedding of the precious blood of the Lamb. The mercy seat on the Ark of the Covenant represented his final, victorious blood-shedding. The incarnate Person of Christ is the place where God's wrath is forevermore turned away from anybody who will sincerely ask God to forgive their sins. (That is what is meant by the word 'propitiation'). The thrilling glory of this gospel is that once we identify with Christ through faith, we have absolutely no judgment to face. Instead of facing a fearful Judge, we face the reconciled face of a loving Father. That is grace! Those saints, now praying to God and singing his praises around the altar, were once as sinful as any of us is, but by grace, they repented and asked God to forgive them. His Holy Spirit took hold of their lives, so that they are now in glory, where they will never face judgment, for Christ took it from them on himself. And we can be where they are.

A Final Choice Is Set Before You

Here is the choice set before every sinner. Either the water of human life will be turned to dead blood for me, or Jesus' blood is shed for me. I either experience some kind of living death through all eternity if I reject Jesus, or he takes all my blood-judgment, life for life, and all my separation in hell is taken on him upon that cross. As I believe and repent, God the Father gives me his Son's purity and heaven in exchange for my sin and endless hell. Is that not wonderful? That is the gospel. God is thoroughly just when sinners believe; he pronounces them holy, and says, 'At the set time, you will come home to heaven to live with me forever.' And God is thoroughly just when sinners reject his Son, and he says 'You must go into a place of judgment and outer darkness.' God is holy both ways. Which will it be for me? There is no third option.

> There is a fountain filled with blood
> drawn from Immanuel's veins;
> and sinners plunged beneath that flood
> lose all their guilty stains.[111]
>
> His hands were pierced, the hands that made
> the mountain range and everglade;
> That washed the stain of sin away
> and changed earth's darkness into day.
>
> His feet were pierced, the feet that trod
> the furthest shining star of God;
> And left their imprint deep and clear
> on every winding pathway here.
>
> His heart was pierced, the heart that burned
> to comfort every heart that yearned;
> And from it came a cleansing flood,
> the river of redeeming blood.
>
> His hands and feet and heart, all three
> were pierced for me on Calvary;
> And here and now to him I bring,
> my hands, feet, heart, an offering.[112]

He that has ears to hear, let him hear what the Spirit says to the churches.

43

THE DISASTER OF IMPENITENCE

Revelation 16:8–11

These four verses bring before us the disaster of impenitence. In other words, it is a total personal disaster to refuse to repent of our sins. One of the greatest gifts of God to the sinful human race is the gift of repentance. Repentance is generally thought of as something we do, and that is true, but repentance is also a divine gift that is given to you directly from heaven. That is what Peter says in Acts 5:31, where he speaks of our repentance as one of the blessings that comes through the crucifixion, resurrection, and going up to glory of our Lord Jesus Christ: 'Thou hast exalted him a Prince and a Savior in Israel to give repentance to his people'.

Repentance Is a Divine Gift

Once Christ took his place on the throne beside his Father, he began to parcel out certain gifts to us on the basis of his finished work. Ephesians 1–2 and 4 speak of the ascension gifts given to us by the Risen Lord with whom the Holy Spirit has united us in an inextricable union. The gifts are always in the context of our union with Christ.

One of the preliminary and foundational gifts that the exalted Jesus conveys to his people is the gift of a penitent spirit. That is, a spirit that seeks forgiveness from God and, with the help of the Holy Spirit, spends a lifetime forsaking sin and following hard after the Lord. Ephesians 4:21–4 specifies our believing and penitent rethinking of everything and the consequent moral changes that follow in our daily lives:

> If so be that ye have heard him, and have been taught by him, as the truth is in Jesus; That ye put off concerning the former conversation [i.e. conduct] the old man, which is corrupt according to the deceitful lusts; And be renewed in the spirit of your mind; And that ye put on the new man, which after God is created in righteousness and true holiness...

Why Repentance Is Necessary for All People

All humans, every child of Adam, with the exception of the Lord Jesus Christ who was born without sin, need this gift of repentance. Repentance means turning from sin to God. All need to do this, because all are born into sin, which has caused us to look away from God in ignorance, distrust, and disobedience. Romans 5:12–21 teaches that in Adam all sinned, and sin brought death. Because we are connected with Adam, we are born into sin, and we need the gift of repentance. As David says: 'I was shapen in iniquity; in sin did my mother conceive me' (Ps. 51:5). Repentance is a necessary step from our fallen condition in Adam to a new relationship to God through Christ, the Last Adam. The Puritans called repentance 'the twin sister of faith.' They go together in a genuine salvation experience, which shows that now we are in Christ; 'the last Adam.'

There is something that the people who are now in heaven and the people who are now in hell have in common: all of them were originally sinners. All were born children of Adam and Eve; all were under the righteous judgment of the Lord. So how did some of them get to heaven, while others descended to a place of outer darkness? What made the difference, since all were sinners?

No Entrance into Heaven without Repentance
Here is what makes the difference. The people who end up in heaven repented and asked God for forgiveness, while those who descend into hell refused to repent and would not seek the forgiveness that God offered them. That was the difference between the Israelites and the Egyptians at the time of the Exodus. Terrible plagues were poured out on the Egyptians to lead them to repentance. As we have seen, there is a connection between some of the ten plagues over Egypt and the terrible judgments that come in Revelation from those destroying angels whom God lets loose. There is a connection, except that the judgments under the angels are far worse than the plagues in Egypt.

But Pharaoh adamantly refused to repent. He would feign repentance for a while to get rid of another plague, but then he would immediately harden his heart against God and his people. According to Romans 9:18, and relevant passages in Exodus (e.g. 7:14), God judicially hardened Pharaoh's heart. But that was a response to Pharaoh's hardening his own heart (Exod. 8:15).

Eventually, Pharaoh gets past the point of any repentance whatsoever in his earthly life, and the destroying angel of death went over all Egypt, so that the firstborn in every household died, from the palace of Pharaoh down to the humblest servant, and even the animals.

Judicial Hardening
But it was different with the Israelites in Goshen. Their Covenant God worked so that they gave the sign of repentance in its Old Testament form. After slaying a sacrificial lamb for their own sins, they smeared its blood on their door posts, and the Angel of Death passed over them, because they appropriated the sacrifice that pointed to the final judgment of sin that would be visited upon 'the Lamb of God slain from the foundation of the world' (Rev. 13:8). The blood was a sign that the Israelites repented of their sins, and believed in God's substitutionary provision. It is not that they were sinless and the Egyptians were sinful. All were sinful in God's eyes, but one group gave the sign of repentance, and they were spared. The others hardened their hearts, refused to repent, and were judged. Romans 9 shows that the electing love of God was behind their choices, yet they made those choices of repentance or impenitence. They were not forced from outside themselves. The mystery of election is that no child of Adam will repent, unless the Lord intervenes to soften their hearts. He is in charge of such matters, but we do what we internally want to do. 'As the tree falls, so shall it lie.'

The Theory of Universalism
Come back to Revelation 16. It is repentance, or lack of it, that determines the final destiny of every human being, and behind that is the electing love of God that prepares some to repent and believe. As Psalm 110:3 says: 'Thy people shall be willing

in the day of thy power.' You could, if you had the eyes of the Lord, go down the street, look at the different people, and foresee that here are some who are on their way to heaven. No power from hell or on earth can stop them from getting there. All the powers of heaven are conspiring that this person walking down the main street outside Wal-Mart is on his or her way to heaven. But if we had the eyes of the Lord, we could see that there are others who look as good as the ones who are on their way to heaven, yet these others will be finally impenitent. They will not ask God for forgiveness under any conditions whatsoever, so they are on their way down to a place of darkness and everlasting grief. That is what determines the final destiny of every human.

Revelation 16:8-11 shows that the modernist theory that every last person is finally going to be saved is not taught in Holy Scripture. The supreme Judge of the universe teaches us in his Word that while a multitude which no man can number will be in heaven praising the Lord, yet a certain number will be eternally lost because they refused to look to God for forgiveness.

We take only two points from this brief text:

1. Apart from God's grace, divine judgments will not soften a sinner's heart (Rev. 16:8-10).
2. Impenitent sinners refuse to see the connection between their sinful natures with their evil deeds, and their pains (Rev. 16:11).

Divine Judgments Will not Soften a Sinner's Heart without God's Grace

Apart from grace, passing through suffering and judgment, even of a major nature, will not soften a sinner's heart. Look at the wicked reaction of the unbelievers in Revelation 16:9 to the judgment of the fourth angel, who had the authority to scorch men with fire—a forewarning or foretaste of the outer burnings: 'And men were scorched with great heat and blasphemed the name of God which had power over these plagues'. They could have turned to Him, and cried out: 'Lord, forgive us, Lord God, have mercy on us'. He has the power to remove the judgment, but instead of asking God to remove the judgment, they curse Him. That is the reaction of a sinner's heart that is not softened by divine grace. Instead of thinking that my sins have caused these sufferings and I need to repent, the typical reaction of a sinner who refuses to look to the cross is to curse and blaspheme Almighty God.

For Whom Is Suffering Beneficial?

But what a difference grace makes in granting us the repentance we need. Psalm 119:71 has this marvelous verse: 'It is good for me that I have been afflicted, for now I keep your word'. Can you imagine that anybody would every say, 'It is good for me that I have been afflicted, that I went through that loss, that I experienced that near disaster, that I felt that pain and these reversals that I thought were so awful at the time'? Instead of arguing, 'Why did God let it happen to me?' I realize that the Lord is using these bad things to get me back in touch with Him, to clarify my vision, and to remove every cloud between us. Then I say: 'Lord, Thy will be done; I want to be in the center of Thy will. And now I am keeping Thy word and have never known such a peace.'

That is what suffering does for the elect, who are granted the gift of repentance. When we have grace, reversals lead to repentance, a drawing closer to God, and sweeter blessing than we ever had before. There are many illustrations of this process in the Bible.

We see it in Psalm 51, a penitential Psalm written after David, a man after God's own heart, got out of the will of God by having relations with a married woman and having her husband killed in the army. He committed adultery and murder, but God sent the prophet Nathan to convict David. After many months of impenitence, David was broken. He freely confessed his sins with tears. God said to him, 'Fear not, thou shalt not die, thy sins are forgiven'. David repented and was eternally forgiven, yet for the rest of his life his family had to reap the tragic consequences of this high-handed disobedience. Thus, he cries out: 'Have mercy upon me God, according to Thy lovingkindness, according to the multitude of Thy tender mercies, blot out my transgressions'.

The Disaster of Blame-shifting
A penitent person calls a sin a sin; an impenitent person blames it on everybody else. There is a whole industry in certain types of counselling that teach you to cope with your problems by blame-shifting. There is a time and place for looking such background issues in the face, but it is a sign of impenitence always to be blame-shifting, rather than facing our own sinful responses and repenting of them.

Revelation 16:9 and 11 teach that no matter how much people suffer they will not become better people unless grace is appropriated by them in that suffering and in those difficulties of their life. There has to be grace, or suffering will not make you a better person; it will make you meaner. Although there are complicated factors to be taken into account in each case, that is how it is with old people. Some people get sweeter and more Christ-like as they get older. They handle their tempers better, and are more gracious and kinder in their seventies, than they were in their forties. Is it not wonderful to see? But others, instead of getting sweeter with the decades, get meaner and harsher, and make life difficult for their families and caretakers. One group has repented and grown closer to the Lord, while the other has consistently refused the grace of God.

A hospital chaplain in Richmond, Virginia told some of us in the 1960s about a family in which there seemed to have been no grace. He was on duty when the body of an elderly man, who had suddenly dropped dead, was brought into hospital. His wife was outside the emergency room, so the chaplain went to speak to her, to see if he could give her any comfort. She looked at him in anger, spat in his face, and cursed God.

Years ago, a fine doctor told me about the difference he had noted in the deathbeds of those who believed in Christ and had repented of their sins, and those who had refused grace throughout their lives. In one case, this Christian doctor witnessed to a patient who was in a terminal condition in hospital. The man rejected his testimony with an oath, and forbade the doctor to speak of it again. This doctor was present when this man was dying. He reported that the man started cursing God and writhing on the bed, before he landed on the floor—dead. The last thing on his lips was cursing the holy God.

Suffering and ailments incidental to going through this world will not in and of themselves make us more Christ-like, unless we appropriate the forgiving grace of God through faith and repentance of our sins. For true Christians, difficulties are used by the providence of the Lord to bring us closer to Christ. It does work unusual graces in our lives. We see how this works in Romans 5:3–5: 'We glory in tribulation also, knowing that tribulation worketh patience and patience experience and experience hope and hope maketh not ashamed because the Love of God is shed abroad in our hearts by the Holy Ghost which is given unto us'. This process of beautification is what happens for those who appropriate the proffered grace of God. Such people become a fountain of encouragement to others all around them.

But the unbelievers in Revelation 16 refuse to humble themselves under any condition. They refuse to give glory to God by repenting. Did you realize that when you repent and believe, you are thereby giving God glory? One of the major ways to glorify God, according to Revelation 16, is to tell the truth about myself, rather than lying and blame-shifting. For instance, in Joshua 7:19, after Achan's sin of having stolen and hidden forbidden treasure from Ai has been discovered, Joshua asks him to make an honest confession of his sin. Joshua uses this significant expression: 'My son, give, I pray thee, glory to the LORD God of Israel, and make confession unto him.' Therefore, it gives God glory when we honestly and humbly cry out to Him: 'Lord, I failed in this area; I wilfully disobeyed your Word. For Jesus' sake, I ask You to forgive me.'

Psalm 51 tells us that God requires truth in the inward parts. When you are truthful about yourself before God, and are transparently specific about your sins, you bring him glory. But in Revelation 16, the unbelievers who had waxed so numerous on earth, refused to glorify God in this way, and in fact cursed Him, rather than admitting what they were like.

The Impenitent Refuse to Connect Their Evil Deeds with Their Pains

People who refuse to repent are determined not to recognise any connection between a life that displeases God and the pains and sores that follow. They say: 'No connection! What do you mean? I'm a nice person! It just happened to me.' But this is to deny the most basic moral category on which this universe is founded: God blesses righteousness and curses sin. That is what the Ten Commandments say: '...visiting the iniquity of the fathers upon the children, to third and fourth generation of them that hate me; and showing mercy unto thousands of them that love me.'

While God curses iniquity, his grace teaches us that the iniquities we have committed have been cursed in Christ, if I will come to him for his help. No curse is left for me, if I come to Christ! But in a moral universe, if I reject the sacrifice Jesus made for my sins, then I must heap lasting condemnation upon my own head.

History Is not an Unplanned Cosmic Game
Materialistic philosophy tends to think that the connections between some kind of unseen fate or luck, and the particularities of what happens to them are purely accidental—it is like a card game or a lottery machine. Their model of how the world works seems to be something like a cosmic game, so that the connections are accidental between where you end and where you started. At the end of life, many will complain that they backed a loser, but that it was not their fault; it was just an accident. They fail to see any moral connection between their deeds in this life, and the pain they are to experience, now or later. If there is a God, then my failures and disappointments are God's fault, not mine. Persisting in such a hard-hearted attitude is an open door to the realm below. Those who refuse to repent can never justly claim that God would not forgive them. God has never ever refused to forgive anyone who sincerely asked Him, but they will never ask. The people being judged in Revelation 16, refused to bow the knee; they refused to admit the connection between the judgments now upon them, and the sins of their own lives. Through it all, they would not ask for divine forgiveness, so the eternal consequences are forever their own responsibility.

How can someone who is by nature self-centered, as we all are from birth, look out from self to Christ in faith and repentance? Many have asked me: how do I know if I have sincerely repented? What if my repentance is imperfect?

The Vicarious Repentance of Christ

The key to repentance is to point to the Lord Jesus Christ, who is our all-sufficient salvation. Think of his baptism at the beginning of his public ministry. What kind of baptism did Jesus undergo? We read that when Jesus went to John the Baptist at the Jordan River, John protested: 'I do not need to baptize You; I need to be baptized by You!' Jesus replied: 'No, suffer it to be so, for thus it behooves us to fulfill all righteousness'. In other words, baptism at the hands of John was for sinners, who needed to repent, and Jesus underwent the baptism of repentance. Jesus was baptized in my place, just as Jesus lived in my place, and died in my place, rose in my place, and even now, is praying for me above.

Why did Jesus undergo the baptism of repentance, since he was not a sinner? Rather, 'he was holy, harmless, and undefiled, separate from sinners' (Heb. 7:26). He underwent baptism because he was standing in the room and the stead of every human who will ever believe in Him. It means that he was even repenting in our place. The great evangelist George Whitefield once said that 'My tears of repentance need to be washed in the blood of Jesus.' Our repentance, insofar as it depends on us, can never be perfect, for there is too much of me in everything I do. But Jesus repents as my holy substitute. He lives a holy life to be given over to me. Jesus dies in my place, taking away my death and hell, giving me his life and heaven. So any sinner, however imperfect his own poor responses to divine grace, who says, 'Lord, forgive me for Jesus' sake', is counted by God as having repented with the perfect repentance of his divine substitute. The Lord Jesus has fulfilled every response that the Covenant of Grace requires from those who are in it. How generous the God of the Covenant is!

The Daily Repentance of the Believer

Christ's perfect repentance being made over to me does not imply that I do not need to live a life of daily repentance. Jesus' call to all his disciples still rings out: 'Take up your cross daily, and follow me' (Luke 9:23). Rather, his vicarious repentance makes the repentance of his people possible and effective. That is the dynamic of the Christian life: God's work makes our work effective, as Paul describes it: 'Work out your own salvation with fear and trembling. For it is God which worketh in you both to will and to do of his good pleasure' (Phil. 2:12–13). All we do: believing, repenting, loving, and obeying is in union with the crucified and risen Christ. We are 'bound in a bundle of life' with him (1 Sam. 25:29), so that it is not possible to separate his working and our working. He is in us, and we are in him (Gal. 2:20). The life of God constantly surges through the souls of his saints, and one aspect of that is faith in God and repentance towards him (Acts 20:21).

On this matter of true repentance, I often think of the life of Fred J. Hay, one of my predecessors in the Presbyterian Church of Dillon, South Carolina, a wonderful old saint, who died shortly after I arrived in Dillon. His wife told me that one of the verses Dr Hay asked her to read to him several times on his deathbed, was Isaiah 1:18. What a contrast this is from the impenitent ones in Revelation 16, who adamantly refuse to repent! 'Come now and let us reason together, saith the Lord. Though your sins be as scarlet, they shall be as white as snow. Though they be red like crimson, they shall be as wool'.

He that has ears to hear, let him hear what the Holy Spirit says to the church.

44

ANATOMY OF COLLAPSE

Revelation 16:10–21

This chapter talks about shaking among the nations—in a sense, the greatest shaking that would ever happen. The shaking comes from the throne (Rev. 16:1), whence God sends out his angels to initiate this bringing down of political systems. That takes us back to Hebrews 12, which gives the background for these terrible shakings spoken of in Revelation 16. Why does God allow the nations to be shaken down? 'That those things which cannot be shaken may remain' (Heb. 12:27). To make any sense of history, we must keep that in mind that God is behind all the shakings that come on the nations.

Changes in the Twenty-First Century
From the twenty-first century, we can look back and see that the twentieth century was a time of tremendous moral decline, accompanied by dislocating political and military shakings, such as had not been seen for a long time. We had two world wars, the rise of Communism and its taking over of Russia in 1917, and then its downfall in 1991. We saw the decline of the Christian control of culture and governments in the West and the simultaneous rise of a new, fervent Christianity in the Third World. In the twenty-first century itself, much shaking has gone on since September 11, 2001. Militant Islam is on people's mental map, where it had once been absent.

Nobody knows what lies ahead. 'We know not what a day may bring forth', much less a year or a decade. Without being certain, it is likely that the Western world is teetering on the verge of tremendous shaking, such as we have not seen since the Great Depression or World War II.

In the midst of such uncertainties, it is a grand time for the Church to manifest her confidence that what lies ahead will not be accidental, but that all is under the direct control of our Sovereign God. This is what Revelation 16 brings before us: behind all these disturbing shakings stands the changeless and omnipotent throne of God.

God's Throne Orchestrates the Shakings
Every time the nations live through a period of shaking, it is not accidental; God is preparing for something to be established after that shaking. God is letting things that oppose him and hinder the kingdom of Christ be shaken down and removed. And while some things are being shaken down and hauled out on trucks to the garbage heap of this world, other things are being built up to replace them. Other things are being established that can never be shaken down.

The only thing that can be shaken down is something that under evil influences has become perverted from its original purpose (like a totalitarian government), and is hindering the advancement of the Kingdom of God. God in his wisdom, with his infinite knowledge of every factor, lets things happen to shake it down. Usually, the evil persons or system have the seeds of their own destruction within themselves. As their evil tendencies grow ever larger, unhealthy and destructive impulses take over the body politic, like a cancer, and wreak havoc with it, so that it is already in a state of collapse before external enemies come against it. Often the severe internal weaknesses of a now evil institution do not show up until shortly before its final collapse.

What Cannot Be Shaken
But God's Church, based on the love of the Father, through the Son, and in the Spirit to sinners, can never be shaken down. Like 'leaven, hidden in meal', the spreading of the truth of the Bible, along with the invisible working of the Holy Spirit among the masses gradually transforms darkness into light, so that the culture begins to experience renewal. As the love of God through the resurrection power of Jesus spreads in various segments of humanity, the strongholds of evil give way. Hence, the kingdom of Christ can never be shaken down. In all the political and military turmoil that hits the world, God is secretly working, so that the powers of darkness lose their ability to stop the spread of the light and to stop the kingdom of Jesus from going forward. 'Where the devil is active, God is more active' (William Still). God is shaking down the powers of evil, to make room for his kingdom to stand taller and spread its beneficent wings further: greater blessing is on the other side of fearsome collapses.

At any one time in history, especially in times of turmoil and transition, nobody could tell you exactly how particular events fit into the big picture of replacing evil structures with good and lasting ones. But perhaps a century or two later, looking back, one can discern much of what God was doing in bringing down powers and nations, and in replacing them by others. Here we are not given that physical sight, but we are given the view of faith, which sees that God is even more active than the servants of the devil.

No matter what happens amongst the nations, God's throne is well established. He will not let the devil and his demons go any further than his eternally beneficent purposes determined before there was a world. God lets things that are displeasing to him be shaken down, in his good time. And the kingdom of love and light, of which we have the privilege of being a part can only be the better established and spread more widely.

A Prayer for Hard Times
Even if hard times are ahead of us, what a joy and privilege we have. We may say, 'Lord, above all else, I want to be on your side, now and ever. I do not know what will happen or what price we may pay before these shakings calm down, but I want to be one of Your people. I want to be part of that movement that cannot be reduced to rubble; I want to be part of something that can only grow more beautiful as we move into eternity. I want to belong to Jesus and to serve Him.' That is the right response to this passage.

In 2003, one of my cousins was at the airport in Kinston, North Carolina, when a terrible explosion at a large plant just across the road killed several people and injured others. Everything shook and the ceiling in the room where she was standing came down. She said she had never had such an emotional experience, to see the whole thing go up like a bomb with a great column of fire, less than a hundred yards away, not knowing what would happen next.

In some ways, this passage is like that sudden, unexpected explosion. God suddenly brings to bear explosive and destructive energy on normal life in the world, with strong institutions, solid buildings, and everybody at work. It's a normal day, the clock is moving, the calendar is in order, and it seems that we are in charge of what is happening in our lives. Suddenly, everything blows up! You stand there not knowing what will come next. That is the picture.

An Orientation to Disasters

One of the purposes of Revelation is to give the people of God some orientation to the disasters that can occur in this world. Then we remember that behind the columns of flame, God is at work.

In Revelation 16:17 the angel was told exactly what to do; he was given word to bring a vial of destructive judgment 'out of the temple': 'There came a great voice out of the temple of heaven from the throne, saying…'. That is the perspective, that God wants us to have as we study these frightening passages of what has happened in the past, which also serve as pictures of what may happen again. We are to remember that God is leading these seeming disasters in a certain direction so that Christ and his people will reach far more lost people, and spread the light of salvation further than before.

With this in mind, we note two points:

1. A vast shaking occurred around AD 70, but Revelation 16 conveys a lasting principle.
2. God still shakes the nations so that the kingdom of light may hasten its holy work.

A Vast Shaking in History

Revelation 16:10 tells us that 'the fifth angel poured out his bowl upon the seat of the beast and his kingdom was full of darkness.' There is an important movement here from what had happened earlier through the action of the first four angels. They brought judgments into nature, such as the sun scorching people, and the waters becoming putrid. The fifth angel, however, brings the judgment of God, not into nature, but into the heart of the political system, which is sold out to the beast and opposed to Christ.

This political judgment unleased by the fifth angel concerned not only unbelieving Judaism in AD 70, but also later political and military governmental systems that set themselves 'against the Lord, and against his anointed' (Ps. 2:2). No matter how rich and mighty they seem, they will be shaken down. A mighty unseen angel from the presence of God is going to pour out a vial of wrath on the seat of the beast and everything will become dark. The oil and money will be gone. Power stations and transportation systems will be turned off. The lights will go off in the presidential palaces and parliamentary headquarters. Rulers will lose their vaunted positions, and be unable to resist those who come to supplant them, and lead the institutions or nations in another direction.

'Land' or 'Earth'?

Some commentators understand the word that is translated as 'earth' in Revelation 16:1, to mean 'land', that is the land of Israel. Thus David Chilton speaks of '…this outpouring of plagues into the Land that has spilled the blood of Christ and his witnesses, the people who have resisted and rejected the Spirit: The old wineskins of Israel are about to split open.'[113]

The coming down of the still powerful Jewish

state, backed to a significant degree by Rome, was highly significant for the young Christian Church. Unbelieving Judaism was still strong in Jerusalem, killing Christians, persecuting the church, and exercising anti-Christian influence across the Mediterranean world. Jerusalem, once the holiest of cities, was acting like the throne of the beast, rejecting Christ and killing his saints, hand-in-glove with the Roman power.

The Lights Go Out for Great Kingdoms

Verse 10b speaks of the lights going out: so that politically, governmentally, economically, a once holy kingdom becomes full of darkness. What does it mean for this text to speak of the lights going out? When Old Testament passages such as Isaiah 13:9-10; Amos 8:9; and Ezekiel 32:7-8 speak of the lights going out and kingdoms becoming dark, they mean that God's judgments have been let loose against particular earthly governments. Great kingdoms and their systems break apart, their leaders lose power, or are killed. The lights go out, and in the confused darkness, somebody else will come in and take over. That happened when the Roman General Titus conquered Jerusalem with devastating warfare in AD 70.

From what we know about the wider scene, God was letting much of the world be shaken in AD 70, about forty years after the Jewish leadership had rejected God's Son and the Romans had crucified Him. Still they refused to repent (Rev. 16:9).

The Bible presents a God who is reluctant to judge. You never, in any true reading of the Bible, get a view of God as a harsh Deity. On the contrary, he has the most tender, Fatherly love; none of us who are fathers has anything to compare with the patience and restraint and compassion and love of our heavenly Father. Would that we did! Isaiah speaks of judgment as being God's 'strange work.' This means that God's normal work is to bless. God says in Ezekiel, 'Why will ye die?' And he says in the Psalms, 'Oh that you would have listened to My voice; than I should have fed you with the finest of the wheat and the honey from the comb'. God delays the execution of his wrath a very long time, to give people time to repent. Romans 2:4 asks: 'Knowest thou not that the goodness of God leadeth thee to repentance?'

Two Ways to Interpret the Delays of God

You and I can take the delays of God in our lives in one of two ways. All of us know that at times we have done things that were sinful, that were far beneath our calling and capacities as believers in Jesus. But God did not publicly call us into account for it. It seems as if he let us by with it. He did not expose us for doing something that was not right. So how do you interpret this?

Honesty. The wise person would say: 'God did not approve of something I did or thought or said that was out of line with his will. Yet, he dealt with me mercifully; he covered it. Therefore, I know what this means: God is calling me to change. He calls me to split with that unworthy behavior pattern. God has given me time to get under the blood of Christ, to appropriate his strength to do right, and with his help I'm going to change.' That is wise, spiritual thinking.

Dangerous Presumption. There is another way to interpret those times when God seems to let you by with something that you know was not right. We can be presumptuous and assume that we are so special that we will always get by with it, or that God will tolerate our disobedience for a while longer. As a minister, I can say that this sort of presumption constitutes a temptation for the ministry. At times we may be tempted to think, 'Since I do so much valuable spiritual work, the

Lord is likely to overlook a few sins on my part.' Then we become even more presumptuous. I suspect this attitude has brought down many an otherwise good minister of the gospel. They foolishly assumed that God would always cover for them. What a mistaken interpretation of the kindly delays of the Lord. How different it would have been if they had seen clearly that the goodness of God, which protected us when we did not deserve it, is intended not to minister to further sin, but to lead us to repentance.

Presumption within First Century Israel
That sort of presumptuous attitude seems to have been widespread within the Jewish state in the years after they had rejected their Messiah. Acts makes clear that many of the priests and Levites did become obedient to the faith. They were forgiven and saved for eternity. But much of the Jewish leadership, and much of the populace, refused to repent. It was a serious sin to have crucified the Son of God, yet his blood is sufficient to cleanse from every sin, including the one that led to his death. If they had repented, God would have forgiven them. The degree of the sin we commit never prevents forgiveness. The only thing that prevents the forgiveness of our heavenly Father, with his tender heart of love, is that we will not repent. Too many in Israel considered that 'being chosen' justified a hard-hearted attitude towards the loving offers of the Son of God.

God did delay his judgments against the Jewish state for a long time. He was graciously offering them time for repentance. But the time came when the Lord in heaven said: 'It is done! Angels, go forth and pour out the cups of wrath on this unbelieving system that continues to reject My Son and continues to trample underfoot the blood shed for them. Now is the time they must be brought down—and let the flames of fire leap high.' God delays his judgments, but there comes a time when a loving, holy God in effect says: 'It is done. Holy angel, go forth; pour out the chalice of wrath against all who are not covered by the atonement of My Son.'

Predicted Details of Jerusalem's Destruction
Revelation 16:12–14 gives prophetic details of Jerusalem's coming destruction under images taken from the Old Testament. To make sense of the details in Revelation, we must interpret many images and symbols from the Old Testament. The real question is: how do the various Old Testament passages where these images and pictures are found understand them? That will help us understand what they mean in the New Testament.

The Euphrates River. For instance, verse 12, speaks of the drying up of the Euphrates River. No doubt, that goes back to Cyrus, who conquered mighty Babylon by means of a marvelous ploy. He took hydraulic engineers, who diverted the channel of the Euphrates River, which normally surrounded Babylon with its protecting waters, so that at night his army marched into Babylon through the river gate. With the waters turned away, they had been able to move the bars on the gate and conquer Babylon.

There are other examples of rivers or seas being 'dried up' in the Old Testament. Exodus tells us that because God caused the Red Sea to part, his children went through dry-shod. He then changed the winds, no doubt directing the angels at work in nature to let loose the waters on Pharaoh's army, thereby drowning them. We know from Joshua that God caused the waters to pile up in the river Jordan when the feet of the priests, bearing the Ark of the Covenant, hit the edge of the waters (actually, at flood time). These waters flew back into a heap, and became like stone, allowing the children of Israel to get across.

God has various ways to dry up rivers or to remove the boundaries of water that have been blocking us or protecting us, as the case may be. Josephus reports in *The Jewish Wars, Book III*, that while the Euphrates did not literally dry up, thousands and thousands of General Titus' troops (probably the main contingent of the Roman army that brought down Jerusalem) managed to get across the Euphrates.[114]

Frogs and Demons. Revelation 16:13-14 gives further details of Jerusalem's downfall. It speaks of three unclean spirits, proceeding out of the mouths of the dragon, the beast, and the false prophet. These are not physical frogs as in the third Egyptian plague, but demonic spirits who are able to perform signs and wonders, to delude those of mankind who refuse the gospel into opposing the victorious Lord in self-suicidal fury.

First Kings 22 tells how evil spirits deluded wicked King Ahab and the otherwise good king of Judah, Hezekiah, into fighting a hopeless battle, where Ahab would be slain, as the judgment of God. Ahab called the prophets and asked: 'Should we go into this battle?' The self-serving crowd of false prophets answered: 'Yes, go up; you shall prosper!' Only one prophet, a true spokesman of God, Micaiah, was willing to face the king's wrath by telling him the unacceptable truth, that he would be a fool to go into this battle. Proud and angry Ahab refused to believe the one true prophet, so Micaiah rolls back the curtains that keep people from seeing the heavenly court and reports what he saw there (in 1 Kings 22:19-22). He said, 'I saw the Lord sitting on his throne, and sending forth lying, demonic spirits into the mouth of these prophets, so that they will delude Ahab and his kingdom because the time of its judgment is ripe'. Thus, the demons tricked Ahab into backing the losing side. That kind of thing would happen again, when against all common sense, those leaders of Jerusalem, who were hardened by rejecting Christ, would foolishly think they could overcome the mighty Roman Empire, and they therefore go into a suicidal rebellion, tricked by demons (i.e. 'the frogs').

The Battle of Armageddon. Verse 16 deals with the battle of Armageddon. Again, we know by the language here that this requires a symbolic interpretation rather than a literal one. There is no literal place of 'Armageddon'. The word is formed of two parts: *har*, in Hebrew, meaning 'mountain', and 'city' or 'place' of Megiddo. But geographically, there is no mountain at Megiddo. It is a plain. So it is not a literal mountain, but it is used to refer to 'a place of defeat'. Megiddo was the place where godly King Josiah was killed by Pharoah Neco, after which Israel plummeted into apostasy, and eventual deportation to Babylon (2 Chron. 35-6). Dean Farrar writes:

> In sum, Mt. Megiddo stands in his mind for a place where lying prophecy and its dupes go to meet their doom; where kings and their armies are misled to their destruction; and where all the tribes of the earth mourn, to see him in power, whom in weakness they had pierced.[115]

It would be like saying in modern language, 'you are going to meet your Waterloo!' Megiddo represents a place of defeat for the disobedient against the kingdom of God. Deborah had defeated the kings of Canaan there in Judges 5; King Ahaziah, the wicked grandson of King Ahab, was killed at this plain of Megiddo (2 Kings 9), as was King Josiah. Kistemaker summarizes the meaning of this reference well:

> I regard the term *Armageddon* as a symbol by which God delivers his people from harm and demonstrates that he has the power and might to overthrow his enemies. He repeatedly showed his faithfulness by rescuing them in both Old Testament and New Testament times. Thus, he sets them free during the final tribulation at the return of Christ. 'It is for this reason that Har-Magedon is the sixth bowl. The seventh is the judgment.'[116]

An Earthquake. Verse 18 speaks of a horrendous earthquake. Is it literal, or is it symbolic? It may be both. Probably it means more than just one earthquake, as in Hebrews 12:25–9. As earthly kingdoms become humanistic and unbelieving, at the right time, God sends forth the invisible angels to pour out wrath upon them, shaking them to their roots. Flames of fire will consume them. At the same time, these earthquakes are not a disaster for the people of God. Instead, they make possible the removal of that which was really opposing the gospel and human life at its best. The shakings remove those powers; their lights go out. Economies, armies and political systems are shaken down in order that the only thing that cannot be shaken may stand and increase in stature: the Kingdom of Christ.

That is what was happening to the unbelieving Judaism of the first century. It had once been of God, but finally turned against Him, and kept rejecting his Son for the forty years God gave them to repent.

The City Split into Three Parts. Verse 19 briefly says that the great city will be split into three parts. This is symbolic, although it refers to reality. What does it mean? If you go back to Ezekiel 5:1–12 we see that Ezekiel was told to cut off his hair and to divide it carefully into three parts. That is what is going to happen to Jerusalem. You know the old saying: 'united we stand, divided we fall'. We know from Josephus that during the Romans' siege under Titus, the Jews divided into three factions. They had thousands of Romans, with their devastating military equipment on the outside besieging the city, and on the inside you had the people divided into three gangs, who started killing each other. Hence, the great city (v. 19), will be split into three parts. That truly happened.

Massive Hailstones. Finally, in verse 21, hailstones about the weight of a talent (approximately 100 pounds), will be thrown down into the rebellious city. The political and religious seat of the kingdom will have to be destroyed. Josephus tells us the Romans used catapults in which one could put huge stones, so that they landed inside the walls of Jerusalem, at the very time that the city was divided up into three gangs. The stones were white, so people could see them and avoid them as they were coming. But the Romans were clever; they painted the stones black and so that it was harder to see them coming. They started bursting houses, roofs, and streets where the people were assembling; killing people in vast numbers. That seems to be a major illustration of verse 21, with the hailstones coming from heaven.

Why is this so significant? Many cities have been destroyed in history. Dresden was bombed at the end of World War II. But this one is so significant because Christianity comes out of Judaism. 'Salvation is of the Jews', as our Lord said. But the Jewish leadership of the first century rejected Him. To use a parable of Jesus, when the Father sent his own Son into the vineyard, they killed Him. God gave them a chance to repent, but instead of repenting, their hearts got harder. Then God hardened their hearts, and let loose the evil demons upon them. He divided them up, at which time the Romans sent in stones and down they came. Therefore, that which could be shaken (apostate Jerusalem), was shaken down, in order that what cannot be shaken—the Christian church—may remain. That was the greatest shaking down that ever occurred in history, to the establishment of the church of the Lord Jesus Christ in the earth.

A Lasting Principle

That tremendous shaking in AD 70 illustrates a principle that, in due season, God himself in his mysterious calendar, lays low those kingdoms and powers who oppose his Son and his church. God lets something happen, till they are shaken down so that his church may thrive. That seems to have been what was happening when Rome fell in the fifth century. My Roman Catholic friends would not agree, but I sincerely believe that what was happening at the end of the Middle Ages, with the Protestant Reformation in the sixteenth century. The Roman church had become so corrupt that it was obscuring the gospel. In its vitals was corrupt immorality. God let it be shaken down, at least in a huge section of Europe, and let the American colonies be founded, as a Reformed, Protestant place. Even the Roman church had to do some reforming after that, because the corrupt system was shaken down by God, and had lost most of Northern Europe.

Modern application?

I must leave this application to you. Christ is going to be victorious, although I do not know the details. Think, for instance, of radical Islam. Ultimately, it cannot stand against the kingdom of light. How will such great powers fall? Who now knows? And what if the Western powers keep on with abortion, and go increasingly into euthanasia, not to mention other economic and political forms of widespread injustice? Unless, they repent, all of them will be shaken down.

John Owen, the great Puritan theologian wrote:

> Although the removal of Mosaical worship and the old church-state be principally intended, which was effected at the coming of Christ, and the promulgation of the gospel from heaven by him, yet all other oppositions to him and his kingdom are included therein; not only those that then were, but all that should ensue unto the end of the world. The 'things that cannot be moved' are to remain and be established against all opposition whatsoever. Wherefore, as the heavens and earth of the idolatrous world were of old shaken and removed, so shall those also of the antichristian world, which at present in many places seem to prevail. All things must give way, whatever may be comprised in the names of heaven and earth here below, unto the gospel, and the kingdom of Christ therein. For if God made way for it by the removal of his own institutions, which he appointed for a season, what else shall hinder its establishment and progress unto the end?[117]

He that ears to hear, let him hear what God says to the church.

45

God's Strategy to Defeat Evil
Revelation 17:1–2

Chapters 17 to 19 constitute a new section of Revelation. These chapters comprise the sixth vision in the book. It is about God's strategy for winning the battle against evil. This sixth vision gives us God's overall battle plan, as to what is going to transpire and how he is going to make it work out victorious for the good and the holy side.

We deal with three points in this introductory chapter:

1. An outline of chapters 17–19: God's strategy for defeating evil and establishing the victory of Christ in all who believe in Him.
2. How to interpret these pictures and figures (Rev. 17:9–10, 15, 18).
3. Introduction to chapter 17 (Rev. 17:1–2).

God's Strategy for Defeating Evil

In earthly wars, even the most brilliant generals and governments can make reasonable plans that may fail on the day of battle. The failure may be owing to one or two factors that nobody could have foreseen, which make things go very poorly. But with God, it is entirely different. God alone has the sovereign power to control the future at every point, without the intervention of any detail unknown to Him, or outside his plan. He is able to lay out an overall strategy, and because he is able to be in charge of every little detail that comes into the battle, his strategy will turn out exactly as he planned; it will be in every point successful.

Look ahead to Revelation 17:17, which unveils the determination of evil powers to destroy Christ and his church, if they can: 'For God hath put in their hearts to fulfil his will, and to agree, and give their kingdom unto the beast, until the words of God shall be fulfilled'.

The Mystery of Evil

Our limited human minds face profound mystery in this verse. Scripture teaches that God does not approve of evil. God never makes people do evil. Indeed, he tells them not to. Yet, because of his infinite wisdom and all-surpassing power, he is able to bring good out of evil, and even during the worst times, he has the devil on a chain. Sometimes he lets him go a long way, so that the devil deceives wicked multitudes, but he will only let him go so far. He will never let the devil raise up an ungodly movement, unless that movement will somehow advance the holy purposes of God, and end up being reduced to dust.

Proverbs 21:1 says, 'The heart of the king is in the hand of the Lord; he turneth it whithersoever he will, like the rivers of water'. God is able to turn the thinking even of ungodly kings and dictators, so that although they seem to get stronger and have great success, they will make the wrong decisions and end up losing. This will occur because God has every heart in his hands, both Christian and pagan. His battle plan will work out successfully down to the smallest detail.

God's Battle Plan
In chapters 17–19, we have the laying out of God's battle plan. It is almost like going into a meeting of the Joint Chiefs of Staff in the Pentagon in Washington, or the military authorities in Whitehall in London, or the Kremlin in Moscow. All is highly confidential, with guards outside the doors, while the officials plan their strategy. Chapter 17 shows the defeat of the prostitute, and the defeat of Babylon the great, which refers to military and political disaster. Chapter 18 speaks of the fall of Babylon and its empire, which is particularly an economic disaster. Then chapter 19 is the good news following two disasters: the celebration of the Wedding Supper of the Lamb, followed by successful war against evil armies and the casting of evil leaders into the lake of fire, irrevocably. This gives us the overall picture of what we will be studying in the next few chapters.

Interpreting These Figures
How are we to interpret these figures or symbols, such as the harlot, the city of Babylon, the many waters, and a beast with seven heads? What are we to understand that to mean? A literal interpretation cannot be right, for the simple reason that chapter 17:15–18 shows that none of these symbols or figures is literal. Of course they mean something real and important, but if you take them literally, you will misunderstand their intended message.

For instance, Revelation 17:9–10 refer to a beast with seven heads. But those same verses tell us that this imagery means two things: seven mountains and seven kings. In verse 18, the prostitute is said to be the great city, while verse 15 speaks of many waters, which refers to multitudes of people. We need to take our understanding of these strange figures from the text of Revelation, and we also have to study how the Old Testament uses such images. In a word, we need to see how the Bible uses these pictures to know what they mean.

Introduction to Chapter 17
In Revelation 17:1–2, which is the beginning of the sixth vision, we come back to God's overall battle strategy between the first coming of Christ and his final return. These first two verses portray the big picture, not only of the future, but also of what God is already doing.

The Sixth Vision
These introductory verses invite us to look at the future, so as to make sense of the present troubles and struggles in the world. This kind of survey of the future is profoundly different from star-gazing or fortune telling, which look to dark powers, and ultimately to the devil, for future guidance. They lead you away from God and the wholesome life he has planned for those who trust him. This is different. God gives this so that we may be caught up in a true vision of life and history, so that we can make sense of the struggle between good and evil all around us. This sixth vision leads us into a fuller and more robust faith in God.

In verse 1, the holy angel says to John, 'Come hither and I will show you'. In other words, I will show you important things that are going to occur, to help you and the church make sense of the trials and troubles of this fallen world. What a privilege it is to be Christian believers; we have information given to us in the Scriptures of what the turmoil, tumult, and wars all mean.

God tells us exactly what we need to know to function as faithful, confident, and fruitful people. He gives us the big picture and the final result. We are told enough to encourage us to keep on in the good fight, but we are not told everything because the Lord wants us to exercise faith in what we cannot see. That means trusting in Him, day by day.

Opposing Sides in the Battle
Next, notice who are the opposing sides in this greatest of all battles, the battle that underlies all other battles that occur between Jesus' first and second coming. It is very helpful to know who your enemy is and what the fight is about. One of the problems our Western governments faced after 2001 was finding out exactly what was Al Qaeda, and where they were. Where did they get the information, and the ability to fly those planes into the World Trade Center and the Pentagon and the fields of Pennsylvania? It is hard to deal with an enemy, if you do not know where he or she is and what they are.

Here we are given an exact picture of the enemy and what to do, and what God is already doing. The two protagonists in this mother of all battles are two women. One is an obscene prostitute, although very attractive and alluring; the other is a pure, beautiful, spotless bride: the bride of Christ, the church of God. It is the same struggle as what you have from the gates of the Garden of Eden, where the seed of the woman, the seed of Eve, the seed of Abraham, the seed of David—ultimately the Lord Jesus Christ, and the seed of the serpent, that huge segment of humanity that sells itself out to oppose God, are in an age-long struggle. In verse 2, you have this terrible prostitute, then in Revelation 19:7, the beautiful, pure, true bride of the Lamb of God.

We are not yet looking at the beautiful bride, however. Chapter 17 concentrates on what happens to the prostitute, and that is the basis of God's battle strategy. What is being laid out in verses 1–2, is why this is a just and a necessary war, for God to judge the prostitute. In merely human wars, sometimes it is difficult to know exactly who is right. But God's Word lays out in these two verses why it is a righteous and holy war in which God deals with what this terrible, powerful harlot represents.

Notice two things here: first of all, what this prostitute stands for, and secondly, what she did.

What this Prostitute Stands for. Once again, we have to go back to the Old Testament to make sense of what Revelation says here about the prostitute. In the Old Testament, three cities are termed 'prostitutes:' Tyre (Isa. 23), Nineveh (Nah. 3), and Jerusalem (Isa. 1; Jer. 2; Ezek. 16). But Revelation 17:5, calls Babylon 'the Mother of Prostitutes'. What does that stand for?

We know that Babylon was destroyed and wiped out, long before Revelation was written. Ruins of it are still there in Iraq. We know where it was, so the 'harlot' of Revelation could not stand for the actual city of Babylon, because there had not been a city there for centuries. Yet Babylon does refer to something very real and dangerous, that God has to oppose and bring down.

Over the ages, this harlot has taken many different forms. As the culture changes, she looks different; she changes with the times; she speaks different languages. But she is always alluring and outwardly very attractive. Scripture describes her purple garments and jewels. Some have thought that she looked obscene or tacky, but purple speaks of royalty, of highly placed aristocratic background, able to afford jewels, and other outward insignia of wealth. She would get in with the top people. This prostitute changes her style in different nations, cultures, and religions. But here is what is constant: she always seeks to lead people away from simple trust in God as Savior and Father. She is always working to get the heart of foolish people away from faith in Christ and a happy relationship to Him. She says, in different ways, 'Do not trust in Christ; come on with me, and I'll give you fun and satisfaction and power'. She is always seeking to get people to prostitute their souls and bodies to the false gods and idols of this world, who always promise quick pleasure.

Herb Schlossberg wrote a perceptive book, *Idols for Destruction; the Conflict of Christian Faith and American Culture*. He brings out that three of our modern culture's most powerful idols are not even recognized by us as idols, which makes them the more deceptive. These idols are money, sex and power. Those 'values' are just as alluring and powerful as any idol, such as an ancient statue of Molech or Buddha. This harlot is always saying, 'Come on, come on; give everything up for the present; you do not know whether there is anything beyond this life. If you will only cast off this Christian value system and quit being bound by this narrow, Biblical viewpoint, I can give you money; sex will be available, and great power'.

That is the first reason that this is a just war. That is why all that God does to bring down this spirit of prostitution that sends men and women into eternal perdition is absolutely necessary in a moral universe.

What this Prostitute Has Done. Secondly, God must proceed against this unclean, destructive spirit, because of what this prostitute has done and is still trying to do. She has lured the kings of the earth to commit fornication with her. She encourages the cultural leadership to reject God's holy way of living as backward Puritanism. 'Rather', she says, 'I will provide you an alternative life and a different way of "salvation," that will make you feel good and affirm your own sense of worth.'

From what Jesus said to the Pharisees, it would appear that they had, without recognizing it, become involved in an adulterous, self-serving spirit that kept them from bowing before the true God, when he appeared in the flesh. In Matthew 12:39 and 16:4, when they demanded from him another sign before they would believe, Jesus said, 'a wicked and adulterous generation seeketh after another sign'.

Ezekiel 23 calls Israel and Judah 'prostitutes'. The whole book of Hosea is about how the Lord had tenderly loved a young woman, but she became unfaithful and adulterous, and lost everything. Hosea shows the continuance and triumph of the redemptive love of God for this corrupted woman, who represents the erring people of God's covenant.

Yet Revelation 17:2 refers to 'the kings of the earth', which would include the leadership of Old Testament and New Testament Israel, as Jesus' remarks in Matthew make clear. But it means more than that. It goes beyond the covenant people of Scripture, to the governing authorities of the whole earth. There is a universal tendency of unredeemed political systems, to try to replace Christ in the affections and values of its people with some aspect of the created order, particularly something that maintains the power of that system over against God. That is what God calls prostitution at its worst. At the right time, he will bring it down with his most severe judgments.

A tragic illustration of what this can entail is the widespread belief that abortion is good for the economy. It gets rid of unwanted children, it saves the parents money, and saves the state from having to educate them. That is the spirit of prostitution. God says, 'Thou shalt not kill', that we are to reproduce offspring, and to cherish them, for 'the fruit of the womb is his reward'.

An old Southern Baptist preacher of a former generation, Robert Greene Lee, had a wonderful sermon entitled *Payday Someday*. It is about Jezebel, and has this memorable line: 'Satan always pays in counterfeit wages.' It looks attractive at first, an easy way to get ahead, have fun, and make some cash. But Satan does not tell you about the shocking price to be paid later!

In terms of the honest preaching of R. G. Lee, we must ask: Has abortion really been good for the economy? Totally apart from the most important moral questions, was it really good for the American economy that more than fifty million innocent babies have been put to death since 1973? Obviously not; the United States is facing a crisis with social security. Too many are retiring and receiving income, while too few are entering the work force to pay into the system, because they have been put to death in the womb. If they were alive, the system would probably be more or less balanced. Their absence means that we have to bring in foreign workers, because we do not have enough of our own people to do the jobs. Satan pays in counterfeit wages.

Is sin ever good for the economy? The only way of long-term blessing, of course, is to do it God's way; but the prostitute says, 'No, I've got a quicker way; let's do it my way.'

Encouragement in Times of Evil

How widespread is this spiritual seduction that has gripped the souls and the bodies of nations that used to be Christian! Can anything stand against this kind of wickedness that clothes itself in the purple garments of legality, covering heinous sin with insincere and false feats of language, yet is choking people to death? Is there anything in the world that could overcome the multitudes that verse 15 speaks of as the 'many waters' that the prostitute is riding on? The following verses of this chapter and Revelation 18–19 are going to show us, as the Old Testament says, that 'the triumph of the wicked is short'. Yes, the grip that evil has on the Western world looks impressive, if not overwhelming. But in this section of Revelation, God says to all who know him and believe in his Word, that he has a successful strategy, a battle plan that cannot fail.

Naturally, the unbelieving world cannot see it, because it requires faith. Therefore, the unbelieving world is going to back the prostitute and the beast. They are backing the losers. Those who thought the Christians were fools, will end up being the fool at the last and will lose everything, not only for time, but for eternity. But to hearts of faith, the resurgence of evil is only the first little step in drawing down the victorious response of a holy God and his angelic messengers. They come in judgment against evil, spiritual prostitution, and national corruption, and in favor of holiness, love, and truth; in favor of the people of Christ. All will be well, and indeed, more than well, if we are on his side.

46

Babylon the Great, Mother of Harlots
Revelation 17:3–6

What John says in Revelation 17:6 is the key to interpreting verses 1–6, as they identify the 'mother of harlots'. It shows her supreme hatred of Christ, and murderous vengeance against his people. These verses are part of a larger section (ch. 17–19), which show us where all this trouble comes from and where it is going. The two protagonists are a very attractive woman—at first look—who turns out to be a powerful harlot, and a beautiful, pure bride. All the conflict in chapters 17 to 19 takes place between the forces marshalled by these two feminine figures: the harlot, seated on the evil beast, and the spotless bride of Christ, washed clean in his blood. The long-standing battle between these two figures determines the underlying story of what is really happening in the world. Revelation 17–19 gives the big picture that provides the meaning of history.

The Mystery of the Conflicts of History

Here in chapter 17, the spotlight of God's Word is focused on the source of world evil. In chapter 17 and 18 the spotlight of the apostle John shines on that figure who is the underlying source of all these evils, moral declines, and world wars between Jesus' first coming at Bethlehem and his last coming on the Final Day. In Revelation, we are given the underlying diagnosis of the universal disease that keeps breaking out in hatred and war. From the daily news you get the symptoms, but here is the diagnosis, given in terms of symbols or patterns. Verses 5 and 7 speak of 'the mystery'. So we may not rest with the literal picture itself, but follow its leading to deeper truth that the holy angels explain.

In this chapter, we concentrate on verses 3–6 concerning 'the mystery of Babylon the Great, the mother of harlots'. Later, we will see the detailed course of her violent career, and how God is going to handle her with fullest justice. For the present, verses 3–6 show us the background explanation for the major source of world evils. We are led to look at this female personification of evil; this alluring, yet horrible harlot.

Four truths brought out in these verses explain what this woman stands for and does. As we look at these four descriptions we get considerable insight into what is going on around us, particularly in times of trouble.

1. Her habitation (Rev. 17:3).
2. Her appearance (Rev. 17:4).
3. Her power (Rev. 17:4 and 6).
4. Her name (Rev. 17:5).

Her Habitation

Two things are said about her habitation: (1) it is in the wilderness, and (2) she is mounted royally on an evil, political, military beast.

'In the Wilderness'

'In the wilderness' represents the world after the fall of Adam, and in him, our entire human race. Adam was first housed in Paradise, in the beautiful Garden of Eden. By sinning, he turned the world from a paradise into a howling wilderness. Romans 5:12 says 'By one man sin entered into the world, and death by sin; and so death passed upon all men, for that all have sinned.' But that was not God's last word, for it is the background to the good news of the gospel.

In 1 Corinthians 15:45, Christ is called 'the last Adam'. In our place, he went into the wilderness to do battle with Satan, as he went through his temptations at the beginning of his ministry. And whereas the first Adam disobeyed, the last Adam, the Head of the church, was completely obedient to the Father. He totally overcame every temptation. By his victory in the wilderness, and then in that final wilderness, which was the cross, where he took our place, he overcame the devil and all his hosts. Thus, Christ began to restore paradise. He did this first, in men's souls on the inside; and later, when the last trumpet shall sound, he shall restore paradise in our bodies and in the whole natural environment.

Although the fallen world is spoken of as a wilderness, yet it remains inhabited, and largely ruled by those who listen to the devil instead of to God, as we see in Psalm 2. In that messianic Psalm, we hear the voice that draws people into this wilderness: "'Why do the heathen rage, and the people imagine a vain thing? The kings of the earth set themselves and the rulers take counsel together against the Lord and against his Anointed," saying, "Let us break their bands asunder and cast away their cords from us" (v. 1–3). The shrill cry of the ungodly world rulers is an exhortation to get rid of God and the constraints of his Word, of his gospel, of his law (all of which they decry as repressive to their wills, and not to be tolerated). Their protest reminds us of the wicked citizens in the parable of Jesus, who said: 'We will not have this man reign over us' (Luke 19:14). 'Let us make our own paradise on earth; why should the Lord be allowed to tell us what to do? Let's conspire against Him, and we can win'. That is what you hear in the wilderness of this fallen world. That is why so many follow that alluring voice into this evil place.

The harlot leads the pack of a fallen, world population that will not submit to God and wishes to establish its own man-centered paradise. Like the Tower of Babel, they would work their way up to heaven, humanistically, by man's power. That is the attitude of the wilderness. Yet in a sense the wilderness is not really a place, because you can live in the most beautiful, rich country in the world, and yet the wilderness be in your heart. That is the point. It is not a physical place, but a God-denying attitude that takes possession of the personality, and of political systems built on ungodliness.

The Harlot Is Royally Seated on the Beast

Notice that this harlot is seated with regal authority, and riding upon the beast. There are different ideas as to who is the beast. It may be the same as the red dragon or the devil, Satan; or it may be the beast that came from the sea. In Revelation 12:3 the beast from the sea and also the red dragon had seven heads and ten horns, as does this beast on which the evil prostitute is mounted. Daniel 7:7, 20 and 24, mentions the power of the beast with ten horns, which seems to refer to the last of the four great world empires that would arise between Daniel's time and the time of the Messiah's coming, a few hundred years later. The last of those four great empires prior to Christ's birth was Rome—a city sitting on seven hills. But it means more than just historical Rome, Babylon, or even unbelieving Jerusalem; it includes all of that, but it also gives us a principle that is in operation throughout the ages. The beast on which the harlot is seated and riding forth with great power, is a principle found in all world empires that deny God's authority over them. It is institutionalized paganism in league with false religion, which is determined to get rid of God and his church. This is confirmed by the fact that this beast on which the harlot is seated, is full of blasphemous names.

> The beast in 13:1 had a blasphemous name on each of the seven heads, but here heads and horns are full of names that ridicule God, his Word, people, church, and kingdom. With his mouth the beast utters blasphemous words and slanders God, heaven, and the saints (13:5–6).[118]

Hatred for God and his Truth

That means actual hatred for the true, holy God and for his Christ. It gets to the point of blasphemy, where people make open fun of the glorious character of God and his plan of salvation. In the 1920s, for instance, the Protestant modernists, many of whom were leading the main-line churches at that time in America, made fun of belief in the blood of Jesus for salvation. They called it a primitive, ignorant, slaughterhouse religion. That is blasphemy! It was the beast. The harlot was working through them. And the blasphemous names on the immoral political system means that they are uttering vile language to assert their denial of God's existence, or at least to say that he has no authority over us.

Her Appearance

We notice the appearance of this terrible harlot in verse 4. It is important to grasp this point, or we will miss a great deal: she does not look terrible at first. She is outwardly beautiful and impressive, majestic to unanointed, unspiritual eyes. She looks wonderful. Paul tells us that Satan is transformed into an *'angel of light'* (1 Cor. 11:14). That is how he comes to you and me; not with a pitchfork, not normally with an ugly face showing you what will happen to you if you follow. Rather, he comes looking sharp and *avant-garde*, slick, powerful, and able to help you. That is the way this awful harlot looks.

Attractive Offers at First Sight

In effect, she says, 'Forget about God and fit in with this system. Look at how powerful and attractive we are. Look at how many beautiful things we can offer you now. It is silly to wait for heaven; you do not even know if there is a heaven. If there is, you do not know if you will get in. But we can offer you almost everything you could ever want, right now. Why bother with heaven and all of that?' That is how Karl Marx, Lenin, and Stalin got such a following. Communism said, 'There is not a God; there is not a heaven; that is the opium of the people. But we can offer you an earthly paradise, if you give our government enough power we will make the world a paradise'. Well, what did they do? The name of their paradise is Siberia. Solzhenitsyn described it very well in his *Gulag Archipelago, Cancer Ward,* and other books. Finally, that man made paradise became so horrible, that even the former communists at last overthrew it. Yet it took about seventy years for people to see what had happened, and to do something about it. Like this sinful woman, it first looked very beautiful to untrained eyes. An ungodly political and religious system usually has outward trappings of power and beauty, and many are foolishly drawn into alliance with it.

Her Power

This great prostitute possesses the power to pretend (1) that she can fill your sinful appetite, and also (2) to make you fear that if you do not go along with her program, she is able to kill those who resist her (Rev. 17:4, 6).

Power to Fill Sinful Appetites

Not all of her claims are pretence: this prostitute does have temporary power from the devil and from the political beast he motivates, to give people drink from a golden cup (Rev. 17:4). It looks fabulous! What this modern world-system can offer me is tremendous! But wait till you see what is inside the cup; it is full of abominations and filthiness of her fornications!

Abomination. Kistemaker has described effectively and accurately the concept of 'abomination':

> The word *abomination* denotes the objects and practices that are acutely offensive to God. Among others, they include the worship of idols, (Deut. 27:15); the wages of prostitution (Deut. 23:18); homosexual acts and sexual perversions (Lev. 18:22; 20:13); witchcraft, casting spells, and divination (Deut. 18:10, 11) ... The golden cup is filled with idolatry to spite and provoke God. But the cup itself is held out to the people at large, who are being seduced to drink its contents. When they do so, they suffer disastrous results, becoming victims of pornography, gambling, extravagance, power, and the craving for celebrity status. The great prostitute occupies a central position in an anti-Christian culture.

A Golden Cup of Deadly Poison. The mention of the golden cup seems to be related to Jeremiah 51:7: 'Babylon hath been a golden cup in the Lord's hand, that made all the earth drunken: the nations have drunken of her wine; therefore the nations are mad'. We ask ourselves: 'Why have the countries gone crazy?' It is because they have been drinking from the golden cup of the ultimate spiritual prostitute, who says: 'This is the way. Do it any way but God's way. Drink this, and you will prosper'. But Jeremiah 51:8 gives you the results that the devil hides from the foolish nations until it is too late: 'Babylon is suddenly fallen and destroyed; howl for her; take balm for her pain, if so be she may be healed'.

We see the vile shadow of the great spiritual prostitute falling with so many living together without being married. Now it seems to be almost totally acceptable. The prostitute draws near us in the halls of science and medicine, by offering us a brave new world through genetic engineering and gene cloning—human cloning—not just Dolly the sheep! How the prostitute has taken so many schools by saying, 'Replace the Bible with humanistic philosophy that comes directly from the beast upon whom I sit'.

By means of the spiritual personification of opposition to God that we find in the prostitute on that beast, we see her offering a beautiful cup filled with fatal poison, which all too many drink. And yet as Jeremiah says in 51:8: 'Take balm for her pain, if so be she may be healed.' Yet one can reach a certain stage of self-inflicted corruption, such that even 'the balm of Gilead' will effect no cure (cf. Jer. 46:8).

Power to Kill those Who Resist Her

Secondly this harlot, in league with the ungodly political beast can do harm to those who refuse to drink her nasty potion. We see in verse 6 that she has motivated evil kingdoms to put many Christians to death. That was true with unbelievers in Jerusalem who killed the brother of the Lord, James, and many another. Peter and Paul were killed by Rome. God sometimes allows the powers of evil a certain amount of physical power over his saints, but he never lets them touch the soul of his saints: that is impossible. The beast and the harlot can never get at the the eternal security of one believer, even of the weakest believer. They cannot do this, but they can, when allowed in God's strange providence, get at their bodies (cf. Matt. 10:28).

Her Name

Revelation 17:5 tells us that the first part of her name is '*Mystery*'. 'Mystery' probably indicates that only God himself understands exactly why he allows evil in these different forms. 'Mystery' means that only God himself knows precisely how he is using the evil he allows to further his final purposes. It's a mystery! Even the horrible actions of spiritual prostitution, in tandem with anti-God world systems will never be able to destroy the elect, and will only advance the purposes of God. It is a wondrous mystery that they cannot do so!

A Greater Mystery than that of Evil

Over against this profound mystery of abominable spiritual, cultural and political prostitution, the New Testament presents another great mystery. 'Great is the mystery of godliness,' says 1 Timothy 3:16. This verse goes on to talk about how Jesus left heaven and became incarnate to reverse the work of the devil. That is an even greater and infinitely more powerful mystery than spiritual prostitution: it is godliness, such as we find eternally established through the completed work of the Lord Jesus Christ.

Verse 6 showed John wondering about the appearance of this at-first, attractive, alluring woman, royally clothed, though soon to be seen as the very personification of evil. Before the holy angel, John was saying, 'I wonder all about this!' Naturally he wonders, because he is a human. And we, who are less in the counsel of God than the apostle John, also wonder about such mysteries. In the next chapter we shall overhear the answer that the angel gives to John, where he reveals a good part of the mystery, and thereby encourages the Lord's servant to look forward with confidence and joy to the fuller unfolding of the plan of God. It will not be long before John will hear the choirs of heaven singing over the final judgment of the great prostitute: 'Alleluia; Salvation, and glory, and honor, and power, unto the Lord our God...' (Rev. 19:1).

47

ANGELIC EXPLANATIONS

Revelation 17:7–11

There is a profound change of atmosphere from Revelation 17:7 down to the end of chapter 19. What changes is the outlook on evil, war, destruction, and desolation. Throughout the book there has been heavy emphasis on the frightening depth and breadth of moral and political evil in this fallen world. We have seen what terrible shapes evil can take in a fallen world: morally, militarily, and politically. But from here we move into the beginning of the victory of God over all this evil.

God takes his time. He lets evil grow and come to a point when all its corruption has been gathered together into a head. Then, at the divinely determined moment, he moves to blot it out definitively.

In that light, we begin surveying the victory of 'the Lamb slain from the foundation of the world', together with his bride, over all the powers of hell. We notice four points:

1. It takes angelic help to know what these visions mean (Rev. 17:7).
2. The angel explains what the beast means (Rev. 17:8, 11).
3. The angel shows the temporary power of this beast (Rev. 17:9–10).
4. The angel shows the true character of this beast in different ages (Rev. 17:9–10).

ANGELIC HELP TO EXPLAIN THESE VISIONS

When John saw the symbolic shapes of the future: a beast, the harlot, seven heads, ten horns, and many waters, he was unable to understand what it meant, until God sent an angel to explain these pictures plainly. There is no doubt that he saw a literal vision, like Nebuchadnezzar and Daniel saw literal visions. But he needed to know exactly what they meant. That is why God sent an angel to explain to John these pictures in a plain way.

In this chapter we look at verses 8-11, which tell us about the beast and the seven heads. The power of Christ is going to let them reach a certain point, and then wipe them out.

THE ANGEL EXPLAINS WHAT THE BEAST MEANS

The rest of chapter, 17 concentrates more on the beast than it does on the evil harlot, who sits astride the beast. Why does the focus pass from the corrupt harlot to the beast on whom she is riding? Here is the reason: the beast, as far as world history is concerned, is more important than the woman, for the woman depends upon the beast. She gets her power from him. The beast is directly motivated by Satan, personified earlier in Revelation as the red dragon. Satan gives the beast his authority (Rev. 13:3).

Changing Visage of Evil
So what is this beast? This beast is empowered by the devil through the ages of history so that he takes different forms. One time the beast appears one way; in another century he looks different; in another historical context, he is yet different again. The beast can veil himself as a kingdom, a tribe, an empire, or even as a democracy. His shape changes over the ages, but what matters is not so much the outward shape of a government, but the heart of the beast. That heart is always the same, no matter what outward shape he takes. Whether it was the Roman Empire, Stalin's Soviet Union, some of the Islamic dictators, or a soul-destroying system masking itself as a democracy, the heart remains the same.

A Parody of the Trinity
Three words or three sayings in verses 8 and 11 explain what the heart of the beast is like, and why he is so wicked. He can never be reformed, but will have to be wiped out by the sovereign power of the Word of God. These words are: he was and is not, yet shall be, and goes into perdition. He was, he is not, yet he will stay around a while, but finally, he is going to be destroyed. These three states of being are a parody of how Revelation 1:4 speaks of the holy Trinity: he was, he is, and he shall be.

Revelation 1:4 recalls Exodus 3:14, where God Almighty says: I am that I am. God always was; God always is; God always shall be. That is the essence of the being of God: he Who is will never pass out of existence. That is why he wins the battle—every battle—against evil. He always is, and of no other being can that truly be said.

What an appalling sign of the perversion of sin, of the twisting of high intelligence, for an angel such as Lucifer was, to think that he could mimic God and say: I was, I am, and I shall be. But this cosmic pretension does not work. Revelation says, 'Yes, the devil expresses these high pretensions of spanning eternity like God himself, but he came into being, and he is going into perdition'. He had a beginning, because he is a creature. He is going to have a terminus for his activities, when he will be cast into the Lake of Fire.

Hence, it is suicidal for anyone to identify with Satan instead of with Christ. To sell out one's immortal soul to fit into the world system, in order to benefit from the temporary things that Satan can offer, is to assure a final landing into the never-ending destruction of the Lake of Fire, where Satan must always be.

God alone always is and always will be, but Satan tries to mimic Him. He who in ape-like fashion vainly tried to become God, said to our first parents in the garden, 'Commit this sin; do not do what God said, and you shall be as gods'. He tempted them with his own sin, wanting to replace God. He came to the Lord Jesus Christ, when Jesus was tempted in the wilderness in Matthew 4:8-10, showed the kingdoms of the world to Christ in a moment: all the nations in their impressive splendor, with their palaces and armies. Satan said, 'Bow down, worship me and I will give you the whole thing'. He was trying to mimic God, even having the temerity to confront the holy Son of God in the flesh. But Jesus said, 'Get thee behind me, Satan, for it is written, thou shalt worship the Lord thy God and him only shalt thou serve'. And Satan had to leave.

Some Governments Seek to Replace God
Let us bring this back to the point of the beast. The beast is empowered by Satan and reflects the

thinking of Satan to a large degree. Being a beast often includes exercising political or religious power that is very influential among the nations of mankind, at any one time. He changes form in different ages. Here is the way we know that a religious or political system is demonic: it seeks to replace God with itself and to create its own values instead of getting them from the Word of God. That is the spirit of the beast. A famous German philosopher, named Hegel, actually said, 'The state is God walking on earth.' The philosopher of Communism, Karl Marx, said that 'Religion is the opiate of the people'. He held that people need to get rid of religion, so as to replace God and the church with an all-powerful, centralized state. Then everything will be so wonderful that you will not even need a state; everything will be a humanistic paradise.

In the United States we feel that the spirit of the beast has not completely taken over, but since the 1960s we have been increasingly feeling the hot breath of the beast saying: 'Do not let God be mentioned in public life. It might offend an atheist or somebody with another religion, who has immigrated here. Do not dare have the Ten Commandments in a court room or read the Bible and pray the Lord's Prayer in a public school'.

Although not everyone agrees with the late R. J. Rushdoony, we can at least appreciate that during the late seventies and early eighties, he did a lot of testifying in cases against people who had Christian schools. He would explain why the laws of America give the right to have different kinds of schools, so that it was not illegal to have a Christian school or a home school. He went all over the country doing this, with considerable success. Once in the early eighties he went to a court, where the judge said at the beginning of the trial, 'Now one thing I will not allow in this court room is any kind of testimony in which you mention the Bible.' The judge went on to say, 'I will consider it contempt of court if you mention any reference to the United States Constitution or to the Declaration of Independence'. What was this judge doing? He was saying, 'There can be nothing above the power of the state, as I interpret it'. Surely, that is the spirit of the beast! There is nothing above the government; what they say is the last word; there is no transcendent law.

The Temporary Power of This Beast

While it is grim to talk about war, it is also encouraging to face reality in the context of this glorious God, who cares and who is in charge, right to this minute. When, in the light of Revelation 17, you look at the worst, you come out encouraged, when you remember who God is and what he is doing. Verses 9 and 10 show us that the beast, the various political systems that hate God and that want to replace God, are only for a time. God sets the time, in his own secret calendar and clock, of how long they shall last.

The End of all Evil Governments

We are not given a vision into the Divine clock, as to how long any particular anti-god system shall last. God does not tell us that, but he does tell us that all political, immoral, and false religionist powers that oppose Christ and his Word, are temporary. They will be destroyed. Revelation 17:11 says that the beast 'is not and shall pass into perdition'. Until the cross of Christ, his bodily resurrection and the pouring out of the Holy Spirit at Pentecost, the beast had massive power over all the nations. But something happened when Christ came to earth, that greatly delimited the power of the beast. He has never had the power since Christ was here that he had before Christ came. He still has power, but it is greatly limited. Jesus said in Luke 10:18, after one of the successful missions of his disciples, winning souls, casting out evil spirits, healing the sick and proclaiming the good news: 'I saw Satan fall like lightning'.

The initiative passes from Satan because of the victory Christ won. Thus, in Matthew 28:18, Jesus says: 'All power is given unto Me, in heaven and on earth'. In Revelation 17:8 we are told that the beast is not. Yet after having received this eventually fatal wound in Christ's atoning resurrection-work, the beast still is allowed to circulate. But it is only for a season that the devil is able to do his work.

We did not know exactly when Communism would be defeated in the Soviet Union. We now know that it lasted, more or less, from 1917 to 1991. Some of us remember when Khrushchev at the U.N., took off his shoe, banged it on the desk, and said: 'We will bury you.' Khrushchev did not think that the mighty power, with all those nuclear weapons of the Soviet Union, would be gone in less than 30 years, but it was. God had a limit to it, and it passed. It was the same with Hitler. He took over Germany in 1933, yet he blew his brains out in 1945, some twelve years later. He had said that the Third Reich was going to last for 1,000 years, but Hitler's timetable was not the same as God's.

Human powers never give up their corrupt control, willingly. But God gives the devil, in these different forms, only a temporary season. Thus he warns us never to sell ourselves out to accommodate any earthly power that seeks to replace him and that refuses to hear his Word. In the end it will lose and we would lose with it.

THE TRUE CHARACTER OF THIS BEAST

The various details related by John about this beast include such things as 'the seven heads'. The holy angel tells John that it means seven hills, and then he says that it means seven kings. Does this mean Rome, a city sitting on seven hills? Yes, it does mean Rome, which was a major power when Revelation was revealed to John. But these seven hills go much further than Rome, to the Roman Empire that was persecuting the church and would destroy Jerusalem. It also speaks about things that will happen long after Rome has been reduced to rubble and lost its world empire.

Similarly, the seven kings could be Roman emperors, yet that does not literally work out, because whether you start with Julius or Augustus, it is hard to get it to work out exactly with the number of the various emperors. I think what it is referring to is all anti-Christian, anti-God governments between the fall of Rome and the coming of Christ in final glory.

Verse 10 says: 'he must continue a short space'. Again, must means God's must. God has put it in his plan that the powers of evil have a certain limited time in which he lets them work. How they hate God; if they could, they would drag him off his throne, and destroy his people. They will continue, but the message of the text is 'for a short space'. Somehow the worst they can do, in that short space that God allows them, is invisibly used to destroy themselves at the right time, so that ultimately they advance God's purposes of grace amongst the nations. Only God knows how to do that!

The Eighth Beast Concentrates Evil

The eighth beast personifies the anti-God heart of the seven previous world powers; he has a beginning, and the good news is that he has an end. But Jesus has no end. Father, Son and Holy Spirit have no beginning and no end. This eighth beast is the concentration of every thing that is evil. His future location is defined in chapter 19 as the Lake of Fire.

The holy angel explains that since God will wind up world history with the destruction of the evil kingdoms and the victory of the cause of Christ, only one thing matters: that men and women make sure they are on the winning side. This is brought out in Revelation 17:8: 'They that dwell on the earth shall wonder, whose names were not written in the book of life from the foundation of the world, when they behold the beast that was, and is not, and yet is'. In other words, they will be amazed when what they were counting on was at last shown to be merely a human, political, and cultural power. It arrayed itself against God, but it is utterly destroyed, so that those who sold themselves out to it lose everything.

The Lamb's Book of Life

We are told that their names were not written in the Lamb's book of life from the foundation of the world. Notice the dramatic contrast. Those whose names were not written in the Lamb's book of life are destroyed with the beast. The contrast is amplified in Ephesians 1:4: 'According as he hath chosen us in Christ before the foundation of the world, that we should be holy and without blame before him in love, having predestinated us unto the adoption of children...'

While at present, none of us can gaze into the Lamb's Book of Life, on the last day we shall see something of defining importance about those who rejected Christ and said: 'We will not have this Man reign over us! We will align ourselves with this political, humanistic power that opposes Scripture and truth'. We will look back and realize that their names were not written in the book of life, but at present, it is a mystery, known only to God. On the other hand, those who are vindicated on the last day, when God says: 'Well done, thou good and faithful servant, enter thou into the joy of thy Lord', will know that they were chosen before the foundation of the world in Christ. That is why they remained faithful, and stood with the Lord, even when the powers of evil in their generation seemed so strong.

God has not told us precisely who is written in this book, and who is not. That is God business. But how can I know of my part in all this? Ephesians 1:12–14 talks about this, 'that we should be to the praise of his glory who first trusted in Christ, in whom ye also trusted after that ye heard the Word of truth and the gospel of your salvation'. In other words: believe the gospel. There are many mysteries, but here is what it comes down to for me to have a secure future: 'Who first trusted in Christ and received the gospel of salvation'. It is very simple: 'For God so loved the world that he gave his only-begotten Son that whosoever believeth in him should not perish, but have everlasting life'. Or as the Philippian jailer said to Paul and Silas, 'Sirs, what must I do to be saved?' They replied, 'Believe on the Lord Jesus Christ and thou shalt be saved'. To know that I am eternally secure, I am never called on to put myself in place of God, so as to get into the mysteries of election; that is hidden in God. But God says, 'I sent My Son into the world, not to condemn the world, but that through him the world might be saved.' People of every class, race, nation, without distinction, are invited to come to Jesus. Anybody that comes to Jesus and asks him to forgive them, and make them clean through his blood, and fill their lives with his Spirit, will never be turned away; they will never be disappointed! They will find security and rest and hope for the future by trusting in the One to Whom, alone, the future belongs.

48

THE FALL OF BABYLON

Revelations 18:1–8

The modern nation of Iraq, which has been the center of war, terror and tumult since the early 1980s, contains the ruins of the ancient city of Babylon, on the banks of the Euphrates River. When John in this passage predicted the downfall of 'Babylon' (probably in the sixties, or as some think, the nineties of the first century), ancient Babylon had been in ruins for centuries. So what does he mean by the coming destruction of 'Babylon', since it had long since been destroyed?

As we answer that question, we notice that chapter 18 has two main divisions: verses 1–8 concern the impending fall of mighty Babylon, and verses 9–24, which we will look at in the next chapter, concerning Babylon after her fall.

To identify the meaning of Babylon, we draw four points out of the first eight verses:

1. What is Babylon? (Rev. 18:2–7).
2. The characteristics of Babylon (Rev. 18:2–3, 5, 7).
3. The certain fate of Babylon (Rev. 18:1, 6, 8).
4. A warning to God's people (Rev. 18:4).

WHAT IS BABYLON?

Since the ancient city of Nebuchadnezzar had lain in ruins for centuries, that historical city cannot literally have been meant by John. Yet it does have a spiritual meaning, with definite analogies to that ancient city-state. Babylon is frequently used in Holy Scripture as a symbol of satanically inspired, humanistic evil, starting with the Tower of Babel in Genesis 11. At that time, people had rejected God. They said, 'Let us build a tower that will reach up to Heaven'. That is, 'We will obtain paradise by our own human efforts in disregard to God.' Babel, where the tongues of humankind were confounded, is somehow connected with the origins of Babylon.

Varying Images of Babylon
Babylon was a potent symbol of evil under the reign of King Nebuchadnezzar, under whom the Jews were led captive. God used Babylon as a rod to punish his own people, and yet he finally breaks the rod, as he always does.

We have already noted that at certain points in Revelation, 'Babylon' could be used to refer to apostate Jerusalem, which had rejected Jesus Christ. It was ripe for the destruction that the Romans would visit upon it in AD 70. 'Babylon' could also refer to the powerful Roman Empire, which was persecuting the Christian Church.

So we can summarize the meaning of Babylon in Biblical usage as referring to a world-wide, humanistic system that is hostile to God; that rejects his Word and refuses to accept the salvation that he offers through his Son.

Like the beast, Babylon can take many different forms. She can look very different, depending on the historical context of a particular age, but at heart, Babylon is always the same.

We saw in chapter 17 that Babylon was said to have been the harlot, polluting large populations with her various types of immorality (17:18). Now in chapter 18, Babylon takes the form of a huge multinational, economic military power. Indeed, stress is laid on the multinational, economic power of Babylon: 'For all the nations have drunk of the wine of her fornication and the merchants of the earth are waxed rich through the abundance of her delicacies' (18:3). This is one of the world's great economic powers, where everything seems just right with the banks and the markets. That is the form of Babylon that we find here.

The Characteristics of Babylon

We are given four characteristics that you always find in 'Babylon', whatever the age.

A Dwelling Place of Demons

We find the first characteristic in a description of Babylon after she has fallen (v. 2). This is what made it fall: it was a dwelling place of demons. Forty years ago, there were people who said there is not a devil and demons are mythical, but I hear fewer and fewer people denying the reality of evil or the reality of demons today. We have seen too much evidence of the existence of evil powers for it to be credible to claim that everything can be explained in terms of an optimistic materialism. But why is Babylon a dwelling place of demons?

Babylon had rejected God and his Word. A culture that rejects God on a large scale loses his divine protection against evil. It is like the principle of diffusion that everybody was taught in physics: 'Nature abhors a vacuum'. We are spiritual beings, and we also cannot stand a vacuum. Cultures have a certain spirituality, be it a good one or a bad one. Cultures cannot stand a spiritual vacuum. When you have the Holy Spirit, he fills the vacuum and prevents a great deal of demonic activity and self-destructive actions among the people. Where the Holy Spirit is strong in a culture, even unbelievers are blessed. They are not saved, but they are kept from many forms of pollution. But when a culture turns its back on God, the Holy Spirit, to some degree, is withdrawn, leaving a vacuum. Guess who rushes in to fill it? The evil one and those fallen created beings, former angels, who now are demons. Thus, Babylon, an important, powerful culture that has rejected the God of the Bible, does not realize how far the demonic realm has taken charge of its activities.

So what would a dwelling place of demons look like? In 1999, in Columbine, Colorado, there was the horrible murdering of students by students. One thing that was not stressed much in the mainline media was that the students who killed the other students were involved in Satanic activity. They were uncomfortable with disclosing the nature of the underlying problem. These people went out and shot innocent school children because they were involved in Satanism.

What would a dwelling place of demons look like? Events like these, or the similar scenes that occurred several years earlier in a school in Dunblane, Scotland, illustrate what a dwelling place of demons looks like. And would it not look like suicide bombings? The Bible says that Satan is a murderer, and when large groups of people have the Holy Spirit, Satan's murderous activity is restrained. But Babylon lacked this restraint, and became a dwelling place of demons.

Rejection of God and his Word for Gross Pleasure

We find the second characteristic of Babylon in verse 3, which changes the form and look of Babylon. The name changes, but the reality is the same. Babylon has rejected God and his Word and wants to put man first. We read of gross sensuality. When people give themselves over to pleasing the senses and obtaining short-term pleasures, it short circuits moral, normal restraint in the public. It speaks here of fornication; money is used to keep up sensual experiences. 'Make me feel good now.'

The New Testament says 'there is pleasure in sin for a season', and nobody could deny that there is a certain kind of pleasure in sensuality. But it is extremely short lived and subject to the law of diminishing returns.

Today we see pornography all around. If you go into an airport to buy a paper at the newsstand, you have to look the other way, because of the magazines on sale. Pornography, from the newsstands to the Internet, is the commercialization of sensuality. It means quick pleasure without regard to lasting relationship and personal purity of thought. It is a lowering of restraint, a turning of one's back on the discipline of one's own life. It is letting the flesh take charge against what my mind tells me is pure and right. It is very tempting to all people.

Gambling is much the same as sensuality. It is a quick kind of monetary pleasure (if and when successful). Gambling seeks to short circuit hard work and realizing you have to restrain present expenses to have money for future investment. It says, we may 'hit it big'. How sad to see people, who do not have much money to waste, in line to buy lottery tickets at the gas stations. It is sensuality and financial greed.

It speaks here of merchants and how rich they got. Their wealth is based on financial greed. It is fine to earn money; you have to do so, or you would starve, and if you earn a little extra, you can help others. That is honorable, but there is a big line between legitimate work and savings, and greed. Greed is a kind of sensuality, a desire to amass money that overrides everything else. It overrides honest dealing with one's workers. It may even override love for family and compassion for the needy. Greed readies a person to ignore God's law. Finally, he goes far enough to deny God's existence and to bow down before a false god of gold and silver, stocks and bonds, lands and annuities, or whatever it may be. Those false gods can give the person who bows down to them no help whatsoever in the hour of death.

An article that seems to be grounded on valid sources compares where America was in 1962 and where we were in 2003.[119]

- SAT scores from 1962 to now are down 10%
- Teen suicide rate among 15 to 19 year olds is up 450% since 1962
- Child abuse is up 2,300%
- Illegal drug use is up 6000%
- Divorce is up 350%
- Births by unmarried girls between the ages of 15 and 19 is up 500%

The argument of the article is that part of the reason we are where we are now is because prayer, Bible reading, and some kind of Christian orientation were removed from the public schools starting in 1962. I cannot prove that this is exactly why these statistics have happened, but it may have something to do with it.

It is impossible for us to live in a spiritual vacuum. You deny God, the Bible, and Christ as Lord, and soon the demons come in and fill that vacuum. What the demons do is to destroy body and soul, whereas the Holy Spirit would be building up body and soul. The destroyer is represented by Babylon.

The Piling Up of Unrepented Sins

The third characteristic of Babylon is the piling up of unrepented sins (v. 5). Again, we might have an image of the Tower of Babel behind this. The builders thought, 'We'll get to Heaven and take over without God.' So they build the bricks higher and higher until God stops it. It is a great pile of unrepented sins, mounting up to Heaven that will cause the devastating judgement of God to fall.

A Holy God has only two possible reactions to sin. None of us are without sin, and if all the book of Revelation had to say is that God judges sin, it would be terrible news for all of us. But it says that God has two reactions to sin, and only two. How he reacts to my sin will be determined by which side I decide to stand on.

First, God forgives sins. But for God to forgive sins, those sins have to be repented of. We have to say to God in sincerity, 'Lord, I am sorry that I have transgressed your law and failed to do what I should have done and failed to be what I should be. I ask your forgiveness through Jesus Christ.' Though humans may never accept such pleas for mercy from one another, the miracle of the grace of God is that he completely and eternally pardons every sin in the book that is printed. Perhaps you say, 'There might be some sin I forgot.' Then, say, 'Lord, forgive me the secret sins, the ones I am not even aware of.' Jeremiah 31:34 tells us, 'Their sins I will remember no more.'

How different that is from what he is saying in Revelation 18:5: 'God hath remembered her iniquities'. Die apart from Christ and then there is a second reaction of God to sin. Because of his holy character, and the heinousness of sin, God must react in this way. He must keep count of those sins we refuse to repent of. Although the modernist theory holds that the very category of sin is ridiculous, and does not matter in the least, their sin still remains, and counts heavily against them. Every sin is like the piling up of bricks. One lives without God for many decades and continues to pile up brick upon brick. This horrendous pile invites the devastating, righteous judgment of a pure and holy God to that which is contrary to his character, unless the sinner sincerely repents.

Suicidal Pride and Self-confidence

The fourth characteristic of Babylon, ancient or modern, is winning pride and suicidal confidence in self (v. 7). Think of a drunkard: the inebriated person thinks that he will win a fight with a much stronger man, so he readily goes into the fray, only to be beaten to pulp. This kind of drunken confidence was the case in ancient Babylon.

What could compare with the hanging gardens of Babylon, with their marvelous architecture and overflowing luxury? But in spite of its economic and military power, such social devilry as the raucous feast of Belshazzar showed Babylon's ripeness for judgment. Any great economic and political power that long enough, widely enough, and deeply enough, denies God by exhibiting these four characteristics of Babylon, is ripe for judgment. Those drunken lords did not know that their deeds were quickly to be avenged. Enemy troops, just outside the city gates, were bending the bars in the river so that they could come through, and destroy the wicked elite later in the evening. 'The bigger they are, the harder they fall.'

The Certain Fate of Babylon

The definite fate of Babylon (v. 1, 6, 8) is so certain that it is spoken of as already accomplished (v. 1–2). It is in the past tense. 'Babylon the great is fallen'. The counting up of sins has already been accomplished; the point of no return has been reached. Revelation 18:8 speaks of Babylon's destruction 'in one hour'. It had probably taken hundreds of years to build this mighty city, but its destruction occurred within one hour.

God Has the Power

Perhaps John was thinking of the mighty Roman Empire, which was persecuting the early Church. What a massive empire it was! It had taken hundreds of years to build, yet it could fall very fast. How could this happen? Verse 8 tells us: because 'the Lord is strong.' Psalm 61:11 tells us: 'God hath spoken once; twice have I heard this; that power belongeth unto God.' God created all things out of nothing, by the word of his power in the space of six days. Anything created by God is limited; he alone is infinite, with boundless power over all he created. When some creaturely power wishes to shake its fist in the face of God, 'he who sits in the heaven shall laugh; the Lord shall have them in derision' (Ps. 2:4). When that happens, 'Thou shalt break them with a rod of iron; thou shalt dash them in pieces like a potter's vessel' (Ps. 2:9). The reason Babylon comes down is simply because the Lord is strong.

A Warning to God's People

God commands his people through John: 'Come out of her, my people, that ye be not partakers of her sins, and that ye receive not of her plagues' (Rev. 18:4). This command was followed by the Christians in Jerusalem before its destruction by the Romans in AD 70.[120] As far as the seven churches of Asia were concerned, they did not have the option of literally leaving the pagan cities in which they were living, but at least the principle applied to them: they were to put Christ first in all their decisions. To do so would mean to split with their culture in many instances. They would refuse to participate in idolatrous practices. They would educate their children in the nurture and admonition of the Lord. They would refrain from much pagan entertainment and honor the Sabbath day. They would never take their ease within the context of paganism.

While such practical holiness would frequently make them uncomfortable with their pagan acquaintances, they would have the sheer joy of knowing that they had 'come out, and not touched the unclean thing' (1 Cor. 6:17). The sacrifice would be more than worth it, for thereby they would find the glad presence of God as their heavenly Father (1 Cor. 6:18), and point the way for pagans to him who alone is the viable alternative to Babylon, which is sure to be destroyed.

49

Two Reactions to the Fall of Babylon

Revelation 18:9–24

We have just looked at the fall of Babylon in Revelation 18:1–8. Now we turn to verses 9–24, where we are given two reactions to the fall of Babylon. In this chapter we are only going to look at the first reaction (v. 9–19), and it is great grief, weeping and wailing. Later we will look at the other reaction, which is great rejoicing (v. 20–24).

As we have already seen, the fall of Babylon, that John foresees here is not the ancient city, but the evil, anti-God system that motivated ancient Babylon, first century unbelieving Jerusalem, classical Rome, and that still motivates many modern nation states. Babylon changes its form, but its heart is always motivated by the desire to replace God with the reign of 'the world, the flesh and the devil.'

The real issue is not geography, but a lasting principle: great world powers that reject God, worship money, and oppress people are doomed to certain judgment by a Holy God in his own time-frame. When great economic and military systems collapse under divine judgment, there are always two different reactions: weeping or rejoicing. Much of the modern world rejoiced when Nazi Germany was brought down, but some of its supporters wept. Much of the world rejoiced when the Soviet Union collapsed, but many who had profited from it were grieved, and would like to restore it.

Revelation 18 brings before us the reaction of grief and anguish by worldly people over the destruction of a mighty and immoral economy that had kept their class prosperous until God brought it down. Some people in North American universities are still grieving that the Soviet Union caved in, for they thought it was the best counterbalance to the influence of Christianity. Hence, we need to look at the psychology of those who grieve when evil systems are overthrown.

We note two points:

1. Why some weep when God removes a massive moral cancer (Rev. 18:9–11)?
2. How much is lost when the judgment of God falls on a powerful economic system (Rev. 18:12–13)?

Why Some Weep when God Removes a Massive Moral Cancer

Why do some people, indeed, many people, weep when God removes a massive moral cancer? Jesus tells us why when he says in Matthew, 'Where a man's treasure is, there will his heart be also.' Kings, wealthy merchants, even sailors are all mentioned in chapter 18 as grieving over Babylon's downfall (v, 9, 11, 17–18). Why were they so upset, literally casting dirt on their heads and weeping? Because that is where their treasure was. The only thing in life that really mattered to them, when you got down to it and discovered how they really felt, was money and power, and what money and power could provide for themselves.

The Proper Place of Money
Money is fine in its proper place. It is intended to be a blessing. In itself, it is certainly not evil. Rather, Paul says, 'the love of money is the root of all evil'. Greed can make us deny what our hearts know is right. It can make us trample down the basic moral laws of God and make us treat people as things. Money and what it can buy, can become an idol replacing the true God in our hearts. When this idol is destroyed, then we lose everything. That is why many weep when the immoral economies and political orders that made them rich and proud, at last go under.

Revelation 18:10 and following show a picture of a world in chaos once the judgment has come. The violent overthrow of cities and states is usually followed by looting and anarchy. Notice, how quickly it all unraveled: 'In one hour, your judgment has come' (v. 10). How quickly it all unraveled! Perhaps monetary systems collapsed so that paper money was no good. Riots break out on every block, great institutional buildings are gutted by fire, and what is left is looted.

The Distress of Material Loss
Verse 11 shows the distress of merchants, because with the economic collapse, the public has no money to buy their goods. Their businesses plummet to bankruptcy. The stock market slumps to zero value. If wealth was all one had lived for, then life would no longer be worth living when the funds are gone. We know that some stock brokers on Wall Street jumped out of their windows in October 1929, when the great Depression began. If their idol was smashed, then everything was lost, so they smashed their own bodies and sent out their souls to face the judgment of the one whom their idols hid from their eyes until it was too late. That sort of reaction is portrayed in Revelation 18, when Babylon the great is fallen.

How Much Is Lost When the Judgment of God Falls on a Powerful economy?
Verses 12–13 list luxury items of rare beauty in a very sophisticated culture: gold, silver, precious jewels, wonderful porcelain, and more ordinary food items, such as wine, oil, flour, livestock, and even human slaves and 'souls of men.' Jerusalem was rich in AD 70 and Rome was rich when it fell in the fifth century, just as the Western world is today.

Kistemaker describes an expensive item that is listed by the *King James Version* as 'thyine wood'. (Modern translations render it 'citrus-scented wood'):

> Citrus-scented wood was so costly, that it was only found in the form of tables in the homes of the most affluent citizens. Cicero bought such a table and reportedly paid 500,000 sesterces, an amount that was sufficient to purchase a large estate. The citron tree grew in North Africa, and 'was much prized for its veining, which in the best specimen simulated the eyes of a peacock's tail, or the stripes of the tiger and the spots of the panther. (Martial, 14:85, etc.)[121]

A number of years ago, a friend of ours in the furniture import/export business was a representative of an exclusive British furniture company that made furniture. He sent us a catalogue of their goods. They did not put in the prices, but I asked him later. There was one conference table made for an Arab oil sheik, a gorgeous work of art. He told me that it had sold for $150,000. That kind of thing is envisioned when Revelation 18 reports that the wealthy, sophisticated city is gutted and reduced to ruble. Beautiful and costly things are lost to the flames or to the barbarians. How could the Lord let such fabulous jewels be trashed into the dust?

Something Is More Important than Material Beauties

The last part of verse 18 gives us a clue when it says that one of the things being trafficked was slaves and souls of men. In the modern world, while we do not generally have slaves, the souls of people can become subservient to a system, so that it alienates them from their true destiny to live to the glory of God. Jesus asked this question in Luke, 'What shall it profit a man, if he gain the whole world and lose his own soul?' Nothing has the value of one immortal soul. We are not just bodies, we are souls in bodies, or embodied spirits. Your body is very important, but there is an immaterial aspect of us, usually called our personality, which continues to exist beyond physical death for all eternity. Our souls shall outlast the stars of the galaxies. When the sun is a charred cinder, your soul will still be. Jesus says material things are good, no reasonable person would be against that, but they do not compare in the slightest with the value of one immortal soul. When material things are put first, beautiful though those things may be in themselves, they may have to be destroyed in order to liberate souls from their tyranny.

What God Is Doing When Cultures Are Destroyed

That is part of what God is doing every time a mighty culture that has rebelled against him consistently is brought down. That was happening when ancient Babylon came down. Indeed, when Belshazzar was killed, it made it possible for a new regime to let the Jews go home after seventy years of captivity. The government of Babylon goes down, and Israel goes home. Blessing came out of the destruction. The principle continues to work throughout world history.

Unbelieving Jerusalem that had rejected Christ, persecuted his prophets, and tried to drown the church in blood was devastated in AD 70. Blessing came out of the destruction of a new form of Babylon. A bad spirit came between the Jews and the Romans, which meant that the Christian church could more fully enter its world wide mission, untrammeled by the persecution of the synagogue. Then Rome collapsed in the fifth century and the blessing that came out of the fall of that Babylon was that the Christian church had freedom to spread the gospel all over Europe, and to develop a new Christian civilization for the next thousand years.

What do we think of the modern day Babylons, the mighty secularism enforced by multi-national economic and political systems in today's world? God's Word warns them all, that all ungodly systems that consistently oppose the Lord and his gospel, must be judged severely.

In all these changes, while idol worshippers will weep at the loss of their material goods, the true Church can lift up her head, for as Jesus says in the gospel, 'her redemption draweth nigh'. Great blessing comes out of the downfall of every ungodly Babylonian type system. This gives us the background to join in the rejoicing of the saints over the destruction of Babylon.

50

Heaven's View of International Disasters

Revelation 18: 20–24

These verses show us heaven's view of major international disasters, such as the bringing down of great powers and at times, their civilizations. How does this look from the perspective of heaven? What is God's vision? What is the reaction of the holy ones in heaven when such things occur?

We will see the viewpoint of heaven as we consider two points:

1. A command to rejoice over Babylon's fall (Rev. 18:20).
2. Why Babylon's fall is good news for the saints (Rev. 18:21–4).

A Divine Command to Rejoice

God commands his saints to rejoice over Babylon's fall: 'Rejoice over her, thou heaven and ye holy apostles and prophets…' (v. 20). Is it proper ever to rejoice over some mighty, seemingly disastrous judgment to a huge group of people? This verse says that under certain conditions it is not only right, but it is even commanded for the saints. Looked at in this way, the collapse of humanistic hope and power is for believers on earth and angels above, very good news. We often do not think of it that way. One reason God tells his beloved people, on earth and in heaven to rejoice when Babylon is cast down, is that he has in due time heard our prayers. In due season, he has answered the specific prayers of his suffering people for vengeance.

Essential Ministry of the Martyrs

In Revelation 6:10–11 we saw the saints who are now in their heavenly home, after having been martyred. 'And they cried with a loud voice saying, How long, O Lord, holy and true…'. God said then, 'Rest a little longer, I am going to do it. Keep praying and trusting.' Now in Revelation 18:20, the glorious Lord from his light-filled throne says to the saints: 'Now I have answered your prayer, so start rejoicing. I knew when the time would be to bring down this judgment on the corrupt, anti-God systems that wanted to blot my church from the face of the earth. Now I have done it at the right time, so be greatly joyful over my answer to your long prayers.'

God does answer the specific prayers of his people for justice in world history, at various junctures as the centuries pass. You never know when it will be, but he uses our prayers to get everything in order, then vengeance falls on those who would blot out the testimony of Christ from the earth.

Ancient Babylon

This happened in historical Babylon itself, the ancient city of the line of Nebuchadnezzar. In Revelation 18:21, John speaks of taking up a great stone like a millstone and casting it into the sea, proclaiming 'Thus with violence shall that great city Babylon be brought down'. It is a direct reference to Jeremiah 51:61–4:

> And Jeremiah said to Seraiah, When thou comest to Babylon and shalt see and shalt read all these words; Then shalt thou say, O Lord, thou has spoken against this place, to cut it off, that none shall remain in it, neither man, nor beast, but that it shall be desolate for ever. And it shall be, when thou hast made an end of reading this book, that thou shalt bind a stone to it, and cast it into the midst of Euphrates; And thou shalt say, Thus shall Babylon sink, and shall not rise from the evil that I will bring upon her; and they shall be weary. Thus far are the words of Jeremiah.

And so in Jeremiah 51, the prophet throws the inspired scroll of his writings, tied to a rock, into the Euphrates (Jer. 51:63). Here in Revelation 18, we notice a massive increase in the size of the rock that was cast into the river. In Jeremiah's time, it was a mere rock, probably no larger than a book, but in Revelation it is a huge millstone that is cast into the sea with violence. The sign that Babylon would be brought down after her persecution of so many surrounding nations was the prophet casting the book with the rock into the Euphrates. When Babylon was brought down, it was the answer to prayers of the believers for long years.

Apostate Jerusalem

Similarly, apostate Jerusalem, which had rejected the Lord Jesus Christ, was brought down, as Jesus had predicted it would be in Luke 19.[122] Jesus prophetically announced its destruction when he beheld the city and wept over it, before passion week. Jesus said (Luke 19:43–4):

> For the days shall come upon thee, that thine enemies shall cast a trench about thee, and compass thee round, and keep thee in on every side, and shall lay thee even with the ground and thy children within thee; and they shall not leave in thee one stone upon another; because thou knewest not the time of thy visitation.

Josephus said that something like a million Jews were killed in AD 70, when the Jerusalem that rejected Jesus, and refused to receive his atonement and resurrection, was utterly destroyed. If Revelation were written before AD 70, then the destruction of spiritual 'Babylon' lay only a handful of years after the Holy Spirit through John made this prediction of coming devastation.

All 'Babylons' Will Be Brought Down

Whether ancient Babylon, or first century Jerusalem, or later forms of godless 'Babylon', God lets her reach a certain point of wickedness, power and corruption and down he brings her in answer to prayers of the humble, seemingly powerless saints. But in fact they are not powerless! We now know that even while the Soviet Union seemed impregnably powerful, an apparently random, humble, scattered and humanly powerless group: the Christian churches, were being used in the plan of God to determine the future of that mighty empire. The churches in the USSR were often persecuted and laid waste by the atheistic government. In many cases, the KGB penetrated the church and were turning in Christians to the central government authorities. Yet, without political power, the suffering church was praying for God to do something. And in 1991, God brought that wicked system down. Yes, they still have problems, but life is not so terrible as it was before 1991.

God has ways to bring down the Babylons of every age. They look different, but the principles are the same. They hate God and persecute his saints, and in due time as the saints are faithful, willing to suffer and keep praying, God knows the right time to hear their prayers. So we must never be discouraged when he takes his time, but stand fast and pray.

Downfall of the French Monarchy
The nineteenth century Virginia theologian, Robert L. Dabney, believed that the great and ancient French monarchy had been broken down as a sort of divine judgment for how they had mistreated the Protestant Huguenots a century earlier.[123] In 1684, the French Monarch, Louis XIV, revoked the Edict of Nantes, which had been made in 1589, allowing the Protestant evangelicals the right to worship according to the Reformed Faith. The king revoked that document, which is one of the reasons Charleston, South Carolina was settled with so many of the French Huguenot families right after 1685. He told the French Protestants they would have to turn Roman Catholic or they would be killed. They did kill vast numbers and drove others out, who came to South Carolina, England, Holland, Switzerland, and elsewhere. These godly and talented Huguenots greatly enriched those countries with their integrity, intelligence and creative abilities.

That was 1685. For a long time it looked like the King of France got by with killing and dispursing the Protestants. Almost exactly 104 years later, after those old protestants had for generations cried and prayed, the French royal house that had so mistreated them was itself destroyed. The revolutionaries of 1789 hated Christianity, and certainly did not think of themselves as doing the work of the Triune God. In their writings and then their laws, they utterly disdained Him. Yet, as with Babylon, and Jerusalem, and later the Roman Empire itself, God used wicked persons to bring down the cruel regimes that had persecuted his church. Not everyone will agree with Dabney, but he believed that in the fall of the French monarchy, another Babylon had been brought down.

Which Way the Western World?
We can see a principle here. Humanistic empires, even if they use the name of God while they are persecuting the saints and going against the Holy Scripture, will join Babylon and be utterly reduced to rubble. This should raise questions about the proudly secularistic nations of the Western world, who are 'making void God's law', and seeking to remove every vestige of Biblical morality from the various nations. American and British people do not normally think of themselves as being in the category of Babylon, monarchical France and the Soviet Union, but are our immoral and materialistic policies and practices very different? If the Western nations persist in their practical atheism and attempts to remove Biblical truth from their populations, they too will experience the same destruction felt by the earlier 'Babylons'.

The saints were told to rejoice when evil empires go down, for the way again is open and free for the gospel of Christ to be preached and lived out. Judgment on wicked persecutors proves that a Holy God cares what happens to his dear people. Although the Heavens seem like brass and God seems silent when so many of his people are being killed, behind the scenes the loving and all-powerful Lord is getting everything into battle formation to strike out against evil agencies. God greatly values the blood of his martyrs. When he deems the right number of martyrdoms to have been filled up, holy vengeance will be unleashed on the systems that killed his people. Then the saints shall greatly rejoice.

Superficiality of 'Political Correctness'
This goes against the modern relativism and the political correctness that is reigning even in evangelical churches. But I want to say this from the Bible: judgment is good news in the sense that it disproves relativism. Relativism says everything is the same. There is no ultimate evil, no ultimate good. It just depends on your opinion, so you cannot judge anybody. While we are never to be harsh or censorious, it does not mean that there are no absolute standards and that judgment will not come against evil. Every time another Babylon comes down, it proves that there is absolute good and evil. There is a standard over the nations to which they will be held accountable. That good will be eternally blessed and evil eternally punished. Divine judgment demonstrates that what we do in this life matters for all eternity. The decisions we make here determine where our souls will dwell forever. That is not popular; I do not hear it very often even in evangelical ministries these days, but the Bible says it is so.

Those who persecute Christians think they are getting by with it; that the Christians are trash. The government has the power. They think there is no God, or that if God exists, he will never judge anybody. He is too nice to do this. In other words, their God is either unholy, or they must feel he pays no attention to what happens here below. On the contrary, the physical bringing down of every sort of Babylon is proof of God's holiness, of his watch-care over every life, and of the eternal consequences of our responses in this space and time to his gospel.

Here in Revelation 18:20, the saints are invited to join in the laughter and gladness of God (Ps. 2), over the divine crushing of wicked opposition, and consequently, the establishment of beauty and truth for all who have followed him through thick and thin. As the hymn says: 'Some through the fire, some through the flood, some through great trials, but all through the blood!' Therefore, the people of God are commanded to rejoice when his judgment falls on these ungodly nations and cultures.

Why Babylon's Fall is Good News
Why is a terrible thing good news? To rejoice at the destruction of a rich civilization seems contrary to reason. In verses 20–22, you find a summary of music, productive work, food production, light in our houses, marriage, ceremonies, joys and normal life. All of these are good things of creation, which have now ceased in the destroyed culture. There must be good reasons why we are asked to rejoice at such cessation of normal cultural activities. Let me mention three reasons from this text why we are to rejoice when God's judgment falls on great, godless Babylon.

Violence
The first reason we should rejoice at Babylon's downfall is the violence (Rev. 18:21, 24) that it practiced so widely and for so long. Babylon changes her face, but there is a constant characteristic in every Babylon. If she persists in her godless schemes to exalt herself by making a

humanistic paradise apart from God's Word, she will use violence on those who dare to resist her projects. That was shown in the stone that was thrown into the sea with violence by the Holy Angel. It was an appropriate retribution for the violence that Babylon practiced.

Notice a solemn thing in verse 24: in Babylon was found the blood of prophets and of saints and all that were slain upon the earth. When British troops went into a major city in the south of Iraq, they went into a large warehouse and found a huge number of boxes containing body parts of people that had been killed some time before. They had been persecuted, slain, and chopped into pieces. We do not know why Saddam's regime kept all those boxes, but the British found them. How much more does God see the blood of his saints in these and other countries.

God never forgets a tear or a drop of blood of any of his people. The shedding of innocent blood always has consequences. Modern theology says there are no consequences to what you do. God is only grace; it doesn't matter what you do. But that is utterly wrong! That is not the God of the Bible, for his Word says that there are serious consequences for the shedding of innocent blood, particularly the blood of his people.

First Samuel 2:30 enunciates a basic principle: 'Them that honor me, I will honor and those who despise me shall be lightly esteemed.' To put it another way, honor begets honor; violence begets violence. That is the law of the harvest. 'Whatsoever a man soweth, that shall he also reap'. Rome killed all those Jews in AD 70 in the destruction of Jerusalem, and Rome was, in turn, destroyed centuries later. The twentieth century has seen, as far as we know, the greatest acts of political violence against the human race at any time since the Lord Jesus Christ walked on the earth. I have never understood why WWI was fought. I do not know how often it is said the flower of European manhood was wiped out in that unnecessary, senseless war. Then along came these depraved dictators, Hitler, Stalin, Mao, and Pol Pot, and the violence continues into this third millennium.

One of God's days, all of the violence of evil states and religious fanatics who get power will be justly and fully avenged, like the throwing of a massive millstone into the ocean, causing a tidal wave to wash out proud civilizations and leave something better. And the saints will rejoice. God really did remember their sufferings, heard their prayers and set it right.

Worship of Wealth
The second reason why Babylon's fall is good news is the worship of wealth. Verse 23 says, 'Merchants were great men.' What does that mean? It means that greatness in that society began to be measured only by how much money you have. Money controlled everything else. It became the god of Society. People's personal value was counted only in the gold and silver that they had.

Think of it this way: as believers, we value people—humble people, big people, small people, and all people. We value them highly because they have the image of God in the soul. That is why we always seek never to mistreat another person, whether it is the enemy or not. But when money becomes the highest value of society, it means that you discount the image of God in your fellow humans, and instead, worship the image of Caesar in a coin, making daily decisions and political choices on that basis. Now when that attitude takes root and spreads through an entire society, holy judgment is sure to follow, and the saints will rejoice at materialism being replaced by a truer, more humane standard of life when the divine judgment hits.

Sorcery

The third reason why it is good news these Babylons should be brought down is their practice of sorcery. The Greek word that is so often used for witchcraft or sorcery in Revelation is *pharmakos*. It is related to 'drugs' and we get from it the pharmacy. In witchcraft, there was always heavy drug usage, that is often tied up with pornography, prostitution, and general loosening of sexual restraints that comes when people become addicted to drugs. The drug culture throughout the Western world has invaded all social classes, from the top to the bottom of society, from the ghetto to the mansion. All the socio-economic classes are dabbling with this kind of thing, assuring that the judgment of God must fall to cut out this dreadful cancer.

It is said that one of the ways the dictator in North Korea maintains his power is by the world-wide sale of illicit drugs. Some of their ambassadors have been arrested for pushing drugs in other countries. North Korea is thought to maintain its economy on *pharmakos*, on drugs, and this is connected, at least indirectly, with what Revelation calls 'sorcery'.

When we think of the huge tide of drugs that comes in every day to the United States from South America (especially Columbia and Mexico), it is sobering to wonder at what point will the judgment come against us if we continue these sorts or practices? God alone knows the answer. Various prophets of the Old Testament made it clear to Israel that part of the reason why she was taken into captivity, was to be purged of immoral, occult drug-related practices. God cleaned her out during seventy years.

Therefore, we can only conclude that the saints must join in with those now in heaven to rejoice as widespread impurity, occult practices and related drug abuse are brought low in the various judgments that God sends. He hears the prayers of his suffering church, and on his schedule, violently removes wicked societies, replacing them by a cleaner, holier standard of social relationships. God knows what he is doing. The important thing for us is to be certain that we are on his side in whatever happens amongst the nations. Then we may, in good time, along with holy apostles and prophets, rejoice over whatever judgment the Lord deems best to send.

51

Hallelujahs in Heaven

Revelation 19: 1–5

In chapters 19 to 22, we get onto Alleluia ground. As we get onto these grounds of divine praise, we note three points from this text:

1. A shift of scene from one world to the other (Rev. 19:1).
2. The Hallelujah Chorus (Rev. 19:1, 3–5).
3. The heavenly choir (Rev. 19:4–5).

A Shift of Scene

Notice the first words in verse 1, 'After these things'. That signals an enormous shift. 'These things' refer to the judgments in chapters 17–18: earthly scenes of devastation, the ruin of the world-corrupting prostitute that had so much power over the establishment, and the bringing down of anti-God, wealthy, powerful Babylon.

The Heavenly Perspective

Now all eyes focus on what is happening in the heavenly realm. He said: 'Stop looking at earth. Look up! I am going to show you what is happening above.' Heaven is the seat of all power and control of everything that happens on earth. Here we glimpse how God, and the ransomed host that are up in heaven, look upon devastating events that occurred in earth's history. The meaning of creation and of history, from beginning to end, appears in true perspective.

Our Limited Earthly Perspective

During this brief earthly pilgrimage, we cannot see very far ahead of our nose. Often we cannot make sense of what is happening around us. Sometimes even in our own lives, it is hard to understand. But up there, all is clear. Have you noticed that when all is clear, in that 'morning without clouds,' all the saints are supremely happy? It makes me think of the old gospel chorus:

> Trials dark on every hand
> and we cannot understand.
> All the way the Lord would lead us
> to the blessed promised land,
> But he'll guide us with his eye;
> and we'll see him in the sky.
>
> We will understand it better by and by
> By and by, when the morning comes,
> when all the saints of God are gathered home,
> We will tell the story of how we've overcome
> We will understand it better, by and by.

It may not be very good poetry or music, but it accurately reflects what you have in this text. So what is the first thing we learn about the viewpoint of the inhabitants of heaven on the terrible scenes that occurred on planet earth in previous chapters? It is that they begin with loud, melodious voices, praising the Lord. View world history as a whole, including the place of our own little lives in it, and all we can do is break forth in oceans of praise. That is what we are going to do.

The Hallelujah Chorus

Every time you turn around in these verses, you find the word Hallelujah. In 1741, G. F. Handel, penned his majestic oratorio, *Messiah*. Tradition records that when King George II heard *Messiah* for the first time in England that as the great choir got to the Hallelujah Chorus, taken from this book of Revelation, the king stood up, and the whole congregation followed. That has become the convention every time the Hallelujah chorus is sung. The tone of Handel's music, as well as the Biblical words he uses from Revelation, capture the strains of the flowing joy of heaven over all that Jesus has accomplished for us to make everything turn out right.

Sometimes our circumstances look dark and events seem to go against us; we wonder how things are going to turn out. Revelation gives us a preview of how, without the slightest fail, it is going to turn out for all of God's people. We shall join the Hallelujah chorus when we look back upon our lives and everything that happened in this world. We are going to be praising the Lord. Nothing could keep us from it.

The Ancient Hebrew Word 'Hallelujah'

The ancient Hebrew term, 'Hallelujah', or 'Alleluia', means 'praise the Lord'. The word was so precious to the worship of God's people across the ages, that the Greek translation of the Old Testament kept the Hebrew. The translators felt they should not translate Hallelujah from Hebrew into Greek. That is the way it is in all the languages of the world. Hallelujah and Amen are too valuable to translate. In a sense, they take us back to the tabernacle, and back to the temple. I have worshipped God in many countries and in different languages; French, Russian, Romanian, and Hungarian; Scottish Gaelic, German, and Korean. I could not speak or understand Korean, or some of these other languages, but in the worship of the people, I could regularly hear this grand Hebrew term, Hallelujah. In every country or island where the Lord has his people, you are going to hear this great liturgical word 'Hallelujah'.

This word so central to Biblical praise, is found in only two books in the Bible: the Book of Psalms and the Book of Revelation. One section of the Psalms (113–118), is known as 'The Hallel'. The Jews still preserve the tradition of singing these Psalms at the Passover to celebrate God's wonderful redemption in rescuing his enslaved people from the bondage of Egypt, through the Passover, through the Red Sea, and into glorious liberty. It was probably the Hallel that Jesus and his disciples were singing at the time of the Lord's Supper. Now that and much else is being sung in heaven. Each time the church on earth sings the Hallelujah, we join ourselves to that grand heavenly chorus. Holy influences from heaven come down every time we praise God, for we read in Psalm 22, this phrase from David: 'Oh thou that inhabitest the praises of Israel'. Every time we praise God, whether in church or at home in private, God comes down and inhabits those praises.

Why so many 'Hallelujahs' in Revelation 19?

Why is 'Hallelujah' used so much in verses 1–5? It is in four of the five verses. The last part of verse 1 explains why: 'Alleluia, salvation and glory and honor and power unto the Lord our God.' At last, salvation has been thoroughly worked through and all has been accomplished. Babylon and the harlot are out of the way; all the thoughts of God's people in this text focus on the blessings wrought out through the salvation Jesus accomplished. It took infinite power to defeat the Devil and our own perverse fallen humanity and to save a condemned, dying world. That powerful salvation translates itself into honor and glory of the God who did it all. Salvation means that God Almighty exerts his holy power to save his people. Millions upon millions, myriads upon myriads, multitudes that no man can number, have had their guilt cancelled and their condemnation replaced through Christ's work. By justification, they have a title to Heaven and eternal glory. He transforms souls, darkened, doubting and hating, into light, faith and triumphant love. In a word, salvation!

This salvation even extends to the physical body. First we grow and then at a certain stage our bodies start aging. We are subject to the laws of decay, written into time, but that is only temporary. God is going to reverse all of that, even for our bodies. 'For the trumpet shall sound and the dead shall be raised incorruptible and we shall be changed. Yes, even our bodies will be all right. You know that gospel hymn:

> When the trumpet of the Lord shall sound
> and time shall be no more,
> and the morning breaks eternal,
> bright and fair;
> When the saved of earth shall gather
> over on that other shore,
> and the roll is called up yonder,
> I'll be there.

A Proper View of the Judgment on the Reprobate
The heavenly congregation also uses the word 'Hallelujah', because the righteous and true judgments of God have properly fallen on the reprobate. All who hated God, all who refused the gospel and persecuted the church, are sent into outward darkness and unsanctified burnings. He has judged the great whore and avenged the blood of his servants at her hand, and her smoke rose up for ever and ever (v. 2–3).

Should we as loving people rejoice at judgment to come? Is that proper? We do well to emulate the attitude of the people in Heaven. They have been made perfect in holiness in a way we have not. Revelation 19 gives an accurate vision of the holiest hearts in all of God's universe. Close to his throne, they could not possibly have any attitude that was not right and pure and true. The holiest hearts, the purest minds, in the entire universe, from God's vantage point, recognize that hell is right and just for those who finally go there. They say 'Hallelujah' as they realize that every wrong has been put right and every righteous action has been properly rewarded. It is hard for us to identify with that while we are on earth, but the holy ones above see clearly that God was exquisitely patient. He gave people so much time to repent, offered them so many opportunities, yet as it says in Hebrews, they trampled under foot the blood. The heavenly ones are singing a song that proves God took his time, but how he did it and why he did it was absolutely right, proper, and true. We can rejoice even over that.

The Heavenly Choir
Look now at who is rejoicing. The twenty-four elders lead the choir. They represent all God's redeemed people down to the end of time. They are home at last and they represent us. Therefore, when we get home, we shall be full of praise. The

last time we met those they represent, they were on earth. Some of them were in terrible shape and in circumstances that nobody would wish to be in unless you knew it was the will of God.

Hebrews 11:35-8 tells us what some of them experienced here before they were translated to heaven: 'Women received their dead raised to life again. And others were tortured, not accepting deliverance, that they might obtain a better resurrection.' The world said, 'Deny Christ, and we will spare you,' but they refused the offer. 'And others had trial of cruel mockings and scourgings, yea, morever, of bonds and imprisonment.' How many believers are in jail throughout the world for the gospel? It is certain that there are many people. 'They were stoned, they were sawn asunder, were tempted, were slain with the sword: they wandered about in sheepskins and goatskins, being destitute, afflicted, tormented. (Of whom the world was not worthy:) they wandered in deserts, and in mountains, and in dens and caves of the earth.'

Angelic Singers
That is how it was, but now look at the light of God reflected from their serene, happy faces! Hear the celestial tones of eternal gladness flowing forth in liquid praise from their hearts and lips. They suffered so much, but now the serenest, gladness flows through them. The angelic orders join these redeemed humans in the great chorus. The four beasts, living creatures, at each corner of God's throne, supremely beautiful angelic beings of massive strength and yet celestial sweetness, worship God, singing his Hallelujahs. How they can sing! Their clarion tones add heavenly qualities to the sounds of the ransomed saints praising the Lord. What a chorus it must be!

Verse 5 says that a voice from the throne invites all believers, great and small, to join this chorus. God's standards for greatness are opposite to pagan standards, so what does 'great and small' mean? It means from kings to field hands; from holy martyrs to repentant prostitutes; from saintly missionaries to murderers, who were converted at the last hour on death row; from believers who lived to be 120 to babies who died in their mother's womb: all professions, all classes, all races, all tongues, all ages join hearts and voices. Everyone who is under the blood of Christ, through truth and faith, makes the vaults of heaven ring with this majestic Hallelujah chorus. Can you imagine it flowing down the streets of gold like a tidal wave of fragrant incense and supernal joy from the crystal sea? What a day! What a song!

A happy Perspective on the Future
As we look ahead, 'we know not what a day may bring forth'. James tells us to be very careful when we say, 'In a year I am going into such and such a city to do this business'. Say, 'If the Lord will', because you do not know how long you will be here, or what will work out. But we can know what we need to know to be happy. I know that I am going to be there 'when the roll is called up yonder' and the Hallelujah chorus breaks forth. Through grace and the mercy of Jesus, I shall be there. You can know that too. Once you know that, you can handle anything else that comes your way on earth, because you are going to join in the gladsome singing on that good day. Then you can say with the chorus in verse 4, 'Amen; thy will be done, so let it be. Amen, Lord, carry it out'. And because you are saying 'Amen, thy will be done', you have to say also along with them, 'Hallelujah, Praise be the Lord!'

52

WORLD HISTORY CONCLUDES WITH A WEDDING

Revelation 19:6–9

This marvelous section of the Bible shows us that world history concludes with a wedding. Have you ever stopped to think about our little lives, and then the big picture of which we are a small part, with the nations and the ages, the rise and fall of empires? What is it finally coming to? This passage shows us that world history is moving towards one great climax, and that is a wedding. Revelation 19 speaks of this final denoument of history as the marriage supper of the Lamb and his bride, the church. You could no more make sense of world history without considering this grand, final wedding than you could handle Algebra without an *x*. This last act of world history that ushers us into eternity, makes sense of everything that went before.

We notice two points from this text.

1. The music that sounds forth at this wedding, (Rev. 19:6–7a).
2. The wedding ceremony itself (Rev. 19:7b–9).

The Music at the Wedding

There is much singing in the Bible. The Book of Psalms is largely singing. You hear singing earlier in Revelation, and here in verses 6–8, we find the last hymn in the Bible. We do not know what the tune will sound like, although we may safely assume that this tune will magnify and massively excel the best tunes sung in any human culture at their best—the sounds of David's harp, Gregorian chant, Bach, Handel, Welsh hymns, Scottish metrical Psalms, and African spirituals. All of these, mingled with the notes of the holy angels, cherubim and seraphim: what a volume of glorious praise it will be!

Three Kinds of Voices

The tones are overheard ahead of time by John, who writes this Book of Revelation. He describes the tones of that great wedding hymn of praise in terms of three kinds of voices: the voice of a great multitude of people and angels, the voice of many waters, and the voice of mighty thunder. Those are the earthly images that he uses to help us grasp by anticipation something of those majestic sounds at the wedding of which we are all going to be a part. If we could think of a massive hurricane without any destruction in its wake, or a powerful thunder storm without any harm; maybe these tones would be something like that, or perhaps the sound of two mighty rivers coming together.

I remember as a child, staying with our family at one of my great-aunts' cottages, down at Fort

Fisher, North Carolina, where the Cape Fear River flows into the Atlantic Ocean. We would walk onto 'the rocks', which had been built as part of the Confederate fortifications. It was kind of a dam across the mouth of the Cape Fear River, so that the water would be deeper for shipping, and so that the Yankees would not be able to attack during the War Between the States. At high tide it was wonderful to watch the waters of the mighty Atlantic pouring across those rocks, where the water of the Cape Fear came and churned into the Atlantic. I will never forget the sounds of these mighty waters coming together. These voices John heard all add up to something like this: majesty, power and glory of God in the echoes of these waters. The sound was not unlike the end of the Lord's Prayer, which concludes with the grand finale: 'for Thine is the Kingdom and the power and the glory'. That doxological phrase was, in a sense, turned into this song in Revelation.

Countless blood-washed saints, together with the angels, lift up their voices in sounds of praise and joy, as though the tones were being poured into the winds, waters, and thunder. Perhaps then we will all recognize that the universe was created for this moment of praise! Beauty upon beauty! Praise upon praise!

This magnificent universal hymn is being lifted up through every corner of the universe for two good reasons. The first reason they are praising so loudly and so beautifully is that the sovereign reign of God is at long last, fully and completely evident to our eyes. And the second reason they are praising with such volume is that history has finally reached its happy culmination.

The First Reason for Praise

Saints and angels are all but bursting wide open with praise, because the reign of God, so often hidden from all but the keenest eyes of faith, is now so visible that no one, saint or sinner, angel or demon, can miss it. What a message: well should we sing: 'Alleluia, for the Lord God omnipotent reigneth!' In particular, his total control of all things is now seen in that he has handled the powers of evil to the fullest. He has put to flight and reduced to rubble the dragon, the beast, and the harlot. Now it is proven beyond question; you do not even need faith to see that wickedness does not pay. Every wrong is at last righted, and every act of faith and goodness is generously rewarded, as God said it would be.

The cynics, skeptics and unbelievers, who scoffed at the existence of God, who made fun of his people, and when they had power even took their lives: these people can now only scream out for the rocks to cover themselves from the shining face of the Lamb, as he comes forth in his glory. Liberals who denied that there would ever be any judgment, and said 'God is not like that'; those who explained away the reality of Hell as being something cooked up by ignorant fundamentalist and primitive thinking, how they tremble as they sink down into the everlasting burnings separated from the one who they denied! They have no more time left to deny the reality of God and the sovereignty of his total control and his final judgments of the affairs of all mankind. What they once proudly denied, they are now subjected to with horror!

But the saints are full of praise, because what they had to accept by faith in times of darkness, now shines brighter than the noonday sun before their eyes. It is not that God was not reigning in their times of darkness. He was in total control even at the high point of Satan's influence over the fallen human race, when the eternal son of God was being crucified by the malicious designs of fallen humanity, motivated by the evil one. Great darkness fell over the land, and the earth itself was shaking. That seems to have been the high point of the worst Satan could do against God and his people. But that was on Friday, and within three days, everything would be different. It would soon be known that never had the Heavenly Father been more in control than at that moment of darkness, which became the pre-ordained sacrifice for the atonement of the sins of the world.

So it was during the persecution of the Church when Revelation was written. The Lord God omnipotent was reigning when the church was under Herod, and under Caesar, but the church could not see it yet with her physical eyes. She had to accept it by faith. Part of what this book was written to do was to encourage the church to believe that God, not the Roman Emperor, nor the Jewish Sanhedrin, was in full control, even when the church was feeling the edge of the sword and the famine. Now in chapter 19, everything is visible and the church sees. Even the lost ones see as they pass into another place.

Sometimes in our lives, especially when we experience disappointments, reversals, betrayals, or things that feel like disasters to us or to our family, we do not feel like proclaiming 'Alleluia, for the Lord God omnipotent reigneth'. That is not how it feels to the flesh, to our besieged minds in hard times. But faith tells us: 'This is the victory that overcometh the world, even our faith' (1 John 5:7). Victorious faith tells us that God is reigning. He is in charge, even during the worst moments of my life. On Easter Sunday morning, the resurrection of the crucified, now glorified body of the Lord Jesus Christ showed us that God was reigning all the way through. Then this magnificent wedding day will demonstrate to an assembled universe in open fashion that the Lord God omnipotent reigneth. On that day and with that ceremony, we will appreciate that all of our dark times were in some way necessary, just like Jesus' crucifixion and its darkness was necessary to get him and his people through to the resurrection morning, when the gates of Heaven would forevermore swing wide open. Our times of darkness have been necessary way stations for us to get to that day of glory, when we shall shine forth with his light, transformed in faith and character as times of darkness did their own mysterious work within us. What a day of singing that will be when all is made clear, and faith melts away into sight.

The Second Reason for Praise

The saints and angels are singing in this majestic harmony, because at last earth's history has finally reached its pre-ordained conclusion: the marriage ceremony of the Lamb and his bride, the church. We read in Ephesians 5 that Christ loved the church and gave himself for her. We read in Revelation 13 that he is the Lamb slain before the foundation of the world. Even before God created the world, it was in his plan to make a world and to create a race of beings who would be like his Son, so they could share fellowship with the Triune God. The Almighty Father planned to give his Son the finest gift a father could give a son: a beautiful bride. So why did God make the world? Why did he put me in it? It was because he wanted his son to have a marvelous bride and he has invited us to be part of that.

That is the meaning of the world. That is where it is all leading. God made us for fellowship with himself, and to know him is eternal life (John 17:3). In the beginning of the story of earth history in Genesis 3, we find that Adam and Eve sinned against God and were put out of the Garden. The Lord used to walk familiarly with them in the cool of the day in the garden. Our original ancestors were in intimate, personal union and communion with the Lord. But their sin ruptured the most precious of all relationships. Yet in the midst of the divine judgment upon man's sin, the gracious Lord gives the first promise of the gospel in Genesis 3:15, through which coming 'seed' he would restore the bond of communion.

From that perspective, we can summarize all the covenants of the Bible as preparatory means of restoring us to communion with our heavenly Father. God says to Abraham, 'I will be your God and a God to your seed and you will be my people'. That is what he says to Moses in the Exodus context, and then to David within the context of Israelite kingship. That is what he says in Jeremiah 31 about the New Covenant: 'I will be your God and you will be my people. I will write my law in your hearts, so that you will directly know me from the inside out'. At long last, here in Revelation, the heavenly Jerusalem comes down and God is with us and we are with him; every covenant of the Bible is gloriously fulfilled in this wedding supper of the Lamb.

THE WEDDING CEREMONY (REV. 19:7B–9)
Having sought to hear some sounds of the music, we now look at the wedding ceremony itself (Rev. 19:7b–9). This wedding ceremony represents the full, final, and happy restoration of the divine–human union and communion. Revelation 19 presents this in terms of the time honored Jewish customs for betrothal and marriage. Kistermaker comments on the Jewish wedding customs at the time the New Testament was written:

> In a Hebrew setting, there was a waiting period between betrothal and wedding, while the bride and bridegroom live separately (Deut. 22:23–4; Matt. 1:18–19). During this period, the two families involved arranged the terms of the dowry. When the sum was paid, the actual wedding followed. On that day, the bridegroom in procession accompanied by friends brought the bride from her parental home to his own home. There the wedding feast was held to celebrate the wedding.[124]

William Hendrickson presents a brief sketch of this nuptial sequence as he applies it to Christ and the church:

> In Christ the bride was *chosen* from eternity. Throughout the entire Old Testament dispensation the wedding was *announced*. Next, the son of God assumed our flesh and blood. The *betrothal* took place. The price - the *dowry* - was paid on Calvary. And now, after an *interval*, which in the eyes of God is but a little while, the Bridegroom returns and 'It has come, the wedding of the Lamb'. The church on earth yearns for this moment. So does the church in heaven.[125]

Two matters are raised in this text about the bride and what she looks like: (1) the beauty of the bride and (2) the blessedness of the bride.

The Beauty of the Bride
Knowing ourselves as well as we do, and other believers as well as we do, it is not always instinctive to think of them (including ourselves) as beautiful. Yet it is profoundly true: every person who has become a believer in the Lord Jesus Christ and looked to him by faith, is clothed in spotless, shining robes. If we could visualize the bride coming down a majestic cathedral aisle, she would need no spotlight to shine on her. She is so full of light herself, although it is a reflected light. The beautiful bride comes down the aisle in the beauty of her linen, white garments, shining out with the splendor that the Lord has imparted

to her, and everyone says, 'Here comes the bride! What a beauty!'

But it was not always this way. Once this bride had been dressed in disgustingly filthy rags that were smelly, and besmirched with her constant trafficking with the world, the flesh and the devil. Her stench came from being part of corrupt, fallen humanity. But in the condescending grace of God, she heard the gospel invitation of Jesus, and came to him by faith for salvation. She went through the cleansing stream of the blood of the Lamb of God shed for sinners. She was transformed from ugly self-centeredness to loving, trusting, confidence and faith in another. She could say, 'Upon a life I did not live, upon a death I did not die, another's life, another's death I stake my whole eternity', and she is transformed into what God sees will turn into most gorgeous beauty: a holy character reflecting God's own purity and goodness.

Verse 8b speaks about this beauty in the bride. It says that the fine linen she wears is the righteousness of the saints. This whole book makes clear that salvation, cleansing, and entrance into heaven is by faith in Christ's blood. It is through grace alone, but that grace always works transforming changes in the character of the person who has faith. The Holy Spirit inhabits the believer and renews his or her character to be zealous for good works. That is 'the righteousness of the saints'. There is a righteousness imputed by faith in Christ, and there is righteousness that transforms us and gives us beauty of character in our relationship to others. That is what is spoken of here (often called 'imparted righteousness'). Indeed, verse 8 says that the good works we do are a donation from God to us. Even our acts of righteousness that come after we believe in Christ and are indwelt by the Holy Spirit are divine donations, through the Holy One who is in us. Although we do good deeds, we are *inwardly* motivated by the Holy Spirit to do so. In addition, God provides *outwardly*, providential opportunities for us to carry out the righteousness of the saints. So the best good works, which do enter into that ultimate beauty of character we present to Jesus, have been a donation from God.

This same truth is stated slightly differently in Ephesians 2:8-9: 'For by grace are you saved through faith and that not of yourselves, it is the gift from God, not of works, lest any man should boast'. And then Ephesians 2:10 says: 'For ye are created in Christ Jesus unto good works, that God hath before ordained that we should walk in them'. God has fore-ordained that we should trust in Christ and be saved through him, and beyond that, that our lives should be focused on God's glory and the needs of others, so that something beautiful should happen in us, as we offer ourselves to do good in this world.

In the light of Jesus' teaching in Matthew 25, we see that the righteous actions of the saints somehow will be transmuted into the beauty of their wedding garments on that last day, and bring their Savior much pleasure. One of the main reasons we should be trying to live honorable, healthy lives, is that it will put more beauty into us and bring pleasure to the divine bridegroom. Your brief life on earth is a daily preparation for the beauty that will be presented through you to the one who deserves it so well on that last day.

Jesus speaks of that last day and its revelation of ultimate beauty in Matthew 25:34-40:

> Then shall the King say unto them on his right hand, Come, ye blessed of my Father, inherit the kingdom prepared for you from the foundation of the world: For I was hungry and ye gave me food: I was thirsty, and ye gave me drink; I was a stranger,

and ye took me in; naked, and ye clothed me; I was sick, and ye visited me: I was in prison, and ye came unto me. Then shall the righteous answer him, saying, Lord, when saw we thee hungry, and fed thee? Or thirsty, and gave thee drink? When saw we thee a stranger, and took thee in? or naked, and clothed thee? Or when saw we thee sick, or in prison, and came unto thee? And the King shall answer and say unto them, Verily I say unto you, Inasmuch as ye have done it unto one of the least of these my brethren ye have done it unto me.

Paul speaks of these beautiful garments as being part of the new life in Christ (Eph. 4:21–4):

If so be that ye have heard him, and have been taught by him, as the truth is in Jesus: That ye put off concerning the former conversation the old man, which is corrupt according to the deceitful lusts; and be renewed in the spirit of your mind; and that ye put on the new man, which after God is created in righteousness and true holiness.

He then goes on to detail how 'the new man' in Christ acts towards others. He does not lie (v. 25); he resolves his anger by seeking reconciliation (v. 26); he does not steal, but works and gives away (v. 28); he uses pure language (v. 29).

In this illustration, the way we treat others can be compared to the clothing we wear in public, and this clothing will shine with something of the light of Christ. Yet the garments the bride of Christ shall wear at the great wedding feast are far more than the character qualities developed in a holy life. They are related to it, so that each individual shines in a unique light, unlike anyone else, yet the wedding garments are more. They must be something like the beautiful robes of white, given by the Lord to the holy martyrs in Revelation 6.[126] The beauty of the bride and her garments is both 'imputed' (divinely gifted from outside her by the great transaction of God's atonement in Christ), and 'imparted' (wrought from within by the Holy Spirit uniting the believer to Christ in his death, resurrection and continuing life). In both cases, all the beauty goes back to Christ, who is ours, and we are His. As a hymn says:

> Jesus, Thy blood and righteousness
> My beauty are, my glorious dress;
> Midst flaming worlds, in these arrayed,
> With joy shall I lift up my head.[127]

The Blessedness of the Bride

The English word 'blessed' is a translation of a word from the original New Testament Greek: *makarios*. A literal translation would probably be 'happy', or 'everything that you could want that would make you glad and full of cheer.' That is what we find here: the true happiness of the bride. What is her supreme happiness? She has been divinely invited, and has accepted the invitation to come into this marriage with the Lamb. That is the ultimate happiness! It is the most supreme joy that could come to a creature made in the image of God. It will be this in all its fullness: to know Him, to be known of Him, to shine out with his beautiful glory and gladness before an assembled universe.

The best experiences we can have on earth: good marriages, professional accomplishments, loving friendships, family lands, and ancestral heritage—all of these at best are pale pointers beyond themselves to the supreme happiness of being part of the bride of Christ on that last glorious day.

A parable that Jesus told about a marriage ceremony is the fitting conclusion to the portrayal of the Wedding Supper of the Lamb. In Matthew 22:8–14, Jesus tells about a King who invited people to a wedding. The people who had been invited, refused to come, and abused those who delivered their invitations. The king responds:

> Then saith he to his servants, The wedding is ready, but they which were bidden were not worthy. Go ye therefore into the highways, and as many as ye shall find, bid to the marriage. So those servants went out into the highways, and gathered together all as many as they found, both bad and good: and the wedding was furnished with guests. And when the King came in to see the guests, he saw there a man which had not on a wedding garment: And he saith unto him, Friend, how camest thou in hither, not having a wedding garment? And he was speechless. Then said the king to the servants, Bind him hand and foot, and take him away, and cast him into outer darkness; there shall be weeping and gnashing of teeth. For many are called, but few are chosen.

Jesus is saying that the doors of the church are open; the gospel calls out to anyone who will take the time to hear it. Part of that gospel is that we are freely invited to this wedding, but we must have on the right clothes if we go in. Having on the right wedding garments makes our welcome secure. The garments are given to us at God's expense. They are donned through faith in Christ, and once the life is turned over to him, the Holy Spirit motivates us to show forth the beautiful righteousness of the saints in our character.

But some people, says Jesus, who hear certain aspects of the divine call, become religious without actually putting on the wedding garment that God offers us through Jesus. They seek to crash the gates on their own merits! They try to get into Heaven without going through the blood of Christ. They want resurrection without death. They seek a crown without first meeting Jesus at the cross. In other words, they depend on their own religious works, as though these were sufficient for entrance into the presence of God. One can be religiously active and look decent, yet never experience the miraculous change of regeneration. What a shock awaits these self-satisfied religious people, as they are numbered among the goats, and sent away from the presence of God (cf. Matt. 7:21–3; 25:41–6).

On that last great day, the inward change rooted in the original regeneration of the believer by the Lord will manifest itself in the outrayed beauty of those wedding garments. Nothing is so important for any mortal than to be ready for that day of ultimate destiny.

If we ask the Lord, he will gladly fulfill in us the promise he made to unclean and unworthy humans, burdened with their own corruption (Matt. 11:28–30):

> Come unto me, all ye that labor and are heavy laden, and I will give you rest. Take my yoke upon you, and learn of me; for I am meek and lowly in heart; and ye shall find rest unto your souls. For my yoke is easy, and my burden is light.

53

The King Conquers the Nations

Revelation 19:10–16

This passage shows us the King, our King, whose head was 'once crowned with thorns, but crowned with glory now', going forth conquering the pagan nations. He transforms many within them and judges others to the glory of God. We look at three points from this passage:

1. When does this victorious battle take place?
2. What does the captain of the host, King of Kings, Lord of Lords, look like?
3. What kind of army is following him?

When Does this Battle Take Place?

The timing of this battle is important to the interpretation of Revelation, for to understand the different segments of this prophecy, we have to seek to identify to what period of history each part refers. Revelation 19:11 says, 'And I saw heaven opened.' That is John speaking from the standpoint of earth. In Revelation 4:1, he uses the same phrase. John had seen the door of heaven opened, so he could get into heaven. But this time the same invisible door is opened, not to let John or anybody else in, but to let the King and his heavenly army come out. But when did this take place or when will it take place? Does it refer to a past event, or to a future event?

When Did the Victorious Battle Begin?

There are good reasons for thinking that Revelation 19:9 and following, is not primarily about the end of history, but rather about what begins to take place once the Lamb of God is crucified, risen, and seated on the throne above, from where he sends down the Holy Spirit on the day of Pentecost. In other words, this action, with the King and his heavenly army coming down, and beginning to take over the nations for the honor of God, has already begun to take place. It began when Christ finished his earthly work, once and for all. For instance, 1 Corinthians 15:25, the great resurrection chapter, says of Christ, after his incarnation, crucifixion, resurrection and ascension, that 'he must reign until he hath put all his enemies under his feet. The last enemy that shall be destroyed is death'. So this section of Revelation 19 fits into 1 Corinthians 15:25, where Christ is taking his reign, and increasingly reigning until finally, on the last day, he swallows up death in victory. Similarly, Hebrews 1 speaks of what Christ does after his crucifixion and resurrection. 'When he had by himself purged our sins, he sat down on the right hand of the Majesty on high' (v. 3). Then, contrasting Christ to the greatest of the angels: 'But to which of the angels said God at any time, "Sit on my right hand, until I make thine enemies thy footstool"?' (v. 13). Revelation 19 pictures this mighty Christ going forth through his Word, and through his Spirit, working through the church to make the enemies of God his footstool. It is a mopping up operation after the glorious earthly work of Christ.

But how could one seriously suggest that the King of Kings and the heavenly host that follow him should already be considered to be conquering the nations? Is that not reserved until the end of time? No, the last day will finish it, but ever since Christ was raised, the Devil suffered a major defeat. He lost the power he had to totally blind the pagan nations. Thus the mission of the church has been going forth and conquering those nations.

Modern Nations Moving Godwards

In *The Next Christendom: the Coming of Global Christianity,* Philip Jenkins shows that an amazing thing has been happening in the twentieth century, especially since the 1960s. While the northern European countries, and to some degree the United States and Canada, have been going away from vital Bible believing Christianity, it has advanced in exponential proportions in what he calls the Southern World. By that he means Africa, much of East Asia, and South America. Christianity is spreading more rapidly than at any other time in history in 'the Southern realm'. There are more Anglicans in Africa, than there are in England and the United States put together. There are far more Presbyterians in Korea than there are in America, Canada, and Scotland put together. And those Anglican Africans and Korean Presbyterians are conservative Bible believers. That is not to mention the rapid spread of Pentecostals and others. Jenkins brings out that some people think that Islam is out stripping Christianity, but in several countries, Christianity is out-stripping Islam, for example in Africa. According to Jenkins, if trends stay the same, by 2050 there should be more than three Christians for every two Muslims across the world.

He points out a notable fact: where Christianity has been slipping, it has been liberal Christianity, that has rejected the truth of Holy Scripture, and the reality of the supernatural. Where Christianity is surging forward, the leadership believe the Bible, and offer Jesus and his supernatural salvation. Such statistics help us to see the big picture, as presented in Revelation 19. The risen Christ, with the merits of his death and the power of his forgiveness and new life, is riding forth 'conquering and to conquer'. He has been doing so since his initial enthronement, and with an increasing tempo since the 1960s.

The period since the 1960s has been the biggest period of Christian evangelism and missions in 2,000 years. It seems that the tempo is speeding up, with multitudes coming to Jesus. Something like 23,000 souls are being won to Christ in Africa every day. Thousands are being converted to the Lord every day in China. It is a partial fulfillment of Isaiah 53, the great passage on the suffering servant, which ends with these words of promise: 'he shall see of the travail of his soul and shall be satisfied.' Jesus did not suffer in vain. His infinite suffering is going to produce the most wonderful fruit in saved men and women. And Jesus' satisfaction is growing all the time, as every elect soul is brought from darkness into the light.

These trends help us understand the question: when does this battle take place? It is taking place now, ever since Jesus ascended the throne. It will only increase and its action will only be completed, on the last day of earth's history. We are in the middle of it, or maybe we are towards the end of it; only the Lord knows.

What Does the Captain Look Like?

What is the appearance of the one who is winning such victories? Verses 11–16 put most emphasis on the captain of this heavenly army. Except for two verses, the spotlight is focused on the victorious Jesus. John sees that it is Christ who makes all the difference to what transpires in world history. That is why Christians have multiplied in 'the Southern realm'. It is because of the captain of the host. 'From victory unto victory, his army shall he lead, till every foe is vanquished, and Christ is Lord indeed'.

As in chapter 1, the mighty Christ is described with symbols, pictures, and images taken from the Old Testament, such as crowns, swords, names, and bright clothing. These images would not make sense if you took them absolutely literally. For example, the image of the Lord Jesus Christ conquering the nations with a sharp metal sword sent out of his mouth is a metaphor or an analogy. John uses a physical picture to help us understand a spiritual reality. So these images that are ascribed to the captain of the host tell us exactly who Christ is now.

Rider on a White Horse

Verse 11 says he is riding a white horse—a victorious steed. In ancient times, a conquering general would ride forth on a beautiful victorious white charger. The color white is important in Revelation. Many traditional Protestants have been brought up in the Puritan tradition, so never made much of the various colors in church life. But in the more liturgical denominations where they do make use of colors, on Good Friday, things around the altar are draped in purple. The purple is speaking of Christ's blood and suffering. Then on Easter Sunday morning, they get up early and take the purple off the cross or altar, and put on white linen. White is the picture of the victory of resurrection. On Easter Sunday, he has arisen and every one is wearing white. In the early church, when people were baptized, they would all wear white garments to their baptism.

Christ is on a white steed. That means he has risen, never to be defeated and those who follow him will, by his victorious power, accomplish exactly what God wants them to accomplish. It will be victorious from God's viewpoint. But what about believers in Sudan whose lives have been cut short by martyrdom? How could we say they accomplished in that short time what the Lord wanted them to accomplish? Their blood will be the seed of the future church; one day it will be one of the biggest and greatest churches in the world. The martyrs in Sudan accomplished exactly what God wanted them to accomplish. Their lives were victorious. The victory must be looked at from the viewpoint of the throne of God. Every life yielded to him will accomplish what the Father wanted it to accomplish, and it will add its own contribution to the final victory of Jesus over the unbelieving nations. In that sense, even the slaughtered martyrs have followed their victorious captain on white horses.

'Faithful and True'

The rider is called 'Faithful and True'. Jesus Christ, the Word of God, faithfully carries out every promise made in the Book, and faithfully executes every threat made in the Book. He says, 'I am the way, the truth and the life.' Jesus could never lie. According to 2 Corinthians 1:20, 'All the promises of God in him are yes, and in him are Amen'. Jesus makes the promises over to us. He will carry them out in so far as our Heavenly Father deems we should partake of them. That is why, when we pray, it is not just a liturgical, ritualistic formula, for us to conclude the prayer: 'through Jesus Christ our Lord', or 'in Jesus name'.

We are saying, 'Lord, anything you said you would do for me in the Bible needs to come through the captain Jesus. Let him make it over to me'.

Battering Down of the Gates of Hell
The risen Christ is aggressive in the one battle that counts: 'he judges and he makes war' (v. 11). Jesus says, 'the Gates of Hell shall not prevail against the Church'. The picture is not of the church as a fortress, cowering behind its walls, with the drawbridge up. Instead, Christ is saying that the devil is trying to hold the nations of pagan unbelievers within his invisible walls of self-serving corruption, and false thinking. His problem is that the Christians, led by their captain, on the basis of the preaching of the gospel, administration of the sacraments, holy living, praying, and evangelism, are constantly invading his territory, and bashing down the gates of Hell, which cannot withstand their onslaught. We are breaking down the stronghold of wickedness on the basis of Jesus' victory. Satan is not winning against us.

Satan seemed to have Africa totally tied up in darkness, until the nineteenth century. Now Africa is close to half Christian. At the rate it is growing, it will soon be the most Christian continent in the world. It looked like Satan had China enveloped in darkness until after 1949. Since then, the numbers of believers in China has multiplied amazingly.

'Eyes as a Flame of Fire'
The next verse describes his eyes 'as a flame of fire'. This is similar to what was said in Revelation 1:14, where Christ sees through all pretense to the real issues of men's hearts and to the plots of demons. He knows exactly what to do to win. Christ sees through, and he pierces right into a person's heart to get next to them.

At times, we see little illustrations of this. In an earlier ministry, I preached one Sunday on a passage from John. I later heard that a certain person had been profoundly offended by the sermon. He walked into a certain place of business and spoke to another member of the church. In anger, he said: 'I believe Dr. Kelly has been making phone calls and found out something I did and denounced me through the pulpit, without calling my name. I think very low of a man that would do something like that'. The business man who answered him, simply replied: 'Have you ever heard of the Holy Spirit?'

What had happened? The risen Christ with eyes of flame, had used his Word to penetrate that man's defenses with the message: 'I know you and you had better change!' Jesus is doing that all the time. If he were not real, the gospel would never have worked. The older I get, the less it worries me if somebody gets upset over a sermon, because I know the Lord may be plowing the ground, and piercing through with his invisible sword the hidden thoughts of the heart.

'Crown him with Many Crowns'
Verse 12 speaks of 'many crowns'. Isaiah 62:2–3 speaks prophetically of the church being 'a crown of glory in the hand of the Lord', and Revelation attributes that crown to the Head and Savior of the Church, the Lord Jesus Christ. Why does this verse speak of many crowns? It seems to refer to a crown for his many kingdoms. We think of the Queen of Great Britain as at the same time the Queen of England, Scotland, Wales, and Northern Ireland. Her one crown represents many realms. Christ has the crown over angels and demons, over departed believers and living believers, over the sea, sky, and stars, over the earth and things under the earth. He is the sovereign one over absolutely every area. As the

hymn says: 'Crown him with many crowns, the Lamb upon his throne.'

'Vesture Dipped in Blood'

Jacob in his prophetic blessings in Genesis 49:11 said that a descendant of Judah 'washed his garments in wine, and his clothes in the blood of grapes'. Isaiah 63:2-3 says, 'he hath trodden the winepress alone' and speaks of his clothes being dipped in blood. Now Revelation 19:13 speaks of 'his vesture dipped in blood'. In this case it is the blood of his enemies.

Sentimental, liberal Christianity denies any judgment. God is a nice, old man, and you can run over him. That is not the God of the Bible; it is an idol. We must call on people to renounce that idol, to break him down, and to come to the true God. This God has given glorious opportunities for people to be saved. He has offered full and free forgiveness at infinite cost to himself, but if we do not accept the blood of the Son of God as sufficient to forgive our sins, then the Holy God says we must pay with our own blood. The choice is clear. It is the mystery of iniquity that some insist on paying with their own blood what Jesus' blood is more than able to pay on their behalf.

'A Sharp Sword out of his Mouth'

Military history shows us that it is easier to smite a nation, than to rule it afterwards. But the Lord Jesus Christ not merely smites Satan's control over nations, he begins to rule those nations.

How does he do it? From the sword that goes forth from his mouth (v. 15). In other words, it is the Word of God which conquers. The written Word of God in the power of the Holy Spirit is able to overcome every wicked institution and to change their motivation, so that they will wish to not remain employed in the way they were previously. The Word goes in and transforms personalities, so that their thinking changes, and they use their resources differently.

That is the case when a godly minister goes into a church where he faces hard-necked unbelievers that are nominal Christians. All the minister has is the written Word of God, and the Holy Spirit, who is given in answer to prayer. The nominal church people have the power and social connections; he has nothing but this Word. But God's Word is what brought the world into existence out of nothing. 'He spoke and the worlds sprang forth'. He arranged the stars in heaven by his Word. He holds everything together, even now—the planets rotating in their orbits and the atoms being held together by his Word. Colossians 1:17 says, 'he is before all things, and by him all things consist.' It was the divine Word and Holy Spirit that raised the body of the Son of God from the dead.

His Word is more than sufficient to accomplish everything needing to be changed in a dead church. If it brought the world into existence, if it raised Jesus from the dead, if it controls everything, why should we worry if all he gives us is the word? It will be victorious if we let it move through our own lives first; then it will overcome every obstacle Satan raises against its progress.

'King of Kings and Lord of Lords'

Verse 16 shows the name on his vesture: 'KING OF KINGS, LORD OF LORDS'. That means absolute, sovereign one over everything else without exception. Philippians 2:10–11 says that the day is coming, 'That at the name of Jesus, every knee shall bow, of things in heaven, of things in earth, and things under the earth; And that every tongue would confess that Jesus Christ is Lord, to the glory of God the Father...' That is the totality of the many crowns that will be brought to Jesus Christ the Lord to the glory of God the Father.

There will be two kinds of bowing on the last day. One is voluntary bowing, in which I acknowledge Jesus as my Lord and Savior. I gladly submit to him. That means you are in the true church. But there is another kind of bowing; it will be a forced bowing, when Satan, his hosts, and all the humans who rejected the gospel are forced down on that last awful day. The ancient Latin hymn, traditionally used in the requiem service, describes it well: '*Dies irae, dies illa...*' We do not understand why a person with a normal mind would reject the gospel, but they will be forced to bow by his mighty, glorious coming.

What Kind of Army Follows Him?

John was tempted to bow down to this holy angel (v. 10). The angel said 'do not do that; worship only God', but adds something that might surprise us: 'We (angels) are your fellow servants'. He means this: 'You are a servant of Christ, and we are servants of Christ; therefore, we are fellows, we are equals'. Think of it! A Christian believer, in God's eyes, is in one sense, equal to a holy angel in moving forward the gospel. Hence, this heavenly army has two components: one is saints, and the other is the holy angels with their majestic power.

Holy Angels

We do not know too much about the angels of God. Hebrews 1:14 describes them as being ministers 'for them who shall be heirs of salvation.' Matthew 18:10 speaks of children having guardian angels. This much seems to be implied by many Biblical passages (e.g. Ps. 34:7): God never sends you forth in his service, unless you are accompanied by an invisible angel. Thus, this heavenly army is made up of saints and angels. We do not see the angels, most of the time, but they are there.

The Saints

Verse 14 ascribes incredible dignity to the saints. These imperfectly sanctified believers, sincerely, humbly, and constantly sought to honor God and to bless others during their earthly pilgrimage, often in very lowly and unrecognized places. Such humble people are classed with majestic angels, and are said to be fellow soldiers with them in the splendid, white-robed heavenly army. That should be no surprise when we take into account: that we are 'seated with Christ in heavenly places' (Eph. 2:6). When we pray in the name of Christ, although still on earth with all our weakness, we are actually praying from within the heavenly sanctuary, the place of ultimate power and influence. Those kinds of prayers change things. When we speak for the Lord, our thoughts and words are winging to heaven and come back with power from the holy sanctuary to those with whom we are speaking. Something like that must be happening when people suspect that the preacher has been making telephone calls to find out their private business! It is the shining of light from God, through the convicting words of an imperfect, but faithful man. It is that way when we do good works for the Lord, and for the relief of the needy around us. Jesus says that giving a cup of cold water is noted in heaven, and will be recognized on the last day. That is why we should not underrate the gift of helps (1 Cor. 12:28). Unrecognized helping, especially of those who are powerless to pay us back, is motivated from heaven, and often brings down with it heavenly influence on those who are blessed by it. Until the last great day, we go forward in his service 'conquering and to conquer'. What a privilege to be his and to serve him and all he puts across our pathway, for he can never fail.

54

The Terrible Reality of Hell
Revelation 19:17–21

Without question, this is one of the most grim and solemn passages, not only in Revelation, but in the entire book of God. It brings before us something the Bible does not hide, which is the terrible reality of Hell. Hell is such an awful state of tormented existence, that preachers tend to avoid preaching about it. I do not know how many thousands of sermons I have preached since my first sermon at age twenty-two, but in all those years I have only once dealt very fully with Hell. The sermon on which this chapter is based was only the second time in twenty-seven years.

Reactions to Preaching on Hell

The first time in 1981, when I dealt in detail with Hell, I was preaching through the Book of Luke, and dealing with the story Christ told of the rich man and Lazarus. One went to heaven and the other to hell. I described a little the rich man suffering in a fiery place, without water, as Jesus said. Some Dillon Presbyterians never again set foot in the church (as long as I was there), after that Sunday morning sermon, which, I believe was preached with love and compassion. Of course, the response to a sermon is always between the person and God, not between the person and the preacher, and some who are at first offended, later rethink, and sincerely repent and believe.

Some older members of First Presbyterian Church in Jackson, Mississippi, told me about one of the grand old pastors there, who preached on hell some sixty years ago in that church. They said this saintly minister literally wept all the way through the sermon that he was preaching on Hell, with a handkerchief in his hand, wiping his eyes, as he went through that solemn message. That is how deeply he felt the truth of it, and how great was his love for sinners. He was truly reflecting Christ, who wept over the unrepentant city of Jerusalem in light of its coming devastation.

These verses brings before us three points:

1. A contrast between two banquets (Rev. 19:9, 17–18).
2. A battle with only one army engaged (Rev. 19:17).
3. The outcome of that battle (Rev. 19:20–21).

A Contrast between two banquets

In a previous chapter we looked at the great banquet towards which all world history is moving: that glorious occasion that makes sense of everything that ever happened in world history—the marriage supper of the Lamb, our heavenly bridegroom, and his blood-washed, now beautified church. It will be a glorious ceremony initiating the benefits of supreme love and everlasting joy: communion with God and fellowship with other believers, when indeed, as the old gospel hymn has it 'the circle is unbroken by and by, with a better home awaiting in the sky.' That will be the greatest banquet of them all!

But this text speaks of another banquet. The history of the world ends with two kinds of banquets: the marriage supper of the Lamb, and this very different banquet that is presented to us in this text. It is a banquet in which the mortal remains of slaughtered infidels are eaten by birds of prey, while their lost souls have been cast into a dark place of everlasting separation. How this happened leads us to the second point.

A BATTLE WITH ONLY ONE ARMY ENGAGED
The strange situation described here is that only one army is in the field. It is the rebellious portion of mankind, operating under the satanically inspired false prophet and the once powerful beast. In this final show down, Almighty God does not call on his armies of saints to be present, although he has such armies. God and God alone devastatingly defeats all the hosts of evil doers and unbelievers.

Destruction without an Army
We are not told here or anywhere else in scripture, what the final battle will be like, only that the two evil world leaders, the false prophet and the beast are disastrously defeated in short order by God himself. That defeat was predicted by the psalmist a thousand years before Christ was on earth. He does not tell us precisely how the Lord 'breaks them with a rod of iron' (Ps. 2:9), but the imagery implies that it must be very quick, and utterly devastating. However, Revelation 19 gives a more detailed picture of the aftermath of this battle, where all the unbelieving talent and ability of the humanistic world system, as well as the systems of false religion in the world, are at last, laid low.

An angel in the sun calls on birds of prey, perhaps like buzzards, to descend and gobble up the decaying flesh of all who opposed God and rejected his gospel (Rev. 19:17). Verses 17–18 recall a similar passage in Ezekiel 39, which was a dim portrayal of this final reality. The fowls, in Ezekiel and particularly here in Revelation 19, eat the bodies of those who made common cause with an unbelieving and God-hating world system.

But what happens to their souls? That is more important than the body, and it brings us to the third point.

THE FINAL OUTCOME OF THE LAST BATTLE
We note first (v. 20), that all evil doers, all who rejected the atonement of Jesus Christ, and who said 'I will not have his blood to wash me of my sins,' are cast into 'a lake of fire, burning with brimstone.' That is, a noxious and horrendous realm, along with the devil, or Satan, the beast and the false prophet. This alludes to Daniel 7:10–11:

> A fiery stream issued and came forth from before God: thousand thousands ministered unto him, and ten thousand times ten thousand stood before him: the judgment was set, and the books were opened. I beheld then, because of the voice of the great words which the horn spake: I beheld, even till the beast was slain, and his body destroyed, and given to the burning flame.

Biblical Descriptions of Hell
This lake of fire, or place of torment, is a terrible place from which there is no exit. It is spoken of

in Scripture as being hot, with no water available (see Luke 16). It is also spoken of as being 'a place of outer darkness'. Jude 6 speaks of 'the blackness and darkness forever' in that place. Apparently the fires give off little or no light as they burn.

The best scriptural theologians have spoken of two kinds of disadvantages in hell: negative disadvantages, and positive disadvantages. In other words, something you are deprived of is the negative, and positive is something added on that causes it to be so awful.

Negative Disadvantages of Hell
The worldly person, who lived only for the temporal advantages of 'the world, the flesh, and the devil', now find that those fleshly pleasures are eternally out of their reach. For instance, a man who died after a life of alcohol abuse, without asking God for pardon, will be forever separated from the comforts of his bottle. Those who never repented of this sin, and only lived for another drink, will eventually find themselves in a place where they will never be able to get another drop of alcohol. Those who sold out their bodies and souls to drugs, unless they repent, will not be able to reach a pill bottle or needle and syringe in that place to which they must go. Those who worshipped fame and political power, rather than God, are now wrapped up in their own darkened, worm-like misery with none to impress. The fires do not give off much light, and there is no communion with anybody else in Hell. They have no one to lord it over, which is what motivates some people in politics. Those who rejected God's plan for sexual purity, find no way to relieve the unmortified appetite that caused them to corrupt other persons and lose their own souls. Modernist ministers, who rejected Holy Scripture, and misled thousands in their congregations, must forever face the consequences of the very Word that they were too sophisticated to believe. Now they know how real it is, but it is forever too late.

Positive Disadvantages in Hell
This text speaks of what we might call positive disadvantages in hell: that is to say, not just the things to be deprived of, but the things that are added to it in that dreadful existence. In a word, the positive disadvantages will be an appropriate and fair punishment to body and soul. God will do it just right; he will not overdo it. He is never cruel. He is always fair and just. Yet, nor will he under-do it.

One of the reasons Paul in Romans 12 tells us not to take vengeance against people who hurt us, is that God himself will take vengeance: 'Vengeance is mine, I will repay, saith the Lord'. Many people think in terms of the optimistic Enlightenment that God will never punish anybody, but Romans 12 says that God will repay. Therefore, do not bear grudges; do not carry hatred over years. Leave them to God. A holy and just God will bring vengeance in a totally appropriate fashion to each one, in accordance with their disobedience of his Word in this earthly life.

Are the Fires of Hell to Be Taken Literally?
This question has been raised all through church history: how literally should we take the fires of Hell? What do they mean? Even a great theologian like John Calvin in the sixteenth century believed they were not literally the same thing as we have on earth, but a way of speaking by analogy or by metaphor,[128] to describe a most unhappy state of existence. Some good interpreters of Scripture believe that the fire may be referring to the unchangeable remorse, grief, and horrible thoughts being visited upon the finally impenitent for ever, like the burning

of fire. I cannot answer the question: how literal are the fires? It may be that the fires are literal, but they are not exactly the same as earthly fires, for an earthly fire will burn up your body. But down there, the reconstituted body (after the resurrection of the lost to which the soul is somehow rejoined), will never be annihilated nor destroyed, nor extinguished by those fires. So it presumably has to be somewhat different, yet it definitely means something most unpleasant. In Luke 16, Jesus, himself describes the rich man in perdition as asking for water. The fires of hell are a way of conveying to our earthly minds a terrible reality of discomfort, displeasure, and extreme misery. The 'torment' is never ending.

No Exit

The most solemn aspect of hell is that there is no end to it. How long does hell last, according to the Bible? The holy Book says that Hell lasts as long as heaven, and uses the same Greek word for the duration of both states of existence. It is difficult for our human minds to grasp that anything could be unchanging, and that there would be no way out of such a place. But that is the teaching of Scripture, to which I must bow down as a servant of God, and proclaim it the way the Bible proclaims it. I have no other choice; I receive the message; I do not create it, or adjust it to fit my understanding or preferences.

Is Eternal Hell Consistent with the Love of God?

As a humble believer, do you think that the Biblical description of Hell is consistent with the love of God? I have had to think about that as I teach it to young ministerial students. The right and reverent approach is to remember that we have to define the Love of God according to the Bible, not according to human theories. If you base your teaching on human theories of love, then you can easily manufacture a God who will not punish anybody. But in that case you have created an idol. An idol of the human mind is not worth following; it will destroy you (see Hosea 8:4). This idol will fail you in the hour of death, for he never existed outside the vain thoughts of some philosophers and bad theologians.

The only God I know is the one in the Holy Bible. He is supreme Love. He loves us so much that he sent the Son of his heart to go through unspeakable abuse and death, even the equivalent punishment of Hell, that we, unworthy, hell-deserving sinners, could be forgiven and taken home to Heaven. That is love! Yet God's fathomless love is joined to spotless, stainless purity, integrity, and holiness. Therefore, his loving holiness requires the eternal putting away out of his presence of all that is contradictory to his character. This he did in the infinite sufferings of Christ in the place of all sinners who will receive it.

The Absurd Perverseness of Sin

This question is frequently raised, to avoid the unpleasant thought of the lasting duration of hell: could not the people in hell eventually repent? From all we can learn in Scripture, the solemn fact is that the people in Hell still do not want God. Of course, they do not like the sufferings of that terrible place: they do not like being separated from the bottle, the pills, political power, or money. But the mystery of iniquity is that even down there, they would never choose to love God, nor would they wish to dwell in the holy places above with the saints, angels, and the ever-blessed Trinity. The perverseness of sin is incomprehensible; it is strange, terrible, and absurd. Those who by their sinful choices in this life become finally cut off from God, do not improve morally; they do not begin to repent of sin, nor to love God. If they did not do so during this earthly life with its opportunities of grace, they surely will not do so in the world to come. In sum, we must think of it this way: what does Jesus, the love of God incarnate tell us about this matter? Surely we can trust in what he says.

Jesus mentions eternal punishment in the Sermon on the Mount (Matt. 5:22). He says: 'But I say unto you that everyone who is angry with his brother shall be in danger of the judgment, and whosoever shall say "Thou fool," shall be in danger of the hell of fire'. Further on he says (Matt. 5:29-30):

> If thy right eye cause thee to stumble, pluck it out and cast if from thee, for it is profitable for thee that one of thy members should perish, and not thy whole body be cast into hell. And if thy right hand cause thee to stumble, cut it off and cast it from thee, for it is profitable for thee that one of thy members should perish and not thy whole body go into hell.

In Matthew 7:23, he will say on judgment day to people who used his name, but did not submit to his Lordship: 'I never knew you; depart from me, ye that work iniquity.' In Matthew 24:51 and 25:30-46, he speaks of an eternal separation of sheep and goats. The goats will be cast 'into outer darkness: there shall be weeping and gnashing of teeth'. Jesus teaches an eternal separation from God, the beautiful saints, and all that is lovely and pure: 'And these shall go away into everlasting punishment, but the righteous into life eternal.'

It comes down to this: if we believe in Jesus, then we by definition accept his teaching on hell, and on everything else. Jesus is Lord of all, or he is not Lord at all. We are not given the prerogative of saying that certain strands of the teachings of Jesus are acceptable to me, but not other strands. That would mean that 'I am Lord', and then I am not saved by his grace. To trust in Jesus means to trust him implicitly and completely; to trust everything he said, which includes taking seriously his warning of this awful reality.

Hell is part of the reality we must face, and to deny reality is a disaster for us, sooner or later. It is said that the captain of the Titanic in 1912, fondly denied that the icebergs could hurt his mighty ship. Hundreds of people paid a high price for his denying that particular reality. You can choose to do that, but one day the ship will come against the reality of the icebergs, and down it goes.

A Kind and Gracious Invitation to Sinners
Through his Word and Spirit, Jesus pleads with every sinner, to lose a right eye, or a right hand, rather than lose his own soul! No bodily benefit, no earthly benefit can compare with the value of your immortal soul. Some Christians live in parts of the world where they lose their jobs for being a Christian, or sometimes even their physical lives. Painful as it is, these true believers choose starvation or imprisonment, rather than lose their precious souls in the awful reality of everlasting hell.

The honored cousin of Jesus, John the Baptist, warned: 'Flee from the wrath to come!' (Luke 3:7). The Governors of North and South Carolina occasionally give orders for all people in coastal areas to evacuate immediately if a very strong hurricane is headed towards the Carolina coast. One must obey the governor to avoid possible drowning. When a house is on fire, the firemen do everything possible to get the children out. There us something worse than hurricanes and earthly fires. It is the solemn reality of the Lake of Fire. And the Apostle John, who knew Jesus so well, says to us all: 'Flee from the wrath to come'.

How can we do that? We flee from the wrath to come by doing something else John the Baptist told us: 'Behold the Lamb of God that taketh away the sin of the world'. That lamb, that innocent holy substitute (the Lord Jesus Christ), who never sinned, takes away the sin of the world. He removes the guilt, which causes hell to be there. On that cross he suffered more of the pains of hell than I deserve. Jesus' suffering evacuated my hell and any one else's who will repent and believe in Him. By looking to Jesus in faith, we not only avoid the second banquet of the condemned, but are given entrance to that first banquet, to the wedding supper of the Lamb, and to all the fellowship, joy, and the gladsome service that will follow. May we all one day, sit down together at the marriage supper of the Lamb!

55

The Millennium

Revelation 20:1–6

Our last chapter was on hell, but we now consider a passage of great hopefulness, which shows us where world history is going for all the redeemed. In these verses, by means of symbols that we can interpret through other parts of the Bible, God shows us precisely what is going on now, and where everything is headed. We deal only with two of the chapters points.

1. The binding of Satan and the millennium (v. 1–3).
2. The saints in heaven (v. 4–6).

The Binding of Satan and the Millennium
Christ could not be reigning over the nations, unless Satan were, to a certain degree, bound, for he would not allow it. Symbols and pictures are used to get this truth across to our human minds.

The first question that we must consider to make sense of this passage is, how are we to interpret this binding of Satan and this thousand year period? What does it really mean in light of the rest of Scripture?

Principles of Biblical Interpretation
One of the most basic principles of biblical interpretation that scholars of all true churches have agreed on, is that we take a difficult passage in Scripture and interpret it in light of the clearer passages. Revelation 20 is one of the most difficult in the Bible, so we turn to the easier passages that speak of similar things. Another principle of biblical interpretation followed by most orthodox Christian scholars is this: we interpret the few in light of the many. In the whole Bible, the millennium or the thousand year period, is never spoken of except here in Revelation 20. This chapter is among the few references. Therefore, we must go to the many, to the other passages in the Bible that speak of the same realities, and thereby interpret the few in light of the many. When we do that, we will be on solid ground.

Revelation, and especially this chapter, is highly symbolic, conveying the truth through pictures and symbols, rather than literally. Symbols convey important historical truth like the parables of Jesus. 'A sower went out to sow and cast the seed on different types of soil'. He did not mean that literally, but was conveying profound truth about the reaction of human personalities to the teaching of the Word of God. So he was speaking in terms of symbols.

Why Symbols in the Bible?

Why does the Bible use symbols? Because we live in bodies and in the natural realm, so God accommodates himself to our limited capacities by using pictures and stories of familiar things, so that we can understand higher spiritual truth. That is especially the case in the book of Daniel, on which Revelation, in many ways, is based. These symbols are not meant to be taken absolutely literally. If I were to say that Jesus' parable of the sower and the seeds was primarily about crops, you would not understand the real meaning. He talks about crops, because we know something about them, with their good and bad soil. Jesus is actually talking about human persons, and how they react to the truth of God. Symbols such as seed on good ground and seed falling on stony ground bring to us the higher truth of what different classes of people do with God's Word.

For instance, we are told in verse 1 that a mighty angel comes down from heaven with a chain in his hand and forcibly takes hold of the enemy of God and humanity, Satan. He binds Satan with a chain, and puts him into a bottomless pit. Surely it is not speaking of a metal chain linked together with steel or iron links, because Satan is a malign spirit, and generally not in a body. What the binding with the chain means is that God sends an angel, who is even more powerful than Satan, to severely limit the activities of the evil one. After he is bound by the action of God through the angels, he is not able to do nearly so much as he was allowed to do before the binding. In that light, the key to the bottomless pit, which is certainly a real place that God keeps at his pleasure for his holy purposes, means that God at times 'lifts off the lid'. He lets the powers of evil out for a while, yet he still keeps them limited. How can he do that? Because he is God. Satan is only a creature: only God is Creator. Everything that God created is infinitely weaker than he is, so he can bind or loose them at his pleasure. The key to the bottomless pit stands for God's power through the angels to keep Satan and his demons from doing everything that they would like to do.

How Long Is the Millennium?

Similarly, when we say 'millennium', it is not literally limited to ten successive centuries. Why is this number used? In terms of biblical numbers, ten is the image for fullness and a thousand is ten times ten times ten, so fullness times fullness times fullness equals a vast number of years, without being a precise chronology of human history.

In Psalm 50 this same number is used in a different context, and there it is not meant literally, either. It says that God 'owns the cattle on a thousand hills'. Does that teach that in this physical world, the only thing God owns would be one thousand hills? If you understand the number literally, then after counting the hills in Europe and America, and reaching one thousand, then God would not own the cattle on hill number 1,001. It could not mean that, for 'the earth is the Lord's and the fullness thereof' (Ps. 24:1). It is a Biblical way of stating that God owns absolutely everything, so 'the cattle on a thousand hills' means the world-wide territory of his limitless domain is beyond our counting. By the same token, a thousand or millennium, means a very large number of years.

When Does the Millennium Begin?

The second question we have to raise about this thousand year period in which the evil one is bound or limited is, when does it begin? When did God limit the power of the Devil over the nations, so that he could deceive them no more (Rev. 20:3)? When was his malign power to keep the nations in spiritual darkness limited? Scripture shows us exactly when it began. It began when the babe was conceived in the womb of the Blessed Virgin Mary, when he lived and died, rose again and ascended to the Father, from where he and the Father poured out the Holy Spirit to the church. That is when the millennium began.

In other words, the reign of Christ over the nations began when he came into this world out of eternity as our Messiah and Redeemer, and began to work on redeeming the cosmos. So, when Christ came, Satan began to be bound.

To What Degree is Satan Bound?

What does it mean for Satan to be bound? Before Jesus' ascension back to the Father, Jesus said 'All power is given unto me' (Matt. 28:18). Then he commissions his church 'to go and teach all nations, baptising them in the name of the Father, the Son and the Holy Ghost.' So, as the risen Lord gives the Great Commission to the church, he makes it clear by 'all power' that a great deal of ancient power had been removed from Satan, and given to Christ. Satan no longer possesses the same amount of power over the nations after Jesus' historic victory. That is why even in Jesus' lifetime when he sent out the seventy, he did not send them to the Gentiles or 'the nations'. Why not? Why did he send them only to the lost sheep of the house of Israel? Because Satan had not yet been bound in his authority to deceive the Gentile nations. But after Jesus was crucified the outpoured, infinite Spirit has limited Satan, so that he can no longer keep the heathen nations from being able to receive the truth. It is after that that Jesus gives the missionary commission to his church, 'to go ye into all the world and preach the gospel'. Immediately after this awesome commission, Jesus gives us this encouragement: 'Lo, I am with you always, even until the end of the age'. In other words, when we go out speaking the gospel truth to lost people, whether in a foreign country or at home, Jesus is with us. Satan is bound insofar as he can no longer keep the church from spreading the truth.

Various Biblical passages speak about this, for example Matthew 12:28-9:

> But if I cast out devils by the Spirit of God, then the kingdom of God is come unto you. [When God's kingdom comes in its fullness in Jesus, Satan's kingdom begins to fall.] Or else how can one enter into a strong man's house, and spoil his goods, except he first bind the strong man? And then he will spoil his house.

When the eternal Son of God came to earth in the flesh, and completed his saving work, he was thereby binding the power of the evil one, so that Satan cannot anymore keep the elect part of the world in the darkness. One of the great effects of Christ's coming is to bind the strong man. The evil one is strong, but there is somebody stronger than the strong man. Christ, the eternal Son of God comes in the flesh and does battle with Satan. He defeats him in principle, until that final day when he will defeat him not only in principle, but totally in every way.

The Demons' Awareness of Who Christ Was

Think about the life of Christ and the various altercations he had with demonic spirits. These spirits were in league with the evil one. They wanted to destroy human life, to make people miserable, sick and crazy, so they could not answer the ends of the existence for which they had been created. The Gospels make it clear that the evil spirits themselves knew who Christ was and were terrified. They could see that Christ had come and was beginning to bind their influence.

For instance, in Mark 1:24, there was a man in the synagogue with an unclean spirit, who cried out even before Jesus had touched him. Similarly in Luke 4:34: 'Let us alone; what have we to do with thee, thou Jesus of Nazareth? Art thou come to destroy us? I know thee who thou art; The Holy One of God. And Jesus rebuked him, saying, Hold thy peace, and come out of him. And when the devil had thrown him in the midst, he came out of him, and hurt him not'.

Jesus, as he binds Satan, liberates depraved human personalities and sets them free. It is the same in Luke 10:18–19 after the seventy returned with joy unto the Lord, saying 'even the Devils are subject unto us through thy name'. Upon their return from the mission to Israel, the seventy proclaimed with great joy: 'Even the devils are subject unto us through thy name'. This indicates that the Lord was already binding Satan. Then Jesus says: 'I beheld Satan as lightning fall from heaven'.

Colossians 2:14–15 makes it clear what is happening in Christ's historic ministry, particularly as he is on the cross: 'Blotting out the handwriting of ordinances that was against us, which was contrary to us, and took it out of the way, nailing it to his cross; And having spoiled principalities and powers, he made a show of them openly, triumphing over them in it.' This indicates that malign powers were defeated in principle in the cross of Christ. When Jesus purged away all of our sins on Calvary, something happened to Satan. The evil one lost his authority to keep people back from God. He was bound by what Jesus did.

Satan's Continuing, but Severely Limited Influence
The influence of Satan in the world has not yet been absolutely and totally removed. That will happen on the last day. Until then, Satan is allowed in the wise and overruling providence of God to do a certain amount of evil, as we see in terrorism, the destructive drug culture, lies, hatred, immorality and wars. But Satan has been severely limited in his ability to deceive entire nations and keep them from believing the gospel. Notice in this regard, Acts 28:28 'Be it known therefore unto you, that the salvation of God is sent unto the Gentiles, and they will hear it'.

Once, the citizens of pagan Britain and Europe were involved in demon worship and other evil practices. But through the work of Christ, the gospel came. Converted Roman soldiers brought the gospel to Britain as early as the first or second century. By the fourth century, the Emperor Constantine (who had been born in England, before going to Rome and being promoted to Emperor), was converted to Christianity, and things in Europe greatly changed. Satan had been bound, and our forefathers were brought out of the darkness. What was said in Acts 28:28 about the pagans outside Israel became true for our own people: 'They will hear it.' That is because Satan is bound in his ability to keep the nations from hearing and to keep them from seeing the saving truth.

The Saints in Heaven
The second division of this chapter (vv. 4–6) brings before us what is going on with the saints who have died. Their deaths were not a final defeat, for the gospel is going forth, and the saving truth of God is being proclaimed. In spite of his murderous activity, Satan is not able to keep the elect from coming to faith in Jesus. Gradually, during this 'thousand year' period, many millions of lost souls are being converted, and lives are changing. Because Satan has been bound, God's church can go to the Gentiles, and they will hear the truth of salvation. Even entire

nations can move Godwards during this long season of Satan's relative binding.

Do the Saints Above Miss Out?

That is what is happening on earth, but what is happening in heaven at the same time? Do the martyred saints miss out on the reigning of Christ on earth? Think of how many Christians are put to death! What about them? Revelation says that they do not miss out on the triumph of Satan's binding and of Christ's reign, because they are sitting on thrones in heaven. Verses 3–4 speak of God being with them, and wiping their tears away, while Revelation 6:9 portrays them as resting and rejoicing in the presence of the heavenly Father, and still interceding for the church on earth.

When we contemplate our deceased ancestors and loved ones, it is a true and wonderful thought that they have never been so active, so happy, so vitally alive, and so busy in good works as they are now in the presence of God. Far from being losers, they are gainers, seated on thrones, and reigning with Christ from that place of beauty and glory. Perhaps a large part of their reigning is through their consecrated prayers. Not only martyrs, but also ordinary Christians who have gone above, are taking part in the priestly, and kingly reign of Jesus Christ through intercession.

Still praying, 'Thy kingdom come'

They are now in a much fuller way than ever they could do on earth, pleading what Jesus taught us in the Lord's Prayer, 'Thy Kingdom Come, thy will be done, lead us not into temptation, but deliver us from evil.' Of course the saints above are impervious to temptation and evil, but so close is their identification with the suffering church on earth, that they take the words the Lord put into its mouth, and make them their own. Their sanctified prayers play a large part in reversing the darkness and sending forth the light on earth.

Psalm 2:8 will summarize their continuing ministry above, in company with the saints still laboring below: 'Ask of me, and I shall give thee the heathen for thine inheritance, and the uttermost part of the earth for thy possession.' These ceaseless and countless petitions from saints above and saints below will, without fail, be gloriously answered, because the triumphant work of Christ has bound Satan from keeping the pagan nations in darkness.

56

Two Deaths and Two Resurrections
Revelation 20:4–6

Revelation 20 illumines the nature of the millennium with its concept of two deaths and two resurrections. As we saw in the last chapter, the millennium refers to the time span between Christ's two comings to earth. It starts with his incarnation, and it will end upon his second glorious, physical return on the last day of world history when he sets up the throne of the final judgment. It is the season provided for the outreach of the church, during which all of the elect will be gathered in from every tribe, tongue, and nation of the world.

We consider two points from this text:

1. The chief purpose of the millennial reign (Rev. 20:4, 6).
2. Two deaths and two resurrections (Rev. 20:5–6).

Chief Purpose of the Millennial Reign
Revelation 20:4–6 focuses on the triumphant nature of the outreach of God's church on earth among the nations, which we studied in the last chapter, but we can usefully add a few more Scriptural references here.

'To Destroy the Works of the Devil'
One of the major reasons for Christ's coming to earth was that 'he might destroy the works of the devil' (1 John 3:8). Hebrews 2:8–16 says much the same, but in another way. We could paraphrase the passage by noting that 'Christ took on flesh and blood in order that through death he might destroy him that hath the power of death, that is the devil, and deliver them who through fear of death, that is in us, were all their lifetime subject to bondage'. People were afraid to die because the devil tormented their consciences with awareness of sin and fear of coming judgment. Therefore, when Jesus came the first time and finished his work on earth, Satan's power was massively curtailed. Jesus in dying, did something to break the power of Satan to manipulate the human conscience through fear of death. That is what this passage means by the symbolic phrase 'the binding of Satan' with a chain for a thousand years. That is a pictorial way of expressing what verses such as those just noted from 1 John and Hebrews are teaching. It does not mean that absolutely all Satan's activity has ceased, but the great authority he had, to keep the nations from seeing God, was broken by the work of Christ.

Good News for Bad Times
Revelation was written to the church at a very difficult time for the people of God. On the

surface it appeared that evil was triumphing and would wipe out the church and its mission to the world. In Revelation, God shines his light on what was happening and on what was going to happen to the church, and through it, to the multitudes of lost men and women. The message given to John shows that while Satan is bound in what he can do, believers in Christ are unbound. They have massively fruitful opportunities to influence the nations in a Godward direction, as the church calls the lost to faith and repentance in the crucified, risen Redeemer.

Revelation 20:1–6 gives us the most encouraging picture from God's viewpoint of the tremendous difference the lives and testimonies of Christians can make in this difficult world. Such passages as this take us beyond the earthly, common sense perspective on the suffering and losses of the church in a difficult world. God says, in effect: 'I want to show you what is really happening beneath the surface and then you are going to see that the future is very different from the way you feel as you are facing chains and swords.' The Word of God then shows us things from the heavenly point of view, and that is the one that finally counts, because that is where the power is.

As medical doctors employ X-rays and CAT Scans to find out what is really happening in parts of the body, they are able to discern what the prognosis for treatment is. If doctors only went by the superficial, outward appearance, they would not know the true physical condition of our bodies. It is much like that in the spiritual realm. To deal with the problems that are there, and to make true progress so that our life counts for something, we must look beneath the surface.

One needs something higher than common sense. Common sense is a good and necessary gift from God, but you have to look higher than that or you cannot ascertain what your life means, where God wants you to go, and what is going to happen in the future. You have to go, not against common sense, but above it. Scripture is what enables you to do that. Holy Scripture alone can give us accurate light on what is happening in the spiritual realm. This is of utmost importance, because if something happens in the spiritual realm, then it comes down and influences the natural and physical realm. When big things or little things happen in the natural realm, it is in reaction to something that happened in the spiritual realm. That is how the world works.

If we Christians only look at the world situation around us, we cannot possibly understand just how much our lives could accomplish. If we get our bearings from the popular culture, or even the intellectual culture, we will quickly grow discouraged, because it looks like corrupt political power, immoral culture and the worship of money are in total control of everything. Then we begin to feel that materialism and even atheism sit on the thrones of power, so that our little lives can really make no difference. Of course, that is just where the devil wants us to be, so that we will give up and let depressing secularism have its way, even in our own household.

But how different is the penetrating view given to us by the holy Word of God. Far from Christians being on the losing side, the One who has total power over the past, present and future, says that we, through faith in Christ, are already on the winning side. Far from the devil controlling more and more of the world, Christ and his saints are slowly, but surely, winning victories. As a result, the nations of mankind will eventually be exactly where God wants them to be in terms of the salvation of individuals and great cultural changes within those nations. That is the good news about the unfolding of this 'millennium' between the two comings of Christ.

Advancing the Kingdom Through Believers

This means that what matters the most in discipling the nations towards faith in Christ, is victorious faith in his true Word, along with a mind and life suffused by the Holy Spirit, who raised Christ from the dead. These spiritual virtues, along with poverty of spirit and service to others, overcome all proud opposition. Satan is bound and God's values are therefore free to bring about supernatural reactions in the realm of personalities that somehow glorify Jesus, save souls, and set back the Kingdom of Evil.

That is what is going on in Revelation 20. The Church of Christ participates in the suffering, but also in the resurrection of her Lord. When the church suffers, she shares in the cross, but she comes through that time of suffering and pruning with ever greater fruitfulness. Thereby, she shares in the resurrection of Christ. That is how the truth spreads. It involves our very beings: we share with Jesus his death and resurrection. Satan is bound, and the resurrection keeps going forward, transforming individual lives, and beginning to push communities, tribes, states and even nations, in a heavenward direction.

The world, insofar as it is still motivated by Satan says exactly the opposite. Living the way Jesus taught us works, although it looks unimpressive to be humble, to pray, patiently to serve, and to wait on God to vindicate us. Jesus says 'Look beneath the surface of things that may appear impressive to worldly thinking: do it my way: the way of bearing the cross and trusting in him who raises the dead, because something is going on all the time when you do it my way. There is a series of deaths and resurrections at work that are going to transform the whole world, if you will trust me enough to do it my way. Just watch what I will do. Realize you are nothing; bow at the foot of the cross; look up to me for forgiveness, power, and guidance. Take up your cross and follow me. Put God first, others next, and yourself last. See what I will with humble instruments do to advance my winning cause'.

It is the victorious outworking of the principle found in Mark 10:42–4 and in 1 Corinthians 1:26–9. Death to the self-life and to love of the things that impress the world always come before the many little resurrections that God's people experience in the life and service of the Lord Jesus. That is God's appointed way of advancing his cause, and of transforming the character of his people.

Two Deaths and Two Resurrections

In this passage, especially verses 5–6, God's way of winning the lost and changing the world during the 'millennium' is worked out in terms of two deaths and two resurrections. From God's point of view, the world is like a huge organism, and at any one time there are deaths and resurrections going on within it. Finally, there is going to be an ultimate death, and a universal, last resurrection that makes glorious sense of all the rest, getting the cosmos to where God wants it to be. Hence, even before the final death and the final resurrection, there is a constant series of deaths and resurrections through which God is working to transform the whole. The chart overleaf should help us to summarize how the principle operates through these realities, centered in Christ, and conveyed to the world through his people, who are in union with him.

Let us look in more detail at these two deaths and two resurrections. The use Revelation makes of these concepts will help us grasp much that God is doing through his church, in union with her Lord, between the two comings of Christ.

First Death	Second Death	First Resurrection	Second Resurrection
• Separation of body and soul (or personality)	• Separation from God of the rejoined body and soul.	• Regeneration of the soul (or personality)	• Reunion of the saved soul with its glorified body.
• Physical and temporary	• Physical and eternal	• Spiritual	• Physical and eternal
• Applies to all humans	• Applies to unbelievers	• Applies to believers only, by the Holy Spirit through faith in Christ.	• Applies to believers only

Two Resurrections

Verse 5 indicates that there are two resurrections for true believers. One is a spiritual resurrection, and one will be a physical resurrection.

First Resurrection (Spiritual). The first resurrection means a new birth, to be born again. It comes about through regeneration by the Holy Spirit, who has set us free from the chains of our fallen nature, so that we exercise faith in Christ. That is to say, a believer is a resurrected person in his or her personality. Resurrection life has already come into your body when you become a believer. Your physical body is dying, yet you already have experience of spiritual resurrection, if you are in union with Christ. This first resurrection is described as 'a new creation' in 1 Corinthians 5:17. Romans 6:4 describes it as the Holy Spirit bringing us into union with Christ in his death and in his resurrection. That happens while we are on earth. That is what it is to be a Christian. John 5:24–5 describes it:

> Verily, Verily, I say unto you, the hour is coming, and now is, when the dead shall hear the voice of the Son of God; and they that hear shall live. For as the Father hath life in himself: so hath he given to the Son to have life in himself.

To say that the dead 'shall hear the voice of God and live' refers to the spiritual resurrection, to the new birth of the personality. A Christian is a risen one in his soul or personality. As Jesus explains to Martha at the tomb of Lazarus: 'I am the resurrection and the life. He that believeth in me though he were dead, yet shall he live and whosoever liveth and believeth in me shall never die. Believest thou this?' (John 11:25). Jesus is saying that if you have faith in him, you are united with him in his resurrection. You have experienced resurrection. We are resurrected in our spirits, and are members of a new 'resurrected humanity'.

But people who refuse to believe in Jesus, are still 'dead in sins and trespasses' (Eph. 2:1). That does not mean that their physical bodies are already lying in the grave. They are active, physically up and going, but the innermost core of their being, and thus, their daily thoughts and activities, are dead in the sense that they are cut off from God. They do not see the truth, they do not see Jesus, or the love and grace of God. They are dead towards God. They have not experienced the first resurrection.

That is what verse 5 means when it says: 'The dead live not again until the thousand years are over'. The spiritually dead never partake of the first resurrection. Those who die rejecting the gospel, are never resurrected in their spirit. They never come alive to God, so they do not have the first resurrection. The first resurrection, the new birth, is only for believers, only for those who come into vital union with the risen Lord.

Second Resurrection (Physical). The first resurrection was spiritual; the second is physical. The bodies of saints shall be raised in glory like the beautiful, transformed risen body of Jesus. That will be our second resurrection. Jesus describes it in John 5:28–9: 'Marvel not at this: for the hour is coming, in which all that are in the graves shall hear his voice. And shall come forth; they that have done good, unto the resurrection of life; and they that have done evil, unto the resurrection of damnation.' Daniel 12:2, says: 'And many of them that sleep in the dust of the earth shall awake, some to everlasting life and some to shame and everlasting contempt.'

The Christian's second resurrection, in which their body comes out of the dust in beauty and power, and their saved soul is reunited with its glorified body, is a thing of loveliness and glory. But the lost, those who lived and died for the world, and rejected the truth of Christ to keep serving self and Satan, will have their bodies raised to shame and contempt. No description is given in Scripture of what the resurrection unto damnation is like. Unlike believers, this is the first and only resurrection for unbelievers.

Two Deaths
Now as there are two resurrections, so there are two deaths. Death is used in these two ways, with two very different meanings, here in Revelation. The first death affects all people, saved and lost.

First Death (Physical). Physical death is the temporary separation of our body and soul. Upon physical death, your personality leaves the body. There are mysteries here, but at least we are told that at the moment of the physical death there ensues a temporary separation between the spirit that animated our body and the body itself. The body goes back to dust; the spirit, if you are saved, goes into the presence of God. If you are lost, it goes into a place separated from God.

The first death, which is temporary separation of body and soul, has no power whatsoever to harm believers. Solemn as death is, it is nothing really frightening for Christians. It is an open door into glory for every believer, where they may rest and reign, praise and pray, until Jesus comes back, and they accompany him in his triumphal train. Then the body will be raised and the souls given back to their bodies.

But even before that august moment, the High Priestly prayer of Jesus in John 17:24 reveals the glory that is already the experience of departed believers: 'Father, I will that they also, whom thou has given me, be with me where I am; that they may behold my glory, which thou hast given me: for thou lovedst me before the foundation of the world.' Paul describes what 'the first death' accomplishes for believers: 'For me to live is Christ, and to die is gain … For I am in a strait betwixt two, having a desire to depart, and to be with Christ; which is far better' (Phil. 1:21, 23).

That is the first death. It comes to unbelievers and believers. In experiencing physical death, we are alike, but that likeness ceases in one split second the other side of death. What the first death brings for believers and unbelievers is completely different.

Second Death (Spiritual). The first (physical) death is not at all terrible for the believer; it is gain for all who are united to Christ. But even the first death is a loss for nonbelievers; they are separated forever from any means of salvation. But what an unspeakable loss is theirs in the second death! For then, in both body and soul, the unsaved will be cut off forever from God and heaven. This is the meaning of spiritual death (the second death). It is not extinction of spirit, but an irrevocable cutting off of their reunited spirits and bodies from the source of life, the fount of love, the original light, the ocean of comfort and joy—the Triune God himself. Nothing could be more logical than to be terrified of the second death, if you refuse to repent and believe in Jesus! That is the most logical emotion you could have: absolute terror.

True believers experience the first death, but never the second death. The second death affects only non-believers. The resurrection to damnation of the nonbeliever means that his or her lost soul and body, which was raised in shame, are reunited, only to be separated eternally from God. They are cast into 'the Lake of Fire' (Rev. 19:20). Yet that second death has absolutely nothing to do with believers. They will never experience it.

To summarize, we note that the millennium in Revelation 20 means that between Christ's two comings, something good is happening beneath the surface, because Satan is now too limited to stop it. Even when the powers of evil put true believers to death, they cannot stop the movement. Out of the pruning comes only more fruit. Out of the blood of the martyrs comes the seed for a larger church. The millennium means that all Christians are alive to God now, and God has the ultimate power. After the gospel events, Satan is extremely limited, but God is ever alive and on the throne. Even when Christians are killed, they go to heaven and sit on a throne, they reign through their prayers and affect what happens on earth now. Believers on earth are given the grace to work with God through many personal crucifixions and resurrections, so that the gospel keeps effectively spreading. Unbelievers die twice and are resurrected once. Believers die once and are resurrected twice. Thus, the future is with them and with God who raises them. Make sure that you are on the winning side and that you become part of the resurrection race.

57
When Things Look Worst, Victory Is At Hand
Revelation 20:7–10

There is a great principle in this text, and it is this: When things look at their worst, victory is at hand. All the wrath that Satan has stirred up in the human race is going to come to a head, as it is set before us in these verses. The worst that the devil, the demons, and mankind can do against the Lord and his church are going to bring stupendous hosannas and hallelujahs to God at the end. That is a wonderful way to look at future history.

We have previously seen that the evil one is, to a large degree, bound. He cannot keep the nations from seeing the light of the gospel when it comes forward. He is bound. But you could not say that Satan has been totally defeated, though that is coming. Verses 7–10 describe his final, total defeat and we focus on one point: the great explosion at the end of the gospel age.

The Great Explosion at the End of the Gospel Age
The gospel age, the age of the spread of Christianity, or the millennium, ends with a great bang, or from the point of view of the church, an awesome explosion. At the conclusion of T. S. Elliot's famous poem, 'The Hollow Men', written sometime before the first World War, he says: 'This is the way the world ends; not with a bang, but a whimper.' Revelation 20:7-10 says exactly the opposite of what Elliott said, although he afterwards became a Christian, and changed his thinking. All the efforts of the Christian church since Jesus was raised from the dead are going to end with a tremendous explosion.

Only God Can Lift the Lid off the Infernal Pit
That is how the world really ends, not with a whimper, but with a bang. Verse 7 says some-thing without which none of this would make sense: God is the one who lets Satan out of his prison, who unbinds the one he formerly bound, through the death and resurrection of his blessed Son. Satan is a powerful, malign spirit being, but he is only a creature. He is limited; he is finite. He could never get loose from his bondage at his own will, until God in his sovereign timing takes off the chains from his hands and feet, opens the door and lets him out. Since the death, resurrection and ascension of Jesus Christ, Satan has been 'chomping at the bit' to get loose from the pit in his full fury and to attack the Christian church head on. But God holds him back until the chosen moment.

There is such a moment. It is a split second that God chose even before he created the world.

When we reach that point, the door of the pit will swing open by the authority of God and Satan will be let loose. God will let him loose. He will not let himself out. He would like to, but he cannot do that.

Verses 9-10 say that when the evil one is let loose, there will be tremendous affects upon the nations on earth, among the heathens and pagans. It will lead almost immediately to a great war. It will be brief, and it will be marked by utter defeat for the hosts of evil. It will last only a few hours, and soon it will be all over. Why would God, who is absolutely good, and dwells in holy light, ever let this malign being out of his infernal prison to mount a world-wide attack on the Christian church? Even though that attack is going to end in complete defeat of Satan, why would God have let him loose at all at the end of the gospel age?

God has a good reason for everything he does, though much of it far surpasses our human understanding. A medical illustration might give us a clue to why he lets loose the evil one. If you have a sore or boil on your hand, leg, or foot, before you get rid of it, it normally has to come to a head; the corruption has to collect in one swelling, in order to clean it out and get rid of it. That is something like the position here. Near the end of the gospel age, God is sovereignly going to let Satan loose from the secret pit to gather into one location all the unconverted enemies of the Lord so they can be taken care of at one time in their corrupt fullness.

Much Unbelief Remains at the End of the Age
If, however, the millennium has been a long period of expanding salvation to the tribes and nations of the world, with the elect gathered in through believing in Jesus, then how would Satan be able to muster so many evil troops? The text speaks of them as 'the sands of the sea'. Here is the answer: Scripture never teaches that even in the best period of the gospel age, even during the greatest Holy Spirit revival, all persons are converted.

The history of revivals such as 'the first Great Awakening' in the 1730s and 1740s, or the great revival of 1858-59, when so many were saved, will show us that still there were plenty of people who were not saved, but instead became angry and infuriated against the revival. Jesus says in his parable of the wheat and the tares that although there is much true wheat in the field, still there are tares—false professors, or unsaved—among the true believers. Thus, one cannot root out the tares until the time of the end, lest the true wheat be torn out of the soil. In his parable of the dragnet, it is clear that even in the end time, when the net is hauled in, there are good and bad fish in it. So Scripture does not teach that the gospel age will ever reach a stage where absolutely every person is saved.

Yet the period spoken of in these verses will constitute a time when the unsaved will assemble in an army, led by Satan. But they shall be quickly and radically defeated, and then cast into the fire, while the wheat is gathered into the Lord's treasury barn, and the good fish are collected out of the net.

'Stand Still, and See the Salvation of the Lord!'
Here is another question: if Satan is let loose to gather all unbelievers together into a vast army, with unregenerate numbers like the sands of the sea, how could the church defeat such a large and vicious host of enemies? Verse 9 gives us a simple answer: the church is not going to be called on to fight on that day. God is not going to ask us for help. God in heaven will defeat them directly, by supernatural action. He casts down fire from the altar of heaven, which eats them up like a moth

flying into a flaming oil well. As Moses said to the children of Israel on the verge of the Red Sea, with Pharaoh's army galloping behind: 'Stand still, and see the salvation of the Lord.' God is going to take care of this final outburst of evil that gathers all the corruption into one spot. He will take care of it in short order with universal victory.

Fire coming down reminds us of how the Lord destroyed Sodom and Gomorra by raining down fire and brimstone, once Lot and his wife and two daughters were taken out of the city by the angels. Fire coming down reminds us of Elijah sitting up on the hill when wicked King Ahab kept sending troops of fifty soldiers to try to kill him. Elijah would call down fire from God, and literally burn up all these troops. We also see fire falling from above, and burning up ships in Revelation 8. When God does it, he does it right. He does it with complete efficiency.

A Definite Date

It is not given us to know exactly when this final confrontation of evil has been programmed by God to take place. Yet, it is just as definite as the day of the creation of the world and as the days that were set for the conception and then the birth of the Lord Jesus Christ, 'In the fullness of time' (Gal. 4:4). How far along are we in the gospel age? Are we near the end? We do not know for certain, but all through this age, Satan and his servants disguise themselves as angels of light. They pretend to be what they are not. They dress themselves up most respectably, but inwardly they are wolves in sheep's clothing. That is how so many wicked governments get into power, and so many corrupt politicians get elected. Sometimes unbelievers become ordained ministers, by pretending to be what they are not. Satan must pretend to be like an angel of light. And the people he motivates also pretend to be clothed in light, with sincere concern for the people.

But at the end of the age it is going to be different. Here is how you are going to know if you are alive on earth when Satan is finally let loose out of the pit and time is about finished: Satan will drop all pretense at doing good. He will throw the sheep's clothing off his wolfish back and bare his teeth. All phony religiosity will be gone. Satan will know how short his time is and he will infuriate his own crowd with the desperate determination to attack God, his laws, and his people openly. They will no longer say, 'we are doing what is good for the people'. Instead of insincere talk, they seek to kill the people of God. Satan and his crowd will suicidally attack the institutions of the Living God. But it will already be over for them. Revelation 20:9 says that they will compass the camp of the saints, that is the church. Before they can put a finger on the walls of salvation guarding the people of God, the Lord of the church will suddenly consume them with a mighty fire that falls from the altars of heaven.

If you should be alive on earth when the forces of evil drop all pretense at being religious, and show what they are as open blasphemers, you will thereby know that the clock of time has all but ticked its last. If Big Ben in London is still chiming and ticking near the houses of Parliament, we can then know that it will only chime a few more times before evil shall be removed, with glory soon to follow. That is the way the world shall end: an explosion of fire that will totally consume the assembled hosts of evil and then the glory that follows for the saints of God.

If that is the worst that can happen to the church, we are still totally surrounded by the walls of salvation. That is the ultimate issue. God may let certain things happen to our body, but never to our soul. And he is even going to give us our bodies back at resurrection. But the worst that could happen to the Church is that Satan and all unbelievers, with all their viciousness and hatred against God, could be temporarily unleashed to try to kill us. When that happens, God is going to lay them waste in a matter of moments with the holy fire from heaven.

Focus on the All-encompassing Providence of God
This teaches us something very important, not only about the end, but even more importantly, about the God who has it all in charge. At the right stroke of the clock, God is going to cast Satan and his hosts into the lake of fire. If God has planned to handle the great explosion of evil with consummate skill and attention, then how much more is he handling lesser kinds of evil that may come on us before the end. We should not let the growth of evil depress us, nor let it overly distress us when things seem to be getting worse. It is true that much of Western culture is becoming atheist, blasphemous, and vile. Not many years ago, in New York, the Arts Council put forward as a work of great art a crucifix in a jar of urine. It was open blasphemy, subsidized by government funds to the Council. While such things should anger us with righteous indignation, they should never get the better of us, nor stress or depress us, because the worst that unregenerate mankind can do is just a foreshadowing of when God lets Satan loose to do his worst.

Remember that at the end, world history is going to work out just as God had planned from the beginning. He is just as much in charge today as he is going to be on the final day. When it begins to look so much worse, we Christians know a secret told us in Revelation 20:7–10; it may well be a sign great victory is very soon to follow. And so Paul says in the conclusion of the great resurrection chapter that because Christ has risen from the dead, he is in a position to subject all things to himself, and that includes the last enemy, death, which shall finally be destroyed (1 Cor. 15:58). On that basis, Paul says, 'Therefore my beloved brethren, be ye stedfast, unmovable, always abounding in the work of the Lord, forasmuch as ye know that your labor is not in vain in the Lord.'

58

The Last Judgment
Revelation 20:11–15

If you have visited some of the medieval European cathedrals, you may remember that as you enter the great gates, the front doors of many of those Romanesque and Gothic cathedrals have over the front door a semi-circular carving that is called in Latin, the Tympanum. It portrays the last judgment, with Christ on the throne, the Holy Angels and the sheep (the saved) on the right hand, and on the left hand, the goats (the lost). When our ancestors walked every Sunday through the front doors of those churches, they were reminded of something that should cast its light over every day life—the great final judgment of the quick and the dead.

Revelation 20:11–15 constitutes the fourth and last part of this chapter. These verses contain the most solemn and awful scene that will ever occur in the long history of humanity: the final judgment and casting into endless Hell of all who rejected God. It will be the largest gathering of human beings in all of history. Not one descendant of Adam and Eve will be missing. Hundreds of millions, indeed, billions, will be assembled before the awesome judgement seat of Almighty God. This will be God's final word on the personal, immortal destiny of every soul who has ever lived.

We look at three points from this extremely solemn text:

1. Who sits on the throne (Rev. 20:11)?
2. Who stands before the throne (Rev. 20:12–13)?
3. Where do they go when the gavel of the judge hits the bar of judgment for the last time (Rev. 20:14–15)?

Who Sits on the Throne?

God Almighty is the only one who sits on the great white throne of majesty and power. He created all things out of nothing by the word of his power. He has controlled providentially everything that ever happened in all the twistings and turnings of history, and of all affairs in the earth and the entire universe. He redeemed what he created by his own blood. He alone is fit to utter the last word over every man, angel, demon, and over the devil himself. The stupendous majesty and limitless power of the sovereign God is indicated in the amazing physical response of the elements when he takes his last seat on that judgment day.

We are told that the earth and the heavens fled from before his face, and there was no place found for them. Mountains, seas, continents, islands, forests, swamps, and deserts scurry away like rats abandoning a sinking ship. The clouds, sun, moon, and stars, constellations and nebulae, evaporate like morning vapor before the rising sun. There are no mountains left to hide sinners from the direct glance of the face of the God who sees through us with burning, holy light. There is now nothing to hide any individual in an assembled universe from the Almighty, whose very existence some of these people spent their whole life trying to deny. All pretense is gone on that day. Each one of us will then be face to face with ultimate and final reality. No escape, no hiding place. The refuge of philosophy and false religion has vanished with the clouds. All is held captive by the face of God.

We are told the sovereign throne is white. This speaks of the absolute purity and stainless, unsullied holiness of the thrice Holy God, whom Isaiah heard in his vision crying out 'Holy, holy, holy is the Lord of Hosts'. God sees every fact exactly as it is, no lies, no excuses: nothing but the total truth about us dare present itself before that great white throne. No doubt the entire Trinity is involved, Father, Son, and Holy Ghost, in the last solemn judgment, but Scripture specifically states that the Father has committed all judgment to the glorified Lord Jesus Christ. Jesus sits on that throne and renders the final judgment of every single person, as we see in Matthew 16:27, Acts 10:42; 17:31, and other places.

Think about Jesus on the throne. What an amazing reversal, just in terms of his face. Isaiah 53 tells us that his face, particularly in the last days of his passion, 'was marred more than any man'. He whose beard was plucked out, and his holy face spat upon and his eyes dim with tears mingled with blood, now sends forth streams of light from his majestic countenance, brighter than the noonday sun. What a change in his face!

Who Stands Before the Throne?

Never in earth's long history has there been an assembly of humanity like this. All of the dead are assembled from every corner of the inhabited universe, seen and unseen. All graves have split open; mausoleums, marble saracophagi, cathedrals crypts, and every crematoria box has given up its prey. Death and Hell have been suddenly and totally emptied of their unhappy inhabitants. The restless sea has given up its dead. All who were drowned in floods, including the flood of Noah; all who sank on ships or were buried at sea; every last one is there; no one is missing.

'Great and Small' Stand Equally Together

Notice, according to the text, that small and great are standing together (Rev. 20:12). Many people on earth pay for the privilege of living in gated communities, and having guards around their houses. That sort of security may be necessary in some cases, but on that day, all will be standing together. Human rank, wealth, and social class will have no relevance whatsoever on that mighty day of wrath. Kings, presidents, prime ministers, emperors, dukes and earls, fearfully stand beside field hands, tractor drivers, janitors, preachers, school teachers, and prison inmates. Wealthy CEO's and medial moguls will be fidgeting beside drug pushers and prostitutes. Owners of castles, palaces and fabulous mansions are in line with folks from trailer parks of Dillon County and the slums of Harlem in New York. 'Small and great', high and low, all are now on the same level, which is the way God always saw them.

Every last one is breathlessly awaiting their sentence from the unerring and righteous judge of men's souls. And that sentence is not long in coming. What a frightening sound will be the opening of the books that have the full life story of every last one of us. This passage mainly deals with those whose names are not written in the Lamb's Book of Life, that is the unsaved. Other verses in scripture tell us that the saved are caught up with Christ, and that their names are found safely recorded in this Lamb's Book of Life. They will be immediately separated from the lost, like wheat from the tares, like the sheep from the goats. They will be forever with the Lord and 'joy unspeakable and full of glory' shall surround them forever more. I will say more about the final joy of the saved when we reach Revelation 21.

WHERE DO THE LOST GO AFTER JUDGMENT? These verses plainly state the destiny of all who finally reject God and his gracious way of salvation. It is always a mystery that some people, who seem to have perfectly normal minds, will fiercely reject the tender grace, mercy and love of God offered to sinners in the gospel. No doubt, their persistent rejection of divine grace is directly related to the depravity of their fallen human nature, yet it is a very hard thing to see someone do this. Though I have taught theology and preached for decades, still I find it very painful and exceedingly strange to see some insist on rejecting God's lovingkindness.

What consequences there are for willfully rejecting the gospel! The Bible does not hide them. All who have refused to have their sins covered by the blood of the Lamb, now stand naked before an entire universe of humanity, with all their sins in view, on their own heads. Many people spend much of their life-time hiding their true self, but on that day, it is all brought out into the open. Some people use alcohol, drugs, sex, and material pleasures to deaden their own conscience, but how alive and how alert will every single conscience be, when all assemble before the great white throne.

A Destiny Determined by Impartial Judgment
This text and the rest of scripture teach that people's destiny in Hell will be objectively and impartially judged, according to the infallible information about them written in the Books of God, which will then be open to view. No one is ever sent into Hell on the basis of an emotional, uncontrolled outburst of Divine anger. God is not like that at all. He is Holy. He is calm. He is righteous. He judges 'according to righteous judgment', not 'mere emotion' or superficial appearances. He infallibly sees through the details and context and circumstances of every life, so he judges all the lost according to their works done while they were on earth.

As Christians, we know that we are not saved by works, but by grace. That is what it means for believers to have their names recorded in the Lamb's Book of Life. The Lamb took their punishment and gave them his righteousness, by the grace of a miraculous transfer (1 Cor. 5:21). But if people refuse grace, they consign themselves to be judged by precisely what they did on earth. That includes their refusal of grace and every other action of their lives, including thoughts and words, as well as missed opportunities to do good. To put it simply, the course of life one lived determines one's position in hell for those who finally refuse all grace.

Hell is a mystery as heaven is a mystery. We are not given very detailed descriptions of heaven or hell in the Bible, and it is best to be reserved when we speak of these final realities. But God does reveal a few significant facts about these real places, that enable us to make some intelligent decisions while there is still time. As for hell, there are many different degrees of suffering and displeasure in that place. How unpleasant hell is, is directly determined by the kind of life one lived while on earth. Jesus said to the cites of Chorazin and Bethsaida that at the day of judgment, it would be far more tolerable for Sodom and Gomorra than for them, because if Sodom and Gomorra had heard what Jesus had to say, they would have repented. In other words, on the last day and following that, Sodom and Gomorra will have a less awful place in Hell than Chorazin and Bethsaida, because the latter had more light than did Sodom and Gomorra.

The Biblical principle is this: 'he to whom much is given, of him shall much be required.' Those who had more privilege will be beaten with many stripes says Jesus in one of his parables; while those who had less privilege shall be beaten with fewer stripes. We do not know exactly what that means, but we do know that there are different positions in hell, determined by what one's life was like on earth. Paul deals with this principle in the first two chapters of Romans. The more light one rejects, the worse hell will be for them. The harder one's heart, the meaner one was, the more evil one committed on earth, the tougher will be the experience of hell for them. Romans 2:5-6 says: 'But after thy hardness and impenitent heart, thy treasurest up unto thyself wrath, against the day of wrath, and revelation of the righteous judgment of God, who will render to every man according to his deeds.'

Avoid Personal Vengance. God is utterly pure and just. We need to keep that in mind, when we think of these things. How righteous God is! Hence the purity of that great white throne! God will never give someone more punishment than they deserve, nor less. That is one good reason why we as Christians must never take vengeance into our own hands against people who may have hurt us, and have not repented. We are to keep in mind that solemn day when all will be put right. This is what Paul says in Romans 12:19: 'Dearly beloved, avenge not yourselves; but rather give place unto wrath; for it is written, "Vengeance is mine; I will repay," saith the Lord.' So hell will be far worse for some than for others.

Do not worry if somebody has done a great deal of wrong, and they seem to be comfortable, with everything going their way. They died rich, and during their life everyone was bowing down to them. They seem to have gone into the other world without having received any punishment, while poor believers suffered and were despised. From our merely human viewpoint, it seems unfair how many lives turn out. If you think only on the human level, you can start being bitter, particularly if someone has done you wrong and escaped punishment. You can carry this anger in your bosom all your days, and lose much joy. Paul says, 'No, think of it this way: you do not need to take vengeance. You even have the freedom to forgive them, and forget it as best you can. God is looking. God will bring them before his throne and he is going to handle it with exquisite justice. Leave it to him. Everything he does, he does well. We will be able then, if not now, to praise him, for his rich mercy to those who accept him, and for his exquisitely right justice to those who reject his grace.

The Lake of Fire
And at the last, after the final session of judgment, death and hell and all who belong there, will be forever cast into the terrible Lake of Fire (v. 14–15). The Lake of Fire seems to be much worse than the temporary hell, or hades, that souls experience

between the death of their bodies and the return of the Lord. It appears to be a shoreless, bottomless, ocean of burning. Dante, in his classical *Inferno*, has these words written over the gates of that awful place: 'Abandon hope, all ye who enter here.' Verse 14 tells us that 'the Lake of Fire' is the same reality as 'the Second Death.' We have seen that the first death is temporary separation of one's body and soul, whereas the second death is the eternal separation of the reunited body and soul of sinners from the glorious presence of God forever and ever.

In our relativistic day, many people (including theologians and preachers) are unwilling to accept that anything can really be that final. They follow the theology of 'Star Wars' in which there is a light side and dark side of the force, but it's all the same thing. In this kind of thinking, if there is a hell, it could not possibly be everlasting. But relativism, Eastern philosophy, New Age thought, and Western liberalism are all deceptions of Satan to lure people to sleep in order to keep them from facing the truth and doing something while there is still time.

It is absolutely necessary to take action, because God is judge of all, and has a holy character. Therefore, right is right, wrong is wrong, and every sin and evil work not put under the blood of Christ by faith, must be justly punished. If God did not do so, he would deny his own holy character.

In Matthew 25, Jesus uses the same words to indicate the duration of hell that he uses to indicate the duration of heaven. Both are real places, and both are never-ending. The decision one makes on earth during this brief life determines forever in which of those places one will always be, 'When the trumpet of the Lord shall sound, and time shall be no more'. Once the lid, so to speak, is placed by the Almighty over the narrow passage leading into the Lake of Fire, there is absolutely no exit. God's word is crystal clear on that point, although there are many details he doesn't tell us.

What a privilege to be still in the land of the living where we can humbly pray for the grace to be given us of faith in Jesus and repentance from our sins. You have at present the opportunity to pray to God about these things. One day, those opportunities will be forever ended. Nothing in my life is one millionth so important, as that I seek Christ's face 'while he may be found, and call upon him while he is near'.

Even for those who believe the Bible and do not reject the grace of God in Christ, it is still difficult to take this into our limited minds. What must it be like for even one soul to be everlastingly separated from God, with no desire to repent, and no possibility of getting out forever and ever? It is a hard truth, and it is not wrong to admit that it is.

Jesus Willingly Took our Hell

But remember, this section of the text is bad news only for those who will not have Jesus on any account, no matter how graciously he is offered. When Jesus was on the cross, one of his seven last words was this, from Psalm 22:1, 'My God, My God, why hast thou forsaken me?' Whatever else that means, it indicates that Jesus took the punishment of our hell upon himself in those moments, and so was separated from his Father, taking upon himself all the pains that we deserve. He swallowed them up and overcame them, and then came out of the tomb with the divine authority to offer us the total, complete, and lasting pardon of all our sin and guilt, from the highest heavens. Isaiah 53:5 says, 'The chastisement of our peace was upon him, and with his stripes we are healed'. What a privilege to think of these two amazing texts. We may think of them as two open doors before us, offering a way out of our sin, death, and hell.

The Right Prayer

The best response to these holy truths is to seek God's help in entering these two doors that are set before us. As we do so, let us say with David these words, which are all any sinner ever need say to avoid hell, and to be received into the highest heavens (Ps. 51:1–10):

> Have mercy upon me, O God, according to thy loving kindness: according unto the multitude of thy tender mercies blot out my transgressions. Wash me thoroughly from mine iniquity, and cleanse me from my sin. For I acknowledge my transgressions: and my sin is ever before me. Against thee, thee only, have I sinned, and done this evil in thy sight: that thou mightest be justified when thou speakest, and clear when thou judgest. Behold, I was shapen in iniquity and in sin did my mother conceive me. Behold, thou desirest truth in the inward parts; and in the hidden part thou shalt make me to know wisdom. Purge me with hyssop, and I shall be clean: wash me, and I shall be whiter than snow. Make me to hear joy and gladness; that the bones which thou hast broken may rejoice. Hide thy face from my sins and blot out all mine iniquities. Create in me a clean heart, O God; and renew a right spirit within me.

59

A Final and Sweeping Victory
Revelation 21:1-8

In modern military history, some wars have been fairly swiftly won, but then after many years of occupation by the victorious troops, there is still much conflict, with deaths on both sides. In such wars, it was not a sweeping victory. What we have in those eight verses is a final and sweeping victory after what could have been a most horrendous war. This last battle sums up every other battle. It brought all evil to a head.

After the glorious fire fell from heaven's altar, it ate up the evil one and his massive unregenerate army, and put them down into a place of eternal separation. That cleared the ground. It swept up the floor, so that the true people of God in Revelation 21 and 22 enjoy the most stupendous victory: that for which the heavens and the earth were originally created, for which Jesus died and arose, and for which all the providence of God has been operating through all the ages. What God has planned and was working towards, and what the Church was cooperating with, has now come to pass in the most real and physical way.

The Covenant of Grace

This passage shows us in particular, the heart of the covenant of grace—the covenant relationship between God and man. The whole Bible is a covenant book and these verses show us what the covenant is most essentially about. It is here that we perceive the beauty of the close and lasting fellowship of the Covenant God and his covenant people: that is what the Bible is all about.

We are going to look at 3 points in this text:

1. The newness of it all (v. 1–4).
2. How the new starts in the old, and is gloriously fulfilled (v. 5–6).
3. How obedient faith gets us into that new world of resurrection, joy, and victory (v. 6–8).

The Newness of It All

Verse 1 speaks of 'a new heaven and a new earth.' Here is an important point of biblical principle: God acts negatively only in order to make room for the positive. Augustine's definition of evil was 'the absence of the good'. God acts in such a way that finally he will remove all evil so there will be nothing but good, whereas the only thing Satan can do is negative. He introduces evil and tries to increase evil. As 1 John tells us, 'he is a murderer from the beginning'. Other passages say that he is a liar, or a destroyer. But in this final battle, God sovereignly worked to remove the source of the trouble.

As we saw in the last two chapters, Satan and his malign host were put away into the Lake of Fire. That grand negative makes way for the most beautiful positive. It is the lasting blessing of a new heaven and new earth, where there is not even a particle of evil.

The Created Order Is not Totally Destroyed

We all know the first heaven and the first earth from our personal experience. They are where we live. We have grown up loving the creational context of our existence. God delights in the creation that he brought into existence, and at the end, he will restore and renew it, rather than annihilate it. They are not totally destroyed. That is a misunderstanding of the end of time. Some people think that because the Bible speaks of fire, everything will be burned up, so that nothing will be left of the old creation, but that is not what Holy Scripture teaches. Rather, the fire is a kind of a purging, like a healing fire, or a cleansing flood. Instead of annihilating, or utterly destroying this heaven and earth in which we live, the holy fire purges and renews them. This is indicated in 2 Peter 3:10–13:

> But the day of the Lord will come as a thief in the night; in the which the heavens shall pass away with a great noise, and the elements shall melt with fervent heat; the earth also and the works that are therein, shall be burned up. Seeing then that those things shall be dissolved, what manner of persons ought ye to be in all holy conversation of godliness. Nevertheless we, according to his promise, look for new heavens and a new earth, wherein dwelleth righteousness.

There will be a thorough purging of everything that is unworthy and defective.

The only analogy we have for this kind of total restoration would be the renewal of our physical bodies. Although our bodies must be laid down in the dust one day, they are not going to be totally annihilated or done away with forever. They are going to be raised up from the dust by the miraculous power of God, as he did with his Son. We do not know just how he raised his Son, nor how he will raise us, but when it happens, there will be a close connection between the body we have now and the new resurrection, or spiritual body he shall give us. There will be profound differences, for there will be transformation, purging, purification, and glorification, but it will be in continuity with the bodies we now have.

Philippians 3:21 shows us something of this mysterious transformation of our dying, physical body, into our ever-living spiritual body. It shows us that the whole created order is to be renewed on the analogy of the resurrection of the body of the believer: Christ 'shall change our vile body, that it may be fashioned like unto his glorious body, according to the working whereby he is able even to subdue all things unto himself.' We have seen people laid out in coffins, and it is hard to imagine that one day they will come out of those coffins, beautifully alive and vital and looking like themselves, except massively better.

How could it happen? The last phrase of Philippians 3:21 simply states: 'According to the working whereby God is able even to subdue all things to himself.' The Omnipotent One can readily gather together what is left of the scattered dust or ashes of the decayed or burned up body. God is able to subdue every part of the cosmos, every piece of the puzzle, and every speck of dust, to himself. The resurrection trumpet sounds, the angels are sent out, the dead are raised, and the entire universe of space and time immediately responds. The holy fires purge the vast environment of stars, skies, seas, and lands. What God does with each body that he raises is a picture of what he will do with the entire heavens and earth.

'No More Sea'
John tells us that 'there was no more sea'. I remember in 1977 visiting two elderly, saintly ladies who attended the same church, where I had regularly gone in Edinburgh. One of them, from the Isle of Lewis, hated to see me go, and as I was leaving, said that she did not know if they would ever see me again. Then she added: 'I was just reading in Revelation something that encourages us as you are going back across the sea, which separates us. Revelation says that 'one day there will be no more sea, nothing to separate us'.

I left their little flat there in Edinburgh with a very uplifted heart. 'No more sea'. That which separates us is going to be absent from the new heaven and new earth.

The sea also speaks of the raging, unstable politics, and national orders of mankind that dare to oppose God and his gospel. Out of that raging sea of unregenerate humanity, came the beast, who opposed Christ. But the beast and all he stood for has been put away into the lake of fire, and now 'there is no more sea'. This means that on that day there is not going to be any evil, anywhere in the world. This is something none of us has ever experienced. All of that will have been put down into the lake of fire that is sealed off from us. We wonder what a world without any evil would be like? What a glorious, happy place! This blessed state of a new heaven and a new earth that has been purged with fire, where there is no evil, is still future, but verse 5 says that we can be certain that day is coming. There will be a new world order, where there is absolutely no defect, evil, or hurt, no pain, sorrow, or tears, because God's promise is faithful and true. The word of mankind is not faithful and true; politicians keep adjusting their promises, and pretending to forget their solemn vows. But God's word is faithful and true. Everything he says he will do. In due season, it will all come to pass.

Three Terms with One Reference
In verse 1 the floor is swept clean. The fire has purged. In verse 2, we see the coming down of 'the holy city,' 'the new Jerusalem,' 'adorned as a bride for her husband'. These three terms are threefold ways of speaking about the same reality. What is that reality? It is the Church, the people of God, from the beginning in the Garden of Eden, from the first promise of the gospel to our fallen mother Eve, down to the last elect person who will believe. These three terms are always speaking about God's church, for which God's Son shed his precious blood to make her clean.

The Old Testament sometimes calls Jerusalem 'the holy city' (Neh. 11:1; Isa. 48:2), but after the inhabitants of Jerusalem rejected Jesus Christ and agreed to his crucifixion, God was no longer dwelling in the city of Jerusalem as he had formerly.

But what happened on the day of Pentecost? The Holy Spirit when he came down, in Acts 2, did not fill the temple of Jerusalem, but rather filled the personalities, the bodies and souls of the men and women who believed in Jesus. Through them he began bringing others into this living relationship. Christian believers are the true temple of God. You can read about it in 1 Corinthians 12:13, where we are all 'baptized by one Spirit into the body of Christ'. That is the New Jerusalem; it is the church. Hebrews 12:22 speaks about a heavenly Jerusalem, or Mount Zion, the city of the living God. It originates by action of God in heaven. The saints go there when they die. On the appointed day, they will come down with their heavenly bridegroom to join those who are caught up from the earth (1 Thess. 4:13–18).

The term, 'the bride,' speaks of the tender intimacy of God and his beloved people: 'A bride adorned for her husband.' Revelation 19:7, Isaiah 49:18, and other places speak of people of God as the bride of Christ. Jesus made this bride beautiful by cleansing her with his own blood (Eph. 5:25–7). The wedding ceremony is about to begin, here in Revelation 21. The bride (the church) and bridegroom (Christ) will be forever together.

Everything that you and I, as normal human beings, have been programmed to want in the very best marriage we could have, will be provided in this lasting relationship, for which all earthly relationships were ordained to prepare. God has made most people so that they wish to be married. It propagates the human race, it spreads the church, it is the foundation of society. But I think an even greater reason that it is in us to want to be married, is that deep inside the soul, we feel a longing for that ultimate relationship that even the best marriage cannot completely convey. Yet human marriage does in some real way picture and represent the sweetness and surpassing joy of what is to be, and what we instinctively long for—this final, glorious, lasting, beautiful, loving and wonderful relationship between God in heaven and all his people.

The Heart of Biblical Covenants

In verse 3 we notice the imposing sound of 'a great voice'. Presumably it is God's voice: 'Behold the tabernacle of God is with men, and he shall dwell among them, and they shall be his people.' That is what the covenants of the Bible are essentially about. In different ways, and in different ages and economies, God says in all of them, 'I will be your God, and you will be my people'.

That was already announced in the first promise of the gospel in Genesis 3:15 to our sinning mother, Eve. God promised to put enmity between her seed (the human race, chosen out for redemption), and the serpent (Satan). That is, I am going to divide you from the serpent, so you can come back to me.

God says to Abraham in Genesis 12, 17, 21, and other places, 'Abraham, fear not, for I am thy shield and exceeding great reward. Walk before me and be thou perfect. I will be a God unto you and your seed'. Then God gave the covenant sign of circumcision, to be cut into the son's flesh at eight days old. Thereby God promised that he was going to include the children of believers. And so it continues, with ever more light being given through different sets of circumstances throughout the Old Testament. Details of the covenants vary, but always, God is their God by grace, and they are his people by grace.

It was signified in the economy of Moses in various ways, such as covering the doorposts of their houses with the blood of the Passover Lamb, and eating together the flesh of the hastily roasted lamb. The taking in to the 'holy of holies' the sins of the people by the High Priest, and then, the bringing out of the Aaronic benediction from that holy place back to the needy people reestablished them as cleansed dwellers in the presence of a Holy God.

We see this same essential point in the covenant with David (e.g. 2 Sam. 7:14), where the Lord promises to establish the throne and lineage of David, from whose line would come the Messiah, the Savior of the world. Everybody in the fellowship of that throne, and ultimately, in the fellowship of the Messiah, who descended from it; all of them are going to be 'my people and I am going to be their God'.

If we read the prophecy of Ezekiel which has so much background to Revelation, we find that its last verses (Ezek. 48:35) speak about the name of that heavenly city, which ultimately becomes the church, and in Hebrew means 'Jehovah is there'.

Only God Can Satisfy the Soul

All the best things that any human being has ever honorably wished for—joy, peace, love, and rewarding service—are all found in God. He is the ocean of all the blessings we have been created to desire the most, and to be motivated by above anything else in our earthly life. Lesser things can encourage us, but lesser things and created things in themselves cannot convey the qualities that we most desire.

Only God can give us the kind of intimate, filial relationship that we, who have been created in his image, need in order to satisfy our body and soul. Verse 4 tells us that given this lasting relationship, something wonderful happens at the gates of eternal bliss: 'And God shall wipe away all tears from their eyes, and there shall be no more death, neither sorrow, nor crying, neither shall there be any more pain for the former things are passed away'. Pain, and the shedding of tears is a sign that something is wrong in the world order that we inhabit. It is caused by sin, and the effect of sin is death. But death is going to be totally put away and cast into the lake of fire at the last judgment, then the room is cleansed and beautified, so that the Lord and his covenant people can forever be together. When death departs, sorrow departs. Pain goes and all that causes grief is no more.

THE NEW STARTS IN THE OLD

To say, as does verse 5, that 'God makes all things new', goes back to the original, perfectly beautiful and sinless creation. God does not negate what he made, even though Satan pockmarked it by sin, as our parents gave in to him. God is not going to destroy what he made. He loves his creation; he loves our bodies and souls. He has already started renewing things, but that process will reach its final sweeping victory only on the last day.

A New Creation

'Behold, I am already making all things new.' That is the force of the original language here. It means that God is already recreating men and women into the image of what he wants them to be. We read in 1 Corinthians 5:17, 'If any man be in Christ, he is a new creation. Behold old things are passed away, all things are become new.' During our earthly experience of salvation, God is already beginning 'the new heavens and the new earth', so that with that resurrection quality of life in our spirits when we become Christians, it is like he resurrects our spirits. That is why we are believers. He has done something supernatural on the inside. Then on the last day, when Satan and death are cast into the lake of fire, he will complete what he has already begun when the Spirit baptized us into union with the risen Christ. One day, he will do that in the very dust of our body, for as Augustine once said, 'In that day, the rapture of the saved soul shall flow over into the glorified body'. Jesus said in John 11, 'I am the resurrection and the life. Whosoever believeth in me shall never die.' This means that in your personality, even though death with its cold fingers can pull down your physical body to the grave, it cannot get your spirit. Through the new birth you are already alive, and one day he will raise up your physical body.

God Sets Your Day of Birth and Day of Death

Verse 6 confirms the truth that the new begins with the old: 'I am Alpha and Omega'. In other words, Christ is the beginning of the alphabet, and the end of the alphabet. In 1 John 1:1, he is 'the Word of life'. He is the first word, the final word (see Heb. 1:2), and everything in between.

He has our future as much in control as he does our past. For some reason, after I was fifty years old, it occurred to me that God was in control the day I was born and in control of the environment I was brought into. In my case, it was a Christian family; not a perfect one, but believing people. He is going to be just as much in control, the day and hour and place of my death. He did it well the first time (when and where I was born), and why should I not be confident that he will do it just as well the second time (when and where I shall die)? Jesus is the Alpha and Omega, the beginning and the end, and he is in charge of our whole pilgrim journey, from beginning to end.

Roots in the future
A well known Greek Orthodox theologian, John Zizioulas, said that we normally think of our roots as being in the past, and it is true. In the Carolinas we often think of how our ancestors came from Scotland in the middle of the eighteenth century. Who they were has shaped us. But a Christian, though he has certain roots in the past that explain his heredity, also has roots in the future. We have roots in heaven. We have roots in resurrection reality, which control us even more than our roots in the past.

OBEDIENT FAITH GETS US TO THE NEW WORLD
How do we take our place in the new world of glory and bliss? A choice is set before us in verses 6b–8. The clear choice we now make while we are alive on earth, determines where we shall be for all eternity. In verses 6b–7, we find a gracious promise to anybody and everybody who will receive it. Then in verse 8, we have a solemn warning.

A Promise
Here is the gracious promise: 'I will give to him that is athirst of the fountain of water of life freely.' It is made by the same Jesus who spoke to the woman at the well of Samaria. She was a prostitute and had lived with five different men. Jesus talks to her in the middle of the day, because she had to go to the well when the other women of the village were not there. They did not like her because she may have been trying to seduce their husbands. She was a sinful person, but God had put a thirst in this woman for something better. Jesus said, 'I can give you water, filling you up on the inside and flowing out to others. You will no longer thirst for this water'. And by faith, she drank that water. We are going to see that woman in heaven. We will not even think of what she did on earth, but rather admire the beauty, holiness, and splendor that will shine out from this former prostitute from Samaria, now a princess in the kingdom of God.

Isaiah 55:1 tells us how free it is. 'Ho, every one that thirsteth, come ye to the waters, and he that hath no money, come ye, buy and eat; yea, come buy wine and milk without money, and without price.' It is free to us sinners, but it was very costly to Jesus, and it is the most valuable of all gifts. Who is thirsty for eternal life? For total pardon of sin, fellowship with God now, and everlasting joy beyond the grave? All you need to get on board is this thirst. Indeed, this very thirst is a gift from God, to orient our souls homewards. What a generous God he is! He causes us to want the gift, and then provides the gift at his own expense.

The promise continues in verse 7, that if we drink of what Jesus has to offer to faith, we shall overcome this world, inherit our share of glory, and live forevermore as God's sons and daughters. What if you could have a stately home, a yacht, a Porsche, hundreds of millions in blue chip stocks, broad lands, and great prestige? All of it would pass away very fast, or you would die, and leave it to somebody else, possibly for them to fight over. Even if you could have all these things, you would not be here many years to enjoy them, even if your health held out. But now this thing that God offers, this eternal life of the pardon, peace and joy will always remain. Nothing could take it from you or from me, or from the weakest person who truly believes in Christ.

A Warning and Promise in One

But there follows a solemn warning to unbelievers about unbelief and disobedience (v. 8), lest they be put away out of the new heaven and the new earth. Those who refused to heed God's warning were put away into the lake of fire. The warning in verse 8 is a warning and a promise. If you take a list of the sins in verse 8 that put people eternally away from God in the lake of fire, you will find that there are multitudes now in heaven who did these very things—fearful, unbelieving, murderers, whoremongers, idolators, and liars. Many of the most beautiful and joyful saints in heaven committed these same sins that put unbelievers in the lake of fire. They are people like David, who committed adultery and murder; Moses, a murderer; Samson, a terrible fornicator; the woman at the well of Samaria, a prostitute. But they are in heaven.

What is the difference? Hebrews 11 mentions those people, including Samson, who we know were sinful, but mentions none of their sins. Why not? Because of their saving faith. Hebrews 11 starts with faith and continues the theme into Hebrews 12, where we are instructed to look in the right direction in order to get to heaven: 'Wherefore… looking unto Jesus, the author and finisher of our faith' (Heb. 12:1–2). Faith means looking to him for forgiveness. The issue determining whether we get into heaven or hell is whether we look to Jesus in faith and repentance. It is not that the people in heaven did not commit sin. They did. It was where they looked after they sinned. They looked in faith to the Lord for pardon, and for a new life in fellowship with Him. In the eternal plan of God, all their sins, that otherwise would have put them into hell, have been transferred to the suffering and hell that Jesus endured on the cross at Calvary. All that is left for those who exercise faith, is to drink from the water of life freely. That is why Hebrews 11 never mentions any of the sins of the heroes of the faith. They are all covered in the blood of the Lamb! That is your only hope! The God who raises the dead can enable you to come and drink of these living waters, if you will seek his help, and 'call upon him while he is near.'

60

How Generous God Is with His Glory!

Revelation 21:9–17

This text shows us how very generous God is to share his glory! It demonstrates the generosity of God with the most precious thing he has, and that is his own glory. How gladly he gives the very best that he has to the sons and daughters of mankind.

Let us note two points in this text:

1. The glory of God (Rev. 21:11).
2. The shape and identity of the New Jerusalem (Rev. 21:9–17).

The Glory of God

A verse from Isaiah, written some six hundred years before Revelation, will bring into focus the remarkable generosity of God, portrayed in verse 11, where he brings down to the Church his very own glory: 'I am the Lord. That is my name and my glory will I not give to another, neither my praise to graven images' (Isa. 42:8).

God's Glory Belongs Only to God

God firmly says through Isaiah that he does not give his glory to another, for his glory is so essential to his deity, that it is not given to another; that is, to anyone less than God. Yet, wonder of all wonders, after Christ has come and done his glorious work we are told in verses 10–11: 'The holy Jerusalem, descending out of heaven from God, having the glory of God, and her light was like unto a stone most precious, even like a jasper stone, clear as crystal...' What a stunning contrast. God says in Isaiah 42, 'I do not give my glory to another', and now 'that great city, the holy Jerusalem' is full of the glory of God. God has given his own divine glory to the Church.

Our Desire for Beauty

This wonderful text seems full of holy light. The text is luminous in showing us how the glory of God, which is the origin of everything that is beautiful, literally comes down to radiate into the Church its loveliness and splendor. God has put in us, by virtue of creation in his image, a deep desire for beauty. We may have different ideas about what is beautiful, but when we see or hear it, we know it. Some of the old classical writers said that beauty is 'the splendor of truth'. Its perfect proportion, harmony, and lack of defect draw us to itself. Some of the Medieval scholastics said that it is 'that which is pleasing to see.' Beauty is more than that, but not less than that. In certain types of older theology and philosophy, the word 'ecstasy' was at time used with beauty. That is, true beauty has an alluring nature: it draws us out of ourselves [Hence, *ec—stasy*; that is, 'to be placed outside' or 'to be drawn out'].

There is in every human a certain reaching out towards beauty. God's glory is the origin of all that is beautiful, for the Triune God shines in the uncreated light of his own transcendent purity, harmony, and loveliness. To be precisely who he is in the three co-equal Persons of Father, Son, and Holy Spirit, in the one, undivided Being of his own reality, is the supreme beauty and source of every other created beauty. This glory, which is an essential aspect of the very essence of God, according to verse 11 comes down, and shines out through the Lord's redeemed church.

'The World Exists for the Church'

Here in Revelation 21 we see that the church is the same as the 'holy Jerusalem, from above'. It has become the dwelling place of God's glory. He, who is zealous for his own glory, gives his glory to the church. That is the meaning, the goal, and the end of human history: God's glory filling and transforming the Church. That is why the ancient Christian writing, *The Shepherd of Hermas*, said: 'The world exists for the church.' That is what Christ prayed for in his high priestly prayer: 'And the glory which thou gavest me I have given them; that they may be one, even as we are one…Father, I will that they also, whom thou hast given me, be with me where I am, that they may behold my glory, which thou hast given me: for thou lovedst me before the foundation of the world' (John 17:22, 24). Surely, this prayer of Christ fulfils the longing expressed in the plea of Moses: 'And let the beauty of the Lord our God be upon us: and establish thou the work of our hands upon us…' (Ps. 90:17).

Shape and Identity of the New Jerusalem

Most of the world is always interested in the continual difficulties in the old, earthly Jerusalem, which has a way of staying in the international news. But what about the New Jerusalem, what is it like? The blessed angel shows John in verse 9, the bride, the Lamb's wife. In the next verse, she is identified as 'the holy Jerusalem' that came down out of heaven from God. That clearly identifies 'the New Jerusalem' as the bride of Christ, which is the Christian church, and the focus of this passage. Everything in world history is getting ready for what God is already doing in his church. That will bring human history and all civilization to its consummation.

Two important points flow from verses 9–10, for they show us how to interpret this passage. First, John, in company with the blessed angel, is using symbols from the Old Testament to teach us the deepest and most significant eternal truths. He does so by means of symbols. In this passage about the New Jerusalem, the true reality to which the holy angel is pointing is not so much a literal city in the shape of a cube, some 1,400 miles around, that floats down from heaven. Rather, it means the absolute beauty and perfection that occurs at the end of history, when God fills his redeemed church with fullness of glory and the joy of his divine love.

The second point of proper interpretation for these verses is this: everything that God has done in the history of creation, and in all his covenant work since then had one goal in mind. This goal includes the reason for which we were born, and the over-arching plan behind everything that is allowed to happen. All events are being shaped to make his church ready for the right moment at the end of time, to be filled with his glory and to illuminate the whole universe. You must understand that to interpret Revelation 21 and 22.

We already referred to some of the Church Fathers who said that God made this world as a nursery for the human race, whom he created in his image, in order to give his Son the best gift a father could give his son: that is a bride. So God made the world out of which he would form a bride to present to his Son. That is especially in view in here, where we see the Lamb's bride.

Preparation for the 'Wedding Supper of the Lamb'
All the Bible is preparing for that greatest of all events. Sin entered the human race very soon after Adam and Eve were created, and chose to sin, giving in to the temptation of the devil. But God promised that the seed of the woman would be the ultimate channel through which redemption would come to the human race. The 'seed of the woman' is Christ and everything that happens after Genesis 3 is making preparation for 'the wedding supper of the Lamb', when the bride, which 'the seed' washed clean in his own blood is presented to her heavenly Bridegroom.

In the Old Testament, Abraham is called out to found the church. Israel is the Old Testament form of the bride of Christ. Adumbrations of this coming wedding are frequently found in the Old Testament. One such foreshadowing is seen in the prophecy of Hosea. Hosea was called by God to marry a beautiful young woman, but she turned out to be very unworthy of his love, and became a prostitute, finally reaching such a low point of moral and financial destitution that she was literally sold into slavery as a worn out prostitute on the slave block.

It is hard for us to believe the next action that Hosea took. Representing God, he went down to the slave market, and bought his corrupted, ruined wife. In the middle of Fayetteville, North Carolina stands the old slave market. It is said that the poor slaves were taken out on those porches of the old, brick Market House to be displayed like merchandise, and bid upon. Perhaps we can visualize Hosea going to something like that slave market. The tender love of God shows through the prophet Hosea, when he buys back his unfaithful, degraded wife, and takes her home. That action was an exhibition of the divine, forgiving, restoring, redeeming grace of God to us sinners. Gomer (Hosea's wife) is a picture of us sinners, taken back in by God.

The bride of Christ in the Old Testament is the same as the one in the New Testament. Look in Isaiah 61:10: 'I will greatly rejoice in the Lord. My soul shall be joyful in my God, for he hath clothed me with the garments of salvation. He hath covered me with the robe of righteousness as a bridegroom decked himself with ornaments and as a bride adorneth herself with her jewels.' Paul often speaks of the church and the corporate body of believers as constituting the Bride of Christ. Then in Ephesians 5, he shows how Christ 'loved the church and gave himself for her that he might wash her and purge her from all her sins and might present her to himself as a spotless, pure, beautiful bride'.

Every event that has occurred in world history, has been preparing for that glad day, when the heavenly Bridegroom takes his bride. You cannot make sense of world history or even of your own life, without realizing that this is finally what God is doing. What a generous, loving God we have!

God's Beauty upon His People
To prepare us for this noble goal, God puts his eternal beauty upon us. Beauty is part of what is meant by God's glory, his radiance, splendor, and loveliness. He puts his divine beauty upon this church. We know all too well the imperfections found in churches, and in individual believers. But this beauty of the church is largely hidden until the

final coming of Christ. Certainly, we see sparkling glints of this beauty in holy character, in helpful lives, and in the honorable Christ-like deeds of Christian people. Rays of the beauty of Jesus still break out from time to time from the members of his church; the world would be Hell if it were not for that. But that largely hidden beauty will have a splendid manifestation on the last day, when Christ comes back in glory with his angel train.

We have seen such a royal and stupendous outburst of beauty in Christian lives as shall enthrall us on that final day. The most wonderful, classical art of the Renaissance and the Middle Ages, the most beautiful architecture, the loveliness of the purple-headed mountains in the Scottish Highlands, the 'wine-dark sea' surrounding the Aegean Island, the snow-covered Swiss Alps, the beautiful face of a gorgeous young woman, a marvelous Bach cantata, or a Mozart sonata—whatever you think of as beauty, will be very little, compared with the splendor of Christ, which shall shine out on that day on his church.

Psalm 45:13, may be a prophecy of this: 'The king's daughter is all glorious within; her clothing is of wrought gold.' The daughter of the King, the church, is first of all, glorious on the inside. You do not see it. She is filled with beauty and glory on the inside, and eventually clothing of wrought gold will become her outer raiment. What beauty we are going to see on that day!

'The Weight of Glory'

C. S. Lewis gave a BBC radio address in the 1940s, entitled 'The Weight of Glory.' In it he says that you do not ever meet any really ordinary person, because every person has been created in the image of God, and therefore has an enormous capacity, for which they never asked. By virtue of being created in God's image, everyone has the capacity at the end of time, to be resplendent with the absolute beauty and glory of God in Christ, when the Lord's work is finished in their lives. God turns on the full light of the risen Christ in them, so that the glory at last shines out in all its radiant, heaven-born splendor. Lewis says that if some ordinary man or woman were sitting beside you on the bus and you could seem them as they are going to look when the glory of Christ fully shines out in public fashion, you would be tempted to bow down and worship. They will look so splendid and marvelous then, but at present, the ordinary saints on earth are like 'the daughter of the king.' They do not yet have the fabulous clothing woven of gold threads, yet they are glorious within. It was that shining out from some of them that encouraged me as a young person and helped lead me along the right way.

Geometrical Shapes and Mathematical Proportions

Now the shape of this finally redeemed church, or holy Jerusalem, is described in verses 12–17 in geometrical and mathematical proportions. These figures bring us back to the point of true interpretation. They are not to be taken literally, but they are employed to point us to something true and important. That is to say, we are not dealing with a literal measurement as to exactly how big heaven is going to be, but with eternal truths that we can get hold of and grasp, only through familiar earthly shapes and numbers taken from the Old Testament.

In verses 12–14, we have a description of the holy city in terms of two sets of twelve: twelve gates and twelve foundations. This is much like Revelation 4, where we find twenty four elders, which meant the twelve patriarchs and the twelve apostles, representing one church throughout both Testaments. Now in Revelation 21, there are twelve gates to the city, that have the names of the twelve sons of Jacob on them.

Remember how the high priest had a breastplate, with twelve different kinds of precious stones in it. Each one of the stones represented one of the twelve tribes of Israel. So when the high priest went into the Holy of Holies once a year on the day of atonement, Yom Kippur, he went in with blood to offer, first for his own sins, and then for the sins of the people. Throughout the priestly action, he was bearing on his heart the twelve tribes of Israel into the immediate presence of God.

Ephesians 2:19–22, explains in a more theological way, the same thing that John shows us symbolically in Revelation 21:

> Now therefore ye are no more strangers and foreigners, but fellow citizens with the saints, and of the household of God; And are built upon the foundation of the apostles and prophets [apostles: New Testament, and prophets: Old Testament], Jesus Christ himself being the chief corner stone; In whom all the building, fitly framed together, groweth unto an holy temple in the Lord: In whom ye also are builded together for an habitation of God through the Spirit.

Verses 15–17 represent what this city, or church, means in geometric terms. Again it is a way of using something that we can understand, as for example, architecture, to convey an eternal truth that is, in a sense beyond human words, until we can see it and enter it. Here the holy city, or church, is represented as a cube. In antiquity, a cube was considered the perfect shape.[129]

For instance, 1 Kings 6:20 describes the shape of the holy of holies: 'And the oracle [that is the holy of holies] in the forepart was twenty cubits in length, and twenty cubits in breadth, and twenty cubits in the height thereof: and he overlaid it with pure gold; and so covered the altar which was of cedar.' In other words, the holy of holies was a cube: 20 cubits x 20 cubits x 20 cubits provide a cube. On that analogy, 12 x 12 = 144, which is the perfect number, derived from twelve apostles multiplied by twelve patriarchs, is also used to describe the general shape and size of the city. It is not meant to limit the size of heaven to any particular earthly mileage system. It is a symbolic way of describing heaven in terms of symmetry and perfection.[130]

The Bride Comes Down from Heaven to Earth

Notice finally, that this beautiful bride or city comes down to earth from heaven (Rev. 21:10). What could that mean? Part of the church is in heaven right now; believers who have died are there. Some of God's people are up there, and some are down here. Others are yet to be born and regenerated before the end. When our Lord Jesus Christ returns in glory, he brings all of his people with him. Those saved souls already in heaven, accompany the Lord downwards, and in that miraculous moment, saved souls are reunited with their now glorified, resurrection bodies, so that 'The dead in Christ shall rise first' (1 Thess. 4:14–15). Immediately, 'We which are alive and remain shall be caught up together with them in the clouds, to meet the Lord in the air' (1 Thess. 4:17). That is how the bride descends from heaven to earth immediately prior to the Great Assize. While the bodies came out of the graves, and went up, nevertheless, once the risen bodies and transformed believers join the returning Christ 'in the clouds', the direction is downwards to the place established below for the Last Judgment.

When this beautiful, perfected, glorified Bride of the Lamb comes down from heaven to earth, we can think of it as a contrast with the Tower of Babel, in Genesis 11. As Dr. Kistermaker writes:

The privilege of living forever in the presence of God is his gracious gift. At one time in human history, people started building the tower of Babel to reach heaven, but God frustrated their efforts (Gen. 11:1–9). It is the city of God that descends to earth, not human beings who decide to link their city to heaven.[131]

The Tower of Babel demonstrates that God always judges and confounds proud humans when they think they can save themselves, and work their way up to God. Throughout the Holy Scriptures we learn that the only way of salvation is for God to come down with his blessing. Our God is always a God who comes down, as he did in the Incarnation of Jesus, and in the descent of the Holy Spirit upon the Church on the day of Pentecost. This is what grace is all about! Our salvation is made real by the God who comes down all the way to where we are, and by his grace, lifts us up to where he is. That is how the Bride was justified, sanctified, and glorified: all, by God's matchless grace! The grace of the Father in and through Christ, and the Holy Spirit, beautifies the Church, and renews the entire cosmos. In the next chapter we will look at the beauty and the light of the New Jerusalem.

61

Our Future Is Filled with Beauty and Light

Revelation 21:18–21

This passage teaches us very good news: that our future is filled with beauty and light. The last chapters of the Bible are about our future, and the New Jerusalem is our future, if we belong to Christ by faith. The New Jerusalem means the redeemed church in all its fullness, all who were redeemed by Christ from beginning to end. Not any one denomination, but all true believers, from Adam and Eve, Abel and Enoch, through to Abraham and the twelve tribes of Israel, the twelve apostles, down through the early church, the medieval church, the reformation church, and to the present. Every true believer in the world, all of the elect, to the end of the age, when the last saint shall be gathered in and time is no more: all of these are included in the New Jerusalem. It is the entire church in heaven and on earth.

If you are saved through faith in Christ, you are in the New Jerusalem; that is your basic identity. You belong to that more than to anything else, for as Paul says, 'Our citizenship is in heaven' (Phil. 3:20). What good news: that realm that God created you to long for the most, is full of beauty and light!

Let us focus on one aspect about our future, as described in Revelation 21:18–21:

1. The beauty of the New Jerusalem itself, and thereby, the beauty that will be upon us.

The Beauty of the New Jerusalem

One of the most serious problems of our secular culture is that people are under the impression that if God exists, he is harsh and ugly. That utterly false impression may be what lies behind the widespread denial of God, or at least the refusal to take him seriously, even where he is not officially denied. What a misrepresentation of the devil! This passage shows us the sheer beauty and goodness and generosity of the Triune God. His beauty and generosity are conveyed in this passage in terms of the beauty of the New Jerusalem: this wonderful city that represents the entire, redeemed church.

Time and again, we have noted that in order to convey to us eternal truth, which always surpasses our limited human understanding, God speaks to us in terms of earthly things with which we are already familiar in daily life, such as gates of pearl and foundation stones of rare jewels. We may not own any, but we have seen them, and we have some sense of how expensive they would be. We know how carefully they must be looked after, such as insuring them, and keeping them in the safety deposit box at the bank. The references to precious stones in this text is a way of showing us how inexpressively beautiful, and unspeakably costly and worthwhile and lovely, is that place which God has in store for us.

Isaiah 64:4 is quoted in 1 Corinthians 2:9: 'But as it is written, "Eye hath not seen, nor ear heard, neither have entered into the heart of man, the things which God hath prepared for them that love him."' The beauty to come surpasses human understanding, but to convey just a little of this beauty, the holy city is described in terms of the rarest, most expensive, most splendid jewels. If you have ever been to the Tower of London, and to see the Crown Jewels you know they are amazing. You may have been in the Castle of Edinburgh, where you saw what they call 'the Honours of Scotland'. Among them is the oldest crown in the British Isles. The Scottish crown is gorgeous and when light shines on it, its jewels reflect a variety of splendid colors. It is a thing of rare beauty.

Beauty Takes Us Outside of Ourselves

Things of earthly beauty have an alluring quality; calling us, to some degree, out of ourselves. Even atheists cannot help admiring Notre Dame of Paris, or perfectly proportioned Salisbury Cathedral, or the Renaissance splendor of St. Peter's Basilica in Rome. Why are so many unbelievers attracted to these beautiful places? Why does Handel's 'Messiah' and Bach's, 'Jesu, Joy of Man's Desiring' move hearts today just as much as they did when they were composed in the eighteenth century? Or think of something as simple as a purple iris or a red azalea in full bloom in early April. These things allure us and draw us out of ourselves. Why?

The answer is simple. By having created us in the image of the beautiful God, who is the supreme and original beauty, we are made to desire beauty. Beautiful things are given to draw us up to God. The famous twentieth century Swiss Catholic theologian, Hans Urs Von Baltasar, once said that 'Beauty does not allow those who are touched by it to belong to themselves.'[132] I suspect that is a large part of the beauty of marital love. In the joys and duties of shared family life, we are touched by beauty and thus drawn out of ourselves, so that we belong to a higher, purer, transforming fellowship, and ultimately to God himself. Archibald Rutledge was the Poet Laureate of South Carolina for many years in the twentieth century. He lived on his ancestral Hampton plantation, near Georgetown, South Carolina. He restored that plantation almost by hand, after he turned fifty years of age. In his little book, *Life's Extras*, Rutledge tells a story about a man who was sick in the coastal village of McClellanville, SC, in the early 1920s:

> I remember one October night, visiting a friend who was lying very sick. There was a full moon that night, and as I walked down the village street on my sad mission, I felt the silvery beauty of it quiet my heart. The world lay lustrous. There was no scrawny bush, nor ugly clod that was not transfigured in that glory. A little breeze over the brimming salt tide brought aromatic marshy odors. It seemed to me that some power was trying to make the beauty take away my sadness. I found my friend no less aware than I was of the beauty of the night. He could look from his window and see the argent glamour of it all. How it flooded the gleaming tide with celestial lights. How it ran long white lances through the thwarty cedars. How it tinged with soft radiance the locust and mimosas. He felt the breeze too, and delighted in the odors that it brought of the happy world beyond his window. As I sat beside him, a mocking bird began to sing in

the moonlight, chanting divinely. I know the song reached our spirits. On the table by the bed were all the necessities of a sick man, but he had small comfort from them. But the moonlight and the hale fragrances and the wild song of the bird; these brought peace to his heart. Long afterward, he said to me. 'Do you remember that night? I thought it would be my last. But from the time the bird song came through that window, I felt that I would get well. I do not talk much about these things, but I felt that all that beauty and peace were really the love of God. I guess he does not love us just with words. He loves us by giving us every thing we need in every way.' Rutledge adds, 'It must be as he says.'[133]

There is a wonderful hymn in the *Church of Scotland Hymnary* that has these lines on the uplifting power of beauty:

> Now all the heavenly splendour
> Breaks forth in starlight tender
> From myriad worlds unknown;
> And man, the marvel seeing,
> Forgets his selfish being,
> For joy of beauty not his own.[134]

That is what this many-jeweled description of New Jerusalem is all about: 'Joy of beauty not our own', yet it will be our own, by the grace of Christ, to whom we become united by faith, so that we are lifted out of the prison of our selfish being, into the purity and loveliness of the life of the Triune God!

Beautiful Materials in 'the New Jerusalem'

Verse 18 starts with the wall, and the building material that constitutes, what we would call today, 'the infrastructure' of the only lasting city. It is the one that Abraham looked for, 'not made with hands, whose builder and maker is God.'

The material of the wall is said to be jasper. One excellent commentator writes that: 'This jasper probably is a variety of quartz in the various colors of green, yellow, brown, and mottled red. It reflects God's glory through this stone; it is truly a picture of indescribable beauty.'[135]

The infrastructure of the New Jerusalem may be like a crystallization of the glory cloud that was over the tabernacle and then in Solomon's temple. If you could turn that glory cloud into crystal, perhaps it would constitute the architectural materials, as it were, of the New Jerusalem. It is almost like the beauty of Christ's face, or the singing of choirs of angels being captured in translucent stone, reflecting the gorgeous colors of a thousand rainbows, or the stunning symphonic harmony of the holy choirs above.

Material Descriptions Take us Higher

These architectural descriptions point us beyond the merely literal, both as concerns the wall, and the city itself. I have read books that start counting out how many miles long and wide it is, taking these measurements absolutely literally. But that is not the point. We are given an indication of its non-literal aspect in what John says in verse 18, 'the city was pure gold, like unto clear glass.' 'Like unto' is a comparative term in English: one thing is somewhat like a different thing.

Literally, one cannot see through gold. But John uses this comparative term 'like unto.' Gold speaks of beauty, rareness, and highest value; but instead of being necessarily composed of the literal chemical composition of gold, the city is 'like unto' the sort of transparent crystal that one can see through. 'Gold, like crystal' seems to be a way of saying that the lovely attributes of God's own being are what gives this city its shape, solidity, and splendor, at which we shall wish to gaze for all eternity; always new, always beautiful.

Augustine in his *Confessions* spoke of God as being '…beauty so old and so new.'[136] That is what New Jerusalem is like, when the presence of God comes down fully in all the believers who are gathered there in the work of Christ: beauty that is always ancient, and always new.

Then the foundations, we read in verses 19–20, 'were garnished with all manner of precious stones.' This again reminds us of the High Priest's breastplate, where the twelve stones show that each tribe was a jewel to God. In like manner, each believer is precious to God, and was represented in the Old Testament by the Aaronic High Priest, and in the New Testament by Jesus Christ, the Melchizedekan High Priest, who appears in heaven itself. These twelve bejeweled foundations take us back to Isaiah 54:11–12: 'O thou afflicted, tossed with tempest, and not comforted, behold, I will lay thy stones with fair colors, and lay thy foundations with sapphires. And I will make windows of agates, and thy gates of carbuncles, and all thy borders of pleasant stones.' Then he puts much the same thing into human terms in the next verse (Isa. 54:13): 'And all thy children shall be taught of the Lord; and great shall be the peace of thy children.' These twelve types of expensive jewels speak not only of the wealth and distinction of that city, but above all of the sheer glory and shining holiness of God, who builds that city through the merits of his Son's blood. It is as though the beauty of God's own personal holiness is crystallized into the foundations of that supernal city: the final home of all the elect.

The splendid colors captured in paintings by Raphael, Rembrandt, and Rubens are probably pale compared to the rich hues and tones of the infrastructure of that heavenly city to come. The twelve gates (Rev. 21:21) are formed each of one vast pearl; perhaps cameo-like beige or a most delicate tan; rarest mother of pearl. The point of these gates is not for defense, for it needs no defense since all enemies are now shut up in the lake of fire. Rather, the gates are for sheer beauty and over-flowing of enjoyment. God is a God of beauty and of joy. God wants us to enjoy him forever. To fulfill that goal, the heavenly city opens up the beauties, and splendors and the gorgeousness of God, and God says, 'Come in here; I will not be without you. I want you to be a part of this. It is all for you.'

Sometimes, at the close of a day, when we say our evening prayers, and think through the day, we may feel that God has been somewhat hard on us. But we are not to assess God in terms of difficult experiences in our life, for when we see the big picture, we realize that God is full of generosity and forgiving grace and pardoning love. We realize that he is such a beautiful, wonderful being, that he has lavished his kindness upon us in Jesus. He invites us to come and share that endless joy and splendor of the New Jerusalem, where his divine attributes of holiness and loveliness shall be, as it were crystallized, and made personal inside each one of us in a different way. The difficult things that come to us are just ways that our loving God is polishing the jewels into which he is making us, so that we can all the more reflect the beauty of the Lord our God and enter into its fullness. Christ's intercession for us will get us through all the polishings and shapings of earthly experiences to share the more fully in his transforming beauty. Let us seek the grace to praise Him, even before we see the final product of exquisite beauty in all of his people.

62

The Light that Will Fill Our Future

Revelation 21:22–27

Having thought of the beauty of the New Jerusalem in the last chapter, we now conclude Revelation by looking at the light that will fill our future. The New Jerusalem, the redeemed Church above, constitutes our future. This passage says that our future will be filled with the most beautiful light.

Often people say of a fine young man or young woman, going off to college, to their first job, or to their marriage: 'He or she has a bright future ahead'. This text promises that every Christian believer has a very bright future waiting for them; one filled with the most beautiful light, based on the transforming presence of the Triune God.

We notice four points in this passage:

1. The new temple (Rev. 21:22).
2. The new source of light (Rev. 21: 23–5).
3. The wealth of the nations brought into the city (Rev. 21:24–6).
4. The absence of the unsaved (Rev. 21:27).

The New Temple

When we finally get to glory, we shall see an amazing thing: there will be no temple, no cathedral or Basilica, no church building at all. They are not needed, because God himself is the Temple in that place. His holy presence is so immediate throughout all that beautiful realm, that there is no longer any need for buildings, altars, communion tables, or baptismal fonts to represent God's grace and presence. He is literally and directly accessible to every last inhabitant of that wonderful place in glory.

God and the Lamb, who shed his blood to give us access to the holy city, are the fullness of everything appointed on earth for worship: the tabernacle, Solomon's temple, and Christian churches over the ages. These temporary accommodations were not an end in themselves. They were very important here in history, and should be reverenced as such, but they are not the end product. They are only a signpost to something much greater.

The Epistle to the Hebrews explains that the tabernacle and the temple in the Old Testament were given to represent who Jesus Christ is, and how his work is accomplished, in his bringing us immediately to God. All priestly activity was to bring us to God, cleansed and restored. Hence, this priestly work has been fully accomplished, and has borne all its fruits in the glorification of the elect. There is no longer any need for a temple in that heavenly realm because God is immediately there, and through Christ's person and work, we have been fully prepared to dwell before his face. Everything the temple and the church ever stood for is fulfilled better than our minds could ever imagine, by the glorious and gracious presence of God filling that place.

A pale illustration would be the comparison of a photograph of a beloved fiancé, who was in another place, before the marriage, with the actual presence of the loved one, once you are married. In their physical absence, the photograph certainly has some value, but once you get married, the photograph is far less important, because now you have the immediate presence of the loved one.

It is somewhat like that here in verse 22. Temple and Church on earth were a picture, a sort of a beneficent shadow of the love and fellowship we shall have with God himself, when we get to the place he has prepared for us. As Jesus said, 'If I go and prepare a place for you, I will come again, and receive you unto myself; that where I am, there you may be also' (John 14:3).

Heaven Has a Church, but no Building

In that everlasting heavenly realm, we could say that there is a Church, but no building. The whole glorified people of God are there with their Lord, but no building is needed. For instance, in the Church, before the Second Coming, we celebrate the Lord's Supper. It speaks of the death of the Lamb, and of our taking part in his death and in his resurrection. But up there we do not have a communion service, because we have the Lamb himself to which the Holy Communion pointed. We have him in his fullest, most personal presence, so that we no longer need to celebrate a representative meal, for we shall have the reality. It is the same with the baptism, which speaks of our incorporation into the body of Christ by the Holy Spirit, through faith. But now the body into which we are incorporated through faith and the Holy Spirit's working is fully and finally united to her head forevermore, no more to part. So we will not need baptism or the Lord's supper in the New Jerusalem. We will have the reality to which these things were pointing.

In the fullest sense, God and the Lamb are the Temple. Their presence, in the bonds of the Holy Spirit, makes that place full of sacred joy and life.

Another way of looking at it would be to say that the whole city itself, the New Jerusalem, all the redeemed people of God, are also part of the temple. The holy of holies in Solomon's temple (as in 1 Kings 6:20), was structured in the shape of a cube. We have seen that a cube was the most perfect architectural form. John describes the New Jerusalem, or the new Church in the glory realm, as being a cube. The most beautiful shape to the ancient mind. In a sense, all believers by sharing in the body of Christ, help to form that temple, which the Lord fills constantly with his over flowing, thrilling love. Believers in that place are never outside the Lord's blessed, immediate presence and all that it means.

No More Sad Goodbyes!

One of its glorious meanings is never saying goodbye; no more partings, and never shedding a parting tear because of the separation of loved ones. Revelation 3:12 refers to it:

> Him that overcometh, will I make a pillar in the temple of my God; and he shall go no more out: and I will write upon him the name of my God, and the name of the city of my God, which is new Jerusalem, which cometh down out of heaven from my God: and I will write upon him my new name.

The same thing, in a different way, is said in Revelation 7:15 and 17. What a wonderful promise: 'They shall no more go out' (Rev. 3:12). This is a family reunion, and includes the most beautiful communion that you would never want to leave, but you will not have to go out from it! You know how it is even in very happy families, where father goes off to work, leaving wife and children at home. You hate to leave them, but you have to go out; it is part of our earthly duty. But in the New Jerusalem, you will not have to go out and leave them. I have spoken to many young women who have to work, who tell me how hard it is to leave a child in a day care center, sometimes with the child crying. But in many cases, she has to go out to make enough money to pay the rent, buy groceries, and pay the light bill. In the New Jerusalem, you never have to go out. Or think of it when you bury a relative. The family and friends are assembled around the grave; after the service, the coffin is covered with dirt, and then you have to leave their physical remains. No more of that, once we get to our heavenly home.

Believers as God's Temple

The Holy City is part of the Temple, and it includes all the redeemed people of God, from Adam and Eve, down to the last believer at the end of time. All of these are part of the temple. Paul speaks of believers being 'temples of God, and that the Spirit dwells in you' (1 Cor. 3:16). That is one of the reasons we should not abuse our bodies, for our bodies are the temples of the Holy Spirit, who dwells within us. Ephesians 2:21–2 states: 'In whom [Christ] all the building fitly framed together groweth unto an holy temple in the Lord: In whom ye also are builded together for an habitation of God through the Spirit.' So God and the Lamb are the temple, but yet he builds his people into union with their Lord and Savior, making them the dwelling place of God.

The New Source of Light

The creational lights: sun, moon, and stars, that we see in the night time skies, are no longer needed as our luminaries. They have been replaced with the beautiful splendor from the Father's uncreated light and the radiance from Christ's lovely face. C. S. Lewis was right when he said that sun, moon, and stars had an important natural purpose for the human race, but that their major purpose is to point above and beyond themselves to the future, when the Star-maker himself will immediately and beneficently shine upon every believer.

The Beauty of Created Light and Uncreated Light 'God is light, and in him there is no darkness at all'. All the radiance of created luminaries were kindled by God, himself. But once their purpose has been fulfilled, they will be surpassed. He, the uncreated, original light, will no longer have use for them, for he will be shining directly upon us himself. Isaiah 60:1–3 speaks of it prophetically, and it seems to be taken up by John here:

> Arise, shine; for thy light is come, and the glory of the Lord is risen upon thee. For, behold, the darkness shall cover the earth, and gross darkness the people: but the Lord shall arise upon thee, and his glory shall be seen upon thee. And the Gentiles shall come to thy light, and kings to the brightness of thy rising.

Then Isaiah 60:19–20 adds:

> The sun shall be no more thy light by day; neither for brightness shall the moon give light unto thee:

but the Lord shall be unto thee an everlasting light, and thy God thy glory. Thy sun shall no more go down; neither shall thy moon withdraw itself: for the Lord shall be thine everlasting light, and the day of thy mourning shall be ended.

Much as we appreciate various forms of created light that shine upon us, one day the created light will be there no longer. It will not be needed. But it will not be like a blackout in some modern city, where lights, air-conditioning (or heat) are off, machines do not work, and general panic ensues. We shall have an even more beautiful, and utterly serene light, such as we have never glimpsed!

The created light is very beautiful. We think of the colors of the rainbow, from infrared to ultraviolet, through to blues, yellows, greens, purples and so on. We are told that black is the absence of color, and that white is the pallet of all the colors together. You can imagine every color, put them, together and mix them up, and it turns out white. Can you imagine how gorgeous must be the uncreated light of God? It is infinitely more gorgeous than any earthly color, whether in nature or art. All of this stunning beauty, coming from the splendor of the nature of the Triune God, shall be constantly shining upon us.

The Wealth of the Nations Brought in Verse 24 indicates that all the best results of the created order and of world history shall be brought with much joy and honor into the New Jerusalem. What do you think that would that be?

Redemption Does not Negate Creation and Culture
Jean-Marc Berthoud, has suggested that what 'the kings of the earth will bring into the holy City' will be the lovely outcome in human life of the different tribal, ethnic, and national cultures as these have been used to shaped and beautify their people, and as these are caught up in the redemptive purposes of God, which also fulfill his original creational purposes. When you become saved, you do not properly split with your culture (except those aspects of it which are directly sinful). The providence of God uses the ethnic culture you are in to shape you in certain directions for his kingdom.

In other words, the greatest wealth of the nations is the character of its people. Daniel 12 promises that the character of these people, especially the soul-winners among them, once they belong to the Lord, are being prepared by God to shine as the stars of the firmament, forever and ever. Mankind is the crown of created order. Since we are made in God's image, we reflect something of God in our humanity. God is the chief treasure of the universe: the Father, the Son and the Holy Spirit, and people, who are created in his image, are the chief ornament of everything that he made. Out of all the works of his hands, the Lord is most delighted with humanity, whom he sent his Son to redeem.

Verse 26 speaks of 'the glory and honor of the nations', and what could that be but the beautiful, multifaceted character of its people? Notice that 'nations' is in the plural. This indicates that there is diversity amongst the nations. There are differences. Each nation, people-group, tribe, or subculture of a nation, represents some valuable gift of God, differently from the others.

The Creator-Redeemer's Delight in Differences
The various tribes and people have, over thousands of years, taken what God gave them by heredity and environment, and developed it in diverse ways, in their own moral and character formation; especially the ones who come to the Lord. One ethnic group represents some beautiful trait that another does not have in exactly the

same way, but that other one shows forth some virtue that is less prominent in the first tribe. It is like the many colors of the rainbow reflecting differing hues of beauty from the cut glass prism that hangs under a grand chandelier. It takes all of these tribes and tongues, peoples and nations throughout history with all their uniqueness and differences, all of them together to show the multi-faceted beauty of God, and the final fruit of his gracious benefits in the history of creation and redemption from beginning to end.

When I saw the movie, *God and Generals*, I thought about the beauty of character of some of the Southern Christian people, 150 years ago, such as General Stonewall Jackson and his wife, Mary Anna Morrison from Charlotte. That motion picture showed the deep Biblical faith, courage, hospitality, kindness, courtesy, and willingness to die for principle, of such Southern folk. That was the most beautiful thing that southern culture, at its best, has produced since Jamestown was founded in 1607. Yes, there have been profoundly negative and sinful sides of Southern culture, but these are not to the point at present, although a price is still being paid for them today.

Verse 26 says that the best product of any culture: northern, southern, western, or eastern, will endure forever. It will be brought into the eternal city of God to glorify him in its own way. Once God's people are in heaven, who won what war in world history will be unimportant. The unique beauty of Christ-like character will be brought into the lasting City by the ransomed souls from every tribe and culture: Atlantic, Pacific, Mediterranean, Caribbean, and all the others. The beauty of Christ-like character they bring into the gates of that city will constitute much of its 'glory and honor.'

We will know then that defeat, suffering, disappointment, pain, and poverty were only invisible tools to shape our own people ever more deeply into the holiness of Christ, who is the delight of the Father's heart. Often as I pass by some of the country graveyards where a number of our ancestors have been buried for hundreds of years, I am thinking: we have not really lost them, nor their faith, nor their character, nor their truest culture. The wealth of their faith, and the glory of Holy Spirit-induced character in their lives one glad day will be paraded through the gates of that city to the honor of God and the Lamb. It was the Lamb who gave them everything they ever had that was worth having. Every group of saved ancestors and their descendants will march through the holy Gates to the thrill of all the other extended families, tribes, and nations. Each one will be praising God for all the others.

God's Universal Love to Every Tribe and Tongue
Every different ethnic group in the world is equally precious to God. His love is absolutely universal: North, South, East, and West, but he ordained the differences, and enjoys them. These differences of the various nations reflect something of his own beauty and wonder; differences that will shine forth most splendidly 'when we all get to heaven'. Every people-group in the world—Han and Chiang people in China; numerous tribes, Nilotic, Bantu, and many others in Africa; descendants in South America of Aztec, Mayas and Incas; Arabs and Copts in Egypt; Sephardic and Askenazic Jews—all who have by divine grace, come to love Jesus, as a group will bring something different from their life experiences in their own cultures, as gifts of honor into that holy city.

Think of what has happened in missions in the twentieth century. How much beauty is going to come out of Africa, China, and Russia, where so many have willingly laid down their lives over the last hundred years, and been killed for their faith and love of Christ. I long to see these beautiful saints from Uganda, Rwanda, Sudan and various parts of China: every tribe and tongue, 'when the saints go marching in' to that eternal city.

An Illustration from Ukraine

Take Ukraine, which I have often visited to teach ministers and ministerial students, as an example. In the Early Middle Ages, Christian missionaries brought the faith to Scythian tribes in what is now Ukraine. Tens of thousands were converted in a short time. Great churches that still stand and many monasteries were built all over Ukraine. They had one particularly godly ruler, Jaroslav the Wise, who built St. Sophia Cathedral that still stands in Kiev. He tried to make Christian education available as widely as he could free of charge. He tithed every penny he got from the wealthy Ukrainian lands, and used part of it to build Christian schools. His marble tomb can still be seen in the Cathedral of St. Sophia.

But after the Communist Revolution in 1917, the Ukrainian and Russian people were under the cross, under a death sentence from 1917 to 1991, like the seventy years of Babylonian captivity of the Jews. But now, the persecuted church of Eastern Europe is beginning to come out from under the dirt. One day, at the end of time, the saints of God as a whole redeemed nation will bring their Christ-like characters, as trophies of honor and glory into the heavenly Jerusalem. What will those glories look like, when the saints from the Ukraine go marching into the New Jerusalem? Will it include especially beautiful singing and poetry, because the Ukrainians are wonderful singers, musicians and poets to this day? Will the marks of seventy plus years of crucifixion as a church for the love of Christ under communism be turned into insignia of splendid beauty in their resurrected bodies and ransomed spirits?

The glories that shall be brought into heaven by the saints of God from the Ukraine will be better and brighter than anything we can now imagine. But we will be there to see it, and we can begin to praise God for it even now. One glad day, the saints will go marching in, and what glory and honor they will bring to the feet of Jesus, who so greatly deserves it. What an honor now, that you and I can either go, or pray and give, to make that day the greatest possible pleasure for the Lord Jesus Christ who gave us his all.

THE UNSAVED ARE OUTSIDE THE CITY

That glorious city is the dwelling place of life, joy, and everything worth having, throughout the endless ages. But this text does not hide the fact that some will forever remain outside it. Why would John mention the fact that there will be some outside the holy city, in the middle of a huge passage on its happy characteristics? Chapters 21 and 22 are all about the beauty of the future, so why would he say something about the ones that we have already been clearly told are outside, in the lake of fire? Why would that be mentioned here in the midst of this joy?

Make the right decision while you still have time
Here is the reason. This Apocalypse, this Book of Revelation, is written to those who are still alive on planet earth. It is written for us in this world. There is still time to repent and believe in Jesus. Exercising faith in Jesus is the only way to get into that city. To live and die rejecting this Savior, means that we will be forever outside. To turn to him in repentance, and to trust him as our salvation, means that we will be forever inside, never having to go out anymore.

63

Forward to the New Garden of Eden
Revelation 22:1–5

Some people know their ancestry well. They can name their ancestors, without missing a generation, for 250 or 300 years. Being able to do that, we may feel a certain connection with our own people, who have gone before. It adds a certain quality and atmosphere to our lives, to be so deeply rooted in the past. But what if we could take the family line all the way back to the beginning of time, to the original couple and their children? What were our people really like? Genesis 1–3 tells us, and Revelation 22 is, in many ways, an explication of Genesis 1–3.

The true history of the human race indicates that first our parents were originally placed in a most beautiful, fragrant garden: a perfect place, where God himself regularly came down to visit them—the Garden of Eden. But when Adam and Eve sinned, they were chased out of that garden, out of that glorious environment for which all of us are made. Angels with flaming swords kept them from going back in to that perfect place, so they could not have access to the tree of life.

Universal Homesickness

There is a sense in which the human race has been homesick ever since we were kicked out of Eden. Much of the world's greatest literature somehow reflects this sense of homelessness and wandering. Classical pagan literature like Homer's *Odyssey* or Virgil's *Aeneid*; or in modern times, the trilogy by Christian writer, J. R. R. Tolkien, *Lord of the Rings*; the early twentieth century novel by Thomas Wolf, *You Can't Go Home Again*; or the novel of Italian soldiers during World War II by Eugenio Corti, *The Red Horse*—all of them convey in different ways this epic sense of homelessness and a deep human sentiment of longing for home.

We were created to be happiest in a wonderful garden, where the Lord himself, our Maker, is immediately present, and we can talk to him in the most friendly way. That is why people cannot be satisfied with what money can buy or with human culture or political power; we can never be fully satisfied, till God opens our way to a place far better than that garden. Scripture says that 'God has set eternity in their hearts'. Something in your heart, almost like a loadstone, draws you up towards eternity, so that nothing less can satisfy.

Old Eden and New Eden

The bad news is that we cannot go back to the old Garden of Eden. Sin brought the curse of separation from God, judgment, and death. It is the source of the problems of the human race. Sin put us out of the place of life and beauty. But the good news is this: a Paradise-like garden, a New Eden, a New Jerusalem, something even better than the old, is waiting to receive every one of us who believes. That is where all believers are going. The reality, for which we were originally created, for which we have always longed, will at last be ours, by virtue of the redeeming work of the Agent of Creation, the Redeemer of the Cosmos: the Father's eternal Son, our Lord Jesus Christ. This beautiful 'New Eden' is described here in pictorial images that help us to get hold of this eternal reality, by means of temporal pictures.

We look at three wonderful realities in that new Garden of Eden or New Jerusalem:

1. The river and the trees (Rev. 22:1–2).
2. The presence of God there (Rev. 22:3).
3. The joy of the saints who are there (Rev. 22:3b–5).

THE RIVER AND THE TREES

In the Garden of Eden springs burst out of the ground to form a river, which divided into four branches and flowed out to water the earth. One of those branches was the River Euphrates, which still flows into Iraq. You will read about it in Genesis 2:10–14. In Revelation 22, the holy angel showed John the river of the water of life, sparkling like crystal. I wonder if this holy angel who showed the heavenly river to John could have been the same one who had, long before, guarded with his flaming sword, the entrance to the Garden of Eden, thereby denying Adam and Eve, and their children, any return to Paradise? Whether or not it was the same one, John tells us that the holy angel he met in the glory realm, took him, and said: now look at this 'the river of the water of life, sparking, like crystal' (Rev. 22:1). This crystal stream did not come from the ground as it did in the old Eden, but 'from the throne of God and of the Lamb.'

In Ezekiel 47, the rivers of living waters flowed out from under the temple door, healing the whole world. But in the New Jerusalem, or New Eden, there is no temple. God is immediately present. The Living God sends out waters of life, a beneficent stream of everything worth having that makes life life, and makes us purified, satisfied and fruitful. It flows out from the presence of God, who is supreme beauty and goodness.

The Living God is the only source of eternal life, as Jesus tells us: 'I am come that they might have life, and have it more abundantly' (John 10:10). Only God, the eternal One, can give you eternal life. The woman Jesus met at the well went back into Samaria and became a soul-winner, who brought other people to meet Jesus (John 4:28–30). Already the living water was flowing from this woman, who had been involved in self-destructive behavior. God forgave her and filled her with his living water, which is just a little stream of what comes out from the throne in the realm of glory and gladness.

John was told earlier in Revelation 7:17 that because 'the Lamb is in the midst of the throne, he shall feed them, and shall lead them to fountains of living water.' He shepherds all of his people, for all eternity. That is why Psalm 23 is so universally beloved. It speaks of our cups 'running over'. Imagine having the most refreshing water—better than the finest, most expensive vintage wine—tenderly, handed to you by Jesus himself.

Trees of Life

On each side of this 'crystal, shining river' (to quote an old gospel hymn) are the most beautiful trees of life. In the original Eden, there was only one tree of life, and it was guarded after the fall by the cherubim with flaming swords. But in the

New Eden, there are forests of trees of life on both sides of that river. This illustrates the principle in Romans 5:20, that 'where sin abounded, there did grace much more abound'. The generosity of God is hard for us to take in. And far from being kept back with a flaming sword from these trees of life in heaven, all the inhabitants of the New Eden, are invited to partake (Rev. 22:14).

The trees bear twelve different luscious fruits, depending on the month (v. 2). There is a variety of interesting delectability in the fruit. That raises a question. In eternity, time does not have its march as it does here, yet John speaks of twelve months with various fruits each year. There are no years in heaven, but the Holy Spirit through John uses time measurement that we experience, to point us to a higher reality that does not deny the created order, but fulfills it. John and the angel use this sense of time in the production of fruit, along with the variety that we will enjoy, to help us grasp the substantial joys to come, including delicious fruit. In eternity the passing of time is no more—no decay, aging, or breaking down—yet there is still great variety and movement, with wonderful things to attract our purified senses.

In Western intellectual culture, we get many of our ideas of eternity from the ancient Greeks, some of which came close to thinking of heaven as frozen in ice, with no movement—more like an immobile marble statue than a living organism. Nothing could be further from the truth. Heaven is full of changing variety. When we get to heaven, we will never have been so alive as we are then. It is a vital place. Heaven is in no sense static or boring, frozen or chiselled. It is the liveliest place you could ever be and it gets better all the time.

Why 'Leaves for Healing'?

The end of verse 2 raises another very interesting question when it says 'the leaves of the trees are for the healing of the nations'. But why does anybody need healing in heaven? Verse 3 clearly states that 'there shall be no more curse.' When the curse is gone, as it is for all who get to heaven through faith in Jesus, there is no more sickness, break down, or death. They are all aspects of the curse that came on our first parents, which are gone once we are in glory. So what does this 'healing of the nations' mean? Why speak of healing a well person? What could this 'healing' have meant?

It is a way of saying that everyone in heaven shall always enjoy the fullness of eternal life, without spiritual or physical break down ever casting its shadow upon them. The living waters and delicious fruits of the trees are health-sustaining and joy-giving. The freshness of the glory you experience once you walk into that happy land, remains fresh, new, and always alluring!

Some years ago, we visited the fountain in St Augustine, Florida, which Ponce De Leon had hoped would be 'the fountain of youth'. He came from Spain to find it, hoping that if he drank its waters, his youth would be perpetually restored. Of course, Ponce De Leon, aged and died. Yet I wonder if the story that came from the ancient Indians may not have been a pale reflection of the higher truth that there is a river of life in the realm of glory, of which we shall one day drink. Our wholeness will always be sustained and increased. It is no doubt health giving. Happy Place!

'Tree of Life' and 'Tree of Death'

Some of the old church fathers, one of them Irenaeus of Lyon, said that the tree of life in Eden pointed to the tree on Calvary, to the old-rugged cross, on which the Son of God shed his blood to remove the curse against us. The cross of death outside the old Jerusalem makes possible for us access to the trees of life in the New Jerusalem. What a wonderful exchange! What generosity!

How could anybody turn their back on such a generous God with his arms wide open to them?

The Presence of God

Verse 3 shows us the chief benefit of the New Eden: 'The throne of the father and the Lamb' are in the midst of that new garden. There is not a temple there, but the whole environment is a temple, consisting of God and his people, who serve him day and night in his temple (Rev. 7:15). 'And that he that sitteth on the throne shall dwell among them.' God is there. That is what makes heaven heaven. And although there are mysteries about it, more than anything else, hell is ultimate separation from God, while heaven is the immediate presence of God. That is the basic difference. In Psalm 16:11, David speaks of the presence of God as what makes heaven heaven, 'In thy presence is fullness of joy. At thy right hand there are pleasures forevermore.' God makes heaven heaven, for he is there.

An elderly cousin once said to me that if I and the family could be present at a particular homecoming at the old church in her home town, 'it would be heavenly'—a wonderful expression. The hardest thing we have to face in our earthly lives is the death of our loved ones. Even when they move away alive, it is not always easy. But what a happy gathering around the throne: all of our redeemed loved ones are there, never more to be separated, torn apart, or to say good bye. The joy of that grandest of all family reunions will never fade, for God, who is an ocean of gladness continually flows over his people. He keeps them together in ever new and happy ways.

The Joy of the Saints

Verses 3b–5 speak of the joy of the saints in the New Eden. It mentions five intriguing details:

1. His servants shall serve Him.
2. His Name shall be on their foreheads.
3. They shall see his face.
4. They shall be bathed in the divine light.
5. They shall reign forever and ever.

'His Servants Shall Serve Him'

The first thing verse 3 tells us about the saints in the New Eden is that 'God's servants shall serve Him.' Did you know that there is work in heaven? We speak about heavenly rest, but there is also work in heaven, because 'his servants shall serve him'. Keep this in mind: there was work before the curse fell on our first parents. What a delightful task it must have been for Adam to use his mind and voice to name the marvelous animals one by one. Adam and Eve must have had great pleasure trimming the Garden, making it just right, and articulating the praises of the rest of the created order over which God had given them dominion.

I wonder if when the Lord walked in the Garden in the cool of the day, and talked to Adam and Eve, whether our first parents ran up to the Holy Presence with thrilling descriptions of how beautiful were the animals, trees, and flowers which he had created? I wonder if they praised God for the movement of the silver fish in the waters, for the stately march of the lions and leopards in the forest, for the rainbow colors of the shrubs, flowers, and trees, and for the blue and aquamarine of the waters? It was all pleasure to speak to God about what a superb job he had done in making all this. It makes us think of some of the beautiful nature songs in the Psalms (65:9):

> Thou visitest the earth, and waterest it: thou greatly enrichest it with the river of God, which is full of water: thou preparest them parched corn, when thou hast so provided for it.

Our Work in Heaven Is no Curse. Yes, the curse made work tiresome and frustrating, but now that the curse is gone, all tiresomeness and frustration is forever taken away from work. We can be creative, and accomplish things without being worn out and frustrated. The saints are called 'his servants.' Often in the Old Testament, the prophets are called 'his servants'. That was an honor; it meant they had immediate access to the King of King, and Lord of Lords. God himself talks to these prophets, his servants, and lets them in on what he is doing and what the future means, and sends them out to tell others. They had immediate access to him who is 'the Word'. He talked to them, and they talked to him. Moses once said: 'Would that all the Lord's people were prophets!' (Num. 11:29). Now in the glory, they all are. We shall talk daily to God. He will tell us new things to say, to do, and to sing. Perhaps everyone will be a composer of music and scores. What hymns of praise shall rise from those who could never carry a note on earth. And each song will be different and will add to the united, harmonious chorus above.

'Rule over Ten Cities.' How will we serve God in other ways? We are only given a shadowy foretaste of what this service to God may be. Jesus said those who are faithful on earth will be told at the end of time 'Be thou ruler over ten cities… be thou ruler over five cities' (Luke 19:17–18). What you do on earth helps prepare you for the responsibilities of creating beautiful things in the life to come. Yet, why does God need anybody to rule over five cities or ten cities? Does he not have infinite power? Could not God rule without our help, even in our glorified state? Of course, God could do it, but that is to misunderstand who God is, for since our creation, he has chosen to involve us in his life and work.

Some people use God's infinite power as an excuse not to pray. Since he is in charge of all things, why pray? But that pretext for not praying indicates a serious misunderstanding of God. It is his immense pleasure to involve his humble creatures in what he wants accomplished, both during this earthly life and in the brighter life to which we are going.

'His Name Shall Be on Their Foreheads'
In verse 4, we are told two more wonderful truths about the saints in the New Eden: 'His name shall be on their foreheads,' and 'They shall see his face'. These expressions go back, to Moses and Aaron.[137] Aaron, the first Jewish High Priest, wore a priestly crown, with the name of the Lord inscribed on its front, when he went into the Holy Place, and as he came out to bless the people. Moses came down from Mount Sinai, after he had received the Ten Commandments, with the glory of God literally shining from the skin of his face. It was so bright, that the people were terrified, and asked him to put on a veil, for they could not take God's Holy light shining directly upon them.

'They Shall See His Face'
In 1 Corinthians 3:18, Paul speaks of Moses coming down from the mountain, with the glory of God on his face, and applies it to all the people of God in Christ: 'But we all, with open [unveiled] face, beholding as in a glass the glory of the Lord, are changed unto the same image from glory to glory, even as by the Spirit of the Lord.' Elsewhere, the apostle John tells us that when we see Jesus, 'We shall be like him, for we shall see him as he is' (1 John 3:2). Then the glory of God will fill us and shine out from us, probably in different ways for each one of us, through all eternity. The gospel hymn asks:

> Face to face with Christ my Saviour,
> Face to face what will it be?
> When with rapture I behold him,
> Jesus Christ who died for me!

All this indicates that we have the glory of God shining from us and his name upon our foreheads. When we get to heaven, it is exactly where we ought to be. It is what we were made for. We are truly members of the Lord's family by his marvelous grace, and by that grace, we have every right to be in that place. It is where we belong. This world is not our home. Heaven is where we will finally be at home. In the spring of 1969, I first met some of our distant Kelly cousins in the Isle of Skye. One of the things they said was, 'You look like us; you think like us'. It is going to be like that for all ransomed believers in the highest heavens. We shall reflect the beauty of Jesus and know that we were made for this place. No more wandering, no more homesickness. Home at last!

Bathed in the Divine Light
The saints will forever bathe in the luxurious, splendid light of the presence of the Triune God (v. 5). Much of our earthly pilgrimage involved darkness, finally leading us through 'the valley of the shadow of death'. You cannot live this earthly life, even as the most consecrated Christian, without passing through times of painful darkness. It is impossible. Believers across the world, go through tragedies on a frequent basis. Earthly life, even for the best Christians, has many dark valleys. But in that place every dark cloud is forever removed. As a hymn says: 'There'll be no dark valley when Jesus comes, to gather his loved ones home!'

This verse draws on Isaiah 60:1–3: 'Arise, shine; for thy light is come, and the glory of the Lord is risen upon thee. For, behold, the darkness shall cover the earth, and gross darkness the people: but the Lord shall arise upon thee, and his glory shall be seen upon thee. And the Gentiles shall come to thy light, and kings to the brightness of thy rising.' This glorious shining is further reflected in the song of the father of John the Baptist, Zacharias, who sings after John is born, pointing to the Christ, whom his son is to herald: 'Blessed be the Lord God of Israel; for he hath visited and redeemed his people...Through the tender mercy of our God; whereby the dayspring from on high hath visited us. To give light to them that sit in the darkness and in the shadow of death, to guide our feet into the way of peace' (Luke 1:68, 78–9). We are not out of the dark valley yet, but Jesus has come to give us light in these dark valleys. When we have to go through them, he will guide us to the way of peace, into the place where there are no dark valleys and all is beautiful light.

'They Shall Reign Forever and Ever'
The last thing said about the saints in the New Eden is that they 'shall reign forever and ever' (v. 5). Adam and Eve reigned awhile, but they soon lost their jobs, having given in to the temptations of Satan. But now the wicked tempter is forever shut up in the lake of fire. He can never bother anyone in heaven. In the glory land, we shall be protected and liberated, to serve the one who loves us most, never to disappoint him, throughout endless ages. Think of serving that kind of God. He is so generous that when you give him something, he insists on giving you back a great deal more. To serve such a beautiful, glorious God is to reign with him in always new creative splendor. Lord, hasten the day!

64

The Last Thing Jesus Said Before He Comes Back

Revelation 22:6–17

From verse 6 to the end of chapter 22, we sense a different atmosphere from all that preceded. In this last section, the risen Lord Jesus Christ, for the most part (except for verses 6b–7, 20), is not portraying scenes in the future. All of that is nearly finished. He has said all he had to say. In these verses, Jesus is putting a question to us, as though we do not need any more information about the future and about what history means now. Here is the question: 'What are you going to do with what I have already told you?' That is how the Son of God concludes the Holy Bible: he puts this momentous question to us.

From Revelation 1:1 to 22:5, Christ has stretched out a vast canvas for our eyes. On it he has given us a basic picture of world events between his first and his last coming. Through John and the holy angels, Christ has portrayed scenes past, present and still future. But from verse 6, instead of adding new events to the ones already told us, Christ summarizes the most important message we can hear between the time he is speaking to John on the Isle of Patmos, and the final hour when the Lord returns in great power and glory. He tells us the most important thing we need to hear: 'Listen to my word; obey what I have said, for all your present happiness and the eternal destiny of your soul and resurrected body will directly depend on what you do with my final word.' In effect, Jesus is saying that he has nothing more to add; nothing more to say to any individual soul beyond this written word that concludes Revelation.

Let us take up three points out of these verses:

1. The final, ultimate authority of the Word of God written (Rev. 22:6).
2. The open nature of this Word (Rev. 22:10).
3. Blessings and warnings of this Word (Rev. 22:7–17).

The Final Authority of the Word of God Written

All that God has given us by divine revelation begins in Genesis and concludes in Revelation. Everything the Lord says is going to come to pass without fail, without slowness, exactly and infallibly just as God pronounced it. These are 'Faithful and true' sayings (v. 6).

Revelation Is not Like Humanistic Relativism

This is the precise opposite of the humanistic relativism in our Western culture. At bottom, everything is just a human opinion, about which no one can be certain. On that basis, no one can tell what is going to happen in the future. Many intellectuals argue that if anyone claims to grasp an absolute truth, they are arrogant, judgmental, and probably dangerous to the society around them, who may not agree with their position.

To say the least, that is how Revelation is written. On the contrary, it says, these are 'true and faithful sayings.' This written message is absolute truth: it is going to come to pass and no man, nor demonic power can prevent it. You may not agree with it, but that will not slow the feet that God sends down the corridor of history. What we are told of the victory of Christ and the defeat of Satan up to this point in Revelation, is just as certain and definite as to its outcome as was the original creation of this world in six days. The original creation happened in God's time, and the consummation of the new creation is destined to happen in God's time. Nothing can stop it.

Meaning of 'Things Which Must Shortly Be Done'
Jesus uses the significant phrase 'the things which must shortly be done' (v. 6b). He is predicting certain things in Revelation that he said would 'happen shortly', which seems to indicate their occurrence is in terms of John's lifetime and those in the seven churches of Asia. In other words, they would come to pass during the lifetime of the generation of people alive when this letter was written. In the early chapters of this volume, we looked at some reasons why it may well be that Revelation could have been written as early as AD 66 or 67, possibly three or four years before the disastrous destruction of Jerusalem and the scattering of the Jews in AD 70. If that early dating of the composition of Revelation is correct (and it is challenged by many substantial scholars), much that Christ warned about through John, as coming 'shortly', may have had its primary reference to the judgment through the Roman armies upon the Jewish State. In that way, the Christian church was confirmed as the instrument through which God would reach the lost, and save the world.

Even with the early date, there is a lasting principle. If we hold that the main reference of the term 'come shortly' means the Lord's coming in AD 70 in judgment upon the old Jewish Church or State, it is also a picture of his last and final coming at the end of time to judge the entire world. Although that last and final coming is a secret, known only to God, it is just as fixed as the time he was be born of the Virgin Mary. The year, the month, the day, the hour, and the split second was fixed before the world was created and time began to run its course.

Predetermined Events and Scepticism
The victorious coming of the Lord is shown to have been long ago precisely determined, in that it was prophesized very early in the Old Testament by Enoch, the seventh from Adam, who said, 'Behold the Lord cometh with ten thousands of his saints to execute judgment upon all...' (Jude 14–15). Revelation 13:8 speaks of Christ as 'the lamb slain before the foundation of the world'. The time that Christ would be crucified outside the city walls of Jerusalem was predetermined; the time Jerusalem would be destroyed, in AD 70 was predetermined, and the time he shall finally return to usher in the great judgment day and the renewal of the entire universe, is also predetermined.

It is not that this clear scriptural teaching concerning predetermined events in the history of redemption is generally acceptable, even in many churches. Peter speaks of widespread unbelief concerning the definite return of the Lord: 'There shall come some in the last days, scoffers, walking after their own lusts, and saying, "Where is the promise of his coming?" For since the fathers fell asleep, all things continue as they were from the beginning of the creation' (2 Pet. 3:3–4).

In other words, there will be people who will argue that because it has been so long since Christ walked on earth, and in all that time he has not come back to conclude history, so history will always go on as it is today. Christ will never literally come back. They laughed at Noah who preached for a hundred years that the flood was coming, says Peter, but one day, the scoffers were no longer laughing. The heavens opened and the waters began to rise, so that everybody who was not in the ark was drowned (2 Pet. 3:6). God had instructed Noah to announce the coming flood, and in spite of humanity's incredulity, at a set time, God did it. Similarly, there is coming a day when the entire world will be judged and overwhelmed, not by water, but by fire. That day is just as certain as the day of creation. Many people do not accept it; some make fun of it, but that is not going to slow down the ticking of the clock, nor the draining of the sands in the hourglass. Every day, every moment, it is coming closer and closer. It is going to happen precisely as it was foretold: no shifting, no evasion, no negotiation, no changing of plans. Jesus said in Matthew 5:17, 'Heaven and earth shall pass away, but my word shall not pass away.' It would be easier for the whole universe to evaporate, than for one jot or tittle, the smallest letter or syllable, of God's holy Word not to be completely, precisely, and definitively fulfilled. That is what the risen Lord reminds us of here, when he calls 'These sayings' 'faithful and true'.

What Revelation predicts is not brilliant human guess-work. It is not the product of human philosophy, or even religion. It is rather, a matter of God revealing to us what is true; the angel 'shows his servants the things which must shortly be done' (Rev. 22:6).

Christ's Authority to Do What He Predicted

Jesus is saying that all he has told his church is going to happen because it directly depends upon God's trustworthiness and omnipotent power to bring it about. This same Jesus says in the Great Commission, 'All power is given unto me in heaven and in earth' (Matt. 28:18). Even now Christ 'is holding all things together' in the entire cosmos (Col. 2:17), and John 1:3 shows that he was the agent of its creation. Jesus has 'the keys of hell and of death' (Rev. 1:18). Therefore, Christ has the infinite, unlimited power to dispose of every fact, every element, every force, and every atom in the universe, so as to carry out to the last detail, what his Word says is going to come to pass.

This authority to carry out all things that he ever announced, is confirmed in Revelation 22:13: 'I am Alpha and Omega, the beginning and the end, the first and the last.' 'I was there; I was the agent of creation, and I will be there at the end to conclude it, just as I have told you.' Nothing is so important as my submitting to what Jesus says here willingly, from my whole heart, while I still have time, for it will all certainly come to pass.

The Open Nature of this Word

What the risen Lord says in verse 10 starkly contrasts with the instructions given to the prophet Daniel, 'But thou, O Daniel, shut up the words, and seal the book, even to the time of the end; many shall run to and fro, and knowledge shall be increased' (Dan. 12:4). Daniel was told to seal much of what God had showed him about the end of the age. But now that the Messiah has come in the flesh, and completed his atoning sacrifice, it is different. Jesus says to John 'And he saith unto me, "Seal not the sayings of the prophecy of this book: for the time is at hand."' (Rev. 22:10).

Why did God, through the angel, tell Daniel to seal the prophecy? And then why did God tell John not to seal it, but to open it up? The answer is given clearly in verse 10: 'the things that must shortly be done'. In the time of Daniel, he is given seventy weeks, that is seventy years times seven—490 years, between Daniel and the appearance of Messiah on earth. God says something like, 'I am not going to make clear many facts about the conclusion of the Messiah's work, until he comes to earth, so as to seal it.'

But now Jesus, the present Messiah, says, 'I have fulfilled the atoning work; I have fulfilled the resurrection work, and now I am getting ready to do something very great that will change the entire cosmos.' The first major thing after his resurrection and ascension, would be that the Jewish state would be broken down, and the Christian church would be established in its world mission. Jesus says, 'I am getting ready to do that, so unseal it, explain ahead of time what I am going to do'. Hence, now in Revelation, the prophecy is opened; it is unsealed for all to see, so that they can take the only proper actions of faith and repentance.

BLESSINGS AND WARNINGS OF REVELATION
In this concluding section of Revelation, and of the whole Bible, God through his Son gives us the promise of blessings, and also expresses severe warnings. The Lord is showing how extremely important it is for us to take absolutely seriously this last portion of the written Word of God. Basically the message to the human race is this: 'Get ready, you cannot avoid what is coming! You have everything to win, or you have everything to lose. Get ready now, while your mind is still working, while I have still graciously given you some time.' To help us get ready, the glorious Christ issues two kinds of last words: warnings and then promised blessings.

Verses 11–12 and 15 contain his warnings: 'He that is unjust or unrighteous, let him be unjust, let him be unjust still: and he that is filthy, let him be filthy still...For without are dogs, and sorcerers, and whoremongers, and murderers, and idolaters, and whosoever loveth and maketh a lie.' We are being warned against the refusal to repent of our sins, which is the greatest disaster that can ever occur for any human being. The worst thing that could happen to you is not to get cancer or to lose your job. These things are difficult, but for God's people, there is always something much better on the other side of such losses. From God's point of view, the only final disaster is refusal to repent of one's sins and believe in Jesus. That is the only real tragedy. The French intellectual, Charles Peguy (an atheist, who became a Christian before World War I), once said that 'the only tragedy is not to be a saint'. Every other lesser tragedy can be used to make us more like Jesus Christ, to get us ready for heaven, to make us a blessing, even when it is painful and hurts. From this perspective, all reversals can have a positive purpose. But here is one that does not: to refuse to repent of my sins, and believe the gospel.

Jesus talks about this when he warns Chorazin and Bethsaida, for having rejected him and his gracious offers (Matt. 11:20–23). On the last day, says Jesus, it is going to be much harder on the two cities where I preached, than it will be for Sodom and Gomorra, for they did not have as much light as was offered to you. Jesus means that the worst thing that can happen to a culture is to hear the gospel, and then refuse to repent and accept the kindly offers of the Lord. Jesus says much the same in the next chapter (Matt. 12:41–2):

> The men of Nineveh [a violent, pagan city] shall rise in judgment with this generation, and shall condemn it; because they repented at the preaching of Jonas; and, behold, a greater than Jonas is here. The queen of the south (that is the Queen of Sheba, or maybe Ethiopia) shall rise up in the judgment with this generation [that is, the crowd that heard Jesus preach], and shall condemn it: for she came from the uttermost parts of the earth to hear the wisdom of Solomon; and, behold, a greater than Solomon is here.

True Faith Always Involves Repentance
True faith in Christ always involves repentance, for it enthrones him as Lord of life, which always entails massive changes, and profoundest repentance. 'That if thou shalt confess with thy mouth the Lord Jesus, and shalt believe in thine heart God has raised him from the dead, thou shalt be saved' (Rom. 10:9). To believe that Jesus is Lord, means I am no longer my own Lord: everything that I am, everything that I have now belongs to God. I recognize that he gave it, and therefore, of right, he should control it. Such rethinking involves repentance, for not having willingly given him our hearts previously, and for having misused his gifts. An old Scottish preacher in the nineteenth century, Colquhoun, used to say that 'the eye of faith always drops tears of repentance'. He also said the tears of repentance always come from an eye of hope and faith. Jesus teaches us that this is what truly matters about our future. The real problem about getting to heaven is not finally our sins, but our refusal to repent of those sins.

Simon Peter denied Jesus, but after the cock crowed the third time, he went out broken-hearted for his betrayal of his Lord, and wept bitterly (Luke 22:62). He repented. After Jesus' resurrection, he met again with Peter, and fully restored him (see John 21). On the contrary, Judas Iscariot felt keen remorse for having betrayed Jesus, but instead of repenting and asking the Lord to forgive him, he took matters into his own hands, and hanged himself.

The Risen Christ Gives the Gift of Repentance
The problem for many people is that they feel that they do not know how to repent, and that they will never be able to do so. Thus, they give up the quest to be put in the right with God through his Son. If that is the case with you, take hold of Acts 5:31, where the apostle says: 'Him hath God exalted with his right hand to be a Prince and a Savior, for to give repentance to Israel, and forgiveness of sins'. Did you know that part of Jesus' victory is that he has the power to give you this gift that you do not have, and cannot create by all your religious efforts? He not only gave you the gift of faith (Eph. 2:8–9), but the Risen One will also give you the gift of repentance. If I did not feel sorry for my sins, what would I do? I would start saying, 'Lord Jesus, you give the gift of repentance. Right now, I do not feel it; I do not have it, I do not deserve it; I do not know how to do it. But please give me that gift from yourself.' You can be certain that the gracious Lord will hear such a prayer, no matter how weak the faith of the one who offers it.

Final Warnings
The risen Christ in verse 15 then warns us of where failure to repent will lead us, that is, 'outside the holy City', or 'shut out from God's heaven'. 'Outside the City' are all these categories of sinners (Rev. 22:15). At a recent social function, I happened to be across the table from a North Carolina Judge, who had just rendered sentence in a murder case. He said that he had sentenced the

murderer to 'life without parole', which means that he will die in prison. This hardened criminal had not shown the slightest tinge of repentance. 'Life without parole' in an imperfect fashion, seems to be a mild reflection of the final judgment of God. Not to repent, especially when we are given the information, with the warning and the gracious promises, assures that we shall be outside the city, with all those horrendous categories of sinners.

Promised Blessings

Blessings are promised in verses 7, 12-14, and 16-17. Note the word in verse 7, 'Behold I come quickly, blessed is he that keepeth the sayings of the prophecy of this book.' It recalls what we started with, 'Blessed is he that readeth' (Rev. 1:3). Blessing is a classical word that means something like 'real happiness', involved in a transmission of God's forgiveness and power. God has made you in his image: God is happy, and part of what you want in the depth of your soul is happiness. Well, Jesus says in this concluding portion of the Holy Scriptures, 'Base the rest of your years on earth on the message of this book and you will ultimately enter into all-surpassing blessedness, or happiness.' This blessedness or happiness brings us 'inside the city' (v. 14). Instead of being kept from the tree of life by the angel with the flaming sword, Jesus takes you by the hand, and leads you in. 'Inside' you may eat of this life giving, health-maintaining, joy, peace, and love. Indeed, all the 'fruit of the spirit' are found on this tree, and Jesus bids us to eat from it.

Blessing or happiness is promised in terms of 'the water of life' (v. 17). Jesus told the woman at the well that, 'whoso believes in me, out of his belly [or inner most being], shall flow rivers of living water' (John 7:38-9). It is the abundant, eternal life given to believers through Jesus, in the Holy Spirit. 'He showed me a pure river of water of life' (v. 1). It is free. We may take 'of the fountain of the water of life freely' (v. 6).

What Is Free to Us Was Infinitely Costly to Christ

It is indeed free to us, but it was infinitely costly to Christ. Paul explains the cost: 'For ye know the grace of the Lord Jesus Christ, that, though he was rich, yet for your sakes he became poor, that ye through his poverty might be rich' (1 Cor. 8:9). Yes, it cost Jesus the impoverishment of leaving beautiful heaven for a wicked earth. In the words of the *Westminster Shorter Catechism*: 'Christ's humiliation consisted in his being born, and that in a low condition, made under the law, undergoing the miseries of this life, the wrath of God, and the cursed death of the cross, in being buried and continuing under the power of death for a time' (28). But it is utterly free to those who in the act of repentance and belief will accept it.

Verse 17 invites 'him that is athirst…to take of the water of life freely.' Come, eat and drink. Jesus has paid the infinitely worthy price for us to drink of this living water that flows from the throne of God and of the Lamb. He now has every right to make it freely available to us. That is exactly what he is doing through this chapter.

65

The Last Words of the Covenant
Revelation 22:18–21

In this text, we find the very last words that God gave to the human race in the Holy Bible. In everyday life when we hear that someone has died, we often ask, 'What were his or her last words, if they are know to have had any?' Stories still pass down in my family about the last words of great-grandparents, and great-great-grandparents. Most people will be eager to know what is contained in a deceased relative's 'Last Will and Testament'. But how much more important are these last words of Revelation, not of someone who is dying, but of the living God, whose holy will shall be carried out in fullest detail from eternity to eternity, by him who is Alpha and Omega, the beginning and the end.

In surveying these final words of Holy Scripture, we note three major points:

1. The completeness of the written Word of God (Rev. 22:18–19).
2. Curses for tampering with the written Word of God (Rev. 22:18–19).
3. Blessings that accompany faithful hearing of the written Word of God (Rev. 22:20–21).

The Completeness of the Written Word of God

This statement concerning the completeness of the written Word of God in verses 18–19 directly recalls some words of Moses in Deuteronomy, which is the last of the first five books of the Bible. Through Moses, God says: 'Ye shall not add unto the word which I command you, neither shall ye diminish ought from it, that ye may keep the commandments of the LORD your God which I command you' (Deut. 4:2). These inspired words of Moses put a holy finality on the first five books of the Bible. With almost the same words, the Apostle John some 1,500 years later, writes the concluding portion of the New Testament, as Moses had written the concluding portion of the Pentateuch. Thus, God, through John, puts a finality not only on the Apocalypse, but on the entire Scripture of which Revelation is the last book: the sixty-sixth book of the Bible.

The first verse of Genesis began with God creating, and the last verse of Scripture ends with the grace of God in Christ, thereby completing everything that God began. The Bible begins with

God and ends with God. The whole thing is the Book of God; the very words of God himself from start to finish, from Genesis 1 to Revelation 22.

The Bible's Teaching on Its Own Inspiration

Paul says as much in 2 Timothy 3:16, where he says 'All scripture is inspired' and the Greek word is *theopneustos*, which literally means 'breathed out by God': a direct product, breathed out by the divine breath of God, operating through the personalities of chosen vessels, who would write it. Peter says much the same in 2 Peter 1:21, 'For the prophecy came not in old time by the will of man: but holy men of God spake as they were moved by the Holy Ghost.' This is to say that the Scriptures did not come by personal investigation, personal philosophy, or human research into history and religion, but rather, 'Holy men of old spake as they were moved by the Holy Ghost.' The Greek word we render 'moved' literally means 'lifted up and carried along,' indicating that the personalities of the writers were lifted up by the Holy Spirit and carried along by him with the supernatural result that what they wrote was exactly what God had intended to be written. He used humans to write the Scriptures, starting with Moses, and ending with John. Through the mysterious inspiration of the Holy Spirit, these chosen people were used to achieve the final goal of producing the divinely intended message from God—the very words he wanted, to such a degree that the sixty-six books of the Bible have one divine author, and speak with his voice. God stands behind every word of the Bible, and will carry it out in every detail, just as he said he would.

The fact that the Scriptures did not come by 'the will of man': that is, by private interpretation, or merely human research, is the answer to the widespread relativism of our culture. Relativism holds that no one can know with absolute certainty what is right, if indeed, anything really is 'right'; that is, the relativists usually deny any absolute standard of morality and truth. But the covenant words of Holy Scripture are predicated on this precise fact: there is something definite, absolute, and clear that you can know, and it comes directly from God, to whom you are eternally accountable for what he says. This word of God will stand firm when heaven and earth have passed away, as Jesus says in Matthew 5:18. Christ, 'the supreme Angel of the Covenant', fulfills in its totality this covenant Word of God, contained in the sixty-six books of the Bible (Matt. 5:17).

Curses for Tampering with the Written Word of God

This passage also announces solemn plagues or curses for anyone who tampers with the written Word of God. They are the worst things that could ever happen to us. Whoever tampers with God's written Word will be denied eternal life, and be finally separated from God and the Holy City, which means that we shall be cast into outer darkness and misery forever. No doubt these curses or plagues can involve penalties during this earthly existence, but these penalties point to far worse penalties beyond this present life.

Good Reasons Why Some Will not Be in Heaven

There are good reasons for excluding from glory those who willfully and viciously violate the covenant Word of Holy Scripture. For instance, verse 15 speaks of murderers, who will be forever excluded from the New Jerusalem. Murder obviously involves violence and hatred of human life. At times it appears that this sort of hatred and violence are motivated by hatred of the true God, who created mankind in his own living image.

One of the reasons murder is so serious is that it strikes out against God himself, by way of his image in people.

In addition to the eternal penalty against such violations of God's Word as murder, there are also dire consequences for those who willfully add to, or take away from, the completed word of God in Scripture.

The Problem of Islam

While most of the world is keenly aware of the plague of radical Islamic terrorism, a clear analysis of what motivates terrorism is harder to find. The answer lies in the origins of Islam. Without for a moment denying the significant difference between different types of Muslims (some are radical, while many others are more tolerant), we must recognize that the founder of Islam began the long career of this new religion by doing exactly what God said not to do: tampering with the Word of God (Deut. 4:2; Rev. 22:18–19).

The founder of Islam, Mohammed, tampered with the Word of God in the seventh century. He had access to both Old and New Testament. So he seems to have taken the Bible, and extracted from the Old Testament certain facts about Abraham (and other, often correct, information), and also extracted from the New Testament certain facts about the Virgin Mary and Jesus, but he rejected the whole Word, and rewrote the divinely given covenant Word. He held, for instance, that Jesus was a prophet, but that he, Mohammed, was the final or 'sealing' prophet, and hence that his words supplanted those of Jesus. He even denied that God was a Father, who had an eternal Son. Thus, he negated the central message of Holy Scripture: the true God is Triune.

What dreadful consequences have flowed from this seventh century tampering with the pure Word of God. One cannot reasonably blame the majority of the world's problems on what Mohammed did to the integrity of the Holy Scriptures, yet a great deal of the frightening and unjust violence that threatens our world today, is the offspring of Mohammed's tampering with the Word of God written.

God Calls Us to Love Those Who Live under Islam

Let me add a word here about our attitude to the Muslims themselves. Although as true and loyal Christian believers, we can never accept a religion that has so seriously tampered with God's Word, still we must never disdain the people who are imprisoned in this anti-Trinitarian system (which, I think, is by far its worst problem). God teaches us to love all people, those inside the church and those outside the church, as Jesus showed in the parable of the Good Samaritan. The Bible even teaches us to love our enemies, then we really show what God is like. Hence, as we think of the hundreds of millions of immortal souls under Islam, we must seek divine grace to care about their eternal welfare. We must love them as best we can, for the sake of Christ, and seek to remove anything in ourselves that would hinder their hearing the gospel. Most of these people have never known anything else from childhood, but the harsh teaching of Mohammed, who did not see God as a communion of holy love amongst three co-equal Persons. Let us pray for them. That is Christ's way for us and for them. Since the Islamic peoples are on the loving heart of God, let us seek the grace to stay so close to the compassionate Christ, that they will also be on our hearts. The God whom we see in Revelation is still on his majestic throne of infinite power and matchless grace, so we must pray in confidence for the people under Islam. God will use our humble prayers for them, and at the right time will accomplish all his will.

The Problem of 'Modernism'

Another source of the evils and tragedies that mar modern culture has done far more damage than Islam could ever accomplish. That is, the eighteenth century Enlightenment denial of the general historicity of God's Word, followed by the nineteenth century replacement of creation by the theory of evolution, followed by twentieth century Protestant (and then later by Roman Catholic) 'Modernism', which gets its bearings from the ideas of the humanistic culture around it, and rejects aspects of the Word of God that do not suit those materialistic cultural concepts. This plague of 'Modernism' is a more pressing question than anything radical Islam has been able to do at its worst. Until we deal with Western apostasy from Christianity, by renewed faith, humble repentance, new devotion to God and eager obedience to Him, we will be in no position to provide to the millions living under Islam, a better and higher way than what they already consider to be the ultimate truth. Relativists cannot win over absolutists, even if those they would like to convince have based their thinking on partially (or seriously) incorrect 'absolutes'. As with Islam, Christians must seek grace to love, yearn over, and pray for those who perish under the false assumptions of Modernism.

Blessings that Accompany Faithful Hearing of God's Written Word

Much blessing will accompany those who harken to the entirety of the written Word of God (v. 20–21). Two specific blessings are promised: first, the coming of Jesus is the greatest blessing, and secondly, to get us ready for that, we are promised the grace of Jesus. These two things are the divine benefits that accompany those who follow the Word.

Jesus' Coming

First, Jesus' coming, like everything else predicted in the written word from Genesis to Revelation, is absolutely definite. Revelation 22:20 speaks of his coming quickly. If Revelation were written before AD 70, this would probably refer to an early type of his coming, when Jerusalem was destroyed and unbelieving Judaism was scattered to make room for the mission of the Christian church to the pagan world. If this is so, then this preliminary coming was a foreshadowing of his final, physical coming on the last day to judge the quick and the dead.

Jesus' last coming is an absolutely definite and fixed day and hour. It is fixed; it is unchangeable. Only God knows the exact date, but the clock is ticking and we cannot doubt that the last day is drawing nigh. What joy his coming will be to all who have loved, and faithfully harkened to God's covenant Word! It will be the bride's wedding day; the final defeat of sin and death and sickness; the reunion of all our redeemed loved ones; the outbreaking of eternal glory; the fulfillment of every holy hope. Then the tumultuous rejoicing of all the holy angels and the redeemed multitudes of humanity will flow like mighty waves of the sea, in billows of praise across the new heavens and the new earth. That is why the very last prayer of scripture is a prayer for this blessed Jesus to come back: 'Surely, I come quickly. Amen. Even so, come Lord Jesus' (v. 20).

'The Grace of the Lord Jesus Christ Be with You'

Secondly, there is another blessing attached to faithful adherence to God's written Word: it is 'the grace of the Lord Jesus Christ.' What a blessing! It includes everything else in it.

What Grace Is

Grace means that God does not deal with you as you deserve, but rather God deals with you as Christ deserves. God takes all my sin, all my poverty, and all my shame and puts them upon Christ, and at the same time, takes Christ's wealth, beauty, joy and worthiness, and puts it all on me. That is grace! St. Augustine called it 'unmerited favor'. It is not far away from us. It is free for the asking to those who humbly accept the promises of God's Word rather than tampering with it. That is what Paul means when he says, 'Being justified freely by his grace through the redemption that is in Christ Jesus' (Rom. 3:24). It is an all-sufficient justification, and full redemption of body and soul, and is free for the taking.

Grace 'with You'

The last words of scripture are addressed to those who humbly receive the covenant Word: this grace 'will be with you all'. Imagine that! When I am praying, this grace is not far removed from me, somewhere up in heaven, but it is down with me, in the room where I am praying. It is where I need it most, when I need it most. That is why my prayers can be heard; not because I am a good and worthy person, but because grace is with me and it opens the gates of heaven for God to hear my prayers. As we struggle through life, facing difficulties, this grace is not far away in a future life; it is wonderfully present in this life, to bring us through these struggles. When I come to die, that grace is not on the other side of the mystic river of death waiting for me, it will be in my bedroom, in my failing body, and with my departing soul. Jesus is with me, and thus his grace is with me in life and in death. And on that final, awesome day of last judgment, when an assembled universe with billions of men and angels stand trembling before the sovereign throne, that grace will be with me, and with every believer, and all will be well, even on that 'day of wrath'!

Thus, the true church gladly adds her confirmation to what God promises he will do! In verse 21, the last word of the Bible is the covenant word 'Amen!' It is what you say when you mean, 'Lord, I set my seal to what you said, I 'amen it'; so let it be; so let it stand; do in my life and in the whole world what you said you would do. Bring it about! Thy will be done!' The right response, is 'Amen', whereupon we set our seal to God's covenant, which is 'ordered in all things, and sure.'

Endnotes

1 See Kenneth L. Gentry, *Before Jerusalem Fell: Dating the Book of Revelation* (American Vision: Atlanta, GA, 1998).
2 Gary DeMar, *Last Days Madness* (American Vision: Atlanta, GA, 1999), especially chapters 2–4, pp. 35–64.
3 These are summarized by R. J. Rushdoony in *Thy Kingdom Come: Studies in Daniel and Revelation* (Thoburn Press: Fairfax, VA, 1978), 92,93.
4 Ibid., 93.
5 Simon J. Kistemaker, *New Testament Commentary: Exposition of the Book of Revelation* (Baker Books: Grand Rapids: Grand Rapids, MI, 2001), 84,85.
6 See Kistemaker, op. cit., 94.
7 See David Chilton, *The Days of Vengeance*, xvii–xviii; 10–20; 85–91.
8 O. Palmer Robertson, *The Christ of the Covenants*.
9 See S. Kistemaker, op. cit., 117,118.
10 S. Kistemaker, op. cit., 121.
11 See D. Chilton, op. cit., 103.
12 S. Kistemaker, op. cit., 124.
13 S. Kistemaker, op. cit., 120,121.
14 S. Kistemaker, op. cit., 127.
15 S. Kistemaker, op. cit., 137,138.
16 S. Kistemaker, op. cit., 149,150.
17 Douglas F. Kelly, *Preachers With Power: Four Stalwarts of the South* (Banner of Truth: Edinburgh, 1992), 134.
18 S. Kistemaker, op. cit., 147,148.
19 D. Chilton, op. cit., 121.
20 S. Kistemaker, op. cit., 159.
21 Ibid., 157.
22 S. Kistemaker, op. cit., 167,168.
23 Ibid., 167.
24 Ibid., 173.
25 Ibid., 172,173.
26 S. Kistemaker, op. cit., 183.
27 D. Chilton, op. cit., 150.
28 D. Chilton, op. cit., 151–154.
29 Ibid., 154–155.
30 S. Kistemaker, op. cit., 189.
31 Ibid., 190-2.
32 D. Chilton, op. cit., 155–160.
33 D. Chilton, op. cit., 183–5.
34 S. Kistemaker, op. cit., 223.
35 D. Chilton, op. cit., 188.
36 Gary DeMar, *End Times Fiction* (Thomas Nelson: Nashville, TN, 2001), 56, 57.
37 See Gary DeMar, *Last Days Madness*, Chapter 4 (43–50).
38 David Chilton, *The Days of Vengeance: An Exposition of the Book of Revelation* (Dominion Press: Tyler, TX, 1990), 188.
39 e.g. Ibid., 189.
40 Loraine Boettner, *The Millennium*.
41 By B. E. Warren in *Celestial Echoes*, R. E. Winsett, ed. (Dayton, TN, 1943), 48.
42 See DeMar, *Last Days Madness*, chapters 10–11 (131–56).
43 D. Chilton, op. cit., 197.
44 S. Kistemaker, op. cit., 244-6.
45 J. Marcellus Kik, *An Escatology of Victory* (Presbyterian & Reformed: Nutley, NJ, 1971), 96ff.
46 Andrew Murray, *With Christ in the School of Prayer*.
47 Simon J. Kistemaker, *Revelation* (Baker Books: Grand Rapids, MI, 2001), 249–50.
48 D. Chilton, op. cit., 214.
49 David Chilton, *The Days of Vengeance*, 207.
50 William Law, *A Serious Call to a Devout and Holy Life* (London: Tenth Edition, 1772), 277.
51 See Christopher Hill, *God's Englishman*.
52 S. Kistemaker, op. cit., 285.
53 See David Chilton, op. cit., 244,245.
54 S. Kistemaker, op. cit., 290.
55 D. Chilton, op. cit., 244.
56 S. Kistemaker, op. cit., 290.
57 S. Kistemaker, op. cit., 295.
58 D. Chilton, op. cit., 243.

Endnotes

59   Ibid., 250–51.
60   Ibid., 251.
61   Ibid.
62   S. Kistemaker, op. cit., 305–7.
63   D. Chilton, op. cit., 259.
64   See Chilton, op. cit. 259–262.
65   D. Chilton, op. cit., 273–4.
66   S. Kistemaker, op. cit., 325.
67   D. Chilton, op. cit., 276–7.
68   Ibid., 281–2.
69   D. Chilton, op. cit., 288–9.
70   S. Kistemaker, op. cit., 351,352.
71   D. Chilton, op. cit., 297–300.
72   Ibid., 303–6.
73   D. Chilton, op. cit., 309,309.
74   William Hendricksen, *More Than Conquerors*.
75   See Chilton, op. cit., 321, where he cites Eusebius, *Ecclesiastical History* iii.v.
76   S. Kistemaker, op. cit., 368.
77   D. Chilton, op. cit., 321.
78   S. Kistemaker, op. cit., 378,379.
79   Ibid., 379.
80   D. Chilton, op. cit., 331,332.
81   Ibid., 331.
82   See Kistemaker, op. cit., 380,381.
83   S. Kistemaker, op. cit., 387.
84   Ibid., 388.
85   D. Chilton, op. cit., 337.
86   S. Kistemaker, op. cit., 388–391.
87   D. Chilton, op. cit., 345.
88   Ibid., 344.
89   Ken Gentry, *The Beast of Revelation*, 34 (quoted in Demar, *Last Days' Madness*, 261).
90   'The Sibyllists had already spoken of Caligula as Beliar (*Carm*. iii.63), and as a serpent. The stories of the serpent which had crawled from Nero's cradle, and of his serpent-amulet...would add significance to the symbolism' (Farrar, *Early Days of Christianity*, 471, note 2)—quoted in Demar, ibid.
91   Gary DeMar, *Last Days' Madness*, 258.
92   F. W. Farrar, *The Early Days of Christianity* (Chicago and New York: Belford, Clarke & Co., 1882), 541, quoted in Chilton, op. cit., 351.
93   D. Chilton, op. cit., 352.
94   S. Kistemaker, op. cit., 396.
95   George Eldon Ladd, *a Commentary on the Revelation to John* (Grand Rapids, MI, 1972), 185.
96   G. DeMar, *End Times Fiction*, 160.
97   Ibid., 164.
98   Question 4.
99   John Owen, *Works*, vol. 6, 382,383.
100 Jonathan Edwards, *Charity and its Fruits*

101 Eusebius, *Ecclesiastical History*, viii.ix.5, cited in Chilton, op. cit., 368.
102 Jock Purves, *Fair Sunshine: Character Studies of the Scottish Covenanters* (Banner of Truth: Edinburgh, 2003), 37.
103 S. Kistemaker, op. cit., 417.
104 Ibid., 418–9.
105 D. Chilton, op. cit., 379–382.
106 Ibid., 384.
107 S. Kistemaker, op. cit., 428.
108 See Kistemaker, op. cit., 437,438.
109 D. Chilton, op. cit., 399.
110 Ibid., 398.
111 By William Cowper, 1771, (found in most hymnals).
112 By D. Wood in *Youth Praise* (1966).
113 D. Chilton, op. cit., 398.
114 D. Chilton, op. cit., 408.
115 F.W. Farrar, *The Early Days of Christianity* (Chicago and New York: Belfors, Clarke & Co., 1882), 555f., quoted in Chilton, op. cit., 406.
116 S. Kistemaker, op. cit., 453.
117 John Owen, *An Exposition of the Epistle to the Hebrews*, W. H. Goold ed., seven vols. (Grand Rapids: Baker Book House, [1855] 1980), vol. 7, 368; quoted in Chilton, op. cit., 414.
118 S. Kistemaker, op. cit., 464.
119 Traditional Values Coalition, Hagerstown, MD.
120 D. Chilton, op. cit., 449.
121 S. Kistemaker, op. cit., 495.
122 D. Chilton, op. cit., 460–2.
123 See Robert L. Dabney, 'The Uses of Church History' in *Discussions Evangelical and Theological*.
124 Hendricksen, *More Than Conquerors*, 181.
125 S. Kistemaker, op. cit., 514.
126 See chapter 16.
127 'Jesus, thy blood and righteousness' by N. L. von Zinzendorf, translated by John Wesley.
128 See Henry Buis, *The Doctrine of Eternal Punishment* (Presbyterian and Reformed: Philadelphia, PA, 1957), 73–80.
129 S. Kistemaker, op. cit., 568.
130 Ibid.
131 S. Kistemaker, op. cit., 564.
132 Edward T. Oakes, *Pattern of Redemption: The Theology of Hans Urs von Balthasar* (Continuum: New York, 1994), 143.
133 Archibald Rutledge, *Life's Extras* (Fleming H. Revell Company: Old Tappan, New Jersey, MCMXXVIII), 14–17.
134 'The Duteous Day Now Closeth', (stanza 2), based on Paul Gerhardt, *The Church Hymnary: Revised Edition* (Oxford University Press: London, 1927), 284.
135 S. Kistemaker, op. cit., 569.
136 Augustine, *Confessions*, X.xxv.(36).
137 See Meredith Kline, *Images of the Spirit* (Baker Book House: Grand Rapids, 1980), 54–5.

Subject Index

abominations, 328
abortion, 268, 299, 322-3
Abraham
    called out to found the church, 409
    covenant promises, 131, 148, 202, 360, 402
    faithful witness, 80
Achan, 309
Adam and Eve
    created perfect, 216
    enmity with serpent, 402
    expelled from the Garden, 326, 359-60, 423, 424
    in Garden of Eden, 426
    nakedness, 86
    and original sin, 305-6
    original sin in Adam, 305, 306
    promise of seed to Eve, 239
    promise to Eve, 239
    temptation, 217
    two Adams, 26
Africa: growth of Christianity, 366, 368
Ahab, 204, 316, 391
Ahaziah, 316
AIDS, 60, 89
Alison, Archibald, 271
Alpha and Omega, 19, 403, 431
altar, 181-2, 184
    of incense, 166, 203, 206-7
'Amen', 153

America
    apostasy, 38, 54
    Christian schools, 333, 339
    church in, 40, 69
    homosexuality in, 60
    power of, 289
    religion in public life, 196, 333, 339
    secularism, 76
Amos, 204
ancestors, 423
Andrews, Lancelot, 271
Angel of the Covenant, 194
angels, 97, 103-4, 370
    angelic singers, 356
    in battle with Satan, 222, 223-4
    binding Satan, 378
    care for human beings, 97-8
    compared with mankind, 103
    ranks of, 103
    reaping, 275-6
    singing, 255
    sounding the trumpet, 165
    see also Mighty Angel; music/singing
animal sacrifices, 293, 302
Anselm of Canterbury, 276
Antipas, 50, 52
Apocalypse, meaning of, 17
apostasy in Western world, 38, 54, 76, 289, 438

Apostles, 96, 104-5, 212
Ark of the Covenant, 213, 291, 303, 315
Armageddon, 316-17
army of the Lamb, 255-8
   obedience, 256-7
   purity, 256
   truthfulness, 257-8
   unity, 257
Athanasius, 265
atheism, 153, 211
Augustine, 134, 399, 439
   Confessions, 94, 160

Baal, 59
Babylon
   dwelling place for demons, 338-9
   fall of ancient city, 348
   fall of: grief, 344-5
   fall of: rejoicing, 347
   power of, 267, 338
   pride, 340
   rejection of God, 339-40
   sorcery, 352
   symobolism, 268, 337-8
   unrepented sins, 340
   violence, 350-1
   worship of wealth, 351-2
Babylon the great, mother of harlots, 325-9
   attractive appearance, 327-8
   the beast, 326-7, 331-2
   golden cup, 328
   mystery, 329
   power, 328-9
   in the wilderness, 326
backsliding, 38
Balaam, 53
Balak, 53
baptism, 248
Barnhouse, Donald Grey, 277
battles in biblical history, 219-20
Baxter, Richard, 262
beast from the land, 243-4
   characteristics, 244-5
   mark of, 244, 246-8
   as Nero, 246-7
   satanic power, 245
beast ridden by the harlot, 326-7, 331-5
   as political/religious power, 332-3
   temporary power of, 333-4
beast with ten horns, 238, 239-40
beauty, 407-8, 409-10
Belshazzar, 279, 345
Berlin Wall, fall of, 167-8, 210
Bernard of Clairvaux, 255
Berthoud, Jean-Marc, 420
Bethlehem, 146
Bethsaida, 396, 432
Bible
   completeness of, 435-6
   inspiration of, 436
   keeping to, 76
   principles of interpretation, 244
   rejection of, 125, 197, 198
   word of God, 435-6
birds of prey, 372
black horseman, 125-6
Blaiklock, 77
blame-shifting, 308
blessedness, 270-1
blessings, 154, 434
blood, 111
   life in, 302
blood-red horseman, 124-5
Bloom, Allen, 57
Boettner, Loraine, 125
Book of Life, 110, 240-1, 335, 395
Boston, Thomas, 162
bottomless pit, 169, 171, 172, 378
bowing to Christ, 369-70
bowl of wrath, 301
breastplate, 93
bright face of Christ, 30
Bunyan, John: *Pilgrim's Progress*, 227

Burnham, Richard, 145
buying and selling, 248-9

Caesars, worship of, 238
Cain and Abel, 219
Calvin, John, 104, 107, 129, 179, 241-2, 373
Cameron, Alan, 89-90
Cameron, Richard, 89-90
carmelian, 93
Carrothers, Merlin R., 235
Ceausescu, Nicolae, 183
centralization in modern world, 18
change, rate of, 18
cherubim, 103
Chilton, David, 124, 147, 232, 313
China, 40, 51, 131, 143, 149, 205, 211
    Fukien Province, 168
Chorazin, 396, 432
Christian care, 76
Christianity
    growth in 'Southern realm', 366
    and other religions, 37-8, 76-7, 153, 231
    out of Judaism, 140, 317-18
    in schools, 333, 339
church
    beauty of God in, 409-10
    bride of Christ, 34-5, 256, 357-63, 401-2, 409, 411-12
    center of world history, 27-8, 33, 34
    in Christ's hand, 36
    destiny controlled by the Lord, 32
    enemies of, 237
    given divine glory, 407
    God's protection of, 231-2, 232-3
    in heaven, 97, 147
    last battle with Satan, 389-90
    missionary commission to, 200, 379
    as New Jerusalem, 408-9
    and number 144000, 254
    participating in Christ's suffering, 385
    praying against evil, 183
    sharing Christ's resurrection, 385
    temptations by Satan, 226-7
    withstanding Satan, 221, 234-5
    world existing for, 408
    see also saints/martyrs
circumcision, 248, 249, 402
clarity of vision, 101, 102-3
Colquhoun, 433
Colson, Charles, 17
Columbine, Colorado, 338
coming in judgment, 21-2, 123-4, 431, 438
    see also second coming
'coming of the Lord', 122-3
'coming', meaning of, 22
commandments of God, 270-1
Communism, 327, 334
confession, 302-3, 433
    see also repentance
covenant of grace, 399
covenant Lord, 41
covenant structure of seven letters, 35
covenant warning, 39-40
covenants, 35, 402-3
creation
    destruction of, 400-1
    new, 403
    through the agency of Christ, 34
criticism, receiving, 53
Cromwell, Oliver, 163
crown of life, 47
crowning, 368-9
crystal river, 424
crystal sea, 100, 101, 280-1
    brightness of, 282
Cullman, Oscar, 229
culture, 177, 420
    corruption of, 178-9
Cybele, 42
Cyrus, 224

Dabney, Robert L., 166, 349
Dan, 146

Daniel, 197, 220, 223, 227, 279, 431-2
Dante, 397
darkness and light, 32
David
    covenant, 402
    as psalmist, 285
    repentance of, 305-6, 308
    and Saul, 219, 285
    shepherd and king, 201, 235
Day of Atonement, 292
death
    door to Christ, 270-1
    fear of, 31-2, 51, 159
    final end of, 403
    and resurrection, 205, 262
    and second death, 47, 385-6
    spiritual death, 386-7
    way to eternal life, 159-60, 262
death of Jesus Christ, 173, 262
Deborah, 316
deism, 104, 111, 185
DeMar, Gary, 22, 122, 246
demonic pit, 175-9
demons, 316, 338
    faith of, 264
    recognition of Christ, 379-80
    see also evil spirits; Satan/devil
dependence on the Lord, 83
diamond, 93
distress, 205-6
divine light, 428
doxologies, 105-6, 212
dragon, 215-16, 217, 218-19
    attacking the church, 229-30
    many-headed, 220
drinking blood, 301-2
drugs, 99, 226, 339, 352
drunkenness, 268, 328, 369

earthquakes, 317
    see also shakings
economic collapse, 344

ecstasy, 408
Edwards, Jonathan, 264
Egypt, 125, 136
    Israel in, 219
    plague of locusts, 177
    plagues, 177, 301, 306
Einstein, Albert, 95
elders, 96
elect/election, 212, 241-2
    number of, 143
    sealed, 141
    see also church; saints/martyrs
Elijah, 204, 205, 287, 391
Elisha, 251
Elliot, T.S., 389
emerald, 94
end of the world, 389, 391-2
enemies of God, harvest of, 275-6
Enlightenment, 217, 234, 438
Enoch, 92, 430
Ephesus, 33-40
    Christ and seven lampstands, 36-7
    churches in Christ's hand, 36, 37
    covenant promise, 40
    covenant warning, 39-40
    hard work of Ephesians, 37
    letter of Ignatius of Antioch to, 40
    loss of zeal, 38-40
    purity of Ephesian faith, 37-8
Ephraim, 146
Esther and Hamon, 219
eternity, 261-2
ethnic differences, 420-2
Euphrates River, 188, 315
Eusebius, 271
evangelism, 228
Evangelism Explosion, 228
evil, 288, 295
    battle against, 319-23
    destruction of, 400-1
    good out of, 319-20

mystery of, 329
in opposition to Jesus, 222-3
origins, 217
and triumph of good, 205-6
in the world, 171-3, 175-9, 189
evil characters, 269
evil spirits, 171, 316
dwelling places for, 338-9
Exodus from Egypt, 201
eye salve, 86
eyes, 101
eyes of flame, 368
Ezekiel, 194

Faber, F.W., 106, 144
face of God, 138
faith
involving repentance, 433
keeping, 270
and sight, 281
union with Christ, 386
'Faithful and True', 367-8
false prophets, 245
Farrar, Dean, 316
fate, 102
fear, 46-7, 50-1, 263-5
hateful fear, 264
loving fear, 264-5
and promise of eternal life, 46-7, 263
feet like brass, 29-30
fire, 167, 280, 390-1
purifying, 400
First Great Awakening, 199, 390
flaming eyes, 29
floods swallowed up, 233, 234
food shortages/prices, 123, 125
foreign visitors, 75
fornication, 339
four beasts, 238-9
four horns, 184
four horsemen, 116-19, 121-6

black rider, 125-6
blood-red rider, 124-5
colors of the horses, 117
Old Testament background, 116-17
pale rider, 126
white horse and rider, 117-19
fourth beast, 220
French monarchy, 349
future
God in control of, 403-4
prdicitons, 356, 430
predestined, 92
predetermined events, 430-1
revealed, 91, 92-3, 320-1
roots in, 404

Gabriel, 103, 223
gambling, 339
Garden of Eden, 40, 326, 423-4
see also New Garden of Eden
Gates of Hell, 368
Gessius Florus, 175
Giradeau, John L., 67
glory given to God, 154, 265-6
glory of God, 407
on Moses' face, 427
Gnosticism, 298
God
beauty of, 93-4
in control, 17, 50-1, 90, 104, 182
eternity of, 106
face of, in Christ, 138
fulfilling his Word, 249-50
glory of, 407
goodness of, 172
holiness, 105, 126, 276, 292-3, 394
honor of, 155
humility of, 162
interest in us, 74
as judge, 58
'King of Nations', 289
at the last judgment, 393-4

445

love of, 126, 276, 295, 299
power, 105-6
protective wings, 231-2
purity, 105, 172
revealed through the visible, 93
strength of, 156
tender care of, 161-2
transcendence of, 90, 93
unchanging, 189
unsearchable, 212
voice, 196
wisdom, 154-5
wrath of, 114-15, 280, 295, 303
see also Lamb of God, Jesus Christ, judgment
Goldberg, Bernard, 231
golden crowns, 98
golden cup, 328
good from evil, 173
gospel, 235-6
    apostolic, 260
    everlasting, 260-1
    origin of word, 260
    response to, 263-6
Gospels, 104
grace, 98, 262, 294, 438-9
    covenant of, 399
    leading to repentance, 307, 308
    rejection of, 395, 432-3
    transforming character, 361
grace abounding, 425
Graham, Franklin, 60
grapes of wrath, 275-6, 277
Great Commission, 114
greed, 339, 344
Green, Åke, 175

hailstones, 317
'Hallel', 354
'Hallelujah', 354
Handel, G.F.: *Messiah*, 354
happiness, 25
harps, 285

harvest, 273-5
    double harvest, 275-6
Hay, Fred J., 310
healing of the nations, 425
heaven *see* New Jerusalem
heaven, open door to, 91
heavenly bodies, 134
heavenly choir, 355-6
    see also music/singing
heavenly and earthly realms, 127
heavenly voices from the throne, 99
heavens rolled up, 137
Hegel, 333
Heidelberg Catechism, 270
hell, 161, 269, 371-6, 395-6
    eternity of, 374
    fires, 373-4
    images of, 372-3
    reality of, 269
    separation from God, 426
Hendriickson, William, 360
Herod, 146, 204
Hezekiah, 316
history
    biblical battles, 219-20
    church at center of, 34
    conclusion in wedding of the Lamb, 359-60
    determined by prayer, 127-8, 134, 165, 181-3
    events pointing to future, 201
    Jesus Christ, Lord of, 17, 33-4
    judgment in, 123-4, 176-7
    Lamb in charge of, 113-14
    meaning of, 34
    and prayers of the martyrs, 127-8
    predestined, 134
Hitler, Adolf, 334
holiness of God, 105, 126, 276, 292-3, 394
Holy of Holies, 291, 411
Holy Spirit, 66, 99, 147
    baptism of, 177
    breathed on the disciples, 66
    inspiring Scripture writers, 436

Subject Index

at Pentecost, 401
raising witnesses, 206
renewing zeal, 66-7
in revivals, 67-8
shedding love of God, 85
sufficiency of, 66-7
transforming character, 361
Homer: *Odyssey*, 33
homesickness, 423
homosexuality, 60
honor, 155
horsemen *see* four horsemen
Hosea, 409
Huguenots, 349
human wickedness, 124-5
   see also evil; sin
humanism, 27-8, 102, 106, 154, 211, 230-1
hymn of praise, 107-12
   book/scroll, 110
   singers, 111-12
   in structure of Revelation, 107-9
   theme of, 109-11
hymn of the victors, 285-9
   content, 287-9
   title, 287-8

'I am that I am', 26, 31, 106, 332
idolatry, 190, 245, 268-9
Ignatius of Antioch, 40, 286
imagery, uses of, 134-5, 320
   see also symbolic language
imparted righteousness, 361
imprisonment of Christians, 90-1
Indonesia, 83, 144
intercession, 207
interpretation of Scripture, 244, 377
Iraq, 337, 351
Islam, 38, 60, 61, 76-7, 143, 211
   Christian attitude to, 437-8
   and terrorism, 49, 171, 437
   view of Christ, 183, 230

Israel, 35, 135
   destruction of, 117, 136, 137
   fulfillment of judgment on, 187-9
   presumption of, 315
   shaken down, 138
   womb for Messiah, 218
Israel in Egypt, 219

Jackson, Stonewall, 166
Jacob, 91, 137, 185
James, 46, 240
Jaroslav the Wise, 422
jasper, 93
Jehoshaphat, 286
Jehu, 210
Jenkin, Philip, 366
Jerusalem
   as Babylon, 268, 348
   destruction of, 22, 116, 119, 125, 147, 187-90
   escape of Christians, 190-1, 232
   first century massacre, 175-6
   'holy city', 401
   images of downfall, 315-17
   lament over, 116
   siege of, 141
   Solomon's temple, 194-5
   split in three parts, 317
   Temple, 202-3
   see also New Jerusalem
Jesus Christ
   as advocate, 222, 225, 302-3
   Alpha and Omega, 19, 403, 431
   the Amen, 79-81
   appearance of, 27-30
   as author of Revelation, 19-20, 25
   baptism, 310
   becoming a human being, 97, 288
   birth, 146, 211, 219-20
   blood of, 288, 303
   casting out evil spirits, 379-80
   cleansing the Temple, 249
   coming in judgment, 21-2, 123-4, 431, 438
   conquering by his word, 20

death,   173, 262, 288, 397
deity,   76, 110-11
dispenser of the Holy Spirit,   66
at Emmaus,   111
enthroned,   210-11, 252, 274, 394
eyes of flame,   57-8, 368
face to face with,   427-8
faithful witness,   79, 80
feeding 5000,   201
First and Last,   31, 41, 43
fulfilling Jewish scriptures,   140
giving repentance,   433
greatnes of,   196-7
harvesting,   274-6
head over government,   26
as High Priest,   28-9
holiness and purity,   73-4
images as rider,   118-19
in Islam,   437
as judge,   58, 394
key keeper,   31-2, 74-5, 126
knocking on the door,   87
last battle,   220
at last judgment,   394
Lord of creation,   42, 80
Lord of personal history,   33
Lord of world history,   17, 19-20, 33-4, 109
man child,   216, 220
meekness,   162
message,   30-2
in the midst of the churches,   20
as Mighty Angel,   194-6
nail prints,   114
only way to God,   153, 292
opposing demons,   222-3
parable of King's wedding,   363-4
parable of last judgment,   361-2
parable of the sower,   377, 378
power of,   431
propitiation for sin,   302, 309
reign on earth,   380-1
and remembrance of his love,   39
restoring paradise,   326

resurrection,   111, 114, 260, 385, 386
rod of iron,   218
ruler of nations,   212, 365, 369-70, 379
sacrifice for all sins,   203, 293, 295, 309, 397
and Satan,   219-20, 224, 225, 326, 332, 379
second Adam,   26, 326
second coming,   39, 92, 123
seed of David,   218
six qualities of,   26, 27
Son of God,   225
Son of Man,   273-4
suffering,   108, 276
with a sword,   49-50
tempted by Satan,   212, 332
time of coming,   122-3
transfiguration,   195, 287
true witness,   79, 80-1
unchanging,   189
vicarious repentance,   310
as victor,   43, 209-10, 224, 365-6, 433
washing feet of Peter,   161-2
on white hoorse,   367
as witness,   204
with the woman at the well,   404, 424, 434
Word of God,   194
'yes' to Bible promises,   80
see also Lamb of God
Jewish festivals,   210
Jews
    first century massacre of,   175-6
    rejection of Christ,   116
    return from exile,   223-4
    scattering,   116
    unbelieving cast out,   202
Jezebel,   59, 204
Job,   222
John, author of Revelation,   17, 19-20, 27, 46, 375
John the Baptist,   113, 204
Jordan River,   315
Joseph (NT),   220
Joseph (OT),   137
Josephus,   125, 176, 188, 189, 202, 301, 316, 348

Joshua, 309, 315
Josiah, 316
Judah, 146
Judas Iscariot, 433
judgment, 58, 121-2, 355
    appropriate to the sin, 299
    and coming, 122-3
    delays in, 314-15
    fitting the crime, 301-2
    as good news, 73
    and goodness of God, 297-8
    in history, 123-4, 176-7, 295-6
    on the impenitent, 300-1
    on Israel, 187-9
    last judgment, 393-8
    and love, 276-7
    and mercy, 293-4
    preached by Christ, 375
    rejection of belief in, 298-9
    shaped by God's character, 298
    waiting for, 139-44
just war, 215

keys, 31-2, 74-5, 126
Kiev, 422
killing of witnesses, 204-5
kingdom of Christ, 26, 312
Kistemaker, Simon
    'abomination', 328
    Armageddon, 317
    book of Revelation, 26
    citrus-scented wood, 344
    conflict with Satan, 247
    evil spirits, 177
    holy city and Babel, 411-12
    Jewish weddings, 360
    time before Jesus returns, 232
    twelve tribes, 146
Knox, John, 179
Korah, Dathan and Abiram, 233, 234
Kruschchev, 334

Ladd, 248
Lake of Fire, 332, 372-3, 396-7
Lamb of God
    army of, 255-8
    blood of, 225
    center of heavenly song, 109
    and enemies of God, 253
    final victor, 252-3
    Lord of history, 113-14, 116, 118, 119
    marriage of, 34, 357-63, 409
    on Mount Zion, 252-3
    opeining the seals, 116, 165
    slain for remission of sins, 111
    victor over evil, 117-18
    worthiness of, 109-10, 112
    wrath of, 114-15, 117-18, 119
Laodicea, 79-87
    Christ the Amen, 79-80
    Christ the faithful witness, 80
    Christ the true witness, 80-1
    eye salve, 86
    lack of good works, 82
    lukewarmness, 81-2
    material and spiritual wealth, 82
    miserable, 83-4
    offer of immediate grace, 84-5
    opening the door to Christ, 87
    promise of mercy, 84
    spiritual blindness, 84
    true gold, 85-6
    unawareness of condition, 83-4
    unfaithfulness of, 81
    water supply of city, 81-2
    white robes, 86
last battle, 220, 372
last judgment, 393-8
    all humanity together, 394-5
    destiny of the lost, 395
    God on the throne, 393-4
    impartiality, 395
    lake of fire, 332, 372-3, 396-7
    white throne, 394

Last Supper, 201, 287
'last trump', 210-11, 397
Law, William, 155
Lazarus, 43, 87, 386
Lee, Robert E., 264
Lee, Robert Greene, 323
Levi, 146
Lewis, C.S., 138, 206, 255, 410, 419
liberal Christianity, 366, 369
life decisions and eternity, 350
life not accidental, 102-3
light, 99, 419-20
   in the darkness, 32, 36
   uncreated, 419-20
lightning and thunder, 99
listening, 20
liturgical colors, 367
living creatures, 101, 102, 103-4
Livingston, John, 67
locusts, 176-7
Lord's Supper, 418
loss and eternal gain, 282-3
Lot, 391
love
   lost and regained, 33, 38-9
   in practice, 58, 76
love of God, 26, 126, 276, 295, 299
Lucifer, 170, 217
Luther, Martin, 178, 179

McKinley, B.B., 256
Magnificat, 263
malignant sores, 301
Mark of the Beast, 0
marking, 247-8
marriage, 256, 402
marriage of Lamb of God, 34, 357-63, 401-2, 409
   beautiful garments, 361-2
   beauty of the bride, 360-2
   blessedness of the bride, 362-3
   reasons for praise, 358-60

   voices of the wedding song, 357-8
   wedding ceremony, 360
Martha, 386
martyrs *see* saints/martyrs
Marx, Karl, 333
materialism, 111, 127, 164
meditating on heaven, 151
mercy, 293
Mercy Seat, 291-2, 293
message of pardon, 32
Messiah, rejection of, 135, 140
Micaiah, 316
Michael, 103, 222, 223-4
Mighty Angel, 194-6, 197-200
   clothed in the cloud, 194-5
   face like the sun, 195
   identified with Christ, 194-5
   legs like pillars of fire, 195
   open book, 195-6, 199
   over land and sea, 196
   rainbow round his head, 195
   roaring like a lion, 195-6
   and things not said, 197-8
military imagery, 22-3
millennium, 377, 378-9
Miriam, 211
missionaries, 224
modern idolatry, 190, 245, 322
modernism, 76, 126, 327, 438
Mohammed, 437
   see also Islam
money, 344, 351-2
Moody, Dwight L., 158
moon, 134
moral law, 298
Moses
   author of Pentateuch, 435
   called by God, 26, 31, 106
   crossing Red Sea, 233, 280
   demonic madness, 189
   and earth opening up, 233

and God's protection, 231
leadership of, 233
prayer for beauty, 408
receiving commandments, 99, 134
sapphire pavement, 280
selection of elders, 96
shining face, 427
songs of, 286-7
Ten Commandments, 269-70
ten plagues, 125, 135, 301
at the transfiguration, 203-4, 287
Mount Sinai, 135, 213, 291
Mount Zion, 252, 401
mouth of Christ, 30
multinational companies, 143
murder, 436-7
Murray, Andrew, 83, 143-4, 300
music/singing, 96-7, 105, 151-6, 210, 255
'Amen' response, 153
in Bible stories, 211
doxologies, 105-6, 212
driving out Satan, 286
hymn of the victors, 285-9
hymns of praise, 107-12, 152, 354-6
'last trump', 210-11
qualities of God, 153
salvation in Christ, 152-3
seven themes of praise, 154-6
songs, 211-13
first, 212
second, 212-13
new song, 254
Muslims, 38
see also Islam
mystery, 329
'mystery of iniquity', 276

name inscribed on forehead, 427
nations
diversity of, 420-2
healing of, 425
Nebuchadnezzar, 245-6, 337, 348

Nero, Emperor, 22, 50, 122, 147, 238
as the beast, 246-7
suicide, 249
Neuhaus, Richard John, 197
new creation, 403
New Garden of Eden, 424-8
crystal river, 424
presence of God, 426
saints, 426
trees of life, 424-5
new heaven and earth, 400-1
New Jerusalem, 408-9, 413-16, 417-22
church, 418
diversity of cultures, 420-1
ethnic differences, 420-2
light, 419-20
no partings, 418-19
no temple, 417-18
proportions and shape, 410-11
uncreated light, 419-20
unsaved outside, 422
Nicolaitans, 37
Nietzsche, 217
Nineveh, 321
Noah, 190, 195, 219, 431
nominal Christianity, 68-9, 71, 72, 369
North Korea, 352
number 666, 246-7
number 144000, 254
number of martyrs, 145-7
derivation of number, 145-7
long-term fulfillment, 147
short-term fulfillment, 147
significance of 1000, 146

obedience, 235, 256-7
offensiveness of gospel, 83
Old Testament, 140, 204
imagery, 134, 136, 137
olive trees, 206
open door, 91
Owen, John, 263-4, 318

Packer, J.I., 261
pagans, 36
pale horseman, 126
palm branches, 151-2
parable of the vineyard, 318
Passover, 201, 287, 306, 402
Patmos, 27
Paul (Saul of Tarsus), 108, 183
   at Ephesus, 38
   death of, 46, 149
   eye problem, 30
   persecuting the church, 183, 230, 252
Peguy, Charles, 432
Pentecost, 147, 401
Pergamos, 49-55
   Christ with a sword, 49-50
   compromise with paganism, 49-50, 53-4
   covenant promises, 54-5
   covenant warning, 53-4
   hidden manna, 54-5
   pagan religion, 50
   renewed faith, 54
   and Roman power, 51-2
   stone with a secret name, 55
   strong points, 51-2
persecution, 43, 51-2, 148, 240, 283
   in Romania, 98-9
persecutors pardoned, 32
perseverence of the saints, 72
Peter, 46, 161-2
   repentance, 433
Pharisees, 43, 322
Philadelphia, 73-8
   Christ the key keeper, 74-5
   commendation, 73, 75-6
   dealing with enemies, 77
   foreign visitors, 75
   holiness and purity of Christ, 73-4
   hour of trial, 77
   keeping to Bible, 76
   pillars of God's house, 77-8
   promises, 77-8
   strength against opposition, 76

Philippines, 145
physical death, 387
physical resurrection, 387
Pilgrim Fathers, 233
Pink, A.W., 112
Plato, 159
Polanyi, Michael, 164
'political correctness', 350
pornography, 339
poverty, 44-5
   of Christians in eastern Europe, 45
   honor for, 44
power, 155-6
praise, 354-5
   power of, 235
   themes of, 154-6
prayer, 115
   against evil, 182-4
   bringing judgement, 181-3, 186, 300
   determining history, 127-8, 134, 165
   and fall of Berlin Wall, 167-8
   in Jesus' name, 115
   of the martyrs, 127-31
   opposed by Satan, 226-8
   perfumed, 166
   persistence in, 300
   and shakings, 133
   through wounds of Christ, 166-7
   to accomplish God's purposes, 163-4, 223-4
   waiting for answer, 139-40, 143-4
   worthiness for, 226-7
preaching, worthiness for, 226
precious stones, 93-4
predestination, 134
predictions, 430
presumption, 314-15
priestly robe, 28-9
priorities, 32
prostitute, 320, 321-2
Protestant Reformation, 142-4, 318
Psalms, 354

public opinion, 239
purging of creation, 400-1

rainbow, 195
reason for being believers, 275
Red Sea, 233, 280
redemption, 52, 109-10
   see also salvation
rejoicing over defeat of Satan, 224-5
relationships, 160
relativism, 57, 153, 270, 350, 397, 436
   and Book of Revelation, 429-30
religions in public behavior, 230-1
religious syncretism, 38, 231
Renwick, James, 46
repentance, 54, 60, 71, 340
   daily, 310
   as divine gift, 305
   gift of risen Christ, 433
   only way to heaven, 306
   and refusal, 189-90, 307-9
   in sackcloth, 204
   through faith, 433
resurrection, 205, 260, 400-1
   'all things new', 403
   of just and lost, 84
   spiritual and bodily, 47-8, 385, 386-7
retribilization, 18
Reuben, 146
Revelation, Book of
   authorship, 19-20
   Christ as author, 19-20, 25
   contemporary interest in, 17-18
   date of writing, 21, 122, 430
   meaning of title, 17
   prophecy opened up, 431-2
   and relativism, 429-30
   structure, 108, 209, 215
revivals, 67-8, 75, 390
   in Wales 1904, 96-7
rich man and Lazarus, 371, 374
right hand, 30

righteousness, 361
rivers dried up, 315-16
rod of iron, 218
Roman Catholic Church, 318
Roman Emperor as god, 42, 50
Roman Empire, 19
   as Babylon, 341
   fall of, 32, 42, 62, 130, 137, 142, 220
   persecution of church, 22, 28, 31, 238-9
   wounding, 249
Romania, 52, 98-9, 183
Rome (city), 128, 334
   temple, 50
rule over cities, 427
Rushdoony, R.J., 333
Russia, 62
Rutherford, Samuel, 255, 293
Rwanda, 148

saints/martyrs
   absence of suffering, 160-1
   chosen by God, 142
   communicating with the Lord, 129-30
   by the crystal sea, 282-3
   death of body, 128
   dignity of, 98-9
   equal with angels, 370
   and fall of Babylon, 347-8
   fellowship, 160
   golden crowns, 98
   harvested by Jesus, 275
   judging the angels, 97
   keeping faith, 270
   and martyrdom in modern world, 131, 143, 144, 145, 148
   names in the Book, 241
   near God, 128
   in New Garden of Eden, 426
   number of, 145-7, 254
   patience of, 269-70
   perseverance, 242
   prayer of, 127-30, 165, 181-3, 186

Subject Index

reigning with Christ, 98
reigning through prayer, 112
repentant sinners, 112, 165-6
sealed with the Spirit, 140-1
supernatural power of, 166
and tribulation, 147-50
unworthiness, 226-8
waiting for divine action, 130-1
wedding garments, 158-9
in white robes, 98, 128-9
salvation, 355
    by believing the gospel, 241-2, 335
    names of saved in the Book, 241, 335
    only through Christ, 153, 405
    and predestination, 241-2, 335
Samson, 405
sanctification, 165-6
Sardis, 65-72
    Christ coming in judgment, 70
    Christ as despenser of the Spirit, 66-7
    Christ holding seven stars, 67
    identity of Christ, 65-6
    love to be rekindled, 66-7
    names of penitents preserved, 71-2
    as nominal Christians, 69-71
    promise of white robes, 71
    security and wealth of, 70
    'Wake Up' call, 70
    warning, 70-1
sardius, 93
Satan/devil, 42, 118, 170-2, 399
    attacking the church, 229-30, 232, 234-5
    binding of, 377, 378, 379
    in the book of Job, 222
    cast out, 224, 338
    and Christ, 219-20
    controlling minds, 226
    in disguise, 391
    fall, 217
    final defeat, 390-1
    hatred of Christians, 230
    and the high priest, 222
    in history, 171-2
    let loose, 389-90
    mimicking God, 332
    opposing prayer, 226-8
    and seed of the woman, 218
    tempter on earth, 226
    tempting Christ, 212
Satanism, 338
Saul (OT), 219, 285
Schaeffer, Francis, 190
Schlossberg, Herb, 322
science, 164
Scottish Covenanters, 46
Scripture *see* Bible
sea, 237-8, 281, 401
seals, 109, 110, 113, 116, 127, 165, 247-8
second coming, 39, 92, 123
second death, 47, 385-6
Second Great Awakening, 75
second vision, 90
secrets, 198
secularism, 196-7, 211, 230
seed of the woman, 218, 239
self-interest, death of, 206
sensuality, 339
seraphim, 103
Sermon on the Mount, 265, 270, 299, 375
serpent, 216, 217, 239
Seth, 219
seven beatitudes, 23, 25
seven churches
    rejecting paganism, 341
    seven letters to, 35
    as stars, 36, 37
seven golden lampstands, 27, 36, 37
seven kings, 334
seven spirits, 26
seven stars, 30, 36, 37
seven-fold candelabra, 99
Shadrach, Meshach and Abednego, 245-6

Subject Index

shakings, 133-8, 311-18
    heavenly bodies, 134, 135-7
    heavens rolled up, 137
    in history, 313
    of kingdoms, 314, 318
    mountains and earth, 134-5, 137
Shem, 219
Shepherd of Hermas, The, 34, 408
Shorter Catechism, 154
sight
    clear or dark, 280-1
    and faith, 281
signs of the future, 279
Silas, 108
sin
    in Adam, 305-6
    and confession, 302-3
    incurring judgment, 114-15, 275-6, 298
    infinite, 276
    and need of forgiveness, 153, 262
    perverseness of, 374-5
    seriousness of, 292
    unrepented, 340
'singing in the air', 96-7
six promises, 23
Sixth King, 22
Smyrna, 41-8
    crown of life, 47
    encouragements to, 46-7
    honored for poverty, 44-5
    Jews in, 42-3
    no criticism of, 44
    pagans government, 42
    promise of eternal life, 46-7
    sources of pressure, 42-3
    tribulation, 41-3, 44-5
    vision of Christ victorious, 41-2, 43
Sodom and Gomorrah, 269, 391, 396, 432
Solomon, 194-5, 210
Solzhenitsyn, Alexander, 36-7, 295, 327
Son of Man
    in midst of the lampstands, 28

origin of title, 28, 273-4
    reaping, 273-4
soul, 127-8, 159, 345
Spanish Armada, 207
spiritual blindness, 84
spiritual death, 386-7, 387-8
spiritual realm, 164-5
spiritual resurrection, 386-7
spiritual vacuum, 338
stars, 134
    falling, 136-7
Stephanas, 257
Stephen, 183, 230, 252
Still, William, 118, 172, 227
strength, 156
structure of Revelation, 108
substitutionary death, 262
Sudan, 83, 144, 148, 205, 367
suffering, 41-2, 102
    of apostles, 46
    of Christ, 45, 108, 111
    of Christians, 45-6, 108, 157
    divine presence in, 45
    final end of, 403
    fruit of, 45
    leading to repentance, 307-8
    and promise of resurrection, 47-8
    redemptive, 52
    as stewardship, 52
    through persecution, 51-2
sun, 134
    turning black, 135-6
Sunday, Billy, 178
sweetness and bitterness, 199
sword, 30, 369
sword of Christ, 49-50, 119
symbolic language, 90, 377-8, 408

tabernacle of heaven, 291-6
    opening, 292
tears wiped away, 403

Temple,   22, 202-3, 213, 417-18
    altars,   203
    buying and selling,   248-9
Ten Boom, Corrie,   142
Ten Commandments,   270, 291-2, 298
Tertullian,   131, 149, 205, 299
thanksgiving,   155
third sign,   279-80
throne
    light from,   99
    power controlling the universe,   95-6
    power of God,   90, 93
    and precious stones,   93-4
Thyatira,   57-63
    appearance of Christ,   57-8
    call to repentance,   60
    Christ with flaming eyes,   57-8
    compromise with pagans,   59-60, 60-1
    covenant warning,   60-1
    'Jezebel',   59, 60
    love of God,   58
    Morning Star as gift,   62-3
    overcomers,   61
    power over nations,   61-2
    spiritual disease,   58-9
Thyatira, church at,   29
time,   122, 185-6, 232
    in answers to prayer,   130
    and delay,   199
    and eternity,   261-2
    in heaven,   425
    of waiting,   139
Tishri,   210
Toffler, Alvin,   18
Ton, Joseph,   52
Tower of Babel,   326, 337, 340, 411-12
transcendence,   164
Transfiguration,   195, 287
tribes of Israel,   104, 411
tribulation,   41-3, 44-5, 147-50
    benefits of,   148-50
    honor for,   44

    no escape from,   44-5
    spreading the word,   148
Trinity,   26, 77, 332
trumpet,   165
trust,   191, 264
truthfulness,   257-8
twelve tribes,   146
twenty-four elders,   96, 105-6, 212
two candlesticks,   206
two seeds,   239
Tyre,   321

Uganda,   131, 148
Ukraine,   422
unbelief, defeat of,   267-8, 390
union with Christ,   386
United Nations,   268
universalism,   306-7
USSR,   130, 143, 211, 232, 233, 334, 343
    churches in,   348-9

veil of the temple,   213
vengeance,   124, 206-7, 373, 396
vesture in blood,   369
violence,   350-1
Virgin Mary,   218, 220, 239, 263
virgins,   256
visible and invisible worlds,   184-5
voice like many waters,   30
voice of the Lord,   92
Von Hugel, Baron,   49
vows,   80

waiting for judgment,   139-44
    for conversions to Christianity,   141-2, 143
    till the end of the age,   142-4
warnings,   432, 433-4
wars,   281-2, 351
water of life,   404, 424, 434
Watts, Isaac,   277
wealth
    and spiritual wealth,   82-3

Subject Index

wedding feast, parable of, 158
Westminster Confession of Faith, 244, 261, 434
white garments, 71, 86, 98, 152
white hairs, 29
white horse, 367
Whitfield, George, 310
Whyte, Alexander, 53
wilderness, 326
wings, 231
wisdom, 154-5
witness: worthiness, 228
witnesses, 204-5
woman at the well, 404, 424, 434
woman given wings, 231
woman taken in adultery, 71
Word of God
    completeness of, 435-6
    as mighty angel, 194-6, 197-8
    as sword, 50, 369
    tampering with, 436-7
work in heaven, 427
world seen from the throne, 101-2
world, troubles in, 281-2
worldly power, 267-8
worship, 105, 265, 288
    and holiness of God, 292-3
wrath of God, 114-15, 280, 295, 375-6

Yom Kippur, 411

Zacharias, 428
zeal: loss of, 38-9
Zizioulas, John, 404

Scripture Index

Old Testament

Genesis
1-3   423
2:10-14   424
3   40, 216, 244, 359, 409
3:5   217
3:15   218, 239, 360, 402
4:25   219
6   219
11   337, 411
11:1-9   412
12   402
15:5   148
15:6   130
15:18   188
17   402
21   402
49:10   185
49:11   369

Exodus
3:14   26, 31, 106, 332
6:8   198
7:14   306
8:15   306
9   301
9:5   26
9:6   26
10:21-3   135
13:12-21   195
13:20–14:31   280
14   195
15   287
19   26
19:4-6   231
19:16   99
19:18   134, 135
20   35, 270, 298
20:2   298
20:4   93
24   280
25   99
40   195

Leviticus
4   184
4:13-21   184
16   166
17   302
18:22   328
20:13   328
23:24   210

Numbers
10   146
10:10   210
11:29   427
16:26-33   233
16:28-33   233
23:10   271
23-4   53
25   53
29:1   210
31   146

Deuteronomy
4:2   435, 437
4:32   253
5   270
5:24-5   298
6:5-9   247
6:15   298
8   35
18:10   328
18:11   328
18:15   204
22:23-4   360
23:18   328
24:17   26
27:15   328
28   35
28:27-8   301
28:34   189
29:29   198, 241
32   287
32:10-11   231
32:40   198

Joshua
1:4   188
7:19   309

Judges
5   316

1 Samuel
2:30   351
25:29   310

2 Samuel
7:14   402

1 Kings
1:34   210
6:20   411, 418
22   316
22:19-22   316

2 Kings
6:15-17   251
9   316
9:13   210

2 Chronicles
20:21-25   286
35-6   316

Nehemiah
11:1   401

Job
1:6   222
1-2   222
2:1   222
9   137
38:7   211

Psalms
2   61, 197, 220, 253, 274, 326, 350
2:2   268, 313
2:4   341
2:8   13, 381
2:8-9   220

Psalms (cont.)
2:9 218, 341, 372
2:9-12 118
2:12 218
5 182
10:15 182
14 184
16:11 426
18:9 123
19:1 106
21:1-2 156
22 92, 294, 354
22:1 397
23 52, 253, 424
24 211
24:1 378
27:1 253
27:8 67, 296
29 196
29:3 196
34:7 370
34:8 55
34:9 149, 264
35:4 182
37:4 156
43:3-5 117
43:4 285
45:6-7 172
45:8 14
45:13 410
46 178
46:1 253
46:8-9 118
50 378
51 307, 309
51:1-10 398
51:5 306
56:8 45
61:11 341
62 83
65:9 426
68:1 182
68:17 146, 188
69 92
72 12
76:10 128, 172
90:17 11, 408
91:1 253
91:4-11 231
96 254
102:25-26 137
103 154
107:16 31
110:1 30
110:3 156, 306
113-118 354
119 99
119:71 307
121 157
130:3 263
130:3-4 263
130:4 263
140:1 182

Proverbs
21:1 320

Ecclesiastes
12:1-2 137

Song of Solomon
5:16 12
6:1 12

Isaiah
1 321
1:18 199, 310
4:5 248
5:24-5 135
6 292
6:1 91
6:1-3 103
7:14 218
9:2 32
9:6 226
13:9-10 314
14:12-15 217
19:1 123
21:11 25
22:22 74
23 321
24 135
26:17-19 218
31:4 91
34:4 137
42 407
42:8 407
43:2 234
44:5 248
44:6 43
48:2 401
49:6 148
49:16 71
49:18 402
49:26 302
53 114, 166, 184, 366, 394
53:3-5 44
53:5 397
53:9 257
53:11 12
54:1 218
54:11-12 416
54:13 416
55 87
55:1 86, 404
57:20 238, 281
60:1-3 419, 428
60:19-20 419
61:10 409
62:2-3 368
63:2-3 369
63:2-4 276
63:9 45
64:4 414

Jeremiah
2 321
4:31 218
6:1 188
15 242
21 223
31 72, 360
31:31-4 35
31:34 340
46:8 328
51 348
51:7 328
51:8 328
51:33 275
51:61-4 348
51:63 348

Ezekiel
1:4-7 103
1:25-8 194
1:26-8 93
1:27-8 195
1:28 100
2-3 199
4:10 125
5:1-12 317
9:1-7 140
14:13 288
16 321
23 322
26:7 188
32:2 136
32:7-8 136, 314
39 372
43:2 30

47 424
48:35 402

Daniel
2:35 28
3 245
7 28, 239
7:3-7 220
7:7 327
7:9 29, 91
7:10-11 372
7:12 28
7:13-14 28, 274
7:20 327
7:24 327
7:25 232
8:9-10 137
8:18 31
9 221
10 185, 223
12 420
12:2 48, 387
12:3 262
12:4 431

Hosea
8:4 374

Joel
2:1 136
3:13 275

Amos
8:9 136, 314

Micah
5 219, 223

Nahum
1:2 135
1:5 135
3 321

Habakkuk

- 1:13 172
- 3 116, 118
- 3:3-8 118

Zephaniah

- 3:13 257

Zechariah

- 3:1-12 222
- 4 99
- 4:1-6 206
- 4:2 26, 27
- 4:8 26
- 6 116, 118
- 12 222

Malachi

- 3:2 138
- 4:4-5 204

NEW TESTAMENT

Matthew

- 1:18-19 360
- 1:20-23 218
- 3:10 212
- 4:8-10 332
- 5 161
- 5:16 265
- 5:17 431, 436
- 5:18 436
- 5:22 375
- 5:29-30 375
- 6:10 26
- 7:21-23 363
- 7:23 375
- 10:28 329
- 10:38 256
- 11:20-23 432
- 11:28-30 363
- 12:28-9 379
- 12:39 322
- 12:41-2 433
- 12:43-5 176
- 13:30 275
- 13:39 275
- 13:40-42 275
- 16:4 322
- 16:27 394
- 17 195
- 18:9 344
- 18:10 370
- 18:11 344
- 18:17-18 344
- 19:27-30 149
- 19:30 45
- 21:12 249
- 21:12-13 249
- 21:19 137
- 22:8-14 362
- 23:36 22
- 24 21, 22, 23, 134, 141, 147, 190, 276
- 24:14 147
- 24:24 245
- 24:31 275
- 24:34 22
- 24:51 375
- 24-5 123, 232
- 25 123, 153, 161, 241, 276, 361, 397
- 25:31-46 29
- 25:34-40 361
- 25:37-40 26
- 25:41-6 363
- 27:51 29
- 28 50, 114, 121
- 28:18 334, 379, 431
- 28:19-20 26
- 28 24:32 122

Mark

- 1:24 380
- 2:2 122
- 4:29 275
- 10:42-4 385
- 13 22, 123, 134, 147

Luke

- 1:50 263
- 1:68 428
- 1:78-9 428
- 3:7 375
- 4:34 380
- 8:26-33 237
- 9:23 310
- 10:17-19 170
- 10:18 13, 222, 333
- 10:18-19 380
- 10:19 178
- 11:2 26
- 12 50
- 13:24-9 202
- 15:1 122
- 16 70, 373, 374
- 19 348
- 19:14 326
- 19:17-18 427
- 19:43-4 348
- 21 22, 123, 134, 141, 147, 190
- 21:30 122
- 22:62 433
- 24 111
- 24:28-32 87

John

- 1 196
- 1:1 194
- 1:3 31, 42, 80, 265, 431
- 1:14 194
- 1:18 26
- 3:16 261
- 3:16-17 148
- 4:28-30 424
- 4:35-38 275
- 5:24 48
- 5:24-5 386
- 5:24-9 48
- 5:28-9 387
- 6 87
- 6:53 40
- 7:38-9 434
- 8 71
- 10 36, 52, 150
- 10:3 30
- 10:10 424
- 10:11 26
- 11 403
- 11:18 122
- 11:25 386
- 12:24 149
- 14 122
- 14:3 418
- 14:8-9 26
- 14:19 262
- 15 45, 202
- 15:2 46
- 16:3 65
- 16:7 66
- 16:8-11 265
- 16:33 147
- 17:3 69, 359
- 17:22 408
- 17:24 387, 408
- 18:36 26
- 19:15 240
- 20 66
- 21 433

Acts of the Apostles

- 1 252
- 1:12 122
- 2 401
- 2:23 173
- 5:31 305, 433
- 7 252
- 7:56 252
- 9:1-9 30
- 9:4 230
- 10:42 394
- 13:48 294
- 14 265
- 14:2-6 42
- 17 265
- 17:25 104
- 17:31 394
- 20 38
- 20:21 310
- 21:26-30 249
- 24:4 122
- 28:28 380

Romans

- 1:4 13
- 1:19-21 93
- 1:21 178
- 1-2 245
- 2:4 314
- 2:5-6 396
- 3:24 439
- 4:25 260
- 5:2 31
- 5:3-5 85, 308

Romans (cont.)

- 5:5 67
- 5:12 326
- 5:12-21 26, 305
- 5:17 262
- 5:20 425
- 6:3-6 202
- 6:4 386
- 6:5 257
- 6:23 262
- 8 87
- 8:11 206
- 8:28 91, 128, 197, 282
- 8:31-9 160
- 8:32 26, 108
- 8:33-9 197
- 8:35-9 178
- 8:38-9 191
- 9 306
- 9:18 306
- 9-11 212
- 10:9 263, 433
- 11 119, 212
- 11:33-6 212
- 12 77, 124, 183, 373
- 12:19 206, 396
- 13 50, 238

1 Corinthians

- 1:2 165, 241
- 1:20 80
- 1:26-9 385
- 1:30 184
- 2:9 414
- 2:14 255
- 3:16 419
- 3:17 202
- 3:18 255, 427
- 4 228
- 4:5-8, 10 228
- 4:16-18 255
- 5 160
- 5:1 159
- 5:7 62, 287
- 5:14 156
- 5:17 386, 403
- 5:21 395
- 6:3 97
- 6:11 112
- 6:17 341
- 6:18 341
- 6:19 202
- 8:9 434
- 11:14 327
- 12:4 27
- 12:13 401
- 12:28 370
- 13 101, 199
- 14:24-5 29
- 15 39, 71, 84, 262
- 15:1-6 260
- 15:17 260
- 15:19 84
- 15:20 257, 262
- 15:23 26
- 15:25 365
- 15:45 26, 326
- 15:52 30
- 15:57-8 162
- 15:58 392
- 16:15 257

2 Corinthians

- 1:20 23, 367
- 3 119
- 4 206
- 4:8-12 205
- 4-5 282
- 5 129, 159
- 11:12 256

Galatians

- 1:12 260
- 2:20 31, 202, 310
- 3:8 148
- 4:4 186, 222, 391
- 4:15 30
- 6:10 26

Ephesians

- 1 87
- 1:4 335
- 1:9-11 92
- 1:10-11 26
- 1:11 282
- 1:12-14 335
- 1-2 305
- 2:1 48, 257, 386
- 2:6 13, 225, 258, 370
- 2:8-9 260, 361, 433
- 2:10 361
- 2:12-15 209
- 2:18 153
- 2:19-22 411
- 2:21-2 419
- 4:8 31
- 4:21-4 305, 362
- 5 359, 409
- 5:25-7 402
- 6 98, 118
- 6 1:13 141
- 6 4:30 141
- 6:11-12 223
- 6:17 30

Philippians

- 1:21 149, 387
- 1:23 387
- 2:9 14
- 2:10-11 369
- 2:12-13 310
- 2:19 122
- 3:20 413
- 3:21 400

Colossians

- 1:15-17 31
- 1:15-18 80
- 1:17 369
- 1:18 26
- 1:24 52, 130
- 2 196
- 2:11-12 248
- 2:14-15 380
- 2:15 13, 31
- 2:17 431
- 3:1-10 71

1 Thessalonians

- 4:13-18 401
- 4:14-15 411
- 4:17 411

2 Thessalonians

- 1:7-9 195
- 2:3-4 238

1 Timothy

- 2:2 26
- 3:16 329
- 5:16 26
- 6:15 25

2 Timothy

- 3:5 67
- 3:12 147
- 3:16 436

Hebrews

- 1 97, 252, 365
- 1:2 403
- 1:3 30, 274
- 1:13 274
- 1:14 97, 370
- 2:8-16 383
- 2:14-15 31
- 2:16 97
- 4:12 29
- 7:25 66, 225
- 7:26 310
- 8 72
- 9:22 111
- 9:22-4 225
- 10:12-13 221
- 10:19-20 228
- 10:22 228
- 10:26-31 117
- 11 61, 112, 405
- 11:35 282
- 11:35-8 356
- 12 138, 143, 311, 405
- 12:1-2 405
- 12:2 67
- 12:22 249, 401
- 12:22-3 252
- 12:25-9 317
- 12:26-7 137, 169
- 12:27 142, 311
- 13:4 256
- 13:12 276

James

1:1	147
1:13	172
2:19	264
4:2	184
4:7	226
5	286
5:14-16	66

1 Peter

1:2-7	242
1:7	85
2:9	32
5:8-9	226

2 Peter

1:21	436
2:4	217
3:3-4	431
3:6	431
3:10-13	400

1 John

1	222
1:1	403
1:2-4	235
1:8	184, 302
1:8-10	241
1:9	199, 302
2	222
2:1	222
2:1-2	303
2:12	222
2:20	86
3:2	40, 97, 138, 427
3:8	118, 383
3:20-21	227
3:22-3	228
4:15	263
4:18	32, 264
5:3	235
5:4	54
5:7	359

Jude

3	270
6	217, 373
14-15	430

Further books of interest from
Christian Focus Publications

GALATIANS
A MENTOR EXPOSITORY COMMENTARY
TERRY L. JOHNSON

ISBN 978-1-85792-882-2

Galatians
A Mentor Expository Commentary
Terry Johnson

"What must I do to be saved?"
This is the message that the book of Galatians seeks to answers. It tells us that there is a gospel message to preach even 2000 years on from when these words were first penned. It presents for us the truth of the gospel, unearthing the central message that righteousness can only be obtained through justification by faith. We are told in no uncertain terms that we cannot have this on our own merit. It considers the original context that there would have been questions as to what of the Jewish custom should be adopted if any as Gentiles joined the church. There were issues that could divide them but above all they needed to preach the gospel and to live lives that were bearing the fruit of God's word in them.

> The fact that Johnson has preached through Galatians gives this book the benefit of strong and insightful application. Johnson clearly explains some of the most difficult passages in Scripture, stalwartly defends evangelical doctrines such "justification by faith alone," and also interacts with newer movements such as Federal Vision Theology and the New Perspective on Paul. This volume will be of help to any pastor or faithful Christian alike.
>
> Greg Gilbert,
> Senior Pastor, Third Avenue Baptist Church, Louisville, Kentucky
> Author of *What is the Gospel?*

> Dr. Johnson's extensive pastoral work, his insights into the Word of God, his demonstrated leadership in preaching, teaching and living the message of the book of Galatians qualifies him as the man for the hour to write this great new commentary. I commend this new Christian Focus commentary by Dr. Johnson to all without hesitation
>
> Michael A. Milton,
> Chancellor/CEO elect, The James M. Baird Jr. Professor of Pastoral Theology,
> Reformed Theological Seminary

> Given current debates over the meaning of law, gospel and justification, a knowledge of Galatians has become essential. Johnson's commentary is essential reading for preachers and lay folk alike.
>
> Derek Thomas,
> Minister of Preaching and Teaching, First Presbyterian Church, Columbia, South Carolina

Terry Johnson is Senior Pastor of the Independent Presbyterian Church in Savannah, Georgia.

ISBN 978-1-85792-283-7

Creation and Change

Genesis 1.1 – 2.4 in the Light of Changing Scientific Paradigms

Douglas F. Kelly

In this book Professor Douglas Kelly persuasively argues for a literal interpretation of the seven day account of creation found in Genesis chapters 1 and 2. He assesses both the biblical details and the scientific data to show that there is a convincing case for this understanding and how it is scientifically viable.

A highly intelligent engagement with these crucial verses with which God declares himself to be a speaking God who is our maker. The discussion is scholarly but accessible, a model of the kind of exegetical theology which the church of our day needs.

Nigel M. De S. Cameron,
President, Center for Policy on Emerging Technologies, Washington DC

Douglas Kelly is a theologian who also displays a deep understanding of science and philosophy. The result is this thoughtful, thorough and well researched book that will be valuable to anyone wishing to dig deeper. I highly recommend Creation and Change.

Walter E. Brown,
Center for Scientific Creation, Phoenix, Arizona

It is an excellent work. I believe it will be an important contribution to the field

John Currid,
Carl McMurray Professor of Old Testament,
Reformed Theological Seminary, Charlotte, North Carolina

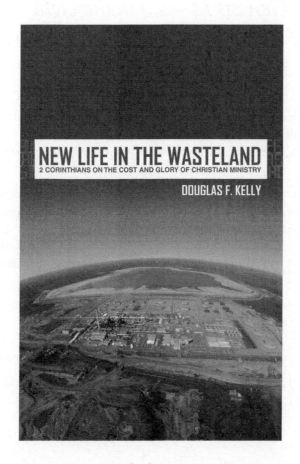

ISBN 978-1-85792-903-4

New Life in the Wasteland

2 Corinthians on the Cost and Glory of Christian Ministry

Douglas F. Kelly

In 2 Corinthians you get a picture of how Paul is a model on how to be a leader in the church. We live with Paul through the problems of overseeing many congregations in different stages of growth. We are given examples of how to deal with many types of disciplinary issues yet throughout it is a great example of the use of authority coupled with humility - two things that the modern world has great difficulties in putting together. If you ask Christian leaders for one of their greatest difficulties in ministry is, it is this, how to lead without arrogance. The answers on how to do that are here.

> Faithful to the text, Douglas brings the meaning of the great themes of 2 Corinthians right into the twenty-first century. His is the gift of lifting the great apostle's thoughts and experiences and transferring them into 'light' and 'salt' for the church today. This is a book for ministers about their congregations; it also a book for congregations about their ministers! Indeed, it will be a hard heart that is not deeply moved and renewed by the reading of *New Life in the Wasteland*.
>
> David Searle

> This book contains much to challenge. It is rich in spiritual teaching. I wish it a wide and attentive reading, and I pray its message will be applied – urgently!
>
> Evangelical Times

> The book is written in a simple, straightforward style, without the use of technical terms. It is rich in vivid illustrations and is easyto read. I warmly commend the book.
>
> Evangelicals Now

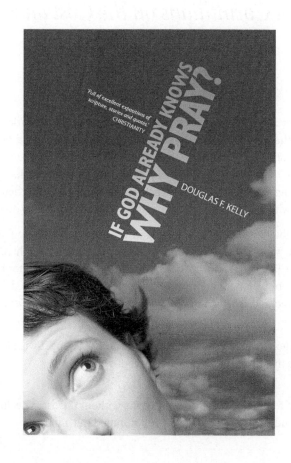

ISBN 978-1-85792-146-5

If God Already Knows Why Pray?

Douglas F. Kelly

Knowing who God is – his character, his plans and why he wants us to pray – are essentials in building our understanding of prayer. Douglas Kelly is a distinguished theologian – he is well qualified to guide us both as a teacher and a fellow traveller, sharing his own setbacks and blessings. One of the biggest questions about prayer is not 'How do you do it?' but rather 'Do we know who we are speaking to?'

Full of excellent expositions of scripture, stories and quotes which time and again focus attention on God.

Trevor Gregory, Christianity

This is a very readable book on an important and difficult subject this is a refreshing book in an age of much flippancy in Christian living and worship.

Monthly Record

It is written for those who find it difficult, in theory or practice, to reconcile our prayers with the sovereignty of God in providence and redemption. He deals with the issues in a way that informs our minds, warms our hearts and moves our wills. He writes with clarity and includes a wealth of memorable and often moving illustrations based on the Bible and personal experience.

Evangelical Times

ISBN 978-1-84550-386-4

Systematic Theology (Volume 1)

Grounded in Holy Scripture and understood in light of the Church

Douglas F. Kelly

"I have written this first volume, thinking of my heritage as both Reformed and Catholic; gladly appropriating crucial insights of the whole people of God over the last two thousand years – Eastern Orthodox, Western Catholic, and Reformation Protestant – as they sought to live out the foundational truths of the inspired Word of God." *Douglas F. Kelly*

> This is the fruit of decades of research, thought and teaching. Kelly's procedure is entirely sound; Scripture is his basis, the primary authority, but he engages throughout the past teaching of the church.. In this he follows in the footsteps of Calvin and the Westminster and the Westminster Assembly. His breadth of coverage is wide.
>
> EVANGELICALS NOW

> I just now completed reading through the entire book you wrote Systematic Theology, vol. 1. I want to express my sincere appreciation for the quality work you have done. You show that you know ancient languages (Hebrew, Greek and Latin) as well as modern languages (French and German). You delve into the Christian fathers of the first few centuries and are familiar with the works of the Reformers and the latest books and articles on Systematic Theology. This is eminent scholarship that lies back of numerous years of study. You have done the Church a favor by writing this book and I personally thank you for this contribution. Excellent work!
>
> SIMON KISTEMAKER,
> Professor of New Testament Emeritus, Reformed Theological Seminary, Orlando, Florida

> Douglas F. Kelly is one of the English-speaking world's leading Reformed theologians. Here we begin to enjoy the fruits of his labors. What a feast it is. Few Protestant theologians in our day know the terrain of the doctrine of the Trinity, and the Person of Christ, as well as Professor Kelly... He is at his best when opening up to us the unrealized importance and glory of these foundational truths about our Savior God. For those who yearn for an orthodox Reformed catholicity, Kelly shows the way forward.
>
> LIGON DUNCAN,
> Senior Minister, First Presbyterian Church, Jackson, Mississippi

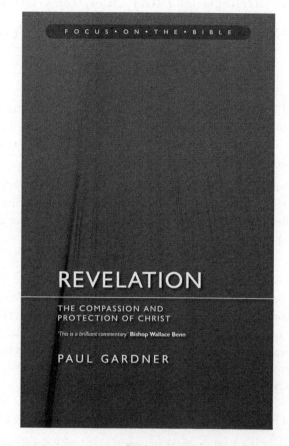

ISBN 978-1-84550-344-4

Revelation

The Compassion and Protection of Christ
PAUL GARDNER

It is ironical that a book called 'the revelation' remains probably the most obscure of all the books of the Bible. Many Christians have never ventured further than the first 3 chapters and others have studied its intricacies and the split churches that resulted wished that they hadn't!

For those who already love the book of Revelation this commentary will take you a little deeper and stimulate thinking about how the teaching should be applied to the modern church.

It is my sincere hope that every evangelical will read this commentary on Revelation. Paul Gardner has given us an in-depth, but clear, approach. He avoids the host of radical interpretations that are available today. His insights into the meaning of this book will touch every dimension of the Christian life.

RICHARD PRATT,
President, Third Millenium Ministries, Orlando, Florida

This perceptive book provides a thorough and totally accessible guide through what has so often seemed a maze of conflicting ideas and interpretations. Here is a detailed explanation, verse by verse, of what the text actually means, exploring its Old Testament roots, unpacking its potent symbolism, but above all applying its message, personally and pastorally to life today.

DAVID JACKMAN,
Engages in a worldwide ministry for Proclamation Trust, London

This is a brilliant commentary that deserves a wide readership. It is lucid, sane, helpful and well applied Revelation is a book of enormous encouragement to Christians and it needs deliverance from the way it has been misused by many. Paul's are a safe pair of hands to guide you through. I warmly and highly recommend this commentary.

WALLACE BENN,
Bishop of Lewes, Sussex, England

Dr Paul Gardner was previously a lecturer in New Testament at Oak Hill Theological College in London and a Rural Dean in the Church of England. After serving as Archdeacon of Exeter for three years, in 2005 Dr. Gardner moved to Atlanta in the United States and now serves as the Senior Minister at Christ Church Presbyterian, Atlanta.

RICHARD BEWES

THE LAMB WINS!

A Guided Tour Through the Book of Revelation

'Makes Revelation leap to life and relevance.' **DON CARSON**

ISBN 978-1-85792-597-5

The Lamb Wins!
A Guided Tour through the Book of Revelation
Richard Bewes

What is the average person to make of the book of Revelation, with its vivid imagery and its apocalyptic visions? Richard Bewes steers his readers through the minefields of controversy and bizarre interpretations. He picks out the great themes and landmarks that are the message of Christ to every generation of believers.

> If the Bible is the book for today's church (and it is), then the Book of Revelation should be the book for today's Church (and it is)....Richard Bewes sweeps us through it with a touch that makes even the back streets seem important and yet keeps the strategic parts in perspective
>
> Michael Baughen,
> Retired Bishop of Chester, Cheshire

> Richard Bewes has captured the central theme of John's Revelation...Written in graceful prose, this little book will make Revelation's central lines of thought leap to life and relevance. It deserves wide circulation.
>
> D. A. Carson,
> Research Professor of New Testament, Trinity Evangelical Divinity School, Deerfield, Illinois

> Richard Bewes has done it again. 'Brilliant' is the word. Here is the best introduction I know to the book of Revelation; profound, yet simple and understandable. I recommend it for every young Christian, in fact for every Christian Bible reader.
>
> Vijay Menon,
> City Evangelist, St Helen's Bishopsgate, London

Richard Bewes was the rector of All Souls, Langham Place in the centre of London for many years. He is an experienced broadcaster, conference speaker and the author of more than twenty books.

Christian Focus Publications

publishes books for all ages

Our mission statement –

STAYING FAITHFUL

In dependence upon God we seek to impact the world through literature faithful to His infallible Word, the Bible. Our aim is to ensure that the Lord Jesus Christ is presented as the only hope to obtain forgiveness of sin, live a useful life and look forward to heaven with Him.

REACHING OUT

Christ's last command requires us to reach out to our world with His gospel. We seek to help fulfil that by publishing books that point people towards Jesus and help them develop a Christ-like maturity. We aim to equip all levels of readers for life, work, ministry and mission.

Books in our adult range are published in three imprints:

Christian Focus contains popular works including biographies, commentaries, basic doctrine and Christian living. Our children's books are also published in this imprint.

Mentor focuses on books written at a level suitable for Bible College and seminary students, pastors, and other serious readers. The imprint includes commentaries, doctrinal studies, examination of current issues and church history.

Christian Heritage contains classic writings from the past.

Christian Focus Publications Ltd,
Geanies House, Fearn, Ross-shire,
IV20 1TW, Scotland, United Kingdom.
www.christianfocus.com